Documents of
Modern Literary Realism

DOCUMENTS OF MODERN LITERARY REALISM

Edited by George J. Becker

PRINCETON, NEW JERSEY

PRINCETON UNIVERSITY PRESS

Printed in the United States of America
by Princeton University Press
Princeton, New Jersey

First PRINCETON PAPERBACK Printing, 1967

Second Printing, 1973

Preface

THE body of discussion of modern literary realism is vast, repetitious, and not infrequently muddle-headed. It is impossible and unnecessary to reproduce it all; it is impossible to select, even for a volume of this compass, to the satisfaction of all who use the book. Therefore the editor owes the reader some indication of the basis on which the selection has been made.

As we read through the nineteenth-century criticism, it quickly becomes evident that there was a first general aspiration toward literature which would have to do directly with contemporary life and observed phenomena and would break away from hackneyed subjects and stereotyped formulas, particularly those of romanticism. It seemed desirable to begin the first section of this collection, "The Impulse toward Realism," with Belinsky's remarks written in 1835, because they clearly take issue with the then regnant philosophy and aesthetics. The section ends at the turn of the century with Galdós's subtle justification of everyday materials in his speech to the Spanish Academy and Dreiser's brief declaration, "True Art Speaks Plainly." The desire for realism continues in this century, but it no longer is the occasion for manifestos.

Because of the imposing bulk and uninhibited voice of Zola, naturalism drew to itself most of the attention of writers and critics from 1870 on. Thus the second section, "The Battle over Naturalism," is heavily weighted with discussions by or about Zola, for the most part published in France. What was said in Italy, Spain, and Germany was largely an echo of the adulatory or acrimonious comments of French men of letters and suffers from being at one remove from the main arena of controversy. It therefore has received little representation. However, I have included a considerable body of discussions originating in England and the United States, both for their critical content and for what they show of the emotional response to realism-naturalism in English-speaking countries.

Except in the United States and other colonial regions the main battle over realism had been fought out by 1900. Thus the third section, "Twentieth-Century Revisions and Evaluations," ignores belated critical fusillades almost entirely and turns to restatements

v

of realistic goals and methods—a fairly limited body of material—
and to overall assessments of the importance of the movement and
the innovations which it brought.

Much of nineteenth-century writing about realism-naturalism
was of an *ad hoc* nature, addressed to a book under review rather
than to the broader implications of the work. Recapitulation of plot
often occupies the greater part of such reviews and has no interest
for us today. Thus nearly all such material has been rejected, the
most notable exception being Sainte-Beuve's famous review of
Madame Bovary, from which some ten pages of narrative summary have, however, been omitted.

In general I have tried to avoid presenting excerpts. The exceptions, in addition to the one just mentioned, are the passage
from Belinsky, a portion of Taine's very long essay on Balzac,
and the section from Proust. In another case it has seemed sufficient to give general standard definitions of socialist realism without extended context.

Another criterion for selection was that the materials presented
should be public, not private, utterances. Letters, diaries, and other
unpublished materials (or published much later as part of an author's complete works) would seem not to qualify as documents
influential in the development of the movement. Again a major
exception has been necessary: the critical statements drawn from
Flaubert's correspondence, which have been of basic importance
in criticism for many decades.

As the title indicates, this book has to do with *literary* realism.
Thus there has been no effort to include statements in the area of
science and philosophy which were the basis of the literary outlook,
or to bring forward analogous statements about arts other than
literature, particularly painting. A number of the writers presented
do in fact go beyond literature in their discussions, thus providing
an incidental glimpse of the breadth of interest and innovation, but
basically it is necessary for the reader to assume the body of opinion and belief which lies beneath and behind the realist-naturalist
movement.

One other limitation may disturb the reader. There is little
about realism in the drama, and nothing about it in poetry. This
limitation has imposed itself. Prose fiction has been the major

vehicle of realism; the important and searching critical discussions have revolved around it almost exclusively. There are here and there a good many remarks about the drama, but not of high critical level. The Zola and Strindberg selections are sufficient to represent this vein. While realism has affected choice of poetic subject and vocabulary, by the very nature of that medium it has never been of central importance.

The order of materials is chronological *within* the first two sections, with one or two exceptions for the sake of obvious convenience. The last section is presented not chronologically but topically, with a rough grouping around the two poles of revision and evaluation.

Unless otherwise indicated, translations are by the editor. Since much of the material had not been previously translated or had been translated only in part, it seemed better to seek consistency in the handling of basic terms and concepts by having a single translator to the extent that was feasible.

The bibliography has been confined to works of general rather than limited or specific literary interest. It makes no pretense of being comprehensive; it does aim to be useful by listing works or articles which have more than a temporary importance and may still be read with profit.

It is the aim of this presentation of documents that they work as the realists expected documents to work: that they speak for themselves and the pattern emerge from the heaped-up data. There has been an effort to avoid bias and to seek representativeness. No point of view has been willfully omitted. If the reader is disturbed by the absence of some document which he considered important, it may be that his memory is at fault. But it may also be that the editor must take refuge in Dr. Johnson's candid and unanswerable excuse—sheer ignorance.

It is not practicable to convey thanks by name to all the persons who have provided help and advice in the making of this book. However, I must acknowledge a grant for secretarial assistance provided by the faculty research fund of Swarthmore College and the tireless and ingenious efforts on the part of the readers' services staff of the College Library in chasing down and procuring obscure publications. I received constant help from the members of the Department of Modern Foreign Languages, especially in the area of Russian literature. Over the years my students in the seminar in Modern Comparative Literature have provided a sounding board to test the meaning and importance of this body of critical doctrine. Above all I am indebted to the patience and meticulousness of my wife, who has held copy and proof in a seemingly endless chain. All these people have tried to keep me from error, and for those errors that remain I have only myself to blame.

Swarthmore, Pa.
December 15, 1962

Contents

Preface   v

Introduction: Modern Realism as a Literary Movement   3

I : THE IMPULSE TOWARD REALISM

VISSARION BELINSKY	On Realistic Poetry	41
N. G. CHERNISHEVSKY	From *Life and Aesthetics*	44
FERNAND DESNOYERS	"On Realism"	80
GUSTAVE FLAUBERT	On Realism	89
EDMOND DURANTY AND CHARLES SAINTE-BEUVE	Two Views of *Madame Bovary*	97
HIPPOLYTE TAINE	"The World of Balzac"	105
GEORGE ELIOT	On Realism	112
EDMOND AND JULES DE GONCOURT	On True Novels	117
OLIVE SCHREINER	On Realism	120
GEORGE BERNARD SHAW	"Ideals and Idealists"	122
WILLIAM DEAN HOWELLS	On Truth in Fiction	129
HAMLIN GARLAND	On Veritism	137
BENITO PÉREZ GALDÓS	Contemporary Society as Novelistic Material	147
THEODORE DREISER	"True Art Speaks Plainly"	154

II : THE BATTLE OVER NATURALISM

EMILE ZOLA	On the Rougon-Macquart Series	159
	"The Experimental Novel"	161
	"Naturalism in the Theatre"	197
J.-K. HUYSMANS	"Emile Zola and *L'Assommoir*"	230

CONTENTS

HENRY JAMES	"Nana"	236
EDMOND DE GONCOURT	Levels of Realism	244
GUY DE MAUPASSANT	"The Lower Elements"	247
HEINRICH AND JULIUS HART	"For and against Zola"	251
EMILIA PARDO BAZÁN	On Spanish Realism	261
LEOPOLDO ALAS	What Naturalism Is Not	266
W. S. LILLY	"The New Naturalism"	275
HAMILTON WRIGHT MABIE	"A Typical Novel"	296
E.-M. DE VOGÜÉ	On Russian and French Realism	310
	"Manifesto of Five against *La Terre*"	344
NATIONAL VIGILANCE ASSOCIATION	"Pernicious Literature"	350
EDMUND GOSSE	"The Limits of Realism in Fiction"	383
AUGUST STRINDBERG	Naturalism in the Theatre	394
PAUL ALEXIS	Naturalism Is Not Dead	407
LEO TOLSTOY	"Guy de Maupassant"	412

III: TWENTIETH-CENTURY REVISIONS AND EVALUATIONS

MALCOLM COWLEY	"A Natural History of American Naturalism"	429
STUART P. SHERMAN	"The Naturalism of Mr. Dreiser"	452
LÉON LEMONNIER	"A Literary Manifesto: The Populist Novel"	465
JAIME BRASIL	On Portuguese Neo-Realism	468
FRIEDRICH ENGELS	On Socialist Realism	483

Contents

MAXIM GORKY
AND OTHERS   On Socialist Realism   486

HECTOR P. AGOSTI   "A Defense of Realism"   489

HENRY JAMES   "Emile Zola"   506

ROGER SHERMAN LOOMIS   "A Defense of Naturalism"   535

MARCEL PROUST   On the Falsity of Realism   549

ARTHUR MC DOWALL   "Conclusions and Applications"   565

PHILIP RAHV   "Notes on the Decline of Naturalism"   579

ERICH HELLER   "The Realistic Fallacy"   591

A Short Bibliography of History and Criticism   599

Index   605

xi

Documents of
Modern Literary Realism

Introduction

Modern Realism as a Literary Movement

THE subject of realism is not especially congenial to the critics of our day. There is one body of opinion that has been against it from the start and has never seen fit to revise its attitude. There is another which has become bored with it and finds that this subject, always rather obvious and even simple-minded, need no longer engage the subtle mind of the literary scholar. Some critics have gone so far as to deny that there was such a thing as a realistic *movement* in literature; others deny the possibility of a realistic work, whatever the literary affiliations of the author; and in concert most critics deny the existence of a realist aesthetic, finding the term pretentious for what is after all mere reportage, not art, and is in addition based on a naive metaphysics. Though the words *realism* and *naturalism* are freely, even rashly, used, there is no general agreement as to what they mean. For many they have come to be merely convenient pejoratives, especially when qualified as *stark, raw, unimaginative, superficial, atheistic*, and more recently *socialist*.

Yet there was a realistic movement, an innovation and an aspiration that shook the academies and the public more deeply than any other literary movement in history. Born in controversy and developed in acrimony, this literary revolution has influenced the literature of every country at some point during the last century and continues to be felt in our day, though no doubt the battle for realism seems almost as remote and as much a *fait accompli* as the battle for romanticism which preceded it. Certainly, and fortunately, contemporary writers have for the most part moved on; they are, after all, the third (and fourth) generation since the high tide of European realism; it would be a pity if they were not attempting something new. Yet whatever our current allegiances and aspirations in literature, our roots are there in the nineteenth century where a massive body of critical discussion remains to remind us of the strenuous and widespread effort at literary renovation. Without too much oversimplification it is possible to say that

3

the writing of our own day may be seen either as a conventional continuation of the realistic mode—so addicted are we that we have not only *Peyton Place* but Peyton Place Revisited—or as a reaction against it which cannot be fully understood unless we are aware of the realistic elements residually present, better perhaps the realistic base on which have been erected a variety of individual and artistically contrived superstructures. *Surrealism* has come and gone, as have other irrealistic efforts; it is difficult to find a term other than post-realistic to describe the writing of our time. To vary the metaphor which Henry James once applied to Zola's novels, realism has proved to be a capacious vessel, capable of carrying a most varied cargo and of being converted to more elegant uses.

One of the favorite gambits of the early opponents of realism was that all the commotion was meaningless, since there was nothing new about it. This is a half-truth which merely confuses matters. Realistic *elements* there have been in most works which have engaged the imagination and interest of readers or hearers. Men seem always to have had a sneaking fondness for the *petit fait vrai* even in the midst of the most elevated or involuted discourse. Heroes and villains, if they were to command belief, had to have some saving touch of nature; adventures had to touch at least on homely soil before they soared off into the stratosphere of myth, allegory, or simple epic hyperbole. What such a half-truth ignores is that realism rarely, if ever, dominated and controlled a whole work before the middle of the nineteenth century; rather it was controlled and its functioning directed by the official aesthetic doctrine of a given time and place, which was never before realistic. For, however secular and down-to-earth may have been the spirit of an occasional writer of the past, never before did the realistic tendency mount to the proportions of a literary movement, to a flood which for a time carried all before it and largely obliterated established literary landmarks.

To be sure, the realists themselves, and notably Zola in his "Naturalism in the Theatre," were for purposes of propaganda quick to claim descent from eighteenth-century figures such as Diderot and Restif de la Bretonne and such immediate predecessors as Balzac and Stendhal. This served a double purpose: it gave them respectable ancestry and it put romanticism in its place as a febrile

Modern Realism as a Literary Movement

and sterile interruption of the main line of literary development. For at the point where modern realism began, romanticism was the enemy, something against which young writers could unite, however much they ultimately differed as to the course literature should follow. The complaints against romanticism are amply documented in this volume; they add up to a very simple observation: the prevailing mode was thin and lifeless because it had lost touch with ordinary, everyday life.

Some critics, however, have seen in realism merely a continuation and extension of the preceding movement. The romantics were expansive. They wanted to import new material into literature and to break the conventions of the classic age. Some of them speedily fell into a new kind of abstraction, but some of them like Wordsworth advocated the use of common subjects and language, and it is the latter strand that is continued in realism. It is perhaps enough to say in answer to this that the Wordsworthian common man was decidedly uncommon by reason of something far more deeply interfused than the realists have ever observed, and that when Wordsworth had a chance to observe, notably in London, he quickly averted his eyes, since what he saw did not square with his *a priori* convictions. It is no doubt true that romantic expansiveness led straight to the area of local color and the primitive, which is one of the avenues to realism but does not necessarily or inevitably come out there. Mérimée in "Mateo Falcone" and "Colomba," for example, seems to be more concerned with costume and strong effects than with observation of human nature. He remains a romantic even though he wrote after Stendhal's various Italian tales, where the interest is in human behavior and not in costume. Certainly interest in the exotic is not enough to bring the two movements together, though it is evident that many of the early advocates of realism would have been content with such an infusion from the picturesque areas of everyday life. Neither does the idea of a return to nature suffice, since the gap between a Wordsworthian conception of nature and that held by the realists is a chasm which permanently separates the two schools.

Therefore, granting that the realists are often overcome by their own exuberance and that Vogüé is not altogether malicious when he suggests that Hugo's *Notre-Dame de Paris* automatically comes to mind as one calls the roll of Zola's novels, what the attempt to make romanticism and realism parts of the same whole overlooks is the sharply different philosophical positions held by the two schools. Romanticism must ultimately be found to rest on an idealist metaphysics and its view of art to be one that is consonant with that metaphysical position. Realism came into being in the ferment of scientific and positivist thinking which characterized the middle of the nineteenth century and was to become what Zola always spoke of as the major current of the age. Realism really did constitute a fresh start because it was based on a new set of assumptions about the universe. It denied that there was a reality of essences or forms which was not accessible to ordinary sense perception, insisting instead that reality be viewed as something immediately at hand, common to ordinary human experience, and open to observation. This attitude demanded that its readers and adherents abandon a host of preconceptions about human nature, about the purposes and mechanism of the universe, and above all about the role of art.

It is not surprising that these new assumptions were continually attacked and denied. So deeply rooted was the idea that it was the function of art to represent the ideal that discussion of the new literature often got no further than an anguished cry that the ideal had been banished, and many English and German critics in particular engaged in astonishing semantic and intellectual acrobatics in an effort somehow to get the ideal back into a literature committed to the representation of the here and now. G. H. Lewes, George Eliot's mentor and friend, provides an interesting example of this effort in an article which he wrote for the *Westminster Review* in October 1858. "Art always aims at the representation of Reality," he asserts, "i.e. of Truth; and no departure from Truth is permissible, except such as inevitably lies in the nature of the medium itself. Realism is thus the basis of all Art, and its antithesis is not Idealism, but *Falsism*."[1] This attitude has never entirely disappeared in spite of the summary treatment given it by such different personalities as Zola and George Bernard Shaw,

[1] Lewes, G. H., "Realism in Art: Recent German Fiction," *Westminster Review* 70: pp. 271-287, October 1858.

6

who saw that it was most often used as an appeal to emotion rather than as the basis for legitimate philosophical argument.

At any rate, as Fernand Desnoyers put it, at last realism came —but it could not come until the change of metaphysical position was sufficiently widespread to support it. To assert specifically when it began is to insure disagreement, yet it seems clear enough that the decade of the 1850's constitutes a kind of watershed. Probably the first use of the term "realism" in England occurred in a *Westminster Review* article on Balzac in 1853, although the phrase "realist school" had been used but not defined in *Fraser's Magazine* two years earlier. The term was new in French in the early 1850's and was often italicized as a neologism. It was in 1855 that the painter Courbet placed the sign "Du Réalisme" over the door of his one-man show. In 1856 Edmond Duranty began a short-lived review called *Réalisme*, and in the following year Champfleury, an enthusiastic supporter of Courbet and the new literature, brought out a volume of critical discussions entitled *Le Réalisme*. The term was launched, though its meaning was still to be defined.

No doubt the works which appeared during that decade are a more important signpost. Tolstoy's *Sevastopol* began to come out in 1856; Flaubert's *Madame Bovary* began serial publication on October 1 of the same year. Tolstoy is demonstrably more of a realist than Pushkin and Gogol, his immediate predecessors in the Russian tradition, and Flaubert is more completely a realist than Balzac and Stendhal, who have often been claimed for the French school. (On this much debated point, the remarks of Count de Vogüé would seem to be definitive.) Let us say of Tolstoy and Flaubert that, whatever their incompleteness as realists, they broke new ground for prose fiction on a basis of observation and objectivity. They more consciously photographed the life around them than did their predecessors, and they took pains that the lens they used should not distort—at any rate not in the old ways. Perhaps we cannot go as far as W. C. Frierson does in asserting that before *Madame Bovary* no novel took as its subject a truly significant human event, but we will do well to remember that for the writers who followed Flaubert that book was a touchstone by which to assess the new literature. The claim that the 1850's are the starting point for the new movement does not rest on the innovations of Tolstoy and Flaubert alone. We must remember that the early works of George Eliot and Anthony Trollope belong to that decade, that for many the appearance of Turgenev's *A Sportsman's Sketches* in 1852 is the true beginning of Russian realism, and that in the United States Whitman's *Leaves of Grass* (1855) had the explosive force of a manifesto in favor of a new literature. We should also remember that by a gratifying coincidence of intellectual history Darwin's *Origin of Species* was published in 1859.

In any event realism came. As William Dean Howells wrote T. S. Perry in 1886, no one invented it; rather it seems spontaneously to have come all at once and everywhere, except in England. As may be inferred from the selections presented in this volume the main battle over realism was waged in France, with subsidiary skirmishes in other countries in which French works were usually the bone of contention. This primary role was due partly to the fact that the French take literary controversy seriously, partly because of the accident that there was a series of French writers of genius who were attempting to write in a new way just at the time when substantial works were needed to define and consolidate the position of realism. It is amusing to read the fears Flaubert expressed in his letters over the fact that Feydeau's *Fanny*, rumored to be a realistic novel, might rob him of the primacy which he expected to gain by *Madame Bovary*. *Fanny* early settled into the rubble of time: it was not so easy to write new or true. Flaubert, in spite of the sparseness of his literary production, did become the bellwether of realism and gathered around him such ones of his countrymen as the Goncourt brothers, the young Zola, and later Maupassant, as well as adventurous foreigners like Turgenev, George Moore, and even Henry James. A succession of works during the 1860's kept the French writers before the public: Flaubert's *Salammbô* and *L'Education sentimentale*, the Goncourts' *Soeur Philomène* and *Germinie Lacerteux* as well as their unsuccessful play, *Henriette Maréchal*, Zola's *Thérèse Raquin* and *Madeleine Férat*.

Flaubert was not of a temperament to be a leader of a school; indeed he distrusted labels and in later life frequently squirmed at being called a realist. The Goncourts (or more particularly Edmond

Modern Realism as a Literary Movement

after his brother's death in 1870) were never slow to assert their
primacy as inventors of the *human document*, but they were not
of a stature to put realism on the highroad of literary domination.
Thus it was that Emile Zola, who among his many talents had a
gift for noisy self-advertisement, rode in with trumpets blowing
and pennants flying to dominate the movement for thirty years.
The twenty novels of the Rougon-Macquart series appeared, usually first in serial form, with great regularity from 1871 to 1893.
The books were timely, since they dealt more than candidly with
the ugly mores of a repudiated regime. They ranged widely among
social milieux, taking seriously the realists' belief that new areas
of experience should be intensively cultivated. Nearly all of them
aroused controversy, and when a number of them were adapted
for the theatre the initial controversies were repeated all over again.
They sold in the hundreds of thousands: the great heaps of the
latest novel in the bookseller's window on publication day were a
challenge to the public, which eagerly responded by carrying them
all away and asking for more. No wonder Goncourt and lesser
writers despaired. Realism, or naturalism as he preferred to call
it, seemed to be the exclusive property of Emile Zola. As the years
went on he was widely and gratifyingly imitated abroad; books
were dedicated to him; his opinion on foreign works was solicited.
For good or ill he stood as the representative of the new movement.
The abuse he received is the measure of the resistance with which
realism was met; the praise and understanding ultimately accorded
him are a measure of its acceptance.

The initial impact of realism had spent itself in France before
the end of the century. "The Manifesto of Five against Zola" in
1887 and Jules Huret's *Enquête* in 1891 indicate the turn of the
tide. Huysmans broke away from the Médan group; Bourget's *Le
Disciple* (1889) attacked the moral premises and influences of
realism. Actually 1893 is often taken as a terminal date: Maupassant and Taine died in that year; the Rougon-Macquart was
completed; and Zola's archenemy Brunetière defeated him in a
contest for a place in the French Academy. The following years
were dominated by the bitterness of the Dreyfus case, in which
Zola intervened with his usual effective flair, but the literary atmosphere had radically changed. After Zola's death in 1902 it

was almost as though there were a tacit conspiracy of silence. Yet, however much in eclipse, realism was not a dead issue in France. The influence of Zola is manifest in the work of Jules Romains and Martin du Gard. The continuing vitality of general realist purposes is attested by the initiators of the populist movement around 1930, and in recent years we have seen what purports to be a neo-realism practiced and upheld by Nathalie Sarraute and Alain Robbe-Grillet.

Russian realism, powerful and permanent as was its example, never excited an equal amount of controversy: there were too many pressing moral and social questions to debate in Russia. It is important to note, however, that Belinsky as early as 1835 discerned the central philosophical core of realism (and used this term well in advance of western writers) and that it was his activity in the 1840's that prepared the way for the important writers who followed; he it was who recognized the worth of Dostoevsky's first novel, *Poor Folk*, and helped to bring about its publication in 1846. Chernishevsky's thesis, though its influence was confined to Russia, was of the highest importance in its implications for realistic art. Not only did he turn his back on idealistic philosophy, but he attempted to find out what the effect of his metaphysical position would be on aesthetics. He attacked the idea that art is superior to reality, considering such an attitude a dilettantish pose. Since the first function of art is the reproduction of nature, its subject matter is therefore life, not beauty, its purpose to bring understanding rather than some sort of vague aesthetic shiver.

This thesis opens the door to and portends the long line of important Russian novels of the second half of the nineteenth century which were concerned about life in its manifold variety and seemed to be oblivious of stylistic or formal questions. Not only were Tolstoy and Turgenev writing in the 1850's, but there were such important works as A. F. Pisemsky's *A Thousand Souls* (1858), a vivid documentary of country life, and Ivan Goncharov's *Oblomov* (1859). There followed the three-fold rivalry of Turgenev, Tolstoy, and Dostoevsky, which made the period from 1860 to Dostoevsky's death in 1880 and the virtual retirement of the other two novelists from literature one of the richest in the literary history of any nation. These writers were in turn followed by

Modern Realism as a Literary Movement

Chekhov and Gorky, who, primarily through the short story and the play, filled out the social panorama by giving attention to marginal and rootless members of the community.

The Russians, it must be repeated, were not theorists; it was their powerful example, rather than Dostoevsky's casual remarks in *The Diary of a Writer* or Tolstoy's moralistic dicta in *What Is Art?* that determined the course of their own literature, which in the 1880's began to have repercussions abroad. It was a French diplomat, Vicomte de Vogüé, author of *Le Roman russe* (1886), who gave his contemporaries a sense of the richness of the new Russian literature. French translations multiplied overnight (the French source accounts for the long-continuing mis-transliterations of Russian names in English); the high seriousness of these works gave heart to the opponents of Zolaesque naturalism, although the die-hard opponents of any literary change found elements of crudeness and morbidity in Tolstoy and Dostoevsky against which they could continue their invective.

Another independent strain of realism was that which appeared in Scandinavia with Ibsen and Björnson as the acknowledged leaders and Georg Brandes as their official apologist. Much of the effort of these men and others like them was to let in some fresh air to the smug, hypocritical, narrow-minded Scandinavian scene (Ibsen's *Pillars of Society* begins with precisely this symbolism), and they found themselves continually engaged in battles with oppressive authority. Brandes indeed inaugurated his series of lectures on the main currents of nineteenth-century literature at the University of Copenhagen in 1871 with the avowed purpose of unsettling the conservatives, his thesis being that "A literature in our day shows it is alive by taking up problems for discussion." Ibsen was more or less run out of Norway and lived in Germany for many years, where he wrote his most truly realistic plays, *Pillars of Society, A Doll's House, Ghosts*, and *An Enemy of the People*, from 1877 to 1882. Because his work met with such resistance at home, he became a sort of symbol of realism in the theatre; the new theatres of the day automatically presented his works at their openings as a clear statement of literary independence.

German participation in the realistic movement leaves much to be desired so far as both critical discussion and the works produced are concerned. Though there were during the middle of the century works of a certain importance in terms of their representation of everyday life, there was also a tendency toward what is called "poetic realism," which inclines toward the sentimental. What the Germans of the 1880's found in the way of inspiration in Ibsen and Zola was, in fact, less a reading of experience that attracted them than a bludgeon with which to batter down the moribund conventions of German writing in the hope that it might be brought back into the mainstream of European literature. Nowhere else is the impulse toward realism so obviously an effort on the part of *les jeunes* to make themselves heard and known, and nowhere else were they so little successful.

Two important periodicals were founded during the 1880's, notably M. G. Conrad's *Die Gesellschaft* in Munich, and in Berlin, after the inauguration of the Freie Bühne, a new theatre, a periodical of the same name, which later became the *Neue Rundschau*. Conrad's journal had the purpose of defending Zola (Conrad was the only one of the group of new German writers who had met the Frenchman, and he made the most of it) and in general of stirring up interest in the new literature. The first volume contained several discussions of Zola of no particular critical insight, such as "Ist Zola unmoralisch?" and "Zolaismus," as well as a discussion of Zola and Daudet written by Conrad himself.

The books of criticism which appeared during these years promised much and delivered little. Carl Bleibtreu's *Revolution der Literatur* (1886) (which was dedicated to Conrad) calls the roll of obscure contemporary writers in the new vein, makes some perfunctory efforts at classification, but ends by plumping for a realism which will seek to penetrate the ideal. The conclusion is that the future of literature belongs to realism alone, but not to pseudo-realism: "For whoever seeks this in it, to set down man's being as a clear outcome of animal instinct, as the mechanical logic of crass egoism—is guilty of the same sin of untruthfulness as the unfeeling server-up of soothing-syrup and the phrase-mongering 'Idealist.' Man is neither a machine nor an animal; rather he has

Modern Realism as a Literary Movement

a mysterious fatal being in which aspiration of the soul and physical instincts are at odds until death and to the death."[2]

Still another pretentious general work is *Die Naturwissenschäftlichen Grundlagen der Poesie: Prolegomena zu einer realistischen Aesthetik* by Wilhelm Bölsche (1887). It supports realism on the general grounds that it will help the mass of mankind to learn to see better, will enable poetry to resume its role of leader to the light, and will help to make men whole. Bölsche thought that Darwinian theory ought to have the same relation to modern literature as that held by mythology in ancient literature. Arno Holz, who belonged to the same Berlin group as Bölsche, produced a number of works including *Die Kunst ihr Wesen und ihre Gesetze* (1891), an article on "Zola als Theoretiker" in *Freie Bühne* in 1890, and "Une Lettre Ouverte à M. Emile Zola," intended to precede a book with the formidable title of *Soziologie der Kunst*, which he later thanks God he never wrote. The article makes the same distinction as that made by the Hart brothers, that Zola as theoretician left much to be desired and indeed wandered close to the boundaries of nonsense. The letter takes issue with Zola on other grounds and is essentially a youthful challenge: "You have made yourself the defender of reality. Very well, I also constitute myself a defender, not against some old romantic, but against you." What is characteristic in varying degree of all these works is that they indicate at most a temporary infatuation with realism without showing much understanding of its full implications, for they are still dominated by the concept of the ideal and contort themselves in the effort to find a way to reintroduce it into some sort of realistic format. The essential problem of the German critics was that they wanted old wine of slightly headier quality in old bottles with new labels.

The most vigorous aspect of German realism was its impact on the theatre. Ibsen's *Ghosts* was first produced in Berlin in 1887 and was chosen for the inaugural performance at the Freie Bühne on September 29, 1889. It was at that theatre on October 20, 1889, that Hauptmann's *Before Sunrise* received its première. Naturalism may be said to have arrived in Germany with this

[2] Bleibtreu, Carl, *Revolution der Literatur*, p. 86; Leipzig, Verlag von Wilhelm Friedrich, 1886.

13

work, but with the exception of *The Weavers* (1892) Hauptmann cannot be said to have continued in this vein, nor did he have important successors.

Parallel with these developments of derivative cast in Germany were those taking place almost exclusively under French influence in Italy, Spain, and Portugal. As early as 1870 Eça de Queiroz, the most important Portuguese realist, whose *O primo Basilio* is the Portuguese *Madame Bovary*, made a speech on realism in Lisbon. In Spain, where there was a strong tendency toward *costumbrismo*—local colorism—the works of Emilia Pardo Bazán, Leopoldo Alas, and Palacio Valdés were considered to participate in the new movement, and were soon powerfully seconded by the novels of Benito Pérez Galdós. In Italy a native brand of realism called *verismo* developed by Luigi Capuana and Giovanni Verga during the 1880's was of considerable importance. In addition to two novels, *I Malavoglia* (*The House by the Medlar Tree*) and *Mastro Don Gesualdo*, the latter also wrote short sketches of Sicilian life collected as *Vita dei Campi* and *Novelle Rusticane*, which are surprisingly undated even today. In a preface to the story, "Gramigna's Mistress," Verga shows his affiliation with the realistic movement when he speaks of this tale as being a "human document" and says it is something he has "picked up along the paths in the countryside, with nearly the same simple and picturesque words that characterize popular narration"; it is "naked and unadulterated fact" undistorted by the lens of the writer. He aspires to a quality of art "When in the novel the affinity and cohesion of its every part will be so complete that the creative process will remain a mystery, like the development of human passions, and the harmony of its elements will be so perfect, the sincerity of its reality so evident, its manner of and its reason for existing so necessary, that the hand of the artist will remain absolutely invisible, then it will have the imprint of an actual happening; the work of art will seem *to have made itself*, to have matured and come into being spontaneously, like a fact of nature, without retaining any point of contact with its author, any stain of original sin."[3]

[3] Verga, Giovanni, "To Salvatore Farina," prefatory letter to "Gramigna's Mistress," *The She-Wolf and Other Stories*, pp. 86-88; University of California Press, 1958. The translation is by Giovanni Cecchetti.

14

Modern Realism as a Literary Movement

All of the writing thus far mentioned converged on the English-speaking world at the same time during the 1880's. Readers must have been stunned by the sudden avalanche of new names with which they were urged to be familiar. It is not surprising that they were wary of conspiracy, especially when the new writers almost always shocked their staid and decorous expectations. The innocent Anglo-Saxons had all at once to reckon not only with Flaubert, Zola, and Maupassant, but with the Russians, the Scandinavians, the Spaniards, and the Italians. The immediate reaction of the British was to withdraw behind their own innocuous brand of realism, punishing Frank Vizetelly for publishing Zola in translation and keeping the relatively inoffensive Ibsen beyond the pale until time and George Bernard Shaw came to his rescue.

In spite of this opposition, which is well represented in this volume, we must bear in mind that there was a strong indigenous tendency toward realism among English writers in the last half of the nineteenth century, only, as David-Sauvageot has wittily observed, it was a narrow, sectarian realism, always watched over by the clergy. Up to a certain point the English writers had exploited the ordinary, the down-to-earth, rather more consistently than had their continental colleagues. The result was that they furnished considerable encouragement abroad without themselves articulating very much that could be construed as a definite revolutionary or renovating realism at home. On the continent there was significant admiration for the realistic achievements of Dickens and Eliot, even though the one was not a realist and the other confined her observations of life within a fairly narrow spectrum of experience. Innovating doctrine and practice had then, in effect, to be imported. Surprisingly enough, Flaubert was not seriously discussed in England until 1878; Zola's works made their way slowly; the Russians were unknown. The first breach—if we except the case of Olive Schreiner, who was herself a foreigner—was attempted by George Moore, who came back from his sojourn in Paris determined to make English literature over in the new model. It cannot be said that he succeeded, though his novel *A Mummer's Wife* (1885) was a respectable effort, and two later works, *Esther Waters* (1894) and *Evelyn Innes* (1898), are more than respectable. Of particular interest historically is his satiric tract, *Literature at Nurse or Circulating Morals* (1885), which in its attack on the philistine morality (and monopoly) of the circulating libraries gives some idea of the impregnability of the fortress of British decorum and conventionality. In the midst of this controversy a critic on the staff of *Lippincott's Magazine* in the United States made a discriminating statement about the situation in both countries in 1887: "The quarrel between the romanticists and the realists is sufficiently amusing in view of the fact that realism in the Anglo-Saxon literature of the present time is simply impossible. No novelist dares to paint life as it really is."

Whether for that reason or because the impact of the new writing was cushioned by the presence of the traditional brand of English realism, there are no English realistic works as imposing as those of French, Russian, or American writers. The pseudonymous Mark Rutherford with his *The Autobiography of Mark Rutherford* and *The Revolution in Tanner's Lane*, the early Somerset Maugham of *Liza of Lambeth* and *Of Human Bondage*, and the Arnold Bennett of the Five Towns novels and stories are about all England has to offer at the end of the century. Indeed, the battle was never fully fought out in England, so that in recent years we have had the anachronistic experience of reliving the battles of the nineteenth century when resentment has arisen over the forthrightness or brutality of such American imports as *From Here to Eternity* and *The Naked and the Dead*.

In the United States the soil was more favorable to the new growth, though the plant had been less carefully tended. The harsh conditions of pioneer life, the breath-taking scale of the physical milieu, the violence of the Civil War, and in the latter part of the century the cruel and impersonal processes of industrialization and the melting pot were new experiences which were not easily bent to conventional formulas and demanded a new reading of life, though, in all honesty, this was not often given. There is much excellent observation in early American fiction—in Cooper, for example—but it is necessarily submerged in a romantic framework. As has been already indicated, Whitman's *Leaves of Grass* in its insistence on the sensuous texture of everyday life was certainly realist in primary impulse, though the increasing idealism of Whitman's thought is like an undertow that pulls it back. As

Modern Realism as a Literary Movement

early as 1862 Rebecca Harding Davis begins her novel *Margaret Howth: A Story of To-Day* with the words: "Let me tell you a story of To-Day,—very homely and narrow in its scope and aim," adding a few pages later: "I want you to go down into this common, every-day drudgery, and consider if there might not be in it also a great warfare." This sense of new subjects that demanded a new method of treatment was to gather force during the succeeding decades but failed of direction because of lack of a model. It was the local colorists, who sought to write true in terms of local scene, who made the first real advance toward realism in this country. Theirs was primarily an act of provincial piety and often broke down in sentimentality, but they did lead the way to observation of the scene immediately around them; they did seek to set down vernacular and sectional modes of speech. To a degree they recognized the inconveniently lawless relation of the sexes, and as the years went on they became more and more uncomfortable over the way economic misery and degradation contradicted the rosy assurances of progress made by official spokesmen.

Into this scene came William Dean Howells, quondam editor of the *Atlantic Monthly* but by the breadth of his experience no regionalist, to be the eloquent champion of the new writing. His removal from Boston to New York in the mid 1880's, which obliquely provided the material for his novel *A Hazard of New Fortunes*, was in itself a recognition that the image of America was broader, less gentle, and more impersonal than what his eyes habitually saw in New England. His early novels had been essentially trivial in their depiction of social situations; his later works, though inadequate, at least encouraged others in the recognition that it was the harsh, teeming, industrialized, urban America which must be their theme and the object of their scrutiny. Moreover, being a man of languages and catholic tastes, he was among the first to discover and value justly the host of European writers who were coming to the fore in the 1880's. For over ten years he used his literary column in *Harper's Magazine* as a pulpit from which to preach the virtues of realism and the merits of the new European writers, drawing upon himself the outrage of conservatives and chauvinists alike. Since he preferred what he called the smiling aspects of life, he favored Tolstoy over Dostoevsky, and Galdós

17

and Pardo Bazán over Zola, but it was he who introduced Verga to American readers, and he championed the right of native novelists to set down what they saw even when it did not accord with his own vision. What his novels failed to provide in the way of forceful example, he more than made up for through his respectability and enthusiasm.

The culmination of the first push toward realism in this country was the abortive publication of Dreiser's *Sister Carrie* in 1900. Moral scruples led the publisher to withdraw the book after review copies had been sent out, and it looked as though honest writing in America had received its quietus, particularly since there was a strong counter-movement in the direction of romanticism as exemplified by historical novels such as Winston Churchill's *The Crisis* and Thomas Dixon's *The Clansman*. Dreiser retired for ten years to the editorship of women's magazines—at the very heart of enemy country—cannily saved money, preserved his aesthetic independence, and so lived to fight another day. He once commented on the situation of the writer at the beginning of his career that "You couldn't write about life as it was; you had to write about it as somebody else thought it was—the ministers and farmers and dullards of the home." His later works and the ultimately revived *Sister Carrie* gradually imposed themselves upon the public by their massive honesty, though there was one more skirmish with the law and Mrs. Grundy over *The "Genius"* in 1915, as a result of which he acquired the formidable support of H. L. Mencken. Whether Dreiser won the battle for American realism, or it was won for him and others by the rapid social changes following the first World War, the dam broke about 1920 with the publication of Anderson's *Winesburg, Ohio*, Lewis's *Main Street*, and Dos Passos's *Three Soldiers*.

Realism came to the United States when it had already spent its force abroad, came at exactly the time when Proust, Mann, Joyce, and Kafka were demonstrating that there were other and more subtly revealing ways of writing. Thus realism in the twentieth century is largely a phenomenon of the literary history of the United States, and to lesser degree of other countries which for various reasons had been cut off from its renovating influence. For reasons that are not altogether clear, American critics have preferred the term "naturalism" and have tended to make their rather sweeping judgments in terms of this word. Perhaps the source of this error comes from a tendency to lean upon Frank Norris and Jack London as archetypal examples and to ignore their differences from Dreiser. The mistake seems to arise from the obvious derivation of Norris from Zola. Though the former denied it, it is easy to demonstrate that his *McTeague* is *L'Assommoir* set in San Francisco and that his *The Octopus* is *Germinal* transferred to the San Joaquin Valley. But there the resemblance ends. What fired Norris's emulation was the non-realistic elements in Zola—the symbols, the gigantism, the tricky effects. There is no evidence at all that he ever undertook to write true; indeed a reading of his jejune criticism in *The Responsibilities of the Novelist* shows that he had little understanding of or sympathy with realist goals and practices.

By coming late to the scene American realism actually escaped some of the mechanical rigor of naturalist determinism. For one thing, the milieu described was more expansive than that of the European writers; the pattern of social causality was less tight because the society was more fluid. It was not possible to show men ground down into the earth with the same inevitability. It is true that lives are destroyed by inner corruption and are all subject to inescapable physical decay and death, facts which no realist dare overlook, but there is rarely the rigorous causality of the naturalist.

When our writers have turned to a doctrine as tight-meshed as naturalism they have almost always convicted themselves of untruth. The best examples are the so-called proletarian novelists of the 1920's and 1930's. They want man to be the hapless victim of circumstance; they want him to be destroyed, and, what is more, destroyed by specific hostile forces, those of capitalism. Thus they contrive a demonstration that becomes ridiculous in its excess, hysterical in its insistence that there is no way out. Or American writers go in the direction of caricature, as did Sinclair Lewis and Erskine Caldwell, to cite two obvious examples. These writers create monsters, ludicrous monsters, who like Thurber's unicorn inhabit one's familiar garden, but are nonetheless monsters for all that. One other way these would-be naturalists are likely to go astray is in trying to introduce too much meaning into their works, to achieve symbolic significance. Richard Wright did this in *Native Son*; James Jones did it in *From Here to Eternity*, not necessarily to the detriment of the novels named but certainly to their detriment as simple realistic statements.

Of particular importance in twentieth-century developments has been the resurgence of realism in countries long subject to repressive intellectual and artistic forces. Italy after more than twenty years of fascism manifested its desire for truth in a brilliant literary and cinematic revival, which in turn has been influential elsewhere. The one important practitioner of realism in Italy between the wars, Ignazio Silone, whose *Fontamara* is one of the classics of the mode, has turned to a less reportorial way of writing, leaving the field to a younger generation of whom Alberto Moravia is the best known. In two respects at least this writer holds the classic realist position: he believes that "the realistic novel should describe anything if it is necessary without any ideological or moral limitations," and he accepts the charge of pessimism, "For to be a man is automatically not to be happy. That is the human situation."[4] Already, however, there are signs that Italian realism is being transformed into something more intricate—something post-realistic—in the work of Moravia himself or in such a significant film as *La Dolce Vita*.

In Spain there is the same straining toward a true report, whatever the official mask of complacency and optimism. Camilo Cela declares that his novel *La Colmena* (*The Hive*) "is nothing but a pale reflection, a humble shadow, of the harsh, intimate, and painful reality of everyday life." Aware of social evil, he is also aware that it "cannot be fought with the poultices of conformity and the plasters of rhetoric and poetry." Asserting that his book "aspires to be no more . . . than a slice of life told step by step, without reticence, without extraneous tragedies, without charity, as life rambles on . . ." he reiterates his belief that this method is the only possible one for the novel today.[5]

One of the concluding selections in this collection is a discussion

[4] See *Saturday Review* 44: pp. 18-19, October 28, 1961, for an interview with Alberto Moravia by Jerry Bauer.

[5] Cela, Camilo José, "Nota a la primera edición," *La Colmena*, Buenos Aires, 1951.

Modern Realism as a Literary Movement

of Portuguese neo-realism by Jaime Brasil. It is an important document because it attests to the vitality of realism in a culture which has been largely deprived of nourishment for three generations. Part of the literary reinvigoration of which the author writes came from Brazilian example, part of it from the amazingly strong residual influence of Zola, and part from the inevitable desire of free men, or men seeking to be free, to look at life, their own lives. The development of neo-realism in Portugal has been facilitated by the fact that the native tradition did include one realist of stature, Eça de Queiroz, but the point of the article is rather that when there is a spontaneous leap toward meaningful literary expression in the twentieth century it must, in default of vital tradition, root in the daily life of its readers, and that prose fiction is still the major vehicle for such exploratory writing.

The most important development of realism in the twentieth century, because it is a major theoretical formulation, is actually anti-realistic and is only cursorily represented in this collection. I refer to socialist realism, a Marxist deviation which has had wide influence outside of Russia. All the Marxist leaders from Engels on down fancied themselves as literary critics, and it is their statements reformulated in official dicta of party and party leaders that constitute a vast though unvaried body of critical statement in communist countries today.

A distinction must first be made between critical realism and socialist realism, that is, between the traditional nineteenth-century variety and that which is officially practiced in Russia today. Critical realism is to be found in Balzac, in Flaubert, in Turgenev and Tolstoy, in fact everywhere that there has been an effort to depict the workings of bourgeois society and to show its ugly and repressive aspects. Such writing, naturally, is a relic of a past when men knew no better and their minds had not yet been freed of chains. Its role is that of precursor, of partial revelation, but it is necessarily incomplete.

Socialist realism, on the other hand, seeks "the truthful, historically concrete representation of reality in its revolutionary development." It is not enough to represent life as it is; it is necessary to show where it is going, and that is toward the inevitable future of the communist society. In short, what is introduced here is a quasi-philosophical, quasi-religious teleological doctrine—the kind of concept that was among the first to be repudiated by the traditional realists of the nineteenth century because of its *a priori* nature. A convenient analogue would be a notion of Christian realism, which would undertake to depict everyday life in terms of a dogmatically asserted "divine, far-off event toward which the whole creation moves." Or to put it in socio-political terms, a depiction based on the manifest destiny of nation or race.

What happens in a situation of this kind is that at one stroke the doors which realism opened to experience in all its variety and contradiction are closed again. Socialist realism can show only that which constitutes, forwards, or impedes this telic motion. It imposes a system of values on the world of the novel or play and determines in advance the position to be taken with respect to human beings and events in this fictive world. It would not be enough, for example, to depict the defeat of Russia by Germany in the First World War as the result of the complex of causes assigned by historians to that event. The defeat must be seen in terms of its instrumentality in effecting the Russian Revolution. Such writing cannot show a man brought up under the old regime struggling for some sort of *modus vivendi* with the new, heroically or desperately surrendering bit by bit his established patterns of thought and action. Rather if such a relict is to be shown at all, he must be presented in the process of conversion, purging himself of error and recognizing the beneficent course of history. It is necessary to have a "positive hero," that is, a construct who represents the ideal, not a transcript of slow-motion actuality, which is all too slow and inept in translating itself into telic motion.

In 1959 there was smuggled out of Russia a little book entitled *On Socialist Realism*, which sharply substantiates the criticism just made. The pseudonymous author, Abram Tertz, points out that socialist realism "starts from an ideal image to which it adapts the living reality." This constitutes showing what should be instead of what is and turns it into a form of romanticism—"revolutionary romanticism" or "active romanticism," as Gorky called it. This direction of soviet literature is not necessarily bad, but it leads the writer into an inherent contradiction of means and aims, since "A socialist, i.e., a purposeful, a religious, art cannot be pro-

Modern Realism as a Literary Movement

duced with the literary method of the nineteenth century called realism." A really faithful representation of life cannot be achieved within a dialectic based on teleological concepts. Thus if socialist realism is to rise to the heights of great world literature, it must give up realism, cease to model itself after, or aspire to the greatness of, nineteenth-century Russian masterpieces, and instead strike out in the direction of the epic and the mythic which is implicit in its premises.[6]

What is interesting about this denunciation is not merely that it has emanated from within Russia, but that obliquely it gives evidence of the powerful control which true realism is able to exercise in the present day. Tertz's critique must certainly be set alongside that of Jean-Paul Sartre, who suggests that the fault of the old realism was its analytical approach to experience, when what is needed—and here his language becomes more than vaguely Marxist—is a new synthetic approach. It is possible that Tertz has pricked that bubble too.

It is the purpose of this collection to enable the reader to reach his own conclusions about what the realists were trying to do, about what they considered significantly new in their writing. Thus to analyze these critical documents in detail would be to defeat the purpose of the book. However, since realism is no more a single thing than was romanticism, it will be useful to indicate the general lines of innovation which it pursued. In retrospect it is possible to discern three major points of emphasis which have been present with fair consistency since the beginning of the movement.

There is first of all realism in the choice of subject matter, the insistence, as Flaubert put it, that "Yvetot donc vaut Constantinople," that the ordinary and near at hand are as suitable for literary treatment as the exotic and remote. Champfleury summed this idea up as "the choice of modern and popular subjects," and the Goncourt brothers in their preface-manifesto to *Germinie Lacerteux* asked whether in the nineteenth century "the people ought to remain under literary interdict and authorial disdain." George Eliot expressed a predilection for the homeliness of Dutch genre

[6] Tertz, Abram, *On Socialist Realism*, New York, Pantheon Books, 1960.

painting, and in general this taste for the humble and the ordinary has been one of the hallmarks of the movement.

The element of reaction against romantic prettifying cannot be overstated. It is an object of irritation for all the early writers in this mode and is well summed up by Edmond Duranty in the inaugural article of his journal *Réalisme* in 1856:

"The litterateurs and versifiers have spoiled artists and the calling of art by their insistence on upholding the noble genre, on acclaiming the noble genre, on shouting that we must poetize and idealize—words which artists have understood as meaning to 'dress up'; that is, never to tolerate nature but to take everything back to an archaic type which has been preciously observed in museums and has been carried to perfection by Annibal Carrache."

The first step, therefore, was that the material used be the product of observation; from a strictly realist point of view an invented proletarian would be as nauseous as an invented fairy princess. This implies an almost inescapable limitation on the range of the individual realist, since he cannot have access to an infinite range of material. Even an indefatigable note-taker like Zola ran into difficulties in this respect, for his accounts of life at the higher social and economic levels do not have the stamp of authenticity that his other works do. It was evidently to Zola that Edmond de Goncourt was referring in his preface to *Les Frères Zemganno* when he stated that the realist begins "with the dregs of nature because the woman and man of the people, nearer to nature and the savage state, are simple uncomplicated creatures, whereas the Parisians of society, those overly-civilized beings whose sharp originality consists entirely of nuances, halftones, and all those impalpable nothings similar to the coquettish and neutral nothings out of which women create distinguished grooming, demand years for one to pierce to them, to know them, to *seize hold* of them—and even the novelist of highest genius, you may be sure, will never apprehend these drawing-room people from the reports of his friends who go into society to bring him back information."

Since most realists have had a middle-class background, it has been natural for them to exploit that material, and in the beginning, when the movement was in reaction against romanticism, such material had the advantage of novelty as well. One need only

Modern Realism as a Literary Movement

mention Flaubert, Howells, Galdós, Bennett, and Farrell to see how effectively such a background has been presented. However, there was also and early a tendency to go downward in the social scale, for reasons such as that stated by Goncourt above. Realism seems to contain a kind of implicit Benthamite assumption that the life lived by the greatest number is somehow the most real. Maupassant said that the writer "should always incline to the mean, to the general rule." The question of where to find it has been variously answered. Emphasis on the lowest common denominator of human experience was in fact what gave Zola his dominant position and made the final breach in the concept of literary decorum.

There was almost immediate protest that the realists were violating their own principles by concentration on "the lower elements," to which Edmond de Goncourt, Maupassant, and Zola all felt constrained to reply. Such an answer is necessarily somewhat ambiguous: of course realism should cover the whole range of human experience, should reach to the drawing room as well as the stable, but at the same time most human behavior takes place at a level rather lower than that admitted by sterile principles of decorum. Where life inhabits there the realist must go if honest observation leads him there. Gorky reports a significant conversation with Tolstoy on this subject in which the latter said to him:

"You've seen many drunken women? Many—my God! You must not write about them, you mustn't."

"Why?"

"Why?" Tolstoy repeated, then continued thoughtfully and slowly: "I don't know. It just slipped out . . . it's a shame to write about filth. But why not write about it? Yes, it's necessary to write about everything, everything."[7]

Reluctantly or eagerly, this has been the attitude of most of the writers who were involved in the realistic movement, until today we have, in fact, largely fulfilled Taine's description (of naturalism specifically) as "a grand inquiry about man, about all situations, all flowerings, all degenerations of human nature."

This tendency of the realists to drift downward in the social or cultural scale arises, then, from their effort to depict the real

[7] Gorky, Maxim, *Reminiscences of Tolstoy, Chekhov, and Andreyev*, p. 54; New York, The Viking Press, 1959.

average, the common, essentially animal man—in terms of latter-day enlightenment, the being largely dominated by the *id*. Contrary to the usual assumption, this is less a labor of love for dirt than it is a response to a sense of duty, a desire to keep the record straight, a sense of irritation and impatience over impediments to understanding and truth. As mentioned earlier, the first step was to shatter the image which the bourgeois reflected to himself, and Flaubert gave us Homais, not to mention Bouvard and Pécuchet. Convinced that the physiological man is the fundamental being, writers next began to linger over the more indelicate phases of human behavior. Sexuality was fully explored and reported. In the fullness of time we could not fail to achieve Leopold Bloom, as well as some all too unrepresentative cases best left to clinical study. This effort can be seen to have moved in two directions: it has sought to depict the average man in reference to a whole society and has therefore taken us to a lower social level and introduced us to people whom we would not like to see in our drawing rooms, as the Victorian critics put it; it has also attempted to portray the average sensual man at any social level, freed from cosmetic touches of decorum and good manners.

Finally, there has been a vigorous exploration of what Dostoevsky called the "underground man." This might be termed a vertical extension of realism as distinguished from the horizontal extension which first characterized the movement. Dostoevsky began it, Freud brought clinical verification, and readers generally, after a first resistance, have been able and eager to add their own verification through introspection. Yet it remains something of an anomaly. Necessary to the complete representation which is the realist's goal, it is nonetheless essentially subjective, incapable of direct documentation, and verifiable in the last analysis only in the consciousness of the reader. However, it need not be invented, and it does add a needed dimension to the representation of total reality.

As we look back over the whole course of the realistic movement, we realize that immediately vast areas of subject matter and of social and economic situation were opened up which had previously been closed to inspection. Not merely were starkly simple milieux shown, but there was an examination of social situations

Modern Realism as a Literary Movement

and processes, such as strikes and wage slavery. Perhaps it was too easy to fall into the convention of depicting the poor servant girl or the girl of the streets, as many of the early writers did, but many other avenues were quickly opened up as Zola methodically charted the life of France under the Second Empire. Urban slum, mine, department store, central market, the stock exchange, and finally the army were instances of materials which had not before been touched. If other writers staked a claim to still other areas from a sense of challenge rather than literary inspiration and risked engaging in a kind of romantic exoticism of the commonplace, there was nonetheless a net gain, for it is in this literary freedom of the city that the strength of twentieth-century literature lies.

Alfred Kazin writes of the great spate of American realism which has been concerned "with the sights and sounds of common life, with transcriptions of the average experience, with reproducing, sometimes parodying, but always participating in, the whole cluster of experiences which make up the native culture."[8] There is no visible end to this stream—especially in those countries where cultural independence is being achieved or newly regained. Even if there are no important areas of human activity left to be explored, there are still areas of personal and social experience to be graphically depicted, and, of course, social forms are themselves in continual flux, necessitating new portrayals.

The effort at accuracy in the description of human behavior and human motives, including transcription of vulgar speech, undoubtedly was of primary importance to many in an ancillary effort to free literature once and for all of taboos having to do with four-letter words and sexuality. The shock effect of this kind of writing was very great; it early aroused the antagonism of the critics and of the courts and inevitably led the injudicious to equate realism with the raw and the sensational. No doubt, on balance, it did clear the way for honest, clear-eyed examination of life, but we cannot overlook the fact that it has begotten, left-handedly, a malodorous crew of novels purporting to show life as it is but in fact capitalizing only on sensationalism. Mary McCarthy com-

[8] Kazin, Alfred, *On Native Grounds*, p. 207; New York, Reynal & Hitchcock, 1942.

ments on this tendency in an interesting fashion in her book *On the Contrary*, where she points out that while the realists are committed to depiction of the ordinary man, some of them tend to become interested in him as literary material only when he becomes news, that is, in essentially uncommon situations.

Whatever the evaluation recent literature will ultimately receive, it can be said that it is richer in content, is more immediate in impact, and ranges more widely over human experience than any literature before it. To be sure, we do too often get nothing but jumbled and pedestrian assemblages of data, yet the motive behind this collector's mania is a vital one: belief in fact as a way to truth is fundamental to realistic writing. There are many who still complain that literature based on fact is leaden-winged, that documentation has killed the historical novel in particular, that the function of literature is to show man what he can be, not what he is. They may ultimately prevail, but even at this late date in the twentieth century literature is still intoxicated with exploring the vast territories to which the realists laid claim.

This sweeping observation leads us to the second aspect of the realistic movement, the innovations in technique which are either part of its doctrine or are derived from it. It should be obvious that the exploration of new subject matter demands also the application of a new method; otherwise the new materials will be anything the author wants to make of them—except realistic. It is here that the hard core of the movement is to be found. The foundation stone is the tenet of objectivity, as forcefully enunciated by Flaubert in his letters, though not perfectly practiced by him. The facts in a realistic work should speak for themselves as they do in life. There should be no authorial voice raised in way of commentary or exhortation, no authorial elbow nudging the reader in the ribs. In fact, it is necessary to avoid "all poetic and rhetorical devices for obscuring the main issue," as W. L. Courtney puts it. Let us admit at once that this is an ideal impossible of complete achievement and go on to demonstrate how it has nonetheless had a profound influence on literature for the last century. It means first of all that the writer takes great pains not to allow any personal prejudice or predilection to divert him from presenting things as they are. He keeps asking himself: Is this the way I

Modern Realism as a Literary Movement

see things, or the way I think I should see them, or the way other people expect me to see them? His ambition is the dispassionate approach of the scientist; his delusion, the one manifested by Zola, that he can actually manipulate data to a conclusion as coldly impersonal as that reached in the laboratory. At his best he serves no interest save that of truth; he has no preconceived view of how things should be; he observes and he states. Granting the impossibility of absolute objectivity, the essential thing is that such a principle eschews fancy and intuition, is reluctant to go beyond the facts, and is zealous in pursuit of all the facts.

Immediately artificialities of plot and characterization go out the window. A realistic novel or play is a dipping into the stream of life and is ideally all middle, without beginning or end. It often quite literally plunges *in medias res* and worries very little about filling in the background. It avoids as the plague—or should avoid —the neat denouement in which everything is tied up in a tinsel Christmas package. Characters appear and disappear without biographical sketch or obituary notice; while they are before us, we learn of them through their words and acts (or through unstructured interior monologue); when they have left the scene those same words and acts should be enough for us to understand them and their fate. The early realists were properly wary of coincidence because of the absurd contrivances of the romantic novelists or the constructors of the well-made play. More recent writers have come to use coincidence as one of the many incalculables of life but without making it crucial to the events depicted. We do not object, for example, when Dreiser permits Sister Carrie to run into Drouet a second time: "as well him as another," we are bound to say.

This slice-of-life approach spells the death of the hero as he has traditionally been presented. The hero is by definition heightened, that is, distorted, for effect. He is a center of good or evil force demanding our identification to an intense degree. But the power or exemplary quality of the realistic novel rests on its typicality. If a single life is presented—and how many realistic works might be given Maupassant's title *Une Vie*—it must be characteristic in its uneventfulness, its mediocrity. In general two lives cannot be used, since this device almost automatically leads to contrast, to setting up an opposition of good and bad, successful and unsuccessful, fertile and sterile. (Yet a diptych is not altogether impossible, as is shown by Moravia's *Two Adolescents*, in which separate stories reinforce each other in a single volume.) What many of the substantial realists have chosen is a kind of spectrum, made up of three lives or more, in which there is no single protagonist and in which no outcome of a life is necessarily more important or better than another. Because Flaubert exhibited three lives in *Madame Bovary*, Tolstoy three young men in *War and Peace*, Dostoevsky three brothers in *The Brothers Karamazov*, Dos Passos three draftees in *Three Soldiers*, the number three has come to have the tyrannical force of a convention and should no doubt be abandoned. The best slice of life, certainly, is achieved with a kind of kaleidoscopic technique, where multitudes, often anonymous, troop across the pages in no fixed pattern. John Dos Passos and Jules Romains have used this effectively in their monster-works, as did James Gould Cozzens in *Guard of Honor* and Theodor Plevier in *Stalingrad*.

The ability to handle crowds has become a kind of artistic touchstone for the realist's skill. Stendhal had suggested the way in his description of the Battle of Waterloo, where Fabrice is inconspicuous against the huge, impersonal landscape of war. Tolstoy and Zola gave even more impressive examples of this, as did Jules Romains in *Men of Good Will*, perhaps the most memorable sections of which are those showing Paris as an entity. It is hardly necessary to observe that the depersonalization brought about by war and urban life, two of the favorite realist subjects, demands this crowd technique.

As a result of their reaction against sentimentality and gigantism in character presentation, the early realists held rigorously to an external view. It was the actions of men that were shown against a background of other men and things. Thoughts and feelings were largely ignored as being merely epiphenomenal accompaniments of external events, wherein lay the effective chain of causality. Zola gave lip-service to the force of both heredity and environment in the Rougon-Macquart, but it was in fact the environment which was capable of minute demonstration. Thus the heaping up of physical data became important: the place in which people reside, the processes of their jobs, the minutiae of daily living were set forth

Modern Realism as a Literary Movement

in painstaking detail. Realistic works are characterized by a physical density which is often overwhelming. We cannot be told that life in the slum stultifies, that contemporary suburban existence is straitening and boring; we must experience it in wearisome repetition, as the slum-dwellers or suburbanites themselves do. The charge of bad writing which has traditionally been brought against the realistic writers stems, in part at least, from this. They do not seek to illuminate by a blinding flash; no neat symbolic part stands for a whole. Rather they patiently, methodically bow us down with the sheer weight of data and characteristic situations. One critic has said that "The painful is, in a sense, the very nerve of representation"; realism does not allow us to escape, since its basic strategy is to implicate the reader almost beyond endurance.

This primitive method is most effective when the subject matter is new and is being explored for the first time. Once the reader, however, has recovered from the crushing novelty of slum or mine or army barracks, he cries out that thought and emotion, however ineffective, are part of the texture of experience and that the author who ignores them has abdicated part of his responsibility. Dostoevsky's famous remark: "They call me a psychologist: it is not true. I am merely a realist in the higher sense of the word, that is, I depict all the depths of the human soul" indicates his automatic recoil from external realism, although in his case it was also a matter of a doctrinal position. Tolstoy also departed in significant degree from externality, but it is Chekhov who was the first, and is still perhaps the only, complete realist in his ability to show both the nagging data of everyday existence and the feeling tone which they evoke on the part of those embroiled in them. This is a delicate technique, since the temptation is to resort to blatant irony in the contrast between fact and fancy, actuality and illusion. When well done, the representation is certainly more accurate, because more complex, but it is to be observed that in Chekhov, who is without doctrinal commitment, the mind, however intimately presented, never moves mountains.

The method of authorial self-effacement necessitates reliance on documentation and observation. When the romantics wished to give the accolade, they praised an author's *invention*. The realist ideal lies at the other extreme: to come as close as possible to *ob-*

served experience. Thus Flaubert was enraptured when, the day after writing the speech used in the *comices agricoles* scene, he found a newspaper report of an actual speech in almost identical terms. Thus Meyer Levin in "A Note on Method" appended to his novel *Citizens* suggests that "by using only actual attested events as materials, the writer reduces the possibility of arriving at false conclusions." Thus there have been a number of attempts to use photography and literary text together as a means of getting closer to actuality. The realist, to be sure, does not rely exclusively or even primarily on notebook or documents. He usually has access to a memory richly stored with sharply recollected experience out of which he may draw a portrayal of a whole social complex as overwhelmingly detailed as Joyce's Dublin or Farrell's South Side of Chicago. And many writers, having depleted this natural resource, have nothing new to say and cease to be realists or perhaps to write at all. This is a penalty of the method.

It must be pointed out also that there are many perils to the maintenance of objectivity, even as it has been delimited above. One of the most interesting of these has to do with imagery. Observing man in his animal behavior, Zola in particular was strongly drawn toward the use of reinforcing animal imagery. Such implied comparisons seem innocent at first glance; certainly they are more in harmony with what is being shown than traditional classical simile or garlands of romantic images about love, death, and immortality. But animal imagery easily becomes a system, a constant and pervasive referent which consistently downgrades every thought and act of the human protagonists. This is a violation of objectivity, since it does not permit the reader to see or judge the characters in any but one dimension. The cat which finishes up the carcass of the goose after the great feast in *L'Assommoir* is perhaps permissible, though it is a pointed commentary, but continuous or central animal metaphors are another story. The reduction to absurdity is to be found in many of the novels of Jack London and most egregiously in Norris's *Vandover and the Brute*.

One of the clearest departures from objectivity, from letting the facts speak for themselves, stems from Zola's practice and has thus had a widespread effect in undermining this tenet. This is the use of symbol and myth as a superstructure which forces the

Modern Realism as a Literary Movement

reader to interpret from an *a priori* standpoint. *Germinal* provides the classic example. The novel describes a period of a year in a typical Flanders mining community; an adequate slice of life is presented by means of a family protagonist (as in Steinbeck's *The Grapes of Wrath*). True, the events shown may be considered slightly abnormal in that they have as center the first strike on the part of the miserable miners, but this is allowable since the strike is shown to grow out of the characteristic conditions of their misery. The strike is a failure; at the end many of the miners are dead and the rest are worse off than they were in the beginning. There is nothing to object to in this bare recital of facts. But the novel in addition has two elements of superstructure which cause the reader to look at those facts from a certain perspective. First, there is a lineup of opposing economic forces which is schematic rather than fully developed and clearly presents the main outlines of the class struggle as laid down by Marx. Second, the ancient myth of death and rebirth is given extensive treatment, the mine becoming a ravenous monster to which annual tribute must be paid, the darkness of the winter of suffering being set off against the burgeoning of spring and the promise of new life for the miners. It is a brilliant performance, but of course it has gone beyond realism. Once the facts presented are attached to some pre-existent body of doctrine or belief or myth, they cease to speak for themselves and speak only as directed.

Finally there is a serious psychological barrier to the maintenance of objectivity. The realistic writer attempts to retrace the steps by which he arrived inductively and empirically at certain generalizations; in other words, he seeks to have his reader participate in the same act of discovery, the same "experiment," as he. The difficulty is that once he has arrived at these generalizations, he is tempted to use them functionally without reproducing the process of induction in later works which he writes. He is in danger of manipulating his data to strengthen them, to simplify and clarify them, and to heighten them as literature—which is essentially what the imposition of a body of myth also does. Though originally he served no interest and adhered to no philosophy of social action, the very process of experience through which he has passed may lead him to feel the necessity of such adherence. In that

33

case, when he retraces his steps, he will do so no longer in an inductive fashion but in a spirit of doctrine. A case in point is that of Maxim Gorky, in youth an admirable practitioner of uncommitted realism, in later life an advocate of "active romanticism," that is, a form of writing which would advance the class struggle. It is a delicate matter to determine the precise point at which realism ends and overt social criticism begins. Certainly great social awareness has been aroused through realist depictions, since the malfunctioning of institutions is inescapably a subject for observation. But criticism and objectivity are at odds with each other and cannot be equated.

The third important aspect of realism, as indicated at the beginning of this discussion, is the philosophical, which seems to rest on a contradiction. It has just been reiterated that the basic ideal of the movement was and is rigorous objectivity; in spite of this it was almost impossible not to take a position, at least implicitly, about man and his fate, particularly since the whole climate of thought in which realism flourished was one of scientism. As Arthur McDowall says, "Realism in art undoubtedly refers us back to a physical, existing reality," which is anterior to and independent of the individual mind. It is sceptical of that whole cluster of things which are associated with traditional theistic belief, such as the soul, telic motion, the power of divine grace, and the whole world of miracle, that is, the events which escape the otherwise ineluctable laws of causality. It is this last term which is the key to the realist position: the universe is observably subject to physical causality; man as a part of the physical continuum is also subject to its laws, and any theory which asserts otherwise is wishful thinking. Thus as the whole of human behavior and experience, in individuals and societies, was examined and portrayed with increasing exactness, realistic writers could not escape making statements about man and the condition of mankind which were in violent opposition to those traditionally accepted. It usually happened that these writers declared that life had no meaning, no telic motion, that man was a creature barely risen from the level of animal behavior and driven by forces over which he had little or no control and in which he could discern no goodness or purpose. As indicated earlier, such a view entailed an absolute denial of

Modern Realism as a Literary Movement

the principle of idealism, which continued to flourish during the nineteenth century in spite of the conquests of science. In the simplest possible terms, while there was no specific official position philosophically maintained by realists, it was inescapable that if they looked around them, if they subjected traditional views to the rigorous test of experimental method and observation, they would collide headlong with the concept of the ideal and would be forced to deny it. Their determinism was a direct reflection in literature of the prevalent mechanistic science of the age. It was expressed directly or indirectly by Flaubert and by Tolstoy; it was denied on *a priori* grounds by Dostoevsky and reconfirmed by Chekhov. It was popularized by Zola, whose novels and whose critical essay "The Experimental Novel" remain the basic embodiment and statement of that point of view, which he denominated naturalism. The position is in general one which was well expressed in this country some thirty years ago by Joseph Wood Krutch in *The Modern Temper* (a position, however, from which he has since receded); it is one which neither revealed religion nor private mysticism can tolerate, and even secular authority is suspicious of it as encouraging to idleness and despair.

There is among journeyman critics a considerable confusion as to the relation of the terms *realism* and *naturalism*, which have been deliberately used almost interchangeably in this book. There are those who equate the latter term with "stark realism," that is, any account which is unpleasant, sordid, and dubious about man's higher nature. It has been widely and loosely used to indicate any of the more forthright recent American realistic writers without regard for their precise philosophical position. Certainly usage may do what it will with a word, but in essence and in origin naturalism is no more than an emphatic and explicit philosophical position taken by some realists, showing man caught in a net from which there can be no escape and degenerating under those circumstances; that is, it is pessimistic materialistic determinism. The naturalists have been noisy about this position; they have made it a prime article of doctrine, but what is significant is that in a quiet way realists for three or four generations have shown fair unanimity in their conclusions, or more exactly in their depictions, since they rarely argue about these matters, and those who have revolted against such conclusions have generally been driven into the area of literary practice which we may loosely label symbolism —that is, to the presentation of data as meaning more or other than they ostensibly do mean.

To repeat, then, realism insists on the existence of limitations on the efficacy of human personality and endeavor, and it places the boundaries of those limitations rather close at hand. It sees in the activities of consciousness little more than the efforts of an organism at adaptation, certainly not an effort of the spirit toward identity with already and eternally existent Platonic ideas. If it makes allowance for random and fortuitous elements in an otherwise causally constituted universe, it generally denies them purpose and is likely to see them as agents of misfortune and destruction rather than of well-being.

Of four kinds of reality, broadly conceived: that of absolute essence as asserted by Plato or the Transcendentalist; that which is unique in individual experience and has its essential being out of time, as asserted by Proust; that which inheres in external phenomena; and that which has its being in some kind of relation between external phenomena and perceiving consciousness—of these kinds of reality, realism-naturalism must flatly deny the first two, and resort to them is, automatically, a rejection of literary realism. It is with the third type that realism began, and although it is subject to exhaustion as material for literature, it has been a prime source of force and interest for a hundred years. The fourth type, some sort of psychological realism, seems infinite in its possibilities, but it must not stray too far from the norm of human experience.

It is scarcely surprising that discussions of literary realism have been beset by serious semantic confusion, since reality means all things to all men. Whatever reality is, it seems safe to say that it is not identical with a work of art and is anterior to it. Realism, then, is a formula of art which, conceiving of reality in a certain way, undertakes to present a simulacrum of it on the basis of more or less fixed rules. It is not possible to argue that we have always had realism in art conceived in these terms, though there may have been abortive tendencies toward it. Now that the thing has existed, we shall no doubt continue to have sporadic instances of it in the future, even though the convention is no longer dominant

Modern Realism as a Literary Movement

and has been superseded. It is not without design that this collection opens with Belinsky's almost wistful statement that there are two kinds of art but that the realistic is best, and ends with Heller's subtle discussion of the two areas both called "real" and his question as to how long we can go on having competing realities. Certainly it would add to ease of discourse in the future if whatever happens next should be given a new name and not be tagged by some variant or permutation of the word "realism."

There is no need to draw up a balance sheet for literary realism, since individual evaluations are bound to vary. There is a general feeling that the expansion of subject matter which it has brought has been clear gain and is largely responsible for the vigor of twentieth-century writing, even when it has gone beyond realism in other respects. The doctrine of objectivity, of seeing things as they are without interpretation or personal point of view, without becoming involved or committed, is today received with coolness. Jean-Paul Sartre has made a sharp attack on the French writers of 1871 because they did nothing to defend the communards,[9] and from one point of view or another realism is always under attack for its failure to defend or promote a set of values, a point of view, that is considered of basic importance. This resolves itself into a question of the function and nature of art: is it consolation, anodyne, propaganda, or revelation?

The most important question, however, is not this but whether so-called realistic art is art at all. Clearly this is in part a matter of definition, and the effort of the realists to extend the boundaries of that definition is plain to see in the many statements in this volume. Complete agreement on this matter is probably not possible, but there should be agreement that a work of art is a made thing without immediate utility, the contemplation of which gives pleasure which is somehow different from the pleasure of the senses. At this point there arises the uncomfortable question as to whether the pleasure from contemplation of nature is not analogous, but even if it is, the realist should not take the position that Chernishevsky seems to take in suggesting that realistic art should somehow seek to reproduce nature in its entirety. And if we wish to

---

[9] Sartre, Jean-Paul, "Présentation des Temps Modernes," *Situations, II,* p. 13; Paris, Gallimard, 1948: "I hold Flaubert and Goncourt responsible for the repression that followed the Commune because they did not write a line to prevent it."

pursue the "I am a camera" metaphor, we must remember that even what the camera presents as art is a made thing in the sense that it is composed or selected—which is certainly verified the moment we consider cinematic art even of the most documentary sort.

As to the superiority or inferiority of realistic art, if we are willing to admit its existence, that is not reducible to demonstration. Historically a preference for it became an article of artistic faith for some writers and readers during several generations, perhaps even for the last century. The more widespread this preference became, the more imperative it was that some one, reversing Belinsky's stand, assert the opposite formula. Virginia Woolf did this in effect in her essay on "Mr. Bennett and Mrs. Brown," and Proust did it with more sweeping negation in the passage on art at the end of *Le Temps retrouvé*.

One promising line of attack on realism, although it has not always been pursued with sincerity, is that suggested by the Italian critic Francesco de Sanctis among others. Believing that such terms as verism, idealism, realism, materialism, and all the other *isms* were essentially pejorative, he asserted his preference for "the pure and not for purism," for "matter and not materialism," for "the true and not verism. These names do not correspond to the truth of things; nature is broader and cannot be contained within them; and the limited brain of man, unable to embrace the whole, takes out one part and calls it the whole."[10]

Perhaps we do hold a position somewhat like that today. We are interested in individual slants on reality, admitting that no one can encompass the whole; we are willing to accept the writer as *maker*, provided, however, that he makes his work out of the stuff of earth. We are less interested in mirror images than we are in fracture or refraction, less willing to accept solid shapes than quicksilver changing outlines. But much of the philosophic attitude of the realists we have assimilated—from them or more likely from the world we live in. Literature is still anchored to that world, where we still twist and turn on that hard bed, too belabored and aching from the stones of fact to be able to escape into dreams.

[10] Sanctis, Francesco de, *Saggi Critici* 3: 296; Bari, Gius. Laterza & Figli, 1957. The remarks on Zola of which this is a part were made in a speech at the Circolo Filologico in Naples in 1879.

Part One

The Impulse toward Realism

On Realistic Poetry[*]

By Vissarion Belinsky

VISSARION GRIGOREVICH BELINSKY (1811-1848) was the early champion in Russia of realistic and socially responsible literature. His personal influence was as important as his critical writings, and his name was constantly invoked during the latter half of the century as the fountainhead of the new Russian literature.

Largely a self-taught man, he was inevitably drawn to the regnant German idealist philosophy. At first a supporter of Schelling's idealism, he saw art as the expression of a universal spirit. He then for some years considered himself an Hegelian, but during the 1840's he increasingly disavowed that position, since in the practical sphere it seemed to condone Tsarist oppression and an immobile social condition. Ivan Turgenev in his "Reminiscences of Pushkin" quotes from an 1859 lecture which he gave on Pushkin in which he characterized Belinsky as "an idealist in the best sense of the word." He says of this apparent mislabeling that "it was impossible to call many things by their right names" at that time, and that moreover he was trying to shake his audience, who thought of Belinsky as "a coarse materialist," into seeing him as a man of positive rather than negative ideas, since Belinsky "negated in the name of his ideal," which was allied to the vital currents of the time—as might be expected, equated by Turgenev with science, progress, civilization, and the West.

The long article on Gogol's stories from which this passage is taken is very early. It is to be observed that in this statement he gives only minimal lip service to the doctrine of the ideal in literature, while enunciating vigorously his belief that life and promise are to be found on the side of the real. He thus early, if only temporarily, escaped from the impasse over the ideal and the real which beset so much of English and German criticism during the latter part of the century. At the same time by his repudiation of "art for art's sake" he set Russian literature firmly on the path of social and moral reference which was to be aptly symbolized by the title of Chernishevsky's novel *What Is to Be Done?*

In this article, which was published in 1835, the word *poetry* must be taken in the inclusive sense of *poetic literature* in general.

◇◇

THUS we have here another aspect of poetry, *realistic* poetry, the poetry of life, the poetry of reality, at last the true and genuine

[*] Belinsky, Vissarion Grigorevich, "O Russkoi Povesti i Povestiakh Gogolia," *Izbrannie sochineniia*, pp. 56-59; Moscow, 1947. This first appeared in the periodical *The Telescope* in the autumn of 1835. The translation is by Linda Gordon.

41

poetry of our time. Its distinct character consists in the fact that it is true to reality; it does not create life anew, but reproduces it, and, like a convex glass, mirrors in itself, from one point of view, life's diverse phenomena, extracting from them those that are necessary to create a full, vivid, and organically unified picture. The size and the limits of the contents of this picture are decisive in judging the greatness of the poetic work. In order to complete the characterization of that which I call *realistic* poetry, I add that its eternal hero, the unchanging object of poetic inspiration, is a human being, an individual, independent, acting freely, a symbol of the world—its final manifestation, the attempts to understand the curious riddle of himself, the final question of his own mind, the ultimate enigma of his own curious aspirations. The key to this riddle, the answer to this question, the resolution of this problem must be full *consciousness*, which is the mystery, the aim and the reason for his existence!

Is it surprising, after this, that this realistic trend in poetry, this close union of art with life has developed primarily in our time? Is it surprising that the distinct characteristic of the newest works of literature in general is a merciless frankness, that life appears in them as if in order to be put to shame, in all nakedness, in all its tremendous ugliness and in all its solemn beauty, as if it were dissected with an anatomist's knife? We demand not the ideal of life, but life as it is. Be it good or bad, we do not wish to adorn it, for we think that in poetic presentation it is equally beautiful in both cases precisely because it is true, and that where there is truth, there is poetry. . . .

Thus poetry may be divided into the *idealistic* and the *realistic*. It would be difficult to decide which of these to give preference. Perhaps each is equal to the other, when it satisfies the conditions of a work of art, that is, when the *idealistic* poetry harmonizes with feeling, and the *realistic* with the truth of life-as-presented-by-it. But it seems that the latter, born as a result of the spirit of our sober time, satisfies the prevailing demands more completely. Here individuality of taste is also very significant. But however that may be, in our time both *idealistic* and *realistic* poetry are equally possible, equally accessible and understandable to all; notwithstanding this, the latter is the poetry of our time *par excellence*, more under-

On Realistic Poetry

standable and accessible to all, more in agreement with the spirit and needs of our time. Now Schiller's "Die Braut von Messina" and "Die Jungfrau von Orleans" will find sympathy and echo; but the most beloved creations of the time will always remain those which reflect faithfully and truly the realities of life.*

* Further on Belinsky asserts that "the novel is more convenient for the literary description of man, seen in his relation to public life, and here, it seems to me, is the secret of its great success, its absolute domination." For, he adds, it is "the task of realistic poetry to extract the poetry of life from the prose of life and to shock the soul with a true picture of this life."

"Life and Aesthetics"*

By N. G. Chernishevsky

NIKOLAI GAVRILOVICH CHERNISHEVSKY (1828-1889) has been a name
to conjure with in Russian aesthetics since the Revolution. His treatise
Life and Aesthetics, of which the following article is the concluding part,
did not appear in English until 1935, when it was published in *International Literature* in four installments. An introduction acclaims Chernishevsky as an "extraordinary Russian critic, novelist, scientist and
revolutionist" who was devoted to problems of art. It points out that
he was admired by Marx and Lenin, and cites the latter's remark, made
in 1908, that "Chernishevsky is the only really great Russian writer
who remained wholly on the level of an integral philosophic materialism
from the fifties to the year 1888 and who rejected the miserable nonsense of the neo-Kantians, positivists, Machians, and other muddlers.
But Chernishevsky was unable, rather it was impossible for him, in
view of the backwardness of Russian life, to rise to the dialectic materialism of Marx and Engels."

Life and Aesthetics was written as a dissertation and published without change in 1853. The preface, which was written thirty-five years
later for a projected reissue of the work—which censorship made impossible—is particularly important for the emphasis it places on the
philosophic currents of the time. Materialism of any kind was forbidden; it was impossible even to mention the name of Feuerbach.
Thus Chernishevsky by looking upon art as a direct representation
of reality was a heretic of the worst order, even though he could claim
to be a disciple of Belinsky. The suspicions of governmental authority
were no doubt correct. Chernishevsky was arrested in 1862 for sub-
versive activity; he wrote his novel *What Is to Be Done?* while in
prison. In 1864 he was sent into exile in Siberia, where he remained
for twenty-one years.

◇◇

PREFACE

IN THE FORTIES most educated people in Russia were greatly interested in German philosophy; our best publicists retold the Russian public, as much as was possible, the ideas dominating there.
Those were the ideas of Hegel and his disciples.

---

* Chernishevsky, Nikolai Gavrilovich, *Life and Aesthetics*, 1853. This was
published in *International Literature* in 1935: "Preface," pp. 51-53, June 1935;
"On the Question of Poetry," pp. 47-66, October 1935. The translation is by
S. D. Kogan with emendations by the editor.

From *Life and Aesthetics*

Now few followers of Hegel have remained in Germany itself; fewer yet in Russia. During Hegel's lifetime the integrity of the system of thought was maintained among his disciples by his personal authority. But even during his lifetime researches appeared in German philosophy in which inferences from his basic ideas were set forth, such as he either ignored or, in extreme cases, even condemned. When the authoritative teacher died the uniformity of thought among his followers began to weaken and in 1835 the Hegelian school split up into three sections: some remained true to the conservative liberalism of their teacher and they formed the section called the center; quite a number began openly to express opinions decisively progressive—they constituted the left section of the Hegelian school; very many of Hegel's disciples were horrified at the brusqueness of their opinions, and, in polemical exchanges with the left, rejected all those progressive elements which were joined to the conservative ones in Hegel's system—this numerous group formed the right section.

In 1846 the author had the opportunity to avail himself of good libraries and to use some money for the purchase of books. Up to that time he had read only such books as can be obtained in provincial cities where there are no decent libraries. He was acquainted with Russian expositions of the Hegelian system, very inadequate ones. When he at last found the opportunity to read Hegel in the original he began a study of these treatises. In the original he liked Hegel even less than he had expected from the Russian expositions. The reason was that the Russian researches in Hegel set forth his system in the spirit of the left section of the Hegelian school. In the original Hegel proved more akin to the philosophers of the seventeenth century and even the scholastics than to the Hegel in the Russian expositions of his system. Reading him was tiring due to the evident uselessness of it for forming a scientific system of thought. Just then one of Feuerbach's main works accidentally fell into the hands of the youth who was desirous of forming such a system of thought. He became a follower of this thinker; and up to the moment when the cares of life distracted him from his scientific researches, he diligently read and reread the works of Feuerbach.

Some six years after he had first made the acquaintance of Feuerbach an occasion arose when the author had to write a scientific treatise. It seemed to him that he could apply Feuerbach's basic ideas to the solution of some problems in fields of knowledge that did not enter into the researches of his teacher.

The subject of the treatise which the author had to write was to be something that related to literature. He conceived the idea of satisfying this condition by an exposition of those conceptions about art and, particularly, poetry, which seemed to him to follow from Feuerbach's ideas. Thus the little book, the preface to which I am here writing, is an attempt to apply Feuerbach's ideas to the solution of the fundamental problems of aesthetics.

The author makes no pretensions whatever to having said anything new or belonging to him personally. He desired to be only an interpreter of Feuerbach's ideas as applied to aesthetics.

Strangely inconsistent with this is the fact that the name of Feuerbach is not mentioned once in the entire treatise. This is due to the fact that it was then impossible to mention this name in any Russian book. The author does not mention Hegel either, although he is continually polemicizing against Hegel's theories of aesthetics then still continuing to dominate Russian literature, but set forth without mention of Hegel's name. This name was then also an inconvenient one to use in the Russian language.

Among the treatises on aesthetics, Fischer's monumental and very erudite book *Aesthetics, or Science of the Beautiful* was then considered the best. Fischer was a left Hegelian but his name was not included among those inconvenient to mention; hence the author mentions him when he finds it necessary to point out against whom he is polemicizing.

Applying Feuerbach's basic ideas to the solution of problems of aesthetics, the author arrives at a system of conceptions completely opposed to the aesthetic theory maintained by Fischer. This corresponds to the relation between the philosophies of Feuerbach and Hegel. It is entirely different from the metaphysical systems, the best of which, scientifically, was the Hegelian one. Kinship of content has disappeared and the only thing that remains is the employment of some terms common to all German systems of philosophy from Kant to Hegel.

Feuerbach's system is of a purely scientific nature.

From *Life and Aesthetics*

But soon after he had worked out his system ill health curtailed his activity. He was not yet old, but he already felt that he would not have time to set forth in conformity with his fundamental scientific ideas, all those special sciences which were then and still are the learned province of so-called philosophers, because of the lack of specialists capable of working out the broad conceptions upon which the solution of the basic questions of these branches of knowledge is based. (To enumerate these sciences by their old names the most important of them are: logic, aesthetics, moral philosophy, the philosophy of history.) That is why he said in the preface to his collected works that these works should be replaced by others, but that he lacked the physical strength to do so. This feeling also explains his sad answer to the question he puts himself: Has not your new point of view become antiquated?—To my regret, yes. *Leider, Leider!*—Has it really become antiquated?—Of course it has, in the sense that the center of research on the broader problems of science should be shifted from the field of special investigations of the theoretical convictions of the masses of the peoples and of learned systems built up on the basis of these popular conceptions, to the field of natural science. But this has not been done yet. Those naturalists who deem themselves builders of all-embracing theories, in reality remain the disciples, and usually poor disciples, of ancient thinkers who have created metaphysical systems, and usually of such thinkers whose systems have long been demolished partly by Schelling and finally by Hegel. It is sufficient to recall that most naturalists attempting to construct broad theories of the laws of action of human thought repeat the metaphysical theories of Kant on the subjectiveness of our knowledge, argue from Kant's words that the forms of our physical sensations are unlike the really existing objects and that consequently things as they really exist and their real properties, their real interrelations, remain unknowable to us, and, if they were knowable, they could not be the object of our thought, which clothes all the material of knowledge in forms differing entirely from the forms of real existence; that the very laws of thought have only a subjective significance, that in reality there is no such thing as what we deem the connection of cause and effect, because there is nothing previous and nothing following, no whole and no parts, and so on

47

and so forth. When the naturalists will cease to talk such and similar metaphysical nonsense they will become capable of working out, and undoubtedly will work out, on the basis of the natural sciences, systems of thought more precise and more complete than those set forth by Feuerbach. For the present, however, the best exposition of scientific conceptions on the so-called fundamental questions engaging human curiosity remains that of Feuerbach.

In general the author claims primacy to only those particular thoughts which refer especially to aesthetics. All thoughts of a broader nature in this booklet belong to Feuerbach.

ON THE QUESTION OF POETRY

Let us now consider poetry, the highest and fullest of all the arts. Its problems include all the theory of art. Poetry stands high above all other arts in its content. All the other arts cannot tell us even a small fraction of what poetry does. But this relation changes completely when we turn our attention to the force and liveliness of the subjective impression produced by poetry and the arts. All other arts, like live reality, act directly on our senses; poetry acts on the imagination. In some people the imagination is more impressionable and alive than in others—but generally speaking, in the normal person the images of the imagination are pale and weak in comparison with impressions of the senses. It therefore follows that in power and clearness of subjective impression poetry is much inferior not only to reality, but even to the other arts. But let us investigate the degree of objective perfection of the form and content of poetry and whether it can compete with nature in this respect.

There is much talk of the "fullness," "individuality," "live definiteness of the persons and characters depicted" by great poets. We are told at the same time that "these are not individual persons but general types"—upon which it would be futile to argue that the most definite, best-drawn person in a poetic work remains only a general, indefinitely outlined sketch to which only the imagination (really, the memory) of the reader lends definite individuality. The image in poetry bears the same relation to the real, live image that the word bears to the object it denotes—it is a pale, general, indefinite hint at reality. In this "generality" of the poetic

From *Life and Aesthetics*

image many see a superiority over the persons presented to us by real life. Such an opinion is based on a supposed conflict between the general significance of a creature and its live individuality, on an assumption that "in becoming individualized, the general loses its generality" in reality and "is raised again to the general only by the power of art divesting the individual of his individuality." Without entering into a metaphysical discussion as to what the real relation is between the general and the particular (which would only lead to the conclusion that the general is only a pale, dead extract of the individual and the relation between them is therefore that of the word and reality), we shall only add that in actuality individual details do not in the least detract from the general significance of an object but, on the contrary, animate and amplify its general significance; that in any event, poetry admits the great superiority of the individual by its attempts to lend live individuality to its images, that it can, nevertheless, by no means attain individuality, but succeeds only in approaching somewhat closer to it and that the merit of a poetic image is determined by how close it approaches it. And so poetry tries to but never can attain what is always to be found in typical persons of real life. It is evident, therefore, that the images of poetry are weak, anemic, indefinite, as compared with the corresponding images in life.

"But how can one find genuinely typical characters in life?" It is enough to put such a question to find it needs no answer, just like questions as to whether one can really find in life good and bad people, spendthrifts, misers, etc., is ice really cold, bread really nutritious, etc. There are people to whom everything has to be shown and proved. But such people cannot be convinced by general arguments in a general work. To them everything has to be proved separately, they can only be convinced by individual examples drawn from among people they know personally and among which, no matter how close the circle, there will always be a few genuinely typical characters. It will hardly help to point out typical characters from among historical personages. Some will say: "Historical characters have been glorified by tradition, by admiration of their contemporaries, the genius of historians or extraordinary cicumstances."

Somewhat later we shall investigate the origin of the opinion that typical characters are depicted much better and more clean-cut in poetry than they occur in real life. At this point let us turn our attention to the process by means of which characters in poetry are "created," as this is what usually is considered the guarantee of greater typicalness of these characters than of natural ones. It is customarily said: "The poet observes a multitude of living individual people; not one of them can serve as a complete type, but he notes that there is something general, typical in each one of them. Casting aside everything individual, he unites all the scattered features of various persons into one artistic whole and this can be called the quintessence of the real characters." Suppose this is all perfectly just, and that it is really so always. But the quintessence is usually entirely unlike the thing itself. Alcohol is not wine. If they follow the rule quoted, "composers" give us the quintessence of heroism or wickedness in the form of wooden characters instead of living people. All, or almost all, young people fall in love—that is their general trait, in all other things they differ—and we should read about youths and maidens that think and talk only about love and do nothing else throughout the novel than suffer or enjoy happiness through love. All older folks like to philosophize—otherwise there is nothing in common among them, all grandmothers dote on their grandchildren, etc.—and so we should have all stories and novels filled with old men who do nothing but philosophize, with grandmothers who do nothing but fondle their grandchildren and so on. Only the recipe is not always adhered to. Before the imagination of the poet "creating" a character there usually stands the image of some real person, and consciously or unconsciously he "reproduces" this person in his typical character. As proof of this we may point to an endless number of works, the principal hero of which is the more or less true portrait of the author himself (for instance, Faust, Don Carlos, Byron's heroes, the heroes and heroines of George Sand, Lenski, Onegin, Pechorin). We should also recall the frequent accusations of novelists of showing "portraits of their acquaintances in their novels." These accusations are usually ridiculed and indignantly denied, but they are only somewhat exaggerated and crudely expressed and not at all essentially unjust.

Conventions on the one hand, and ordinary tendencies of peo-

From *Life and Aesthetics*

ple to independence, to "create and not copy," on the other, compel the author to alter the characters he takes from life and depict them somewhat inexactly. Besides, the character taken from life has to act in the novel in circumstances entirely different from those that surrounded him in reality and this alters the external semblance. All these alterations, however, do not prevent the character from remaining essentially a copied and not a created portrait, not an original. It may be argued, that though it is true that a real person serves as the prototype for a poetic character, the poet "raises the character to general significance." This is usually superfluous, as the original is already of general significance in its individuality. One should only be able to understand—and this is one of the features of poetic genius—the essence of the character of the real person, see him with penetrating eyes. It is also necessary to understand and feel how the person would act and feel in the situation in which he will be placed by the author—and this is another phase of poetic genius. In the third place, the ability is required to depict the character just as the author conceives him —perhaps the most characteristic trait of poetic genius. To understand, be able intuitively to comprehend and convey—this is the poet's problem when he attempts to depict most characters. The question as to what "raising to ideal significance" and "poetic idealization of the prose and discrepancies of life" represents will be discussed later. We do not in the least doubt the fact that there are many characters in works of fiction which cannot be called portraits but have been entirely "created" by the poet. But this is not at all due to the fact that there are no corresponding models in life but to an entirely different reason—most frequently simply lack of remembrance or insufficient acquaintance. If the live particulars have vanished from the poet's memory, only a general, abstract idea of the character remains there, or it may happen that the poet knows too little about the typical character for it to appear as a live individual in his imagination, and he is compelled to fill in the general outline and put shading on the sketch. But such entirely fictitious characters almost never strike us as living persons.

In general, the more we know about the poet's life and the people he came in contact with, the more we find portraits of living people in his works. It can hardly be disputed that there has always been less of the "created" in the characters depicted by authors than of the copied-from-nature. It is hard not to reach the conclusion that with respect to his characters, the poet is almost always only the historian or the author of their biographies. It is, of course, self-evident, that we do not mean to say by this that every word spoken by Mephistopheles was actually heard by Goethe. Not only a poet of genius, even an ordinary story-teller is able to add similar expressions, an appropriate introduction and transitions.

From Life?

There is much more "independent invention" or "fiction"—as we prefer to call what is usually termed more proudly "creation" —in the events described by the poet, in the plot, its development and denouement—although it is easily demonstrated that the plots of novels, stories, etc., are usually borrowed from life or anecdotes and various sorts of stories (take, for instance, all Pushkin's prose tales: *The Captain's Daughter* is based on an anecdote, so is *Dubrovski, Queen of Spades, The Shot*, etc.). But the plot alone is not sufficient to lend a novel or story high poetic value—one must know how to utilize a plot. Hence, disregarding the question of "independence" of the plot, we shall turn our attention to the question as to whether the "poetry" of poetic works with regard to the plot as it appears upon full development, is of a higher order than the real occurrence. As an aid in arriving at a final decision we shall put a number of questions, though most of them answer themselves. 1) Are there any poetic occurrences in life, are there any dramas, novels, comedies, tragedies, farces, in real life?— Every minute. 2) Are these occurrences truly poetic in their development and denouement? Do they possess artistic fullness and completeness in real life?—This depends; sometimes yes, but often not. There are many occurrences in which a strictly poetic viewpoint can find nothing to carp at with respect to art. This point can be settled by the first reading of a well-written book on history or an evening spent in the company of a man who has seen much in his lifetime. It can finally be settled by a random issue of an English or French court newspaper. 3) Are there any occurrences

From *Life and Aesthetics*

among these finished poetic ones that could, without introducing any changes, be repeated under the title of "drama," "tragedy," "novel," and so on?—Very many. True, many real occurrences are incredible, are based on very rare and extraordinary situations or concatenations of circumstances, and therefore resemble a fable or labored fiction in their natural form (which only goes to prove that real life may be too dramatic for drama, too poetic for poetry). But there are other occurrences in which, with all their being so remarkable, there is nothing eccentric or incredible, and the entire chain of circumstances, the entire progress and development of what is called the plot, are very simple. 4) Have real occurrences a "general" side to them such as is essential to a poetic work?— Of course, there is such a side to every occurrence that deserves the attention of any thoughtful person; and there are many such occurrences.

One cannot but admit that there are many occurrences in life which one only has to know about, understand, and be able to recount and in the pure prosaic story of the historian, biographer, or collector of anecdotes these tales differ from "poetic works" only in greater brevity, less development of scenes, and fewer descriptions and other such minor points. And this is the essential difference between poetic works and the precise prosaic recounting of actual occurrences. Greater fullness of detail or what in poorer writing is called "rhetorical expansion" is really all that can be claimed for the superiority of poetry over the true story. We have as little regard for rhetoric as anyone; but allowing for all the needs of the human heart, we are ready to admit the importance of such poetic expansion, seeing how general it is, inasmuch as we see a tendency towards it in poetry everywhere. Besides, in life these details always exist, and they are necessary for real develop‧ ment although entirely unessential to the story itself; hence, they should also have their place in poetry. There is only the difference that while in life details are never an empty distension of a matter, such details in poetry are all too often merely rhetoric or mechanical distension of the story. Is not Shakespeare superb just because he dispenses with all such circumlocutions in his best scenes? But how much of it there is even in Shakespeare, Goethe, and Schiller! It seems to us (perhaps due to prepossession in favor of one's own) that Russian poetry has in itself the germ of distaste for lengthening a story by mechanical selection of details. The narratives of Pushkin, Lermontov, and Gogol have one common trait—briefness and rapid action.

Thus we can say in general that in plot, types, and fullness of characterization poetic works are far inferior to life. There are only two things in which poetic works might be superior to life—in decoration of a story by the addition of effective accessories and in making the characters harmonize more with the events in which they take part.

We have stated that painting more frequently gives a group surroundings appropriate to the essence of a scene than nature does. Similarly poetry more frequently than nature makes the moving forces of events appear in people whose characters correspond more nearly to the spirit of the event. In life, petty people by nature are frequently the prime movers of events tragic, dramatic, etc. A miserable rake, sometimes not even really a bad fellow, may cause a chain of terrible events. A person whom one would by no means consider wicked, may shatter the happiness of many and be the cause of more grief than has been caused by an Iago or Mephistopheles. In poetry, on the contrary, wicked deeds are usually committed by wicked people, good deeds by good people. In life one is often at a loss whom to blame and whom to praise. In poetry honor and shame are usually justly and definitely distributed. Only is this a merit or a fault? Sometimes it is one, sometimes the other—generally it is a fault. We shall not touch upon the question at this time that the result of such a procedure is idealization or, more simply, exaggeration both of the good and the bad, because we have not yet discussed the significance of art and it would be premature to say that idealization is either a fault or a virtue. We must say, however, that the result of a constant effort to make the character correspond to the nature of the event in poetry is monotony: characters and even action become standardized. With variety in the nature of the characters events essentially similar would acquire a difference in nuance, as happens in life, which is always different, always new; in poetry, however, one often comes across repetitions. It has become customary nowadays to ridicule embellishments not essential to the subject matter

From *Life and Aesthetics*

or to the final purpose; nevertheless, an apt phrase, a brilliant metaphor, thousands of embellishments introduced to lend outward brilliance to a book, are still an important factor in evoking favorable opinion. With respect to embellishments, outward brilliance, intricacy, etc., we have never disputed the superiority of fiction over reality. But one has only to point out such an apparent merit of a story or drama for these to lose favor in the eyes of people of taste and transfer such works from the province of "art" to that of "artificiality."

Exaggerations About Art

Our analysis has thus shown that art may have the advantage over reality only in two or three insignificant details while in everything essential it remains far behind life. The only thing that may be held against our analysis is that it limited itself to general points of view without entering into detail or reference to examples. When one considers how strongly entrenched the opinion is that the beauty of a work of art is supposedly greater than beauty in nature, the briefness of our analysis may really be a fault; this opinion is, however, so shaky, the exponents of it so contradict themselves at every step, that it would only seem necessary to call attention to how unjust this opinion is for everyone to see that beauty in real life is superior to any product of the "creative" imagination. But if this is so, what is the basis or, rather, what are the subjective reasons for the exaggerated opinion of the high merit of works of art?

The prime source of this opinion is the natural human inclination to prize difficult accomplishments and rare things. No one prizes the pure pronunciation of a Frenchman speaking French or of a German speaking German—"it came to him easily and is no rarity." But when a Frenchman speaks German tolerably well, or a German French, it is considered an accomplishment and gives the person the right to some respect for it. Why? In the first place because it is something rare, in the second place, because it is the result of years of effort.

As a matter of fact, every Frenchman who has had the benefit of a decent literary or worldly education speaks an excellent French —but how strict are our requirements in such a case? The least noticeable trace of provincial accent—the least inelegant phrase—and we conclude that "the gentleman has a poor command of his native tongue." A Russian speaking French betrays in every sound that a completely pure French pronunciation is beyond him, always discloses that it is a tongue foreign to him—by his choice of words, construction of phrase, in the entire structure of his speech—but we forgive him all that, do not notice it and sometimes even declare that "this Russian speaks French better than a Frenchman does" without even the least intention of comparing his speech to a native Frenchman's, but only with that of other Russians also endeavoring to speak French. And he probably does speak the language much better than the others but much worse than any Frenchman—that is quite evident to anyone that understands such matters. Many people, however, are actually misled by the hyperbolic expression.

The same thing happens in the aesthetic judgment of the products of nature and of art. The least actual or even imagined deficiency in a product of nature gives a shock to aesthetics, makes it a subject of much talk, and the aestheticians are ready to forget all the good features and beauty. What is there to prize in these? —they cost no effort! In a work of art this same deficiency may be a hundredfold more crude and surrounded by many other deficiencies to boot; but we do not notice it or, if we do, we forgive it all and exclaim: "The sun also has its spots."

As a matter of fact works of art should only be compared with one another in determining their relative merits. Some will prove better than others and in admiration of their beauty (relative, to be sure) we exclaim: "They are more beautiful than nature and life themselves! The beauties of nature pale before the beauties of art!" Only this admiration is biased—it grants more than justice warrants: we prize difficult accomplishment—which is fine; but we should not forget the essential inherent merits which do not depend upon the degree of difficulty encountered. We are positively unjust when we give difficulty of accomplishment preference over inherent merit. Life and nature produce beauty without design and such beauty really comes without effort and hence without merit in our eyes, without any rights to our sympathy or to condescension. And why condescend when there is so much beauty in reality?

From *Life and Aesthetics*

"Everything not completely beautiful in reality is bad; everything in the least tolerable in art is excellent"—there is the rule that governs our judgment.

To prove how highly we prize difficulty of accomplishment and how much that which comes by itself, without any effort on our part, loses in our eyes, we shall consider photography. Among camera portraits there may be many not only perfectly true ones, but even such as transmit perfectly the expression of the face— but do we prize them? It would even sound strange to hear any apologies for camera portraits. Another example: what high regard calligraphy was once held in! Nevertheless, even a moderately well printed book is much more beautiful than any manuscript. But who ever stopped to admire the art of typography and who will not spend a thousandfold more praise on a beautiful manuscript than on a really well-printed book which may be much more beautiful than the manuscript? What is easy interests us very little, even though its inherent beauty may far exceed the product of hard endeavor. It is understood, of course, that even from this point of view we are only subjectively right: "reality produces beauty without effort" only means that no effort is made in this case on the part of the human will. In fact, however, the beautiful and the unbeautiful, the great and the small, are the result of the greatest possible application of energy, knowing no rest and no fatigue. But we have no interest in efforts made and struggles taking place without our participation and outside our consciousness. We should know nothing of them—we only value human energy, only value man.

And this is the second source of our bias for works of art: they are human products. That is why we are all proud of them, considering them something near to our own selves. They are evidence of the human mind, of human power and so, dear to us. All, except the French, can see that there is a great difference between Shakespeare and Corneille or Racine. Only the French still draw comparisons between them. It is hard to realize that "ours is not the height of perfection." There will be many Russians ready to maintain that Pushkin is a universal poet—some would even maintain that Pushkin is superior to Byron—thus man always values most highly his own things. Just as a people exaggerates the merit of its own poet so man as a whole exaggerates the value of poetry generally.

The reasons for partiality to art discussed so far deserve all respect because they are natural ones. How is man not to respect human labor, not to love man, and not to prize the products which bear witness to human intellect and power? The third reason for human partiality to art, however, hardly deserves such respect. The thing is, art flatters our artificial tastes. We are thoroughly aware of the artificiality of the life and manners, the customs and the entire mode of thinking of the period of Louis XIV. We have come closer to nature. We understand and value nature more than society of the seventeenth century did. Nevertheless, we are still at odds with nature. Our habits, manners, our entire mode of life and consequently also our entire mode of thought are still very artificial. It is hard to see the failings of one's age, particularly if they have become smaller than previously. Instead of noting how much refined artificiality there is in us, we only note that the nineteenth century has, in this respect, grown better than the seventeenth, that there is more understanding of nature. We forget that an illness abated is not yet perfect health.

Our artificiality is noticeable in everything, beginning with our clothes, which everyone laughs at and everyone nevertheless wears, and ending with our food, spiced to mask and make utterly unrecognizable the natural taste; in the refinements of our oral language and the subtleties of our literary language, which continues to decorate itself with antitheses, witticisms, with profound reflections on trite themes and learned remarks on the human heart in the manner of Corneille and Racine in fiction and in the manner of Johannes Müller in historical works. Works of art flatter all our petty requirements which originate in our love of artificiality. And then how we still love to "wash" nature, just as the seventeenth century liked to dress it; but to go into this would lead us far astray in discussion of what is "filthy" and to what extent it is permissible in art. Minute dressing of details still prevails in works of art and the object of such a procedure is not to make the details harmonize with the spirit of the whole but only to make each one of them more interesting or beautiful by itself, almost always at the expense of the work as a whole, its credibility and naturalness.

From *Life and Aesthetics*

There prevails a petty chasing after effect in individual words, phrases, and episodes, coloring of characters and action, not in natural but rather in sharp colors. Works of art are both more petty than anything we meet in life or nature and at the same time more effective. Is it to be wondered at that the opinion prevails that art is more beautiful than life or nature in which there is so little artificiality and to which the effort to awaken interest is foreign?

Art Is not Life

Life and nature are superior to art, but art endeavors to suit our bents while reality cannot be subjected to our desires to see everything in the light that suits us best or to answer to our often biased conceptions. Of the many cases of such catering to prevailing ideas we shall point out one: many require a satirical work to contain characters "on which the heart could rest with love"—which is a very natural desire: but reality very frequently presents a contrary spectacle, with many occurrences in which there is not a single positive character. Art almost always complies with this requirement and, in Russian literature at least, we know no writer, except Gogol, who does not. And in Gogol the lack of "positive" characters is compensated for by "elevated, lyrical" digressions. Another example—Man is inclined to be sentimental. Life and nature do not share this inclination. Works of art, however, almost universally cater to this inclination in a greater or lesser degree. Both requirements mentioned are due to human limitations. Real life and nature are above these limitations. Works of art, submitting to these limitations and thus descending below reality and often becoming banal and commonplace, come closer to common human needs and thus gain in man's eyes. "But, in such a case, you yourself admit that works of art are better and fuller than objective reality, that they correspond to human nature; hence to man they are better than the product of nature." This conclusion suffers from a lack of precision in the formulation of it. The thing is—artificially developed man has many artificial needs, needs distorted to the point of falseness, to the point of being fantastic. Such needs cannot be fully satisfied because they are not, essentially, natural needs but the dreamings of a distorted imagination. They cannot be catered to without becoming ridiculous and contemptible to the very man that is being catered to because, instinctively, he feels that these requirements should not be satisfied. Thus the public, and the aesthetics following it, demands "positive" characters and sentimentality, and then the same public laughs in scorn at works of art which cater to these wishes. To cater to man's caprices is not yet to satisfy his needs. The first and foremost of these needs is truth. But thus far we have spoken only of the sources of origin and content. But the impression produced upon us by art and reality are also of great importance; the merits of things are also judged by the strength of such impressions.

We have seen that the impressions produced by works of art are much weaker than impressions produced by life. This does not require any further proof. The work of art, however, is in a much more favorable position in this respect, which might influence one not used to analyse the causes of his sensations to conclude that art, in itself, produces a greater effect than living reality. Against our will, reality seems to us most of the time inept, inappropriate. We go visiting, for instance, not in order to enjoy human beauty, observe human nature, or watch the drama of life—we often start out with a mind full of cares and a heart closed to all impressions. But who ever goes to a picture gallery for any reason but to enjoy beautiful paintings? Who turns to a novel for aught but to immerse himself in the plot and the characters depicted there? Our attention to the beauties and majesty of nature is usually almost forced. Nature must itself, if it can, attract our eyes towards some entirely different object, must penetrate our hearts occupied with other matters, by force. Towards reality our attitude is like that towards a boring guest who persists in demanding our attention— we try to shut ourselves away from it. But there are times when our hearts begin to feel empty due to this very inattention to reality; then we turn to art, seeking solace there—we turn into solicitous persons ourselves.

Life's way is strewn with golden coins, only we do not notice them because we are absorbed in our aims and do not look at the road under our feet. And when we do notice them we cannot stop to pick them up because the vehicle of life carries us relentlessly on. Such is our attitude towards reality. But here we have come to a station and walk about waiting impatiently for our conveyance,

From *Life and Aesthetics*

and here we examine every nail attentively, though it may not even be worth any attention. Such is our attitude towards art. Not to speak of the fact that everyone must evaluate life for himself because life presents to each individual sides invisible to others, and the opinion of society as a whole is not known—while works of art are judged by all of society. The beauties and majesty of nature are seldom patent and few value things that are not talked about generally. The beauties of life are like a bar of gold without a proof stamp—many refuse to handle it because they cannot distinguish it from a bar of brass. Works of art are like a currency bill—it has very little inherent value but all society vouches for its conventional value and consequently everyone holds it precious and very few have a clear idea that all its value is lent to it by the fact that it represents a quantity of gold.

When we observe nature it captivates us by itself, as something independent of anything else, and seldom lets us wander in thought into our subjective world, into our past. But when we observe a work of art there is complete freedom for subjective recollections and it usually serves only as a pretext for conscious or unconscious dreamings and associations. When we witness a tragic scene in reality we forget all about ourselves, while when we read about the tragic end of someone in a novel our memory evokes, clearly or vaguely, all dangerous situations we have been in ourselves and that we know about our friends. The power of art, particularly poetry, is usually the power of recollection. A work of art is particularly suited to evoke our recollections by virtue of its unfinished, indefinite nature, because it is usually "something general" and not a live individual image or event. If we are shown a finished portrait of a person that does not resemble anyone we know, we coldly turn away with perhaps the remark "rather clever." But when we are shown a barely sketched indefinite figure in which no one will positively recognize anyone—this poor weak sketch will call to our minds some dear features. And while .we turn coldly away from a face full of beauty and expression, we are enchanted with an insignificant sketch because it recalls someone close to us and, by association, recalls ourselves to us. The strength of art is in generalities.

There is another side to works of art which to inexperienced and nearsighted people makes art seem superior to life and nature—it is that in them everything is put out for show, explained by the author himself. In life and nature one has to uncover things oneself. The strength of art here is the strength of commentary, but of this we shall speak later.

We have thus found many reasons why art is preferred to reality, but they all only explain why this is so without justifying such preference. Since we cannot agree that art is superior, nay, even the equal of reality in either merit of content or execution, we cannot, of course, acquiesce to the generally prevailing view on the needs which give rise to art and its ultimate aim. The prevalent opinion on the origin of art can be stated as follows: "Man is governed by an invincible desire for beauty but cannot find any true beauty in objective reality. He is thus compelled himself to create objects or works that satisfy his requirements or that are truly beautiful." Or, to use the special terminology of the ruling school: "The idea of beauty, not being realized by reality, is realized in works of art." This must be analysed for the real meaning of the incomplete and one-sided hints intended here. "Man desires beauty"; but if we are to understand by beauty what is here defined —the full correspondence of form and idea—then, not art alone but all human activity is to be inferred as resulting from this desire for beauty as the basic principle of this activity, and, according to this school of thought, the tendency to unity of image and idea. This is the formal basis of all technical development, all labor applied to the creation and perfection of all things necessary to us. In making art the result of the desire for beauty we confuse two distinct meanings of the word art: 1) fine arts (poetry, music, etc.) and 2) the ability or effort to do anything well. Only the latter is a result of the tendency towards unity of form and idea. If, however, we understand by beauty (as we see it) that in which man sees life, it is evident that the desire for beauty will result in a joyous love of everything living and is most fully satisfied by live reality. "Man does not find anything truly and fully beautiful in reality." We have tried to show how unjust this statement is, that the activity of our imagination is awakened not by the defects of beauty in life but by its absence, that beauty in life is truly and fully beautiful but that it, alas, is not always patent to our eyes. If

From *Life and Aesthetics*

works of art were the result of our desire for perfection and disdain of everything imperfect, man should long ago have given up all attempts at art as futile because works of art are always lacking in perfection. Anyone dissatisfied with beauty in life and nature will be even less satisfied with beauty created by art. It is thus impossible to agree with the customary explanation of the meaning of art. There are hints there, however, that might be considered just, if properly interpreted. This is the statement that "man is not satisfied by beauty in reality because such beauty is not enough"—and this is just, only misconstrued, and requires explanation.

The sea is beautiful. As we look at it, it does not occur to us that it is unsatisfactory in an aesthetic sense. But not everyone lives near the sea. Many live through their lifetime without an opportunity to glimpse the sea. They should also like to enjoy the sight of the sea, and to them paintings of the sea are interesting. It is of course better to look at the sea itself rather than at a picture of it, but when the best is not to be had the next best will do; when one cannot get the original one must needs be satisfied with a substitute. Even those that have the possibility of enjoying the sea itself cannot always see it when they should like; then they recall it to their imagination. But the imagination is feeble, it needs support, needs a spur, and in order to revive their recollections of the sea, to see it more clearly in their imagination, they look at pictures of the sea. This is the only aim and value of very many (in fact most) works of art: to make it possible to get even some idea of the beautiful in reality for those people that have no opportunity of enjoying it directly; to serve as a spur to the memory, to revive and strengthen recollections of real beauties seen and which one loves to recollect. (For the present we shall not discuss the statement that "beauty is the essential content of art"; below, we shall substitute another term for the word "beauty" in this expression, a term which defines the content of art much more precisely and fully, in our opinion.)

To sum up, therefore, the first function of art, a function of all works of art without exception, is the reproduction of life and nature. The relation of such works to reality is the same as that of the engraving to the picture from which it is taken, the relation of

63

the portrait to the face it represents. An engraving is made of a picture not because the picture is a bad one and the engraving is to improve it, but, on the contrary, just because the picture is a good one. Similarly reality is reproduced by art not to improve it and round off its imperfections, not because the reality itself is not beautiful, but on the contrary, precisely because it is beautiful. The engraving is not an improvement on the picture from which it was made: similarly the work of art does not approach the beauty or majesty of reality. But there is only one picture and it can be enjoyed only by those fortunate enough to visit the gallery where it is hung—the engraving is broadcast in hundreds of copies all over the world and many can enjoy it whenever and wherever they please, without leaving their chamber or rising from their chair. Similarly a thing of beauty in reality is not always available to everyone's enjoyment and cannot be enjoyed at all times, the reproduction (feeble, crude, it is true, but nevertheless a reproduction) by art is always and everywhere available. Say a portrait is made of one dear to us—it is not for the purpose of improving the features (the face is dear to us with all its imperfections) but to make it possible for us to enjoy looking at this face even when the original is not near us. Such then is the purpose of art—it does not improve reality, does not beautify it, it reproduces it, serves as its substitute.

Art Is a Copy of Nature

So, the first purpose of art is to reproduce reality. Without the least pretensions of having, by this, added anything new to the history of aesthetics, we nevertheless think that the formula "art is the reproduction of reality" means something entirely different than the pseudo-classic "theory of imitation of nature" of the seventeenth-eighteenth centuries. So that this distinction between our view on art and the theory of imitation of nature may not rest upon our bare statement, we shall quote an analysis of the latter theory from one of the best books on the now ruling system of aesthetics. This analysis will in the first place serve to show the difference between the idea it refutes and those propounded by us, and in the second place, it will reveal what is lacking in our

64

From *Life and Aesthetics*

first definition of art as a reproducing activity, and thus lead us to a more precise development of the conception of art.

"In defining art as the imitation of nature only its formal purpose is touched upon. According to this definition art should endeavor to copy as closely as possible what already exists in the external world. Such repetition must be acknowledged futile, as life and nature already give us that which art is supposed to. But more than this—to imitate nature is a vain endeavor which must fall far short of its aim as in imitating nature, art, with the limited means at its disposal, can only give an illusion instead of truth, and instead of something really alive, only a dead mask."

Here we note first of all that the phrases: "art is the reproduction of reality" and "art is imitation of nature" define only the formal principle of art. In order to define the content of art our first conclusion, regarding the purpose of art, must be amplified—and this we shall proceed to do below. The second objection raised does not apply to our views. It is evident from our previous analysis that the reproduction or "repetition" by art of things and phenomena in nature is by no means useless—on the contrary, it is a necessary activity. As to the statement that such repetition is a futile effort which falls far short of achieving its purpose, it must be remarked that this objection has force only if it is assumed that art would compete with reality and not merely serve as a substitute. But this is precisely what we have been arguing: art cannot stand up in comparison with reality and hasn't the lively interest of reality. We may consider this indisputable.

But the statement "art is the reproduction of reality" requires amplification before it can be termed a rounded definition of art. However, though this statement does not exhaustively define the conception of art, it is true as far as it goes and objections to it can only be raised issuing from the unspoken requirements that art must be more perfect than reality. We have tried to show the objective untenability of this view and we believe we have succeeded in revealing its subjective origin. Let us now see whether the further objections to the theory of imitation are applicable to our views.

"Complete success in imitating nature being impossible, there only remains the self-satisfied enjoyment of the relative success of this trick. But this pleasure cools off in proportion as the imitation begins to resemble the original, even turning to satiation or disdain. There are portraits which, as is said, resemble the original to a disgusting degree. An imitation of the nightingale's song most excellently rendered turns into a disgusting bore as soon as we grow aware that this is not the song of a nightingale but an imitation produced by some human imitator—because we are entitled to expect different music from a human being. Such tricks of skillful imitation of nature are comparable to the art of the trickster who could throw lentils through an opening no larger than the lentil without missing once and whom Alexander the Great rewarded."

These remarks are perfectly just, but they refer to the useless and senseless copying of what is not worthy of attention, or to the depiction of empty externalities void of all content. (Alas, how many famed works of art deserve such bitter but merited ridicule!) Only subject matter worthy of the attention of thoughtful men can save art from the reproach that it is the empty amusement which it only all too frequently is. An artistic form will not save a work from contempt or a smile of commiseration at best, if its underlying idea does not give a positive answer to the question, "Was it worth bothering about?" The useless has no claims on our respect. "Man is his own purpose"—but man's activities must have their purpose in human needs and not in themselves. That is why a useless imitation evokes all the greater disdain the more successful it is: "Why spend so much time and energy?"—is our reaction, and we feel, "What a pity to spend such perfection of technique on such comparatively useless subject matter." The boredom and disgust brought on by the trickster who so successfully imitates a nightingale's song is explained by the very remarks about it contained in the quotation. It is a pitiful thing for a man not to understand that he is to sing human songs and not exercise himself in cascades and trills which have any sense only in the song of a nightingale and lose all value when repeated by human beings.

From *Life and Aesthetics*

As regards portraits resembling the original to the point of disgust —this should be understood as follows: any copy, to be true, must convey the essential features of the original. A portrait which does not reproduce the main and most expressive features of a face is not a good portrait. But when all the petty details of a face are drawn in sharply the face on the portrait appears deformed, dead—is it any wonder it awakens disdain? One frequently hears objections to photographic copies of reality, but would it not be better to say only that copying, like all human activities, requires talent, the ability to distinguish between the essential and the unessential? "Dead copying" is the usual phrase. But one cannot copy well if the dead mechanism is not directed by live thought. A correct facsimile cannot be made of an ordinary manuscript without understanding the copied letters.

Before going into the essential subject matter of art in order to complete our definition we must stop a moment on the relations between the theory of "reproduction" and the theory of "imitation." The conception of art we advocate issues from the point of view of later German aesthetics which is a result of the dialectic process whose direction is determined by the ideas of modern science generally. It is thus most intimately connected with two systems of ideas—those of the beginning of the present century and those of the last decades. Any other relation is merely accidental and has no genetic influence upon it. But while the ideas of ancient thinkers cannot affect modern thought due to the development of science, one cannot but see that in many cases modern conceptions prove similar to those of previous ages. There is a particular resemblance to Greek thought. There is a similar situation with respect to aesthetics. Our definition of the formal principle of art is akin to that which was prevalent with the Greeks and can be found in Plato, Aristotle, and most certainly in the expressions of Democritus. Pseudo-classic theory actually did understand art as imitation of reality for the purpose of fooling our senses. But this is an abuse belonging only to periods of spoiled tastes.

Form and Content

We shall now attempt to amplify the definition of art proposed by us and go over to the discussion of the subject matter of art rather than its form.

It is usually maintained that the subject matter of art is beauty. But this confines the sphere of art to too close limits. Even if we should agree to include the sublime and the comic as elements of beauty, very many works of art would still fall outside the bounds of a definition including the beautiful, the sublime, the comic. In painting: pictures of domestic life in which there may be no beautiful or comic figure, pictures of old folks that cannot be said to excel in beauty, etc., etc. In music such a division would be even more difficult. Suppose we consider marches and pathetic compositions sublime, compositions breathing love and gaiety beautiful, and many songs comic; there will still remain a vast number of compositions that cannot be labeled one or the other or the third without great tension. What are sad songs? Are they sublime because they express grief? Or beautiful because they express tenderness? But less than any other art, poetry lends itself to such a classification. Its sphere is that of all life and nature. The points of view of the poet are as varied as those of the thinker contemplating phenomena of the most diverse nature—and the thinker finds much in reality besides the beautiful, the sublime, and the comic. Not every grief reaches the point of the tragic, not every joy that of grace or of the comic. The mere fact that works of poetry no longer can fit into the old subdivisions is proof of the fact that the subject of poetry is not exhausted by the three elements enumerated. Dramatic poetry does not depict only the tragic or the comic as can be seen from the fact that, in addition to the comedy and the tragedy, the drama came into existence. Instead of the primarily sublime epic came the novel with all its numerous ramifications. For most of our modern lyric plays no classification could be found in the older forms which would cover their subject matter adequately. Hundreds of labels are inadequate—so they cannot evidently embrace all works of art (according to subject matter, not form, which must always be beautiful).

The simplest way to untangle this knot is to realize that the sphere of art is not limited to beauty and its so-called elements, and that reality (life and nature) interests man not as a scientist but simply as a human being. What is generally interesting in reality is the subject matter of art. Beauty, tragedy, comedy—these are only three more definite elements out of thousands, to

From *Life and Aesthetics*

enumerate which would be to enumerate all emotions. More detailed proof of the correctness of our conception of the subject matter of art is hardly necessary as, though aesthetics usually includes a more restricted definition of the subject matter of art, the conception we propose prevails in fact, i.e., with artists and poets themselves who constantly express this both in life and literature. If it is sometimes considered necessary to define beauty as the preponderating or, to be more exact, as the only essential subject matter of art, the true reason for this is to be found in the lack of distinction between the conception of beauty as the object of art, and beautiful form, which is a necessary attribute of all works of art.

This formal beauty or unity of idea and image, subject matter and form, is not, however, any special property that distinguishes art from other branches of human endeavor. The activities of man always have a purpose and this constitutes the essence of the activity. The degree to which our activity corresponds to the purpose we wish to achieve by it is a measure of the value of the activity. Every human work is valued according to the degree of perfection of achievement. This is a law which holds for all—trades, business, scientific research, etc. It also applies to works of art. The artist (whether consciously or unconsciously does not matter) tries to reproduce for us some phase of life. It is quite self-evident that the merit of his work will depend upon how successful he is in accomplishing his purpose. "A work of art endeavors to achieve harmony of idea and image" no more and no less than the product of the shoemaker, the jeweller, the engineer or the product of moral determination. "Everything done must be done well" is what the phrase "harmony of idea and image" means.

To sum up then, beauty as unity of idea and image is not at all a characteristic peculiarity of art in the aesthetic sense. "Unity of idea and image" defines only one, formal side of art, and has nothing to do with its subject matter. It speaks of *how* and not of what is shown. But we have already noted that what is important in this phrase is the word "image"—it tells us that art expresses ideas not in the abstract but in live individual facts. When we say "art is the reproduction of life and nature," we say the same thing, because there is nothing abstract in life and nature. Every-

69

thing is concrete there. The reproduction must convey as nearly as possible the essence of the thing reproduced. Hence the creations of art should be least abstract and expressed concretely in live pictures and individual images whenever possible. (Whether art can achieve this completely is quite another question. Painting, sculpture, and music do.) Poetry neither can nor should always bother too much about plastic details—it is quite sufficient when the poetic work as a whole is plastic. Too great attention to plastic details may be harmful to the unity of the whole, as when details are given too bold a relief, but what is even more important, such attention to details distracts the artist's attention from the essentials. Beauty of form, which is unity of idea and image, is something common to all human endeavor and not a peculiarity of art (in the aesthetic sense), and is entirely distinct from the idea of beauty as an object of art, as a thing of joy in the world of reality. Confusion of beauty of form, which is a necessary property of works of art, and beauty, which is one of many things art aims at, has been one of the main reasons for the unfortunate abuses we find in art. "The object of art is beauty at all costs, art has no other object." But what is most beautiful? In human life—beauty and love; in nature—it is hard to say just what, there is so much beauty there. Hence, aptly or not, every poetic work must be filled with descriptions of nature—the more descriptions, the more beauty in the given work. But love and beauty are still lovelier, so (mostly irrelevantly) love is put in the foreground of every play, novel, story, etc. Irrelevant descriptions of nature are not so bad yet— they can be simply omitted, as they are just pinned on. But what is one to do with a love plot? It cannot be omitted because to it, as a base, everything is tied with Gordian knots; without it everything loses all connection and sense. Not to mention the fact that the string of the lovelorn, ever-suffering or triumphing, makes thousands of stories intolerably monotonous; nor the fact that these love adventures and descriptions of beauty take away space that should be devoted to more essential things. More than that: the custom of depicting love and always love makes poets forget that life has also other sides that interest man much more, generally. All poetry and the life it depicts assume a sort of rose-colored tone. Instead of a serious depiction of human life, very many works

From *Life and Aesthetics*

represent an extremely young (to refrain from more exact adjectives) view of life and the poet a young, very young, person, whose stories are of interest to people of a similar spiritual or physiological age. To people who have outgrown the golden age of early youth, such art begins to lose prestige; it seems to them an amusement somewhat mawkish to mature folks and not altogether harmless to the young. We have not the least intention of barring love from poetry; only aesthetics should require the poet to talk of love only when that is what he wants to talk about. Why must it occupy the foreground when something altogether different, other sides of life entirely, is in question? Why, for instance, must love occupy the foreground in novels which are really devoted to the life and manners of a given people or given classes in a given period? Books on history, psychology, ethnography, also speak of love—only in its proper place, just as about all other matters. Walter Scott's historical novels are all based on love adventures—what for? Was love the main occupation of society or the main moving force of the period dealt with? "But the novels of Walter Scott are antiquated." Well, the more modern novels of Dickens are just as full, aptly and inaptly, with love, while George Sand's novels of village life, where again love is not at all the main subject, are just as full of love. A rule seldom followed by poets is to "write about what you want to write." Love, relevantly or irrelevantly—this is the first harmful result for art due to the idea that "the subject matter of art is beauty." The second harmful result, closely tied up with the first, is artificiality. Racine and Madame Deshoulières are a laughing stock nowadays, but modern art has not advanced much beyond them with respect to simplicity and naturalness of the springs of action and naturalness of dialogue. To this day the characters are divided into heroes and villains, and how smoothly, elegantly, and eloquently they speak! The monologues and dialogues in modern novels are only little inferior to pseudo-classic tragedy. "In works of art everything must be wrapt in beauty"— and one of the conditions of beauty is that all details must be developed out of the plot. So we are given profoundly conceived plans of action, such as are almost never even thought of by people in real life, and if the character does sometimes act instinctively, unpremeditatedly, the author considers it his bounden duty to explain it as an idiosyncrasy of character, while the critics remain dissatisfied with this "unmotivated action." As if actions were always motivated by idiosyncrasies of character and not by the general nature of the human heart and circumstances. "Beauty requires rounded characters"—and instead of five people, diverse in their typicalness, the dramatist or novelist gives us motionless statues. "Beauty in a work of art requires elegance of dialogue"—and instead of living speech we are given artificial discussions in which the speakers show their natures by hook and by crook. The result is boresome monotony in poetic works. The characters are stereotyped, the action develops according to definite rules, from the very first pages one can surmise what will happen later and not only what but even how it will happen.

Also an Explanation of Life

But let us return to the question of the essential significance of art. The first and most important feature of all works of art is, as we have said, the reproduction of things that occur in real life and are of interest to man. By real life we, of course, understand not only man's relation to the objects and creatures of the objective world, but also man's inner life. A person sometimes lives in dreams; those dreams then, to him, acquire (to some extent and for a given time) the semblance of something objective. Oftener yet, a person lives in the world of his emotions. Such emotional states, if they reach a point of becoming interesting, are reproduced by art. This we mention only to show that our definition also embraces the imaginative side of art.

But we have also said that art has another significance, besides the reproduction of life—that of explaining life. To some extent this can be said of all the arts. One only has to call attention to some things (which is what art always does) for them to become understandable or even to make life more comprehensible. In this sense painting does not differ from a story about an object, except perhaps in that art achieves this purpose much better than a simple, particularly a scientific, description of the thing. We get more easily interested, understand a thing better, when it is given a live form than when we are given a dry description of it. Cooper's novels did more to acquaint the world with the life of savages than

From *Life and Aesthetics*

any ethnographical studies or discussions on the importance of such studies. But while all art points out new and interesting things in life, poetry necessarily emphasizes the essential features of things. Painting reproduces a thing with all particulars, sculpture also— poetry cannot embrace too many details and, perforce omitting a great deal, concentrates our attention on the features retained. This is what gives rise to the idea of the superiority of poetic pictures over reality. Every word, however, does the same thing to what it represents. In the word (the concept) also, all irrelevant features of what it represents are omitted and only the essential features are left. To the inexperienced thinker the word may be clearer than the thing it represents—but such clearness is only weakness. We do not wish to deny the usefulness of popularizations, but the Tappe *History of Russia* for children is not an improvement over the *History of Russia* by Karamazin, from which it was adapted. In a poetic work an event or an object may be easier to understand than the same thing in life, but we can only grant poetry the merit of a clear and lively picture of life, but not of something independent that can fully rival life itself. It must be added that every prose story does the same thing as poetry. The concentration of attention on the essential features of things is not a characteristic peculiarity of poetry but of human speech generally.

The essential significance of art is the reproduction of what interests us in reality. But interested in life, one cannot, consciously or unconsciously, express one's opinion of it. The poet or artist cannot cease to be human in general and hence to express his opinion of the things he depicts. He expresses it in his work—and this is the new significance of a work of art by virtue of which art becomes a moral activity of man. There are people whose opinions on the phenomena of life are expressed almost solely by exhibiting a predisposition in favor of certain phases of reality, avoiding the others. These are the people whose activity of mind is feeble. When such a person turns out to be a poet or artist, his work has no significance other than that he is reproducing what he likes best. But, when a person whose mental activity is strongly roused by problems arising out of observation of life happens to be gifted with artistic talent, his work, consciously or unconsciously, expresses an endeavor to pass live judgment on things that interest him (and also his contemporaries—because a thoughtful man cannot be interested in things which are of no interest also to others). In his paintings, novels, poems, or dramas questions about life that bother thinking men will be put or solved. His works will be composed, so to speak, on themes proposed by life.

Such tendencies find vent in all arts (in painting, for instance, one can point out pictures of episodes and many historical pictures), but they develop principally in poetry, which represents the best medium for expressing definite thoughts. The artist then becomes a thinker and the work of art, while remaining such, acquires a scientific significance. It is self-evident that in this respect there is nothing to correspond to it in real life—except in form. As regards content, the questions themselves that are dealt with, these can be found in real life only as unpremeditated ones. Let us suppose a work of art develops the thought that "a temporary defection is not fatal to a strong nature" or that "one extreme calls out another," or that a person falls out with himself, or, if you please, the struggle of passion and higher aspirations (we are listing the principal ideas that have been attributed to *Faust*). Does not real life present instances in which the same principles are developed? Is not high wisdom obtained by observation of life? Is not science a simple abstraction of life, resolving life into formulas? Everything dealt with by science and art can be found in life, only in a fuller, more perfect form, with all living particulars in which the true meaning of the thing really lies and which frequently is not understood by science and art and even more frequently cannot be embraced by them. The events of real life are all true, do not suffer from carelessness and biased narrowness of view, which haunt every human work. Life is fuller, truer, is a greater teacher and even more artistic than any work of science or poetry. Only life does not stop to explain its events, does not bother about deducing axioms; this is done by art and science. True, the deductions are not complete, the ideas one-sided as compared with life, but they were produced by men of genius without whose aid our deductions would be even more one-sided, even poorer. Art (poetry) and science are a handbook for the beginner in the study of life. Their purpose is to teach us to read

From *Life and Aesthetics*

the original and then serve for reference from time to time. Science does not pretend to do anything else. Nor do poets claim anything more in their cursory remarks on their work. Only aesthetics continues to claim that art is superior to life and reality.

Summing up all we have said so far, we get the following view on art: the essential function of art is to reproduce everything that interests man in life. Frequently, especially in poetry, the attempt to explain life, to express an opinion on its phenomena, comes to the foreground. The relation of art to life is that of history; the only difference in content is that history tells of the life of humanity scrupulously adhering to facts—art tells of the life of humanity with more concern for psychological and moral truth than for facts. The first task of history is to reproduce life; the second— which not all historians accomplish—is to explain life. When he does not concern himself with the second task the historian stays a mere recorder of events and his work only serves as material for the real historian or to be read only out of curiosity. In attacking the second task, the historian becomes a thinker and his work thus acquires scientific merit. The same can be said of art. History has no pretensions to compete with real historical life—acknowledges that its pictures are pale, incomplete, more or less inexact or one-sided, at any rate. Aesthetics should admit that art likewise, and for the same reasons, cannot pretend to compete with reality, particularly to exceed it in beauty.

But what happens to creative imagination, if we are to adopt such a view of art? What role does it play? We shall not stop to discuss the origin of the artist's license to alter what the poet has seen or heard. This is evident from the purpose of poetic creation of which we require a truthful reproduction of a definite phase of life and not of any individual event. But let us investigate why there is need for the imagination to interfere (by means of association) and alter the perceptions of our senses to create something new in form. Let us assume the poet takes up an occurrence he knows thoroughly out of his own life (this is not frequent— usually many quite important details remain obscure and for coherence the story must be amplified by the imagination). Let us also assume that this occurrence is a perfectly complete one artistically, so that the mere retelling of it will produce a completely artistic product—in other words we choose a case when the interference of the creative imagination seems unimportant or irrelevant to the matter in hand. But for artistic completeness of the story many such details are nevertheless necessary. So they must be borrowed from other situations which the poet's memory has retained (for instance, conversation, description of the surroundings, etc.). True, the amplification of the story by such details does not change it and the variance of the story from the occurrence itself is limited, for the present, to form. But the interference of the imagination is not limited to this. In reality the occurrence was tangled up with other events which were only externally interwoven with the main story, but when we begin to disentangle the story we are interested in from the irrelevant elements, we find lapses in it marring its living fullness. Again the poet must supply material to cover these lapses. More than that—in disentangling the story, he not only robs many elements of their fullness, he frequently alters their very nature and the episode looks entirely different than it did before. In order to retain its essential character the poet is compelled to alter many particulars whose real significance depended upon the actual circumstances and is lost in the isolated circumstances of the story. The activity of the creative imagination is thus hampered very little by our conception of art.

But the object of our investigation is art as an objective product rather than as the subjective activity of the poet. We cannot therefore in this essay enter into the various relations of the poet to his material. We have indicated one such relationship, least favorable to the independence of the poet, and found that, adopting our view on art, the poet has not lost the essential characteristic which pertains not to the poet or artist in particular, but to man and human activity generally—the essential human right and property of considering objective reality as the rightful field of his activity. Under other circumstances, there is even more room for interference on the part of the creative imagination. Say, when not all the details of the story are known to the poet, as when he knows about the situation (and the characters) only from the tales of others, always rather one-sided, inexact, and artistically incomplete, at least as far as the poet personally is concerned. It must, however, be

From *Life and Aesthetics*

remembered, that the necessity to combine and alter things does not arise because real life did not contain the phenomena which the poet or artist wishes to depict, and contain them in a much fuller form than they can receive in the work of art. The necessity arises from the circumstance that the picture of life does not belong to the same sphere as real life. The difference has its origin in the fact that the poet does not have at his disposal the same means as life possesses. When an opera is transposed for the piano, it loses much and the better part of the detailed effects—there is much in the human voice or the full orchestra which cannot possibly be transferred to the comparatively poor, dead instrument which is supposed to reproduce the opera. In the transposition, therefore, much has to be altered, added or changed.

The essence of our discussion has been the defence of reality as compared with imagination, the attempt to prove that works of art cannot but lose by a comparison with live reality. Does this mean to humble art? In the sense that art is *inferior* to real life in artistic perfection—yes. But to protest against panegyrics does not mean to disparage. Science does not pretend to superiority over nature, and this is not to its shame. Art should not pretend to superiority over life—this would not humiliate it. Science is not ashamed to declare that its aim is to comprehend and explain nature, to then apply its explanations for the good of humanity. Let art also not be ashamed to acknowledge that its aim is to compensate man in cases when he has no opportunity to enjoy the full aesthetic pleasure of reality in accordance with its powers and in reproducing it, try to explain it.

Let art be content with its high and beautiful purpose of replacing reality to some extent in its absence and being a text book of life.

Reality is greater than dreams and essential significance more important than fantastic pretensions.

The author's task has been to investigate the aesthetic relation between works of art and the phenomena of life, and find whether the prevalent opinion that the truly beautiful, which is supposed to be the essential content of works of art, does not exist in objective reality and is only to be found in art. Intimately connected with

77

this question is that of the definition of beauty and of the content of art. Upon investigating the question as to what beauty is, the author came to the conclusion that beauty is life. Upon this it became necessary to investigate the conceptions of the sublime and the tragic which, as beauty is usually defined, are supposed to be elements of it. We found that the sublime and the beautiful are objects of art entirely independent of each other. This was an important step towards the solution of the question as to what constitutes art. But if beauty is life, the question of the aesthetic relation between beauty in art and beauty in life solves itself. Having reached the conclusion that art cannot have its origin in man's dissatisfaction with beauty in reality, we had to discover what needs do give rise to art and investigate its real significance. This investigation brought us to the following conclusion:

1. The definition of beauty as "the complete manifestation of the idea in an individual phenomenon" does not stand up under criticism. It is too broad and defines the formal tendency of every human activity.

2. The true definition of beauty is "beauty is life." That seems beautiful to man, in which he sees life as he understands it. A beautiful object is one that recalls life.

3. Such objective beauty, or beauty in its essence, should be distinguished from perfection of form, which consists of the unity of idea and form, or of the object's answering its purpose to perfection.

4. The sublime does not at all affect man in that it evokes in him the idea of the absolute—it never does that.

5. That seems sublime to man which is much greater than anything, or more powerful than any phenomenon it is compared to.

6. The tragic has nothing essentially in common with the idea of fate or necessity. In real life tragedy is most commonly accidental, does not follow as a necessary consequence of preceding events. The necessity in which art clothes tragedy is a consequence of the usual principle governing works of art—that "the denouement must flow from the plot," or the irrelevant subjection of the poet to the conceptions of fate.

7. According to the ideas of modern European culture tragedy is "the terrible in man's life."

From *Life and Aesthetics*

8. The sublime (and its element—the tragic) is not a variation of beauty. The ideas of the sublime and the beautiful are entirely distinct. They have no inner connection, nor are they inwardly contradictory.

9. Reality is not only more alive but also more perfect than imagination. The images of the imagination are only a pale and most generally an unsuccessful subterfuge for reality.

10. Beauty in objective reality is thoroughly beautiful.

11. Beauty in objective reality completely satisfies man.

12. Art does not at all arise out of man's need to improve upon beauty as it is in reality.

13. The creations of art are inferior in beauty to reality not only because the impression created by reality is more lively; they are inferior in beauty (just as in the sublime, tragical or comical) also from an aesthetic viewpoint.

14. The field of art is not limited to beauty in the aesthetic sense of the word, beauty in its live essence, and not only to perfection of form; art reproduces everything in life that is of interest to man.

15. Perfection of form (unity of idea and form) is not a trait characteristic only of art in the aesthetic sense of the term (fine art); beauty as unity of idea and image, or the complete embodiment of the idea is the aim of art in the widest possible sense of the term or of "skill," in fact, the aim of all practical activities of man.

16. The need which gives rise to art in the aesthetic sense of the term (fine art) is the same as that which clearly comes to the fore in portrait painting. A portrait is not painted because the features of the original do not satisfy us, but to help our memory recall the living person when we are not in his presence and give people that have never seen the original some idea of him. With its reproductions, art only reminds us of what is interesting in life and endeavors to acquaint us to some extent with those interesting phases of life which we have had no opportunity to experience or observe ourselves in reality.

17. The reproduction of life is the general characteristic feature of art, its essence. Works of art also often have another purpose —to explain life. They also often express judgment on the phenomena of life.

"On Realism"*

By Fernand Desnoyers

FERNAND DESNOYERS (1828-1889) was a man of letters who early indicated his dissatisfaction with the prevailing romantic mode and his
eagerness for new developments in literature and painting. In 1855
the rather vague aspirations toward sincerity and freedom in art for
which he stood were crystallized somewhat by reason of the controversy generated by the withdrawal of Courbet's paintings from a retrospective show at the Exposition Universelle. Courbet set up his own
exhibition on the Avenue Montaigne nearby, placing over the door a
placard inscribed with the simple but provocative label *Du Réalisme*.
This was also the title of the preface to the catalogue-prospectus which
was a statement of his aims in the form of a manifesto. Champfleury
naturally defended Courbet during the ensuing public argument, writing an article for the journal *L'Artiste* which so outraged one Charles
Perrier that he replied in a long letter which asserted the incompatibility of Courbet's works with what he had understood Champfleury and
others to mean by realism. Courbet, he says, stands for "a system of
painting which consists in exalting and magnifying one of the *real*
aspects of nature, I am speaking of matter, to the detriment of another
side, which is equally real, that is, spirit." Material representation lacks
style and it lacks the idealization of objects, both of which are indispensable to art. Ugliness, in his opinion, can exist "only on condition of being, from a certain point of view, a diaphanous veil through
which spirit may shine."

Desnoyers' article, which appeared in *L'Artiste* in December 1855,
would seem to be the culmination of this dispute and a general attack
on the idealist and romantic position. He assails the banality of romantic art, the hollowness of its conventions, and the insincerity and
sterility of its practitioners, taking the position set forth by Courbet
in his manifesto that the artist must be himself without deference to
isms or schools.

◇◇

THIS article is neither a defense of a client nor a plea for an
individual; it is a manifesto, a profession of faith. Like a grammar
or a course in mathematics, it begins with a definition: Realism is
the true depiction of objects.

* Desnoyers, Fernand, "Du Réalisme," *L'Artiste*, pp. 197-200, December 9,
1855.

"On Realism"

There is no *true* depiction without color, vital spirit, life and animation, without features and feeling. It would therefore be stupid to apply the preceding definition to mechanical art: vital spirit is depicted only by vital spirit, whence it follows that for many men of letters it would be impossible to depict a live man.

(Perhaps some intelligent readers will consider it pointless to *defend* an art the basis of which is truth and which accepts all manifestations of the human spirit on condition that they be sincere and individual, that they emanate from imagination or memory, from reflection or observation. However, it is necessary to *defend*, since there is an *attack*.)

The landscape artist who does not know how to fill his picture with air and who is only able to render color exactly is not only not a realistic painter, but is not a painter at all; for *the features, the vital spirit, the life* of a landscape is air.

The writer who can depict men and things only by the aid of known and conventional means is not a realistic writer; he is not a writer at all.

The word *realist* has been used only to distinguish the artist who is sincere and clear-sighted from the one who obstinately, in good or bad faith, looks at things through colored glasses.

Since the word truth puts everybody in agreement and since everybody approves of the word, even liars, we must admit that, without being an apologist for ugliness and evil, realism has the right to represent whatever exists and whatever we see.

For Venus rarely appears, and the diaphanous nymphs and the gods with silver bows fled our woods and skies a long time ago and took refuge in certain books and pictures.

Now no one is denied the right to like what is false, ridiculous, or faded and to call it the ideal and poetry; but it is permissible to deny that this mythology is our world, in which it is perhaps high time we took a look around.

Moreover, poetry itself is misused. It is served up with every kind of sauce, and this is not a situation where it may be said that the sauce makes the pudding.

Poetry grows like the grass between the paving stones of Paris. It is sparse, and whenever a blade does appear, the flat-footed quickly crush it. Let us leave poetry alone! Every age, every being has its own; yet there is only one. Take your choice. For my part, I believe that the poetry which everybody believes he has in his pocket is to be found in the ugly just as much as in the beautiful, in the fantastic just as much as in the real, provided that the poetry be naive and carry conviction and that its form be sincere. Ugliness or beauty is a matter for the painter or poet; it is for him to decide and choose; but one thing is sure, poetry, like Realism, can be found only in what exists, in what is to be seen, smelled, heard, and dreamed, provided you don't dream deliberately. It is odd that people have made a special effort to hold Realism back as if it had invented the depiction of the ugly. Who can show me a poet or painter whose work does not contain some monsters and many horrors? Shakespeare or Rembrandt? Raphael even or Homer? Persius or Rubens? Veronese or Rabelais? Most of the unbelievable deformities and hideous enormities, all that is disgusting, horrible, or frightening, was imagined or painted by the great artists of the past. Racine himself took pleasure in the depiction of the evil passions and hateful monsters that the watery plain spews forth. It is less pardonable for Albert Dürer to have shown us the atrocious faces of the diluvian Israelites than for present-day painters to show us the nudities of the day, which are certainly less frightful than the ones we generally meet and which in any case could not justifiably be reproached as painting of the ugly since they shine forth in the midst of nature, in verdure full of color and nuances. If we were to satisfy the taste of so-called lovers of the beautiful, would it not be necessary to put a seal on impure manners and on noses which are not straight? Let them pick up a looking-glass, then, and stay at home. Antiquity especially, and mythology, which is much more true than people think, abound in abominations. The most repulsive types—painted or printed—are to be found in libraries and museums; no critics become frightened by them. Let the realists enjoy the same liberty! If the men in greatcoats who parade before our eyes are not handsome, so much the worse! That's not a reason for putting a frock coat on Narcissus or Apollo. I demand for painting and for literature the same rights as mirrors have.

Our adventures nowadays are no less astonishing, diverting, and incredible than those of the past. There are even plenty of bourgeois whose existence will arouse as much curiosity some centuries hence as that of Mercury and good old Jupiter. Faces that we meet are as grotesque as many of the heads which have come down to us from Greek art, and the Paris Stock Exchange resembles the Parthenon. That ought to encourage amateurs, members of the academy, and *conservatives* to leave Claros and Trezene for a moment, to descend from Olympus and the two-humped mountain, where love of the beautiful has confined them for so long.

There are others of equal utility who persist in strolling in the alleys of Watteau parks. The chestnut trees of these gentlemen are still in bloom in November; there is always the rustle of silk in the pomaded greenery, and the flowers smell of vanilla and patchouli; the water gushing up over the shrubbery never loses its irisy look in a rainbow sky.

As for the romantics, now that they have given up exterminating the Atreus family, their hidalgo moustaches look no different from those of veterans of the guard. The plumes on their hats and the ribbons on their doublets have faded. It is in vain that they take Parisian shutters for Seville jalousies and hum an Andalusian air in tremulous voice; no sigh comes through the blinds, behind which is to be heard no rustle of startled dress surprised by some ghost of Bartholo. The Rue de Rivoli like a sword has cut through old Paris from end to end. It was only there that the Romantics could dream of the Middle Ages! All they have left is their daggers, scrap iron, the click of which is to be heard only in the adventures of D'Artagnan; but even the newspaper in which these adventures appear is as deserted as a bar where the quality of the drinks has deteriorated!

A few young enthusiasts are still running after adventure; alas, even the city police pay no attention. Paris street urchins yell in pursuit of the last romantics. But soon these waggish scamps are out of breath. Then to protect themselves from irony and to escape the law of retaliation, they feel the need to *produce some works.* *Exegi monumentum* seems to them to be their law; they submit to it and catch at their memories in the air like flies. Then they journey out on the Saint-Denis plain and into the Bois de Boulogne. The sight of nature moves them; they shed sweet tears which cause great oaks to grow and willows full of singing birds. Under the greenery they make love to amorous ballet dancers and devoted dress-makers, who brew a cup of tea from the buds of these same willows. When winter comes they can no longer kiss *under* the leaves, for the ones that remain are leaves of paper and they must write *on* them. Then, like nightingales in this, they can no longer sing.

Their continual scratching at their foreheads brings forth not Minerva but myriads of dancers who renounce society to give themselves to literature. These newcomers always give the impression they are dancing the polka. Most of them are rich and what is called a good catch. They cultivate literature, first to spite their mothers, who soon cannot resist their glory in flowing facile style; then they get into the public press with both feet, and the fops become little pedants. They pass judgment on serious books with the mannerisms of handsome dancers; through their waltzing they become influential and gather a circle around them in the vestibule on opening nights. They have organized their quadrille.

Then come the professors, who are called master and who give courses in art, as if literature and painting could be taught! Old journalists preserve French conversation. It is only among them that courtliness with patch on face and hoop skirt on back makes its curtsy to fine talk. They are the last straggling troupe who have faithfully received the traditions of the eighteenth century. They talk about Voltaire and Diderot and make an effort to adopt their mannerisms. They are homesick for the Café Procope, and the tearing down of the Café de la Régence makes them think of the ruins of Carthage and Pompeii and the decline of their own country. Fortunately the gas lights at Lepelletier's shine out to them as a beacon of hope. It is the last ray of light from the sacred spring.

There are also some new romantics, and they are no less strange. They draw up a charter in the manner of the famous Preface to *Cromwell*, which the generation of 1830 is still talking about. They have invented industrial literature, Crampton poetry. They maintain that the best way to give new life to literature is to sing the benefits of gas and the sewing machine. With the result that inventors and important business men would have no need of advertising. Books would be handbooks and guides. Why didn't our ancestors think of this? We would have fine epic poems on the candle and prodigious novels and paintings about the potato.

However, among this group you find a few leaders who are more irritating and exaggerated than others. One of them, whom Messers Delaville and Luce de Lancival (master of the Academician Villemain) would have called a pamphleteer, has a reputation as a man of wit in the card room. He obtains preferment, holds his head high, and like Fra Diavolo wears a cloak with dashing effect. Your eye tries to find the bulge of his dagger in the folds of the cloak. It is evident that he only owes his proud manner, his attitude of thrust-back shoulders, to the good opinion of himself which his energy inspires; if writing were done by blows of the fist, he would certainly be a Hercules. One day this critic asked a question about the meaning of the word *Realism* in his column. Unfortunately, the column, having no dictionary, was unable to answer him, and he was reduced to admiring a collection of popular songs, so-called, whose author is beginning to be served up at dessert at important dinners. This young man sings at the piano, is the delight of ladies, and, as they do at the Folies Nouvelles, plays ravishing operettas all by himself. He is the thing in society. People say of him: Yesterday we had that delicious X.

The couplets of this agreeable being find favor with two dramatists. The first has taken his art seriously and for a long time has been trying to make over the poetry of Corneille, Racine, and André Chénier in his own manner out of hatred for romanticism. His great success has led him to try something else. Now, assuming the attitude of a Molière, he is trying to fashion a comic sock. Saint Crispin does not inspire him and the enterprise is going badly.

As for the other dramatist, the coldness of the modern theatre has warmed his bile. His face has become completely flushed and he has set to work, determined to renew the old Gallic sprightliness. No doubt this sprightliness gave pleasure to our ancestors. It makes me think of the *Gallic spirit*, which, not knowing where to hide in a time when rents are so high, has lodged in the head of a *young writer*, in the phrase of certain weekly reviews. The follies this *Gallic spirit* causes the *young writer* to commit are incalculable. However, they cannot refuse the Prix de Rome to this *Gallic spirit*. Realist painting has excited its weapons; the *Gallic spirit* maliciously riddles Courbet's *La Baigneuse* with grains of dirty salt.

Another man of wit, though not reputed to be completely French, is no less sparkling, for he has been effervescing since 1825 and belongs to the famous blossoming of 1830. He writes *verses* as another would write—verses. It costs him no effort. Unlike the people who buy his work—for people do buy his productions—this marvelous improviser and prestidigitator believes that wit is everywhere, even in his own pockets; if Realism succeeds in being as witty as he is, his approbation is not in doubt. But this witty mind skips along too quickly for anyone to catch him; it is better to let him go; at the rate he is going, it will not be long, etc., etc.

All these people, who believe only in the past, constitute a huge carnival. Their armor, doublets, hose, and peplums are not becoming to present-day people. Their frippery is mildewed, faded, worn thin, and full of holes; nothing fits. However, this army of artists and men of letters, painters and critics, are present at the representation of everything that is created, in germ or in harvest, and shake their heads as they talk of the Greeks, the Romans, the Germans, the English, etc., and of the *flowering* of 1830, indistinguishable from those bald heads who on important evenings at the Théâtre-Français, cough out the names of Molé, Mourel, and Mlle Mars.

That is what art has come to. Discussed and invaded by these distinguished men of wit, these delightful talkers, whose books entitled *Petites Nouvelles, Petites Causeries, Revues de Paris, Coups d'épingle*, etc., bring joy to the provincial heart. These golden or silver poets who are as ephemeral as that unhappy mania for Chinese vases; these lovers of the *pretty*, the inventors of the *damp* laugh, and others who illuminate their sentences with adjectives of every color; these old romantics as out of date as the dead they celebrate in their ballads; these new romantics who cannot make the grade in spite of their locomotives; these pedants and unemployed ushers who set themselves up as judges and critics instead of going off and getting themselves killed in the Crimea; these denizens of bars who brood over their beer as they meditate profound works; these stupid and ignorant journalists who ex-

"On Realism"

press opinions which belong to everybody; these founders of reviews, and pretty gentlemen who assume the name of journalist in order to make an impression on women of easy virtue and blackmail them for love; these amateurs in short, bourgeois and men of elegance, graduates of the Collège Bourbon in particular whom the Faculty of Law rejects and sends out into the society of men of letters. So much for literature.

As for painting and sculpture, they are overwhelmed by traditions and imitations, by the Academy, and by foreign lands, as music is by the din of drums and brasses.

At last Realism *is coming*!

It is through this underbrush, this battle of the Cimbri, this Pandemonium of Greek temples, lyres, and jews' harps, of alhambras and sickly oaks, of boleros, of silly sonnets, of golden odes, of rusty daggers, rapiers, and weekly columns, of hamadryads in the moonlight and the tenderness of Venus, of marriages in the manner of M. Scribe, of witty caricatures and unretouched photographs, of canes and false collars, of toothless discussions and criticisms, of tottery traditions, of ill-fitting customs and couplets addressed to the public, that Realism has made a breach.

Can you imagine the din made by so many people pushed, knocked down, rolling over one another, tumbling down from Helicon, from the Rue de Bréda, from the Chaussée d'Antin and all the academies? How many articles, imprecations, and odes, how much red, gold, blue, yellow, green, and black have rushed in agitation out of frames and newspapers!

And why all this commotion? Because Realism tells people: We have always been Greek, Latin, English, German, Spanish, etc.; why don't we try to be ourselves, even if we are ugly? Let us write and paint only what is, or at least what we see, what we know, what we have experienced. Let us have no masters or disciples! A strange school, isn't it, in which there are no masters or disciples and the only principles are independence, sincerity, and individuality!*

* It is interesting to compare Courbet's brief manifesto:

REALISM

The label of realist has been imposed on me just as the label of romantic was imposed on the men of 1830. Labels have never, in any age, given a very

87

accurate idea of things; if it were otherwise, the works would be superfluous.

Without discussing the appropriateness, more or less justified, of a designation which nobody, it is to be hoped, has taken very seriously, I shall confine myself to a few words of explanation in order to prevent misunderstanding.

I have studied the art of the ancients and of the moderns without adherence to a system and without prejudice. It was not my wish to imitate the one or to copy the other; nor was it my idea to attain the idle goal of *art for art's sake*! No! I simply wished to draw from a knowledge of the whole tradition a reasoned and independent sense of my own individuality.

To know in order to create, that was my idea. To be capable of depicting the manners, ideas, and appearance of my time as I see it, in short, to produce living art, that is my goal.

On Realism*

By Gustave Flaubert

GUSTAVE FLAUBERT (1821-1880) was the somewhat reluctant leader of the realistic school in France. As his disciple, Guy de Maupassant, wrote a generation later: "The appearance of *Madame Bovary* [serially in the *Revue de Paris* beginning October 1, 1856; in book form, 1857] was a revolution in literature. . . . Gustave Flaubert, on the contrary [in comparison with Balzac], proceeding by penetration much more than by intuition, brought, in a language that was admirable and new, precise, sober, and sonorous, a study of human life that was profound, surprising, and complete.

"This was no longer the novel as it had been written by the very greatest, a novel where you are always somewhat aware of the author and his imagination, a novel capable of being classified as tragic, sentimental, passionate, or homely, a novel where the writer's intentions, opinions, and ways of thinking show themselves. It was life itself making an appearance. . . ."

It is true that today we see Flaubert as the fountainhead of symbolist as well as realist practices by reason of his image and symbol patterns, his exasperated obsession about nuances of language, and his general concern with producing a beautiful, non-utilitarian object. His break with the past is no less sharp for all that: he felt that contemporary literature was drowning in emotion and gothicism; like Ibsen, he wished to open the windows and let in fresh air. Moreover, the very content of *Madame Bovary* makes it from one standpoint a polemic against romantic philosophy and attitudes. From the time he began to write this work Flaubert was highly conscious of the innovations he was attempting and of the difficulty of breaking away from conventional ways of fabulation. Thus in his letters during this period (chiefly to Louise Colet, his mistress and a writer who suffered from romantic logorrhea) he set forth unsystematically a number of statements about what the new way of writing should be. These remarks, along with later observations in his correspondence, have come to be one of the important *loci critici* of modern literature.

There are three main doctrines enunciated by Flaubert: First, subject is not important; in his words, "Yvetot donc vaut Constantinople." Second, the author must withdraw from his work, maintaining rigid objectivity and impassivity. Third, literature does not preach but shows. There is a fourth doctrine, that of making a beautiful work out

* Flaubert, Gustave, *Oeuvres Complètes, Correspondance*, vols. II-VIII, *passim*; Paris, Louis Conard, 1926-1933.

of nothing, or as nearly nothing as possible, which is certainly not a realistic idea and has indeed led writers in a counter-direction.

In addition to *Madame Bovary* Flaubert wrote *L'Education sentimentale* (1869), an account of an education in disillusionment, which is also something of an archetypal work. His *Salammbô* (1862) may be said to have opened the doors of the historical novel to realism, though Flaubert in a letter to the Goncourts confessed that due to the paucity of documents "Reality is almost impossible in such a subject." Yet, when attacked on that point by Sainte-Beuve, he defended himself stoutly and at length. "Un Coeur Simple" (1877), a novella which tells the short and simple annals of a poor servant woman, exhibits another favorite realistic subject. The unfinished and posthumously published *Bouvard et Pécuchet* is a novelistic encyclopedia of human stupidity and mediocrity.

◇◇

"YESTERDAY EVENING I began my novel. I now foresee difficulties of style which frighten me to death. Being simple is not so easy. I am afraid of falling into Paul de Kock's manner or of writing Chateaubriandized Balzac." (II, 316, To Louise Colet, September ?, 1851)

"I twist and turn; I scratch myself. My novel is having trouble getting under way. I suffer from abscesses of style, and phrases itch at me without coming out. What a heavy oar a pen is, and what a heavy current an idea becomes when it must be dug into! I fret so much about it that I am greatly amused. Today I passed the whole day with the windows open and the sun on the river in the greatest serenity. I have written one page and sketched out three others. In a couple of weeks I hope to have hit my stride; the colors in which I dip my brush are so new to me that I open my eyes in astonishment." (II, 326, To Louise Colet, end of October, 1851)

"What strikes me as beautiful, what I should like to do, is a book about nothing, a book without external attachments, which would hold together by itself through the internal force of its style . . . a book which would have practically no subject, or at least one in which the subject would be almost invisible, if that is possible." (II, 345, To Louise Colet, January 16, 1852)

". . . I think you can have no idea of the kind of book I am writing. In my other books I was slovenly; in this I am trying to be impeccable and to follow a geometrically straight line. No lyricism, no comments, the author's personality absent. It will make dreary reading; it will contain atrocious things of misery and sordidness." (II, 361, To Louise Colet, February 1, 1852)

"I am in a completely different world now, that of attentive observation of the dullest details. My eyes are fixed on the spores of mildew growing on the soul. It is a long way from there to the mythological and theological pyrotechnics of *Saint Anthony*. And just as the subject is different, so do I write in an entirely different manner. In my book I do not want there to be *a single* movement, or *a single* reflection of the author." (II, 365, To Louise Colet, February 8, 1852)

"... The whole value of my book, if it has any, will be in my having been able to walk straight ahead on a hair hung between the double abysses of lyricism and vulgarity (which I want to fuse into an analytical narrative)." (II, 372, To Louise Colet, March 21, 1852)

"... If *Bovary* is worth anything, it won't lack heart. Irony, however, seems to me to dominate life. Is this why, when I was weeping, I often used to go and look at myself in the mirror? This tendency to look down upon oneself from above is perhaps the source of all virtue." (II, 407, To Louise Colet, May 9, 1852)

"The same thing is true in art. Passion does not make poetry, and the more personal you are, the more feeble you will be. I have always sinned in that direction myself; that's because I have always put myself into everything I have written. For example, it was I who was there in place of *Saint Anthony*; the *Temptation* was for me and not for the reader. *The less you feel a thing the more you are likely to express it as it is* (as it is *always* in itself, in its essence, freed of all ephemeral contingent elements). But you have to have the ability *to make yourself feel it*. This ability is nothing other than genius: to have your model constantly posing before you." (II, 461-462, To Louise Colet, July 6, 1852)

"... The books which I am most ambitious to write are precisely those for which I have the least competence. In this sense *Bovary* will be an unheard of *tour de force*, of which I alone will ever be aware: subject, character, effect, etc., everything comes from out-side me. That should make me take a great step forward later on. In writing this book I am like a man who would try to play the piano with lead balls on each finger. But when I have learned my fingering, if I happen upon a tune to my taste and can play with my arms raised up, perhaps I shall do something good. I think, moreover, that in this respect I am on the right track. What you do is not for yourself but for others. Art has no bones to pick with the artist. So much the worse if he does not like red, green, or yellow; all colors are beautiful; it's a matter of painting them." (III, 3-4, To Louise Colet, July 27, 1852)

"One writes with his head. If the heart warms it, so much the better, but it doesn't do to say so. It ought to be an invisible fire, and thereby we avoid amusing the public with ourselves, which I find horrible or too naive, and with the personality of the writer, which always reduces a work." (III, 50, To Louise Colet, November 16, 1852).

". . . I believe my *Bovary* is going to go all right, but I am ham-pered by my propensity for metaphor, which definitely dominates me too much. I am devoured by comparisons as one is by lice, and I spend all my time squashing them; my sentences swarm with them." (III, 79, To Louise Colet, December 27, 1852)

". . . Then let's try to see things as they are and not seek to have more intelligence than God Himself. In days gone by people thought that only sugar cane yielded sugar. Nowadays they get it from practically everything; it's the same way with poetry. Let's extract it from no matter what, for it is latent in everything and everywhere; there's not an atom of matter that does not contain thought. So let's become accustomed to considering the world as a work of art, the ways of which we must reproduce in our works." (III, 138, To Louise Colet, March 27, 1853)

". . . That's what is so fine about the natural sciences: they don't wish to prove anything. Therefore what breadth of fact and what an immensity for thought! We must treat men like mastodons and crocodiles. Does anyone fly into a passion about the horns of the former or the jaws of the latter? Show them, stuff them, put them in solution, that's enough, but appreciate them, no. And what are you yourselves, you little toads?" (III, 154, To Louise Colet, March 31, 1853)

"If the book I am writing with so much trouble comes out well, by its very existence I shall have established these two truths, which to me are axiomatic; first, that poetry is purely subjective, that in literature there are no fine artistic subjects, that therefore Yvetot is worth just as much as Constantinople; and that consequently one subject is as good as another. *It is up to the artist to raise everything*; he is like a pump, he has a big tube in him which goes down to the vitals of things to the deepest layers." (III, 249, To Louise Colet, June 26, 1853)

". . . He [Leconte de Lisle] does not see the *moral density* which there is in certain ugly things. Thus his writing lacks life, and *even relief*, though he does have color. Relief comes from a deep view, *from penetration, from the objective.* For exterior reality must enter into us, almost make us cry out with it, if we are to reproduce it well. When we have our model sharp before us, we always write well, and where indeed is the true more clearly visible than in these fine exhibitions of human misery?" (III, 269, To Louise Colet, July 8, 1853)

"Today I had a great success. You know that yesterday *we* had the *good fortune* to have M. Saint-Arnaud with us. Well, this morning in the *Journal de Rouen* I found a sentence in the mayor's speech to him which the evening before I had written *textually* in Bovary (in a speech by the prefect at the agricultural fair). Not only were there the same idea and the same words, but even the same *assonances* of style. I don't deny that this sort of thing gives me pleasure. When literature has the precision of results of an exact science, that's going some." (III, 285-286, To Louise Colet, July 22, 1853)

". . . Let us always bear in mind that impersonality is a sign of strength. Let us absorb the objective; let it circulate in us, until it is externalized in such a way that no one can understand this marvelous chemistry. Our hearts should serve only to understand the hearts of others. Let us be magnifying mirrors of external truth." (III, 383-384, To Louise Colet, November 6, 1853)

". . . How stupid and false all works of the imagination are made by preoccupation with morality! I concern myself a great deal with criticism. The novel I am writing sharpens that faculty in me, for it is a work of criticism above all, or rather of anatomy. The reader will not be aware, I hope, of all the psychological work concealed beneath the form, but he will feel its effect." (IV, 3, To Louise Colet, January 1854)

". . . there is not in this book *one* movement in my name, and the personality of the author is *completely* absent." (IV, 36, To Louise Colet, March 19, 1854)

"Don't you believe that this ignoble reality, the depiction of which disgusts you, also sickens my heart to an equal extent? If you knew me better, you would know that I execrate ordinary life. I have always withdrawn from it as much as I could. But aesthetically I wanted, this time, and only this time, to get hold of it to the very bottom. Thus I have undertaken it in an heroic manner —by that I mean minute, meticulous—accepting everything, saying everything, depicting everything—a most ambitious statement." (IV, 125, To Laurent-Pichat, October 2, 1856)

"I will admit to you that all that is of complete indifference to me. The morality of Art lies in its very beauty, and I value style first and above all, and then Truth. I believe that I have put as much of literature and *decorum* as possible—given the subject naturally—into my portrayal of middle-class manners and into my depiction of the character of a naturally corrupt woman." (IV, 136, To Louis Bonenfant, December 12, 1856)

". . . *Madame Bovary* contains nothing from life. It is a *completely invented* story. I have put into it nothing of my feelings or of my experience. The illusion (if there is one) comes, on the contrary, from the *impersonality* of the work. It is one of my principles that you must not *write yourself*. The artist ought to be in his work like God in creation, invisible and omnipotent. He should be felt everywhere but not be seen.*

* Taine in a letter written in June 1854 (*Correspondance* II: 66) made a re-

94

On Realism

"Art ought, moreover, to rise above personal feelings and nervous susceptibilities! It is time to give it the precision of the physical sciences, by means of a pitiless method! Nonetheless for me the major difficulty continues to be style, form, the indefinable Beautiful *resulting from the conception itself*; this is the splendor of Truth, as Plato said." (IV, 164-165, To Mademoiselle Leroyer de Chantepie, March 18, 1857)

". . . The novel has been nothing but the exposition of the personality of the author, and indeed I would say this of all literature in general, with the exception of two or three men perhaps. However, the moral sciences must take a new path and proceed, as do the physical sciences, in an atmosphere of impartiality." (IV, 243, To Mademoiselle Leroyer de Chantepie, December 12, 1857)

"I do not believe (unlike you) that there is anything good to be done with the character of *the ideal Artist*. It would be a monster. Art is not made for the depiction of exceptions, and then too I feel an absolute abhorrence about putting anything of my feelings down on paper. I believe, even, that a novelist *does not have the right to express his opinion* on anything whatsoever." (V, 253, To George Sand, December 5-6, 1866)

"I expressed myself badly when I said 'one must not write with the heart.' I meant to say: one ought not let his personality intrude. I believe that Great Art is scientific and impersonal. By an effort of the mind you must put yourself into your characters, not draw them to you. That, at least, is the method. . . ." (V, 257, To George Sand, December 16, 1866)

"Is it not time to bring Justice into Art? The impartiality of painting would then reach the majesty of the law—and the precision of science!" (V, 397, To George Sand, August 10, 1868)

---

markably similar statement about the necessity of the author's withdrawal:

". . . now a narrative ought to set down the facts, all the facts, in detail, but they should be set down completely bare. The author must not intervene and interject a tirade every twenty lines, as Balzac did. He should disappear; I detest a painter who always puts himself in his picture. Beyle avoids reflections and commentaries. This merit produces some obscurity. Without their being explained to him, the reader must get hold of the connections and contrasts of feeling which are so delicate, so strong, in characters who are so original, on so large a scale. . . ."

"I have just finished your horrible and beautiful book! [*La For-tune des Rougon*] I am still stunned by it. It is so powerful! Very powerful!

"I take exception only to the preface. I feel that it spoils your work, which is so impartial and so lofty. In it you tell your secret, which is going too far in candor, and you express your own opin-ion, something a novelist has no right to do, according to my (per-sonal) literary theory.

"That is the *extent* of my objections.

"But you have a strong talent, and you are a fine fellow." (vi, 314-315, To Emile Zola, December 1, 1871)

"As for revealing my personal opinion about the people whom I introduce on the scene, no, no, a thousand times no! I do not feel I have that right. If the reader is not able to draw from a book the morality which is to be found there, it is because the reader is an imbecile or because the book is *false* from the standpoint of exactness. For if a thing is true, it is good. Obscene books are not even immoral, since they lack truth. Things don't happen 'like that' in life.

"But note that I hate what is conventionally called *realism*, al-though people regard me as one of its high priests. Try to figure that out!" (vii, 285, To George Sand, February 6, 1876)

". . . Reality, as I see it, should only be a springboard. Our friends [Daudet and Zola] are convinced that by itself it is the whole State. Such materialism makes me angry, and almost every Monday I am overcome by irritation as I read good old Zola's column. After the Realists we have the Naturalists and the Im-pressionists. What progress!" (vii, 359, To Turgenev, November 8, 1877)

"Art is not reality. Whatever else you do, you must choose from the elements which the latter furnishes." (viii, 224, To J.-K. Huys-mans, February-March 1879)

Two Views of *Madame Bovary*

By Edmond Duranty and
Charles Augustin Sainte-Beuve

LOUIS-EDMOND DURANTY (1833-1880), a member of the Champfleury group, is remembered chiefly for his editorship (with Jules Assézat) of a short-lived review *Réalisme* from July 10, 1856, to May 1857— a period coinciding almost exactly with *Madame Bovary*'s baptism of fire. Many of the articles in *Réalisme* have the detonative effect of manifestos though they are largely directed *against* "litterateurs and versifiers," the upholders of the noble genre, rather than toward any clearcut description of the new literature for which they plead. In the first issue Duranty announces that "Romanticism is dead; it is MM. Vacquerie and Hugo who sing the last song that will be sung at its grave before it is buried forever." He chants that "We must have a revolution," and finds its forerunner in Balzac:

> "Observe: that was Balzac's great secret. Copy: that is the secret of the great painters.
>
> "If the word realism is new, the thing is not. Realism has existed as long as literature has existed; with its rays it has illumined the works of many geniuses who have followed after each other and it has made their fortune. The day has come when it is recognized and has been given a name."

When forced to discontinue the review for lack of support, Duranty lists all the authors it had been his intention to discuss, with Balzac and Stendhal in the vanguard but including practically every important French or English writer of the preceding century who had any realistic qualities—with the surprising exception of Jane Austen.

There is irony in the fact that this avowed champion of the new literature gave *Madame Bovary* a remarkably cool response, dismissing it as cold and mathematical, whereas Charles Augustin Sainte-Beuve (1804-1869), the leading critic of the day and a man essentially traditional in his sympathies who had been notably unresponsive to Balzac, gave the book a warm though discriminating reception in his "Lundi" for May 4, 1857. The accolade with which the review concludes: "Anatomists and physiologists, I find you everywhere!" is important for the recognition that the very impersonality which Duranty condemned is a source of power and for the tacit encouragement which it gave later novelists in their scientific pretensions. Sainte-Beuve, however, does raise one strong objection to the novel as a whole: "the good is too much absent," a charge often repeated by

those who believed in the consolatory and anodyne nature of literature.

It may well be that a passing remark made by Charles Baudelaire
(1821-1867) in his review of *Madame Bovary* indicates the essential
difference of these two responses: "Champfleury, in a charming, in-
fantile spirit, dabbled happily in the picturesque; he trained a pair of
poetic binoculars (more poetic than he thought) on the burlesque or
touching accidents and hazards of street scenes and family life. But out
of originality or weakness of sight, voluntarily or through inner necessity, he neglected the ordinary, which is the meeting place of the crowd,
the public rendezvous of eloquence." Clearly Duranty suffered from
the same limitations as Champfleury.

◇◇

Madame Bovary, a novel by Gustave Flaubert, shows obstinacy
in description. It makes one think of a line drawing, to such a degree is it made with a compass and meticulous exactitude: calculated, worked over, everything at right angles, and totally dry
and arid. We are told that the author spent several years working
on it. Indeed its details have been set down one by one, each given
the same value; each street, each house, each room, each brook,
each blade of grass is fully described; each character when he arrives on scene makes preliminary remarks on a host of useless and
uninteresting topics, merely for the sake of bringing out his level
of intelligence. As a result of this system of obstinate description,
the novel is presented almost entirely in *gestures*: not a hand, not
a foot, not a facial muscle moves without two or three lines or more
of description. In this novel there is no emotion, no feeling, no
life, only the great force of an arithmetician who has calculated
and assembled what there can be in the way of gestures, steps,
and inequalities of terrain in *given* characters, events, and landscapes. This book is a literary application of the mathematics of
probability. I am speaking here for those who have been able to
read through it. The style is uneven, as always happens with a man
who writes *artistically* without *feeling*: here imitation, there lyricism, never anything personal.—I repeat, always material *description* and never *impression*. It seems to me pointless even to consider the point of view of this book, which the aforementioned
faults deprive of all interest.—Before this novel appeared, people

On *Madame Bovary*

thought it would be better.—*An excess of study* cannot take the place of the spontaneity which comes from feeling.*

I am not unmindful of the fact that this work was the object of a debate quite different from a literary debate, but I recall above all the conclusions and the wisdom of the judges. Henceforth the work belongs to art, and to art alone; it is subject only to the judgment of criticism, which may exercise complete independence in talking about it.

It may and it should. We often take great pains to bring things of the past to life, to resuscitate ancient authors whose works scarcely anyone reads any more but to which we impart a shred of interest and a semblance of life. Yet when real and living works pass before us, within our reach, in full sail with flags flying, as though they were saying: *"What have you to say of us?"* then if we are really critics, if in our veins there is a drop of that blood that animated the Popes, Boileaus, Johnsons, Jeffreys, and Hazlitts, or even simply M. de La Harpe, we crackle with impatience, become irritated at always keeping silent; we burn to state our opinions, to salute these newcomers as they go by or to give them a lively charge of gunfire. Long ago Pindar said in reference to poetry: Long live old wine and young songs! —Young songs also include tonight's play and today's novel; these are what youth talks about the instant they appear.

I did not read *Madame Bovary* in the form in which it first appeared in the periodical where it was initially published in installments. However striking the installments were, it was bound to lose by this; above all the general idea, the conception, was bound to suffer. Having come to a stop with a bold scene, the reader asked himself: *What will be next?* He could see the work as a rank growth and impute to the author intentions which he did not have. A continuous reading puts each scene in proper perspective. *Madame Bovary* is a book above all, a composed and meditated book in which everything holds together, in which nothing is left to the chance stroke of the pen, and in which the author, or better the artist, has achieved what he wished from beginning to end.

The author has evidently lived much in the country and in the

* Duranty, Edmond, *Réalisme*, no. 5, pp. 79-80, March 15, 1857.

Norman region, which he describes with incomparable fidelity. This is remarkable! When people live a great deal in the country, when they know nature so well and are so able to depict it, they do so out of a general love for it or at least out of a desire to show it as beautiful, above all after they have left it. They are led to make it a framework for a well-being and happiness for which they feel nostalgia, at times idyllic and completely idealized. Saint-Pierre was bored to death on Mauritius as long as he lived there, but once away from there, at a distance, he saw only the beauty of its landscapes, the sweetness and peace of its valleys. In that setting he placed characters of his choice, and produced *Paul and Virginia*. Without going to Bernardin de Saint-Pierre's extreme, Madame Sand, who was perhaps at first bored in her region of Berry, later chose to show us its more attractive aspects; she did not disenchant us—far from it—with the banks of the Creuse. Even when she introduced characters dominated by theories and passions into the scene there was an amplitude of atmosphere that was pastoral, rural, and poetic in the manner of the Ancients. Here, with the author of *Madame Bovary*, we come upon another way of doing things, another sort of inspiration, and, to tell the truth, we encounter another generation. The ideal has disappeared; the lyrical spring has dried up. We have turned away from it. A severe and pitiless truthfulness has come even to art as the last word of experience. The author of *Madame Bovary* has, then, lived in the provinces, in the country, in the small town and the little city; he has not passed through on a spring day like La Bruyère's traveler who, from a hilltop, sketches his dream like a painting on the slope of the hill; he has really lived there. Now what did he see there? Meanness, misery, pretentiousness, stupidity, routine, monotony, and boredom, and he will tell us so. This landscape which is so true, so frank, and breathes the lively genius of the place will serve him only as a setting for beings who are vulgar, banal, stupidly ambitious, completely ignorant or semi-literate, and who are lovers without delicacy. The only distinguished nature to be cast there, the only one capable of dreams and aspiration toward another world will be as though stifled and uprooted; as a result of suffering, of finding no one with whom to communicate, she will change and become corrupt, and, pursuing false dreams and

On *Madame Bovary*

absent joys, she will step by step arrive at ruin and perdition. Is that moral? Is that consoling? The author seems not to have asked himself this question. He asked only one thing: Is that true? It is to be assumed that he must have observed something of this sort with his own eyes, or at least he has chosen to condense into a tightly linked depiction the result of his various observations against a background of bitterness and irony.

Another singularity which is equally remarkable! Among all his very real and very living characters there is not one who may be supposed to be what the author would himself like to be; not one has received his careful depiction for any purpose other than to be shown with full precision and rawness; none has received the gentle forbearance you would offer to a friend. The author has completely abstained; he is only there to see everything, to show everything, and to say everything, but in no corner of the novel do you get even a glimpse of his profile. The work is completely impersonal. This is a great proof of force. . . .

In the last half of the work, which is no less studied and no less exactly expressed than the first, I must indicate one weakness which is all too evident: certainly without the author's having intended it but as an effect of his method, which consists of describing everything and insisting on everything that occurs, there are details which are very sharp, scabrous, and stimulating to the sensory emotions; he should absolutely not have gone so far. A book after all is not and could never be reality itself. There are times when description, if prolonged, compromises the aim, I will not say of the moralist, but of the austere artist. I know that M. Flaubert's feeling continues to be very sharp and ironical even in the most risqué and daring passages. The tone is never one that is tender or seeks to make the reader an accomplice: basically nothing could be less tempting. But the book is read by a French reader, who was born with a smutty mind and finds this quality wherever he can.

The terrible end to which Madame Bovary comes, her punishment if you wish to call it that, her death, are presented and laid before us in inexorable detail. The author has not been afraid to strike the ringing bronze until it grates upon the nerves. The end of M. Bovary, which comes soon after, is touching and arouses our interest in that poor excellent man. I have mentioned the natural and terribly true expressions which are uttered. In his sorrow over the loss of his wife, concerning whose wrongdoing he has closed his eyes as far as possible, Bovary continues to think of everything in relation to her, and, about this time receiving Léon's marriage announcement, he bursts out: "How happy my poor wife would have been!" Soon after, when he has found the packet of letters from Léon as well as from Rodolphe, he forgives everything; he continues to love the ungrateful and unworthy one whom he has lost, and he dies of grief.

At certain points in these situations it would have taken very little to add the ideal to reality, to let the character undergo some alteration. Thus for Charles Bovary toward the end, had the sculptor wished it, it would have taken only a quick pressure of the thumb on the hardening clay at once to transform a vulgar head into a noble and tender figure. The reader would have allowed this and almost demanded it. But the author always refused; he did not wish to do this.

In the midst of his despairing grief Father Rouault, who has arrived post-haste and has just buried his daughter, makes a peasant utterance which is grotesque and sublime in its naturalness: each year he had been accustomed to send Charles Bovary a turkey in memory of the mending of his broken leg; as he leaves Charles with tears in his eyes, he tells him as a last expression of feeling: "Don't worry; you will always get your turkey."

While I am well aware of the conviction which constitutes the very method and *poetic art* of the author, there is one reproach which I must make against his book. It is that the good is too much absent; not a single character represents it. Little Justin, M. Homais's apprentice, the sole being who is devoted, disinterested, and able to love in silence, is scarcely noticeable. Why not place in the book one character whose nature is such as to console and soothe the reader with the sight of goodness, why not allow him one friend? Why deserve to be told: "Moralist, you know everything, but you are cruel." Certainly the book has a moral quality: the author has not sought it, but it is there for the reader to discern, and it is indeed terrifying. However, is it the office of art to be unwilling to console, to be unwilling to admit any element of clemency and sweetness under the excuse of being more true? Moreover, if truth alone is sought, it is not entirely and necessarily to be found only on the side of evil, on the side of human stupidity and perversity. In provincial lives, where there are so many vexations, persecutions, sickly ambitions, and petty annoyances, there are also good and beautiful souls who have remained innocent and are better preserved than elsewhere and more meditative; there is modesty and resignation and devotion lasting for many years: who among us does not know of examples? You have labored in vain, however true your characters, if you assemble them somewhat deliberately and bring together with your art the maimed and the ridiculous. Why not provide the good in one figure at least, on one charming or venerable face? In the depths of a province in central France I have known a woman who was still young, endowed with superior intelligence, ardent in heart, and bored; married but without children, having no child to rear and love, what did she do to occupy her overflowing mind and soul? She adopted those around her. She undertook to be an active benefactress, a civilizing force in the rather wild region where fate had placed her. She taught reading and moral culture to the children of the villagers, who often lived scattered about at great distances. In her benevolence she sometimes went a league and a half on foot; her pupil, for his part, did the same, and they held their lesson on a path, under a tree, on a heath. Such souls exist in the provinces and the country: why not show them too? That provides relief and consolation, and the view of humanity is only the more complete.

That is my objection to a book which I value very highly, however, for its merits: observation, style (except for a few blemishes), design, and composition.

In every respect the book carries the signature of the times in which it has appeared. Begun, they say, several years ago, its appearance is very timely today. It is decidedly a book to read after listening to the clean, sharp dialogue of a comedy by Alexandre Dumas Fils or applauding *Les Faux Bonshommes* between two articles by Taine. For in many places, and in varied forms, I believe I recognize the signs of the new literature: science, spirit of observation, maturity, force, a bit of harshness. These are characteristics which seem to attach to the leaders of the new generation. Son and brother of distinguished doctors, M. Gustave Flaubert holds the pen as others wield the scalpel. Anatomists and physiologists, I find you everywhere!*

* Sainte-Beuve, Charles Augustin, "Madame Bovary par M. Gustave Flaubert," *Causeries du Lundi*, pp. 346-363 (Monday May 4, 1857) ; Paris, Garnier Frères, n.d. Ten pages of narrative summary are omitted.

"The World of Balzac"*

By Hippolyte Taine

HIPPOLYTE TAINE (1828-1893) may be called the philosopher of the realistic movement. As a student at the Ecole Normale Supérieure he was enamored of science and positive philosophy; some years later he for a time studied physiology and natural science and did dissections at the Ecole de Médicine. When he was denied a degree in philosophy, he turned to literature and produced a dissertation cn La Fontaine. Through opposition of the government and orthodox circles he was denied a place in the educational establishment. Thus he was forced into free-lance scholarship and writing until he was given a chair in aesthetics and art history at the Ecole des Beaux Arts, where he lectured for twenty years. His various books kept pace with the developing of the new movement in literature, his *History of English Literature* in 1864 and *On Intelligence* in 1870 being of tremendous influence on his contemporaries. This article on Balzac in 1858 and a similar one on Stendhal in 1864 were also influential in molding the critical tastes of the day.

In Taine's view all knowledge derived from experience, and notions of the intellectual apprehension of essences were intolerable. In general he took the abstract or idiosyncratic man of the romantics and replaced him in the physical world, subject to an inflexible determinism. In the preface to the *History of English Literature* he set forth the famous formula that literature is determined by race, milieu, and momentum (of literary and cultural forces). A year later he wrote that the function of the novel is to show us what we are, while that of criticism is to show what we have been. Both of them are now "a grand inquiry on man, on all the varieties, situations, flowerings, and degenerations of human nature." He was the implacable enemy of abstractions in the moral sciences, where he considered his approach that of a physiologist. He tended to reduce psychological phenomena to a physiological level; he thought of the novel as basically an accumulation of data which through the operation of scientific laws would fall into inevitable patterns. The similarity of these observations with what Zola sets forth at length in *Le Roman Expérimental* shows how much the naturalists derived from Taine.

In 1863 one Monsignor Dupanloup, Bishop of Orléans, published a little tract entitled *Warning to Youth and the Fathers of Families concerning Attacks on Religion by Some Contemporary Writers*. In

* Taine, Hippolyte, "Balzac," *Nouveaux Essais de culture et de l'histoire*, pp. 1-94; Paris, Hachette, n.d. The portion here translated is pp. 48-53, 62-65. The article appeared originally in *Le Journal des Débats*, February-March 1858.

this he complained that the writers in question were not obscure persons but men of talent who enjoyed a considerable position in the world of learning: two of them were professors at the Collège de France (Renan and Maury) ; another, M. Taine, had recently been a candidate for an important chair at the Ecole Polytechnique; and another, M. Littré, "has got his doctrines into a famous medical dictionary, which was composed at the beginning of the century by two honorable scientists but is now to be found, altered and corrupted by him, in the hands of all the youth in the medical schools." He continues and points up his charge against these leaders of the revolution in thought:

> "They all labor at a common task, the overthrow of Christianity ; but it is not only Christ and the Gospel that they attack; along with Christian belief their systems are battering down and undermining all the basic truths, God, the soul, the future life, and the whole moral and social order."

In spite of continued opposition from such quarters of orthodoxy and tradition Taine was elected to the French Academy, though his deterministic rigor continued to give offense.

◇◇

IN HIS PREFACE to *La Comédie humaine* Balzac sets forth his intention to write the *natural history* of man; his talents were in harmony with his plan, which accounts for the kinds and features of his characters: like father, like offspring. When we know how an artist invents, we can predict his inventions.

In the eyes of the naturalist man is not a reasoning creature who is independent, superior, healthy in himself, capable of achieving truth and virtue by his own efforts, but a simple force, of the same order as other creatures, receiving from circumstance his degree and his direction. He likes man for himself; that is why at all levels, in all occupations he likes him; provided that he sees him in action, he is satisfied. He is as glad to dissect an octopus as an elephant; he is as eager to analyze a doorkeeper as a minister of state. For him there is nothing unclean. He understands and handles forces; that gives him pleasure, and he has no other; he does not say: what a fine sight! but what a fine subject! And fine subjects are odd beings, important to science, capable of putting some notable type into relief, or some unusual deformation, so as to reveal new and broad laws. He has scarcely any concern for purity or grace; to his eyes a toad is as important as a butter-fly; a bat interests him as much as a nightingale. If you are deli-cate, do not open his book; he will describe things to you as they are—that is, very ugly—crudely, without softening or embellish-ing anything; if he does embellish, it is in a strange manner; since he likes natural forces, and likes only them, he exhibits the gran-diose deformities, the maladies, and the monstrosities which those forces produce when they are stepped up.

The ideal is lacking in the naturalist; it is even more lacking in the naturalist Balzac. We have seen that he has nothing of the quick and lively imagination by which Shakespeare touches and handles the loosened threads which link beings together; he is heavy-handed, painfully and obstinately sunk into his dungheap of science, busy counting the fibres he is dissecting, with such a litter of tools and variety of repulsive preparations that when he emerges from his cellar and comes back to the light, he retains the smell of the laboratory in which he has been buried. He lacks true nobility; delicate matters escape him; his anatomist's hands soil chaste natures; he makes ugliness more ugly.—But he tri-umphs when it is a matter of depicting base existences; then he is immersed in the ignoble, where he dwells without repug-nance; with inner satisfaction he follows household worries and financial manipulations. With an equal contentment he fol-lows the development of exploits of force. He is armed with brutality and calculation; reflection has provided him with know-ing combinations; his roughness frees him from fear of shocking people. Nobody is better able to depict beasts of prey, little or big. —Such is the mold into which his nature directs and encloses him; he is a powerful, heavy artist who has as his servants and masters the tastes and talents of the naturalist. In this capacity he copies the real, he likes the monstrous on a large scale; he depicts baseness and force better than other things. These are the materials which will form up his characters, making some imperfect and 'others admirable, according to how their substance fits or resists the mold into which they must enter.

I.

At the very bottom of the scale are workmen and provincials.

In former times they were shown only as grotesque, exaggerated to bring a laugh, or negligently sketched in at a corner of a picture. Balzac describes them seriously; he is interested in them; they are his favorites, and he is right, for with them he is in his proper domain. They are the proper object of the naturalist. They are the species of society, like the species of nature. Each of them has his instincts, his needs, his coat of arms, his distinctive features. Trades produce varieties of men, just as climate produces varieties of animals; the attitude which they impose on the soul, being constant, becomes definitive; the faculties and inclinations which they restrict tend to diminish; those which they exercise grow; the primitive natural man disappears; there remains a being warped and strengthened, formed and deformed, made ugly but capable of living.—That this is repulsive is of little importance; these acquired deformities please Balzac's mind. He likes to go into the kitchen, the shop, the old-clothes store; he draws back from no odor or dirt; his senses are gross. For better or worse, he is at ease among these people; there he finds stupidity in full flower, prickly and base vanity, and above all, interest. Nothing diverts him from these people, or rather everything draws him to them; he is at his best in matters of money; it is the great human motivating force, especially among the lower depths where man must calculate, heap up, and scheme for the sake of his life. Balzac participates in this thirst for gain; he enlists our sympathy for it, and embellishes it by the skill and patience of the combinations which he gives to it. His systematic power and his frank love for human ugliness have constructed the epic of business and money.—Thence those provincial drawing rooms where people stupefied by their occupations and by idleness come, in worn-out frock coats and stiff cravats, to talk about available positions and the weather; stifling rooms where every idea perishes or becomes moldy, where prejudice bristles, where the ridiculous is exhibited, where cupidity and amour-propre, made shrill by waiting, make deadly assault on the conquest of priority or place by means of a hundred basenesses, a thousand maneuvers.—Thence those ministerial offices where the employes become irritable, brutalized, or resigned, some of them bound within mania, makers of puns or of collections, others inert and chewing their pens, others restless as monkeys in a cage, practical jokers and babblers, others withdrawn into their stupidity like snails in their shells, happy to write out their papers in a fine round irreproachable hand, most of them family men who crawl through the mire in order to pocket a tip or an advancement.—Thence those shops spattered by the mud of Paris, deafened by the jangle of carriages, darkened by the sad fog, where little tradespeople, pale and flaccid, pass thirty years tying up packages, persecuting their clerks, making inventory, lying and smiling.—Thence above all those little newspapers, the cruelest of Balzac's depictions, where they sell truth and above all lies, where intelligence is retailed at so much an hour and so much a line, "absolutely as you light an argand lamp," where the writer, harassed by need, hungry for money, forced to write, works like a machine, grinds out art, despises everything, despises himself, and finds forgetfulness only in orgies of the mind and of the senses.—Thence his prisons, his boarding houses, his Paris, his provinces, and his varied but unvarying depiction of human deformity and cupidity.—At bottom they please him; they are his heroes, for it is they whom he crowns: Scapin, whom he calls Rastignac, becomes a minister of state; Turcaret, whom he calls Nucingen, becomes a peer of France and thirty times a millionaire. Most of his scoundrels finally become rich, titled, powerful, become deputies, attorneys general, prefects, counts. The gilding is a sort of aureole, the only one of which they are capable; taking his cue from society and nature, Balzac poses them complacently in their dress coats. . . .

Indeed his ideal lies elsewhere. His doctors have no greater pleasure than the discovery of a strange or forgotten malady; he is a doctor and does as they do. He has many times described passions against nature of a kind that cannot even be indicated here. He has depicted with infinite detail and a sort of poetic enthusiasm the execrable vermin who swarm and teem in the Parisian mud, the Cibots, the Rémonencqs, the Mme Nourissons, the Fraisiers, poisonous creatures of the dark depths who, enlarged by the concentrated light of his microscope, exhibit the multiple arsenal of their weapons and the diabolic brilliance of their corruption. He has sought out in every corner and every mire unhealthy and strange creatures who live outside the law and nature, gamblers, go-betweens, gypsies, usurerers, convicts, spies; he has so completely penetrated their beings, he has so strongly seized upon their springs of action, he has shown their nature to be so necessary and their actions so inevitable, that as you detest them you admire them, and your imagination which would like to turn away from them cannot do so.—They are in short the heroes of the naturalist and rude artist whom nothing disgusts; they are the curiosities of his gallery. You pass quickly by his indelicate honest women, his emphatic preachers, his nebulous or talkative great men; the beautiful is not to be found there: a natural history museum is not an art gallery. But you stop before his workmen and his businessmen, each one displayed in his glass cabinet, exhibiting arrested or excessive development, which places him with his species. You stop before his men of wit, dazzling, perverted, and disgusting; before his sick women, his provincial gossips, his lady authors and his women of the street; before his virtuous men, set forth like the others by means of his sad anatomical method, and all of whom derive their virtues from their prejudices, their manias, their calculations, or their vices; before eccentric or deformed beings whom he has kept back so as to display them as his choice pieces. Wait a moment longer, and he will raise the curtain and you will see in a special hall monsters of special quality: he loves them better than the little ones.

The Big Characters

If you believe that in human nature the essential element is reason, you will take reason as your hero and you will depict generosity and virtue. If your eyes turn to the external envelope and are interested only in the body, you will choose the body as your ideal, and you will depict voluptuous flesh and vigorous muscles. If you see in sensibility the important part of man, you will see beauty only in lively emotion and you will depict falling tears and delicate sentiments. Your opinion about nature will dictate your opinion about beauty; your idea about the real man will form your idea of the ideal man; your philosophy will direct your art.—Thus it is that the philosophy of Balzac has directed the art of Balzac. He considered man as a force: he took force as his ideal. He freed it of its fetters; he has shown it complete, free, disengaged from reason which keeps it from hurting itself, indifferent to justice which keeps it from harming others; he has made it larger, has nourished it, has spread it out and put it on view in the foreground, as hero and sovereign, in monomaniacs and in scoundrels.

On Realism*

By George Eliot

THE REPUTATION of George Eliot (1819-1880) as a realist has had its ups and downs of fortune. For a time in the 1880's when French naturalism was at its height she was cited on every hand as an example of what true and balanced realism ought to be. Today she is looked upon as at best a precursor, as one who by partially satisfying the desire of English readers for truth prevented the realistic movement from going any further in that country. Lord David Cecil, on the other hand, calls her "the first modern novelist," though he recognizes the limit of her scope since she makes no "excursions into the uncomfortable regions of the animal passions."

Her emphasis is on the true and the normal depiction, as indicated in this passage from *Adam Bede*. Her novels are dense with the homely details of everyday life, and these are no incidental adornment but the very texture of which the works are made. She has a strong sense of causality as it operates in both the psychological and sociological spheres. She will not allow strokes of fortune and coincidence; she does not shy away from an unhappy ending, as is evident from the fates of Hetty Sorel and Maggie and Tom Tulliver.

Where she fails to live up to the requirements of the reader today would seem to be in the persistent intrusion of the omniscient author and in a rigidity of moral values, both of which seem to contradict the intention of the realist to set things down as they are and let the reader draw his own conclusions. She believes that character is fate but that there is room for free will; by her insistence on envisaging characters almost exclusively in their moral aspects she somehow straitens the view of existence which the realists battled long to enlarge.

◇◇◇

"This Rector of Broxton is little better than a pagan!" I hear one of my lady readers exclaim. "How much more edifying it would have been if you had made him give Arthur some truly spiritual advice. You might have put into his mouth the most beautiful things—quite as good as reading a sermon."

Certainly I could, if I held it the highest vocation of the novelist to represent things as they never have been and never will be. Then,

* Eliot, George, *Adam Bede*, Chap. XVII, pp. 129-132. (In *The Best-Known Novels of George Eliot*, Random House [Modern Library] n.d.)

of course, I might refashion life and character entirely after my own liking; and I might select the most unexceptionable type of clergyman, and put my own admirable opinions into his mouth on all occasions. But it happens, on the contrary, that my strongest effort is to avoid any such arbitrary picture, and to give no more than a faithful account of men and things as they have mirrored themselves in my mind. The mirror is doubtless defective; the outlines will sometimes be disturbed, the reflection faint or confused; but I feel as much bound to tell you as precisely as I can what that reflection is, as if I were in the witness-box narrating my experience on oath.

Sixty years ago—it is a long time, so no wonder things have changed—all clergymen were not zealous; indeed there is reason to believe that the number of zealous clergymen was small, and it is probable that if one among the small minority had owned the livings of Broxton and Hayslope in the year 1799, you would have liked him no better than you like Mr. Irwine. Ten to one, you would have thought him a tasteless, indiscreet, methodistical man. It is so very rarely that facts hit that nice medium required by our own enlightened opinions and refined taste! Perhaps you will say, "Do improve the facts a little, then: make them more accordant with those correct views which it is our privilege to possess. The world is not just what we like; do touch it up with a tasteful pencil, and make believe that it is not quite such a mixed, entangled affair. Let all people who hold unexceptionable opinions act unexceptionably. Let your most faulty characters always be on the wrong side, and your virtuous ones on the right. Then we shall see at a glance whom we are to condemn, and whom we are to approve. Then we shall be able to admire, without the slightest disturbance of our prepossessions: we shall hate and despise with that true ruminant relish which belongs to undoubting confidence."

But, my good friend, what will you do then with your fellow-parishioner who opposes your husband in the vestry?—with your newly-appointed vicar, whose style of preaching you find painfully below that of his regretted predecessor?—with the honest servant who worries your soul with her one failing?—with your neighbor, Mrs. Green, who was really kind to you in your last illness, but has said several ill-natured things about you since your convalescence?

—nay, with your excellent husband himself, who has other irritating habits besides that of not wiping his shoes? These fellow-mortals, every one, must be accepted as they are; you can neither straighten their noses, nor brighten their wit, nor rectify their dispositions; and it is these people—amongst whom your life is passed—that it is needful you should tolerate, pity, and love: it is these more or less ugly, stupid, inconsistent people, whose movements of goodness you should be able to admire—for whom you should cherish all possible hopes, all possible patience. And I would not, even if I had the choice, be the clever novelist who could create a world so much better than this, in which we get up in the morning to do our daily work, that you would be likely to turn a harder, colder eye on the dusty streets and the common green fields—on the real breathing men and women, who can be chilled by your indifference or injured by your prejudice; who can be cheered and helped onward by your fellow-feeling, your forbearance, your outspoken, brave justice.

So I am content to tell my simple story, without trying to make things seem better than they were; dreading nothing, indeed, but falsity, which, in spite of one's best efforts, there is reason to dread. Falsehood is so easy, truth so difficult. The pencil is conscious of a delightful facility in drawing a griffin—the longer the claws, and the larger the wings, the better; but that marvelous facility which we mistook for genius is apt to forsake us when we want to draw a real unexaggerated lion. Examine your words well, and you will find that even when you have no motive to be false, it is a very hard thing to say the exact truth, even about your own immediate feelings—much harder than to say something fine about them which is *not* the exact truth.

It is for this rare, precious quality of truthfulness that I delight in many Dutch paintings, which lofty-minded people despise. I find a source of delicious sympathy in these faithful pictures of a monotonous homely existence, which has been the fate of so many more among my fellow-mortals than a life of pomp or of absolute indigence, of tragic suffering or of world-stirring actions. I turn, without shrinking, from cloud-borne angels, from prophets, sibyls, and heroic warriors, to an old woman bending over her flower-pot, or eating her solitary dinner, while the noonday light, softened

On Realism

perhaps by a screen of leaves, falls on her mob-cap, and just touches the rim of her spinning-wheel, and her stone jug, and all those cheap common things which are the precious necessaries of life to her;—or I turn to that village wedding, kept between four brown walls, where an awkward bridegroom opens the dance with a high-shouldered, broad-faced bride, while elderly and middle-aged friends look on, with very irregular noses and lips, and probably with quart-pots in their hands, but with an expression of unmistakable contentment and good-will. "Foh!" says my idealistic friend, "what vulgar details! What good is there in taking all these pains to give an exact likeness of old women and clowns? What a low phase of life!—what clumsy, ugly people!"

But bless us, things may be lovable that are not altogether handsome, I hope? I am not at all sure that the majority of the human race have not been ugly, and even among those "lords of their kind," the British, squat figures, ill-shapen nostrils, and dingy complexions are not startling exceptions. Yet there is a great deal of family love among us. I have a friend or two whose class of features is such that the Apollo curl on the summit of their brows would be decidedly trying; yet to my certain knowledge tender hearts have beaten for them, and their miniatures—flattering, but still not lovely—are kissed in secret by motherly lips. I have seen many an excellent matron, who could never in her best days have been handsome, and yet she had a packet of love-letters in a private drawer, and sweet children showered kisses on her sallow cheeks. And I believe there have been plenty of young heroes, of middle stature and feeble beards, who have felt quite sure they could never love anything more insignificant than a Diana, and yet have found themselves in middle life happily settled with a wife who waddles. Yes! thank God; human feeling is like the mighty rivers that bless the earth: it does not wait for beauty—it flows with resistless force and brings beauty with it.

All honour and reverence to the divine beauty of form! Let us cultivate it to the utmost in men, women, and children—in our gardens and in our houses. But let us love that other beauty too, which lies in no secret of proportion, but in the secret of deep human sympathy. Paint us an angel, if you can, with a floating violet robe, and a face paled by the celestial light; paint us yet oftener a

Madonna, turning her mild face upward and opening her arms to welcome the divine glory; but do not impose on us any aesthetic rules which shall banish from the region of Art those old women scraping carrots with their work-worn hands, those heavy clowns taking holiday in a dingy pothouse, those rounded backs and stupid weather-beaten faces that have bent over the spade and done the rough work of the world—those homes with their tin pans, their brown pitchers, their rough curs, and their clusters of onions. In this world there are so many of these common, coarse people, who have no picturesque sentimental wretchedness! It is so needful we should remember their existence, else we may happen to leave them quite out of our religion and philosophy, and frame lofty theories which only fit a world of extremes. Therefore let Art always remind us of them; therefore let us always have men ready to give the loving pains of a life to the faithful representing of commonplace things—men who see beauty in these commonplace things, and delight in showing how kindly the light of heaven falls on them. There are few prophets in the world; few sublimely beautiful women; few heroes. I can't afford to give all my love and reverence to such rarities; I want a great deal of those feelings for my everyday fellow-men, especially for the few in the foreground of the great multitude, whose faces I know, whose hands I touch, for whom I have to make my way with kindly courtesy. Neither are picturesque lazzaroni or romantic criminals half so frequent as your common labourer, who gets his own bread, and eats it vulgarly but creditably with his own pocket-knife. It is more needful that I should have a fibre of sympathy connecting me with that vulgar citizen who weighs out my sugar in a vilely-assorted cravat and waistcoat, than with the handsomest rascal in red scarf and green feathers;—more needful that my heart should swell with loving admiration at some trait of gentle goodness in the faulty people who sit at the same hearth with me, or in the clergyman of my own parish, who is perhaps rather too corpulent, and in other respects is not an Oberlin or a Tillotson, than at the deeds of heroes whom I shall never know except by hearsay, or at the sublimest abstract of all clerical graces that was ever conceived by an able novelist.

On True Novels*

By Edmond and Jules de Goncourt

EDMOND (1822-1896) AND JULES (1830-1870) DE GONCOURT represent a somewhat independent strand of French realism. Though less renowned today than Flaubert and Zola, they share with the latter the position of leaders of the new movement. More psychological in content, more impressionistic in technique, their novels did not evoke the solid social situations of a Flaubert or a Zola. They were always interested in what they called "écriture artiste," asserting that "The ideal of the novel is to give, with art, the liveliest impression of human truth, whatever it may be."

Aristocratic by taste as well as background, they were interested in a realism of the *haut monde*, as the preface to *Les Frères Zemganno* suggests. Nonetheless this early preface-manifesto to *Germinie Lacerteux* is a ringing assertion of the necessity of depicting lower levels of experience. This novel is based on the life of their own corrupt servant; other works from a comparable milieu such as *Henriette Maréchal* and *La Fille Elisa* (written by Edmond alone) demanded many expeditions into the *bas quartiers* of Paris to gather what the brothers called *documents humains*.

Loyal throughout his life to Flaubert, Turgenev, and Daudet, Edmond was always somewhat jealous of Zola, who he thought had robbed him of the leadership and fame which were his due. Certainly the Goncourts' works never aroused the furore that Zola's did and never sold in the tens of thousands. The production of *Henriette Maréchal* in 1865 was a resounding failure, whereas Zola's plays some fifteen years later met with considerable success—Edmond remarking with some justice that Zola was the beneficiary of their pioneer efforts.

Edmond de Goncourt will no doubt be remembered less for his novels or his works on French and Japanese art than for the Academy which bears his name and annually awards an important literary prize. Above all he will be remembered for the incomparable *Journal*, begun by him and Jules on December 2, 1851, and carried on by Edmond alone until his death in July 1896. It provides a detailed account of literary and artistic life in Paris during the four decades of the realistic-naturalistic movement; even more, in its many vignettes of Parisian life and particularly in its account of the siege and the Commune in 1870-1871 it shows Edmond as a reporter par excellence, presenting factual detail with a richness far greater than what appears in the novels.

* Goncourt, Edmond and Jules de, "Préface," *Germinie Lacerteux*, Paris, 1865.

Paris, October 1864

We must ask the public's pardon for giving it this book, and warn it as to what it will find there.

The public loves false novels; this is a true one.

It loves books which pretend to move in polite society; this book comes from the streets.

It loves smutty little works, prostitutes' memoirs, alcove confessions, erotic dirt, scandal adjusting its dress in a picture in a bookstore window: what it is about to read is severe and pure. It must not expect the decolleté photograph of Pleasure; what follows is a clinical study of love.

The public also loves vapid and consoling reading, adventures that end happily, imaginings which upset neither its digestion nor its serenity: this book with its sad and violent distraction is bound to challenge its habits and upset its hygiene.

Why then did we write it? Was it simply to shock the public and offend its taste?

No.

Living in the nineteenth century, in a time of universal suffrage, democracy, and liberalism, we asked ourselves whether what are called "the lower classes" did not have a right to the Novel, whether this world beneath a world, the people, must remain under literary interdict and the disdain of authors, who up to now have kept silence about whatever heart and soul the people might have. We asked ourselves whether in this era of equality in which we live there could still be, for writer or for reader, any classes too unworthy, any miseries too low, any dramas too foul-mouthed, any catastrophes insufficiently noble in their terror. We became curious to know whether Tragedy, the conventional form of a forgotten literature and a vanished society, was really dead; whether in a country lacking castes and legal aristocracy the misfortunes of the little people and the poor could arouse interest, emotion, and pity to the same degree as the misfortunes of the great and rich; whether, in a word, the tears which are shed below could evoke tears as readily as those which are shed on high.

These thoughts caused us to venture our humble novel *Soeur Philomène* in 1861; now they bring about the publication of our *Germinie Lacerteux*.

118

On True Novels

Now, it is of little importance whether this book be calumniated. In the present day when the Novel is expanding and growing, when it begins to be the great serious, impassioned, living form of literary study and social examination, when by means of analysis and psychological research it is becoming contemporary Moral History, in the present day when the Novel has undertaken the studies and obligations of science, it can demand the liberties and freedom of science. Let it seek Art and Truth; let it show to the happy people of Paris misery which should not be forgotten; let it show to people of fashion what Sisters of Charity do not shrink from, what the Queens of olden days let their children see in the hospitals—human suffering, immediate and alive, which teaches charity; let the Novel have that religion to which the past century gave that broad and encompassing name, *Humanity*. Such a consciousness will suffice it. Its right lies there.

On Realism[*]

By Olive Schreiner

OLIVE SCHREINER (1855-1920) was an independent advocate of realism, and an alien one. Born in South Africa and entirely self-educated, she wrote *The Story of an African Farm* about the life and background that she knew. Unable to publish the book in South Africa, she went to England in 1881 to seek a publisher there. Chapman & Hall undertook to do the book, and George Meredith, their chief reader, helped her rewrite it. She published it in 1883 under the pseudonym of Ralph Iron.

This is her only important contribution to literature, though *Trooper Peter Halket of Mashonaland* (1897) caused a considerable stir for its attack on Cecil Rhodes. In general Olive Schreiner was caught up in the various causes and currents of advanced thought of the time. She was critical of Christianity and an advocate of the cause of women's rights. Like many a realist after her she quickly exhausted her literary vein since she could write only of life with which she was intimately acquainted.

◇◇

I HAVE to thank cordially the public and my critics for the reception they have given this little book.

Dealing with a subject that is far removed from the round of English daily life, it of necessity lacks the charm that hangs about the ideal representation of familiar things, and its reception has therefore been the more kindly.

A word of explanation is necessary. Two strangers appear on the scene, and some have fancied that in the second they have again the first, who returns in a new guise. Why this should be we cannot tell; unless there is a feeling that a man should not appear on the scene, and then disappear, leaving behind him no more substantial trace than a mere book; that he should return later on as husband or lover, to fill some more important part than that of the mere stimulator of thought.

Human life may be painted according to two methods. There is the stage method. According to that each character is duly mar-

* Schreiner, Olive, "Preface," *The Story of an African Farm* (second edition), London, 1883. Reprinted by permission of Ernest Benn Limited.

On Realism

shalled at first, and ticketed; we know with an immutable certainty that at the right crises each one will reappear and act his part, and, when the curtain falls, all will stand before it bowing. There is a sense of satisfaction in this, and of completeness. But there is another method—the method of the life we all lead. Here nothing can be prophesied. There is a strange coming and going of feet. Men appear, act and re-act upon each other, and pass away. When the crisis comes the man who would fit it does not return. When the curtain falls no one is ready. When the footlights are brightest they are blown out; and what the name of the play is no one knows. If there sits a spectator who knows, he sits so high that the players in the gaslight cannot hear his breathing. Life may be painted to either method; but the methods are different. The canons of criticism that bear upon the one cut cruelly upon the other.

It has been suggested by a kind critic that he would better have liked the little book if it had been a history of wild adventure; of cattle driven into inaccessible "kranzes" by Bushmen; "of encounters with ravening lions, and hair-breadth escapes." This could not be. Such works are best written in Piccadilly or in the Strand: there the gifts of the creative imagination, untrammelled by contact with any fact, may spread their wings.

But, should one sit down to paint the scenes among which he has grown, he will find that the facts creep in upon him. Those brilliant phases and shapes which the imagination sees in far-off lands are not for him to portray. Sadly he must squeeze the colour from his brush, and dip it into the grey pigments around him. He must paint what lies before him.

June, 1883   R . I R O N

"Ideals and Idealists"*

By George Bernard Shaw

GEORGE BERNARD SHAW (1856-1950) capitalized in his numerous writings on the work of demolition which had been carried on by the early realists and other advanced thinkers of the late nineteenth century. A socialist, he was one of the founders of the Fabian Society; as music critic, he was a partisan of Wagner; as drama critic, it was natural that he should espouse the cause of Ibsen and Strindberg. Only incidentally interested in realism as a literary movement, he approved its use of everyday materials, pointing out that when "Ibsen began to make plays the art of the dramatist had shrunk to the art of contriving situations." Also he applauded the abandonment of the pure hero or villain and the suppression of coincidence and accident, since "no accident, however sanguinary, can produce a moment of real drama." His first plays, *Widowers' Houses* (1892) and *Mrs. Warren's Profession* (written in 1893 but banned from public performance in England until 1924), show a strong general influence of Ibsen's subject matter and ideas, though they also manifest the typical Shavian twist for the sake of shock value. *Man and Superman* (1903) departs even further from realism, and in general that tag is not applicable to Shaw, who ranged over a wide gamut of dramatic experiment.

His book on Ibsen was the result of a lecture given to the Fabian Society as part of a series on Socialism in Contemporary Literature in the summer of 1890. Relieved that his stint was over, he put it aside, but was soon embroiled in the controversy which greeted the production of Ibsen's plays in England. He therefore expanded it into a book which, like the speech, was "purposely couched . . . in the most provocative terms." After Ibsen's death he rewrote it in order to take the last plays into account. He suggested at that time that the words "idols and idolatry" might well be substituted for "ideals and idealists," and it is clearly Ibsen's attack on received ideas which Shaw delights in espousing and enlarging in this book. He takes realistic doctrine for granted, as he does an increase in human strength and wisdom which he considers ascribable to new writers like Ibsen, Strindberg, Tolstoy, Gorky, Chekhov, and Brieux. A preface written in 1922 continues to grant them wisdom but doubts that human beings have profited very much from it, since the first World War can be described as a war of ideals.

* Shaw, George Bernard, "Ideals and Idealists," *The Quintessence of Ibsenism*, London. 1891. This chapter is reprinted by permission of the Public Trustee and The Society of Authors.

"Ideals and Idealists"

WE have seen that as Man grows through the ages, he finds himself bolder by the growth of his courage: that is, of his spirit (for so the common people name it), and dares more and more to love and trust instead of to fear and fight. But his courage has other effects: he also raises himself from mere consciousness to knowledge by daring more and more to face facts and tell himself the truth. For in his infancy of helplessness and terror he could not face the inexorable; and facts being of all things the most inexorable, he masked all the threatening ones as fast as he discovered them; so that now every mask requires a hero to tear it off. The king of terrors, Death, was the Arch-Inexorable: Man could not bear the dread of that. He must persuade himself that Death can be propitiated, circumvented, abolished. How he fixed the mask of personal immortality on the face of Death for this purpose we all know. And he did the like with all disagreeables as long as they remained inevitable. Otherwise he must have gone mad with terror of the grim shapes around him, headed by the skeleton with the scythe and hourglass. The masks were his ideals, as he called them; and what, he would ask, would life be without ideals? Thus he became an idealist, and remained so until he dared to begin pulling the masks off and looking the spectres in the face —dared, that is, to be more and more a realist. But all men are not equally brave; and the greatest terror prevailed whenever some realist bolder than the rest laid hands on a mask which they did not yet dare to do without.

We have plenty of these masks around us still: some of them more fantastic than any of the Sandwich islanders' masks in the British Museum. In our novels and romances especially we see the most beautiful of all the masks: those devised to disguise the brutalities of the sexual instinct in the earlier stages of its development, and to soften the rigorous aspect of the iron laws by which Society regulates its gratification. When the social organism becomes bent on civilization, it has to force marriage and family life on the individual, because it can perpetuate itself in no other way whilst love is still known only by fitful glimpses, the basis of sexual relationship being in the main mere physical appetite. Under these circumstances men try to graft pleasure on necessity by desperately pretending that the institution forced upon them is a congenial one, making it a point of public decency to assume always that men spontaneously love their kindred better than their chance acquaintances, and that the woman once desired is always desired: also that the family is woman's proper sphere, and that no really womanly woman ever forms an attachment, or even knows what it means, until she is requested to do so by a man. Now if anyone's childhood has been embittered by the dislike of his mother and the ill-temper of his father; if his wife has ceased to care for him and he is heartily tired of his wife; if his brother is going to law with him over the division of the family property, and his son acting in studied defiance of his plans and wishes, it is hard for him to persuade himself that passion is eternal and that blood is thicker than water. Yet if he tells himself the truth, all his life seems a waste and a failure by the light of it. It comes then to this, that his neighbors must either agree with him that the whole system is a mistake, and discard it for a new one, which cannot possibly happen until social organization so far outgrows the institution that Society can perpetuate itself without it; or else they must keep him in countenance by resolutely making believe that all the illusions with which it has been masked are realities.

For the sake of precision, let us imagine a community of a thousand persons, organized for the perpetuation of the species on the basis of the British family as we know it at present. Seven hundred of them, we will suppose, find the British family arrangement quite good enough for them. Two hundred and ninety-nine find it a failure, but must put up with it since they are in a minority. The remaining person occupies a position to be explained presently. The 299 failures will not have the courage to face the fact that they are irremediable failures, since they cannot prevent the 700 satisfied ones from coercing them into conformity with the marriage law. They will accordingly try to persuade themselves that, whatever their own particular domestic arrangements may be, the family is a beautiful and holy natural institution. For the fox not only declares that the grapes he cannot get are sour: he also insists that the sloes he *can* get are sweet. Now observe what has happened. The family as it really is is a conventional arrangement, legally enforced, which the majority, because it happens to suit them, think good enough for the minority, whom it happens not to suit at all. The family as a beautiful and holy natural institution is only a fancy picture of what every family would have to be if everybody was to be suited, invented by the minority as a mask for the reality, which in its nakedness is intolerable to them. We call this sort of fancy picture an Ideal; and the policy of forcing individuals to act on the assumption that all ideals are real, and to recognize and accept such action as standard moral conduct, absolutely valid under all circumstances, contrary conduct or any advocacy of it being discountenanced and punished as immoral, may therefore be described as the policy of Idealism. Our 299 domestic failures are therefore become idealists as to marriage; and in proclaiming the ideal in fiction, poetry, pulpit and platform oratory, and serious private conversation, they will far outdo the 700 who comfortably accept marriage as a matter of course, never dreaming of calling it an "institution," much less a holy and beautiful one, and being pretty plainly of opinion that Idealism is a crackbrained fuss about nothing. The idealists, hurt by this, will retort by calling them Philistines. We then have our society classified as 700 Philistines and 299 idealists, leaving one man unclassified: the man strong enough to face the truth the idealists are shirking.

Such a man says of marriage, "This thing is a failure for many of us. It is insufferable that two human beings, having entered into relations which only warm affection can render tolerable, should be forced to maintain them after such affections have ceased to exist, or in spite of the fact that they have never arisen. The alleged natural attractions and repulsions upon which the family ideal is based do not exist; and it is historically false that the family was founded for the purpose of satisfying them. Let us provide otherwise for the social ends which the family subserves, and then abolish its compulsory character altogether." What will be the attitude of the rest to this outspoken man? The Philistines will simply think him mad. But the idealists will be terrified beyond measure at the proclamation of their hidden thought—at the presence of the traitor among the conspirators of silence—at the rending of the beautiful veil they and their poets have woven to hide the unbearable face of the truth. They will crucify him, burn him, violate their own ideals of family affection by taking his children away from him, ostracize him, brand him as immoral, profligate, filthy, and appeal against him to the despised Philistines, specially idealized for the occasion as Society. How far they will proceed against him depends on how far his courage exceeds theirs. At his worst, they call him cynic and paradoxer: at his best they do their utmost to ruin him if not to take his life. Thus, purblindly courageous moralists like Mandeville and Larochefoucauld, who merely state unpleasant facts without denying the validity of current ideals, and who indeed depend on those ideals to make their statements piquant, get off with nothing worse than this name of cynic, the free use of which is a familiar mark of the zealous idealist. But take the case of the man who has already served us as an example: Shelley. The idealists did not call Shelley a cynic: they called him a fiend until they invented a new illusion to enable them to enjoy the beauty of his lyrics, this illusion being nothing less than the pretence that since he was at bottom an idealist himself, his ideals must be identical with those of Tennyson and Longfellow, neither of whom ever wrote a line in which some highly respectable ideal was not implicit.

Here the admission that Shelley, the realist, was an idealist too, seems to spoil the whole argument. And it certainly spoils its verbal consistency. For we unfortunately use this word ideal indifferently to denote both the institution which the ideal masks and the mask itself, thereby producing desperate confusion of thought, since the institution may be an effete and poisonous one, whilst the mask may be, and indeed generally is, an image of what we would fain have in its place. If the existing facts, with their masks on, are to be called ideals, and the future possibilities which the masks depict are also to be called ideals—if, again, the man who is defending existing institutions by maintaining their identity with their masks is to be confounded under one name with the man who is striving to realize the future possibilities by tearing the mask and the thing masked asunder, then the position cannot be intelligibly described by mortal pen: you and I, reader, will be at cross purposes at every sentence unless you allow me to distinguish pioneers like Shelley and Ibsen as realists from the idealists of my imaginary community of one thousand. If you ask why I have not allotted

the terms the other way, and called Shelley and Ibsen idealists
and the conventionalists realists, I reply that Ibsen himself, though
he has not formally made the distinction, has so repeatedly harped
on conventions and conventionalists as ideals and idealists that if
I were now perversely to call them realities and realists, I should
confuse readers of *The Wild Duck* and *Rosmersholm* more than
I should help them. Doubtless I shall be reproached for puzzling
people by thus limiting the meaning of the term ideal. But what,
I ask, is that inevitable passing perplexity compared to the inextricable tangle I must produce if I follow the custom, and use the
word indiscriminately in its two violently incompatible senses?
If the term realist is objected to on account of some of its modern
associations, I can only recommend you, if you must associate it
with something else than my own description of its meaning (I
do not deal in definitions), to associate it, not with Zola and Maupassant, but with Plato.

Now let us return to our community of 700 Philistines, 299
idealists, and 1 realist. The mere verbal ambiguity against which
I have just provided is as nothing beside that which comes of any
attempt to express the relations of these three sections, simple as
they are, in terms of the ordinary systems of reason and duty.
The idealist, higher in the ascent of evolution than the Philistine,
yet hates the highest and strikes at him with a dread and rancor
of which the easy-going Philistine is guiltless. The man who has
risen above the danger and the fear that his acquisitiveness will
lead him to theft, his temper to murder, and his affections to de-
bauchery: this is he who is denounced as an arch-scoundrel and
libertine, and thus confounded with the lowest because he is the
highest. And it is not the ignorant and stupid who maintain this
error, but the literate and the cultured. When the true prophet
speaks, he is proved to be both rascal and idiot, not by those who
have never read of how foolishly such learned demonstrations have
come off in the past, but by those who have themselves written
volumes on the crucifixions, the burnings, the stonings, the headings and hangings, the Siberia transportations, the calumny and
ostracism which have been the lot of the pioneer as well as of the
camp follower. It is from men of established literary reputation
that we learn that William Blake was mad, that Shelley was spoiled

by living in a low set, that Robert Owen was a man who did not know the world, that Ruskin was incapable of comprehending political economy, that Zola was a mere blackguard, and that Ibsen was "a Zola with a wooden leg." The great musician, accepted by the unskilled listener, is vilified by his fellow-musicians: it was the musical culture of Europe that pronounced Wagner the inferior of Mendelssohn and Meyerbeer. The great artist finds his foes among the painters, and not among the men in the street: it was the Royal Academy which placed forgotten nobodies above Burne Jones. It is not rational that it should be so; but it is so, for all that.

The realist at last loses patience with ideals altogether, and sees in them only something to blind us, something to numb us, something to murder self in us, something whereby, instead of resisting death, we can disarm it by committing suicide. The idealist, who has taken refuge with the ideals because he hates himself and is ashamed of himself, thinks that all this is so much the better. The realist, who has come to have a deep respect for himself and faith in the validity of his own will, thinks it is so much the worse. To the one, human nature, naturally corrupt, is held back from ruinous excesses only by self-denying conformity to the ideals. To the other these ideals are only swaddling clothes which man has outgrown, and which insufferably impede his movements. No wonder the two cannot agree. The idealist says, "Realism means egotism; and egotism means depravity." The realist declares that when a man abnegates the will to live and be free in a world of the living and free, seeking only to conform to ideals for the sake of being, not himself, but "a good man," then he is morally dead and rotten, and must be left unheeded to abide his resurrection, if that by good luck arrive before his bodily death. Unfortunately this is the sort of speech that nobody but a realist understands. It will be more amusing as well as more convincing to take an actual example of an idealist criticizing a realist.

On Truth in Fiction*

By William Dean Howells

WILLIAM DEAN HOWELLS (1837-1920) may be said to have fought the battle for realism in this country before 1900 almost singlehanded. Associated with the *Atlantic Monthly* from 1866 to 1881 and editor-in-chief for the last nine years of that period, associated with *Harper's Monthly* from 1886 on, by nature sympathetic with the new literature as it arose in other countries, he used his pre-eminent editorial position to proclaim his sympathies and to encourage young American writers who wanted to cast loose from convention and write what they saw and knew.

In January 1886 Howells took over the "Editor's Study" section in *Harper's* and used it as a pulpit from which to disseminate knowledge about the new European writers. The French were already fairly well-known, and in any case he was lukewarm toward them, but the Scandinavians, Russians, Spaniards, and Italians he championed fervently month after month, bringing most of them to American attention for the first time. To be sure, it was "the smiling aspects of life" in these writers which most attracted Howells, and it was Tolstoy above all whom he extolled almost to the point of deification. His catholicity of taste and his sharp remarks about American provincialism quickly irritated the literary chauvinists, and his gentle effort at persuasion often met with bitter and intemperate rejoinder. Maurice Thompson, writing in *America* for August 15, 1889, attacked Howells for his assumption that "the American taste in fiction is far below that of France, Spain, Portugal or Russia." Thompson's position forced him to assert: "I do not believe Tolstoi is great in any way. . . . His novels are rude, raw, without art, interminable, garrulous, and vicious." "But for Mr. Howells' sake," he continued, "let us admit that Tolstoi is the genius of Russia, and that Zola, or, not to make it too strong, that Flaubert is the autocrat of French art in fiction; still it remains true that no one of these is fit to set the pace for American culture or for American creative imagination. Every true patriot (not of the eagle-soaring, Fourth o' July sort) has the right to resent the presentation of an alien model for his work."

Criticism and Fiction (1891) from which the selection below is drawn, is largely a reworking of the materials which had appeared in *Harper's* during the preceding five years and is by no means a profound or systematically reasoned work. A reviewer in the *Atlantic*

---

* Howells, William Dean, *Criticism and Fiction*, pp. 1-17; Harper and Brothers, 1891. The materials in this volume were reprinted with very little change from the author's "Editor's Study" department in *Harper's Magazine*.

for October 1891 complains that in it Howells is shrill and intemperate and that he has set up "a Russian idol in place of our native gods." He feels that it is possible to be in sympathy with Howells's demand for truth "without in the least believing that the portrayers of human life who are using fiction as a vehicle for conveying their diseased or hopeless views upon the character of civilization and the destiny of man are any more close to the truth than men and women who, taking great delight in life, and unvisited by dreadful visions of the future, have built in their imagination from the materials lying about them beautiful palaces of art."

While Howells was castigated beyond his deserts by the generation which emerged after 1920, it is true that as novelist he failed to provide a definitive and forceful example of realism in the way that Flaubert did because of the gingerly and tentative manner in which he approached basic issues of experience. His early works are fragile and somewhat tedious comedies of manners. *A Modern Instance* (1881) and *The Rise of Silas Lapham* (1885) are honest efforts to come to grips with changing values and social forms. The five social novels written from 1887 to 1893, of which *A Hazard of New Fortunes* (1890) is the most significant, are an attempt to analyze the new society in which money values have become paramount. But they all fail to convey the sense of blind, impersonal force which is the mark of the great realistic novels.

◇◇

THE question of a final criterion for the appreciation of art is one that perpetually recurs to those interested in any sort of aesthetic endeavor. Mr. John Addington Symonds, in a chapter of The Renaissance in Italy treating of the Bolognese school of painting, which once had so great cry, and was vaunted the supreme exemplar of the grand style, but which he now believes fallen into lasting contempt for its emptiness and soullessness, seeks to determine whether there can be an enduring criterion or not; and his conclusion is applicable to literature as to the other arts. "Our hope," he says, "with regard to the unity of taste in the future then is, that all sentimental or academical seekings after the ideal having been abandoned, momentary theories founded upon idiosyncratic or temporary partialities exploded, and nothing accepted but what is solid and positive, the scientific spirit shall make men progressively more and more conscious of these bleibende Verhältnisse, more and more capable of living in the whole; also, that

On Truth in Fiction

in proportion as we gain a firmer hold upon our own place in the world, we shall come to comprehend with more instinctive certitude what is simple, natural, and honest, welcoming with gladness all artistic products that exhibit these qualities. The perception of the enlightened man will then be the task of a healthy person who has made himself acquainted with the laws of evolution in art and in society, and is able to test the excellence of work in any stage from immaturity to decadence by discerning what there is of truth, sincerity, and natural vigor in it."

I

That is to say, as I understand, that moods and tastes and fashions change; people fancy now this and now that; but what is unpretentious and what is true is always beautiful and good, and nothing else is so. This is not saying that fantastic and monstrous and artificial things do not please; everybody knows that they do please immensely for a time, and then, after the lapse of a much longer time, they have the charm of the rococo. Nothing is more curious than the charm that fashion has. Fashion in women's dress, almost every fashion, is somehow delightful, else it would never have been the fashion; but if any one will look through a collection of old fashion plates, he must own that most fashions have been ugly. A few, which could be readily instanced, have been very pretty, and even beautiful, but it is doubtful if these have pleased the greatest number of people. The ugly delights as well as the beautiful, and not merely because the ugly in fashion is associated with the young loveliness of the women who wear the ugly fashions, and wins a grace from them, not because the vast majority of mankind are tasteless, but for some cause that is not perhaps ascertainable. It is quite as likely to return in the fashions of our clothes and houses and furniture, and poetry and fiction and painting, as the beautiful, and it may be from an instinctive or a reasoned sense of this that some of the extreme naturalists have refused to make the old discrimination against it, or to regard the ugly as any less worthy of celebration in art than the beautiful; some of them, in fact, seem to regard it as rather more worthy, if anything. Possibly there is no absolutely ugly, no absolutely beautiful; or possibly the ugly contains always an element of the beautiful better adapted to the general appreciation than the more perfectly beautiful. This is a somewhat discouraging conjecture, but I offer it for no more than it is worth; and I do not pin my faith to the saying of one whom I heard denying, the other day, that a thing of beauty was a joy forever. He contended that Keats's line should have read, "Some things of beauty are sometimes joys forever," and that any assertion beyond this was too hazardous.

II

I should, indeed, prefer another line of Keats's, if I were to profess any formulated creed, and should feel much safer with his "Beauty is Truth, Truth Beauty," than even with my friend's reformation of the more quoted verse. It brings us back to the solid ground taken by Mr. Symonds, which is not essentially different from that taken in the great Mr. Burke's Essay on the Sublime and the Beautiful—a singularly modern book, considering how long ago it was wrote (as the great Mr. Steele would have written the participle a little longer ago), and full of a certain well-mannered and agreeable instruction. In some things it is of that droll little eighteenth-century world, when philosophy had got the neat little universe into the hollow of its hand, and knew just what it was, and what it was for; but it is quite without arrogance. "As for those called critics," the author says, "they have generally sought the rule of the arts in the wrong place; they have sought among poems, pictures, engravings, statues, and buildings; but art can never give the rules that make an art. This is, I believe, the reason why artists in general, and poets principally, have been confined in so narrow a circle; they have been rather imitators of one another than of nature. Critics follow them, and therefore can do little as guides. I can judge but poorly of anything while I measure it by no other standard than itself. The true standard of the arts is in every man's power; and an easy observation of the most common, sometimes of the meanest things, in nature will give the truest lights, where the greatest sagacity and industry that slights such observation must leave us in the dark, or, what is worse, amuse and mislead us by false lights."

If this should happen to be true—and it certainly commends itself to acceptance—it might portend an immediate danger to the

On Truth in Fiction

vested interests of criticism, only that it was written a hundred years ago; and we shall probably have the "sagacity and industry that slights the observation" of nature long enough yet to allow most critics the time to learn some more useful trade than criticism as they pursue it. Nevertheless, I am in hopes that the communistic era in taste foreshadowed by Burke is approaching, and that it will occur within the lives of men now overawed by the foolish old superstition that literature and art are anything but the expression of life, and are to be judged by any other test than that of their fidelity to it. The time is coming, I hope, when each new author, each new artist, will be considered, not in his proportion to any other author or artist, but in his relation to the human nature, known to us all, which it is his privilege, his high duty, to interpret. "The true standard of the artist is in every man's power" already, as Burke says; Michelangelo's "light of the piazza," the glance of the common eye, is and always was the best light on a statue; Goethe's "boys and blackbirds" have in all ages been the real connoisseurs of berries; but hitherto the mass of common men have been afraid to apply their own simplicity, naturalness, and honesty to the appreciation of the beautiful. They have always cast about for the instruction of some one who professed to know better, and who browbeat wholesome common-sense into the self-distrust that ends in sophistication. They have fallen generally to the worst of this bad species, and have been "amused and misled" (how pretty that quaint old use of amuse is!) "by the false lights" of critical vanity and self-righteousness. They have been taught to compare what they see and what they read, not with the things that they have observed and known, but with the things that some other artist or writer has done. Especially if they have themselves the artistic impulse in any direction they are taught to form themselves, not upon life, but upon the masters who became masters only by forming themselves upon life. The seeds of death are planted in them, and they can produce only the still-born, the academic. They are not told to take their work into the public square and see if it seems true to the chance passer, but to test it by the work of the very men who refused and decried any other test of their own work. The young writer who attempts to report the phrase and carriage of every-day life, who tries to tell just how he has heard men talk and seen them look, is made to feel guilty of something low and unworthy by the stupid people who would like to have him show how Shakespeare's men talked and looked, or Scott's, or Thackeray's, or Balzac's, or Hawthorne's, or Dickens's; he is instructed to idealize his personages, that is, to take the life-likeness out of them, and put the book-likeness into them. He is approached in the spirit of wretched pedantry into which learning, much or little, always decays when it withdraws itself and stands apart from experience in an attitude of imagined superiority, and which would say with the same confidence to the scientist: "I see that you are looking at a grasshopper there which you have found in the grass, and I suppose you intend to describe it. Now don't waste your time and sin against culture in that way. I've got a grasshopper here, which has been evolved at considerable pains and expense out of the grasshopper in general; in fact, it's a type. It's made up of wire and card-board, very prettily painted in a conventional tint, and it's perfectly indestructible. It isn't very much like a real grasshopper, but it's a great deal nicer, and it's served to represent the notion of a grasshopper ever since man emerged from barbarism. You may say that it's artificial. Well, it is artificial; but then it's ideal too; and what you want to do is to cultivate the ideal. You'll find the books full of my kind of grasshopper, and scarcely a trace of yours in any of them. The thing that you are proposing to do is commonplace; but if you say that it isn't commonplace, for the very reason that it hasn't been done before, you'll have to admit that it's photographic."

As I said, I hope the time is coming when not only the artist, but the common, average man, who always "has the standard of the arts in his power," will have also the courage to apply it, and will reject the ideal grasshopper wherever he finds it, in science, in literature, in art, because it is not "simple, natural, and honest," because it is not like a real grasshopper. But I will own that I think the time is yet far off, and that the people who have been brought up on the ideal grasshopper, the heroic grasshopper, the impassioned grasshopper, the self-devoted, adventureful, good old romantic card-board grasshopper, must die out before the simple, honest, and natural grasshopper can have a fair field. I am in no haste to compass the end of these good people, whom I find in the

On Truth in Fiction

mean time very amusing. It is delightful to meet one of them, either in print or out of it—some sweet elderly lady or excellent gentleman whose youth was pastured on the literature of thirty or forty years ago—and to witness the confidence with which they preach their favorite authors as all the law and the prophets. They have commonly read little or nothing since, or, if they have, they have judged it by a standard taken from these authors, and never dreamed of judging it by nature; they are destitute of the documents in the case of the later writers; they suppose that Balzac was the beginning of realism, and that Zola is its wicked end; they are quite ignorant, but they are ready to talk you down, if you differ from them, with an assumption of knowledge sufficient for any occasion. The horror, the resentment, with which they receive any question of their literary saints is genuine; you descend at once very far in the moral and social scale, and anything short of offensive personality is too good for you; it is expressed to you that you are one to be avoided, and put down even a little lower than you have naturally fallen.

These worthy persons are not to blame; it is part of their intellectual mission to represent the petrifaction of taste, and to preserve an image of a smaller and cruder and emptier world than we now live in, a world which was feeling its way towards the simple, the natural, the honest, but was a good deal "amused and misled" by lights now no longer mistakable for heavenly luminaries. They belong to a time, just passing away, when certain authors were considered authorities in certain kinds, when they must be accepted entire and not questioned in any particular. Now we are beginning to see and to say that no author is an authority except in those moments when he held his ear close to Nature's lips and caught her very accent. These moments are not continuous with any authors in the past, and they are rare with all. Therefore I am not afraid to say now that the greatest classics are sometimes not at all great, and that we can profit by them only when we hold them, like our meanest contemporaries, to a strict accounting, and verify their work by the standard of the arts which we all have in our power, the simple, the natural, and the honest.

Those good people, those curious and interesting if somewhat musty back-numbers, must always have a hero, an idol of some sort, and it is droll to find Balzac, who suffered from their sort such bitter scorn and hate for his realism while he was alive, now become a fetich in his turn, to be shaken in the faces of those who will not blindly worship him. But it is no new thing in the history of literature: whatever is established is sacred with those who do not think. At the beginning of this century, when romance was making the same fight against effete classicism which realism is making to-day against effete romanticism, the Italian poet Monti declared that "the romantic was the cold grave of the Beautiful," just as the realistic is now supposed to be. The romantic of that day and the real of this are in certain degree the same. Romanticism then sought, as realism seeks now, to widen the bounds of sympathy, to level every barrier against aesthetic freedom, to escape from the paralysis of tradition. It exhausted itself in this impulse; and it remained for realism to assert that fidelity to experience and probability of motive are essential conditions of great imaginative literature. It is not a new theory, but it has never before universally characterized literary endeavor. When realism becomes false to itself, when it heaps up facts merely, and maps life, instead of picturing it, realism will perish too. Every true realist instinctively knows this, and it is perhaps the reason why he is careful of every fact, and feels himself bound to express or to indicate its meaning at the risk of over-moralizing. In life he finds nothing insignificant; all tells for destiny and character; nothing that God has made is contemptible. He cannot look upon human life and declare this thing or that thing unworthy of notice, any more than the scientist can declare a fact of the material world beneath the dignity of his inquiry. He feels in every nerve the equality of things and the unity of men; his soul is exalted, not by vain shows and shadows and ideals, but by realities, in which alone the truth lives. In criticism it is his business to break the images of false gods and misshapen heroes, to take away the poor silly toys that many grown people would still like to play with. He cannot keep terms with Jack the Giant-killer or Puss in Boots, under any name or in any place, even when they reappear as the convict Vautrec, or the Marquis de Montrivaut, or the Sworn Thirteen Noblemen. He must say to himself that Balzac, when he imagined these monsters, was not Balzac, he was Dumas; he was not realistic, he was romantic.

On Veritism*

By Hamlin Garland

HAMLIN GARLAND (1860-1940) was one of the native writers whom William Dean Howells encouraged to write truthfully of the American scene. Indeed he is a classic case of the writer who was precipitated into realism by a desire to keep the record straight. Born in Wisconsin and reared on what he called "the middle border," Garland did not go East until he was twenty-one. He went back to North Dakota in 1883 to take up a claim, but returned East once more the following year.

It was the disparity between farm life on the frontier as he knew it and the romantic accounts of the West appearing in fiction that impelled Garland to write his collection of short stories *Main-Travelled Roads* (1891), which illustrate the drabness and frustration of the farmer's life. In the same year B. O. Flower, the crusading editor of the *Arena*, sent him on a tour of the West to investigate the situation of the farmer and farm-laborer. Out of this background arose three propagandistic novels, *A Member of the Third House, A Spoil of Office*, and *Jason Edwards: An Average Man*, all published in 1892. Much later he produced *A Son of the Middle Border* (1914-1917) and *Trail-Makers of the Middle Border* (1926), which, in his words, "present the homely everyday history of a group of migrating families from 1840 to 1895," and "are as true to the home-life of the prairie and the plains as my memory will permit." Memory, softened by the passage of years, presents these materials in a much gentler light than that cast upon them in 1891.

In 1894 appeared a book of criticism, *Crumbling Idols*, in which he pleads the cause of what he preferred to call "veritism" instead of realism. His description is vague and essentially hortatory:

> "This *theory* of the veritist is, after all, a statement of his passion for truth and for individual expression. The passion does not spring from theory; the theory rises from the love of the verities, which seems to increase day by day all over the Western world.
>
> "The veritist, therefore, must not be taken to be dogmatic, only, so far as he is personally concerned. He is occupied in stating his sincere convictions, believing that only in that way is the cause of truth advanced. He addresses himself to the mind prepared to listen. He destroys by displacement, not by attacking directly."

* Garland, Hamlin, *Crumbling Idols: Twelve Essays on Art and Literature,* pp. vii-ix: "A Personal Word," and pp. 3-18: I "Provincialism"; Chicago, Stone and Kimball, 1894.

The position advanced can scarcely be called *theoretical*; rather it is a naive plea for literary independence both from the Old World and from the East, and is almost Whitmanesque in its enthusiasm and orotundity of style. Nonetheless it is a clear expression of the spontaneous desire for realism in a new country whose life and experience are falsified and stunted by existing literary conventions.

Unhappily Garland did not long pursue the realistic vein, but turned to a polemical, sentimental, or romantic treatment of western subjects. Whether this was from economic necessity or innate preference remains a question.

◇◇◇

A PERSONAL WORD

THIS book is not a history; it is not a formal essay: it is a series of suggestions.

I do not assume to speak for any one but myself,—being an individualist,—and the power of this writing to destroy or build rests upon its reasonableness, simply. It does not carry with it the weight of any literary hierarchy.

It is intended to weaken the hold of conventionalism upon the youthful artist. It aims also to be constructive, by its statement and insistent re-statement that American art, to be enduring and worthy, must be original and creative, not imitative.

My contention is not against literary artists of the past, but against fetichism. Literary prostration is as hopeless and sterile as prostration before Baal or Isis or Vishnu. It is fitter to stand erect in these days.

Youth should study the past, not to get away from the present, but to understand the present and to anticipate the future. I believe in the mighty pivotal present. I believe in the living, not the dead. The men and women around me interest me more than the saints and heroes of other centuries.

I do not advocate an exchange of masters, but freedom from masters. Life, Nature,—these should be our teachers. They are masters who do not enslave.

Youth should be free from the dominion of the dead; therefore I defend the individual right of the modern creative mind to create

On Veritism

in the image of life, and not in the image of any literary master, living or dead.

There came a young man to Monet, saying, "Master, teach me to paint." To which Monet replied, "I do not teach painting; I make paintings. There never has been, and there never will be, but one teacher; there she is!" and with one sweep of his arm he showed the young man the splendor of meadow and sunlight. "Go, learn of her, and listen to all that she will say to you. If she says nothing, enter a notary's office and copy papers; that, at least, is not dishonorable, and is better than copying nymphs."

It is this spirit which is reinvigorating art in every nation of Europe; and shall we sit down and copy the last epics of feudalism, and repeat the dying echoes of Romance?

I. PROVINCIALISM

The history of American literature is the history of provincialism slowly becoming less all-pervasive—the history of the slow development of a distinctive utterance.

By provincialism I mean dependence upon a mother country for models of art production. This is the sense in which Taine or Véron would use the word. The "provincialism" which the conservative deplores is not provincialism, but the beginning of an indigenous literature.

"The true makers of national literature," writes Posnet, in his "Comparative Literature," "are the actions and thoughts of the nation itself. The place of these can never be taken by the sympathies of a cultured class too wide to be national, or those of a central academy too refined to be provincial. Provincialism is no ban to a truly national literature."

Using the word "provincialism," therefore, from the point of view of the central academy, we have had too little of it. That is to say, our colonial writers, and our writers from 1800 on to 1860, had too little to do with the life of the American people, and too much concern with British critics. Using it in its literary sense of dependence upon England and classic models, we have had too much of it. It has kept us timidly imitating the great writers of a nation far separated from us naturally in its social and literary ideals.

The whole development can be epitomized thus: Here on the eastern shore of America lay a chain of colonies predominantly English, soon to be provinces. Like all colonies, they looked back to their mother-country for support and encouragement in intellectual affairs as in material things. They did not presume to think for themselves. But the Revolution taught them something. It strengthened the feeling of separate identity and responsibility. It liberated them in politics, but left them still provincial (dependent) in literary and religious things. There still remained some truth in the British sneer, that American poets and artists were merely shadows or doubles successively of Pope, of Scott, of Byron, of Wordsworth, and of Tennyson. In all the space between the Revolution and the Civil War, American poets reflected the American taste fairly well, but the spirit and form of their work (with a few notable exceptions) was imitative.

Here and there song was sung, from the sincere wish to embody American life and characteristic American thought. Each generation grew less timid, and more manly and individual. The Civil War came on, and was an immense factor in building up freedom from old-world models, and in developing native literature. National feeling had an immense widening and deepening. From the interior of America, men and women rose almost at once to make American literature take on vitality and character.

American life had been lived, but not embodied in art. Native utterance had been overawed and silenced by academic English judgments; but this began to change after the Civil War. The new field began to make itself felt, not all at once, but by degrees, through "Snow-bound" and "The Biglow Papers" and "The Tales of the Argonauts" and the "Songs of the Sierras." But while this change was growing, there was coming in Eastern cities the spirit of a central academy that was to stand in precisely the same relation to the interior of America that London formerly occupied with regard to the whole country.

It may be that New York is to threaten and overawe the interior of America, as Paris reigns over the French provinces. The work of Mistral and the *Felibrige* may be needed with us to keep original genius from being silenced or distorted by a central academy which

On Veritism

is based upon tradition rather than upon life and nature. Decentralization may come to be needed here, as in Europe.

The evolutionist explains the past by the study of laws operative in the present, and by survivals of ancient conditions obscurely placed in modern things, like sinking icebergs in a southern sea. The attitude of mind (once universal with Americans) which measured everything by British standards, and timidly put new wine into old bottles, can still be found among the academic devotees and their disciples. They are survivals of a conception of life and literature once universal.

The change which has taken place can be specifically illustrated in the West. That is to say, the general terms which could be applied to the whole country up to the time of the Civil War can be applied specifically to the middle West to-day. As a Western man, I think I may speak freely, without being charged with undue prejudice toward the States I name.

The school-bred West, broadly speaking, is as provincial in its art as it is assertive of Americanism in politics. The books it reads, the pictures it buys, are nearly all of the conventional sort, or, worse yet, imitations of the conventional. Its literary clubs valiantly discuss dead issues in English literature, and vote in majority against the indigenous and the democratic. They have much to say of the ideal and the universal in literature, quite in the manner of their academical instructors.

The lower ranks of Western readers, as everywhere, devour some millions of tons of romantic love-stories, or stories of detectives or Indians. It is a curious thing to contrast the bold assertion of the political exhorter of "America for Americans" with the enslavement of our readers and writers to various shades of imitative forms of feudalistic literature. America is not yet democratic in art, whatever it may claim to be in politics.

These facts are not to be quarrelled about, they are to be studied. They are signs of life, and not of death. It is better that these people should read such things than nothing at all. They will rise out of it. They can be influenced, but they must be approached on the side of life, and not by way of the academic. They are ready to support and be helped by the art which springs from life.

It is the great intelligent middle class of America, curiously enough, who are apparently most provincial. With them the verdict of the world is all-important. Their education has been just sufficient to make them distrustful of their own judgment. They are largely the product of our schools. They have been taught to believe that Shakespeare ended the drama, that Scott has closed the novel, that the English language is the greatest in the world, and that all other literatures are curious, but not at all to be ranked in power and humanity with the English literature, etc., etc.

I speak advisedly of these things, because I have been through this instruction, which is well-nigh universal. This class is the largest class in America, and makes up the great body of school-bred Westerners. They sustain with a sort of desperation all the tenets of the conservative and romantic criticism in which they have been instructed.

It can almost be stated as a rule without an exception that in our colleges there is no chair of English literature which is not dominated by conservative criticism, and where sneering allusion to modern writers is not daily made. The pupil is taught to worship the past, and is kept blind to the mighty literary movements of his own time. If he comes to understand Ibsen, Tolstoy, Björnson, Howells, Whitman, he must do it outside his instruction.

This instruction is well meaning, but it is benumbing to the faculties. It is essentially hopeless. It blinds the eyes of youth to the power and beauty of the life and literature around him. It worships the past, despises the present, and fears the future. Such teaching is profoundly pessimistic, because it sees literary ideals changing. It has not yet seen that metamorphosis is the law of all living things. It has not yet risen to the perception that the question for America to settle is not whether it can produce something *greater* than the past, but whether it shall produce something *different* from the past. Our task is not to imitate, but to create.

Instruction of this kind inevitably deflects the natural bent of the young artist, or discourages attempt altogether. It is the opposite of education; that is, it represses rather than *leads out* the distinctive individuality of the student.

These conservative ideas affect the local newspapers, and their literary columns are too often full of the same gloomy comment. They are timidly negative when not partisanly conservative. They

On Veritism

can safely praise Ruskin and Carlyle, and repeat an old slur on Browning or Whitman.

There is also a class of critics who can launch into two-column criticisms of a new edition of "Rasselas," and leave unread a great novel by Tolstoy, or a new translation of Brand, or a new novel by Howells. Their judgment is worthless to detect truth and beauty in a work of art close at hand. They wait for the judgment of the East, of London.

The American youth is continually called upon by such critics to take Addison or Scott or Dickens or Shakespeare as a model. Such instruction leads naturally to the creation of blank-verse tragedies on Columbus and Washington,—a species of work which seems to the radical the crowning absurdity of misplaced effort.

Thus, the American youth is everywhere turned away from the very material which he could best handle, which he knows most about, and which he really loves most,—material which would make him individual, and fill him with hope and energy. The Western poet and novelist is not taught to see the beauty and significance of life near at hand. He is rather blinded to it by his instruction.

He turns away from the marvellous changes which border-life subtends in its mighty rush toward civilization. He does not see the wealth of material which lies at his hand, in the mixture of races going on with inconceivable celerity everywhere in America, but with especial picturesqueness in the West. If he sees it, he has not the courage to write of it.

If, here and there, one has reached some such perception, he voices it timidly, with an apologetic look in his eye.

The whole matter appears to me to be a question of individuality. I feel that Véron has stated this truth better than any other man. In his assault upon the central academy he says, in substance, "Education should not conventionalize, should not mass together; it should individualize."

The Western youth, like the average school-bred American, lacks the courage of his real conviction. He really prefers the modern writer, the modern painter, but he feels bound to falsify in regard to his real mind. As a creative intelligence, he lacks the courage to honestly investigate his surroundings, and then stand

143

by his judgment. Both as reader and writer, he dreads the Eastern comment. It is pitiful to see his eagerness to conform; he will even go beyond his teachers in conforming. Thus he starts wrong. His standards of comparison are wrong. He is forced into writing to please somebody else, which is fatal to high art.

To perceive the force of all this, and the real hopelessness of instruction according to conventional models, we have only to observe how little that is distinctive has been produced by the great Western middle States,—say Wisconsin, Illinois, and Iowa. Of what does its writing consist?

A multitude of little newspapers, first of all, full of local news; and larger newspapers that are political organs, with some little attention to literature on their inside pages. Their judgments are mainly conservative, but here and there in their news columns one finds sketches of life so vivid one wonders why writers so true and imaginative are not recognized and encouraged.

The most of the short stories in these papers, however, are absolutely colorless, where they are not pirated exotics. In all that they call "literature" these papers generally reflect what they believe to be the correct thing in literary judgment. In their unconscious moments they are fine and true.

Art, they think, is something far away, and literary subjects must be something select and very civilized. And yet for forty years an infinite drama has been going on in those wide spaces of the West,—a drama that is as thrilling, as full of heart and hope and battle, as any that ever surrounded any man; a life that was unlike any ever seen on the earth, and which should have produced its characteristic literature, its native art chronicle.

As for myself, I am overwhelmed by the majesty, the immensity, the infinite charm of the life that goes on around me. Themes are crying out to be written. Take, for a single example, the history of the lumbering district of the northern lakes,—a picturesque and peculiar life, that through a period of thirty years has been continually changing in all but a few of its essential features; and yet this life has had only superficial representation in the sketches of the tourist or reporter; its inner heart has not been uttered.

The subtle changes of thought and of life that have come with the rise of a city like St. Paul or Minneapolis; the life of the great

On Veritism

saw-mills and shingle-mills; and the river-life of the upper Mississippi are all fine subjects. So are the river towns like Dubuque and Davenport, with their survivals of French life reaching down to the present year, and thus far unrecorded.

Then there is the mixture of races; the coming in of the German, the Scandinavian; the marked yet subtle changes in their character. Then there is the building of railroads, with all their trickery and false promises and worthless bonds; the rise of millionnaires; the deepening of social contrasts. In short, there is a great heterogeneous, shifting, brave population, a land teeming with unrecorded and infinite drama.

It is only to the superficial observer that this country seems colorless and dull; to the veritist it is full of burning interest, greatest possibilities. I instance these localities because I know something special about them; but the same words apply to Pennsylvania, Ohio, or Kentucky. And yet how few writers of national reputation this eventful century-long march of civilization has produced!

We have had the figures, the dates, the bare history, the dime-novel statement of pioneer life, but how few real novels! How few accurate studies of speech and life! There it lies, ready to be put into the novel and the drama, and upon canvas; and it must be done by those born into it. Joaquin Miller has given us lines of splendid poetry touching this life, and Edward Eggleston, Joseph Kirkland, Opie Read, Octave Thanet, have dealt more or less faithfully with certain phases of it; but mainly the mighty West, with its swarming millions, remains undelineated in the novel, the drama, and the poem.

The causes of it, as I have indicated, are twofold: first, lack of a market; and, second, lack of perception. This lack of perception of the art-possibilities of common American life has been due to several causes. Hard life, toil, lack of leisure, have deadened and calloused the perceiving mind, making life hard, dull, and uninteresting. But, beyond this, the right perception has been lacking on the part of instructors and critics. Everything has really tended to repress or distort the art-feeling of the young man or woman. They have been taught to imitate, not to create.

But at last conditions are changing. All over the West young people are coming on who see that every literature in the past was at its best creative and not imitative. Here and there a paper or magazine lends itself to the work of encouraging the young writer in original work. They are likely to err now on the side of flattery. Criticism should be helpful, not indiscriminate either in praise or blame.

And more than this, in every town of the interior there are groups of people whose firmness of conviction and broad culture make them the controlling power in all local literary work. They are reading the most modern literature, and their judgments are not dependent upon New York or London, though they find themselves in full harmony with progressive artists everywhere. They are clearly in the minority, but they are a growing company everywhere, and their influence is felt by every writer of the progressive group.

Contemporary Society as Novelistic Material*

By Benito Pérez Galdós

BENITO PÉREZ GALDÓS (1843-1920) was the leading Spanish realist, though he left no work to rank with the major achievements of the movement or to become part of the broad body of European literature. Beginning with two historical novels in 1871, he turned to what he called the *Episodios nacionales*, popularized historical narratives which in effect taught the national history to the people of Spain. The first two series, consisting of twenty volumes, appeared from 1873 to 1879; the last three series, after 1898; in all there were forty-six volumes recapitulating Spanish history from the time of the Napoleonic wars to the late nineteenth century and describing the life of the people in infinitely varied detail. As Galdós wrote: "The intimate entanglements and encounters of people who never aspired to the judgment of posterity are a branch of that same tree which provides the lumber of history with which we erect the structure of the external life of peoples—of their princes, social changes, laws, and condition of war and peace. Joining both kinds of wood together as best we can, we erect a lofty scaffolding from which we see in luminous perspective the body, soul, and temper of a nation."

In the interval between the two groups of historical works he wrote his contemporary novels, which are partly realistic, partly tendentious in the beginning and which incline to the symbolic and abstract toward the end of his career. The most notable of these are *La Desheredada* (1881), *Tormento* (1884), *La de Bringas* (1884), *Fortunata y Jacinta* (1886-1887), *Realidad* (1889), and *Misericordia* (1897).

Galdós never purged himself completely of the claptrap of the romantic plot. On the other hand, his works are rich in sharp observation of everyday life. Even in the historical works it was the ordinary and the contemporary at which he aimed. This position is taken with subtle indirection in the speech here presented—a speech made to the ultraconservative members of the Spanish Academy at the time of his induction—in which he attempts to lead them first to a recognition of the inevitability of social change and then to persuade them of the literary potential of such material. The result, he argues, is movement away from the stereotype to the freshly observed and memorably individual. Whatever his effect upon his auditors, this is the direction in which the important Spanish writers have gone.

* Pérez Galdós, Benito, *Discursos leídos ante la Real Academia en la recepción pública del Sr. D. Benito Pérez Galdós*, pp. 5-16; Madrid, 1897. Translated with the permission of Doña Maria Pérez Galdós, Uda de Verde, and The Sociedad General de Autores de España.

Contemporary society as novelistic material, that is the topic on which I propose to venture certain opinions before you. Instead of turning to books and their immediate authors, I turn to the supreme author who inspires them, who indeed engenders them, and who, after the transmutation which the created material undergoes at our hands, returns to take the books in its hands for the purpose of judging them; I turn to the prime author of the work of art, the public, the human race, to whom I do not hesitate to ascribe the adjective *common,* thereby indicating the masses at a mediocre level of ideas and feelings; yes, to the common people, first and last material of all works of art, because they, as humanity, give us passions, characters, and language, and afterwards, as public, ask us for tales out of those elements which they have given us so that we may artistically recreate their own image, with the result that, beginning by being our models, they end by being our judges.

I wish, then, briefly to examine that *nature,* speaking in pictorial terms, which, in extension behind ours, tells us and indeed commands us to paint it, begging us in forceful terms to recreate the portrait it contains or incur the wrath of severe criticism. I face it courageously, and yet I admit in all truth that the frown of this model and its unfriendly face also disturb me greatly, though the fright is not as great as that I experience in the library. Social erudition is easier of acquisition than bibliographical and is within the reach of imperfectly cultivated minds. Examining the conditions of the social milieu in which we live as source of literary works, the first thing I note about the masses to which we belong is the slackening of all principles of unity. The great and powerful energies of social cohesion are not what they were; nor is it easy to see what forces will replace them in the government and direction of the human family. We have only a firm conviction that these forces must reassert themselves, but the predictions of Science and the divinations of Poetry are as yet without the power or knowledge to raise the veil which conceals the key to our future destinies.

The lack of unity is such that even in political life, naturally organized in disciplined groups, there is clear evidence of the dissolution of those large families formed by the enthusiasm of constituencies, by traditional affinities, or by more or less clear-cut principles. Just to complete this process, we also witness the disappearance of fanaticism, which once bound enormous masses of people in tight groups, and made their feelings, their conduct, and even their faces uniform, whence there resulted generic characters of easy access to Art, which made use of them over a long period of time. The falling apart of political life is the echo we hear near at hand of that terrible *ripping of the fabric* which sounds from one end to the other of the social body like a voice of panic clamoring for dissolution. It might be said that society is reaching a point on its road where it sees itself surrounded by huge rocks which block its way. Various crevices open up in the hard and awful rock, indicating to us paths or exits which perhaps would lead to unobstructed regions. We have heard tales, no doubt, of indefatigable travelers who have been directed by supernatural voices from on high: *this way shall ye go, and this way only.* But supernatural voices do not strike our ears, and the wisest among us are entangled in endless controversies as to what can or may be the opening or the crevice by which we shall be able to escape from this fearful pit in which we suffocate as we go round and round.

Some who intrepidly rush into this or that defile return in despair, saying that they have seen only shadows and tangles of briars which bar their steps; others seek by patient labor to open a way with pickaxes or to break up the rock by the action of explosives; but all of us in the end lament in noisy discord that we have come to a stop at an impasse from which we see no way out, though there must be one, since we surely do not have to remain here until the end of time.

Among the panic-stricken crowd, which invents a thousand tricks to conceal from itself its own sadness, there is to be noted a breakdown of those ancient social classes forged by history which have been powerful in organization right up to our own times. Common people and aristocracy are both losing their traditional characteristics, on the one hand by the diffusion of wealth, on the other by the progress of education, and the distance we still have to go before the basic classes lose their physiognomy will be traversed rapidly. The so-called middle class, which as yet has no positive existence, is only a shapeless agglomeration of individuals drawn from the upper and lower categories, the product, we might say, of the decomposition of both groups: of the common people, on their way up; of the aristocracy, on their way down, the deserters from both groups establishing themselves in that middle zone of learning, official careers, and business, which is coming to be the vanguard of political and municipal life. This enormous mass without a character of its own, which absorbs and monopolizes all of life, subjecting it to endless regulations, legislating frenziedly on everything without leaving out things of the spirit, which are the exclusive domain of the soul, will in the end absorb the deteriorated remains of the classes at either pole, the traditional depositories of the basic feelings. When this happens, there will be discerned at the center of this chaotic mass a fermentation from which will issue social forms which we cannot yet guess at, vigorous unities which we cannot succeed in defining in the confusion and bewilderment in which we live.

The result is, from what I have indicated vaguely with my natural laziness of expression, that in the sphere of Art generic types, which symbolized major groupings of the human family, are disappearing and losing life and color. Even human faces are not what they were, though it would seem ridiculous to say so. You will no longer find those faces which, like masks molded by the conventionalism of custom, represented the passions, the ridiculous, the vices and the virtues. The little which the people retain of the typical and picturesque is fading and becoming obliterated; even in language we notice the same tendency away from the typical, leading to uniformity of diction and similarity of speech on the part of everybody. At the same time urbanization is slowly destroying the peculiar physiognomy of each city; and if in the country there is still preserved in people and things a distinctive profile of popular stamp, this will be worn away by the continual progress of the leveling roller which flattens every eminence, and will go on flattening until it produces the longed-for equality of forms in all things spiritual and material.

While this leveling is taking place, Art offers us a strange phenomenon which demonstrates the inconsistency of ideas in the present-day world. In other eras changes of literary opinion manifested themselves over long periods of time with the majestic

Contemporary Society as Novelistic Material

slowness of all historical process. Even in the generation preceding our own we saw the romantic evolution last long enough to produce a multitude of vigorous works; and to indicate the change in aesthetic ideas, the literary forms which followed romanticism were slow in presenting themselves with vigor and lived for many years, which today seem to us like centuries, when we consider the rapidity with which our tastes are now transformed. We have come to a time when aesthetic opinion, that social rhythm not unlike the ebb and flow of the sea, changes with such capricious speed that if an author lets two or three years pass between imagining and publishing his work, it may well happen that it is out of date the day it appears. For if in the scientific realm the rapidity with which inventions follow each other, or the applications of physical agencies, makes today's marvels seem commonplace tomorrow and causes every new discovery to be immediately put in the shade by new marvels of mechanics and industry, in the same way in literature, unstable aesthetic opinion seems to be the rule, and we continually see it change before our eyes, fleeting and whimsical, like fashions in clothing. And thus, in the shortest time, we leap from nebulous idealism to the extremes of naturalism; today we love minute details, tomorrow broad and vigorous lines; we are equally ready to see the source of beauty in poorly assimilated philosophical reasoning and in ardent inherited beliefs.

To sum up: the same evolutionary confusion that we note in society, the prime material of novelistic art, is to be found in the latter by the uncertainty of its ideals, by the variability of its forms, by the timidity with which it makes use of profoundly human data; and when society turns into a public, that is, when after having been the inspirer of Art, it looks at it with the eyes of a judge, it betrays the same uncertainty in its opinions, with the result that critics are no less confused than authors.

But do not believe that I have any intention of drawing a pessimistic conclusion from these facts, and asserting that from this social breakdown there must ensue a period of anemia and death for narrative art. Certainly the lack of unity in social organization deprives us of generic characters, types that society itself provides in outline, as if they were already the first imprint of artistic handling. But in the measure that generalized characterization of persons and things is effaced, their human models appear more clear, and it is in them that the novelist ought to study life in order to achieve the fruits of an Art that is great and lasting. Wise criticism cannot fail to recognize that when the ideas and feelings of a society appear in very clear-cut categories it seems that those characters arrive in the realm of Art already touched with a certain mannerism or conventionalism. With the breakdown of categories masks fall at one blow and faces appear in their true purity. Types are lost, but man is better revealed to us, and Art is directed solely to giving to imaginary beings a life that is more human than social. And no one is unaware that, when we work with purely human materials, the force of genius to express life has to be greater and its effort more profound and difficult, as the plastic representation of the nude is a greater undertaking than the representation of a figure draped with clothes, however scanty they may be. And in proportion to the difficulty, no doubt, the value of the artistic product increases, so that if in periods of powerful principles of unity it shines forth with vivid social meaning, in the unhappy days of transition and evolution it can and ought to be profoundly human.

I find I have come to a point where the ideas which I am setting forth, without dogmatic arrogance, lead me to an affirmation which some might believe false and paradoxical, namely: that the lack of principles of unity encourages a flowering of literature, an affirmation which logically would destroy the legend of the so-called *Golden Age* in this and other literatures. The fact is that general literary history does not permit us to assert in an absolute manner that divine Poetry and the sister arts prosper more luxuriantly in periods of unity than in periods of confusion. Perhaps the opposite could be proved after investigating the life of peoples with penetrating criticism, making more use of private documentation than of the accounts of the old History, which was usually artificial and composed. That emphatic narrative, somewhat touched with delusions of grandeur, speaks to us by tenacious preference of the high powers of the State, of wars, intrigues, and courtly favors, of marriages and quarrels between families of kings and princes, leaving in shadow the deepest emotions which stir the soul of the social body. Taking this into account, I do not believe it beside the point to point out that in the so-called *Golden Age* there was a notice-

Contemporary Society as Novelistic Material

able amount of official history or fiction of the palace, the work of salaried chroniclers or official historians, more concerned with the composition of their work than with internal political truth. They give value only to what are or appear to be culminating actions and are unconcerned with the true feelings and thoughts of the people as being prosaic and trivial data.

I am well aware that this is a subject for careful examination, and if I were to attempt to unravel it, I would incur my own censure for throwing myself into a work before whose formidable difficulty I have asserted my own incapacity in the first paragraphs of this discourse. With patience and with books at hand, all might be proved, and I would attempt to demonstrate what I have indicated above if more force than my desires did not show my incapacity to summon up ancient and modern texts. I therefore leave it to others to elucidate this point, and conclude by saying that the present-day social situation with all its confusion and nervous disquietude has not been sterile for the novel in Spain, and that perhaps this very confusion and uncertainty have favored the development of so fine an art. We cannot foresee how far the present disintegration will go. But we may affirm that narrative literature does not have to be lost just because the old social organisms die or are transformed. Perhaps new forms will appear; perhaps works of extraordinary power and beauty which will serve as harbingers of future ideals or as a farewell to those of the past, as the *Quixote* is a farewell to the world of chivalry. Be that as it may, human genius lives in all environments and produces its flowers alike before the happy portals of resplendent monuments and among sad and desolate ruins.

I have spoken.

"True Art Speaks Plainly"*

By Theodore Dreiser

THEODORE DREISER (1871-1945) was the American Zola. It was the power and magnitude of his example which finally brought realism to this country. He attracted to himself almost as much vituperation as did his French predecessor, though he was without the latter's skill at or joy in verbal brawling.

Dreiser's effort as novelist was to show the forces that actually molded lives in the United States and to describe the patterns which they followed. Deeply influenced by the scientific ideas of his youth, he concentrated on the struggling organism in its efforts to secure life or achieve adaptation in an indifferent, amoral environment. Because he was more aware of social flux than was Zola, and especially of a peculiarly American social mobility, his works seem less tightly deterministic than those of the French naturalists. There is even a note of brooding wonder at the impenetrable mystery at the center of the shifting web of phenomena.

For his examples of typical human lives Dreiser did not go as far down in the social scale as the naturalists generally did. His *Sister Carrie* (1900) is an account of an ordinary farm girl who comes to Chicago, goes wrong, and prospers. This was so upsetting a reversal of traditional morality that the pusillanimous publisher decided to withdraw the book after the review copies had been sent out. Dreiser weathered this blow, bided his time, and in 1911 published *Jennie Gerhardt*, a story of a kept woman which was even less conciliatory, though slightly more sentimental, than the first novel. He then turned to the business tycoon for his major portrait, devoting the three volumes of his Trilogy of Desire (*The Financier*, 1912; *The Titan*, 1914; and *The Stoic*, 1947) to an analysis of the predatory appetites of Frank Cowperwood, showing them as developing from and responsive to the times in which he lived. The last major work was *An American Tragedy* (1925), in which he turned to the obverse of the coin, showing a hapless youth who is a predestined victim of social forces which Cowperwood knew so well how to master—temporarily.

Dreiser was only incidentally a critic, and the present selection states half of all he ever had to say: that is, that the official descriptions of life from pulpit, rostrum, or printed page did not square with life as he had experienced or observed it. This position is reiterated in the pamphlet *Life, Art and America* (1917), when, still smarting from his brush with the forces of Comstockery over *The "Genius"*, he assails

---

* Dreiser, Theodore, "True Art Speaks Plainly," *Booklovers Magazine* 1: p. 129, February 1903. Reprinted by permission of the Dreiser Trust.

the forces of philistinism for making it impossible to get a correct idea of "what might be called the mental abcs of life." The result is that America has failed to produce writers who treat life seriously, and he calls the roll of Turgenev, Maupassant, Flaubert, Taine, Sainte-Beuve, the Goncourts, Ibsen, Chekhov, Shaw, Hauptmann, and Brieux as examples of what we have failed to achieve. The name of Zola is significantly absent from the list. Dreiser always maintained that his was an independent literary development and that he had come to Zola after his own attitude was fully formed.

The other half of Dreiser's critical doctrine was an insistence that art did not preach, that it was a simple inquiry without *parti pris*. There has been some confusion on this point, since he was well known as a social activist after 1930 and, indeed, joined the Communist party six months before his death. The works bear out his claim to impartiality. He provides the facts; any judgment and subsequent action comes from the reader.

In 1944 Dreiser received the award of the American Academy for his works and for his "courage and integrity in breaking trail as a pioneer in the presentation in fiction of real human beings and a real America."

◇◇◇

THE sum and substance of literary as well as social morality may be expressed in three words—tell the truth. It matters not how the tongues of the critics may wag, or the voices of a partially developed and highly conventionalized society may complain, the business of the author, as well as of other workers upon this earth, is to say what he knows to be true, and, having said as much, to abide the result with patience.

Truth is what is; and the seeing of what is, the realization of truth. To express what we see honestly and without subterfuge: this is morality as well as art.

What the so-called judges of the truth or morality are really inveighing against most of the time is not the discussion of mere sexual lewdness, for no work with that as a basis could possibly succeed, but the disturbing and destroying of their own little theories concerning life, which in some cases may be nothing more than a quiet acceptance of things as they are without any regard to the well-being of the future. Life for them is made up of a variety of interesting but immutable forms and any attempt either to picture any of the wretched results of modern social conditions or to assail the critical defenders of the same is naturally looked upon with contempt or aversion.

It is true that the rallying cry of the critics against so-called immoral literature is that the mental virtue of the reader must be preserved; but this has become a house of refuge to which every form of social injustice hurries for protection. The influence of intellectual ignorance and physical and moral greed upon personal virtue produces the chief tragedies of the age, and yet the objection to the discussion of the sex question is so great as to almost prevent the handling of the theme entirely.

Immoral! Immoral! Under this cloak hide the vices of wealth as well as the vast unspoken blackness of poverty and ignorance; and between them must walk the little novelist, choosing neither truth nor beauty, but some half-conceived phase of life that bears no honest relationship to either the whole of nature or to man.

The impossibility of any such theory of literature having weight with the true artist must be apparent to every clear reasoning mind. Life is not made up of any one phase or condition of being, nor can man's interest possibly be so confined.

The extent of all reality is the realm of the author's pen, and a true picture of life, honestly and reverentially set down, is both moral and artistic whether it offends the conventions or not.*

* In an article "On the New Humanists" Dreiser at the height of his career made a self-evaluation of importance:

"Personally I appear to be charged with being a realist. I accept the insult but with reservations. For I fear I do not run true to type—do not march with any clan. Rather I see myself as a highly temperamental individual compelled to see life through the various veils or fogs of my own lacks, predilections and what you will, yet seeking honestly always to set down that which I imagine I see. I am told by some that it agrees with what they see. By others not. But what I think I see is beauty and ugliness, mystery and some little clarity, in minor things, tenderness and terrific brutality, ignorance sodden and hopeless and some admirable wisdom, malice and charity, honesty and dishonesty, aspiration and complete and discouraging insensitivity and indifference." (*New York World*, May 9, 1930)

Part Two

The Battle Over Naturalism

On the Rougon-Macquart Series[*]

By Emile Zola

EMILE ZOLA (1840-1902) is the colossus of the realistic movement, both by reason of his formidable ability to engage in verbal combat on behalf of naturalism and because of his impressive Rougon-Macquart series in twenty volumes, which dominated the literary scene from the appearance of *The Fortunes of the Rougon Family* in 1871 until the publication of *Dr. Pascal* in 1893. The extent of his importance will be evident from the frequency with which his name is invoked, in praise or derogation, in this volume.

His first novel, *Thérèse Raquin* (1867), raised a storm of protest which the author countered in a preface to the second edition in 1868. He asserts that he has sought to study temperament, not character: "I chose characters completely dominated by their nerves and their blood, deprived of free-will, pushed to each action of their lives by the fatality of their flesh." His goal was scientific—experimental, although he did not yet use the word: "I have simply done on living bodies the work of analysis which surgeons perform on corpses." He shrugs off charges of pornography and immorality as meaningless, since he has written out of "pure scientific curiosity." Competent critics would see that the novel in its employment of scientific analysis is using "the modern method, the universal instrument of inquiry of which this age makes use with such ardor to open up the future. Whatever their conclusions, they would admit my point of departure, the study of temperament and the profound modifications of the organisms under the pressure of environment and circumstance."

The themes here stated were repeated and developed in later utterances with one important addition: the social utility of naturalistic works. There is all too much evidence that Zola's scientific culture was superficial and that he drew uncritically from current works which supported his bias toward a crude materialist determinism, especially from Dr. Claude Bernard's *Experimental Medicine*. It is to be noted that even before encountering Bernard's work he conceived of the Rougon-Macquart series in terms of strict interplay of heredity and environment, *à la* Taine; indeed he used Bernard as a basis for theoretical argument after the fact.

Although the first novel in the series appeared in 1871, it was not until publication of *L'Assommoir*, the seventh novel, in 1877 that Zola's success was assured. This work was powerful, original, and well observed; more than any other of the author's works it stands

[*] Zola, Emile, "Préface," *La Fortune des Rougon*, Paris, 1871.

for naturalism. Its success was capped by that of *Nana* two years later and by the performance of a play drawn from it. Then in 1880 Zola and a band of younger literary men published *Les Soirées de Médan*, a collection of naturalistic short stories having events of the Franco-Prussian war as their common basis. Having reached this apogee of success as novelist, dramatist, and leader of a school, it is not surprising that Zola, in the eleven works of the Rougon-Macquart which appeared after 1880, did not consistently maintain the standard expected by his public. It was *La Terre* in 1887 that finally provoked a storm of protest which led to the *Manifesto of Five*, a public signal of Zola's decline. Whatever the trailing off of some of the later works, it must be remembered that *Germinal* (1885) and *La Débâcle* (1892) are with *L'Assommoir* the greatest of his novels.

Since he had outraged the Church by his three novels *Paris, Rome*, and *Lourdes*; the Army by *La Débâcle* and by his dramatic efforts in behalf of Captain Alfred Dreyfus; and the Academy and university establishment by his brutal literary innovations, it is not surprising that Zola's name was rarely mentioned in right-thinking circles for many years after his death. It has always been, however, a rallying cry in other countries where the literary revolution was still in progress, and it is of considerable significance that several volumes about Zola have been published in Latin America in the last two decades.

The first of the three articles that follow is the preface which accompanied the publication of the first volume in the Rougon-Macquart series in 1871. The other two, "The Experimental Novel" and "Naturalism in the Theatre," first appeared in Russian in *The Messenger of Europe*, a St. Petersburg newspaper to which Turgenev had secured entree for Zola. Along with other pieces they made up the content of the volume entitled *Le Roman expérimental*, which was published in 1880, when Zola in the full flush of success was claiming the world for naturalism. The first is important for the statement of the author's scientific-philosophic position; the second gives a comprehensive statement of the relation of naturalism to writers of both the preceding and current literary generations.

I WANT to explain how a family, a small group of human beings, comports itself in a society, flowering to give birth to ten, twenty individuals, who, at first glance, seem very dissimilar, but who upon analysis are seen to be intimately bound one to the other. Heredity has its laws, like weight.

Taking into account the two-fold question of temperaments and environments, I shall try to find and trace out the thread which leads mathematically from one man to another. And when I have all the threads, when I hold a whole social group in my hands, I shall show this group in action, as the actor of an historical era. I shall create it acting in the complexity of its efforts. I shall analyze at the same time both the total will of its individual members and the general drive of the whole body.

The Rougon-Macquart—the group, the family, whom I propose to study—has as its prime characteristic the overflow of appetite, the broad upthrust of our age, which flings itself into enjoyments. Physiologically the members of this family are the slow working-out of accidents to the blood and nervous system which occur in a race after a first organic lesion, according to the environment determining in each of the individuals of this race sentiments, desires, passions, all the natural and instinctive human manifestations whose products take on the conventional names of virtues and vices. Historically they originate in the lower classes, spread out through all of contemporary society, climb to every eminence under that essentially modern impulsion which the lower classes receive on their way through the whole social body; by means of their individual dramas they thus constitute a narrative of the Second Empire from the ambuscade of the coup d'état to the betrayal at Sedan.

For three years I had been assembling the documents for this grandiose work, and the present volume had indeed been written, when the fall of the Bonapartes, which I had need of as artist and which I always had considered the fated end of the drama, without daring to think it would come so soon, took place and gave me the terrible and necessary denouement for my work. It is as of today complete; it whirls within a closed circle; it becomes a picture of a dead reign, of a strange epoch of folly and of shame.

This work, which will be made up of numerous episodes, is therefore to my mind The Natural and Social History of a Family under the Second Empire. And the first episode, *The Fortunes of the Rougons*, ought to be called by its scientific title, *The Origins*.

Paris
July 1, 1871

"The Experimental Novel"*

By Emile Zola

IN MY WRITING on literary subjects I have often discussed the experimental method as applied to the novel and the drama. The return to nature, the naturalistic evolution, which is the main current of our age, is gradually drawing all manifestations of human intelligence into a single scientific course. However, the idea of literature determined by science is likely to be surprising unless clearly defined and understood. It therefore seems useful to be explicit about what the experimental novel means, as I see it.

My remarks on this subject will be only an adaptation, for the experimental method has been set forth with force and marvelous clarity by Claude Bernard in his *Introduction to the Study of Experimental Medicine*. This book by a scientist of decisive authority will provide me with a solid base. In it the whole question is treated, and I shall confine myself to giving such quotations from it as are necessary as irrefutable arguments. This discussion therefore will be no more than a compilation of texts; for on all points I intend to fall back on Claude Bernard. Usually it will be sufficient for me to replace the word "doctor" by the word "novelist" in order to make my thought clear and to bring to it the rigor of scientific truth.

What has led me to choose the *Introduction* is the fact that to many people medicine, like the novel, is still an art. All his life Claude Bernard worked and fought to set medicine on the road of science. With him we see the first stammerings of a science disengaging itself slowly from empiricism and coming to rest on truth, thanks to the experimental method. Claude Bernard demonstrates that this method as applied in the study of inanimate bodies, in chemistry and physics, ought equally to be used in the study of living bodies, in physiology and medicine. I shall attempt to prove in my turn that if the experimental method leads to knowledge of physical life, it may also lead to knowledge of passional and in-

* Zola, "Le Roman Expérimental," *Le Roman expérimental*, Paris, 1880.

tellectual life. It is only a question of gradation on the same scale from chemistry to physiology, and then from physiology to anthropology and sociology. The experimental novel comes at the end.

For greater clearness I shall briefly summarize the *Introduction* here. The reader will better comprehend the application I make of my quotations by knowing the plan of the work and the material which it treats.

Claude Bernard, after asserting that medicine will in the future follow the road of science by relying on physiology, using the scientific method, first sets forth the differences that exist between the observational sciences and the experimental sciences. He comes to the conclusion that fundamentally an experiment is nothing but a forced observation. All experimental reasoning is based on doubt, for the experimenter should have no preconceived idea about nature and should always maintain an open mind. He merely accepts phenomena which occur once they are verified.

Then in the second section he begins his real subject by demonstrating that the spontaneity of living bodies does not preclude the use of experimentation. The difference comes only from the fact that an inanimate body is to be found in the common external environment whereas the elements of higher organisms exist in an interior and highly developed environment, though one which is also endowed with the same constant physio-chemical properties as the external environment. Thus there is absolute determinism in the conditions of existence of natural phenomena both for living beings and for inert matter. By "determinism" he means the cause which determines the appearance of phenomena. This proximate cause, as he calls it, is nothing but the physical and material condition of the existence or manifestation of phenomena. The goal of the experimental method, the end of all scientific research, is therefore identical for living beings and for inert bodies: it consists in finding the relations which link any phenomenon whatsoever to its proximate cause, in other words, in determining the conditions necessary for the occurrence of this phenomenon. Experimental science should not concern itself with the *why* of things; it explains the *how*, nothing more.

After setting forth the experimental conditions common to living bodies and inert bodies, Claude Bernard goes on to the experimental considerations special to living bodies. The great and unique difference is that in the organism of living beings a harmonious ensemble of phenomena is to be considered. He then treats of the technique of experimentation to be used on living beings, of vivisection, the preparatory anatomical conditions, the choice of animals, the employment of mathematics in the study of phenomena, and the physiological laboratory.

Finally, in the last part of the *Introduction*, Claude Bernard gives examples of experimental physiological investigation in support of the ideas he has formulated. He then gives examples of a critique for experimental physiology and ends by showing the philosophical obstacles that experimental medicine encounters. In the first rank he places the false application of physiology to medicine and scientific ignorance, as well as certain illusions of the medical mind. He concludes by saying that empirical medicine and experimental medicine, far from being incompatible, should on the contrary be inseparable from each other. The last assertion of the book is that experimental medicine is not dependent on any medical doctrine or philosophical system.

Such, very simply, is the skeleton of the *Introduction* divested of its flesh. I hope this rapid summary will suffice to fill in the gaps that my method of discussion will inevitably leave; for naturally I shall take from the book only those quotations necessary to define and comment on the experimental novel. I repeat that this is only the foundation on which I base my case, a foundation most rich in arguments and proofs of all sorts. Even though stammering, experimental medicine alone can give us an exact idea of experimental literature, which, still in embryo, has not even begun to stammer.

I

The first question above all to consider is this: Is experimentation possible in literature, where heretofore observation alone seems to have been used?

Claude Bernard has a long discussion of observation and experiment. There is a very sharp line of demarcation between them. Here it is: "We give the name of *observer* to him who applies simple or complex procedures of investigation to the study of phenomena which he does not cause to vary and which he merely collects as they are provided by nature; we give the name of *experimenter* to him who uses simple or complex procedures of investigation to vary or modify natural phenomena for whatever purpose, and to make them appear in circumstances and under conditions not found in nature." For example, astronomy is a science of observation, because we cannot imagine an astronomer acting on the stars; whereas chemistry is an experimental science since the chemist acts on nature and modifies it. According to Claude Bernard, this is the only really important distinction between the observer and the experimenter.

I cannot follow him into his discussion of the various definitions given in the past. As I have said, he concludes that an experiment is basically only a provoked observation. I quote: "In the experimental method, the search for facts—that is, investigation—is always accompanied by reasoning, with the result that usually the experimenter sets up an experiment in order to control or verify the value of an experimental idea. Thus we may say that in this case the experiment is a forced observation to provide a control."

In addition, to be able to find out what there may be of observation and of experimentation in the naturalist novel, I need only the following passages:

"The observer sets down purely and simply the phenomena he has before his eyes. . . . He ought to be the photographer of phenomena; his observation ought to represent nature exactly. . . . He listens to nature and writes at her dictation. But once the fact is set down and the phenomenon is carefully observed, ideas come into play, reasoning intervenes, and the experimenter appears in order to interpret the phenomenon. The experimenter is he who, by virtue of a more or less probable but anticipatory interpretation of observed phenomena, institutes an experiment in such manner that in the logical framework of prevision, it furnishes a result which serves as a control for the hypothesis or preconceived idea. . . . From the moment that the result of the experiment is manifest, the experimenter confronts a true observation which he has induced, one which he must set down without preconceived idea like any other observation. The experimenter ought thus to disappear or rather transform himself instantly into observer, and it is only after he has set down the results of the experiment in absolutely the same fashion as he would an ordinary observation that his mind will once more proceed to reason, compare, and judge whether the experimental hypothesis has been verified or invalidated by these same results."

There you have the whole procedure. It is somewhat complicated, and Claude Bernard is led to say: "When all this takes place at once in the head of a scientist who is an investigator in a science as confused as medicine still is, there is such a tangle between what results from observation and what belongs to experiment that it would be impossible and indeed useless to try to analyze each of these terms in their inextricable mingling." In short, we can say that observation "shows," and experiment "informs."

Now, coming back to the novel, we can see equally well that the novelist is both observer and experimenter. The observer in him presents data as he has observed them, determines the point of departure, establishes the solid ground on which his characters will stand and his phenomena take place. Then the experimenter appears and institutes the experiment, that is, sets the characters of a particular story in motion, in order to show that the series of events therein will be those demanded by the determinism of the phenomena under study. It is almost always an experiment "in order to see," as Claude Bernard puts it. The novelist starts out in search of a truth. I shall take as an example the figure of Baron Hulot in Balzac's *La Cousine Bette*. The general fact observed by Balzac is the ravages that a man's amorous nature produces in himself, his family, and society. Once he has chosen his subject, he has departed from observed facts, for he has initiated his experiment by subjecting Hulot to a series of tests, having him pass through various situations in order to show how the mechanism of his passion works. It is therefore evident that we here have not only observation but also experimentation, since Balzac does not restrict himself to being a photographer of facts gathered by himself, but he intervenes directly to place his character in conditions over which he maintains control. The problem is to learn what such and such a passion, acting in such and such a milieu under such and such circumstances, will bring about in terms of the individual and of society; and an experimental novel, such as *La*

"The Experimental Novel"

Cousine Bette, for example, is simply the record of the experiment which the novelist repeats before the eyes of the public. In short, the whole operation consists of taking facts from nature, then studying the mechanism of the data by acting on them through a modification of circumstances and environment without ever departing from the laws of nature. At the end there is knowledge, scientific knowledge, of man in his individual and social action.

To be sure, we are here far from the certainties of chemistry, or even physiology. We do not yet know the reactive agents which will break up the passions and permit us to analyze them. Often in this study I shall remind the reader that the experimental novel is even younger than experimental medicine, which, however, has scarcely been born. But I do not intend to set forth achieved results; I desire simply to give a clear exposition of a method. If the experimental novelist still gropes his way in the most obscure and complex of sciences, that does not prevent that science from existing. It is undeniable that the naturalistic novel, such as we know it at this time, is a true experiment which the novelist makes on men, with the support of observation.

Moreover, this opinion is not mine alone, but is equally that of Claude Bernard. He says somewhere: "In the conduct of their lives men do nothing but make experiments on one another." And what is more conclusive, here is the whole theory of the experimental novel: "When we reason about our own acts, we have a certain guide, for we have consciousness of what we think and what we feel. But if we wish to judge the acts of another man and know the motives of his action, it is quite a different thing. No doubt we have before our eyes the movements of such a man and his behavior, which are, we are sure, modes of expression of his sensibility and will. In addition, we admit that there is a necessary rapport between his acts and their cause; but what is that cause? We do not feel it in ourselves; we are not conscious of it as in ourselves; we are thus obliged to interpret it, to suppose it on the basis of the movements we see and the words we hear. Thus we must use the acts of this man as controls one upon the other; we consider how he acts under a given condition, and in short we have recourse to the experimental method." All that I have advanced above is summed up in that last sentence, which is by a scientist.

I shall also quote an image of Claude Bernard's which has greatly struck me: "The experimenter is the examining magistrate of nature." We novelists are the examining magistrates of men and their passions.

But see how things begin to clear up when you take the position of the experimental method in the novel, with all the scientific rigor of the physical sciences. A stupid reproach made against us naturalist writers is that we wish to be merely photographers. In vain have we asserted that we accept temperament and personal expression; people go right on answering us with imbecile arguments about the impossibility of the strictly true, about the necessity of arrangement of facts to make any work of art whatever. Well, with the application of the experimental method to the novel all argument comes to an end. The idea of experiment carries with it the idea of modification. We begin certainly with true facts which are our indestructible base; but to show the mechanism of the facts, we have to produce and direct the phenomena; that is our part of invention and genius in the work. Thus without having recourse to questions of form and style, which I shall examine later, I state right here that when we use the experimental method we must modify nature without departing from nature. If the reader will recall the definition: "Observation shows, experiment instructs," we can henceforth claim for our works the high instruction of experiment.

Far from being diminished, the writer is hereby singularly increased. An experiment, even the most simple one, is always based on an idea, which in turn comes from observation. As Claude Bernard says, "The experimental idea is in no way arbitrary or purely imaginary; it must always have a basis in observed reality, that is, in nature." It is on this idea and on scepticism that he rests his whole method. "The appearance of the experimental idea," he says further on, "is quite spontaneous and completely individual in nature; it is an individual sentiment, a *quid proprium*, which constitutes the originality, the inventiveness, the genius of each man." Next, scepticism is necessary as the great scientific lever, "The sceptic is the true scientist; he doubts only himself and his interpretations but he believes in science; he even admits, in the experimental sciences, an absolute criterion or principle, the determinism of phenomena, absolute in the phenomena of living beings as in those of inert bodies." Thus instead of binding the novelist tightly, the experimental method leaves to him all his intelligence as thinker and all his genius as creator. He must see, understand, invent. An observed fact will bring forth the idea of the experiment to try, of the novel to write, in order to arrive at complete knowledge of a truth. Then, when he has discussed and laid out the plan of his experiment, he will at all times judge the results with the freedom of intelligence of a man who accepts only facts in conformity with the determinism of phenomena. He has begun in doubt in order to arrive at absolute knowledge; he does not cease to doubt until the mechanism of passion, taken to pieces and put back together again by him, functions according to laws fixed by nature. There is no broader or freer task for human intelligence. We shall see later the miserable state of the scholastics, the systematizers and theoreticians of the ideal, in comparison with the triumph of the experimenters.

I sum up this first section by repeating that the naturalistic novelists observe and experiment, and that their whole task begins in the doubt which they hold concerning obscure truths, inexplicable phenomena, until an experimental idea suddenly arouses their genius and impels them to make an experiment, in order to analyze the facts and become master of them.

II

Such then is the experimental method. But it has long been denied that this method can be applied to living bodies. This is the important point which I am going to examine with the help of Claude Bernard. The chain of reasoning will be very simple: if the experimental method has been capable of extension from chemistry and physics to physiology and medicine, then it can be carried from physiology to the naturalist novel.*

* Compare Taine's statement in *Histoire de la littérature anglaise* (I: xv; Hachette, 1885):
"Whether the data are physical or moral makes no difference; they always have causes; there are causes for ambition, courage, truthfulness, just as there are for digestion, muscular movement, or animal heat. Vice and virtue are prod-

To cite only one scientist, Cuvier maintained that experimentation, while applicable to inert bodies, could not be used with living bodies; according to him, physiology had to be purely a science of anatomical observation and deduction. The vitalists still posit a vital force which in living bodies is in constant struggle with physio-chemical forces and neutralizes their action. Claude Bernard, on the contrary, denies the existence of any mysterious force and asserts that experimentation is applicable everywhere: "I do not propose," he says, "to establish that the science of life phenomena can have other bases than the science of phenomena of inert bodies and that there is in this regard any difference between the principles of the biological sciences and the physio-chemical sciences. In fact the goal which the experimental method sets for itself is the same everywhere; it consists of linking by experiment natural phenomena to their conditions of existence or to their proximate causes."

It seems to me unnecessary to enter into the complex explanation and reasoning of Claude Bernard. I have said that he insisted on the existence of an internal milieu in the living being. "In experimentation on inert bodies," he says, "one has to take only one milieu into account: that is the external cosmic milieu; whereas in the higher living bodies there are at least two milieux to consider: the external or extra-organic and the internal or intra-organic. The complexity arising from the existence of an intra-organic milieu is the sole reason for the great difficulties we encounter in experimental determination of phenomena of life and in the application of measures capable of modifying it." He goes on from there to prove that there are fixed laws for the interior physiological elements as there are fixed laws for the chemical elements in the exterior milieu. Thus one may experiment on the living being just as on the inert body; it is a question merely of achieving the desired conditions.

I insist on this because, I repeat, the important point of the matter is there. Claude Bernard, writing about the vitalists, says this: "They consider life to be a mysterious and supernatural influence which acts arbitrarily and freed from all determinism, and

---

ucts like vitriol and sugar, and any complex phenomenon develops from the relationship of simpler phenomena on which it is based."

"The Experimental Novel"

they berate as materialists all those who make an effort to bring vital phenomena under determined organic physio-chemical conditions. Those are false ideas which it is not easy to root out once they have lodged themselves in the mind; only the progress of science will make them disappear." And he sets down this axiom: "In living bodies as well as in inert bodies the conditions of existence of every phenomenon are determined in an absolute fashion."

I limit my remarks so as not to complicate the reasoning unduly. This then is the progress of science. In the last century a more exact application of the experimental method has created chemistry and physics, which disengage themselves from the irrational and the supernatural. Thanks to analysis, it has been discovered that there are fixed laws; we become masters of phenomena. Then we push ahead another step. Living bodies, in which the vitalists still admitted a mysterious influence, are in their turn brought and reduced to the general mechanism of matter. Science proves that the conditions of existence of all phenomena are the same for living bodies as for inert bodies; and thenceforth physiology takes on little by little the certainty of chemistry and physics. But are we to stop there? Evidently not. When we shall have proved that man's body is a machine, when we shall someday be able to take it to pieces and put it together again at the will of the experimenter, we shall then have to go on to the passional and intellectual acts of man. Then we shall enter into a domain which up to now has belonged to philosophy and literature; that will be the decisive conquest by science of the hypotheses of the philosophers and writers. We have experimental chemistry and physics; we shall have experimental physiology; later still we shall have the experimental novel. That is a progress which imposes itself, the last term of which it is easy to foresee even now. Everything holds together; it was necessary to start with the determinism of inert bodies in order to arrive at the determinism of living bodies; and since scientists like Claude Bernard now show that fixed laws govern the human body we can assert without fear of mistake that the day will come when the laws of thought and the passions will be formulated in their turn. One and the same determinism must govern the stone in the road and the brain of man.

This opinion is stated in the *Introduction*. I cannot repeat too often that I am taking all my arguments from Claude Bernard. After explaining that the most specialized phenomena can be the result of the more and more complex union or association of organized elements, he writes this: "I am convinced that the obstacles which surround experimental study of psychological phenomena are in large part due to difficulties of this kind; for, in spite of their marvelous nature and the delicacy of their manifestations, it is impossible, as I see it, not to bring cerebral phenomena, like all the phenomena of living bodies, under the laws of a scientific determinism." That is clear. Later, no doubt, science will discover the determinism of all the cerebral and sensory manifestations of man.

From that time on science will therefore enter into the domain of us novelists, who are now the analysts of man in his individual and social action. By our observations and our experiments we continue the task of the physiologist, who has continued that of the physicist and the chemist. To a certain extent we are doing scientific psychology, as a complement to scientific physiology; and to complete the evolution we have only to bring to our studies of the nature of man the decisive tool of the experimental method. In short, we must operate with characters, passions, human and social data as the chemist and the physicist work on inert bodies, as the physiologist works on living bodies. Determinism governs everything. It is scientific investigation; it is experimental reasoning that combats one by one the hypotheses of the idealists and will replace novels of pure imagination by novels of observation and experiment.

Certainly I have no intention of formulating laws at this point. In the present state of the science of man confusion and obscurity are still too great for us to risk the least synthesis. All that we can say is that there is an absolute determinism for all human phenomena. From that point on investigation is a duty. We have the method; we must go forward even if a whole lifetime of effort produces the conquest of only a tiny bit of truth. Consider physiology: Claude Bernard made great discoveries, and he died admitting that he knew nothing, or nearly nothing. On each page he confesses the difficulties of his task. "In phenomenal relations," he says, "as nature offers them to us there always reigns a more or

"The Experimental Novel"

less considerable complexity. In this respect the complexity of mineral phenomena is much less great than that of vital phenomena; that is why sciences studying inert bodies have come into being so much more quickly. In living bodies the phenomena are of enormous complexity, and in addition the mobility of the vital properties makes them much more difficult to get hold of and determine." What should we say then of the difficulties which the experimental novel may expect to meet, since it takes from physiology its studies on the most complex and delicate organs and treats of the most elevated manifestations of man as individual and as member of society? Evidently analysis becomes even more complicated here. Thus if physiology is just being constituted today, it is natural that the experimental novel is only at its very beginning. It may be foreseen as a fated consequence of the scientific evolution of the age; but it is impossible to base it on certain laws. When Claude Bernard speaks "of the limited and precarious truths of biological science," we may well confess that the truths of the science of man with respect to the mechanism of the mind and passions are even more precarious and limited. We are still babbling; we are the latest comers; but that should merely be an additional spur to push us to exact studies as soon as we have the tool, the experimental method, and our goal is very clear, to know the determinism of phenomena and to make ourselves masters of those phenomena.

Without risking the formulation of laws, I believe that the question of heredity has a great influence in the intellectual and passional behavior of man. I also accord a considerable importance to environment. Here it would be necessary first to consider Darwin's theories; but this is only a general study of the experimental method as applied to the novel, and I would be lost if I tried to go into detail. I shall simply say a word about environments. We have just seen the decisive importance given by Claude Bernard to the study of intra-organic environment, which must be taken into account if we are to find out the determinism of phenomena among living beings. Very well! in the study of a family, of a group of living beings, I believe the social environment also has capital importance. One day physiology will no doubt explain the mechanism of thought and the passions; we shall know how the individual machine of a man works, how he thinks, how he loves, how he goes from reason to passion to madness; but these phenomena, these data of the mechanism of the organs acting under the influence of the internal environment do not occur outside in isolation and in a vacuum. Man is not alone; he lives in a society, in a social milieu, and hence for us novelists the social milieu endlessly modifies phenomena. Indeed our great study is there, on the reciprocal influence of society on the individual and of the individual on society. For the physiologist the external environment and the internal environment are purely chemical and physical, which permits him to discover their laws easily. We have not reached the point of being able to prove that the social milieu also is nothing but chemical and physical. It certainly is, or rather it is the variable product of a group of living beings who themselves are absolutely subject to physical and chemical laws which govern living bodies just as much as inert bodies. Thus we shall see that we can act on the social environment by acting on the phenomena over which we shall have control in man. And that is what makes the experimental novel: to have the mechanism of phenomena in men, to show the working of the intellectual and sensory manifestations as physiology will explain them to us under the influences of heredity and the surrounding circumstances, then to show man living in the social milieu which he himself has produced, which he modifies every day, and in the midst of which he in his turn undergoes continuous modification. Therefore we lean heavily on physiology; we take man in isolation from the hands of the physiologist in order to carry forward the solution of the problem and resolve scientifically the question of knowing how men behave themselves once they are in society.

These general ideas are enough to guide us today. Later on when science will have gone forward, when the experimental novel will have given decisive results, some critic will make a definitive statement of what I merely sketch out today.

Moreover, Claude Bernard confesses how difficult the application of the scientific method is to living beings. "The living being," he says, "above all among the higher animals, never falls into physiochemical indifference toward the external environment; he undergoes incessant movement, an organic evolution in appearance spon-

"The Experimental Novel"

taneous and constant, and although that evolution has need of external circumstances to manifest itself, it is nonetheless independent in its progress and in its modality." And he concludes as I have said: "In résumé, it is only in the physio-chemical conditions of the internal milieu that we will find the determinism of the external phenomena of life." But whatever the complexities which present themselves, even when special phenomena occur, the application of the experimental method remains rigorous. "If vital phenomena are more complex than and apparently different from those of inert bodies, they only present this difference by virtue of conditions, determined or determinable, which are proper to them. Thus if the vital sciences should differ from the others by their applications and their special laws, this makes no difference to the scientific method."

I must still say a word about the limits which Claude Bernard sets for science. As he sees it, we shall always be ignorant of the *why* of things; we can know only the *how*. He expresses this in these terms: "The nature of our minds leads us to seek out the essence or the *why* of things. In that respect we aim further than the goal which it is given us to attain; for experience soon teaches us that we may not go further than the *how*, that is, beyond the proximate cause or the conditions of existence of phenomena." Further on he gives this example: "If we cannot know *why* opium and its derivatives induce sleep, we shall be able to know the mechanism of that sleep and know *how* opium or its principles produce sleep; for sleep takes place only because the active substance comes in contact with certain organic elements which it modifies." And the practical conclusion from this: "Science has precisely the privilege of teaching us what we do not know, by substituting reason and experiment for feeling, and by showing us clearly the limits of our present knowledge. But by a marvelous compensation, in the measure that science thus reduces our pride she increases our power." All these considerations are strictly applicable to the experimental novel. So as not to stray into philosophical speculations, so as to replace idealist hypotheses by the slow conquest of the unknown, it must refrain from searching for the *why* of things. That is its exact role; from that it draws, as we shall see, its raison d'être and its morality.

175

I have then reached this point: the experimental novel is a result of the scientific evolution of the age; it continues and completes physiology, which itself leans on physics and chemistry; for the study of the abstract, the metaphysical man, it substitutes study of the natural man subject to physio-chemical laws and determined by the influences of environment; in a word it is the literature of our scientific age, just as classic and romantic literature corresponded to an age of scholasticism and theology. Now I turn to the major question of application and of morality.

III

The goal of the experimental method, in physiology and in medicine, is to study phenomena in order to control them. Claude Bernard on each page of the *Introduction* comes back to this idea. As he says: "All natural philosophy is summed up in that: to know the laws of phenomena. The whole experimental problem boils down to this: to predict and direct phenomena." Farther on he gives an example: "It will not suffice the experimental doctor, as it does the empirical doctor, to know that quinine cures fever; what is important above all to him is to know what the fever is and to understand the way in which quinine cures it. All that is of importance to the experimental doctor of medicine because as soon as he knows that, the cure of fever by quinine will no longer be an isolated empirical fact but a scientific fact. This fact will then relate to the conditions which tie it to other phenomena, and we will be thus led to knowledge of the laws of the organism and to the possibility of controlling its manifestations." The example becomes striking in the case of scabies. "Today when the cause of scabies is known and determined experimentally, everything has become scientific, and empiricism has disappeared. We always and without exception effect a cure when we place ourselves in the experimental conditions known to attain this goal."

This then is the goal, this the morality of physiology and of experimental medicine: to master life in order to direct it. Let us imagine that science has made progress, that the conquest of the unknown is complete: the scientific age that Claude Bernard dreamed of will be realized. Then medicine will be master of illness; it will provide sure cures; it will act on living beings for the happiness and vigor of the species. We shall enter into an age where all-powerful man will have mastered nature and will use its laws to make the greatest possible sum of justice and liberty reign on this earth. There is no goal more noble, more elevated, more grandiose. That is the role of intelligence: to penetrate the why of things in order to become superior to things and reduce them to the state of obedient mechanisms.

Fine! This dream of the physiologist and the experimental doctor of medicine is also that of the novelist who applies the experimental method to the natural and social study of man. Our goal is theirs; we wish, we too, to be masters of the phenomena of intellectual and personal elements in order to direct them. We are, in short, experimental moralists showing by experiment in what fashion a passion behaves in a social milieu. The day when we have an understanding of the mechanism of this passion we will be able to treat it and reduce it or at least render it as inoffensive as possible. That is where the utility and the high morality of our naturalist works lie; they experiment on man, take apart and put together the human machine piece by piece in order to make it function under the influence of environment. When time shall have passed, when we shall have the laws, we shall have only to act on individuals and milieux if we wish to reach better social conditions. This is how we carry on practical sociology, how our labors aid the political and economic sciences. I do not know, I repeat, any work which is more noble or of wider application. To be master of good and evil, to regulate life, to regulate society, in the long run to resolve all the problems of socialism, above all to bring a solid foundation to justice by experimentally resolving questions of criminality, is that not to do the most useful and moral human work?

Let us compare for a moment the task of the idealist novelists with our own; and here the word idealist indicates the writers who leave observation and experiment to base their works on the supernatural and the irrational, who in a word admit mysterious forces outside the determinism of phenomena. Claude Bernard will answer for me once more: "What differentiates experimental reasoning from scholastic reasoning is the fecundity of the one and the sterility of the other. It is precisely the scholastic who believes he has absolute certainty who gets nowhere; that is understandable, because by an absolute principle he places himself outside nature in which all is relative. On the contrary, it is the experimenter who always doubts and does not believe that he has absolute certainty about anything who succeeds in mastering the phenomena which surround him and in extending his power over nature." A little later I shall return to this question of the ideal, which is, in sum, only the question of indeterminism. Claude Bernard says rightly: "The intellectual conquest of man consists in making indeterminism diminish and recede in the measure that, with aid of the experimental method, he wins ground for determinism." The true work for us experimental novelists is there, to go from the known to the unknown in order to master nature; whereas the idealist novelists remain in the unknown by prejudice, by all sorts of religious and philosophical prejudices, on the stupefying pretext that the unknown is more noble and more beautiful than the known. If our task, at times cruel, if our terrible pictures had need of excuse, I should once more find in Claude Bernard this decisive argument: "We shall never arrive at really fruitful and enlightening generalizations on vital phenomena except by experimenting in the hospital, the operating room, and the laboratory, in the fetid and palpitant ground of life. . . . If it were necessary to give a comparison which expressed my feeling about the science of life, I would say that it is a superb drawing room shining with light at which we can arrive only by passing through a long and frightful kitchen."

I insist on the term experimental moralists which I have used as applied to naturalist novelists. One page of the *Introduction* struck me above all, the one on which the author speaks of the vital circle. I quote: "The muscular and nervous organs support the activity of the organs that prepare blood; but blood in its turn nourishes the organs which produce it. There you have an organic or social solidarity which maintains a sort of perpetual motion until derangement or cessation of the action of a necessary vital element breaks the equilibrium or brings a disturbance or stoppage in the working of the animal machine. The problem of the experimental doctor of medicine consists therefore in finding the simple determinism of an organic derangement, that is, getting hold of the initial phenomenon. We shall see how a dislocation or the apparently most complex derangement of the organism may be traced to a simple initial determinism which then produces the most complex determinisms." Here we need only change the words experimental doctor for experimental novelist and the whole passage will apply exactly to our naturalist literature. The social circle is identical to the vital circle: in society as in the human body there is a solidarity which links the different members, the different organs together so that if an organ becomes infected many others are tainted, and a very complex illness becomes evident. Thus in our novels when we experiment on a grave infection which poisons society we proceed like the experimental doctor; we seek to find the simple initial determinism in order to arrive at the complex determinism which has ensued. I take up once more the example of Baron Hulot in *La Cousine Bette*. See the final result, the denouement of the novel: an entire family destroyed, all sorts of secondary dramas occurring under the action of Hulot's amorous temperament. It is in that temperament that the initial determinism is to be found. One member, Hulot, becomes gangrenous and at once everything around him is corrupted, the social circle is impaired, the health of society is compromised. That is why Balzac has insisted so much on Baron Hulot, has analyzed him with such scrupulous care! The experiment bears upon him above all because it was a question of mastering the phenomenon of this passion in order to direct it; admit that it is possible to cure Hulot, or at least hold him in and make him inoffensive, at once the drama has no more raison d'être, equilibrium has been re-established, or, better, the health of the social body. Thus naturalist novelists are in fact experimental moralists.

So I now come to the great reproach that may be heaped upon naturalist novelists in calling them fatalists. How many times people have tried to prove to us that from the moment we no longer accepted free will, from the moment we saw man as no more than an animal machine acting under the influence of heredity and environment, we were falling into a gross fatalism, we were reducing humanity to the level of a herd driven along by the stick of destiny! It is necessary to be accurate: we are not fatalists, we are determinists, which is not the same thing. Claude Bernard explains the two terms very well: "We have given the name of determinism to the proximate or determining cause of phenomena. We do not ever act on the essence of the phenomena of nature, but only on their determinism, and by the fact alone that we act on it determinism differs from fatalism, on which we could not act. Fatalism presupposes the necessary manifestation of a phenomenon independent of its conditions, whereas determinism is the necessary condition of a phenomenon, the manifestation of which is not forced. Once the search for the determinism of phenomena is posed as the fundamental principle of the experimental method, there is no more materialism, or spiritualism, or brute matter, or living matter; there are only phenomena whose conditions must be determined, that is, the circumstances which play the role of proximate cause in relation to the phenomena." This is decisive. We merely apply this method in our novels, and we are therefore determinists who, experimentally, seek to determine the conditions of phenomena without ever in our investigations going outside the laws of nature. As Claude Bernard says so well, as soon as we can act and do act on the determinism of phenomena, in modifying environment, for example, we are not fatalists.

That then is the moral role of the experimental novelist well defined. I have often said that we did not have to draw a conclusion from our works, and that means that the works carry their conclusions within them. An experimenter does not have to make conclusions, for that is precisely what the experiment does for him. If necessary he will repeat the experiment a hundred times before the public; he will explain it, but he will have no occasion to become indignant or to give his personal approval: such is the truth, such is the mechanism of phenomena; it is for society always to produce or not to produce this phenomenon if the result is useful or dangerous to it. I have said elsewhere that you cannot imagine a scientist becoming angry against nitrogen because nitrogen is hostile to life; he gets rid of nitrogen, when it is harmful, that is all. Since our power is not the same as that of the scientists, since we are experimenters without being practitioners, we must be content to seek out the determinism of social phenomena, leaving to legislators, to those with power of application, the task sooner or later of directing these phenomena in such a way as to develop the good and reduce the bad from the standpoint of human utility.

I sum up our role as experimental moralists. We show the mechanism of the useful or the harmful; we disengage the determinism of human and social phenomena so that we may one day control and direct these phenomena. In a word, we work with the whole age at that great task which is the conquest of nature, the unleashing of man's power. And consider alongside ours the work of the idealist writers, who lean on the irrational and the supernatural, each of whose bursts of enthusiasm is followed by a deep descent into metaphysical chaos. It is we who have strength; it is we who have morality.

I V

What made me choose the *Introduction*, as I said, is that medicine is still considered by many to be an art. Claude Bernard proves that it ought to be a science, and in his book we are present at the birth of a science, a sight which is very instructive in itself, and which proves to us that the scientific domain is widening and taking over all manifestations of human intelligence. Since medicine, which was an art, is becoming a science, why should not literature itself become a science, thanks to the experimental method?

It is to be remarked that everything is of a piece, that if the domain of the experimental doctor of medicine is the human body in the phenomena of its organs, in a normal state or in a pathological state, our own domain is equally the human body in its cerebral and sensory phenomena, in a healthy or diseased state. If we no longer have the metaphysical man of the classic age, we must indeed bear in mind the new ideas about nature and life that our age is making for itself. We continue inevitably, I repeat, the task of the physiologist and the doctor, who carried on that of the physicist and chemist. Thus we enter into science. I pass over questions of feeling and form, which I will consider later.

See first of all what Claude Bernard says of medicine: "Certain doctors think that medicine can only be conjectural, and they conclude from this that the doctor is an artist who ought to supplement the indeterminism of particular cases with his genius, his personal touch. Those are anti-scientific ideas against which we must exert all our strength because they contribute to leaving medicine in the stunted state in which it has been for so long a time. All the sciences necessarily began by being conjectural; today in every science there are still conjectural areas. Medicine is still nearly everywhere conjectural, that I do not deny; I wish only to say that modern science ought to make an effort to get out of that provisional state which does not constitute a definitive scientific state, for medicine any more than for the other sciences. The scientific state will take longer to achieve and will be more difficult to reach in medicine, because of the complexity of the phenomena; but the goal of the doctor-scientist is in his science, as in all others, to bring indeterminism to determinism." The mechanism of the birth and development of a science is all there. We still treat the doctor as an artist because in medicine there is an enormous area left open to conjecture. Naturally the novelist will be more deserving of this title of artist, since he is even more mired in indeterminism. If Claude Bernard confesses that the complexity of phenomena will for a long time prevent medicine from achieving a scientific state, what then will be the case for the experimental novel, where the phenomena are still more complex? But that will not prevent the novel from entering on the road of science and obeying the general evolution of the age.

Moreover, Claude Bernard himself has indicated the evolution of the human mind: "The human mind," he says, "at various periods of its evolution has passed successively through feeling, reason, and experiment. First, feeling alone imposing itself on reason created the truths of faith, that is, theology. Reason or philosophy, then becoming mistress, brought forth scholasticism. Finally experiment, that is, study of natural phenomena, taught man that the truths of the external world were not formulated in the first instance either in feeling or in reason. They are only indispensable guides; but to obtain truths we must necessarily go down into the objective reality of things where they are concealed under their phenomenal form. Thus it is that in the natural progress of things there appeared the experimental method, which sums up everything and which leans in turn on the three branches of this immutable tripod: feeling, reason, and experiment. In the search for truth by means of this method, feeling always has the initiative, it engenders the *a priori* idea or intuition; reason or reasoning later develops the idea and deduces its logical consequences. But if feeling must be clarified by the light of reason, reason in its turn must be guided by experiment."

I have quoted this entire page because it is of the greatest importance. It shows clearly the role of the novelist's personality in the experimental novel, outside of style. From the moment that feeling is the point of departure for the experimental method, with reason intervening to lead to experiment and to be controlled by it, the genius of the experimenter dominates everything; and it is, moreover, because of this that the experimental method, inert in other hands, has become so powerful a tool in the hands of Claude Bernard. I have just used the word: the method is only a tool; it is the workman, it is the idea which he brings which makes the masterpiece. I have already quoted these lines: "It is a particular feeling, a *quid proprium* which constitutes the originality, the invention, or the genius of each one." That is then the part reserved to genius in the experimental novel. As Claude Bernard also says: "The idea is the seed; the method is the soil which enables it to develop, prosper, and give its best fruit according to its nature." Everything then is reduced to a question of method. If you remain in an *a priori* idea, and in feeling, without the support of reason and without the verification of experiment, you are a poet, you risk hypotheses that prove nothing, you carry on a struggle in indeterminism painfully and uselessly, often in a harmful way. Listen to these lines from the *Introduction*: "Man is naturally metaphysical and proud; he has believed that the ideal creations of his mind which correspond to his feelings also represent reality. From which it follows that the experimental method is not at all primitive and natural to man, that it is only after having wandered for a long time in theological and scholastic discussions that he has finished by recognizing the sterility of his efforts on that path. Man then perceives that he does not dictate laws to nature because he does not himself possess the knowledge and the criteria of external things; and he understands that to arrive at truth he must on the contrary study natural laws and subject his ideas, if not his reason, to experiment, that is, to the criterion of fact." What then happens to genius in the experimental novelist? It remains genius, the *a priori* idea, only if it is controlled by experiment. Naturally experiment cannot destroy genius; on the contrary it confirms it. In the case of a poet, for him to have genius is it necessary that his feelings, his *a priori* ideas, be false? Evidently not, for the genius of a man will be all the greater if experiment proves also the truth of his personal idea. Truly only an age of lyricism, of romantic malady, would have taught us to measure the genius of a man by the quantity of stupidities and follies that he has put in circulation. I end by saying that henceforth in our scientific age, experiment ought to provide proof of genius.

Our quarrel with the idealist writers is there. They start always from some irrational source or other, such as revelation, tradition, or conventional authority. As Claude Bernard says: "We must admit nothing occult; there are only phenomena and the conditions of phenomena." We the naturalist writers subject each datum to observation and to experiment; whereas the idealist writers allow mysterious influences which escape analysis and thus are based on the unknown outside the laws of nature. Scientifically the question of the ideal is reducible to a question of indeterminism and determinism. All that we do not know, all that is still beyond us, is the ideal, and the goal of our human effort is each day to diminish the ideal, to win truth from the unknown. We are all idealists, if by that is understood that we are all concerned with the ideal. Only what I call idealists is those who take refuge in the unknown out of pleasure in being there, whose taste is only for the most risky hypotheses, who disdain subjecting them to the control of experiment under the pretext that truth is in them and not in things. They, I repeat, carry on a vain and harmful labor, while the observer and the experimenter are the only ones who work toward the power and happiness of man by making him bit by bit the master of nature. There is no nobility, no dignity, no beauty, no morality in not knowing, in lying, in pretending that the further you go into error and confusion the greater you are. The only great and moral works are true works.

The only thing we should accept is what I call the spur of the ideal. Certainly our science is still very small alongside the immense mass of things which we do not know. That immense unknown which surrounds us should only inspire us with a desire

"The Experimental Novel"

to pierce it, to explain it, thanks to scientific methods. And this is not a matter merely for scientists; all manifestations of human intelligence are of one order, all our efforts converge on the need of making ourselves masters of truth. Claude Bernard expresses this very well when he writes: "The sciences each possess, if not a special method, at least special procedures, and in addition they make reciprocal use of each other's instruments. Mathematics serves as a tool to physics, chemistry, and biology within various limits; physics and chemistry serve as powerful instruments for physiology and medicine. In this mutual aid that the sciences lend each other it is very necessary to distinguish the scientist who makes each science go ahead from him who makes use of it. The physicist and the chemist are not mathematicians because they use computation; the physiologist is not a chemist or a physicist because he uses chemical reactive agents or physical instruments, any more than the chemist and the physicist are physiologists because they study the composition or the properties of certain liquids and animal or vegetable tissues." That is the reply that Claude Bernard makes for us naturalist novelists to critics who have made fun of our pretensions to science. We are not chemists, or physicists, or physiologists; we are simply novelists who lean on the sciences. Certainly we have no pretensions about making discoveries in physiology—which we do not practice; only, having to study man, we believe we cannot avoid taking account of new physiological truths. And I will add that novelists are certainly the workers who depend on the greatest number of sciences at one time, for they treat of everything and they have to know everything, since the novel has become a general inquiry into nature and man. That is why we were led to apply the experimental method to our work as soon as that method became the most powerful tool of investigation. We are the culmination of investigation; we throw ourselves into the conquest of the ideal by making use of all of human knowledge.

It must be clearly understood here that I am talking of the *how* of things, not the *why*. To an experimental scientist the ideal which he seeks to diminish, the indeterminism, is never anywhere except in the *how*. He leaves the other ideal, that of the *why*, to the philosophers, since he despairs of ever knowing it. I believe that the experimental novelists ought equally to avoid preoccupation with that unknown, if they wish to avoid losing themselves in the follies of the poets and philosophers. They have already a sufficiently broad task, to seek to know the mechanism of nature, without bothering themselves for a moment with the origin of this mechanism. If someday we come to know it, it will no doubt be thanks to the method, and it is better therefore to begin at the beginning, with the study of phenomena, instead of hoping for a sudden revelation that will give us the secret of the world. We are workers—we leave to the speculators the unknown of the *why* in which they have been struggling in vain for centuries—to confine ourselves to the unknown of the *how*, which each day diminishes before our investigation. The only ideal that should exist for us experimental novelists is that which we can conquer.

However, in the slow conquest of the unknown which surrounds us, we humbly confess the state of ignorance in which we are. We begin to go ahead, nothing more; and our only true strength is in the method. Claude Bernard, after confessing that experimental medicine still stammers, does not hesitate in practice to leave a large place to empirical medicine. "Basically," he says, "empiricism, that is, observation or fortuitous experiment, has been the origin of all the sciences. In the complicated sciences of humanity empiricism will necessarily govern practice much longer than in the simple sciences." And he is quite willing to agree that at the bedside of a sick person, when the determinism of the pathological phenomenon is not discovered, the best thing is still to act empirically; which, moreover, is in the normal order of our knowledge, since empiricism inevitably precedes the scientific state of knowledge. Certainly if doctors must confine themselves to empiricism in nearly every case, we ought all the more to hold ourselves there as well, we novelists whose science is more complex and less fixed. I say once again it is not a question of creating out of whole cloth the science of man, as individual and as social being; it is a matter of making it emerge fumblingly and gradually from the darkness in which we are concerning ourselves, happy when in the midst of so many errors we can fix on a truth. We experiment; that means that we ought for a long time still to employ the false in order to arrive at the true.

186

"The Experimental Novel"

That is the feeling of the strong. Claude Bernard vigorously fights against those who wish to see only an artist in the doctor. He is aware of the habitual objection of those who affect to regard experimental medicine "as a theoretical conception in which nothing at the moment justifies its practical reality because no fact indicates that we may reach in medicine the scientific precision of the experimental sciences." But he does not allow himself to be troubled; he shows that "experimental medicine is only the natural flowering of practical medical investigation, directed by a scientific mind." And this is his conclusion: "No doubt, we are far from the time when medicine will become scientific; but that does not prevent us from conceiving the possibility and of making every effort to reach it while seeking even today to introduce into medicine the method which will take us there."

All that, I am never too tired to repeat, applies exactly to the experimental novel. Set down the word "novel" in place of the word "medicine" and the passage continues to be true.

I shall address to the young literary generation which is growing up these great and strong words by Claude Bernard. I know none which are more virile. "Medicine is destined to emerge bit by bit from empiricism, and it will emerge in the same way as all the other sciences, by means of the experimental method. This deep conviction sustains and directs my scientific life. I am deaf to the voice of doctors who ask that someone explain to them measles and scarlatina experimentally, and think they have thereby found an argument against the use of the experimental method in medicine. These discouraging and negative objections emanate in general from systematic minds or lazy ones which prefer to rest on their systems or to sleep in darkness instead of working and making an effort to emerge from it. The experimental direction which medicine is taking today is definitive. In fact there is to be found no evidence of the ephemeral influence of any personal system whatever; it is the result of the scientific evolution of medicine itself. These are my convictions in this regard which I seek to make penetrate the minds of the young doctors who follow my courses at the Collège de France. . . . Above all it is important to inspire young men with the scientific spirit and initiate them into the ideas and tendencies of the modern sciences."

I have often written the same words and given the same advice, which I repeat here. "The experimental method alone can make the novel emerge from the lies and errors in which it drags along. My whole literary life has been directed by this conviction. I am deaf to the voices of critics who ask me to formulate the laws of heredity in characters and the laws of the influence of environment; those who make these negative and discouraging objections address them to me only through laziness of mind, through stubborn devotion to tradition, by more or less conscious attachment to philosophical and religious beliefs. . . . The experimental direction which the novel is taking is clear-cut today. This is in no sense the effect of any ephemeral influence or personal system; it is the result of scientific evolution, of the study of man itself. These are my convictions on this point which I seek to make penetrate the minds of the young writers who read what I write, for I believe that above all it is necessary to inspire them with the scientific spirit and to initiate them into the ideas and tendencies of the modern sciences."

v

Before concluding, there are certain secondary points that I want to treat.

What it is necessary to emphasize above all is the impersonal nature of the method. Claude Bernard was reproached for affecting the allures of an innovator, and he replied with his high intelligence: "I have certainly no pretention of being the first to propose the application of physiology to medicine. That has been recommended for a long time, and numerous efforts have been made in that direction. In my work and in my teaching at the Collège de France I therefore only pursue an idea which is already bringing results when applied to medicine." That is what I have answered myself when people have pretended that I pose as an innovator, as the leader of a school. I have said that I brought nothing, that I was simply trying, in my novels and my criticism, to apply the scientific method, which has been in use for a long time. But naturally people have pretended not to understand me, and they have kept on talking about my vanity and my ignorance.

What I have repeated twenty times, that naturalism is not a

personal fantasy, that it was the basic intellectual movement of the age, Claude Bernard said also, with more authority, and perhaps he will be believed. "The revolution that the experimental method has brought to the sciences," he writes, "consists in having substituted a scientific criterion for personal authority. The strength of the experimental method is that it depends only on itself, because it contains in itself its criterion, which is experiment. It recognizes no other authority than that of facts; it has freed itself of personal authority." Consequently no more theory. "The idea should always remain independent; it should not be enchained, either by scientific beliefs or by philosophical or religious beliefs. We must be bold and free in our ideas; we must follow our feelings and not be stopped too much by childish fear of contradictory theories. . . . We must modify a theory to adapt it to nature, and not nature in order to adapt it to a theory." From that comes an incomparable breadth. "The experimental method is the scientific method which produces liberty of thought. It shakes off not only the philosophical and theological yoke but it also admits no personal scientific authority. It is in no way pride or boastfulness; the experimenter, on the contrary, does an act of humility in denying personal authority, for he also doubts his own knowledge and subjects the authority of men to that of experiment and the laws of nature."

That is why I have said so often that naturalism was not a school, that, for example, it was not incarnated in the genius of one man or in the mania of a group, like romanticism, that it consisted simply in the application of the experimental method to the study of nature and of man. From that starting-point there is only a vast evolution, one forward march in which everybody is a worker according to his genius. All theories are admitted, and the theory which carries the day is the one which explains the most. There is no literary or scientific path which is wider or straighter. Everyone, large and small, moves there freely, working at the common task of investigation, each at his specialty, and recognizing no other authority than that of facts, proved by experiment. Therefore in naturalism it would be impossible for there to be either innovators or leaders of a school. There are simply workmen, some of whom are more powerful than others.

Claude Bernard thus expresses the scepticism which should be adopted toward theories. "You must have robust faith and not believe; I shall explain myself by saying that in science you must believe firmly in principles and doubt formulas; in fact, on the one hand, we are sure that determinism exists, yet we are never sure that we have got hold of it. You must be unshakable on matters of principle in experimental science (determinism), yet not believe absolutely in theories." I shall also quote the following passage in which he announces the end of systems. "Experimental medicine is not a new system of medicine, but, on the contrary, the negation of all systems. In fact, the coming of experimental medicine will result in making individual views disappear from science and replacing them by impersonal and general theories which will merely be, as in the other sciences, a regular and reasoned coordination of the facts furnished by experiment." It will be exactly the same for the experimental novel.

If Claude Bernard defends himself against the charge of being an innovator, or rather an inventor, who brings his own personal theory, he comes back with equal frequency to the danger of a scientist's becoming concerned about philosophical systems. "For the experimental physiologist," he says, "should have neither spiritualism nor materialism. These words belong to a natural philosophy which is antiquated; they will fall into disuse through the very progress of science. We shall never know either mind or matter, and if this were the occasion, I could easily show that on the one hand as on the other, you quickly reach scientific negations, whence it results that all considerations of this nature are idle and useless. For us there are only phenomena to study, the material conditions of their manifestations to know, and the laws of these manifestations to determine." I have said that in the experimental novel the best thing for us is to hold to this strictly scientific point of view if we wish our studies to have a solid basis. Don't go beyond the *how*, don't get involved in the *why*. However, it is certain that we cannot always escape from this need of our intelligence, from the restless curiosity which leads us to wish to know the essence of things. I say that then we must accept the philosophical system which is best adapted to the current state of the sciences, but simply from a speculative point of view. For example, transformism is presently the most rational system, the one most di-

"The Experimental Novel"

rectly based on our knowledge of nature. Behind a science, behind any manifestation whatever of human intelligence, there is always, whatever Claude Bernard may say, a more or less clear-cut philosophical system. We cannot attach ourselves to it devoutly and still keep to the facts, ready to modify the system if the facts demand it. But the system exists nonetheless, all the more vigorously in proportion as the science is less advanced and less solidly based. For us experimental novelists who are still at the stammering stage, hypothesis is fatal. Indeed I shall shortly concern myself with the role of hypothesis in literature.

Moreover, even if Claude Bernard in practice pushes away philosophical systems, he recognizes the necessity of philosophy. "From the scientific point of view, philosophy represents the eternal aspiration of human reason toward knowledge of the unknown. Therefore philosophers always busy themselves with controversial questions of very abstract nature, at the upper limits of science. Thus they communicate to scientific thought a movement which vivifies and ennobles it; they strengthen the mind in developing it by a general intellectual gymnastics, at the same time that they carry it ceaselessly back toward the solution of basic problems; thus they maintain a thirst for the unknown and the sacred fire of research which must never die out in a scientist." That is a fine passage, but philosophers have never been told more clearly that their hypotheses are pure poetry. Claude Bernard evidently considers philosophers, among whom he flatters himself he has many friends, like musicians of genius, whose music encourages scientists during their work and inspires the sacred fire of great discoveries. As for philosophers, left to themselves, they would sing forever and never find a truth.

Up to this point I have neglected the question of form in naturalist writing, but this is what gives literature its special quality. Not only does genius for the writer reside in feeling, in the *a priori* idea, but also in the form, in the style. However, the question of rhetoric and the question of method are distinct. And naturalism, I repeat, consists uniquely in the experimental method, in observation and experiment applied to literature. Rhetoric for the moment has no place here. Let us fix the method, which should be general; then let us accept in letters all the rhetorics which may be produced; let us regard them as the expression of the literary temperaments of the writers.

If anyone wants my forthright opinion, it is that today an exaggerated emphasis is given to form. I could say a great deal on this subject, but that would carry me beyond the limits of this study. At bottom it is my opinion that the method reaches to form itself, that language is nothing but logic, a natural and scientific construction. He who writes best will not be he who sets off on the wildest gallop among hypotheses, but he who walks straight among truths. Today we are rotten with lyricism, we wrongly believe that a great style is made of a sublime disorder, always ready to tumble over into madness; a great style is made of logic and clarity.

Thus Claude Bernard, who assigns to philosophers the role of musicians playing the *Marseillaise* of hypotheses while the scientists make their assault on the unknown, has much the same idea of artists and writers. I have noticed that many scientists, and the greatest among them, very jealous of the scientific certainty which they have as their possession, wish therefore to shut literature up in the realm of the ideal. They themselves seem to feel the need of a recreation of lies, after their exacting labors, and take pleasure among the most hazardous hypotheses, among fictions which they know to be perfectly false and ridiculous. These are a tune on the flute which they allow to be played to them. Thus Claude Bernard is right in saying: "Artistic and literary productions never age, in the sense that they are expressions of immutable sentiments like human nature." In fact, form is sufficient to immortalize a work; the spectacle of a powerful individuality interpreting nature in superb language will be interesting throughout the ages; however, we will also always read a great scientist from this same standpoint, because the spectacle of a great scientist who has been able to write well is every bit as interesting as that of a great poet. This scientist may have been mistaken in his hypotheses, but he will remain on a footing of equality with the poet, who certainly is equally mistaken. What must be said is that our domain is not made up solely of immutable feelings like human nature, for there is also the matter of bringing into play the true mechanism of these feelings. We have not exhausted our material when we have

"The Experimental Novel"

described anger, avarice, love; all of nature and all of man belongs to us, not only as phenomena but as causes of phenomena. I am aware that this is an immense field to which they have wished to bar our entry; but we have broken down the barriers and we now triumph on that field. That is why I do not accept the following statement by Claude Bernard: "In the arts and letters personality dominates everything. There it is a matter of spontaneous creation of the mind, which has nothing in common with the observation of natural phenomena, in the course of which our minds must create nothing." Here I find one of our most illustrious scientists under the necessity of denying literature entrance into the realm of science. I know of what kind of letters he is speaking, when he defines a literary work as "a spontaneous creation of the mind, which has nothing in common with the observation of natural phenomena." No doubt he is thinking of lyric poetry, for he would not have written those words if he had been thinking of the experimental novel, of the works of Balzac and Stendhal. I can only repeat what I have said: if we except form and style, the experimental novelist is nothing but a special kind of scientist, who uses the tools of other scientists, observation and analysis. Our domain is the same as that of the physiologists, except that it is more vast. Like them we operate on man, for everything leads us to believe, and Claude Bernard recognizes it himself, that cerebral phenomena may be determined like other phenomena. It is true that Claude Bernard can tell us that we are floating on pure hypothesis; but it would be ill-founded to conclude from that that we shall never arrive at the truth, for he fought all his life to make a science of medicine, which the preponderant majority of his colleagues consider an art.

Now let us define the experimental novelist clearly. Claude Bernard gives the following definition for the artist: "What is an artist? He is a man who realizes in a work of art an idea or a feeling personal to him." I absolutely repudiate that definition. Thus if I portrayed a man walking on his head, I would make a work of art, if that was my personal feeling. I would be a fool, that is all. It is therefore necessary to add that the personal feeling of the artist must be subject to the control of truth. In this way we arrive at hypothesis. The artist has the same starting point as the scientist; he stands before nature, has an *a priori* idea, and works

193

in line with that idea. There only does he diverge from the scientist if he carries his idea out to the end without verifying its exactness by observation and experiment. We might call experimental artists those who take account of experiment; but then we would have to say that they are no longer artists the moment that we consider art as the sum total of personal error which the artist puts in his study of nature. I have set it down that, in my opinion, the personality of the artist could only be in the *a priori* idea and in the form. It can not be in a stubborn pursuit of the false. I also believe that it may be in the hypothesis, but here we must understand each other.

It has often been said that writers should break a path for scientists. That is true, for we have just seen in the *Introduction* that hypothesis and empiricism precede and prepare the scientific state, which is established in the last analysis by the experimental method. Man began by risking certain explanations of phenomena; poets have expressed their feelings and scientists have come along later to control hypotheses and establish the truth. It is always the role of pioneers that Claude Bernard assigns to philosophers. It is a noble role, and writers still have the duty to fulfill it today. However, it must be understood that every time a truth is fixed by scientists, writers must immediately abandon their hypothesis and adopt this truth; otherwise they will remain by predilection in error, with no good to anybody. This is how science, in the measure that it goes forward, furnishes us writers with solid ground on which we must stand before soaring off into new hypotheses. In short, every phenomenon which is explained destroys the hypothesis which it replaces, and it is then necessary to carry the hypothesis further into the new unknown which then appears. I shall take a very simple example to make myself clearer: It is proved that the earth goes around the sun: what would we think of a poet who adopted the ancient belief that the sun went around the earth? Evidently the poet, if he wishes to risk a personal explanation of a fact, will have to choose one for which the cause is not yet known. That then is what an hypothesis ought to be for us experimental novelists; we must strictly accept determined facts, hazard about them no personal sentiments, which would be ridiculous, go all the way in accepting the ground won by science; then, and then

"The Experimental Novel"

only, can we exercise our intuition before the unknown and go ahead of science, reconciled to being mistaken on occasion, happy if we secure some documents for the solution of problems. Moreover, I am here using Claude Bernard's practical program, his acceptance of empiricism as a necessary fumbling. Thus in our experimental novel we may very well risk hypotheses on questions of heredity and the influence of environment, after having shown respect for what science today knows on these subjects. We shall prepare the way, we shall furnish data from observation, human documents, which will become very useful. A great lyric poet exclaimed not so long ago that ours was the century of prophets. Yes, if you wish; only it must be understood that prophets do not rest on the irrational or the supernatural. It is evident that if prophets are to put the most elementary notions in doubt, arrange nature with a strange philosophical and religious sauce, take the side of the metaphysical man, confuse and obscure everything, then prophets, in spite of their rhetorical genius, will never be anything but gigantic ignoramuses, ignorant of the fact that you get wet when you jump into the water. In our age of science, prophecy is a delicate mission, since people no longer believe in revealed truths and since in order to foresee the unknown it is necessary to begin by knowing the known.

This is the conclusion toward which I have been moving: if I were to define the experimental novel, I would not say, as Claude Bernard does, that a literary work is entirely in the area of personal feeling, for, as I see it, the personal feeling is only the first impulsion. Afterward nature is there and exerts her power, at least that part of nature whose secrets science has delivered up to us and about which we no longer have the right to lie. The experimental novelist is therefore he who accepts proved facts, who shows in man and society the mechanism of the phenomena which science has mastered, and who lets his personal sentiments enter in only concerning those phenomena whose determinism is not yet fixed, while he tries to control this personal sentiment, this *a priori* idea, as well as he can by observation and experiment.

I would not be able to conceive of our naturalist literature in any other terms. I have spoken only of the experimental novel, but I am firmly convinced that the method, after it has triumphed in history and criticism, will triumph everywhere, in the drama and even in poetry. It is an inevitable development. Whatever people may say, literature does not exist only in the writer; it is also in the nature which it depicts and in the man whom it studies. Now if scientists change their ideas about nature, if they find the true mechanism of life, they force us to follow them, to go ahead of them even to play our role in the new hypotheses. The metaphysical man is dead; our whole domain is transformed with the coming of the physiological man. No doubt the wrath of Achilles or the love of Dido will continue to be eternally beautiful portrayals; but now we need to analyze wrath and love and see exactly how these passions function in the human being. The point of view is new; it has become experimental instead of philosophical. In short, everything is summed up in this great fact: the experimental method, in letters as well as in science, is on its way to understanding natural phenomena, both individual and social, for which up to now metaphysics has given us only irrational and supernatural explanations.

"Naturalism in the Theatre"*

By Emile Zola

I

To BEGIN with, is there any need for me to explain what I mean by "naturalism"? People have severely reproached me for the use of this word; they still pretend not to understand it. It is easy to make jokes about matters of this kind. However, I am glad to answer them, for you cannot bring too much light to criticism.

It appears that my great crime is to have invented and launched a new word to designate a literary school which is as old as the world. To begin with, I do not believe that I invented this word, which was already in use in several foreign literatures; at most I applied it to the present-day development of our own national literature. Then, it is asserted, naturalism dates back to the first written works. Well, who ever said the contrary? That merely proves that it comes from the very vitals of humanity. All criticism from Aristotle to Boileau, it is added, has set forth the principle that a work ought to be based on truth. Now that delights me and provides me with new arguments. The naturalist school, by the very admission of those who make sport of it and attack it, rests therefore on indestructible foundations. It is not the caprice of one man or the collective folly of a group; it has sprung from the eternal core of things, from the necessity felt by every writer to take nature as his basis. Very well, we are agreed on that. Let us go on from there.

Well, then, they say to me, why all this noise; why do you pose as an innovator, as a source of revelation? Here is where the misunderstanding begins. I am simply an observer who sets down facts. It is only the empiricists who provide invented formulas. Scientists are content to go forward step by step with the support of the experimental method. I certainly do not have a new religion in my pocket. I reveal nothing, for I do not believe in revelation;

* Zola, Emile, "Le Naturalisme au Théâtre," *Le Roman expérimental*, Paris, 1880.

197

I invent nothing, because I believe it is more valuable to obey the impulsion of humanity, the continuous evolution which carries us along. My whole role as critic consists therefore in studying where we have come from and where we are. When I risk predicting where we are going, that is pure speculation on my part, the drawing of logical conclusions. On the basis of what has been and what is I believe that I am able to say what will be. That is all I am trying to do. It is ridiculous to ascribe some other role to me, to set me on a rock to speak as pontiff and prophet, posing as the leader of a school and addressing God in the familiar second person.

But this new word, this terrible word, naturalism? No doubt people would like me to have used Aristotle's language. He spoke of truth in art, and that ought to be enough for me. If only I would accept the eternal nature of things and not try to create the world a second time, I would not need a new term. Now really are people making fun of me? Does not the eternal nature of things take on various forms in accordance with changing epochs and civilizations? Has not each people for the last six thousand years interpreted and given names in its own way to things which have come from the common source? I will admit for the moment that Homer was a naturalist poet; but our novelists are not naturalists in his manner. Between the two literary epochs there is an abyss. To deny this is to speak in absolute terms, to erase history at one stroke, to confuse everything and to ignore the constant evolution of the human spirit. Certainly a work will never be more than a corner of nature seen through a temperament. However, if we leave it at that, we shall not get far. As soon as we consider literary history, we will necessarily encounter foreign elements, manners, events, intellectual movements which modify, arrest, or hurry literatures forward. My personal opinion is that naturalism dates from the first line written by man. Then and there the question of truth was raised. If you conceive of humanity as an army on the march through the ages, pushing toward the conquest of truth in the midst of miseries and infirmities, you ought to put the scientists and the writers in the foremost rank. It is from this point of view that universal history ought to be written, not from the point of view of an absolute ideal, of a common aesthetic measuring stick, which is perfectly ridiculous. Now it is evident that I cannot go back that far, cannot undertake so colossal a task and examine the marches and countermarches of writers of all nations, describing through what darkness and what dawns they have traveled. I have had to limit myself; I have confined myself to the last century, that marvelous flowering of intelligence, that prodigious movement which has brought forth our contemporary society. And it is precisely there that I have seen the triumphant affirmation of naturalism and found the word. The chain goes confusedly back through the ages; it is enough to take hold of it in the eighteenth century and follow it up to our day. Let us forget Aristotle; let us forget Boileau. A special word was necessary to designate an evolution which quite evidently began at the beginning of the world but which at last reached its decisive development in the midst of the circumstances most favorable to it.

Therefore let us pause at the eighteenth century. It was a superb flowering. One fact towers over everything: the creation of a method. Up to that time scientists proceeded like poets, by means of individual fantasy, by strokes of genius. Certain of them discovered truths, in a haphazard manner; but these were scattered truths, linked together in no way and mixed with the grossest kind of errors. They wanted to create science out of whole cloth, as you rhyme a poem; they superimposed it on nature by means of empirical formulas, by metaphysical considerations which today would dumbfound us. And then a very tiny circumstance broke up this sterile field in which nothing was growing. One day a scientist bethought himself of experimenting before he set forth a conclusion. He gave up the so-called acquired truths; he went back to first causes, to the study of bodies, to observation of data. Like the child who goes to school, he consented to humble himself, to spell out nature before he was able to read it fluently. That was a revolution! Science disengaged itself from empiricism; the method consisted in going from the known to the unknown. You began with an observed fact; you then went forward from observation to observation, avoiding any conclusion until you possessed the necessary elements. In short, instead of beginning with a synthesis, you began with analysis; you no longer hoped to wrest truth from nature by a sort of divination or revelation; you studied long and patiently, going from the simple to the complex, until you knew the whole mechanism. The tool had been found; the method was to consolidate and expand all the sciences.

Indeed that soon became evident. Thanks to minute and exact observation, the natural sciences were firmly established. To cite only anatomy, it opened up a whole new world; each day it revealed a bit of the secret of life. Other sciences were created, such as chemistry and physics. Today they are still very young, but they are growing and are leading us to truth in a movement that is sometimes disturbing because of its rapidity. I cannot examine every science in this way. It is enough to mention cosmography and geology, which have struck such a terrible blow at the fables of religion. The flowering has been general and it is still going on.

But everything in a civilization is tied together. When one part of the human spirit receives an impetus, the shock spreads and quickly produces a complete evolution. The sciences, which up to that time had borrowed a share of imagination from letters, were the first to free themselves from fantasy and return to nature; then letters in their turn followed the sciences and also adopted the experimental method. The great philosophic movement of the eighteenth century was a vast inquiry; it was often groping, but its constant goal was to subject all human problems to scrutiny and to resolve them. In history, in criticism, the study of data and milieux replaced the old scholastic rules. In purely literary works nature intervened and was soon regnant with Rousseau and his school. Trees, waters, mountains, and the great forests became beings and again took their place in the mechanism of the world; man was no longer an intellectual abstraction, nature determined and completed him. Diderot above all is the great figure of the century; he perceived all the truths; he went in advance of his age, making continual war on the worm-eaten edifice of conventions and rules. What a magnificent outburst in that age, what a colossal labor, out of which our society has sprung—a new era from which will be dated the age into which humanity now enters with nature for its base and the method as its tool.

Very well, then, it is this evolution that I have called naturalism, and I consider that no more accurate word could be used. Naturalism is the return to nature; it is that operation which the scientists made the day they decided to start with the study of bodies and phenomena, to base their work on experiment, and to proceed by means of analysis. Naturalism, in letters, is equally a return to nature and to man; it is direct observation, exact anatomy, the acceptance and depiction of what is. The writer and the scientist have had the same task. Both have had to replace abstractions with realities, empirical formulas with rigorous analysis. Thus no more abstract characters in books, no more lying inventions, no more absolutes, but real characters with true histories, and the relativity of everyday life. It was a matter of starting all over again, of coming to know man at the very sources of his being, before drawing conclusions in the manner of the idealists, who invented types; and writers henceforth had only to take hold of the construction at the base, providing as many human documents as possible and presenting them in logical order. That is naturalism, which originated in the first thinking brain, if you will, but the broadest development of which—the definitive one no doubt—took place in the last century.

So considerable a development of the human spirit could not occur without a social upheaval. The French Revolution was this overturn, this tempest which was to sweep away the old order so as to leave the ground clear for the new. We are starting this new world; we are the direct heirs of naturalism in all things, in politics as in philosophy, in science as in literature and art. I broaden the scope of this word naturalism because it is really the whole age, the movement of the contemporary mind, the force which carries us along and which works for the future. The history of these last one hundred and fifty years proves it, and one very typical phenomenon is the momentary divagation of minds in the wake of Rousseau and Chateaubriand, that singular outburst of romanticism at the very threshold of an age of science. I pause over this for a moment, for there are valuable observations to be made about it.

It is rare for a revolution to be carried out under conditions of calm and good sense. Minds go off the track; imaginations become frightened, gloomy, and peopled with phantoms. After the rude shocks at the end of the last century and under the emotional and disturbed influence of Rousseau, you see poets taking melancholy and fatal poses. They do not know where they are being led; they throw themselves into bitterness, contemplation, and extraordinary reveries. Yet they too have felt the breath of the Revolution. Thus they too are rebels. They bring the rebellion of color, of passion, of fantasy; they speak of a violent breach of the rules and of renewing the language by a flood of lyric poetry, which is striking and superb. Moreover, truth has touched them; they demand local color; they seek to revive dead ages. All of romanticism is there. It is a violent reaction against classical literature; it is the first rebellious application to literature that writers make of their regained liberty. They break windows, they become intoxicated with their shouts, they rush into excess out of a need for protest. The movement is so irresistible that it carries everything along with it; not only does literature blaze up, but painting, sculpture, and even music become romantic. Romanticism triumphs and imposes its rule. Confronted with what is so general and so powerful a manifestation, for a moment you can believe that this literary and artistic formula has been established for a long time. The classic formula endured for two centuries at least; why should not the romantic formula which has replaced it have equally long life? And you are surprised when you perceive after a quarter of a century that romanticism is in its last agony, slowly dying its fine death. Then truth makes its appearance. The romantic movement was definitely only a minor skirmish. Some poets and novelists of immense talent, a whole generation possessed of magnificent élan, have managed to go off on a false scent. But the age does not belong to those overexcited dreamers, to those soldiers of the dawn, who are blinded by the rising sun. They stood for nothing clear-cut; they were only the avant-garde, whose mission was to clear the way, to affirm the conquest by their excesses. The age belonged to the naturalists, to the direct descendants of Diderot, whose solid battalions came later and were to found a true State. The chain was renewed; naturalism triumphed with Balzac. After the violent catastrophes of its infancy the century finally took the broad highway which it was to follow. This crisis of romanticism was bound to occur, for it corresponded to the social catastrophe of the French Revolution, just as I would compare triumphant naturalism to the Republic which is now in process of being established by science and reason.

That then is where we are today. Romanticism, which corresponded to nothing lasting, which was simply an anxious nostalgia for the old order and a bugle call to battle, collapsed before naturalism, which returned with renewed strength, the all-powerful master, giving direction to the age of which it is the very life breath. Is it necessary to indicate its manifestations in every situation? It rises from the earth on which we walk; it grows every hour; it penetrates and animates everything. It is the motive power of our productions, the pivot on which our society turns. You find it in the sciences, which quietly continued their forward march during the folly of romanticism; you find it in all manifestations of intelligence as it frees itself more and more from romantic influences, which for a time seemed to have submerged it. It is renovating the arts, sculpture and especially painting; it is broadening criticism and history; it asserts itself in the novel. Indeed it is through the novel, through Balzac and Stendhal, that it goes back beyond romanticism and visibly links the chain with the eighteenth century. The novel is its domain, its field of battle and of victory. It seems to have taken over the novel in order to demonstrate the power of its method, the impact of the true, the inexhaustible novelty of human documents. Finally it is now taking over the stage and is beginning to transform the theatre, which is inevitably the last stronghold of convention. When it has triumphed there its evolution will be complete; the classic formula will be definitely and solidly replaced by the naturalist formula, which is the formula of the new social state.

I have felt it necessary to emphasize and explain the meaning of this word naturalism at such length inasmuch as people pretend not to understand it. But now I shall narrow the discussion: I wish simply to study the naturalistic movement in the theatre. However, I must first speak of the contemporary novel, since I need a point of comparison. We are going to see where the novel is today and where the theatre is. The conclusion will then be easy.

II

In my frequent conversations with foreign writers I have found that they all share the same astonishment. They are better situated than we to judge the main currents of our literature, for they see us from a distance and are removed from our daily battles. They are astonished that we have two absolutely separate literatures, the novel and the drama. Nothing like this exists among neighboring peoples. In France it seems that for more than half a century literature has been cut in two; the novel has gone to one side, while the theatre has remained on the other, and between them a gulf of ever-increasing depth has been dug. Let us look at this situation for a moment, as it is both singular and informative. Our running criticism—I speak of the newspaper writers whose difficult task it is to criticize new plays from day to day—operates on the principle that a novel and a dramatic work have nothing in common, either in form or method. It even goes so far as to declare that there are two styles, the style of the drama and the style of the novel, and that a subject which may be handled in a novel cannot be put on the stage. Which amounts to saying, as foreigners do, that we have two literatures. This is quite true: the critics are merely stating a fact. But there is the question as to whether they do not help this unfortunate situation along by transforming this fact into a law and by saying that this is so because it cannot be otherwise. We are continually inclined to subject everything to rule, to codify everything. The worst of it is that when we have strangled ourselves with rules and conventions, we then have to make superhuman efforts to break through those bonds.

Thus we have two literatures, which are dissimilar in all respects. When a novelist wants to try his hand at a play, he arouses distrust; people shrug their shoulders. Did not Balzac himself fail? It is true that M. Octave Feuillet succeeded. I am going to allow myself to track this matter down so as to try to resolve it logically. Let us first consider the contemporary novel.

Victor Hugo wrote poetry, even when he descended to prose. Alexander Dumas the elder was only a prodigious teller of tales. George Sand recounted to us her imaginary reveries in facile, felicitous language. I shall not go back to those writers who belong to the superb romantic outburst and have left no direct descendants. I mean to say that their influence is no longer felt today except by reaction, in a way which I shall determine later on. The sources of our contemporary novel are to be found in Balzac and Stendhal. That is where they are to be sought out and examined. Both writers escaped the madness of romanticism, Balzac in spite of him-

"Naturalism in the Theatre"

self and Stendhal by the prejudice of a superior man. While people were acclaiming the triumph of the lyricists, while Victor Hugo was noisily being crowned king of literature, those two were dying in misery, almost in obscurity, disdained and neglected by the public. But in their works they left the naturalist formula of the age, and it was to come about that a whole posterity would rise from their tombs whereas the romantic school would die of anemia and would cease to be embodied in anyone except an illustrious old man, to whom out of respect no one told the truth.

This is only a quick résumé. It is not necessary to dilate on the new formula brought us by Balzac and Stendhal. Through the novel they made the sort of inquiry that scientists were making through science. They no longer imagined; they no longer fabulized. Their task consisted of taking man and dissecting and analyzing him in flesh and brain. Stendhal remained above all a psychologist. Balzac more particularly studied temperaments, reconstituted milieux, amassed human documents, taking for himself the title of doctor of social sciences. Compare *Le Père Goriot* or *La Cousine Bette* with novels that preceded them, with those of the seventeenth or eighteenth century, and you will perceive what a development the naturalistic novel has made. The word novel alone has been kept, and that is a great mistake, for it has lost all meaning.

Now I must discriminate between the descendants of Balzac and Stendhal. First, there is M. Gustave Flaubert, and it was he who was to bring the present-day formula to completeness. It is here that we shall find the recoil of romantic influence of which I spoke above. One of the sources of Balzac's bitterness was that he did not have the dazzling form of Victor Hugo. He was accused of writing badly, which made him very unhappy. On occasion he would attempt to compete with showy lyricism, for example when he wrote *La Femme de trente ans* and *Le Lys dans la vallée*; but this effort achieved very little, for this prodigious author was never a greater writer than when he maintained his strong, abundant style. With M. Gustave Flaubert the naturalistic formula passed into the hands of a perfect artist. It solidified and took on the hardness and brilliance of marble. M. Gustave Flaubert grew up in full romanticism. All of his affections were for the movement of 1830. When he published *Madame Bovary* it was as a challenge to the realism of that day, which prided itself on writing badly. He set out to prove that one could tell of the provincial lower-middle class with the amplitude and power with which Homer told of Greek heroes. Happily, however, the work reached out in another direction. Whether M. Gustave Flaubert wished it or not, he brought to naturalism the final strength that it needed, the perfect and imperishable form which helps a work to live. Henceforth the formula was fixed. There was nothing for newcomers to do but follow the broad way of truth through art. Novelists would pursue Balzac's inquiry, would advance always further in their analysis of man under the influence of environment; only they would at the same time be artists. They would have originality and knowledge of form; they would give truth a revivifying power through the intense vitality of their style.

At the same time as M. Gustave Flaubert, Messers Edmond and Jules de Goncourt were striving for this striking quality of form. They did not derive from romanticism. There was nothing Latin, nothing classical about them; they invented their language; they noted down their sensations as artists sick from art with incredible intensity. In *Germinie Lacerteux* they were the first to study the common people of Paris, depicting the suburbs and the desolate landscape of the outlying areas, daring to say everything in a refined language which gave true life to people and things. They had a very great influence on the current group of naturalist novelists. If we found our solid base, our exact method, in M. Gustave Flaubert, it must be added that we have all been stimulated by the Messers de Goncourt's new language, which is as penetrating as a symphony, giving to objects the nervous tension of our age and going further than the written phrase by adding color, sound, and perfume to dictionary words. I am not passing judgment; I am merely making a statement. My sole purpose is here to set down the sources of the contemporary novel and to explain what it is and why it is that way.

These then are the clearly discernible sources. At the top of the list, Balzac and Stendhal, a physiologist and a psychologist, freed from the rhetoric of romanticism, which was primarily an insurrection of rhetoricians. Then between us and these two ancestors, M. Gustave Flaubert on the one hand and Messers Edmond and

"Naturalism in the Theatre"

Jules de Goncourt on the other, bringing the science of style and fixing the formula in a new rhetoric. The naturalist novel is there. I shall not speak of its present practitioners. It will be enough for me to indicate the basic characteristics of this type of novel.

I have said that the naturalist novel is simply an inquiry into nature, beings, and things. It therefore no longer directs its ingenuity toward a fable which is well invented and developed according to certain rules. The imagination no longer has a function; intrigue is of little importance to the novelist, who is not concerned about exposition, or complication, or denouement. I mean that he does not intervene to diminish or add to reality, nor does he construct a fabric out of whole cloth according to the needs of a preconceived idea. We begin with the idea that nature is all we need; it is necessary to accept her as she is, without modifying her or diminishing her in any respect; she is sufficiently beautiful and great to provide a beginning, a middle, and an end. Instead of imagining an adventure, complicating it, and arranging a series of theatrical effects to lead to a final conclusion, we simply take from life the story of a being or group of beings whose acts we faithfully set down. The work becomes an official record, nothing more; its only merit is that of exact observation, of the more or less profound penetration of analysis, of the logical concatenation of facts. On occasion it is not even a whole life, with a beginning and an end, that is being told; it is only a shred of existence, a few years from the life of a man or a woman, a single page of human history, which has attracted the novelist in the same way that the special study of a body may interest a chemist. The novel, then, no longer has limiting boundaries; it has invaded and dispossessed the other genres. Like science it is master of the world. It attempts all subjects, writes history, treats of physiology and psychology, soars to the highest poetry, studies the most varied questions: politics, the social economy, religion, manners. All of nature is its domain. It moves there freely, adopting the form which pleases it, taking the tone it judges best, no longer subject to any bounds. We are far removed from the novel as our forefathers understood it, a work of pure imagination whose goal was limited to charming and distracting readers. In the old rhetorics the novel was placed at the very foot of the scale between the fable and light verse.

Serious men disdained it and left it to the women as a frivolous and compromising recreation. This opinion still persists in the provinces and in certain academic circles. The truth is that masterpieces of the contemporary novel have much more to say about man and nature than serious works of philosophy, history, and criticism. The modern instrument lies there.

I pass on to another characteristic of the naturalist novel. It is impersonal: I mean that the novelist is only a stenographer who forbids himself to judge or to draw conclusions. He confines himself to the strict role of a scientist who exposes facts, goes clear to the end of an analysis without risking synthesis. The facts are thus and so, the experiment tried under such and such conditions gives such and such results; and he leaves it at that, for if he were to go beyond phenomena he would enter into the area of hypothesis, and that would be probabilities and not science. Very well! the novelist likewise must confine himself to observed data and to the scrupulous study of nature if he is to avoid straying into lying conclusions. Thus he disappears; he keeps his emotion to himself; he simply sets forth what he has seen. That is reality: shudder or laugh at it, draw from it some lesson or other if you will; the sole task of the author has been to put true documents before your eyes. Moreover, there is an artistic justification for this moral impersonality of a work. Impassioned or tender intervention on the part of the novelist diminishes a novel by destroying sharpness of outline, by introducing elements foreign to the facts, which undermines their scientific value. You cannot imagine a chemist getting angry at nitrogen because that element is hostile to life, or tenderly sympathizing with oxygen for the opposite reason. Likewise a novelist who feels a need to become indignant against vice and to applaud virtue spoils the documents which he sets forth, for his intervention is as embarrassing as it is useless. The work loses its power; it is no longer a marble page hewn from a block of reality; it is material that has been worked over, remolded by the emotion of the author, an emotion which is subject to all prejudice and error. A true work will be eternal, whereas a work of emotion only tickles the fancy of an age.

Thus, like the scientist, the naturalist novelist never intervenes. This moral impersonality of a work is of capital importance, for it

"Naturalism in the Theatre"

raises the question of morality in the novel. We are violently reproached with being immoral because we place scoundrels and
honest men on scene without judging either of them. The whole
quarrel centers about this. Scoundrels are permitted on condition
that they be punished at the end or at least receive the crushing
weight of our anger and disgust. As for honest men, they deserve
here and there to receive a few lines of praise and encouragement.
Our impassivity, our tranquil attitude as analysts in the face of
evil and good is completely culpable. And so people end by saying
that we lie when we become too true. What! an endless series of
rogues; not a single sympathetic character! It is here that the
theory of the sympathetic character appears. There must be some
sympathetic characters in order to help nature along. No longer do
people ask merely that we prefer virtue; they demand that we
embellish virtue and make it lovable. Thus in presenting a character we must select, picking out his good points and passing over
the bad ones in silence; it would be even more commendable if
we invented characters out of whole cloth and poured them into
the conventional molds of good form and honor. For that purpose
there are ready-made types which can be introduced into an action
without any trouble. These are sympathetic characters, ideal conceptions of men and women, whose purpose is to compensate for
the unfortunate impression made by true characters taken from
nature. As people see it, our error in all this is to accept nothing
but nature and to be unwilling to correct what is by what should
be. Absolute honesty is no more to be found than is absolute health.
There is a residuum of the human beast in everybody, as there is
an element of illness. Thus those very pure young girls and honorable young men we find in certain novels simply do not stand up;
if they have their feet on earth it is necessary to tell everything
about them. We say everything: we no longer select, we do not
idealize; and that is why people accuse us of taking pleasure in
dirt. In short, the question of morality in the novel is reducible to
these two opinions: the idealists assert that it is necessary to lie
in order to be moral; the naturalists affirm that it is not possible
to be moral outside the truth. As a matter of fact, nothing is so
dangerous as the romantic vein; such works, depicting the world
in false colors, throw imaginations out of gear and lead people

astray—and I pass over the hypocrisy of outward decorum, the abominations which are concealed under a covering of flowers. With us these dangers disappear. We teach the bitter science of life; we give the lofty lesson of the real. Here is what exists: try to come to terms with it. We are only scientists, analysts, anatomists—I emphasize this once more—and our works have the certainty, the solidity, and the practical application of works of science. I know of no school which is more moral or more austere.

Such is the naturalist novel today. It has triumphed; all novelists are coming over to it, even those who attempted to kill it in embryo. It is an old, old story: at first people jeer and get angry, then they end in imitation. Success is what it takes to determine a new tendency. Moreover, now that the shaking up has been accomplished, you will see the movement grow broader and broader. A new literary age is about to begin.

III

I turn now to our contemporary theatre. We have just examined the state of the novel; now we must look at the situation of dramatic literature. But first of all I shall rapidly recall the main lines of development of the French theatre.

At the beginning we find formless plays, dialogues between two or three characters at most, which were performed in the public square. Then theatres were built, and comedy and tragedy were born under the influence of the classical Renaissance. Great geniuses consecrated this formula: Corneille, Molière, Racine. They were the product of the age in which they lived. The tragedy and comedy of that day, with inflexible rules, court etiquette, generous and noble bearing, philosophical dissertations, and oratorical eloquence were the exact image of the contemporary society. And this identity, this close relationship of the dramatic formula and the social milieu was so true that for two centuries the formula remained pretty much the same. It did not lose its rigidity; it did not give way until during the eighteenth century with Voltaire and Beaumarchais. The old society was then deeply disturbed; the winds which shook it touched the theatre. There was a greater desire for action, a muffled revolt against the rules, a vague return to nature. Even at that period Diderot and Mercier established the basis of the naturalist theatre in straightforward fashion. Unfortunately neither of them produced a master work which would establish a new formula. Moreover, the classic formula had such solidity on the ground of the old monarchy that it was not completely carried away by the tempest of the Revolution. It persisted for a time, though weakened, bastardized, and slipping into insipidity and imbecility. Then occurred the romantic insurrection which had been developing for many years, and romantic drama finally cut short the death agonies of tragedy. Victor Hugo put in the final blow and reaped the benefit of a victory to which many others had contributed. It is to be remarked that through the logical necessity of the struggle romantic drama became the opposite of tragedy; it opposed passion to duty, action to recitative, color to psychological analysis, and the middle ages to classical antiquity. This was the striking antithesis which assured it of its triumph. It was necessary for tragedy to disappear; its hour had come, for it was no longer the product of the social environment, and the drama brought the necessary liberty by a violent clearing of the ground. But today it would appear that its role was no more than that. It was only a superb affirmation of the nothingness of the rules and of the need for life. In spite of all the commotion it stirred up it remained the rebellious child of tragedy. Like the latter it lied, it costumed facts and characters with an exaggeration at which we smile today; and like the latter it had its rules, its conventional plots and effects, which were all the more irritating because of their greater falseness. To sum up, just one more rhetoric had made its appearance in the theatre. Thus romantic drama was not destined to have as long a reign as tragedy had had. After completing its revolutionary task, it expired, suddenly exhausted, leaving the ground clear for reconstruction. The history of the theatre is thus the same as that of the novel. After the necessary crisis of romanticism we see the tradition of naturalism reappear, the ideas of Diderot and Mercier asserted more and more. The new social situation, born of the Revolution, gradually fixes the new dramatic formula after much groping, many backward and forward steps. This work was fated. It took place and is still taking place through force of circumstances, and it will stop only when the evolution is complete. The naturalistic formula will be for our age what the classic formula has been to past ages.

Thus we come down to our own times. Here I find considerable activity and an extraordinary expenditure of talent. It is an immense workshop in which everyone is working feverishly. Things are still confused; there is much lost effort; few strokes are hard and straight, but the spectacle is nonetheless marvelous. And what must be set down is that all the workmen are striving for the definitive triumph of naturalism, even those who appear to fight it. They participate willy-nilly in the main movement of the age; perforce they must go where it is going. Since none of them so far is of sufficient stature by an effort of genius to establish the new formula in the theatre all by himself, you might say that they have shared the task, each in turn giving his support at a predetermined point. We shall look at the best known of them at work.

I have been violently accused of insulting our leading playwrights. That is a legend which is developing. It is in vain that I protest that I have spoken of the great and small in broad terms in relation to a general body of ideas; current criticism continues to insist that my personal setbacks have made me fierce toward my more successful colleagues. I pass over that kind of remark, since it does not deserve a reply. But I am going to attempt to judge of our luminaries, examining the place they hold and the role they play in our dramatic literature. That will explain my attitude once more.

First let us look at M. Victorien Sardou. He is the current representative of the comedy of intrigue. The heir of Scribe, he has renewed the old tricks and has pushed scenic art to the point of prestidigitation. Such a theatre is a continuing and increasingly emphatic reaction against the former classic theatre. As soon as action takes precedence over talk, as soon as events are more important than characters, you have slid over to complicated intrigue, to marionettes pulled by a string, to continual peripeties, and to unexpected denouements. Scribe was a milestone in the history of our dramatic literature: he exaggerated the new principle of action, making it the only thing of importance and deploying his extraordinary abilities as a maker to invent a whole code of laws and formulas. That was inevitable, for reactions always run to extremes. What has long been called the genre theatre is, then, in origin nothing but an exaggeration of the principle of action at the expense of depiction of character and analysis of feeling. There has been a divagation from truth, though the effort was to get back to it. The breaking of the rules has been followed by the invention of other rules, which are even more false and ridiculous. The well-made play—I mean one constructed on a certain balanced and symmetrical pattern—has become a strange, amusing toy which has diverted all of Europe along with us. It is with this that the popularity of our repertory begins abroad, where it is received with the same infatuated enthusiasm as are our luxury goods. To-day the well-made play has undergone a slight change. M. Victorien Sardou is less careful about the cabinet work, but if he has enlarged the framework and increased the sleight-of-hand, he nonetheless remains the representative of action in the theatre, of frenetic action which dominates and crushes everything else. His great quality is movement; he does not have life but movement, reckless movement which sweeps his characters along and even on occasion gives the illusion of life. They seem to be alive, but they are really only well set up, moving like perfect mechanical tops. Ingenuity and deftness, a flair for actuality, great scenic skill, a special ability in the handling of episodes, small details presented in prodigal and lively fashion: such are the principal qualities of M. Sardou. But his observation is superficial; the human documents which he provides are shop-worn and only superficially patched up; the world into which he takes us is a papier-mâché world that is inhabited by puppets. In each of his works you feel the solid earth slip away from you; there is always some unacceptable intrigue, some false sentiment pushed to an extreme, which serves as pivot of the piece, or else there is an extraordinary complication of action which a magic word will dissolve at the end. Life comports itself differently. Even if we accept the necessary exaggerations of the farce, we should prefer more amplitude and simplicity in the means. But we never get anything except outrageously enlarged vaudeville skits, the comic force of which comes entirely from caricature. I mean that laughter does not rise from the accuracy of the observation but from the grimaces of the characters. There is no need for me to cite examples. You have seen the little town depicted by M. Victorien Sardou in *Les Bourgeois de Pont-Arcy*. The key to his observation is there: silhouettes which are scarcely freshened up, jokes that are current in the newspapers, remarks that are on everybody's lips. Compare this with Balzac's little towns. *Rabagas*, in which the satire is often excellent, is spoiled by a bit of amorous intrigue of the most mediocre sort. *La Famille Benoiton*, in which certain caricatures are very amusing, also has its flaw, the famous letters, those letters which are found everywhere in M. Sardou's repertory and which are as necessary to him as thimble-rigging tricks are to a conjuror. He has been tremendously successful, which was to be expected, and I consider that fine. Notice, in fact, that if he usually passes to one side of truth, he nonetheless has been of singular service to the cause of naturalism. He is one of those workmen of whom I spoke who are of their time, who work within the limits of their capacity according to a formula which they have not had the genius to adopt completely. His personal contribution is exactitude of setting, the greatest possible exactness in material representation of everyday existence. If he fakes in filling in his framework, he does nonetheless provide the framework, and that is already something. For my part, his significance is to be found there above all. He came at the right time; he has given the public a taste for life and pictures cut from reality.

I pass on to M. Alexandre Dumas the younger. Certainly he has done an even better job. He is one of the most powerful workers for naturalism. He just barely failed to find the complete formula and bring it to realization. To him we owe physiological studies in the theatre; so far he alone has dared to show sexuality in the young girl and the beast in the man. *La Visite de noces*, certain scenes in *Le Demi-Monde* and *Le Fils naturel*, show absolutely remarkable analysis and rigorous truth. They are fresh and excellent human documents, something very rare in our modern repertory. It is evident that I am not niggardly in my praise of M. Dumas Fils. Only I admire him on the basis of a body of principles which force me also to be very severe toward him. As I see it, there is a crisis in his career: he has developed a philosophical flaw and has experienced a deplorable need to be didactic, to preach and to convert. Having made himself God's substitute on earth, he has allowed the strangest ideas from his imagination to spoil his faculty of observation. He departs from human documents in order to reach extra-human conclusions and incredible situations in the wild blue yonder of fantasy. Consider *La Femme de Claude, L'Etrangère*, and other plays. Nor is this all: wit has spoiled M. Dumas. A man of genius is not witty, and it takes a man of genius to establish the naturalist formula in magisterial fashion. M. Dumas has lent his wit to all his characters; the men, the women, even the children in his plays utter witticisms, those famous *mots* which have often been the basis of his success. There is nothing more false or more wearisome; this destroys all truth of dialogue. Finally, M. Dumas, who is above all what we call a man of the theatre, never hesitates between reality and the exigencies of staging; he wrings the neck of reality. His theory is that truth is not very important so long as you are logical. A play becomes a problem to solve. You start at one point and you have to arrive at another point without irritating the public, and the victory is complete if you have been skillful and forceful enough to leap over obstacles and carry the public along with you, even against its will. The spectators can protest later, shout about the lack of verisimilitude, and carry on a debate; nonetheless they have belonged to the author for an evening. The whole of M. Dumas's theatrical art is covered by this theory, which he continually puts into practice. He triumphs in paradox, in inverisimilitude, in the most useless and risky theses by the force of his wrists alone. He who has been touched by the breath of naturalism and has written such sharply observed scenes never recoils, however, from a fiction if he needs it to increase his effect or merely to provide a framework. He provides the most annoying mixture of perceived reality and baroque invention. Not one of his plays escapes this double tendency. Recall the incredible story of Clara Vignot in *Le Fils naturel*, and in *L'Etrangère* the astonishing story of the Virgin of Evil. I cite these at random. You might say that M. Dumas makes use of the true only as a platform from which to leap into the void. Something blinds him. He never takes us into a world that we know; the milieu is always painfully factitious; the characters lose all natural accent and do not stand on the ground. This is not existence with its amplitude, its nuances, its simple goodheartedness; it is an address to the court, an argument, something cold, dry, and brittle, where there is no air. The philosopher has killed the observer, that is my conclusion, and the man of the theatre has finished off the philosopher. It's too bad.

I come to M. Emile Augier. He is the current master of the French stage. It is his effort which has been the most constant and the most regular. We must remember the attacks which the romantics directed against him; they called him the poet of good sense; they made fun of his poems, not daring to make fun of the poetry of Molière. The truth was that M. Emile Augier embarrassed the romantics, for they felt in him a powerful adversary, a writer who was linked with the French tradition before the insurrection of 1830. With him the new formula grew: exact observation, real life put on the stage, depiction of our society in a sober and correct language. M. Emile Augier's first works, dramas and comedies in verse, had the great merit of deriving from the classic theatre; they had the same simplicity of intrigue, as in *Philiberte*, for example, where the story of an ugly woman who became charming and whom every one courted was enough to fill three acts without the least complication. They were also characterized by illumination of character, a vigorous good nature, and quiet yet powerful development in which complication and denouement sprang from feeling alone. My conviction is that the naturalist formula will only be the development of this classic formula as it is broadened and adapted to our milieu. Later on M. Emile Augier asserted his personality still more. Once he turned to prose and a freer depiction of our contemporary society he could not escape reaching the naturalistic formula. I should like to cite particularly *Les Lionnes pauvres, Le Mariage d'Olympe, Maître Guérin, Le Gendre de M. Poirier*, and his two comedies which have made the biggest hit, *Les Effrontés* and *Le Fils de Giboyer*. They are very remarkable works, all of which to some degree at least in some scenes realize the new theatre, the theatre of our age. Notary Guérin's final impenitence is very new and very true in effect; in *Le Gendre de M. Poirier* there is an excellent characterization of the bourgeois who has become rich; Giboyer is a strange creation, accurate enough in tone as he moves about in a society which is depicted with great satiric verve. The strength

216

"Naturalism in the Theatre"

of M. Emile Augier, that which makes him superior, is that he is more human than M. Dumas Fils. This human side places him on solid ground; with him you are not afraid of leaping into the void; he is settled firmly, less brilliant perhaps but more able to inspire confidence. What then has kept M. Augier from being the long-awaited genius, the genius destined to establish the naturalist formula? Why, I say, does he remain only the wisest and strongest of the workmen of the present day? In my opinion it is because he has not known how to free himself sufficiently from conventions, clichés, and ready-made characters. His drama is continually diminished by stereotypes, slick portraits, as they say in the painters' studios. Thus it is not unusual in his comedies to find the immaculate young girl who is very rich and does not want to get married because she resents being married for her money. The young men are likewise models of honor and loyalty, sobbing when they learn that their fathers have made fortunes by unscrupulous means. In a word, the sympathetic character triumphs, I mean the ideal type of good and fine sentiments which is always formed in the same mold, a veritable symbol, a hieratic characterization outside of all true observation. There is Captain Guérin, that model of military men, whose uniform helps him at the denouement; there is Giboyer's son, that archangel of delicacy but born of a tainted father, and there is Giboyer himself, so tender in his baseness; there is Henri, Charrier's son is *Les Effrontés*, who pledges restitution because his father has been involved in a shady deal and who prevails on the latter to reimburse the people whom he has bilked. That is all very fine and very touching; only as a human document it is very debatable. Nature is not so sharply defined in good and evil. You can only accept these sympathetic characters as a source of contrast and consolation. And that is not all. M. Emile Augier often modifies a character by a touch of his wand. The formula is well known: a denouement is needed and a character is transformed after a striking scene. Look at the denouement of *Le Gendre de M. Poirier*, for example, to cite only one. Truly it is too convenient; it is not that easy to turn a dark man into a light one. From the standpoint of valid observation these brusque changes are deplorable; a temperament is consistent all the way and is subject only to slow changes, which demand extremely minute analysis. Thus the best figures of M. Emile Augier, those who will no doubt endure because they are the most complete and the most logical, seem to me to be the notary Guérin and Pommeau, in *Les Lionnes pauvres*. The denouements of the two plays are very fine, with their large opening onto reality and the implacable march of life going its way beyond the sorrows and joys of each day. As I reread *Les Lionnes pauvres* I thought of Mme Marneffe, married to an honest man. Compare Séraphine to Mme Marneffe; compare M. Emile Augier and Balzac for a moment, and you will understand why, in spite of these good qualities, M. Emile Augier has not established the new formula in the theatre. His hand has not been sufficiently daring or vigorous to thrust away the conventions which encumber the stage. His plays are too mixed; none of them impose themselves with the decisive originality of genius. He straddles the fence; he will remain in the history of our dramatic literature as a level-headed, sensible pioneer.

I should like to mention M. Eugène Labiche, whose comic verve has been so fresh; Messers Meilhac and Halévy, those fine observers of Parisian life; M. Gondinet, who has succeeded in outmoding Scribe's formula by means of his witty tableaux, which are handled outside of all action. But it is enough that I have explained my position in respect to our three most celebrated dramatic authors. I admire their talent very much and the different qualities which they possess. Only, I repeat, I judge them from the standpoint of a body of ideas and seek to determine the place and the role of their works in the literary movement of the age.

IV

Now that the elements are known, I have in hand all the necessary documents for a discussion and conclusion. On the one hand, we have seen what the naturalist novel is at the present time; on the other, we have just set forth what the leading dramatists have made of our theatre. There only remains the setting up of a parallel.

Nobody denies that in a literature all genres are linked together and move forward in unison. When a gust of wind has passed and a shock has been given, there is a general impulse toward a common goal. The romantic rebellion was a striking example of this unity of movement under a specific influence. I have shown that the

"Naturalism in the Theatre"

power of impulsion in this age is naturalism. Today that force is more and more accentuated and precipitate, and everything must obey it. The novel and the drama are swept along. Only it has happened that the development has been much more rapid in the novel; naturalism is triumphing there whereas it is only faintly to be discerned on the stage. That was inevitable. The theatre has always been the last fortress of convention, for many reasons, which I shall have to explain. This, then, is my point: the naturalist formula, henceforth complete and established in the novel, is far from being so in the theatre, and I conclude from that that it will have to reach completion, that sooner or later it will take on scientific rigor. If not, the theatre will collapse, will become more and more impoverished.

People have been deeply irritated by me and have cried out: "But what do you want? What are you waiting for? Hasn't this development taken place? Haven't Messers Emile Augier, Dumas Fils, and Victorien Sardou pushed observation and depiction of our society as far as it will go? Let's stop. We have already gone too far into the realities of this world." First of all, it is naive to want to call a halt; nothing is stable in a society, everything is borne along in continuous movement. We go willy-nilly where we must go. Then I submit that the development in the theatre, far from being complete, has barely begun. So far we have seen only the first tentative efforts. We have had to wait for certain ideas to come to the fore, for the public to become used to them, and for the power of circumstance to destroy obstacles one by one. In my rapid discussion of Messers Victorien Sardou, Dumas Fils, and Emile Augier, I have tried to show why I consider them merely workmen who clear the way and not creators or geniuses who build a monument. Therefore after them I expect something more.

The other thing which arouses indignation and so many facile pleasantries is, however, very simple. We have only to reread Balzac, M. Gustave Flaubert, and Messers de Goncourt, in short, the naturalist novelists. I am waiting for dramatists to place on the stage men of flesh and bone who are taken from reality and analyzed scientifically without lying. I am waiting for them to rid us of fictitious characters, of those conventional symbols of virtue and vice who have no value as human documents. I am waiting to see environment determine characters and for characters to be shown acting in accordance with the logic of fact in combination with the logic of their own temperaments. I am waiting for the time when there will be no more conjuring tricks, of any sort, no more strokes of a magic wand which transforms things and beings from one moment to the next. I am waiting for them to stop telling us unacceptable stories and to stop spoiling accurate observation by romantic incidents, the effect of which is to destroy even the good parts of a play. I am waiting for them to abandon banal recipes, worn-out formulas, tears, and facile laughter. I am waiting for a dramatic work which, purged of declamation and free of fine language and pretty sentiments, has the high morality of truth and the terrible lesson of sincere inquiry. In short, I am waiting for the evolution which has occurred in the novel to be accomplished in the theatre, waiting for the day when they both go back to the same spring of science and modern art, to the study of nature, to human anatomy, to the depiction of life in an exact transcript, which will be all the more original and powerful in that no one has yet dared to attempt it on the stage.

That is what I am waiting for. People shrug their shoulders and reply with a laugh that I shall wait forever. Their decisive argument is that this sort of thing is not to be demanded of the theatre. The theatre is not the novel. It has given us what it can. That is all, and we must be content.

Very well, we have come to the crux of the quarrel. We are in collision with the theatre's conditions of existence. What I demand is impossible, which amounts to saying that lies are necessary on the stage, that a play must have its romantic incidents, that it must rotate in equilibrium around certain situations and reach a denouement at a certain time. And then there are various technical matters: analysis is boring; spectators demand action, always action; then there is the visual quality of the stage—an action must take place there in three hours, whatever its length; and also characters take on individuality, which necessitates a fictitious scene. I do not cite all the arguments but come to the role of the public, which is considerable. The public wants this, the public does not want that; it would not tolerate too much truth, it demands four sympathetic puppets to one real character taken

"Naturalism in the Theatre"

from life. In short, the theatre is the domain of convention: everything about it is conventional, from the stage set and footlights which illuminate the actors from below to the characters who are pulled about by strings. Truth may appear there only in small doses adroitly distributed. People go so far even as to swear that the theatre would no longer have any role to play if it ceased to be an amusing lie destined to console spectators in the evening for the painful realities of the day.

I am familiar with this line of reasoning, and I shall attempt to answer it shortly in my conclusion. It is evident that each genre has its own conditions of existence. A novel which one reads at home with his feet on the fender is different from a play which is to be performed before two thousand spectators. The novelist has time and space before him: he may play truant as much as he wishes; if he so pleases, he may take a hundred pages for a leisurely analysis of a character; he may describe setting as long as he desires; he may interrupt his narrative, turn back in time, change scene twenty times; in short, he is the absolute master of his material. The dramatic author, on the contrary, is bound by a rigid framework; he is subject to necessities of many kinds; he moves about only amid obstacles. In other words, there is the situation of the isolated reader as against that of spectators in the mass: the isolated reader accepts everything and goes where you wish to lead him, even when he gets angry, whereas spectators in the mass are subject to shame, fright, and other expressions of sensibility which must be taken into account if one is not to court failure. This is all true, and it is precisely for this reason that the theatre is the last citadel of convention, as I said above. If the naturalist movement had not encountered a difficult terrain in the theatre—ground so encumbered with obstacles—it would already have achieved the impact and success that it has had in the novel. By reason of the conditions of its existence the theatre was bound to be the last, the most difficult, and the most disputed conquest of the spirit of truth.

I should like to remark here that the development of any age is necessarily incarnated in a particular literary genre. It is quite evident that the seventeenth century is given body in the dramatic formula. The theatre in that day was of incomparable brilliance to the detriment of lyric poetry and the novel. The reason was that the theatre then responded with exactness to the spirit of the age. It abstracted man from nature, studied him with the philosophic tools of the time; it had the balance of a pompous rhetoric and the polished manners of a society which had reached full maturity. It was the product of the soil, the written formula into which the civilization of that time could flow with the most ease and perfection. Compare our age to that and you will feel the decisive reasons which made Balzac a great novelist instead of a great dramatist. The spirit of the nineteenth century, with its return to nature and its need for exact inquiry, was deserting the stage, where too many conventions hindered it, and began to assert itself in the novel, where the boundaries were without limit. It is thus that, scientifically, the novel became the form par excellence of our age and the first path on which naturalism was to triumph. Today it is the novelists who are the literary princes of the times; they have language and method; they are in the vanguard, shoulder to shoulder with science. If the seventeenth century has remained the age of the theatre, the nineteenth century will be the age of the novel.

Let me admit for a moment that current criticism is right when it asserts that naturalism is impossible in the theatre. That is understood. Convention is inflexible there; there we must always lie. We are condemned forever to the tricks of M. Sardou, to the theses and wit of M. Dumas Fils, to the sympathetic characters of M. Emile Augier. We can go no further than the talent of these authors; we must accept them as the glories of our age in the theatre. They are what they are because of the demands of the theatre. If they have gone no further, if they have not been more responsive to the great current of truth which sweeps us along, it is because the theatre has forbidden it. Within the theatre is a barrier which blocks the way to the strongest. Very well! But then it is the theatre that we condemn; it is against the theatre that we must strike a mortal blow. We shall crush it beneath the novel; we shall assign it an inferior position; we shall make it contemptible and futile in the eyes of generations to come. What do you expect us to do with the theatre, we workers for truth, we anatomists, analysts, researchers of life, and compilers of human documents, if you prove to us that we cannot bring our method and our tools

"Naturalism in the Theatre"

to it? Truly, the theatre lives only by conventions; it has to lie; it refuses to yield to our experimental literature! Very well, the age will leave the theatre to one side; it will abandon it to the public amusers, and carry on its superb and grandiose task elsewhere. It is you who pronounce this verdict; it is you who are killing the theatre. It is very evident that the naturalist evolution will broaden more and more, for it is the intellectual current of the age. Novels will probe deeper and deeper and will bring us newer and more accurate documents, but the theatre will daily flounder more and more ineptly among its romantic fictions, its threadbare intrigues, its tricks of the trade. The situation will become all the more annoying because the public will certainly develop a taste for reality through reading novels. Such a development is already discernible, and it will move with vigor. The time will come when the public will shrug its shoulders and itself demand a renovation. Either the theatre will be naturalistic or it will cease to be: such is my formal conclusion.

And is this situation not already evident today? The whole new literary generation is turning away from the theatre. Ask the beginners of twenty-five—I am speaking of those who have a real literary temperament—and they will all show disdain for the theatre; they will speak of popular authors with a lightness which will arouse your indignation. To them the theatre is an inferior genre. This derives solely from the fact that it does not offer them the ground of which they have need; in it they find neither enough liberty nor enough truth. They are all flocking to the novel. But if the theatre were captured tomorrow by some stroke of genius, you would see what an impetus would be given. When I wrote somewhere that the stage was empty, I meant that it had not yet produced its Balzac. You cannot, in good faith, compare Messers Sardou, Dumas, or Augier with Balzac; all of our dramatic authors heaped on top of each other would not equal his stature. Very well, the stage will remain empty, from this standpoint, so long as there is not a master who, by affirming the new formula, causes the coming generation to fall in behind him.

v

And yet I am the one with the most robust faith in the future of our theatre. Now I cease to admit the correctness of current criticism when it says that naturalism is impossible on the stage. I am going to discuss the conditions under which the movement will surely make itself felt there.

No, it is not true that the theatre will remain stationary; it is not true that present conventions are the basic conditions of its existence. Everything goes forward, I repeat; everything goes forward in the same direction. Today's authors will be surpassed; they cannot have the presumption to fix dramatic literature forever. What they have stammered forth, others will assert vigorously, and this will not destroy the theatre; on the contrary, it will enter on a broader and straighter path. In every age the forward march has been denied; newcomers have been refused the power and the right to do what their elders have not done. But that has been futile anger, impotent blindness. Social and literary evolutions have an irresistible force; they easily jump over enormous obstacles which people think unpassable. Let the theatre be what it will today; tomorrow it will be what it must be. And when that happens, everybody will consider it natural.

Here I am engaging in deduction; I make no pretense of having the same scientific rigor as before. What I have reasoned from the facts I have set forth. Now I shall be content to predict. The evolution is taking place, that is certain. But will it go to the right or left? I am not too sure. We can reason about it; that is all.

Moreover, it is certain that the theatre will always have its special conditions of existence. The novel, thanks to its free form, will perhaps remain the chief tool of the age, whereas the theatre will only follow it and complete the development. We must not forget the marvelous power of the theatre, its immediate effect upon the spectators. There is no better instrument for propaganda. If therefore the novel is read by the fireside, at several sittings, with a patient tolerance of the most long-drawn-out details, the naturalist dramatist must remind himself that above all he has nothing to do with an isolated reader but is concerned with a crowd which has need of clarity and conciseness. I see no reason why the naturalist formula cannot adjust itself to this conciseness and clarity. It will merely be a matter of changing the construction, the skeleton of the work. The novel analyzes at length with a minuteness of detail in which nothing is forgotten; the theatre will analyze as briefly as it wishes by means of actions and words. In Balzac a word, an exclamation, is often enough to give the whole character. Such an utterance is the best kind of theatre. As for what the characters do, that is analysis in action, the most striking kind of analysis that can be made. When we have got rid of trifling intrigue and the childish game of tying up complicated threads so that we may have the pleasure of untying them later, when a play is nothing but a true and logical story, we shall by that very achievement have entered upon a full analysis; we shall perforce analyze the double influence of characters on action and action on characters. This is what has often led me to say that the naturalistic formula took us to the very source of our national theatre, the classic formula. It is precisely in the tragedies of Corneille and the comedies of Molière that we find the continuous analysis of character that I am demanding; intrigue is of secondary importance; the work is a long dialogue dissertation about man. Only, instead of making man abstract, I would like him to be placed once more in nature, in his proper environment, and I would like the analysis to be extended to all the physical and social causes which determine him. In a word, the classic formula seems good to me on condition that within it the scientific method be applied to a study of contemporary society, just as chemistry studies bodies and their properties.

As for the long descriptions of the novel, it is evident that they cannot be brought to the stage. Naturalist novelists describe a great deal, not for the pleasure of description as they are accused of doing, but because their formula demands that they make their characters circumstantial and complete by means of environment. For them man is no longer the intellectual abstraction he was considered to be in the seventeenth century; he is a thinking animal, who is part of the totality of nature and is subject to the multiple influences of the soil from which he has sprung and on which he lives. That is why a climate, a region, a horizon, a room often have decisive importance. The novelist therefore does not separate his character from the atmosphere in which he moves; he does not describe out of a need for rhetoric, like the didactic poets, like Delille, for example; he simply notes down at each step the material conditions under which his people act and his data occur, in order to be absolutely complete, in order that his inquiry bear upon his whole world and evoke reality in its entirety. But it is not necessary to take description into the theatre; it is to be found there naturally. Is not the set a continuous description, which can be much more exact and striking than description provided in a novel? People say it is only painted cardboard; in fact, it is, but in a novel it is even less than painted cardboard; it is blackened paper, yet an illusion is created. After the stage settings so surprising in their truth and so powerful in their relief which we have recently seen in our theatres, it is no longer possible to deny the possibility of evoking the reality of milieux on stage. It is now up to dramatic authors to make use of this reality. They will furnish the characters and the data; the stage designers, on their indications, will furnish the description with as great exactness as is necessary. Therefore a dramatist has only to make use of milieux in the same way as novelists do, since he can realize and show them. I will add that, since the theatre is a material evocation of life, milieux have always been imposed upon it. Only in the seventeenth century, since nature did not count and man was pure intelligence, the settings remained vague: a temple peristyle, some room or other, a public square. Today the naturalist movement has brought greater and greater exactness to settings. This has taken place slowly but inevitably. Indeed this provides evidence of the quiet effect naturalism has had on the theatre since the beginning of the century. I cannot go into this matter of settings and accessories with any thoroughness; it is enough to declare that description is not only possible on stage but is there by reason of necessity, is imposed as an essential condition of existence.

There is no need, I think, to speak of change of scene. Unity of place has not been observed for a long time. Dramatic authors are not uneasy about covering a whole existence or taking the spectators from one end of the world to the other. Here convention continues to rule, as it does, moreover, in the novel, where the writer covers a hundred leagues sometimes from one line to the next. It is the same for the problem of time. You have to trick. An action which would take two weeks, for example, has to be contained in the three hours you take to read a novel or listen to a play. We are

"Naturalism in the Theatre"

not the creative force which governs the world; we are only creators at second hand, analyzing, summing up, almost always fumbling, successful and acclaimed as geniuses when we can bring out a single ray of truth.

I come to language. People claim that there is a special style for the theatre. They want this to be completely different from spoken conversation, more sonorous, more vigorous, written in a higher key, and many-faceted, no doubt so that the facets will catch the light from the chandeliers. In our day, for example, M. Dumas Fils has the reputation of being a great dramatic author. He is famous for his witty sayings. They go off like fireworks and fall in sprays to the applause of the spectators. Moreover, all his charters speak the same language, the language of the witty Parisian, teeming with paradoxes, aiming continually at effect, dry and blunt. I do not deny the striking quality of this language, though it has little solidity, but I do deny its truth. Nothing is so tiring as this continual titter of phrase. I should like something more supple, more natural. Such language is at once too well written and not well written enough. The true stylists of the age are the novelists; you must look for impeccable, vital, original style in M. Gustave Flaubert and the Messers de Goncourt. When you compare the prose of M. Dumas to that of these great prose writers, it is seen to have no correctness, or color, or movement. What I should like to see in the theatre would be a résumé of spoken language. If a conversation with its repetitions, its longueurs, its useless words cannot be brought to the stage, it would be possible to keep the tempo and tone of conversation, the distinctive utterance of each speaker, reality, in short, raised to the necessary point. Messers de Goncourt made a curious attempt of this kind in *Henriette Maréchal*, that play which no one wanted to listen to and which nobody knows. Greek actors used to speak into a bronze tube; under Louis XIV comedians sang their roles in a singsong tone in order to give them more pomp; today we are content to say that there is a language of the theatre which is more sonorous and is punctuated with explosive phrases. You see that there is progress. Some day it will be perceived that the best style in the theatre is the one which best reproduces spoken conversation, which puts the right word in the right place with the value it ought to have. Naturalist novelists have already written excellent models of dialogue, with language reduced to the strictly useful.

There remains the question of sympathetic characters. I do not conceal the fact that it is of capital importance. The public remains cold when we do not satisfy its need for an ideal of loyalty and honor. A play where there are only living people taken from reality seems to it dark, austere, and generally exasperating. It is over this point above all that the battle of naturalism is joined. We shall have to be patient. At present a vast amount of quiet influence is being exercised on spectators; bit by bit, under the impulsion of the spirit of the age, they are coming to accept the audacity of real depictions and even to find these to their taste. When they can no longer endure certain lies, we shall be close to having won them over. The works of the novelists are already laying the groundwork by accustoming readers to this. The day will come when it will be enough that a master reveal himself in the theatre for it to become evident that there is a public ready to become passionate in favor of the true. This will be a matter of tact and vigor. We will see then that the most elevated and most useful lessons are in the depiction of what is, not in repetitious generalities or bravura airs about virtue that are sung for the pleasure of the ears alone.

Here then we have the two formulas in opposition: the naturalist formula which makes the theatre the study and depiction of life, and the conventional formula which makes it purely an amusement of the mind, an intellectual speculation, an art of equilibrium and symmetry governed by a certain code. At bottom it all depends on the idea we have of what literature is, and of dramatic literature in particular. If we admit that literature is only an inquiry into beings and things made by original minds, we are naturalists; if we insist that literature is a scaffolding imposed upon the true, that a writer ought to make use of observation in order to launch forth into invention and arrangement, we are idealists and proclaim the necessity of convention. I have just been struck by an example. *Le Fils naturel* of M. Dumas Fils has lately been put on again at the Comédie Française. A critic is suddenly fired with enthusiasm, and away he goes. Good heavens, but it is well made, is admirably planed, grooved, glued, and bolted together. What a pretty piece of mechanism it is! And one piece is beautifully adjusted to mesh with another piece, which in turn sets the whole mechanism in motion! The critic preens himself; he cannot find words sufficiently full of praise to express the pleasure he gets from this gadget. Wouldn't you think he was talking about a toy, a puzzle, which he is proud of scrambling and putting together again? As for me, I am unmoved by *Le Fils naturel*. Why is that? Am I more stupid than the critic? I do not think so. Only I have no taste for clock-work, and I am very fond of truth. Yes, to be sure, it is a pretty mechanism. But I should like it to be glorious with life; I should like life, with its thrill, its amplitude, its power. I should like all of life.

And I add that we shall have all of life in the theatre as we already have it in the novel. That so-called logic of present-day plays, that symmetry, that balance established in the void by methods of reasoning which come from ancient metaphysics will fall before the natural logic of facts and of beings as they behave in reality. In the place of a theatre of fabrication we shall have a theatre of observation. How will this evolution be accomplished? That is what tomorrow will tell us. I have attempted to foresee it, but I leave to genius the task of realizing it. I have already given my conclusion: our theatre will be naturalistic or it will cease to be.

Now that I have tried to sum up the ensemble of my ideas, may I hope that people will no longer ascribe to me statements that I never made? In my critical opinions will they continue to see I know not what ridiculous inflation of vanity or need of hateful reprisal? I am only the most convinced soldier of the true. If I am mistaken, my judgments are there, in print, and in fifty years I shall be judged in my turn. I can then be accused of injustice, of blindness, of futile violence. I accept the verdict of the future.

"Emile Zola and *L'Assommoir*"*

By J.-K. Huysmans

JORIS-KARL HUYSMANS (1848-1907) was one of the original members
of Zola's Médan group and a leading naturalist in the early part of
his career. His novel *Marthe; histoire d'une fille* (1876) was admired
by Zola and brought the two writers into close relationship. *Les Soeurs
Vatard* (1879), which was dedicated to Zola, and *En ménage* (1881)
are typical naturalist works, as is "Sac au Dos," the story Huysmans
contributed to *Les Soirées de Médan*. The encomium of Zola here
presented was published in *L'Actualité* of Brussels in 1877 shortly
after the resounding success of *L'Assommoir* and represents a vigorous
assertion of the claims of the new movement, though the terms are
reminiscent of Zola's earlier prefaces. Beginning with *A rebours*
(1884), however, Huysmans turned more and more against naturalism
and ultimately became one of its foremost opponents, though he continued to be a champion of the Impressionistic school in painting, his
L'Art moderne (1882) being a pioneer work on that subject.

The opening chapter of the novel *Là-Bas* (1891) contains a discussion of naturalism which is a document in its own right. It begins
with a dialogue between des Hermies and Durtal on the subject, the
former castigating naturalism without reserve, the latter defending it
in increasingly lukewarm fashion. Des Hermies assails it on various
grounds:

> "I do not reproach naturalism for its prison terms or its
> vocabulary of the latrine and the doss-house, for that would
> be unjust and absurd; first of all, certain subjects call for
> such language, and moreover with the gravel of speech and
> the tar of words it is possible to raise up huge and powerful
> works, as Zola's *L'Assommoir* proves. No, the problem is
> different: what I hold against naturalism is not the heavy
> strokes of its crude style, but the filthiness of its ideas. What
> I hold against it is that it has incarnated materialism in lit-
> erature and has glorified the democracy of art!
>
> "Yes, say what you will, what an infamous intellectual
> theory it is, what a shabby and narrow system! To desire
> confinement in the prison of the flesh, to reject the supra-
> sensible, to deny dreams, not even to understand that the
> uniqueness of art begins where the senses are no longer of
> use!

* Huysmans, J.-K., "Emile Zola et L'Assommoir," *Oeuvres Complètes* II: pp.
159-166; Paris, n.d. First published in 1876.

"Emile Zola and *L'Assommoir*"

"You shrug your shoulders, but, look, what has your naturalism seen in all the discouraging mysteries which surround us? Nothing. When it has been a matter of explaining any of the passions, when it has been necessary to probe a spiritual abscess or cleanse even the least purulent sores of the soul, it has ascribed everything to appetite and instinct. Rut and mania are its only diagnoses. In short, it has confined its researches below the navel and has babbled stupidly when it came near the genitals. It provides a truss for the feelings, sells bandages for the soul, and that is all!

"And you must realize, Durtal, that it is not only clumsy and obtuse; it is stinking, for it has extolled this atrocious modern life, has boasted of the new Americanism of morals, and has arrived at a eulogy of brute force and an apotheosis of the strongbox. Through a prodigy of humility it has come to revere the nauseous tastes of the mob, and by that very fact has repudiated style, has rejected all lofty thought, all aspiration toward the supernatural and the invisible. It has come to stand for bourgeois ideas so patly that I swear it seems to be the product of the coupling of Lisa, the pork-butcher woman in *Le Ventre de Paris*, and of Homais!"

Durtal attempts a reply:

"Materialism is as repugnant to me as it is to you, but that is no reason to deny the unforgettable services that the naturalists have rendered art, for after all it was they who rid us of the inhuman puppets of romanticism and pulled literature out of a stick-in-the-mud idealism and the inanition of an old maid crazy from celibacy! In short, following Balzac, they have created visible and palpable beings and have placed them in harmonious relation with their surroundings. They have aided in the development of the language which was begun by the romantics; they have known real laughter, and at times they have even had the gift of tears. And indeed they have not always been fanatically in pursuit of the baseness of which you speak!"

Left to himself, Durtal realizes that he has long been troubled by the inadequacies of naturalism:

"Certainly naturalism, confined to monotonous studies of mediocre beings, making its way through interminable inventories of drawing rooms and fields, led us straight to the most complete sterility if we were honest and clear-sighted, and in the contrary case to the most tedious twaddle and the most wearisome repetitions. But outside of naturalism Durtal did not see any possibility for the novel except by return to the hollow nonsense of the romantics, to the downy works of Cherbuliez and Feuillet and their kind, or to the lachrymose little tales of Theuriet, Sand, and company.

"Then what? And Durtal, his back to the wall, struggled with confused theories, uncertain postulations, which were difficult to construct, hard to delimit, impossible to fill in. He did not succeed in defining to himself what he felt, or rather he came out at an impasse which he feared to enter.

"It was necessary, he told himself, to keep the veracity of the document, the precision of detail, the ample, responsive language of realism, but at the same time it was necessary to sink shafts into the soul and to be unwilling to explain the mysterious by sickness of the senses. If it could be done, the novel should divide itself into two parts, which would none-theless be soldered together, or rather fused, as they are in life—that of the soul and that of the body—and concern itself with their interactions, their conflict, their harmonious relation. In short, it was necessary to follow the highway so deeply furrowed by Zola, but it would be necessary to trace another route, a parallel road in the air, by which to reach things out beyond in time and space, in fact, to create a spiritualist naturalism. . . .

"And he came to feel that des Hermies was right. It was true, there was nothing left standing in the confusion of lit-erature; nothing except a need for the supernatural which, in default of more elevated ideas, stumbled off in all directions as best it could into spiritism and the occult."

To a considerable extent this last statement characterizes what Huysmans did. Jean des Esseintes in *A rebours* is an archetype of the decadent hero. The later works are drawn toward decadence, Satanism, symbolism, and religious mysticism, which on occasion gave them a *succès de scandale* and helped at least to demonstrate that there were other ways of writing, other kinds of experience to pre-sent than what had been hallowed by Zola.

◇◇◇

PERHAPS it would not be without value to define those words which are interpreted in such diverse ways: *realism* and *natural-ism*. According to some and, it must be admitted, according to the most widely received opinion, realism would seem to consist in choosing the most abject and trivial subjects, the most repulsive and lascivious descriptions, in a word, in bringing to light the sores of society. After removing the ointment and bandages which cover the most horrible sores, naturalism would seem to have only one goal, that of probing them to their frightful depths in public.

Green pustules or rosy flesh, it makes little difference to us; we touch them both, because they both exist, because the boor merits study just as much as the most perfect of men, because fallen women swarm in our cities and have a right there just as much as honest women. Society has two faces: we show them both; we make use of all the colors of the palette, of black as well as blue; we admire Ribera and Watteau without distinction, because both had style, because both created living works! Whatever may be said, we do not prefer vice to virtue, corruption to modesty; we applaud equally the rough, spicy novel and the sweet, tender novel, if they have both been observed, have been lived.

No, we are not sectarians; we are men who believe that writers like painters ought to be of their time; we are artists thirsty for modernity; we wish the burial of cloak and sword romances; we wish to be rid of the hand-me-downs and cast-offs of former times, to be rid of all those Greek and Hindu rigadoons; we do not throw down those so-called masterpieces with which we have been gorged to the point of nausea; we do not shatter statues of reputed fame; we simply pass them by; we go into the street, the living, swarming street, into hotel rooms as well as into palaces, into empty lots as well as proud forests; we want to try to avoid doing what the romantics did, making puppets more beautiful than nature, which have to be wound up again every three or four pages and are seen as vague and large by means of an optical illusion; we wish to try to set on their own feet beings in flesh and blood, beings that speak the language they were taught, beings in short who palpitate with life. We wish to try to explain the passions which drive them, and, as soon as they well up and break through, show them growing bit by bit and dying in the course of time or croaking with a cry that bursts from the lips! Given a man and a woman as subjects for study, we wish to make them act in a milieu which has been observed and rendered with minute care for details; we wish to demonstrate, if it can be done, the mechanism of their virtues and their vices, to dissect the love, indifference, or hate that result from the casual or continued contact of these two beings; we are the showmen, sad or gay, of animals!

It is true that our novels do not always come to a tidy end, in accordance with the usual formulas, by marriage or death; our novels support no thesis and, most of the time, reach no conclusions, that is also true.

But art has nothing to do with political theories and social utopias; a novel is not a rostrum; a novel is not a sermon, and I think that an artist ought to avoid as the plague all such rubbishy verbiage.

I shall be even more explicit about conventional formulas.

As I see it, literature up to this time has been wrong in concerning itself only with exceptions. Love, as novelists and poets show it to us, love which kills, leads to suicide or madness, is, when you get down to it, only an unusual case. That this curious case be noted, observed, rendered, I have no objection, since it exists, but that real life, the life that nearly all of us lead, should not be studied, should not provide the subject of a work on the pretext that it does not abound in furious passions, that it contains no situation made tense or lively here and there by knife thrusts and bottles of laudanum, by jeremiads on fate or grandeur of soul, which are admirable in a book but unconvincing in reality, that I find absurd. He who has sobbed for one woman and married another experiences no regret and grows thick about the middle. That man, I insist, seems to me just as great, just as interesting to put on the stage as Werther, that imbecile who mutters poetry by Ossian when he is gay and kills himself for Lotte when he is sad!

And believe me, the public is coming around to those novels where imagination gives way to analysis, to those novels whose plot is so uncomplicated that the upset reader exclaims: But nothing happens! This is because, thank God, we are already far from the time when the crowd, idolatrous of Dumas Père and Sue, despised Balzac! They are weary today of porcelain doll heroines who throw themselves and their horses into an abyss; they are weary of all the litanies in imitation of the Legouvés, Sandeaus, and so forth; they are weary to the point of disgust at all the affectations chanted by Sistine choirs!

"Emile Zola and *L'Assommoir*"

Yes, the public has come over to virile works. The success of *L'Assommoir* is proof of this. Oh! I know, prudishness and stupidity at bay make a terrible outcry: we want books that are chaste and comforting; life is sad enough, why show it as it is? Write observed and modest novels like those of Dickens, novels which are entertaining and in which virtue triumphs in the apotheosis of the last few pages.

And I say, for all that finally makes me indignant! I say that art cannot confine itself to celebrating the marriage of worthy young men and amiable maidens who timidly lower their eyes and bite the ends of their fingers; art cannot be limited to repeating the role established by Dickens: to bring a tear to the eyes of families gathered together in the evening and to lighten the tedium of convalescence. Art has nothing to do, I repeat loud and firmly, with shame or shamelessness. A novel that is dirty is a novel that is badly written, and that is all there is to it. I admire *Mademoiselle de Maupin* because it was sculpted by an artist, and I feel disgust rise to my lips when I read that sodden ignominy: *Mademoiselle Giraud, ma femme!*

To the preceding reflections I shall add that when you make a book living and true it is difficult not to make it moral. Vice engenders its own punishment itself; licentiousness is punished more by the consequences which arise from it than by laws drawn up against it:—to write true is to write morally. To sum up what I have said, naturalism is the study of created beings, the study of the consequences resulting from the contact or impact of these beings on each other; naturalism is, using M. Zola's expression, the patient study of reality in which the whole is derived from the observation of details.

"Nana"*

By Henry James

HENRY JAMES (1843-1916) was during his lifetime generally labeled a realist. This was due in part to his early association with the Flaubert circle, but in larger degree to the evident innovating spirit in which he approached the novel. Today we see his art as springing from the same ferment that produced realism but rising above it or going beyond it in important respects. He is in much the same position as such post-realists as Proust and Joyce: he assimilated what he needed from the realistic movement but went on to a highly individual art.

An essay on "The Art of Fiction," published in *Longman's Magazine* for September 1884 and often reprinted, has been characterized as a kind of manifesto in behalf of the new novel. In it James asserts that "the only reason for the existence of a novel is that it does attempt to represent life." Fiction, like history, finds its subject matter "stored up in documents and records." This apparently realistic position is denied, however, by the assertion that "A novel is in its broadest definition a personal, a direct impression of life: that, to begin with, constitutes its value, which is greater or less according to the intensity of the impression." As further resistance against the realistic strait jacket he insists: "Humanity is immense, and reality has a myriad forms; the most one can affirm is that some of the flowers of fiction have the odor of it, and others have not; as for telling you in advance how your nosegay should be composed, that is another affair." Believing in artistic independence, he thus counsels the young novelist: "All life belongs to you, and do not listen either to those who would shut you up into corners of it and tell you that it is only here and there that art inhabits, or to those who would persuade you that this heavenly messenger wings her way outside of life altogether, breathing a superfine air, and turning away her head from the truth of things."

Certainly James was sympathetic to the realistic tendency; for example, he hailed *Madame Bovary* as a "revelation of what the imagination may accomplish under a powerful impulse to mirror the unmitigated realities of life." And in his own insistence on "rendering," that is, on presenting dramatically, his practice coincided with the general realistic tendency.

The essential difference between James and the realists lies in his relative disregard of external data and his preference for depicting

* James, Henry, "Nana," *The Future of the Novel: Essays on the Art of Fiction*, pp. 89-96; Vintage Books, 1956. This essay originally appeared in *The Parisian*, February 26, 1880, and is reprinted with the permission of Paul R. Reynolds & Son, New York, and John Farquharson Ltd., London.

subtle shifts of perception, attitude, and values. This is not to deny that there can be a realism of mental experience, but most realists find James's presentation too rarefied, too abstracted from materiality. They take exception too to an intricacy and convolution of novelistic pattern as being a subtle kind of intervention on the part of the artist. The latter charge, to be sure, is one that is also to be brought against Flaubert.

Roderick Hudson, his first novel, appeared in 1876; *The American* in 1877; *The Portrait of a Lady* in 1881; and *The Bostonians* and *The Princess Casamassima* in 1886. These early works were thus in direct competition with the novels of Zola and the newly discovered Russians. It is not surprising that they seemed bloodless and unrooted in actuality by comparison, and that the names of Howells and James were often bracketed as exponents of the pedestrian school.

James as critic has been immensely influential in this century precisely because of his independent position and example. The theory of the novel as it is now constituted derives very largely from the comments he made in his critical writings, especially in the prefaces to his own works. He never addressed himself directly to an evaluation of realistic writing; yet, while it is clear that he thought its official doctrines were restrictive, if not misguided, he could show remarkable sympathy for a way of writing of which he disapproved.

◇◇◇

M. ZOLA'S new novel has been immensely talked about for the last six months; but we may doubt whether, now that we are in complete possession of it, its fame will further increase. It is a difficult book to read; we have to push our way through it very much as we did through *L'Assommoir*, with the difference that in *L'Assommoir* our perseverance, our patience, were constantly rewarded, and that in *Nana*, these qualities have to content themselves with the usual recompense of virtue, the simple sense of duty accomplished. I do not mean, indeed, by this allusion to duty that there is any moral obligation to read *Nana*; I simply mean that such an exertion may have been felt to be due to M. Zola by those who have been interested in his general attempt. His general attempt is highly interesting, and *Nana* is the latest illustration of it. It is far from being the most successful one; the obstacles to the reader's enjoyment are numerous and constant. It is true that, if we rightly understand him, enjoyment forms no part of the emotion to which M. Zola appeals; in the eyes of "naturalism" enjoyment is a frivolous, a superficial, a contemptible sentiment. It is difficult, however, to express conveniently by any other term the reader's measure of the entertainment afforded by a work of art. If we talk of interest, instead of enjoyment, the thing does not better our case—as it certainly does not better M. Zola's. The obstacles to interest in *Nana* constitute a formidable body, and the most comprehensive way to express them is to say that the work is inconceivably and inordinately dull. M. Zola (if we again understand him) will probably say that it is a privilege, or even a duty, of naturalism to be dull, and to a certain extent this is doubtless a very lawful plea. It is not an absolutely fatal defect for a novel not to be amusing, as we may see by the example of several important works. *Wilhelm Meister* is not a sprightly composition, and yet *Wilhelm Meister* stands in the front rank of novels. *Romola* is a very easy book to lay down, and yet *Romola* is full of beauty and truth. *Clarissa Harlowe* discourages the most robust persistence, and yet, paradoxical as it seems, *Clarissa Harlowe* is deeply interesting. It is obvious, therefore, that there is something to be said for dullness; and this something is perhaps, primarily, that there is dullness and dullness. That of which *Nana* is so truly a specimen, is of a peculiarly unredeemed and unleavened quality; it lacks that human savor, that finer meaning which carries it off in the productions I just mentioned. What *Nana* means it will take a very ingenious apologist to set forth. I speak, of course, of the impression it produces on English readers; into the deep mystery of the French taste in such matters it would be presumptuous for one of these to attempt to penetrate. The other element that stops the English reader's way is that monstrous uncleanness to which—to the credit of human nature in whatever degree it may seem desirable to determine—it is probably not unjust to attribute a part of the facility with which the volume before us has reached, on the day of its being offered for sale by retail, a thirty-ninth edition. M. Zola's uncleanness is not a thing to linger upon, but it is a thing to speak of, for it strikes us as an extremely curious phenomenon. In this respect *Nana* has little to envy its predecessors. The book is, perhaps, not pervaded by that ferociously bad smell which blows through *L'Assommoir* like an emanation from an open drain and makes the perusal of the history of Gervaise and

"Nana"

Coupeau very much such an ordeal as a crossing of the Channel in a November gale; but in these matters comparisons are as difficult as they are unprofitable, and *Nana* is, in all conscience, untidy enough. To say the book is indecent, is to make use of a term which (always, if we understand him), M. Zola holds to mean nothing and to prove nothing. Decency and indecency, morality and immorality, beauty and ugliness, are conceptions with which "naturalism" has nothing to do; in M. Zola's system these distinctions are void, these allusions are idle. The only business of naturalism is to be—natural, and therefore, instead of saying of *Nana* that it contains a great deal of filth, we should simply say of it that it contains a great deal of nature. Once upon a time a rather pretentious person, whose moral tone had been corrupted by evil communications, and who lived among a set of people equally pretentious, but regrettably low-minded, being in conversation with another person, a lady of great robustness of judgment and directness of utterance, made use constantly, in a somewhat cynical and pessimistic sense, of the expression, "the world—the world." At last the distinguished listener could bear it no longer, and abruptly made reply: "My poor lady, do you call that corner of a pig-sty in which you happen to live, *the world?*" Some such answer as this we are moved to make to M. Zola's naturalism. Does he call that vision of things of which *Nana* is a representation, *nature?* The mighty mother, in her blooming richness, seems to blush from brow to chin at the insult! On what authority does M. Zola represent nature to us as a combination of the cesspool and the house of prostitution? On what authority does he represent foulness rather than fairness as the sign that we are to know her by? On the authority of his predilections alone; and this is his great trouble and the weak point of his incontestably remarkable talent. This is the point that, as we said just now, makes the singular foulness of his imagination worth touching upon, and which, we should suppose, will do much towards preserving his works for the curious contemplation of the psychologist and the historian of literature. Never was such foulness so spontaneous and so complete, and never was it united with qualities so superior to itself and intrinsically so respectable. M. Zola is an artist, and this is supposed to be a safeguard; and, indeed, never surely was any other artist so dirty as M. Zola! Other performers may have been so, but they were not artists; other such exhibitions may have taken place, but they have not taken place between the covers of a book—and especially of a book containing so much of vigorous and estimable effort. We have no space to devote to a general consideration of M. Zola's theory of the business of a novelist, or to the question of naturalism at large—much further than to say that the system on which the series of *Les Rougons-Macquart* has been written, contains, to our sense, a great deal of very solid ground. M. Zola's attempt is an extremely fine one; it deserves a great deal of respect and deference, and though his theory is constantly at odds with itself, we could, at a pinch, go a long way with it without quarreling. What we quarrel with is his application of it—is the fact that he presents us with his decoction of "nature" in a vessel unfit for the purpose, a receptacle lamentably, fatally in need of scouring (though no scouring, apparently, would be really effective), and in which no article intended for intellectual consumption should ever be served up. Reality is the object of M. Zola's efforts, and it is because we agree with him in appreciating it highly that we protest against its being discredited. In a time when literary taste has turned, to a regrettable degree, to the vulgar and the insipid, it is of high importance that realism should not be compromised. Nothing tends more to compromise it than to represent it as necessarily allied to the impure. That the pure and the impure are for M. Zola, as conditions of taste, vain words, and exploded ideas, only proves that his advocacy does more to injure an excellent cause than to serve it. It takes a very good cause to carry a *Nana* on its back, and if realism breaks down, and the conventional comes in again with a rush, we may know the reason why. The real has not a single shade more affinity with an unclean vessel than with a clean one, and M. Zola's system, carried to its utmost expression, can dispense as little with taste and tact as the floweriest mannerism of a less analytic age. Go as far as we will, so long as we abide in literature, the thing remains always a question of taste, and we can never leave taste behind without leaving behind, by the same stroke, the very grounds on which we appeal, the whole human side of the business. Taste, in its intellectual applications, is the most human faculty we possess, and as the novel may be said to be the most human form of art, it is a poor speculation to put the two things out of conceit of each other. Calling it naturalism will never make it profitable. It is perfectly easy to agree with M. Zola, who has taken his stand with more emphasis than is necessary; for the matter reduces itself to a question of application. It is impossible to see why the question of application is less urgent in naturalism than at any other point of the scale, or why, if naturalism is, as M. Zola claims, a method of observation, it can be followed without delicacy or tact. There are all sorts of things to be said about it; it costs us no effort whatever to admit in the briefest terms that it is an admirable invention, and full of promise; but we stand aghast at the want of tact it has taken to make so unreadable a book as *Nana*.

To us English readers, I venture to think, the subject is very interesting, because it raises questions which no one apparently has the energy or the good faith to raise among ourselves. (It is of distinctly serious readers only that I speak, and *Nana* is to be recommended exclusively to such as have a very robust appetite for a moral.) A novelist with a system, a passionate conviction, a great plan—incontestable attributes of M. Zola—is not now to be easily found in England or the United States, where the storyteller's art is almost exclusively feminine, is mainly in the hands of timid (even when very accomplished) women, whose acquaintance with life is severely restricted, and who are not conspicuous for general views. The novel, moreover, among ourselves, is almost always addressed to young unmarried ladies, or at least always assumes them to be a large part of the novelist's public. This fact, to a French storyteller, appears, of course, a damnable restriction, and M. Zola would probably decline to take *au sérieux* any work produced under such unnatural conditions. Half of life is a sealed book to young unmarried ladies, and how can a novel be worth anything that deals only with half of life? How can a portrait be painted (in any way to be recognizable) of half a face? It is not in one eye, but in the two eyes together that the expression resides, and it is the combination of features that constitutes the human identity. These objections are perfectly valid, and it may be said that our English system is a good thing for virgins and boys, and a bad thing for the novel itself, when the novel is regarded as something more than a simple *jeu d'esprit*, and considered as a composition that treats of life at large and helps us to *know*. But under these unnatural conditions and insufferable restrictions a variety of admirable works have been produced; Thackeray, Dickens, George Eliot, have all had an eye to the innocent classes. The fact is anomalous, and the advocates of naturalism must make the best of it. In fact, I believe they have little relish for the writers I have mentioned. They find that something or other is grievously wanting in their productions—as it most assuredly is! They complain that such writers are not serious. They are not so, certainly, as M. Zola is so; but there are many different ways of being serious. That of the author of *L'Assommoir*, of *La Conquête de Plassans*, of *La Faute de L'Abbé Mouret* may, as I say, with all its merits and defects taken together, suggest a great many things to English readers. They must admire the largeness of his attempt and the richness of his intention. They must admire, very often, the brilliancy of his execution. *L'Assommoir*, in spite of its fetid atmosphere, is full of magnificent passages and episodes, and the sustained power of the whole thing, the art of carrying a weight, is extraordinary. What will strike the English reader of M. Zola at large, however, and what will strike the English reader of *Nana*, if he have stoutness of stomach enough to advance in the book, is the extraordinary absence of humor, the dryness, the solemnity, the air of tension and effort. M. Zola disapproves greatly of wit; he thinks it is an impertinence in a novel, and he would probably disapprove of humor if he *knew* what it is. There is no indication in all his works that he has a suspicion of this; and what tricks the absence of a sense of it plays him! What a mess it has made of this admirable *Nana*! The presence of it, even in a limited degree, would have operated, to some extent, as a disinfectant, and if M. Zola had had a more genial fancy he would also have had a cleaner one. Is it not also owing to the absence of a sense of humor that this last and most violent expression of the realistic faith is extraordinarily wanting in reality? Anything less illusory than the pictures, the people, the indecencies of *Nana*, could not well be imagined. The falling-off from *L'Assommoir* in this respect can hardly be exaggerated. The human note is completely absent, the perception of character, of the way that people feel and think and act, is helplessly, hopelessly at fault; so that it becomes almost grotesque at last to see the writer trying to drive before him a herd of figures that never for an instant stand on their legs. This is what saves us in England, in spite of our artistic levity and the presence of the young ladies—this fact that we are by disposition better psychologists, that we have, as a general thing, a deeper, more delicate perception of the play of character and the state of the soul. This is what often gives an interest to works conceived on a much narrower program than those of M. Zola—makes them more touching and more real, although the apparatus and the machinery of reality may, superficially, appear to be wanting. French novelists are at bottom, with all their extra freedom, a good deal more conventional than our own; and *Nana*, with the prodigious freedom that her author has taken, never, to my sense, leaves for a moment the region of the conventional. The figure of the brutal *fille*, without a conscience or a soul, with nothing but devouring appetites and impudences, has become the stalest of the stock properties of French fiction, and M. Zola's treatment has here imparted to her no touch of superior verity. He is welcome to draw as many figures of the same type as he finds necessary, if he will only make them human; this is as good a way of making a contribution to our knowledge of ourselves as another. It is not his choice of subject that has shocked us; it is the melancholy dryness of his execution, which gives us all the bad taste of a disagreeable dish and none of the nourishment.

Levels of Realism*

By Edmond de Goncourt

THIS and the following selection by Guy de Maupassant are both concerned with the attack on naturalism as being too prone to choose its subject-matter from the lowest human strata. By aesthetic preference Goncourt was bound to disavow such a predilection, but it is interesting that Zola too (in a letter to Georges Renard on May 10, 1884, about his book *Le Naturalisme contemporain*) takes a not dissimilar position:

> "Nearly everywhere I go along with you. A single reproach: you see us too much shut up in the low, the gross, the common. . . . That is where you have been influenced by the legend, which makes us pay for certain noisy successes by having only such success seen in our works. The truth is that we have tried to handle all levels, though in each, to be sure, pursuing a physiological study.

> "Now I do not accept your conclusion without reservation. We have never chased what you call *the ideal* out of men, and it is useless to try to bring it back. Then, too, I would be more comfortable if you would replace this term, the ideal, by that of *hypothesis*, which is its scientific equivalent. Of course I anticipate the inevitable reaction, but I believe it will be more against our rhetoric than against our formula. It is romanticism which will finally be destroyed in us, whereas naturalism will become more simple and more quiet. This will be less a reaction than a pacification, than an enlargement. This is what I have always said. Perhaps that is what you meant, but I was disturbed by the ideal turning up on the last page, like a young girl's dream, contradicting the judgment of our age and the scientific rigor of all the rest."

◇◇◇

WE CAN publish books like *L'Assommoir* and *Germinie Lacerteux* and agitate and stir up part of the public. Yes! but to me the successes of these books are only brilliant avant-garde skirmishes and the great battle which will decide the victory of realism, of naturalism, of *studies from nature* in literature, will not occur on the ground that the authors of those two novels have chosen. The

---

* Goncourt, Edmond de, "Préface," *Les Frères Zemganno*, Paris, 1879.

Levels of Realism

day when the cruel analysis that my friend M. Zola, and perhaps I myself, have brought to the depiction of the lower depths of society will be taken up by a writer of talent and used for the representation of men and women of the world in environments of education and distinction—only then will classicism and its followers be killed.

It was my brother's and my ambition to write the realistic novel of the elegant world. Realism, to use a fighting word, does not in fact have as its sole mission the description of what is low, what is repugnant, what stinks; it came into the world also to set down in *artistic* writing what is elevated, what is pretty, what smells good, and also to give a representation of refined people and rich things: all this through a conscientious and rigorous study of beauty, one not conventional or imaginative but like that which the new school has made of ugliness in recent years.

But people ask me, why did you not write that novel? why did you not at least attempt it? Well, there you are! . . . We began with the dregs of humanity because the woman and man of the people, nearer to nature and the savage state, are simple and uncomplicated creatures, whereas the Parisians of society, those overly civilized beings whose sharp originality consists entirely of nuances, half tones, all those impalpable nothings similar to the coquettish and neutral nothings out of which women create distinguished grooming, demand years for one to pierce to them, to know them, to *seize hold* of them—and even the novelist of highest genius, you may be sure, will never apprehend these drawing-room people from the reports of his friends who go into society to bring him back information.

Moreover, everything surrounding these Parisians is long, difficult, diplomatically laborious to grasp. An observer can get hold of a workman's interior in one visit; to get hold of a Parisian drawing room you must wear out the silk of its chairs in order to surprise its soul and receive the full confession of its rosewood and gilt.

These men and women, and even the milieu in which they live, can be captured only through an immense storing up of observation, by innumerable notes taken through a lorgnette, by the amassing of a collection of *human documents*, like those heaps of pocket sketches which, assembled at a painter's death, represent his life-time of work. For let me say it aloud, human documents alone make good books: books in which there are real human beings on two legs.

This plan for a novel which was to take place in high society, on the most quintessential social levels, for which we were slowly and patiently assembling the delicate and fugitive materials, I abandoned after my brother's death, since I was convinced it was impossible to succeed alone. . . . Then I took it up again . . . and it is above all the novel that I want to publish. But will I do it now at my age? It is unlikely . . . and the purpose of this preface is to tell the young that the success of realism will lie there and only there, not any longer on the level of the *literary canaille*, which has now been exhausted by their predecessors.

As for *Les Frères Zemganno*, the novel which I am publishing today, it is an attempt at poetic reality. Readers complain of the harsh emotions which contemporary writers bring them with their brutal reality; they scarcely suspect that those who make that reality suffer from it quite differently and sometimes remain nervously ill for weeks on account of the book which has been painfully and dolorously brought forth. Well, this year I found myself in one of those aging, sickly periods of life, cowardly before the poignant and anguishing labor of my other books, in a state of soul where truth too true was antipathetic to me also!—and this time I have written a work of imagination out of dreams mingled with memory.

"The Lower Elements"*

By Guy de Maupassant

GUY DE MAUPASSANT (1850-1893) is one of the most important writers of the realistic movement in France, particularly by reason of his short stories, though such novels as *Une Vie* (1883), *Bel-Ami* (1885), and *Pierre et Jean* (1888) are of lasting interest. A disciple of Flaubert, who taught him to write, he was also an original member of Zola's Médan group, contributing the famous story "Boule de Suif" to *Les Soirées de Médan*.

Not primarily a critic and to some degree disdainful of his role as man of letters, Maupassant's pronouncements are unsystematic and even contradictory. The present article, published in *Le Gaulois* for July 28, 1882, is noteworthy for its advocacy of realistic freedom of subject as well as for the recognition that novelists should not all write in the same way but rather as they see things. The preface to *Pierre et Jean*, which has been often reprinted, is a much more random and diffuse declaration converging on the doctrine of the writer's independence. In it Maupassant shows himself open to variety by saying: "Today we have the symbolists? Why not? Their artistic dream is respectable; and what is particularly interesting about them is that they know and proclaim the extreme difficulty of art."

In the preface just cited he repeats some of the remarks made in this article and amplifies other commonplaces about realism: ". . . the novelist who undertakes to give us an exact image of life must carefully avoid all plotting of events which appear to him exceptional. His goal is not to tell us a story, amuse us, or affect our emotions, but to make us think, to make us understand the deep-seated and hidden meaning of events." Thus his skill will "not consist in emotion or charm, in an engrossing beginning or a moving catastrophe, but in the adroit grouping of little constant facts from which the basic meaning of the book will be drawn." He concedes that even in this kind of writing it is necessary to select, "which is a first assault on the theory of the whole truth." However, he does not believe this invalidates the basic realistic position: "To write true therefore consists in giving the complete illusion of truth by following the ordinary logic of facts and not in transcribing them servilely in the randomness of their sequence." He admits the legitimacy of the novel of analysis but expresses his own preference for the method of objectivity, which he qualifies as an "ugly word," where the writers try to give "an exact representation

* Maupassant, Guy de, "Les Bas Fonds," *Oeuvres Complètes Illustrées* 15: pp. 73-75; Librairie de France, 1934-1938. The article originally appeared in *Le Gaulois* for July 28, 1882.

247

of what takes place in life, carefully avoiding all complicated explanations, all dissertations on motives, and confining themselves to making
people and events pass before our eyes. They believe that psychology
ought to be hidden in a book as in reality it is hidden beneath the
facts of existence."

The short story should be the ideal vehicle of the realist, since it is
short enough to need no structuring in its presentation of a moment
of existence. In fact, Maupassant often structured his stories in the
interest of ironic deflation or reversal, as is all too evident in "La Pa-
rure" ("The Diamond Necklace"). His ironic tone seems to us today a
little too pat, a little too glib. George Moore was no doubt right when
he wrote that Maupassant "did with Flaubert's style what he did
with Flaubert's thought, he popularized both."

◇◇◇

M. ALBERT WOLFF, in his lively criticism of the interests of the
young literary school, reproaches it for studying nothing but the
lower elements and adds with complete reasonableness: "But these
words (lower elements) do not imply exclusively a study of prostitutes and drunkards, who in such literature are graciously called
sluts and stinkers. The lower elements of society come into being
with the undermining of character, the collapse of honor, whatever
the level on which this occurs. What a vast terrain is therefore open
to the observation of the novelist! We have the lower elements of
the aristocracy, of the middle class, of the artists, financiers, and
workingmen. . . ."

Then, taking me personally to task, M. Wolff reproaches me for
not having replied frankly to Francisque Sarcey the other day.
Putting personal questions to one side, I claim the absolute right
of the novelist to choose his subject as he sees fit. Today, with M.
Wolff's permission, I am going to express my complete agreement
on this matter of the lower elements.

The mania for the lower elements, which is decidedly the vogue,
is only an excessively violent reaction against the exaggerated
idealism that preceded it.

Novelists today, it is clear, claim to write true novels. This
principle being allowed and this artistic ideal having been set forth
(and every age has its own principle), the exclusive and continual
study of what is called the lower elements would be as illogical as
the continual representation of a practically perfect world.

"The Lower Elements"

What difference would there be between a work in which all the characters were the very image of goodness and one in which they were all low and criminal? None. In the one as in the other there would exist a bias toward good or toward evil which would in no way be in harmony with the expressed intention to reproduce life, that is, to be more balanced, more just, more lifelike than life itself.

In the novel as our elders understood it, the search was for the exceptions, the fantasies of existence, for rare and involved adventures. The world they created was certainly not human, but it was very pleasant to the imagination. Their way of writing has been called "idealist art or method."

In the novel as it is understood today the effort is to banish the exceptional. We wish, so to speak, to hit the mean level of human events, to draw a general philosophy from it, or rather to derive general ideas from the facts, habits, ways of behavior, and experiences which are most widespread.

Hence the necessity to observe with impartiality and independence.

Life has its byways which the novelist must ignore, given the current approach. The imperious necessities of art must often make him sacrifice strict truth to simple but logical verisimilitude.

Now accidents are of frequent occurrence. People are injured on trains and swallowed up in the ocean, and passersby are hit by chimney pots in a high wind. But what novelist of the new school would dare, in the course of his story, suppress a principal character by one of these random accidents.

If you consider the life of every man to be a novel, each time a man dies in such fashion the novel has been broken off abruptly by nature. In such cases we do not have the right to copy nature. For we should always incline to the mean, to the general rule.

Thus to see in humanity only one class of people (be it high or low), one type of feelings, one sole order of events, is certainly a mark of narrowness of mind, a sign of intellectual myopia.

Balzac, whom all of us invoke as an example, whatever our interests, because his mind is as varied as it is broad—Balzac considered humanity in groups, facts in blocks; he catalogued people and passions in broad categories.

If today we seem to overuse the microscope and always study

the same human insect, so much the worse for us. This indicates that we are incapable of showing our talents on a larger scale.

But let us take reassurance. The present literary school will no doubt gradually expand the limits of its studies and rid itself of this bias above all.

When you look at it closely, the persistent representation of "lower elements" is, in fact, only a protest against adherence to a poetical view of things.

All sentimental literature has from far back lived in the belief that there existed sentiments and things which were essentially noble and poetic and that only these feelings and things could supply subjects to the writer.

For centuries poets sang only about maidens, stars, springtime, and flowers. In the drama the baser passions, like hatred and jealousy, were presented as having something elevated and magnificent.

Today we laugh at those who sing of the dew, for we have come to understand that all actions and all things are of equal interest to art; but once this truth was discovered, writers, in a spirit of reaction, stubbornly depicted only what was the opposite of what had been depicted before that time. When this crisis is over, and it is about to come to an end, novelists will view with just eye and balanced mind all people and all facts, and their works, in proportion to their talent, will take life in all its manifestations in the widest possible embrace.

It is precisely in the effort to get rid of literary prejudice that there have been created other prejudices which are merely the opposite of the first.

If there is a motto that the modern novelist ought to take as his own, one that sums up what he is attempting in a few words, is it not this:

"I do not wish anything human to be alien to me"?

"For and Against Zola"*

By Heinrich and Julius Hart

HEINRICH (1855-1906) and JULIUS (1859-1930) HART, though themselves chiefly writers in a lyrical vein, are important representatives of the group of young German writers who in the 1880's attempted to revitalize their national literature through affiliation with naturalism. They were active members of a Berlin group which included Otto Brahm, Wilhelm Bölsche, and Arno Holz. They contributed to the anthology *Moderne Dichter-Charaktere* (1885) and were members of the avant-garde literary club "Durch." Their most important venture was *Kritische Waffengänge*, which for the two years of its existence (1882-1884) carried on a campaign for naturalism. They later edited two other short-lived periodicals, the *Berliner Monatshefte* (1885) and the *Kritisches Jahrbuch* (1889), and wrote for the *Freie Bühne* after 1890.

Primarily they were concerned with breaking down the sterile, conventional qualities of German literature and the narrow philistinism of the critics. Since in their view "no material, including the indecorous and the commonplace, is in itself unpoetic," they were chiefly interested in the naturalists because of the example they brought of a close study of life. This position is, in fact, the logical one which we find throughout the history of the realistic movement—a seizing on the new literature as life-giving examples of expansion and modernity. It is a position echoed by their colleague Carl Bleibtreu, who defined realism as "that direction of art which renounces all cloud-cuckoo-lands and does its utmost to hold to the ground of reality as a reflection of life." In their acceptance of such a broadened base for literature they also largely avoided concern for the preservation of ideality which stultified much of German criticism during the debate over realism.

This does not mean they were uncritical of Zola. They found him to be a much better novelist than theoretician. They refused to go along with his materialist determinism and attacked his simplistic view of human nature as gross as well as limited. Like Emilia Pardo Bazán in Spain, they insisted that Germany would wear her realism with a difference and that essentially all she need do was to go back to the life-giving source of all virtue—in their eyes, Goethe.

◇◇◇

IN HIS BOOK *The Koran* Sterne speaks of the relationship of poetry to science and art in the following terms: "I maintain that

* Hart, Heinrich and Julius, "Für und gegen Zola," *Kritische Waffengänge* 2: pp. 44-55, Leipzig, 1882.

251

poetry is neither art nor science. Arts and sciences may be taught, poetry cannot." (Goethe mistranslates this by saying: "Arts and sciences may be understood by thought.") "Poetry is inspiration; it was already implanted in the soul when it first began to stir. On that account we should not call it either art or science but genius."

This remark goes much too far if it seeks to remove poetry from all connection with the arts—for these too cannot be taught in their deepest essence—but it is legitimate as a challenge to criticism to probe more deeply into the nature of poetry than it usually does.

Poetry is art; indeed in it all the other arts find a second being —the dance in stylistic and metric movement; music in rhythm and rhyme, as well as in the tonal quality of words; painting in description; the plastic arts in individual characters, and architecture in symmetry of structure—but there is more than art in poetry, for it is at the same time science, with which it shares dominion over speech and thought (*Faust, Hamlet, The Divine Comedy*), and again more than science, since it is also religion, with which it has a common mystical source (Angelus Silesius, Oschelaleddin Rumi, Ponce de Leon, Juan de la Cruz), and again more than religion, since it appropriates to itself all spheres, religion, science, art, and nature.

A similar view of poetry is also arrived at by Wilhelm von Humboldt when (in a discussion of *Hermann and Dorothea*) he speaks of a something in poetry "that goes beyond art"; likewise by Schelling, who (in his *System of Transcendental Idealism*) asserts: "It is to be expected that just as philosophy was born of poetry in the childhood of the sciences, and carries all of them with her toward their fulfillment so she will bring them back with her as a broad stream into the common ocean of poetry from which they came." No less by Solger, for in *Erwin* he characterizes poetry as the art which alone expresses ideas in their truth, in their essence; and also by Weisse (*Aesthetik*, vol. II, p. 352); by Hegel, according to whom (see his *Aesthetik*) poetry is the absolute, true art of the spirit, as well as the expression of the spirit; and likewise by Goethe and Jean Paul. Now in spite of the fact that poets and aestheticians are at one on this point in assigning to poetic genius a territory as boundless and uncircumscribed as the spirit itself,

"For and against Zola"

as endless as nature, for the most part our critics, like those elsewhere, persist in opposing every new and individual literary phenomenon from the position of narrow-minded philistinism, outworn pedantry, and rigid regard for rules. But does it make any difference if you judge a character, an action, a creation not in terms of its own being but applying the measuring stick of the trivial, the conventional to it, if you consider Bismarck's career from the standpoint of the schoolmaster, the Wars of Liberation from the viewpoint of a Mennonite, Rubens' *Last Judgment* through the eyes of a boarding-school miss? That would be pedantic, that would be narrow-minded, that would be philistine, wouldn't it? Now almost the same thing is occurring in the battle over so-called naturalism which has recently burst out in France, Denmark, and Norway, and which is spreading to Germany as well. Emile Zola has had to bear the brunt of this attack since his novels give sharpest expression to the naturalist trend and by their recklessness drive to despair the innocent Germans, who in all that they write think first of the innocent young girls of their acquaintance. Those reviewers who simply call Zola a "dirty fellow" I can ignore, for they have scarcely read him—and there is no need to pay attention to outright calumny—but there is another body of critics who recognize the powerful talent of the author and who only deplore that—perhaps that his characters are overdrawn, that his novels lack artistic development and concentration, that his descriptions tend more toward quantity than quality? Nothing of the sort. They deplore the fact that Zola in portraying men from the depths of society does not first send them through a steam bath, that he does not first dip them in eau de cologne and then put them in clean linen and black suits, instead of presenting them as they really are and letting them speak as no doubt they do speak in their miserable holes. And why do they deplore this? Because words like *derrière, merde*, etc., are never used in polite society, because dirty and unseemly scenes are normally offensive to good manners, because our reading public must be considered to belong to decent society. Stop! That is the first error these people make. Does the creative writer really address himself to the reader as a man in society, as a being bound by prejudice, decorum, and conventional lies, or does he address himself to man as such, released from the mundane defects of folly and prejudice? Certainly to the latter, for otherwise the representation of purity of soul and holy peace, as in Goethe's *Iphigenia* or a Raphael madonna, would make no impression, since such purity stands as far above "decent" sensibility as the exhibition of the commonplace is perhaps beneath it. That is unquestionably a fundamental error which speaks volumes about the aesthetic theories of such critics, about their confusion over the relation of what is common in actuality to artistic representation, about the validity of decorum as a limit of the poetically allowable.

When in his day in *The Inspector General* and *Dead Souls* Gogol depicted the social ills of Russia as stark and shocking as his eyes had seen them, critics rushed forth to sneer and hurl their anathemas against the heretic whose art was a shrill cry of reality without any reconciling, harmonizing, illuminating structure. Now criticism has long since given way; Gogol belongs to the recognized great of Russian literature; but criticism has learned nothing from this and similar cases. Such critics, in whose limited view the only goal of poetry is pleasure, chiefly instructive pleasure, still condemn his works and decry them as treason to the ideals of poetry. Against such an attitude I call to my aid the idea which I abstracted above from the most eminent creators of poetry, namely, that poetry can have no other task than to mirror the whole world, or in the meaning of Aristotle's *mimesis*, to mirror and reshape it. What the poet depicts is a matter of indifference; what is important is that he depict as poet. To be sure, in the very choice of material, he may betray a higher or lower degree of talent, but it remains true that no material, including the indecorous and the commonplace, is in itself unpoetic.

Schasler remarks in his critical history of aesthetics that "The spiritually ugly (the indecorous, etc.) has nothing to do with art; on the other hand, the ugly can be characteristic, even the object, of the most artistically complete representation." And elsewhere he says: "Now in a certain sense Dutch genre painting may be called ugly when we point to the objective content alone. But this external appearance is not the essence of art, but merely the way that certain materials are conceived of by a culture at a given stage of its

"For and against Zola"

development and the manner in which they are technically handled." There you are! It comes back to a question of the *how*, not the *what*. All right, our opponents object, it may be conceded that the poet may also depict the ordinary but then he must touch it up and give it a form which does not violate propriety. Now after a long struggle to free poetry from the grip of morality, the sterile, shadowy sister of morality, propriety, slips in through the back door accompanied by Rudolf Gottschall and Paul Lindau. Look, you fine gentlemen; stop firing; you will quickly range too far and bring into disrepute not only the poetry which threatens to endanger the purity of a fifteen-year-old girl—from Ovid's elegies, the fabliaux of the troubadours, the tales of Boccaccio, and the *Celestina* of the Spaniard Rojas to Goethe's elegies—but you will make it impossible for us to write poetry at all, for who in the long run can avoid writing a line which will offend nobody either among the godly or the godless, among the asses or the foxes. It will be best, then, not to ignore the old witch, but to strike her dead before she finds occasion to do greater harm. If any demand is to be made of the poets, let it be only the one which is made of all earthly creatures, that their creations have a truly moral and humanistic effect; the means used to achieve such an effect we must leave to them. And Zola's novels, particularly the most embattled of them, *L'Assommoir* and *Nana*, will have no such moral effect! These frightful tragedies of man's rottenness will not bring that *katharsis* of the passions in the way Aristotle tells us is the sole aim of tragedy! Oh, the pitiful souls who can experience such poetic works and only be concerned whether everything is in conformity with decorum, whether all the strong effects, which in Zola no less than in the Walpurgis scene of *Faust* are a necessary part of the whole effect, would be acceptable in the drawing room! Is the poet then to be allowed only the freedom of the drawing room and not even the freedom of philistine society, not even the freedom of the beer hall! Indeed, we have strayed far from German idealism—true idealism, which is open-minded, all-embracing, and hostile to every pedantry and unnatural limitation. The idealism of Gottschall and Conforten is like a Spanish lace boot, trimmed with a thousand regulations; it holds everything earthy and hearty in horror; it changes "Poetry should bring modern life before our eyes" to

255

"Its material is to be chosen from the past three hundred years," and its greatest achievement is that of recasting the old Odin verse saga in rhyme. A caricature, a caricature of idealism, but not the thing itself! As far as I am concerned, I willingly confess that I had rather the dark side of life be treated with sovereign humor, but this preference will in no way prevent me from recognizing the special quality of a Zola as fully legitimate and powerful, and will never lead me to decry a great talent on the grounds of decorum. Just as we judge a successful statesman by his deeds and not by the style of his utterances, so we value a poet by his poetic skill and the aesthetic effects he achieves. However, in the case of Zola it is worthwhile to examine the ways in which he offends against the spirit of poetry—for example, his heaping up of descriptive details, his poverty of invention, and his excessive use of sordid material—since these offenses derive from the author's theory, which is as original as it is false.

This theory of Zola's has been developed in several essays such as "Le Roman Expérimental," "Lettre à la Jeunesse," "Du Roman," "De la Critique," and "Le Naturalisme au Théâtre." Its main points run as follows:

"The return to nature, the naturalistic evolution, which is the main current of our age, is gradually drawing all manifestations of human intelligence into a single scientific course." Literature also, particularly the novel, must follow this movement of the times and transform itself from art to science. The way such a development can occur has been indicated by the development of medicine, which is often considered to be an art by many doctors and laymen, but which as a result of Claude Bernard's epoch-making work, *Introduction to the Study of Experimental Medicine*, has been turned onto the path of science. The experimental method must be applied (according to Bernard) not only to inorganic bodies, as in chemistry and physics, but also to the study of living bodies, as in physiology and medicine, and further (according to Zola) to the investigation of human passions and sensibility, in the novel, for example. The following proposition and example serve to clarify this position.

Proposition: "The novelist is both observer and experimenter.

"For and against Zola"

The observer in him presents data as he has observed them, determines the point of departure, and establishes the solid ground on which his characters will stand and his phenomena take place. Then the experimenter appears and institutes the experiment, that is, sets the characters of a particular story in motion, in order to show that the series of events therein will be those demanded by the determinism of the phenomena under study."

Example: "Baron Hulot in Balzac's *La Cousine Bette*. The general fact observed by Balzac was the ravages that a man's amorous nature produces in himself, his family, and society. Then he initiated his experiment by subjecting Hulot to a series of tests, having him pass through various situations in order to show how the mechanism of his passion works."

In other words, the novelist is the examining magistrate in the area of human passions. But it is to be expected that the experimental method will triumph not only in the novel but also in the drama and, yes, even in poetry, for experimental literature is precisely the literature of our scientific age, just as romantic and classical poetry were the expression of ages of scholasticism and theology.

Indeed it is really not necessary to set down the main points, in order to make clear the foundations of Zola's system, the web of one-sidedness, false assumptions, misstatements, and half truths on which it rests. Zola the novelist is henceforth a star, Zola the theoretician at best a clouded star. Historically the rise of French naturalism is easily understood: it arose as a result of the well-known reaction against the falsehood and bombast of Victor Hugo, Dumas, and Sue, but the reaction is so strong that literature now stands in danger of being engulfed in the contrary system and thus of giving birth once more to new lies and shallowness instead of bombast. That is, moreover, quite natural when people, like Zola, have scarcely any idea that any other literature than the French exists. For they generally call Victor Hugo "the greatest of the lyric poets," and in a book on literary aesthetics of 414 pages mention perhaps two or three names that belong to a cultural tradition other than that of the French. As a result of such blindness there easily arises a one-sidedness by which the novel and poetry are looked upon as two different areas, and the lyric is considered an idealistic hollow toy, and such people venture to base a new aesthetic on principles which are certainly in need of examination in view of their lack of evidence. If Emile Zola had only read one of those poems of Goethe which are as natural as nature itself, it is certain that light would have fallen upon his confused conception of poetry and would have dissipated all the gloomy clouds. It is amusing how Zola builds on Claude Bernard. Since medicine has recently been "raised" from art to science, so must the novel also become a science. Chemistry and physics are concerned with inorganic matter, medicine and physiology with the organic; therefore it is left to a science of the soul to deal with its passions and feelings. That science must be the experimental novel. No, good sir, you have completely overlooked psychology. The progression is very simple: physics, physiology, psychology. The novel has no place there. Where does it belong? Why, naturally, with poetry. Claude Bernard sees that clearly; he says expressly: "In the arts and letters personality dominates everything. There it is a matter of spontaneous creation of the mind, which has nothing in common with the observation and setting down of natural phenomena, in the course of which our minds must create nothing." That is unquestionably a true and profound conception which readily overthrows Zola's flimsy structure. Science investigates, analyzes, and probes nature, but poetry creates according to nature, creates a second nature, making use of the first in the way an artisan makes use of raw materials.

The Wallenstein whom science sets before us is at best a well-preserved corpse; the Wallenstein of poetry is, however, a completely new man, a living being, with whom history has little more in common than the garment, the outer shell. Now how does Zola get around the remarks of Claude Bernard, whom he represents as an infallible authority? He answers somewhat testily: "Here I find one of our most illustrious scientists under the necessity of denying literature entrance into the realm of science. No doubt he has a low opinion of the lyric, for he would not have written those words if he had been thinking of the experimental novel, of Balzac and Stendhal." The basis for this assumption? Wishful thinking on Zola's part, nothing else. Zola has involuntarily stated the authority for this wish in every comparison he has made in which he asserts that "naturalism" in literature is the expression of our scientific age, just as classicism and romanticism were an expression of the scholastic and the theological. Now classical and romantic poetry were neither scholasticism nor theology as such, but rather incorporated the spirit of these; so it may rightly be inferred that the poetry of the present time must not become natural science but must merely draw from it. That is a proper attitude; but by every step that it goes beyond this there will be a whittling away of poetry, as was the case with the false idealism of Zola's opponents. However unique we may consider the development of the novel to be, it will never become a textbook of pathology, as Zola would have it. Science seeks to extract the universal from individual cases and to dissolve them in general understanding; the novel, and poetry also, seek above all to express the universal in particulars and to embody them in form. With thoughtful discrimination Jean Paul challenges the poet not to imitate nature but to copy from nature. So we can understand that it is entirely possible to learn from poetic works but only as we learn from nature, whereas we can learn nothing from science, but only through science. Poetry does not even have the relation to science that childish perception has to adult understanding; both are co-ordinate areas of perception and understanding which grow and expand together, without one's doing harm to the other.

"The mystery of poetry from the hand of truth!" That is the principle of all pure poetry, which is undermined by any one-sidedness—and at those unique and insufficiently valued moments when we can accept Zola's theories as well as his novels as eternally valid there is certainly the ring of truth. But look how most of our German writers daily sin against this principle! Untruthfulness of speech, thoughts, action, characters, world views has almost become the norm for the majority of our writers of novels and plays. How seldom do we encounter a figure about whom we can say from the heart what we ought to be able to say about any poetic creation: *Tat twam asi*—that is you? How seldom are we able to discover a shoot from the tree of truth, of free, bold, strong humanity? By narrow restrictions our literature has been reduced to a mere women's literature, yes, perhaps rather a young girls' literature. What does not please the coddled, prudish, silly products of a petty education is forbidden; what pleases them will be our guide. We have already succeeded in bringing it about that serious, deeply spiritual words from the eternal greatness and beauty of true poetry are laughed at as effusions of a crazy idealism and that criticism which refuses to employ the reading standards of young girls, which refuses to make a narrow-minded ox into a contented cow, is considered to have gone berserk. Now there is no need to be despondent about this. Every great age of history is followed by an exhaustion of the spirit, and even more of sensibility and imagination, and naturally this process fulfills itself most visibly in the history of literature. Practically our whole body of decadent literature is essentially nothing more than a recrudescence of classicism, an artificial, literature-derived reproduction, in no sense an original outburst of nature, in no sense an outwelling from a living spring. What it lacks is not sensibility in general, but rather primal feeling, flowing from the heart of nature, in other words, genius, naturalism in the highest sense of the word as opposed to formalism, that which in Hellenic times reached its fullest flower and was imported into our literature by Goethe, the poet of *Iphigenia*. Such formalism is a necessary stage of development, but in the present day when it has reached its limits it must again be passed through and absorbed by the naturalism of genius. It is in this sense that I wish to be understood when I say that we must once more attach ourselves to the young Goethe, the creator of *Werther* and *Faust*, for there we find not merely truth, as in Zola, but poetry-impregnated truth. Only then will our poetry find the proper mean between earth-fresh realism and the higher idealism, between cosmopolitan humanism and self-conscious nationalism, between thoughtful manliness and deep-welling emotion; only then will it reach the highest point and, creating out of the full spring of actuality, transfigure primitive, many-faceted nature in the light of the ideal. Various ones of our poets, such as Hamerling, Gottfried Keller, and others, stand already on the ground of this new literary spirit—I have no fear that they will prove to be a vanguard without an army.

On Spanish Realism*

By Emilia Pardo Bazán

COUNTESS EMILIA PARDO BAZÁN (1858-1921) was a leading exponent of realism in Spain, an advocate of what was called Catholic realism. The preface here presented sets forth in brief a position which was elaborated in a series of articles published in *La Epoca* in 1882 under the general title of *The Burning Question*.

This longer work, which surveys the course of European fiction practically from its beginnings, presents a firm philosophic and aesthetic position. She refuses to allow realism and naturalism to be considered as identical. The latter she considers invalid because of its materialistic determinism, which she calls its capital vice, whereas realism offers a much broader and more perfect theory, making allowance for both body and soul. The movement is of basic importance also because it provides an exact instrument which measures the moral state of a nation. As a Spaniard she appeals to her Spanish readers to be hospitable to realistic works, for the tendency they manifest is indigenous to the Spanish soil which produced the *Quixote*.

Looking back on *La cuestión palpitante* in 1891, the author recalls that though it had been her intention to write not "a catechism of a school," but a dispassionate exposition of theories which had been wrongly understood, the work embroiled her in prolonged and vigorous controversy. In addition to substantial answers in the periodical press, three books appeared in reply. These were *La cuestión palpitante: Cartas a la Sra Doña Emilia Pardo Bazán* by J. Barcia Caballero, 1884, which was favorable; and *La novela moderna, cartas criticas,* by Juan B. Pastor Aicart, 1886, and *Apuntes sobre el nuevo arte de escribir novelas* by Juan Valera, 1887, which were unfavorable. Her one regret in retrospect is that she did not consider the Russian realistic novel, which was virtually unknown in Spain at that time. This omission she repaired, however, in a series of lectures given at the Ateneo in 1887 which were published under the title of *La revolución y la novela en Rusia*.

Less famous today than her contemporary Pérez Galdós, Countess Pardo Bazán enjoyed an exalted place in Spanish letters during her lifetime. Denied election to the Spanish Academy because she was a woman, she did receive the honor of the chair of modern romance literature at the University of Madrid. In addition to *Un viaje de novios* she is particularly well-known for the novels *Los pazos de Ulloa* (1886) and *La madre naturaleza* (1887).

* Pardo Bazán, Emilia, "Prefacio," *Un viaje de novios*, Madrid, 1881. Translated by permission of Doña Maria de las Nieves Quiroga y Pardo Bazán, Condesa de Torre de Cela, and the Sociedad General de Autores de España.

IN SEPTEMBER of last year, 1880, medical science ordered me to drink the waters of Vichy at their source, and for that purpose having to cross all of France and Spain, I thought I would set down the events of the journey in a notebook with a view to publication. Then I recalled the boredom and irritation that hybrid little travel works usually cause me, those "Impressions" and "Diaries" in which the author sets down for us his ecstasies before a cathedral or a vista and itemizes the tips he gave the waiter or the salad on which he dined, with other facts no less worthy of passing into history and being immortalized in marble and in bronze. Stimulated by this consideration, I decided to write a novel, since the lands through which I travelled would make a good setting for a story.

That would be enough in the way of prologue and explanation of my novel, which merits or demands no more; but now that I am writing I am eager to make a few points which, if not indispensable, are at least not out of place here. Anyone who finds them irritating may easily skip over them and go on without delay to the first chapter of *Un viaje de novios*; God grant that he does not find the remedy worse than the illness.

Every age has its literary battles, which on occasion are engagements all along the line—like the conflict between classicism and romanticism—while others take place on more restricted grounds. Unless I am greatly mistaken, today's ground is the novel and the drama, and abroad the novel above all. Lyric poetry, for example, enjoys such liberty that it might border on anarchy without anyone's taking fright, whereas the French school of novelists which has raised the banner of realism or naturalism is a topic of agitated discussion and rouses both sharp criticism and heated defense. Its products go all over the globe, badly translated and even worse understood, but assured of sale in an incalculable number of editions. It is good form to be shocked by these works and it is very certain that those who are the most shocked are by no means the ones who read them least. To the expert in things literary all this indicates something original and individual, a new phase in literary development, a sign of vitality, and on that account it is more in need of careful examination than everlasting condemnation or blind praise.

On Spanish Realism

From this battle one fruitful principle has already emerged, and I consider it of utmost importance that the novel has ceased to be a work of mere entertainment, a means of passing a few hours pleasantly, and has been raised to the level of social, psychological, historical analysis—in short, a study. From this is to be drawn a conclusion that will surprise many: namely, that observation and analysis are no less necessary to the novelist than the trappings of imagination. For, in fact, if we reduce the novel to the level of mere lively inventiveness, our ideal would seem to be something like *Las sergas de Esplandián* or *The Thousand and One Nights.* Today—it is no longer possible to doubt it—the novel is drawn from life, and the only thing the author puts into it is his own particular way of seeing real things: just as two people referring to the same authentic fact render it with different language and style. Thanks to this recognition of the boundaries of the true, realism can enter, head high, into the domain of literature.

It is proper to add that the latest and much discussed French genre seems to me a realistic tendency, but off base and twisted in a number of respects. There are realisms within realism, and I think this one is deficient, or rather is excessive, in boasting that it points the direction of right rules and durable influence in literature. The unhealthy taste of the public has perverted writers with money and applause, and they ascribe to their own ability what is really due to the low nature and indelicacy of their readers. It is not the most perfect and real naturalistic novels that have achieved the greatest vogue and sales, but those that describe the most licentious behavior and provide the most free and highly colored pictures. How much may authors step up the dosage? Formerly they reached fame with scandal and talent, or with talent alone; now at times scandal replaces talent. Even Zola says this: the number of editions of a book is not proof of merit but of success.

I do not condemn the patient, minute, exact observation which is distinctive of the modern French school; on the contrary I praise it; but I disapprove, as artistic aberration, the systematic and preferential choice of repugnant or shameful data, the excessive and at times boring prolixity of description, and, above all, a defect which I am not sure the critics have noticed: the perpetual solemnity and sadness, the undeviating grim, gloomy look, the lack of a note of joy and of grace and ease in style and idea. To me Zola, with his immense talent, is the most hypochondriac of all the writers we have ever had or will have; a Heraclitus who does not like a handkerchief, a Jeremiah who bewails the downfall of a country through a coup d'état at the same pitch as the ruin of a warehouse full of foreign merchandise. And since the novel is the imitation of human life par excellence, it is proper that in it, as in our own existences, tears and laughter, the basis of the eternal tragicomedy of the world, should take their turn. These brand-new realists consign the dagger and the poison of the romantic school to oblivion, but they drag on stage faces a thousand times more surly and frightful.

Oh, how healthy, true and beautiful is our national realism, our most glorious tradition of Spanish art! Our realism, which weeps and laughs in the *Celestina* and the *Quixote*, in the pictures of Velásquez and Goya, in the comic dramatic vein of Tirso and Ramón de la Cruz! A realism that is indirect and unconscious, and for that reason finished and full of inspiration; not disdainful of idealism, and, thanks to it, legitimate and profoundly human, so that like man himself, it contains spirit and matter, heaven and earth! When I consider that even today, in our low estate, when literature scarcely provides its practitioners with a crumb of bitter bread, when there is scarcely any public to read or applaud, we still have novelists who are in no way inferior in style, or invention, or indeed in perspicacious observation to their colleagues in France and England (countries where the writing of good novels is a profession, not only honorable but lucrative), I am proud of the abilities of our race at the same time that I am unhappy over the niggardly reward that Spanish talent receives, and I am mortified at the shameful preference sometimes shown by the multitude for the rantings and pessimistic raving of Zola when we have in Spain Galdós, Pereda, Alarcón and others whom I leave out only so as not to make the list too long.

If it occurs to critics to call this novel of mine realistic, as they did its elder sister *Pascual López*, I beg them, out of charity, not to link me with trans-Pyrenean realism but to our own, the only one that satisfies me and the one in which I wish to live and die. So great is my respect and love for our national models that, better

On Spanish Realism

to imitate them and to saturate myself with them, I gave *Pascual López* an archaic savor, which was praised to the skies by the benevolence of some and condemned by others, but which in my humble opinion was not at all out of place in a work intending— as far as possible in our day and in so far as I have talent—to recall the highly seasoned and never very weighty picaresque genre. I should not have to excuse myself for using the same style in *Un viaje de novios*, which is closer to the modern novel of local color, so-called.

I might also defend myself in advance against the other charge that is sometimes made against me by ill-humored critics. There are those who believe that the novel ought to prove, demonstrate, or correct something, at the end castigating vice and crowning virtue, in the manner of little stories written for children. This is a demand to which painters, architects, and sculptors are not subject: so far as I know no one blamed Velásquez because his *Hilanderas* or *Meninas* provided no edifying lesson. Only the writer, with a slap on the fingers, is commanded to lay the lash on society but with such dissimulation that his discipline may be taken for a caress and people may mend their ways by means of entertainment. I must declare that in art I like the indirect instruction which comes from beauty, but that I abhor the moral pills wrapped up in literary gold paper. Between the cold and shocking shamelessness of the ultranaturalistic writers and the sentimental homilies of the authors who take a pulpit in their hands and go about the world preaching I have no choice; I can do without either. This judgment may seem lax to some and unduly strict to others; for my part it is enough to know that, in practice, it is what was professed by Cervantes, Goethe, Balzac, and Dickens.

You will pardon me, kind reader, for having dragged such illustrious names in by the hair in connection with my own insignificant writings. It is possible that sight of a pond may recall the ocean; but the pond remains a pond. Even if it knows this and is unhappy over its own littleness, God made it no larger and it must practice the resignation that you will need if you are to peruse these pages.

What Naturalism Is Not[*]

By Leopoldo Alas

LEOPOLDO ALAS (1852-1901), who wrote under the name of "Clarín," was a powerful voice in the renovation of Spanish literature at the end of the nineteenth century. Professor of law at the University of Oviedo, he was also a critic and novelist of stature, two novels, *La regenta* (1884-1885) and *Su único hijo* (1890), being important contributions to the movement he defended. He published his *Benito Pérez Galdós* in 1889 and his critical writings of more fugitive nature were collected as *Folletos literarios* (1886-1891).

In 1883, when Countess Pardo Bazán's *La cuestión palpitante* was about to appear in book form (the so-called second edition), Alas let her know through a friend that he would like to provide a preface. What he wrote is an unusually clear, succinct, and basically uncontroversial view of the goals of the movement, though he does place himself in a dubious position at one point by denying that naturalism is pessimistic. The eight-button gloves of which he speaks may become the countess, but what he shows on his own account is a tight fist raised in challenge. His sharp statement gives us some idea of the literary passions which even so mild a book raised in Spain.

◊◊

A FEW DAYS ago an illustrious academician called naturalism the *dirty hands* of literature; and now we have a white and very beautiful hand, one of those which do not offend since they are distinguished and are covered with fragrant eight-button gloves, which has come to defend with golden pen what the author of *The Three-Cornered Hat* has so harshly denounced.

However, to be exact, it is possible that what is defended in this book is not the same as what Señor Alarcón attacks, just as the windmills attacked by Don Quixote were not the giants which he saw.

It is difficult enough to cope with the fact that naturalism is not what its enemies imagine it to be without having to consider its lack of conformity with the idea that many of its adherents have of it, for they are likely to show the rashness of faith of the blind.

[*] Alas, Leopoldo, "Prólogo de la segunda edición," *La cuestión palpitante*, in Emilia Pardo Bazán, *Obras completas* I: pp. 27-41, Madrid, 1891. Translated by permission of the heirs of the author and the Sociedad General de Autores de España.

What Naturalism Is Not

In Spain, and perhaps abroad, new ideas are likely to begin to decay before they are ripe: when Spaniards who are capable of thinking on their own account have not yet been convinced of anything, the mob is at the end of the street already misunderstanding what the others have not yet begun to understand aright. The bad thing about the vulgar is not that it belongs to the masses, but that it belongs to the worst, who are the most numerous. Ideas which have been vulgarized lose their majesty, like popularity-seeking kings. For it is one thing to propagate an idea and quite another to vulgarize it. Natural science vulgarized has given as its fruit the absurd novels of Verne and the books of Figuier. Positivism, when it reaches the cafés, indeed even the taverns, is nothing more than vulgar blasphemy, with a few technical terms added.

Literary naturalism, which so far has been accepted in Spain by very few serious people, spreads easily, like a fire in an oil depot, among trivial people who are fond of risqué reading. It is clear that naturalism is not what such enthusiasts, more sympathetic than judicious, believe and pronounce it to be. According to them naturalism can put idealism to flight five times an hour. What naturalism is, in its own terms, Señor Alarcón has not yet managed to understand, and what is more to be regretted, neither has Señor Campoamor. To the latter it is the imitation of what is repugnant to the senses; to Alarcón it is . . . just the opposite.

The book to which these remarks serve as preface is one of the best expositions of the doctrines of this new literary tendency which is so much calumniated by friends and foes.

What is naturalism? He who reads the chapters that follow in good faith and without bias, and is prepared by acquaintance with the principal works among the many to which reference is made, will be able to give an exact answer to this question, or very nearly so.

I am here going to limit myself on this subject to saying something about what naturalism is not, reserving the greater part of my natural enthusiasm for the deserved praise of the lady who has written the present book. For, to tell the truth, if naturalism is clear to me, even more clear is the skill of so discreet an advocate, who recalls to me another of the same sex portrayed by Shakespeare in *The Merchant of Venice*.

267

Naturalism is not the imitation of what is offensive to the senses, most esteemed poet, Señor Campoamor; because naturalism does not and cannot copy sensation, which is where repugnance lies. If literary naturalism spreads before Señor Campoamor smells, colors, forms, sounds, tastes, and tactile sensations which disgust him, he has a right to complain, although at the expense of the tastes of others (since the smells, tastes, forms, colors, and contacts which disgust the eminent poet may well be agreeable to others). But the fact is that literature cannot consist in such sensations or in their imitation. Sensations can be imitated only by sensations of the same order. Thus literature has been able to describe the Milan plague and the gripes suffered by Sancho at the fulling mill without fear of contagion or bad odors. The charge of nausea brought against naturalism is therefore in bad faith.

Naturalism likewise is not the constant repetition of descriptions whose goal is to represent to the imagination images of ugly, vile, and miserable objects. Anything that exists in the world may enter into a work of literature, but it will not do so because it is ugly but by reason of the fact that it exists. If on occasion a naturalistic writer through bad judgment has exaggerated this liberty in the choice of materials, losing his way in description of the insignificant, this fault is not chargeable to the new literary tendency.

Naturalism is not subordinate to positivism, or limited in its procedures to observation and experiment in the abstract, narrow, and logically false sense in which such aspects of method are understood by the illustrious Claude Bernard. It is true that Zola in the worst of his critical works has said something to this effect; but he himself later wrote what amounted to a correction; and in any event naturalism is not responsible for Zola's systematic exaggeration.

Naturalism is not pessimism, whatever the eminent philosopher and critic González Serrano may say, even if he is joined in that opinion by the powerful intelligence of Doña Emilia Pardo Bazan, the author of this book. It is true that Zola speaks on occasion— for example, in his criticism of *The Temptation of St. Anthony*—of what Leopardi called "the utter vanity of everything"; but this does not occur in a novel; it is a critic's opinion. And although it may be demonstrated, though I doubt it, that the novels of Zola

What Naturalism Is Not

and Flaubert prove that their authors were pessimists, that does not prove that naturalism, a school, or rather a purely and exclusively literary tendency, is strictly bound to deterministic ideas about the causes and goals of life. No serious literary theory permits the dragging in of metaphysics, least of all naturalism, which in its perfect imitation of reality abstains from giving a lecture, from depicting things as they are depicted by inventors of philosophies of history, who make them say what the author wants them to say: naturalism, like life, contains instruction, but it does not mount a pulpit; he who deduces pessimism from a good naturalistic book carries pessimism within him; he will draw the same conclusion from his experience of life. If it is the book itself which forcefully imposes this conclusion upon us, then the book may be either good or bad, but it is not in this respect naturalistic. To depict the misery of life is not to be a pessimist. A realization that there is much sorrow in the world is perhaps the result of exact observation.

Naturalism is not an exclusive, closed doctrine, as many say: it does not rule out other tendencies. It is rather a literary opportunism; it believes modestly that the literature which is most suited to modern life is the kind it champions. Naturalism does not absolutely condemn the good works which may be called idealistic; it does condemn idealism as a literary doctrine because the latter denies it the right to existence.

Naturalism is not a collection of rules for writing novels, as many unwary people have thought. Although it denies the chimerical abstractions of a kind of aesthetic psychology which speaks of myths of inspiration, afflatus, genius, rapture, artistic disorder and other sometimes immoral inventions; although it concedes much to the forces of work, good sense, reflection, and study, it is far from denying to the foolish the right of turning themselves into artists or of entering its temple. All who wish to do so may come to naturalism at any time but in this rite Mass is not sung by any comer; the faithful listen and are silent. This is forgotten, or not known, by many gentlemen, who, having grasped hastily and ill what the new literary movement demands, join and start writing novels, full of good intentions and disposed to follow the dogma and the discipline of naturalism in everything. But *fides sine operibus nulla est.* Among these authors there are those who have it in mind to count the stars and all the grains of sand in the sea in order to write the perfect naturalistic work. Naturalistic novels with maps have already been written; and there is sure to be someone who will plan a political novel, naturalistic as well, in which with the idea of making the protagonist a deputy he will set down the electoral laws and the census. It is too bad that such aberrations are not merely excesses of ingenuity, but are also the product of fawning mediocrities who, thanks to the freedom of social intercourse, think that, having rubbed shoulders everywhere with men of talent, even to the point of talking to them, they may dare undertake the same enterprises.

Now it is time to stop talking about naturalism and to speak of the illustrious writer who defends it in so masterly a way, though not without many reservations arising from the confusions I have already referred to.

There is no need for me to extol the merits of Emilia Pardo Bazán, for they are well known. I shall set them down simply as an indication of the great value of her vote on the *burning question.* There are still those who deny women the right to be writers. Indeed, women who write badly are not very agreeable, but the same is true of men. In Spain, it must be confessed, women who write poetry and prose ordinarily do not do a good job of it. Even today there are many women who write for the public who are so many calamities for literature, in spite of which I kiss their feet. Even of those whom a certain part of the public praises I would be able to say only offensive words, if I were forced to express myself. In my opinion there are two Spanish women writers who are the glorious exception to this unhappy general rule; I refer to the illustrious and never sufficiently praised Doña Concepción Arenal and to the lady who wrote *La cuestión palpitante.*

The Spanish woman of letters is usually no better educated than the Spanish woman who is unconcerned with literature: she gives everything over to imagination and feeling and tries to supplement talent by tender emotion. The worst of it is that these lady writers do not always follow the moral precepts which they teach any better than ordinary women. Emilia Pardo Bazán, who is cautious in her exercise of imagination, has cultivated the sciences and the

What Naturalism Is Not

arts and is learned in many matters and speaks five or six living languages. Proof that she studies much and thinks well is to be found in her historical-philosophical works, such as the memoir on Feijóo, her examination of the Christian epics, her book on St. Francis, and many others. Her novels *Pascual López* and *Un viaje de novios* are the principal spokesmen for the strength of her imagination. This last work has given its author a place among the leading novelists of the current renascence. But in *La cuestión palpitante* Señora Pardo Bazán undertakes a road that has never been followed by our women of letters: that of contemporary criticism. And in what fashion! with what courage! A profound, sincere, impartial spirit, without bias, without feeling any need to play a role in the comedy of that literature that calls itself classical, Emilia Pardo by studying what today is called literary naturalism, both in her own novels and in the works of criticism that set forth her doctrines, forces us to recognize that there is something new asking for a just evaluation, something of value which is condemned with mannered disdain and without examination by so many cloying and indolent men of letters who think only of savoring the crumbs of glory or vainglory which the public grants them out of kindly generosity.

It is sad to think that in Spain good faith and sincerity hardly appear in literature. The same affectation customarily found in the style and composition of works of the imagination is present in thought and feeling: people think ready-made thoughts just as they speak ready-made phrases. And there is no one to hoot pitilessly at the vanity of academics who affect the uniform of men of letters, or ridicule them with crushing satire. Literature thus becomes the toy of children and the recipient of senile dotage. Naturalism has been received here with the ostentation of ignorance and the rudeness of ill-reared grandees, with that disdain which those who boast of noble descent show toward talent without a pedigree. One critic has gone so far as to tell us that we are enthusiastic over naturalism because . . . we have read so little! That none of this is new, that there were naturalists in Greece, or indeed in China, that everything is natural without ceasing to be ideal, and vice versa, and that the best thing to do is to admire nothing in literature.

La cuestión palpitante shows that there is someone in Spain to-day who has read widely and thought a great deal and still recognizes that naturalism is right in many respects and seeks necessary reforms in literature to make it accord with the spirit of the age.

Emilia Pardo is a Catholic, a sincerely religious woman; she loves classical literature; she fervently studies the periods of our beautiful national romantic literature, and yet she is aware, because she sees clearly, that naturalism has made an opportune and timely appearance. Such and such a theory of a given author may have to be combated; a given novelist may have to be condemned for exaggeration or systematic spirit, but to deny that naturalism is a ferment which works for the good of literature is absurd, is to fly in the face of the evidence.

The sympathetic, courageous, and highly discreet author of this book is aware of what she is letting herself in for by publishing it. I know even more about it: I know that there are those who will pour on her, even though she is a woman, all the brutality of aroused ill-feeling; I know that they will not pardon her for working so effectively as propagandist for a critical position, that she will alienate many admirers of certain wilted flowers that pass for jewels of our contemporary literature. This does not matter. The older literature, that still wears knee-breeches on solemn occasions and dances a sort of minuet at *receptions* and *baptisms* of those it admits to its academies, has a right to the follies of senility. Our pseudo-classical writers, who pass their lives rubbing and shining the rust of the language, remind me of a certain poor old woman in a famous contemporary novel. Having lost her mind, she has a mania for cleanliness and does nothing but rub chains and trinkets until they shine as spotless as the sun. Our *classical* men of letters, yesterday's romantics, sigh out their longing for a badly understood idealism and, lacking the talent to say anything new, amuse themselves by shining up their jewels of yesteryear and cleaning them over and over again like the poor old woman. May they rest in peace!

Saddest of all is the fact that some of the young, desiring to inherit little niches in the academic world, praise these maniacs, turn up their noses at the new, and keep turning over old papers—while reading Zola in translation!

What Naturalism Is Not

Having viewed such a miserable state of affairs, how can we fail to admire and praise with enthusiasm one who disdains the flattery that seduces others and dares to provoke such rancor, to go against so many prejudices, and to suffer so many rebuffs, sacrificing everything to truth and sincerity of taste, a virtue which in this country is confused with bad tone and even with ill-breeding?

You decadent *aesthetes*, who divide everything into three parts, and do not read novels, and then speak of objective and subjective literature as though you were saying something; you insipid pseudo-classicists, who do not understand why the world does not admire your verses to Phyllis and Amaryllis and scorn the modern French authors because they are full of gallicisms; you badly paid reviewers, who translate the Sarceys, Vérons, and Brunetières and send these bits to Spain in your *Paris Letters*, without taking into account the rancors, revenges, and envies of these critics, who are idealists but by no means ideal; you metaphysical hack-writers, extemporizing men of erudition, shoddy imitators, reckless apostles, disoriented novelists, creaking dramatists . . . read, read all of *La cuestión palpitante*, so that you might learn something and (what is more important) perhaps forget your preconceptions, your pedantry, your blind anger, your tenacity in error, your injustice, your impudence, and your sordid calculation.

Some newspaper, which the visionary considers *idealistic*, will say of this book "that it is an effort to stir up a vigorous polemic about literature."

Would that it were so! But no. In Spain neither books nor lampoons arouse polemics.

What the book will arouse is much quiet rancor.

Here men of letters of any importance are not accustomed to discussion. They prefer to take vengeance by skinning the enemy aloud.

I should add that what will be most irritating to many is not the defense of certain doctrines but the praise of certain persons.

Would that what I say in behalf of Emilia Pardo Bazán might give certain male and female writers a deadly case of jaundice— all those writers of the weak sex, since in literary envy there is always something of the *eternal feminine!*

"The New Naturalism"*

By W. S. Lilly

THIS REVIEW, which appeared in the *Fortnightly Review* for August
1, 1885, is an almost perfect example of the stereotyped thinking with
which the claims of the new literature were met in England and the
United States, and for that matter in the rest of the western world.
It begins with prejudice and recounts with irony, never meeting the
innovating doctrines on their own grounds. The red herring of vivisection which the author draws across the trail would be a show-piece
of the irrelevant if it were not for the limitations of understanding
which it reveals.

The appeal is largely to emotion, to fear that the foundations of
civilization are endangered: when the ideal is slain a mortal stroke
has been given the moral life of the world. For example, "What M.
Zola inherits from Diderot is the dogma that there is nothing sacred
in man or in the universe, and the nauseous bestiality which is the
outcome of that persuasion." Or the new naturalism is characterized
as "the most popular literary outcome of the doctrine which denies the
personality, liberty, and spirituality of man and the objective foundation on which these rest, which empties him of the moral sense, the
feeling of the infinite, the aspiration towards the Absolute, which makes
of him nothing more than a sequence of action and reaction, and the
first and last word of which is sensism." It is but a step from these
inflammatory words to the enflamed action of the National Vigilance
Committee.

◇◇◇

IN THE month of February, 1881, the Ambigu Theatre in Paris
was the scene of what an enthusiastic spectator pronounced to be
the highest effort as yet made by Naturalism in the dramatic art.
The piece represented was M. Zola's *Nana*, adapted for the stage
by M. Busnach. The aim of the playwright had been to put the
story of the courtesan's life and death before the audience with
complete "reality." For this purpose the resources of the stage
decorator had been taxed to the utmost, the result being nine
tableaux, beyond which, it was proudly contended, the force of
scenic illusion could no further go. The first exhibited a *cabinet de*

---

*Lilly, W. S., "The New Naturalism," *Fortnightly Review* 38: pp. 240-256,
August 1, 1885.

toilette, where the heroine was revealed to us "au saut du lit, décoiffée, en peignoir de damas foncé sur une jupe de satin rose." The second introduced us to the *salon* of a great lady, much commended by my admiring friend as a marvellous reproduction. Not less marvellous was the third *tableau*, which took us behind the scenes of the *Théâtre des Variétés*; while the fourth, which presented the ruins of Chaumont, with the paths winding through the vines, the rustic bridge over a stream of real water in which a real man fell—happily he was clad in mackintosh underneath—to say nothing of artificial sunlight and an artificial nightingale, excited the spectators to almost lyrical enthusiasm, and was with one voice glorified as of a quite adorable poetry. Next came a drawing-room furnished *à la japonaise*, a species of upholstery just then in the height of fashion; after that a racecourse with real horses, and then a boudoir hung with real blue satin. In the eighth *tableau* a noble town house was burnt to the ground before our eyes. The ninth and last was a perfect copy of a room at the *Grand Hôtel*, in which Nana lay dying of confluent small-pox. Yes, there she lay, "un tas d'humeur et de sang, une pelletée de chair corrompue"; and the thrill of horror which rang through the house bore witness to the fidelity with which the "marchands de maquillage," aided by the doctors of the theatre, had imitated the ravages of the dire disease. Such was the realistic representation of the harlot's progress wherewith our eyes were feasted. The dialogue, judiciously adapted from the pages of M. Zola's fiction, was a fitting accompaniment to it. Of course nothing savouring of imagination or sentiment was uttered by any of the *dramatis personae*. Reality was the great law which the playwright proposed to follow, and it is not exactly imagination or sentiment that seasons the talk of the *lupanar*. "On s'ennuyait à crever," observes M. Zola, in his account of a famous supper given by his heroine. M. Busnach, in this respect, as in others, had kept faithfully to his original. It seemed to me, indeed, that both the master and the disciple had here somewhat overshot their mark. I thought of Dr. Johnson's account of Thomas Sheridan: "Why, sir, Sherry is dull, naturally dull. But it must have taken him a great deal of pains to have become what we now see him. Such an excess of stupidity, sir, is not in nature." The utter inanity of the piece was relieved only by a few cynical speeches—

"mots raides" they are called in the jargon of the day—put for the most part, if my memory is not at fault, into the mouth of Nana's *bonne*. This is one of them which may serve as a specimen of the rest. "Elle n'est donc plus au théâtre, Nana?" some one asks her. And she replies, "Non, le théâtre, c'est bon quand on commence; après, ça fait perdre trop de temps."

M. Zola, I believe, regards *Nana* as his masterpiece, and only the other day he warmly expressed his unbounded admiration of his friend's dramatic version. "Ce rôle de Nana," he writes, "est superbe, car il tient tout le clavier humain." I do not propose just now to discuss the value of this estimate. I wish rather to consider what is the significance of the movement of which *Nana*, whether in the original form of a novel or in M. Busnach's theatrical adaptation, may be taken as a typical instance. It has received the name of the New Naturalism, and it is very widely spread. M. Zola and his disciples unquestionably constitute the most popular school of contemporary French fiction. And Italy in this, as in most other things, servilely copies the fashion of France. In both countries the dramatic stage has for years been more and more given over to *costumiers*, mechanicians, and others whose function it is to speak to the eye. In both, as was recently stated by a caterer of theatrical amusements who well knew his business, "l'idéal de jambes est très recherché." It is an "ideal" which appears to be much in request with the British public also. "I am a dealer in legs" is said to have been the account of himself given by one of the most successful of our London managers, whose candour at all events is respectable. English fiction too, if it has produced nothing which can rival M. Zola's compositions, has at least shown more than a tendency to imitate them from afar. And translations of that author's most characteristic works have been published in periodicals which, I am informed, are largely read. The New Naturalism, then, whatever our feelings towards it may be, is well worthy of the attention of the student of man and society. And as M. Zola is confessedly its great luminary—"Zola, comme un soleil en nos ans a paru"—it will be well in the first instance to consider the account of it which that master has provided in his volume *Le Roman Expérimental*.

The great aim and object of the New Naturalism, according to M. Zola, is a return to nature. The novelist, the dramatist, he says,

"The New Naturalism"

ought to be the photographers of phenomena. Their business is to study the world—to observe, to analyse humanity as they find it. But this is best done in its most vulgar types. The human animal —"la bête humaine," a phrase which our author employs with damnable iteration—is the same in all social varieties and conditions. Look at the revelations which sensational trials occasionally make of the highest classes, showing how little they, in truth, differ in their ethos from the lowest. Everywhere at the bottom there is filth (*l'ordure*). Those proceedings in the courts of justice which from time to time bring it to the surface—like an abscess—are merely an experimental novel unfolding itself, chapter after chapter, before the public. Now the business of the novelist or the dramatist is to do scientifically what is there done fortuitously. He should display the real mechanism of life. A simple monograph, a page of existence, the story of a single fact, such is what the novel and the play are more and more becoming. The artist in experimental fiction is, apart from questions of style and form, merely a specialist, a *savant* who employs the same instruments as other *savants*, observation and analysis. His domain is that of the physiologist. Only it is more vast. To be master of the mechanism of human phenomena, to exhibit the machinery (*les rouages*) of intellectual and sensual manifestations, as physiology shall explain them, under the influences of heredity and environment, then to show the living man in the social order which he has himself produced, which he daily modifies, and in the bosom of which he undergoes a constant transformation—such is the theory of the experimental novel. In like manner the experimental drama must be a material evocation of life on the stage; and who can now doubt the possibility of effecting this by the art of the scene-painter and the upholsterer? No: "après les décors si puissants de relief, si surprenants de vérité" (possibly M. Zola was thinking of the nine *tableaux* in *Nana* which I have described) "on ne peut nier la possibilité d'évoquer à la scène la réalité des milieux." So too the language must be real—the language of the street—*un morceau de rue*. The old notion of a style differing from that of common life, more sonorous, more nervous, more highly pitched, more finely cut, is an abomination to M. Zola, and it must be allowed that he scrupulously avoids it. With equal care he eschews idealism and poetry, which he calls lyricism, and of which, he tells us, literature is "rotting." Invention must be used as sparingly as possible and confined to the plot, which, however, is to be scrupulously kept within the limits of every-day life. The rest he will have to be mere copying—a transcript of facts. Formerly the greatest compliment you could pay a novelist or playwright was to say, "He has a great deal of imagination." If such a speech were addressed to M. Zola he would regard himself as a very ill-used gentleman.

Such, in M. Zola's own words, is the theory of the novelistic and dramatic art, as of all other art, presented to us by the New Naturalism. It may be worth while before we go further to see how the matter was judged of by the Old. To do this effectually I shall have to touch upon a grave subject which will take us into a very different sphere from that tenanted by Nana and her company; for here, as in most other controversies, if we follow them far enough, the issue turns upon a question of philosophy. There is nothing new in M. Zola's contention that the novelist, the dramatist, and the worker in all other arts must conform to nature. Art is nothing but the minister, the interpreter of nature; its function to create the image and symbol of that which is. Further, all art is essentially one. The instruments of the painter, the sculptor, the musician, the poet—I use the last word in its widest literary sense—are diverse. Their aim is identical: to body forth by the brush, by the chisel, by the concord of sweet sounds, by ordered words, something which they discern "in the high reason of their fancies" more clearly than the multitude; and the value of their work is precisely in accordance with its truth. I do not know who has given more admirable expression to this great principle than Pope in his *Essay on Criticism*, that marvellous production of a boy of sixteen, which alone would furnish sufficient evidence of his transcendent genius.

> "First follow Nature, and your judgment frame
> By her just judgment, which is still the same.
> Unerring Nature, still divinely bright,
> One clear, unchanged, and universal light,
> Life, force, and beauty must to all impart,
> At once the source, and end, and test of art."

"The New Naturalism"

The Old Naturalism is at one, then, with the New in proposing conformity to nature as its great law. Where the two differ is in the meaning which they set upon the words "conformity to nature." Formerly men looked upon phenomena as the visible expression of an invisible reality. Thus to our Aryan ancestors the universe was no dead thing. Its substance was held to be intelligence. It was, to adapt Goethe's phrase, "the garment of life which the Deity wears." Its beauty, its bounty, its terror were revelations. The hymns wherein the rishis "sought out the thousand-branched mystery, through the vision of their hearts," were attributed to "the promptings of the thoughtful gods." So in ancient Hellas, the sense of the beautiful was the sense of the divine. The poetic gift was conceived of as inspiration. When Homer said, ἄειδε, θεά—"Sing, O goddess!"—he meant what he said. Visible loveliness was referred to an invisible type. Phidias was no mere copyist of phenomena; he worked from within. "Ipsius in mente insidebat species pulchritudinis eximia quaedam," Cicero well says. Again, Christianity, accentuating the conflict between the inferior instincts and the higher aspirations, between the spiritual and the material, and proclaiming the absolute supremacy of the soul, compelled even things of the contrary order to put on the semblance of the supersensuous. I need not dwell upon what is so familiar. Speaking generally we may say, that from the very dawn of the intellectual development of our race until the middle of the last century, men had looked upon external nature as a veil, a parable, a sacrament. The conviction that behind the world of form, of colour, of extension there is a reality of which phenomena are the shadows was the life of the Old Naturalism. And the function of art was conceived of as being the union of spiritual substance and material symbol. To eliminate the accidental, the transitory, the superfluous, to penetrate through innumerable vain details, that rank parasitic growth, "heavy as frost and deep almost as life," to find the type and to body it forth —such was the office of the artist. This view has been succinctly stated by Balzac in his profoundly philosophic study, *Le Chef-d'oeuvre Inconnu.* "The mission of art," he makes Maître Frenhofer say, "is not to copy nature, but to express it. We have to seize the spirit, the soul, the physiognomy of things. Effects! They are but the accidents of life, not life itself." But art was held to be life, to be idealised creation. And this in its latest form of the novel as much as in its earliest of painting. Springing into notice in the last century, romantic fiction has gradually taken a large place in the literature of our age as one, and perhaps the most distinctive, of its legitimate forms. It is, in fact, mainly a development of the drama. The modern novel might with strict accuracy be called an unacted play, and the modern play an acted novel. Both have been regarded as essentially works of imagination, and so as subject to the same great laws and immutable principles which rule throughout the whole domain of art. So much as to the difference between the Old and the New Naturalism. The one was poetical, and in dealing with the commonest realities of life was "quick to recognise the moral properties and scope of things," using sensible forms to body forth their inner significance. The other claims to be scientific, and declining to recognise in nature anything which cannot be analysed, or dissected, or vivisected, proposes as its object the study of the human animal—*la bête humaine*—subject to the action of its environment, the compulsion of heredity, the fatality of instinct. The one is dominated by the ideal, and in a true sense is, and cannot help being, religious. The other is strictly materialistic and frankly professes atheism. M. Zola is not surprised that "classicalists" and "romanticists" "drag him in the mud." "I quite see the reason," he writes. "It is because we deny their *bon Dieu*, we empty their heaven, we take no account of the ideal, we do not refer everything to that abstraction." Even the cult of beauty he repudiates as heartily as all other worship. It is "suspect" to him, as holding of Theism. "That religion," he tells us, "does not exist apart from the others. The pretended Beautiful, the Absolute Perfection, fixed according to a certain standard, is only the outward expression of the Deity that men dream of and adore"; which, to be sure, is true enough. Not less decisively does he cast aside ethical considerations. You have nothing to do with them, he tells his disciples. Sympathy with good or hatred of evil are as much out of place in your work as would be a chemist's anger against nitrogen as inimical to life, or his admiration of oxygen for a contrary reason. Your aim should be to produce a composition—he might have written decomposition—which logically classifies and correctly values the facts. His disciples have given heed to him. And when we consider the wide popularity enjoyed by him and them, it must be allowed that he has correctly apprehended and successfully interpreted a tendency of modern thought.

This, indeed, is the claim which he makes. And it is but fair to him—and will, moreover, be instructive—to hear his own apology for his method. I shall give it as I find it in his volume *Le Roman Expérimental*, and although I am obliged to compress into few words what he has said in many, he would, I feel sure, allow that my exposition does him no injustice. M. Zola holds, then, that the time in which we are living is essentially a New Age. Its spirit is "scientific." Now a civilisation is all of a piece (tout se tient dans une civilisation). The great movement of the last century was a vast inquiry—often nothing more than a groping—after reality; its effect being to state afresh the problems of human life and human society. Everywhere there has been a return to nature, to reality. In politics it has assumed the form of Democracy; in metaphysics of Positivism; in art of Naturalism. You may call it generally the Naturalistic Evolution. It means everywhere the banishment of sentiment, of imagination, of empirical doctrines, of poetic idealism; the recognition of facts cognisable by the senses, which are the only facts; and the adoption of the experimental method. Analysis and experience, the study of environment and mechanism —such is everywhere the course to be followed. The new democratic society is merely a collection of organised beings existing upon earth in certain conditions—of *bêtes humaines*, who know that they are human beasts, and do not pretend to be anything else, who are well aware that the old religious conceptions which regarded them as something else are cunningly devised fables. The republic, as it happily exists in France, is the best type of human government—*le gouvernement humain par excellence*—resting, as it does, upon universal suffrage, determined by the majority of facts, and so corresponding with the observed and analysed wants of the *bêtes humaines*, who make up the nation. Now every definitive and stable government must have a literature. And the New Naturalism supplies the fitting literature for this government, since it is the expression, in the intellectual domain, of the causes of which the Third Republic is the political and social outcome. Yes, he assures us, literature must become pathological or it will cease to exist. "Pathological?" does the reader exclaim? Even so. Literature in general, and in particular the novel and the drama. M. Zola has devoted a long, and, I must say, a very ingenious, essay to prove that the writer of fiction must follow the latest methods adopted by the student of experimental medicine. Art must disappear from the novel and the drama. The science of the vivisector is to take its place. In this way, he tells us, we shall arrive at practical sociology: our craft will become an auxiliary to the political and economical sciences. "I know of no labour," he adds, "more noble or of larger application. To be master of good and evil, to regulate society, to solve in the long run all the social problems, above all to furnish justice with solid foundations by determining experimentally questions of criminal law—is not that the most useful, the most moral, of human tasks?" Thus does he magnify his office. He disclaims, however, the honour of having introduced this new spirit into the novel and the drama. For his great forefather he claims Diderot, whom he accounts the most considerable figure of the eighteenth century, and very much in advance of it. One work of the *philosophes*, he thinks—a work to a great extent unconsciously executed—was to break up the old classical form of French literature, Voltaire, great destroyer as he was, being its last representative. Upon its ruins two new schools arose, the school of Diderot and the school of Rousseau, the latter essentially idealist, the former frankly positivist. Rousseau appears to him the literary ancestor of Madame de Staël, Victor Hugo, and George Sand. On the other hand, Stendhal and Balzac, Gustave Flaubert and himself, he regards as the literary successors of Diderot.

This is in substance M. Zola's apology for himself and his school. And it must be admitted that there is a great deal of truth in it. There is also a great deal which is not true. Thus I do not deny that M. Zola does in some sort represent the literary movement initiated by Diderot, and so may claim to be of his house and lineage. It has been said that the philosophy of Materialism always issues in mere filth. M. Zola furnishes a good illustration of the saying. Diderot, of course, was filthy enough, but he was something more. Sometimes the scintillations of his vast genius almost blind us to his obscenity. The Caliban of the eighteenth century, while his backward voice utters foul speeches in sad abundance, his forward voice discourses on occasion admirably well. Take for example his famous dictum which strikes at the root of M. Zola's doctrine of art: "Il faut que l'artiste ait dans son imagination quelque chose d'ultérieur à la nature." What M. Zola inherits from Diderot is the dogma that there is nothing sacred in man or in the universe, and the nauseous bestiality which is the outcome of that persuasion. His claim to number Stendhal and Gustave Flaubert among the prophets of experimental fiction appears to me to rest upon an even slenderer foundation. M. Zola professes to be nothing but a physiologist. Now, Stendhal was anything but a physiologist. M. Taine has well pointed out that sentiments, traits of character, vicissitudes of the soul, in a word, psychology, constituted the domain in which he worked. Again, how little Flaubert can be brought within the experimental formula is forcibly shown by a recent writer. "He has been represented as a realist, a naturalist," we read in M. du Camp's *Souvenirs*. "There are those who have sought to see in him a literary surgeon, dissecting the passions and making a kind of *post mortem* of the human heart. He was the first to shrug his shoulders at this sort of thing. He was in truth a poet (*un lyrique*)." Yes, a poet; not indeed of a high order, for of the deepest founts of inspiration he never drank; but a great master of literary form, which he was wont to account the whole secret of his art. And what shall we say of M. Zola's attempt to shelter himself and his method under the name of Balzac? He tells us, "Balzac was the great master of the real." True; the greatest certainly in the literature of France. But there is all the difference in the world between M. Zola's unimaginative realism and Balzac's imaginative reality. Balzac is no mere copyist from the streets. To him, as to every artist worthy of the name, the living model is a means, not an end; and he was, primarily and before all else an artist, ever working in the spirit of his own dictum that art is idealised creation. An artist is one who reproduces the world in his own image and likeness. And in the *Comédie Humaine* we have a colossal fresco in which the society of the first half of the century is painted for us with pitiless accuracy and terrible pathos as by the brush of Michael Angelo—a Titanesque work, described with equal grandeur and truth by Victor Hugo in his superb funeral oration on its author as "livre vivant, lumineux, profond, où l'on voit aller et venir, et marcher, et se mouvoir, avec je ne sais quoi d'effaré et de terrible, mêlé au réel, toute notre civilisation contemporaine; livre qui est l'observation et qui est l'imagination; et qui par moments, à travers toutes les réalités brusquement et largement déchirées, laisse tout à coup entrevoir le plus sombre et le plus tragique idéal." Like the great Florentine, Balzac was indeed an anatomist, and owed his vast technical skill to dissection; and, like him, he parades his science too much. But where the scalpel has destroyed, his brush recreates; and with what accuracy of detail, what force of conception, what depth of colour, what prophetic divination! His figures present that almost perfect union of type with character which is the highest note of the poet. They are instinct with life; they become to us, as they were to him, more real than the men and women of the phenomenal world; and no wonder, for genius holds of the noumenal. I know, and I by no means seek to extenuate, the blots which disfigure the work of this incomparable master. The ideal with him too often falls into the mud. King as he is among French artists in romantic fiction, his royal robes cover a cancer at the heart. M. Zola is wholly eaten up by that cancerous taint. Above the mud he never rises; it is his native element. So much has he in common with the author of the *Comédie Humaine*. "L'imagination de Balzac m'irrite," he complains. No wonder. But it is precisely that rich and puissant imagination which specially marks off Balzac from the "experimental" school. M. Zola seems, indeed, to have caught a glimpse of this verity. "Peut-être," he writes, "si Balzac pourrait nous lire, nous renierait-t-il" :—

> "Thus he, for then a ray of reason stole
> Half through the solid darkness of his soul."

M. Zola's literary pedigree must then, I think, be pronounced for the most part spurious. But the parallel which he has drawn between his school in literature and the school in medicine of which Claude Bernard was the great light, appears to be fair enough. The attempt to determine ethical and jurisprudential problems by means of physiological fiction seems entitled to precisely the same amount of respect as the attempt to discover the secrets of physical life by torturing animals in a physiological laboratory. The theory of the vivisectionist, succinctly stated, amounts to this, that by the observation of symptoms artificially produced in sound animal organisms, we may arrive at a knowledge of the causes of natural symptoms in unsound human organisms; for example, that by studying the phenomena of death by heat in a rabbit baked alive, we may understand the mechanism of febrile disturbances in a man. This theory obviously rests upon the confusion of two entirely different sciences, physiology, the science of healthy life, and pathology, the science of unhealthy states—a confusion which, in the words of the late Professor Bufalini, "has caused both science in general, and medicine in particular, the greatest evils, for it has blotted out the indirect treatment of disease and has extinguished the best method of diagnosis, substituting for it one which is perfectly arbitrary and conjectural." It is difficult to conceive of anything more senseless and unscientific than an attempt to interpret morbid states and morbid phenomena by physiological theories, to develop the laws of nature by mutilating the structure of conscient organic beings—every one of them an integral system of most complicated nervous network—to illustrate the modifications which spring up in a disease by processes which are foreign to natural influences. I say nothing of the confusion which also arises from the perfect dissimilarity between the functions and diseases of man and of the lower animals. But, indeed, the history of medicine is largely a history of human folly. Its so-called science in every age has consisted to a lamentable extent of mere aberrations from common sense. We live in an era of vivisection. And the voice of reason is as ineffectual against that ghastly shibboleth as it was against the vomiting of the emetic era, the evacuation of the purging era, the depletion of the bleeding era, the poisoning of the mercurial era and of the iodide of potassium era. Certain it is that the whole race of vivisectors, from the first until now, have not discovered one single agent for the cure of any malady, nor established any therapeutic fact or theory helpful in the smallest degree for the treatment of disease, nor contributed at all to the advance of scientific surgery. Certain it is that some of the most ferocious vivisections upon record—those, for example, of Dr. Bennett and Dr. Rutherford on the biliary secretion of the dog—have issued in mere fallacy and absurdity. Certain it is, as has been pointed out with great plainness of speech by Professor Koch, that the vast series of experiments in splenic fever performed by M. Pasteur have yielded results which are worse than valueless, so insufficient and so evanescent is the immunity against natural infection conferred by his preventive inoculation, and so grave are the dangers which it develops for man and other non-inoculated animals. And there is not the slightest reason for believing that the new vaccine of rabies, prepared in the laboratory of the same *savant*, by similar processes, will be one whit more efficacious. Nor let it be said that it is arrogant for a layman like myself to express so confident an opinion upon a matter lying within the domain of medicine and surgery. Here the question is of no esoteric mystery. It is purely of fact. And any mind trained to weigh and appreciate evidence according to the admirable rules followed in our courts of law is in a far better position to judge of it than a mind destitute of that discipline, warped by professional prejudices and fettered by medical etiquette. A practitioner who refuses the vivisection shibboleth is in great danger of being put out of the synagogue. And although, as I know well, there are many of his brethren who share the convictions of Mr. Lawson Tait, there are few who have shown the courage displayed by that eminent surgeon when three years ago he read before the Birmingham Philosophical Society his masterly paper—it may be perused in the third volume of the Society's *Transactions*—wherein, going through the specific claims made for vivisectional experiments as a means for the advancement of medical science, he demonstrated their hollowness and untenableness. The similar claims made by M. Zola for his experimental method in literature are just as empty; the results obtainable by his researches in the latrine and brothel are of precisely the same value as those which the vivisector derives from the torture trough. "The problem," M. Zola tells us, "is to know what a certain passion, acting in a certain environment, and in certain circumstances, will produce as regards the individual and society. And the way to solve it is to take the facts in nature, then to study their mechanism by bringing to bear upon them the modifications of circumstances and environments. Just as M. Claude Bernard transferred the experimental method from chemistry to medicine, so I transfer it from medicine to the drama and the novel." Quite so. And, we may add, as the vivisector confounds two distinct sciences, physiology and pathology, so does M. Zola confound two sciences as distinct, physiology and ethics. And as the vivisector, in the study of phenomena arbitrarily produced in certain organisms, seeks the explanation of natural phenomena in very different organisms, due to quite other causes, so does M. Zola take his types from one variety of the human species, place them in certain arbitrary conditions, mutilate them at his pleasure, and then pretend to draw from them conclusions as to the action of the passions in the lives of men. True it is that the experimental medicine of M. Paul Bert and the experimental morality of M. Zola are analogous. And true it is that they are both as false in theory, and as worthless and worse in results, as they are vile and debasing in practice. "Trahit sua quemque voluptas." Remonstrances are wasted upon the artist in filth or upon the artist in torture. Nor is it by any means the first time in the world's history that obscenity and cruelty—the natural, the inevitable results of Materialism—have sought to conceal their foul and hideous lineaments under the mask of science.

And now let us come to the main point of M. Zola's vindication of himself. He is but the poor minister of a great movement of the human intellect. The literary evolution of which his school is an instrument is merely part of a vast naturalistic transformation, that for a century has been remaking European society. In an age grown "scientific," the novel, the drama must become scientific too, and must keep to matter of fact and the needs and instincts of the *bête humaine*. "Nous avons tué l'idéal," says Massimilla Doni sadly, in Balzac's *Gambara*. Yes, exults M. Zola, we have killed the ideal; it is the great achievement of the age. For the future, in art, as in philosophy and politics, we must be altogether experimental and altogether materialist. Hence the literature which he provides supplies a want. He claims, as we have seen, that it is the only appropriate form of fiction for the Third Republic, and argues that the Third Republic will do well to recognise that truth, and to find in *Nana* the poetry of universal suffrage. The time has come, he says, to bring the Republic and literature face to face; to see what the one should expect from the other; to examine whether we, analysts, anatomists, collectors of human documents, *savants* who admit no authority but that of "fact," should find in the republicans of the present hour friends or enemies. For himself he does not doubt that the existence of the Third Republic is involved in the question. And, availing himself of the famous phrase of M. Thiers, he declares prophetically, "La République sera naturaliste ou elle ne sera pas." Whatever may be the value of M. Zola's vaticination, his contention that the fiction of his school is a popular literary expression of that movement which in the political order has issued in Jacobinism, seems to me unquestionably true. The spirit which exhibits Nana in all the foulness of her life and the horror of her death for the admiration of contemporary Paris, is the same which a century ago exalted a naked prostitute on the altar of Notre Dame as the living image of the Deity worshipped with human sacrifices in the Place de la Révolution. If we would apprehend the practical value of any idea we must consider it, not as expounded by the great masters, but as it lives and works in the minds of the common people. No system of philosophy which makes its way into credit is without influence upon the masses, absolutely unacquainted though they must necessarily be with its formal expression. Insensibly it descends among them, and modifies their instincts, their sentiments, their beliefs. We know that all matter is in constant flux, that, physically considered, we have nothing of our own. I have often thought that this may have its counterpart in the intellectual order. However that may be, the especial value of the writings of M. Zola and his school seems to me that they are the most popular literary outcome of the doctrine which denies the personality, liberty, and spirituality of man and the objective foundation on which these rest, which empties him of the moral sense, the feeling of the infinite, the aspiration towards the Absolute, which makes of him nothing more than a sequence of action and reaction, and the first and last word of which is sensism. Now, I am far from denying that this view of humanity may be presented—as a matter of fact it often has been—with great literary skill and adorned with graces not its own. M. Zola has done us this service; he has reduced it to its ultimate, its most vulgar resolution. He has supplied the most pregnant illustration known to me in literature that "the visible when it rests not upon the invisible becomes bestial."

The bestial, or something lower. I use the word with some reluctance, for it is unfair to the beasts. If we weigh the matter well, wherein lies the chief difference between civilised man and animals, human and other, beneath him in the scale of being? is it not in the power of apprehending more the bare phenomena, of perceiving the ideal? I say human or other; for I do not see how we can deny this perception altogether to non-human animals. Consider the religious ideal in the dog. Define religion how you will, as the sense of duty, the sense of reverence and love for one of a higher order, a blind sense of dependence, self-renunciation, consciousness of relationship to the worshipped object, the feeling of a dog for his master—who, as Lord Bacon says, is to him instead of a god or *melior natura*—answers to all these tests. This by the way. My present point is that the condition of advance in the scale of being is not merely or chiefly the subjugation of the external world, but emancipation from the tyranny of the senses: that the great criterion of elevation in the order of existence is whether the higher or lower self, to borrow a distinction from Aristotle, is dominant: the self of the appetites and passions, or the self of the reason and moral nature. The true law of progress is to

> "Move upwards, working out the beast,
> And let the ape and tiger die."

The New Naturalism does just the reverse of this. It eliminates from man all but the ape and tiger. It leaves of him nothing but the *bête humaine*, more subtle than any beast of the field, but cursed above all beasts of the field. It is beyond question—look at France if you want overwhelming demonstration of it—that the issue of what M. Zola calls the Naturalistic Evolution is the banishing from human life of all that gives it glory and honour: the victory of fact over principle, of mechanism over imagination, of appetites, dignified as rights, over duties, of sensation over intellect, of the belly over the heart, of fatalism over moral freedom, of brute force over justice, in a word, of matter over mind. Tell me not of its industrial triumphs in which Philistia finds a crown of rejoicing; think rather of the cost at which they are purchased. Emerson has said that there is something cruel in the aspect of any great mechanical work. Cruel indeed is the effect of machinery upon the working man. Consider how it destroys the elegance and pic-turesqueness of his labour; how it makes of him a mere "hand," a subordinate adjunct to a structure of wood and iron; how it con-demns him to a life-long servitude of weariness and disgust, with no scope for personal initiation, no field for the exercise of one faculty of the soul. This much-vaunted industrialism is largely materialism in its most ignominious form. It is that industry with-out art which Mr. Ruskin has well called brutality.

What, then, is the true mission of the artist in such an age as this? Surely not to merge art in physical science, which is its per-ceptual living contradiction; but in the midst of the ugly and sordid realities of daily life to present that image of a fairer and better world, the desire of which springs eternal in the human breast. Certain it is that the spirit of man cannot be long content with that which has not been touched and hallowed by the ideal. And surely as existence becomes more and more materialised, and glory and loveliness die away from it, and the sphere of mechanical necessity enlarges, and the kingdom of dulness rules among men, the mission of the artist will become of ever higher importance, of ever deeper sanctity, as the minister of the supersensuous, the transcendental, the eternal. Rightly has Schopenhauer conceived of the function of art—it is, perhaps, the most valuable part of his philosophy— as the deliverance of man from the chain of vulgar realities which binds us to this phenomenal world, by presenting the things that have true being, the permanent essential forms, immutable and ever true, the disinterested contemplation of which is as the shadow of a great rock in a weary land, the pure timeless subjects of knowl-edge independent of all relations; the revealing to us of the thing in itself, or, as I would venture to say after Plato, of Him who alone hath life and immortality in Himself. Such would seem to be the true mission of the artist, as at all times, so especially in this new age. And it holds of the novel and the play no less than of the higher departments of art. No less, but rather more. When Balzac or Thackeray, George Eliot or George Sand is the storyteller, we are all listeners, the wise and learned as well as the ignorant and foolish. But the writer of romantic fiction is especially the minister of the ideal to the multitude, who, as they gaze on the masterpieces of the painter and the sculptor, having eyes see not, who have no ears to hear the message of the poet, the philosopher, the musician. Mr. Carlyle scornfully abandons to him "children, minors, and semifatuous persons." Well, but, Mr. Carlyle himself being judge, children, minors, and semifatuous persons constitute the vast majority of "our own flesh and blood." "Twenty-five millions, chiefly fools!" Perhaps. Yet we may be quite sure that in the most foolish the heart does not exist that has never throbbed with a deep emotion, nor the intellect that has never harboured a true thought, nor the imagination that has never nursed a dream of beauty. In the dullest, the least cultivated, as in the most richly endowed and highly disciplined of our race, we may discern what the historian of Materialism confesses to be, "the same necessity, the same transcendental root of our nature, which leads us to fashion a world of the ideal, whither we may escape from the limitations of the senses, to find there the home of our spirit."

"The man of letters has a cure of souls," a great French writer has well said. This is particularly true of those who work in that department of romantic fiction, the influence of which in this age is so great and is ever increasing. It is their vocation to refine, to elevate, to moralise. And here comes in the essential difference between their function and that of the physicist. To physical science nothing is filthy or impure. The student in its domain takes all the facts and catalogues them in the order of their importance, reducing them to formulas. He deals with matter. Ethics is a sphere into which he does not enter. Far other is it with the writer of fiction. In the first place he is not concerned with all the facts. His work is essentially poetical, and the primary duty of the poet is choice, which is governed by those eternal laws, those necessary conventions ruling throughout the domain of art. The great ethical principles of reserve, shame, reverence, which have their endless applications in civilised life, prescribe limits to imagination as to action. There are moods of thought which do not yield in heinousness to the worst deeds—moods of madness, suicidal and polluting. To leave them in the dark is to help towards suppressing them. And this is a sacred duty. "We are bound to reticence," says George Eliot, "most of all by that reverence for the highest efforts of our common nature, which commands us to bury its lowest fatalities, its invincible remnants of the brute, its most agonizing struggles with temptation, in unbroken silence." The main theme of the novelist, the dramatist, is ever the passion of love—the most common, the most imperious of human sentiments. But love is not to him what it is to the physiologist—a mere animal impulse which man has in common with moths and mollusca. His task is to extract from human life, even in its commonest aspects, its most vulgar realities, what it contains of secret beauty; to lift it to the level of art, not to degrade art to its level. And so he is concerned with this most potent and universal instinct, as transformed, in greater or less degree, by the imaginative faculty; whether, dealing with it in its illicit manifestations, he exhibits it as the blight and bane of life, or depicts it in its pure and worthy expression—"the bulwark of patience, the tutor of honour, the perfectness of praise." His ethos comes out in the treatment of his subject rather than in his personnages, his plot, or his *dénouement*. It is easy to conceive of a work of fiction in which all the characters should be evil, but which should be severely ethical in its tone. An hour passed in Dante's Inferno does but intensify our longing to enter his Paradiso. Unquestionably this general canon may be laid down, that the depicting of deformity and evil is admissible only as it brings into stronger relief beauty and virtue; that when the sensuous impression overpowers the spiritual, we have a bad book. Certainly the drama or the novel of modern life must be true to life; it may not put darkness for light, nor light for darkness; it must represent the darkness and the light as they are. A work of imagination should not obtrude the moral sentiment. To employ it for the establishment of a thesis is fatally to pervert it from its true function. Flaubert was well warranted when he wrote, "Une oeuvre d'art qui cherche à prouver quelque chose est nulle par cela seul." Let the literary artist body forth things as they are in this confused drama of existence, subject only to the reservations which the essential laws of art impose. Those "bad good books," as they have been well called, which depict things as they are not, stand condemned by the first principle of literary ethics, for they are wanting in the primary condition of morality, which is truth. Balzac has profoundly observed, "Great works of imagination subsist by their

passionate side. But passion is excess, is evil. The writer has nobly
accomplished his task when, not putting aside this essential element
of all literary work, he accompanies it with a great lesson. The
really immoral book," he justly adds, "is that which saps the
bases of property, religion, justice"—in other words, which ignores
or denies the spiritual nature of men, whereon these essential foundations of civilisation rest. And he elsewhere sums the matter up
in the proposition that to moralise his epoch is the end which
every literary artist should propose to himself. How far this great
master contributed to moralise his epoch, how far he is open to
the impeachment that his virtue is after all but an obscene virtue,
are questions which must not detain us now. What I would insist
on is the great principle which he so well states that the true value
of any work of art is its ethical value, and that the measure of its
ethical value is its correspondence with the truth of things. But
the true is the ideal; the phenomenal is not the real, but its perpetual antithesis. A generation nourished on Kant should not need
to be reminded how pregnant is that old aphorism of Hellenic wisdom that the senses are very indifferent witnesses of truth; that
what meets them is merely an expression, adapted to our imperfect
apprehensive powers, of eternal verities, which eye hath not seen
nor ear heard, for they are beyond the reach of our limited per-
ceptive organs. Those verities are the true domain of the artist in
fiction as of all artists. He is essentially a psychologist; and it is precisely in the degree that the physiognomy, gestures, words, actions
of his characters interpret truly the innumerable sentiments which
make up the life of the soul that he is veracious; for the soul is the
great human reality; man's moral being is the dominant fact about
him. Balzac's piercing eyes discerned this truth clearly enough;
and he has formulated it with admirable succinctness in the introduction to the *Comédie Humaine*: "Un roman a pour loi de tendre
vers le beau idéal." Yes; this is the great law of romantic fiction.
The ultimate test in judging of it ever is, whether there is any
high thought, any true ideal, which serves as the centre of the
fable and informs the composition. If, and in so far as, there is, it
may be pronounced artistic, ethical, true. And here M. Zola's
"masterpiece" shall help me to a comparison which will serve to
illustrate my meaning and to conclude this paper. In *Nana* there

is not a vestige of the *beau idéal*. Blank and crude materialism, the trivial, the foul, the base of animal life, is the staple of the book from beginning to end. The heroine, whose *rôle* M. Zola deems to embrace the whole keyboard of human existence, is "a beast, no more," indeed, rather less. Even her affection for her child is merely the instinct of a beast, and not so pure or touching as the devotion of a bitch to its puppies. A movement of prurient curiosity, a spasm of concupiscence, a thrill of physical horror—these are the highest emotions which the book excites. That such literature can possess the slightest interest for any one who has not sunk to Nana's spiritual level is inconceivable; and herein is the appalling significance of its popularity. And now turn to another work of French fiction which in many respects offers a close parallel to *Nana*: I mean the *Dame aux Camélias*. Here, too, the heroine is a courtesan, and the author has placed her before us with rigorous realism, in all the ignominy of her life and the tragedy of her death, nay, in all the loathsome horror of a two months' burial. Here, too, are details in sad abundance, repulsive, I do not say to delicacy, but to decency, the author, true to the tradition of uncleanness so firmly established in France, not shrinking from minute description of things which it is a shame even to speak of. Still, with whatever reservations, the *Dame aux Camélias* is a work of art, not a mere obscene photograph. Why? Because it is informed by a true ideal. In spite of Marguerite's shameful trade—and the shame of it can be no more vividly painted than she has herself painted it—there is still an ethical element in her. The wants and impulses of the *bête humaine* have not quite killed her soul. She is yet capable of generosity, of self-sacrifice, of morality; for what is morality but the victory of the higher self over the lower? It is this that, in some sort, redeems the book in which her story is told, in spite of its crudity and grossness and hideousness. So far as it is informed by this ideal, so far does it conform to the great law which rules in art, and in the world of which art is the counterfeit presentment. It is the ideal which keeps the world from putrefaction. Slay it, and you have dealt a mortal stroke at the world's moral life. But that is an achievement beyond the power of the Naturalistic Evolution:

"The New Naturalism"

"For it is, as the air, invulnerable,
  And our vain blows malicious mockery."

It manifests itself to our reason as the law of things. And in its power to draw the hearts of men—a power far transcending any possessed by the highest truths sought out by physical science—it bears witness to the divine in man; it bears witness to itself as a pathway into the transcendental, the noumenal, the only real.

"A Typical Novel"*

By Hamilton Wright Mabie

IN AN AGE when American periodicals headlined their reviews of novels as "Zola's Stinkpot" or "A Filthy Book" the temperate tone and judicious analysis of Hamilton Wright Mabie (1845-1916) comes as a great relief. As a man of letters he belonged to the Genteel Tradition and was bound to repudiate all that naturalism stood for on grounds of both taste and spiritual view. In 1879 he joined the staff of the *Christian Union*, which later became the *Outlook*, and after a term as literary editor, he held the post of associate editor until his death. For a time he was also a contributing editor of the *Ladies' Home Journal* and was one of the editors of the Library of the World's Best Literature. His writing consisted of stories for children and many inspirational discussions of major works and authors of the past.

The essay here reprinted appeared in the *Andover Review* for November 1885. It is noteworthy, first, for its bracketing of Howells and Henry James as exemplars of realistic writing and proof of the lack of vitalizing imagination which characterizes that school. More important is his belief that the new and "theoretical realism of the day" raises issues which go "to the very bottom of our conceptions of life and art." It challenges the traditional idea of art as revelation, and so undermines the time-honored view of the world that it may be called "practical atheism applied to art." Both views are cogently stated and stand as admirable expressions of the aesthetic and moral views against which the realists were determined to prevail.

◇◇

IN "The Rise of Silas Lapham" Mr. Howells has given us his best and his most characteristic work; none of his earlier stories discloses so clearly the quality and resources of his gift or his conception of the novelist's art. As an expression of personal power and as a type of the dominant school of contemporary fiction in this country and in France, whence the special impulse of recent realism has come, this latest work of a very accomplished and conscientious writer deserves the most careful and dispassionate study. If Mr. Howells's work possessed no higher claim upon attention, its evident fidelity to a constantly advancing ideal of workmanship

* Mabie, Hamilton Wright, "A Typical Novel," *Andover Review* 4: pp. 417-429, November 1885.

would command genuine respect and admiration; whatever else one misses in it, there is no lack of the earnestness which concentrates a man's full power on the thing in hand, nor of the sensitive literary conscience which permits no relaxation of strength on subordinate parts, but exacts in every detail the skill and care which are lavished on the most critical unfoldings of plot or disclosures of character. Mr. Howells evidently leaves nothing to the chance suggestion of an inspired moment, and takes nothing for granted; he verifies every insight by observation, fortifies every general statement by careful study of facts, and puts his whole force into every detail of his work. In spite of its evident danger in any save the strongest hands, there is a tonic quality in this exacting conscientiousness which writers of a different school often lack, and the absence of which is betrayed by hasty, unbalanced, and incomplete workmanship. It is this quality which discovers itself more and more distinctly in Mr. Howells's novels in a constant development of native gifts, a stronger grasp of facts, and a more comprehensive dealing with the problems of character and social life to which he has given attention. In fact, this popular novelist is giving thoughtful readers of his books a kind of inspiration in the quiet but resolute progress of his gift and his art; a progress stimulated, no doubt, by success, but made possible and constant by fidelity to a high and disinterested ideal.

Nor has Mr. Howells spent his whole force on mere workmanship; he has made a no less strenuous endeavor to enlarge his knowledge of life, his grasp of its complicated problems, his insight into the forces and impulses which are the sources of action and character. If he has failed to touch the deepest issues, and to lay bare the more obscure and subtle movements of passion and purpose, it has been through no intellectual willfulness or lassitude; he has patiently and unweariedly followed such clews as he has been able to discover, and he has resolutely held himself open to the claims of new themes and the revelations of fresh contacts with life. The limitations of his work are also the limitations of his insight and his imagination, and this fact, fully understood in all its bearing, makes any effort to point out those limitations ungracious in appearance and distasteful in performance; if personal feeling were to control in such matters, one would content himself with an expression of hearty admiration for work so full of character, and of sincere gratitude for a delicate intellectual pleasure so varied and so sustained. The evidence of a deepened movement of thought is obvious to the most hasty backward glance from "The Rise of Silas Lapham" and "A Modern Instance" to "Their Wedding Journey" and "A Chance Acquaintance." In the early stories there is the lightness of touch, the diffused and delicate humor, which have never yet failed Mr. Howells; but there is little depth of sentiment, and almost no attempt to strike below the surface. These slight but very delightful tales discover the easy and graceful play of a force which deals with trifles as seriously as if it were handling the deepest and most significant problems of life. Seriousness is, indeed, the habitual mood of this novelist, and in his early stories it was the one prophetic element which they contained. There is a progressive evolution of power through "The Lady of the Aroostook," "The Undiscovered Country," "Dr. Breen's Practice," and "A Modern Instance"; each story in turn shows the novelist more intent upon his work, more resolute to hold his gift to its largest uses, more determined to see widely and deeply. His purpose grows steadily more serious, and his work gains correspondingly in substance and solidity. The problems of character which he sets before himself for solution become more complex and difficult, and, while there is nowhere a really decisive closing with life in a determined struggle to wring from it its secret, there is an evident purpose to grapple with realities and to keep in sympathy and touch with vital experiences.

In "The Rise of Silas Lapham" Mr. Howells has made a study of social conditions and contrasts everywhere present in society in this country; not, perhaps, so sharply defined elsewhere as in Boston, but to be discovered with more or less definiteness of outline in all our older communities. His quick instinct has fastened upon a stage of social evolution with which everybody is familiar and in which everybody is interested. The aspect of social life presented in this story is well-nigh universal; it is real, it is vital, and it is not without deep significance; in dealing with it Mr. Howells has approached actual life more nearly, touched it more deeply, and expressed it more strongly than in any of his previous stories. The skill of his earliest work loses nothing in his latest; it is less evident because it is more unconscious and, therefore, more genuine and effective. There is the same humor, restrained and held in check by the major interests of the story, but touching here and there an idiosyncrasy, an inconsistency, a weakness, with all the old pungency and charm; a humor which is, in fact, the most real and the most distinctive of all Mr. Howells's gifts. There is, also, stronger grasp of situations, bolder portraiture of character, more rapid and dramatic movement of narrative. Still more important is the fact that in this novel life is presented with more of dramatic dignity and completeness than in any of Mr. Howells's other stories; there is a truer and nobler movement of human nature in it; and the characters are far less superficial, inconsequential, and unimportant than their predecessors; if not the highest types, they have a certain force and dignity which make us respect them, and make it worth while to write about them. Add to these characterizations of "The Rise of Silas Lapham" the statement that Mr. Howells has never shown more complete mastery of his art in dealing with his materials; that his style has never had more simplicity and directness, more solidity and substance, and it will be conceded that the sum total of excellence which even a reader who dissents from its underlying conception and method discovers in this story is by no means inconsiderable; is, indeed, such as to entitle it to very high praise, and to give added permanence and expansion to a literary reputation which, from the standpoint of popularity at least, stood in small need of these things.

And yet, when all this has been said, and said heartily, it must be added that "The Rise of Silas Lapham" is an unsatisfactory story; defective in power, in reality, and in the vitalizing atmosphere of imagination. No one is absorbed by it, nor moved by it; one takes it up with pleasure, reads it with interest, and lays it down without regret. It throws no spell over us; creates no illusion for us, leaves us indifferent spectators of an entertaining drama of social life. The novelist wrote it in a cool, deliberate mood, and it leaves the reader cold when he has finished it. The appearance and action of life are in it, but not the warmth; the frame, the organism, are admirable, but the divine inbreathing which would have given the body a soul has been withheld. Everything that art could do has been done, but the vital spark has not been transmitted. Mr.

Howells never identifies himself with his characters; never becomes one with them in the vital fellowship and communion of the imagination; he constructs them with infinite patience and skill, but he never, for a moment, loses consciousness of his own individuality. He is cool and collected in all the emotional crises of his stories; indeed, it is often at such moments that one feels the presence of a diffused satire, as if the weakness of the men and women whom he is describing excited a little scorn in the critical mind of the novelist. The severest penalty of the persistent analytic mood is borne by the writer in the slight paralysis of feeling which comes upon him at the very moment when the pulse should beat a little faster of its own motion; in the subtle skepticism which pervades his work, unconsciously to himself, and like a slight frost takes the bloom off all fine emotions and actions. There are passages in Mr. Howells's stories in reading which one cannot repress a feeling of honest indignation at what is nothing more nor less than a refined parody of genuine feeling, sometimes of the most pathetic experience. Is Mr. Howells ashamed of life in its outcries of pain and regret? Does he shrink from these unpremeditated and unconventional revelations of character as vulgar, provincial, inartistic; or does he fail to comprehend them? Certainly the cool, skillful hand which lifts the curtain upon Silas Lapham's weakness and sorrows does not tremble for an instant with any contagious emotion; and whenever the reader begins to warm a little, a slight turn of satire, a cool phrase or two of analysis, a faint suggestion that the writer doubts whether it is worth while, clears the air again. Perhaps nothing more decisive on this point could be said of Mr. Howells's stories than that one can read them aloud without faltering at the most pathetic passages; the latent distrust of all strong feeling in them makes one a little shy of his own emotion.

This failure to close with the facts of life, to press one's heart against them as well as to pursue and penetrate them with one's thought; this lack of unforced and triumphant faith in the worth, the dignity, and the significance for art of human experience in its whole range; this failure of the imagination to bridge the chasm between the real and the fictitious reproduction of it, are simply fatal to all great and abiding work. Without faith, which is the very ground upon which the true artist stands; without love, which

"A Typical Novel"

is both inspiration and revelation to him, a true art is impossible. Without faith there would never have come out of the world of the imagination such figures as Jeanie Deans, Colonel Newcome, Eugénie Grandet, Père Goriot, and Hester Prynne; without love —large, warm, generous sympathy with all that life is and means —the secret of these noble creations would never have been disclosed. Mr. Howells and Daudet practice alike the art of a refined realism, but what a distance separates the Nabob from Silas Lapham! Daudet is false to his theory and true to his art; life touches him deeply, fills him with reverence, and he can no more rid himself of the imagination than he can part the light from the flower upon which it falls. The Nabob might have suggested a similar treatment of Silas Lapham. How tenderly, how reverently, with what a sense of pathos, through what a mist of tears, Daudet uncovers to us the weakness and sorrows of Jansoulet! The Nabob is always touched by a soft light from the novelist's heart; poor Silas Lapham shivers in a perpetual east wind. Imagine the "Vicar of Wakefield" treated in the same spirit, and the fatal defect of Mr. Howells's attitude towards life is apparent at a glance.

The disposition to treat life lightly and skeptically, to doubt its capacity for real and lasting achievement, to stand apart from it and study it coolly and in detail with dispassionate and scientific impartiality, is at bottom decisive evidence of lack of power; that is, of the dramatic power which alone is able to reproduce life in noble dramatic forms. A refined realism strives to make up in patience what it lacks in genius; to make observation do the work of insight; to make analysis take the place of synthesis of character, and "a more analytic consideration of the appearance of things" —to quote Mr. James—the place of a resolute and masterly grasp of characters and situations. The method of the realism illustrated in "The Rise of Silas Lapham" is external, and, so far as any strong grasp of life is concerned, necessarily superficial. It is an endeavor to enter into the recesses of character, and learn its secret, not by insight, the method of the imagination, but by observation, the method of science; and it is an endeavor to reproduce that character under the forms of art, not by identification with it, and the genuine and almost unconscious evolution which follows, but by skillful adjustment of traits, emotions, passions, and activities which are the result of studies more or less conscientiously carried on. The patience and work involved in the making of some novels constructed on this method are beyond praise; but they must not make us blind to the fact that no method can take the place of original power, and that genius in some form—faith, sympathy, insight, imagination—is absolutely essential in all true art. The hesitation, the repression of emotion, the absence of color, are significant, not of a noble restraint of power, a wise husbanding of resources for the critical moment and situation, but of a lack of the spontaneity and overflow of a great force. Ruskin finely says that when we stand before a true work of art we feel ourselves in the presence, not of a great effort, but of a great force. In most of the novels of realism it is the effort which impresses us, and not the power. In Turgénieff and Björnson, masters of the art of realism, and yet always superior to it, the repression and restraint are charged with power; one feels behind them an intensity of thought and feeling that is at times absolutely painful. No such sensation overtakes one in reading "The Rise of Silas Lapham" or "The Bostonians"; there is no throb of life here; the pulse of feeling, if it beats at all, is imperceptible; and of the free and joyous play of that supreme force which we call genius there is absolutely not one gleam. If either novelist possessed it, no method, however rigidly practiced, could wholly confine it; it would flame like lightning, as in Björnson, or suffuse and penetrate all things with latent heat, as in Turgénieff, or touch all life with a soft, poetic radiance, as in Daudet.

Mr. Howells has said, in substance, that realism is the only literary movement of the day which has any vitality in it, and certainly no one represents this tendency on its finer side more perfectly than himself. Its virtues and its defects are very clearly brought out in his work: its clearness of sight, its fixed adherence to fact, its reliance upon honest work; and, on the other hand, its hardness, its lack of vitality, its paralysis of the finer feelings and higher aspirations, its fundamental defect on the side of the imagination. Realism is crowding the world of fiction with commonplace people; people whom one would positively avoid coming in contact with in real life; people without native sweetness or strength, without acquired culture or accomplishment, without that

"A Typical Novel"

touch of the ideal which makes the commonplace significant and worthy of study. To the large, typical characters of the older novels has succeeded a generation of feeble, irresolute, unimportant men and women whose careers are of no moment to themselves, and wholly destitute of interest to us. The analysis of motives that were never worth an hour's serious study, the grave portraiture of frivolous, superficial, and often vulgar conceptions of life, the careful scrutiny of characters without force, beauty, aspiration, or any of the elements which touch and teach men, has become wearisome, and will sooner or later set in motion a powerful reaction. One cannot but regret such a comparative waste of delicate, and often genuine, art; it is as if Michael Angelo had given us the meaningless faces of the Roman fops of his time instead of the heads of Moses and Hercules.

It is certainly a mental or a moral disease which makes such trivial themes attractive to men of real talent. The "storm and stress" period returns at intervals, and, in spite of its extravagances of feeling, is respectable because of the real force and promise that are in it; one has a certain amount of patience with Werther, and with the hero of Schiller's "Robbers." But our modern misanthrope gropes feebly about for some clew to the mystery of his existence, and, not finding it ready to hand, snuffs out the flame of life in obedience, not to an honest conviction of the hopelessness of things, but because something goes wrong at the moment. Here is the modern hero skillfully displayed on a small canvas:—

"Vane walked up to Central Park, and returned to dress for dinner. Where was he to dine? The Club was the best place to meet people. His lodgings were dark, and he had some difficulty in finding a match; then he dropped one of his shirt-studs on the floor, and had to grope for it. Another one broke, and he threw open the drawer of his shaving-stand, impatiently, to find one to replace it. Lying in the drawer was an old revolver he had brought from Minnesota two years before. He took it out, placed the muzzle at his chest, and drew the trigger. As he fell to the floor, he turned over upon his side, holding up his hands before his eyes."

If such diseased and irresolute youths as Vane were the refuge of weak but ambitious writers groping for subjects with which to illustrate their own feebleness, there would be no significance in the fact; there is deep significance, however, in the fact that the man who wrote this story has genuine strength and skill. That such a character as Vane should attract such a writer, that Mr. James's stories should uniformly convey the impression, not of the tragic pathos of life, but of its general futility, that Mr. Howells should, for the most part, concern himself with men and women of very slender endowments and very superficial conceptions of life, are phenomena which lead us very directly to a conclusion somewhat similar to that reached by Mr. Stedman, after a survey of the present condition of poetry in this country, in his article on the "Twilight of the Poets" in a recent issue of the "Century Magazine." The work of the younger generation of American poets, in the judgment of this acute and accomplished critic, is full of the resources of a delicate art, and not without qualities of individual insight and imagination; but, as a whole, it lacks vigor, variety, grasp, and power. It is an interlude between the poetic activities of a generation now fast becoming silent and a generation not yet come to the moment of expression. Fiction has, however, a better outlook than poetry; there are already in the field novelists to whom life and art speak as of old with one voice, and who are illustrating under new forms those imperishable truths of character and destiny, the presence of which lifts the most obscure life into the realm of art, and the absence of which leaves life without a meaning, and devoid of all interest. It is very significant that realism either fails to grasp life firmly and present it powerfully, or else seizes upon its ignoble aspects; its vigor is mainly on the side of moral pathology.

The great name of Balzac is a word of power among the realists; and yet it is not easy to find in this master of fiction on a great scale either the principles or the method of the writers who profess to stand in direct line of succession from him. His realism was of that genuine order which underlies the noblest art of every age; it studies with most patient eye, and reproduces with most patient hand, the facts of life, in order that it may the more powerfully and the more faithfully discover the general law, the universal fact, which are the sole concern of art, behind them. The "more analytic consideration of the appearance of things" which one finds in Balzac is accompanied by a more powerful irradiation of the imagination. It is easy to understand Zola when he says "l'imagination de Balzac m'irrite"; it is just this imagination, this penetration of the real with the ideal, which makes the *Comédie Humaine* such a revelation of the age, such a marvelous reproduction of the complex life of the most complex epoch of history. The Naturalism of Zola, which is not psychological but physiological, which reduces life to its lowest factors, has little in common with the art of Balzac, which found all methods and facts inadequate for the complete illustration of the sublime, all-embracing fact of life. Naturalism is worthy of study, not only because of the great place it fills in contemporary literature, but because it is the logical result of realism, and, by exaggeration, makes the defects and limitations of realism more apparent.

The issue between the theoretical realism of the day and the older and eternal realism of fidelity to nature as the basis of all art is the more momentous because it is concealed in many cases by so much nice skill, and so much subtlety and refinement of talent. The divergence between the two is in the nature of a great gulf fixed in the very constitution of things; it goes to the very bottom of our conceptions of life and art. To see nature with clear eyes, and to reproduce nature with deep and genuine fidelity, is the common aim of the old and the new realism; the radical character of the difference between them is made clear by the fact that the realists of the new school deny the existence in nature of the things which the older realists have held to be deepest and truest. The new realism is not dissent from a particular method; it is a fundamental skepticism of the essential reality of the old ends and subjects of art. It strikes at the very root of the universal art growth of the world: adherence to its fundamental precepts would have made Greek art an impossibility; would have cut the ground from under Aeschylus, Sophocles, and Euripides; would have prevented the new growth of art and literature in the Renaissance; would have paralyzed the old English drama, the classical French drama, and the late but splendid flowering of the German genius from Lessing to Heine. If the truth lies with modern realism, we must discard all those masters by whom the generations have lived and died, and seek out other teachers and shrines. Realism writes failure and barrenness across the culture of the world as the hand once wrote a similar judgment on the walls of an Assyrian palace. Fortunately, the parallel fails at the vital point; it requires a stronger faith than realism is able to furnish to identify the inspiration of the modern and the ancient interpreter, to discover in Zola the successor of Daniel.

The older art of the world is based on the conception that life is at bottom a revelation; that human growth under all conditions has a spiritual law back of it; that human relations of all kinds have spiritual types behind them; and that the discovery of these universal facts, and the clear, noble embodiment of them in various forms, is the office of genius and the end of art. The unique quality of the Greek race lay in its power to make these universal, permanent elements of life controlling. This is the secret of its marvelous and imperishable influence upon the minds of men. This was the work for which it was so lavishly endowed with genius. The art instinct among the Greeks was so universal and so controlling that all individual thought, feeling, and living seemed to be a kind of transparent medium for the revelation of elements and qualities which are common to the race. What was personal, isolated, unrelated to universal life has largely disappeared, and there remains a revelation, not of Greek character, but of human life of unequaled range and perfection. Every great Greek character is a type as truly as every Greek statue; and it is the typical quality which lifts the whole race into the realm of art. But modern realism knows nothing of any revelation in human life; of any spiritual facts of which its facts are significant; of any spiritual laws to which they conform in the unbroken order of the Universe. It does more than ignore these things; it denies them. Under the conditions which it imposes art can see nothing but the isolated physical fact before it; there are no mysterious forces in the soil under it; there is no infinite blue heaven over it. It forms no part of a universal order; it discovers no common law; it can never be a type of a great class. It is, in a word, practical atheism applied to art. It not only empties the world of the Ideal, but, as Zola frankly says, it denies "the good God"; it dismisses the old heaven of aspiration and possible fulfillment as an idle dream; it destroys the significance of life and the interpretative quality of art.

Such was not the conception of the great Balzac. With characteristic acuteness and clearness he puts the whole issue in a paragraph: "A writer who placed before his mind the duty of exact reproduction might become a painter of human types more or less faithful, successful, courageous, and patient; he might be the annalist of the dramas of private life, the archaeologist of the social fabric, the sponsor of trades and professions, the registrar of good and evil. And yet to merit the applause at which all artists should aim, ought he not also to study the reasons—or the reason—of the conditions of social life; ought he not to seize the hidden meaning of this vast accretion of beings, of passions, of events? Finally, having sought—I will not say found—this reason, this social mainspring, is he not bound to study natural law, and *discover why and when Society approached or swerved away from the eternal principles of truth and beauty?*" And he adds, to the same end, "History does not, like the novel, hold up the law of a higher ideal. History is, or should be, the world as it has been; the novel—to use a saying of Madame Necker, one of the remarkable minds of the last century—*should paint a possible better world.*" Readers of Balzac do not need to be told that his work, defective as it is on the side of moral insight, is still a commanding interpretation of life because it penetrates through individual fact to the universal fact, and through particular instances to the common law. It is only when one sees clearly this denial of the spiritual side of life, and sees it in all its results, that one understands why Naturalism inevitably portrays the repellant, and a refined realism the superficial, aspects of life. In this pregnant fact lies the secret of its rigidity, its coldness, its inevitable barrenness. A natural method, a true and vital conception, are always capable of further expansion. Is there anything beyond Zola? He has pressed his theory so far that even his hottest adherents see no step left for another to take. The energetic Naturalist—a man of great force and splendid working power—has left his followers not a single fig leaf to be plucked off the shameless nudity of the "bête humaine"—the human animal—in the delineation of which he rivals the skill of Barye. It is equally difficult to imagine any further progress along the lines of a refined realism; it has brought us face to face with the hard, isolated facts of life, and, having discarded the only faculty that can penetrate those facts to their depths and set them in the large order of the higher reason, there remains nothing more to be done by it. Materialism in art reaches its limits so soon that it never really gets into the field at all.

This denial of the imagination, this effort to discard it entirely and banish it into the region of moribund superstitions, is at bottom a confession of weakness. It is the refuge of writers who have inherited the skill, but not the impulse, of the great literary creators, and who are driven, unconsciously no doubt, to adopt a theory of art which makes the most of their strength and demands the least of their weakness. It is a new illustration of the old tendency to elevate individual limitations into universal laws, and to make the art bend to the man rather than the man to the art. We need not concern ourselves about the imagination, as if any man, or body of men, could discard it, or, for any long time, even obscure it; the imagination may safely be left to care for itself; what we need to concern ourselves about is the fact that we are on the wrong road, and that men of genius, unconsciously mistaking the way along which the sign-boards have all been carefully misplaced, may lose time and heart in the struggle to free themselves from misleading aims. We are in great danger of coming to accept as work of the first order that which has no claim to any such distinction, and adopt as the standards of the noblest literary art the very delightful but very inadequate creations of some of our contemporary writers. It is always wisest to face the truth; if the poets of the time lack the qualities which go to the making of great singers, let us acknowledge the fact and make the best of it; if our realistic novelists are more skillful than powerful, more adroit and entertaining than original and inspiring, let us admit this fact also. But, in the name and for the sake of art, let us decline to accept these charming story-tellers as the peers of the great masters, and, above all, let us refuse to impose their individual limitations upon the great novelists of the future. "The Rise of Silas Lapham" and the novels of its class are additions to the literature of fiction for which we are grateful; but it is a great injustice to them and to their writers to insist upon placing them side by side with the great novels of the past.

What is needed now, in fiction as in poetry, is a revitalization of the imagination and a return to implicit and triumphant faith in it. The results of the scientific movement are misread by men of literary genius no less than by religious people; in the end, they will be found to serve the noblest uses of art no less than of religion. Their first effect is, indeed, to paralyze all superficial faiths and inspirations, by disturbing the order of facts upon which these rested, or from which they were derived; but, in the end, it will be found that the new order of the universe has under it a harmony of sublime conceptions such as no art has ever yet so much as dreamed of, and no religion ever yet grasped with clearness and certainty. Science not only leaves the imagination untouched, but adds indefinitely to the material with which it works. The more intelligent study of facts which it has made possible and inevitable purifies and enlarges in a corresponding degree the conceptions which underlie them, and will add in the end immeasurably to the scope and majesty of life. The hour is fast approaching for a new movement of the imagination; a new world awaits interpretation and reproduction in art at its hands. The first effects of the scientific tendency, evident in the uncertain note of contemporary poetry and the defective insight of realistic fiction, must not be mistaken for the final effects; it is this mistake which gives our poetry its elegiac note and our fiction its general confession of the futility of all things. Great works of art never come from hands afflicted with this kind of paralysis. The real outcome of the scientific spirit is something very different from the interpretation of realism; for its interpreters and prophets the time is fast approaching, and no blindness and faint-heartedness of this generation will delay their coming when the hour is ripe. They, too, will be realists as all the great artists have been; realists like Dante and Shakespeare; like Balzac and Thackeray; like the wise Goethe, who held resolutely to the fact because of the law behind it, who saw that the Real and the Ideal are one in the divine order of the universe, and whose clear glance into the appearance of things made him the more loyal to the Whole, the Good, and the True.

On Russian and French Realism*

By E.-M. de Vogüé

VICOMTE EUGÈNE-MELCHIOR DE VOGÜÉ (1848-1910) was secretary
at the French Embassy in St. Petersburg from 1876 to 1882. While
there he learned the Russian language, married a Russian wife, and
generally immersed himself in Russian culture, so that he became the
first important interpreter of that country to the West. As early as
1879 he wrote a review of the recently translated *War and Peace* for
the *Revue des Deux Mondes*. Between October 1883 and June 1886
he published six more general articles which were then reworked to
form *Le Roman russe*, published in the latter year.

This book caused a tremendous stir in intellectual circles and may
be considered of basic importance to the development of nineteenth-
century literature. Up until this time comparatively little was known
in France, or the rest of Europe, about the Russian novelists other than
Turgenev. It is true that Ernest Dupuy had published *Les Grands
Maîtres de la littérature russe* in 1885, but he omitted Pushkin and
Dostoevsky from his discussion and was not very probing in his study
of Gogol, Turgenev, and Tolstoy. Translations of Tolstoy's and Dostoevsky's works which had begun to appear in 1884 and 1885 were
received with little enthusiasm by the public. Vogüé's writings changed
all that. Over 20,000 copies of *War and Peace* were sold after the article on Tolstoy came out in 1884. The book itself produced a flood of
translations and a never-ending, though by no means unanimous, literary argument about the merits of the prodigious figures from the
East.

Even more important than the new territories which Vogüé opened
up to exploration was the polemic impact of the book. It was clearly
designed as a weapon against the regnant naturalism in France. Although an admirer of Taine and aware of the persuasiveness of posi-
tivistic thought, Vogüé was by his sympathies a traditionalist in religion, politics, and literature. Naturalism alarmed and affronted him
by its lack of any idealistic leavening; its preoccupation with the base
and the sordid seemed to him not only to degrade the individual
reader but to block the spiritual rebirth which defeated France must
undergo in order to reach greatness again. This is the argument of the
long preface (drawn from the concluding article in the series), which
has not previously been translated into English in its entirety.

* Vogüé, E.-M. de, "Préface," *Le Roman russe*, pp. vii-lv; Paris, Librairie
Plon, 1886.

On Russian and French Realism

In offering this book to the people, every day more numerous, who are interested in Russian literature, I owe them certain explanations about the object, the goal, and the voluntary gaps in these essays. The region in which we are going to travel is vast and barely explored; the whole has not yet been surveyed, a few roads have been cut through more or less at random; it is necessary to tell whoever undertakes this journey why it is our preference to visit such and such a province, why we ignore others.

In this volume he will not find a history of literature, a full, didactic treatise on the subject. Such a work does not yet exist in Russia and would be premature in France. I was tempted to do it, and might have made the attempt if I had sought only the approval of the learned world. My ambition is different. For literary reasons —I shall mention them later on—and for reasons of another sort which I shall pass over, since everyone can guess them, I believe that we must work to bring the two countries together by a mutual understanding of things of the spirit. Between two peoples as between two men there cannot be close friendship and solidarity except through the contact of minds.

In seeking to achieve this result it is prudent to keep the public's inertia in mind; you cannot stimulate appetite in people if you give them indigestion right off. They want to be slowly inducted into new knowledge, to be caught in the snare of their pleasure and forced to instruct themselves in order better to enjoy this pleasure. Let us examine this feeling of the public: if we were to try constraint, we would not reform them and would fail to serve the superior interests to which I have referred. If we were to be just toward the dead and the living, a history of Russian literature would have to cite, for the last century alone, a long list of names which are strange to our ears and of works which no translation has made known. It would be necessary to write about the political and social history of the last three reigns, which alone could explain the literature, though it is as untouched as is the latter. Without such preparation empty syllables would beat the air and leave no impression on the mind of the Western reader; these names would resemble maps of the evening sky, catalogues of the invisible stars set down by astronomers for a few of the initiate.

It has seemed to me preferable to proceed in another fashion, in the manner of the naturalist who wishes to inform us about a new land. He does not linger over the intermediate and uninteresting areas; he goes straight to the heart of the country, to the regions of special interest. There among the numerous samples of flora and fauna which vie for his choice, he makes a note of the species common to all parts of the world brought in by chance or industry; he passes rapidly over fossil or degenerate varieties, which have only an historical interest; his interest is in local and vigorous families, characteristic of their land and climate; among these he chooses certain individual-types, outstanding for their perfect development. These are the objects he offers for our examination, as the most suitable to reveal to us the present and special conditions of life in this corner of the planet.

Such is my plan. I shall recall briefly the origins of Russian literature, its limited promise, since it was for a long time subject to foreign domination, and its emancipation during the present century. From that moment the humble family of writers became a multitude and a power; its richness is now an embarrassment, as formerly its poverty was. I shall pay close attention to several figures who sum up the features of that unknown multitude. This method is especially legitimate in considering Russia because individual differences are less sharp among these young masses still largely undifferentiated and subject to uniform development. Go through a hundred villages between Petersburg and Moscow: by their features, attitudes, and costumes all the people you will meet seem to come from the same mold. As in most very new civilizations personal effort has not disengaged them from collective ties; a few portraits chosen at random will depict all these brothers. The same is true of their minds: one soul is representative of many more souls than among us. By multiplying documents, we would only give an impression of monotony.

This first series of studies is devoted in large part to the four contemporary novelists who are without equal and who have already been brought to the attention of Europe by partial translations. These archetypal writers will offer us a sharp and complete cross-section of the national genius which we are seeking to discover. I have attempted to show in them the man as well as the work, and in the two together the expression of a society. Ques-

On Russian and French Realism

tions of art have their interest and their greatness; but there is even more interest and grandeur in the secret which they aid me to seek out, the secret of that mysterious entity, Russia. Without great regard for rules of literary composition I have gathered everything which served my design: biographical details, personal recollections, digressions on matters of history and politics, without which nothing would be intelligible in the moral evolution of so recondite a country. There is perhaps only one rule, that of lighting up by every available means the object which is being exhibited, of illuminating it and making it understood in all its facets.

To this end I have used and abused comparisons between Russian writers and those of other countries who are more familiar to us. This is by no means through vanity of facile erudition. I know the danger of such analogies; they always limp; but in order to give a glimpse of the unknown there is still only one rapid and sure method, comparison with the known. It would have been necessary to give long and obscure explanation to characterize a man or a work: a name with which we are acquainted replaces that; it evokes at once in everyone's mind a whole literary physiognomy which is closely related to what we are studying. It is the image which lights up the text and permits us at one glance to classify the newcomers by order of family and precedence. Later we can make the discriminations necessary to bring out the differences between those things which have momentarily been made similar.

Some people will be surprised that I seek to find the secret of Russia in her novelists. For reasons which will be seen later, philosophy, history, the eloquence of the pulpit and the bar—I do not add of the rostrum—are genres almost entirely absent in this young literature. What would be found in other countries under these arbitrary headings, in Russia finds its way into the broad framework of poetry and the novel, the two forms of expression which are natural to the national thought, the only ones which are compatible with the exigencies of a censorship which was formerly uncompromising and is today still quick to take offense. Ideas slip through the pliant mesh of fiction only under disguise; but they do all slip through, and the fiction which shelters them takes on the significance of doctrinal treatises.

Of these two sovereign forms, one, poetry, dominated the beginning of the century; the other, the novel, has dislodged the first and has carried all before it for the last forty years.

Dominated by the great name of Pushkin, the Russians consider the romantic period as the time of their greatest intellectual glory. I at first agreed with them and directed my labors toward poetry. Two reasons have made me change my opinion. On the one hand, it was too wild an enterprise to talk about works of which nothing could be exhibited; it is like trying to catch hold of clouds that pass in another sky. The Russian poets are not translated and never will be. A lyric poem is a thing living with a furtive life that resides in the arrangement of words; you cannot transplant that life into an alien body. Sometime ago I was reading a Russian translation—quite exact and proper—of Musset's *Nuits*; it gave me the same pleasure as the corpse of a beautiful woman; the soul had departed, the aroma which constitutes the whole value of those divine syllables. The problem is even more insoluble when the exchange takes place between the most poetic idiom of Europe and the one which is least poetic. Certain lines of Pushkin and Lermontov are the most beautiful that I know in the world; when their debris is caught in a colorless rag of prose what remains is a banal thought. People have tried, and will try again; the result is not worth the effort.

On the other hand, I do not believe that romantic poetry is the most original manifestation of the Russian spirit. In giving it first place in their literary history their critics bow to the prestige of the past and the enthusiasm of youth. Time falsifies critical estimation to the detriment of the present; it makes venerable everything that is remote. A foreigner is perhaps better placed to perceive the judgment of the future; distance does for him the office of the years; it gives him a perspective which places the objects to be compared in a position of equality upon the same scale.

When the literary reckoning of the century is settled, I believe that the great novelists of the last forty years will be seen to be of greater worth to Russia than her poets. With them she has for the first time gone in advance of literary movements of the West instead of following them; she has at last found an aesthetic and nuances of thought which are her own. This is what made me de-

On Russian and French Realism

cide to examine the novel first for the scattered traits of the Russian genius.

Ten years of arduous acquaintance with the works of the Russian genius have suggested a few reflections on its particular characteristics, on the part which it is proper to assign it in the present labors of the human spirit. Since the novel alone undertakes to pose all the problems of the national life, it is not astonishing that I rely on light fiction in order to discuss grave subjects and to tie together certain general ideas. We are going to see the Russians plead the cause of realism with new arguments, with better arguments, to my mind, than those of their emulators in the West. It is a great controversy; at the present time it constitutes the basis of all the literary differences of opinion in the civilized world; and under the banner of literature it reveals the most basic conceptions of our contemporaries. Before introducing the Russian writers as principal party in this dispute, I should like to sum up the debate in all freedom and sincerity.

I

Classical literature considered man at the summit of humanity, in great transports of passion, as protagonist in a very noble, very simple drama; in that drama the actors divided certain roles of good and evil, of happiness or suffering, roles in harmony with ideal and absolute conceptions about a higher life, in which the springs of the soul were stretched entirely toward a single goal. In short, the classical man was the *hero* whom alone all primitive literatures considered worthy of attention. The action of this hero corresponded to a group of religious, monarchical, social, and moral ideas, the foundation on which the human family had rested since its most ancient attempts at organization. In enlarging his personages for good or evil, the classical poet was proposing an example of what should or should not be, rather than an instance of what existed in reality.

Insensibly during the last century other views came to prevail. They have brought about an art of observation rather than of imagination, one which boasts that it observes life as it is in its wholeness and complexity with the least possible prejudice on the part of the artist. It takes men under ordinary conditions, shows characters in the course of their everyday existence, average and changing. Jealous of the rigor of scientific procedure, the writer proposes to instruct us by a perpetual analysis of feelings and of acts rather than to divert or move us by intrigue and exhibition of the passions. Classical art imitated a king who governed, punished, rewarded, chose his favorites among an aristocratic elite, and imposed on them conventions of elegance, morality, and seemly speech. The new art seeks to imitate nature in its unconsciousness, its moral indifference, its lack of choice; it expresses the triumph of the collectivity over the individual, of the crowd over the hero, of the relative over the absolute. It has been called realist, naturalist: would it perhaps be enough to call it democratic?

No, it would be too short-sighted to stop at the apparent root of our literature. The change in the political order is only one episode in the universal and prodigious change which is taking place. Observe the work of the human spirit in all its applications for the last century; you might describe it as a legion of workmen occupied in turning over an enormous pyramid which rested on its point, so as to set it once more on its base. Man has occupied himself anew with explaining the universe; he has perceived that the existence, greatness, and evil of that universe come from the incessant labor of the infinitely small. While institutions were handing over the government of states to the multitude, the sciences were turning the government of the world over to atoms. Everywhere in the analysis of physical and moral phenomena, the ancient causes have been decomposed and, so to speak, broken to pieces; for the brusque and simple agencies, proceeding with great powerful blows, which once upon a time explained the revolutions of the globe, history, and the soul, there has been substituted the constant evolution of tiny, obscure beings.

It is as though there were an inevitable slope down which the modern spirit goes as soon as it begins to move. Does it seek the origins of creation? No longer is there a masterpiece wholly constructed in six days by the sudden operation of a demiurge. Vapor which condenses, drops of water, molecules slowly agglomerated for myriads of centuries, that is the humble beginning of the planets; and the beginning of life, the light sigh of beings without name, swarming in a piece of mud. Do we seek an explanation of the successive transformations of the globe? Volcanoes, floods, great cataclysms have played only a feeble part in this; it is the work of anonymous and imperceptible agents, a grain of sand rolled by a rivulet through days without number, a coral reef which becomes a continent through the work of micro-organisms, the little people patiently at work at the bottom of the ocean. If we turn to our own mechanism, we have certainly been curtailed of our glory; all this marvelous machinery is only a chain of cells, a man today, tomorrow a blade of grass or a worm; everything, even that bit of grey substance from which at this moment I draw my ideas about the world. Consulted about the breakdown of this machine, medical science like the others concludes with the universal explanation; it is not great movements of our humors which destroy us; the little creatures eat us away, the works of life and death are confided to an invisible animality. The discovery is of such importance that we begin to wonder whether the future, instead of designating our century by the name of some rare genius, will not call it the century of microbes; no word would better render our features or the meaning of our passage through the generations.

The moral sciences undergo the disturbance communicated by the natural sciences. History receives the deposition of peoples and pushes into the background the only witnesses which it used to listen to, kings, ministers, and captains; going through her necropolises, she is less willing to pause before pompous monuments, she goes among the mass of forgotten tombs, trying to catch their murmur. To illuminate the course of events a few dominant wills are not sufficient; the spirit of a race, its passions and hidden miseries, the chain of minute facts, such are the materials with which we reconstruct the past. There is the same preoccupation on the part of the psychologist, who studies the secrets of the soul; human personality appears to him as the resultant of a long series of accumulated sensations and acts, as a sensitive and variable instrument, always influenced by environment.

Is there any need to insist on the application of these tendencies to practical life? Leveling of classes, division of fortunes, universal suffrage, equal liberties and obligations before the law, before the fiscal authorities, in the barracks and in the school, all the consequences of this principle may be summed up in the word democracy, which is the banner of our times. Even sixty years ago they were saying that democracy was running at full banks; today the river has become a sea, a sea which has risen all over Europe. Here and there islands seem to be preserved, more solid rocks on which you still see thrones, shreds of feudal constitutions, remnants of privileged castes; but to these castes and to these thrones the most clear-seeing know that the sea mounts. Their only hope, and nothing forbids it, is that democratic organization be compatible with the forms of monarchy; we shall find in Russia a patriarchal democracy growing in the shadow of absolute power.

Not content to change the political structure of states, the irresistible spirit transforms all the functions of their organization; it substitutes association for the individual in most enterprises; it changes the base of public wealth by multiplying institutions of credit and issues of securities, by putting thus into every purse a delegation on the common treasure; and it modifies the conditions of industry and subordinates them to the exigencies of the greatest number.—I make no claim to an exhaustive demonstration; I could continue for a long time verifying this inflexible law in the bowels of the earth, in the body of man, and in the obscurities of his soul, in the scientist's laboratory and the administrator's office; everywhere it overturns ancient principles of knowledge and action, it brings us to the observation of one and the same fact: the handing over of the world to the infinitely small.

Literature, that confession of societies, could not remain aloof from the general change of direction; first by instinct, then by doctrine, it has regulated its methods and its ideal by the new spirit. Its first efforts at reformation were uncertain and awkward; romanticism, we must recognize today, was a bastard product; it breathed revolt, a bad condition in which to be as calm and strong as nature. In reaction against the classical hero, it sought its characters by preference in the lower levels of society; but since without being aware of it, it was still permeated by the classic spirit, the monsters which it invented became heroes again upside down: its convicts, courtesans, beggars were more windy and more hollow than the kings and princesses of olden times. The declamatory theme had changed, but not the declamation. We quickly got tired of it. We asked writers for representations of the world which were more sincere and more in keeping with the teachings of positive science, which every day was gaining ground; we wished in their books to find a sense of the complexity of life, of people, and of ideas, and that sense of relationship which in our time has replaced a taste for the absolute. Then realism was born; it took over all European literatures, it reigns among them as master at this hour, with the various nuances that we are going to compare. Its literary program was traced out for it by the universal revolution, some of the effects of which I have just called to mind; but only an understanding of the causes which produced this revolution could give it a philosophical program.

What were these causes? In France, with admirable fatuity, we imagined that these great changes in the human soul were due to certain philosophers who wrote the *Encyclopédie*, to a few malcontents who destroyed the Bastille, and so on. We thought that emancipated reason had alone accomplished this miracle and displaced the axis of the universe. The man of this century has gained a confidence in himself which is highly excusable. By a magnificent twofold effort his intelligence has penetrated most of the enigmas of nature, and his will has freed him from most of the social burdens which weighed upon his predecessors. The rational mechanism of the world has at last appeared to him: he has broken it down into its primary elements and its generative laws; and since, at the same time, he has proclaimed the liberty of his person in this world subject to science, man has believed himself destined to possess all knowledge and all power. Formerly the little area that fell within his grasp was surrounded by an immense, mysterious zone where the poor ignorant creature found at once a torment for his reason and ground for his hopes. Diminished, having receded far back, this belt of shadows sown with stars seemed suppressed. It was decided to take no more account of it. In the explanation of things as in the conduct of life, he threw out all the ancient thoughts that inhabited this higher domain, that is, the whole divine order. The most creditable scientific truths were often irreconcilable with the gross anthropomorphism of our ancestors, with their ideas on creation, history, and the relation of man and God. And religious feeling seemed inseparable from the temporary interpretations which were identified with it. Besides, why seek for doubtful causes when the functioning of the universe and of man was becoming so clear to the physicist and the physiologist? Why have a master up above, when we no longer recognized one here below? The least of God's wrongs was to be useless. Fine intelligences affirmed it, and all mediocre minds were convinced of it. The eighteenth century had inaugurated the cult of reason: for a moment people experienced the drunkenness of the millennium.

Then came the eternal disillusionment, the periodic ruin of all that man builds on the hollow foundation of his reason. On the one hand, he had to admit that in extending his domain he had extended his outlook, and that beyond the circle of truths which had been conquered the abyss of ignorance reappeared, just as vast, just as irritating as before. On the other hand, expérience taught him that under the oppression of natural laws political laws were able to do very little in behalf of this liberty; subject of a despot or citizen of a republic, after the declaration of his rights as before, he found himself to be the miserable slave that he is, weakened by his passions, limited in the attainment of all his desires by material fatality; he had to admit that the finest charter does not erase a single line of suffering from the forehead of the unfortunate, does not give a morsel of bread to the starving man. His extravagant presumption vanished away. He saw himself fallen back into the uncertainties and servitudes which will forever be his lot; better equipped and better educated, no doubt, but what does it matter? Nature seems to have calculated a rigorous balance, the equilibrium of which she constantly redresses, between our conquests and our needs, the latter increasing with the means to satisfy them. In this great disenchantment the old instincts came to life again; man sought above him for a superhuman power to implore, but there no longer was one.

Everything conspired to make the divorce from the traditions of the past irreparable: pride of reason, persuaded of its omnipotence, as well as the distressed resistance of orthodoxy.—Pride has never welled up more haughtily than in this age when we declare ourselves so little and so weak in relation to the enormousness of the universe. It is common to find the infatuation of a Nebuchadnezzar or a Nero in the back-premises of shops. By a very in-

structive contradiction, attachment to our senses has grown with
the universal doubt which has shaken all opinions. All the wise men
having decided that the new explanations of the world were contradictory to religious explanations, pride refused to review the judgment.

Defenders of orthodoxy have scarcely facilitated a reconciliation.
They have not always understood that their doctrine was the
source of all progress and that they diverted that spring from its
natural gradient in carrying on hand-to-hand combat with the
discoveries of the sciences and the mutations of the political order.
Orthodoxies rarely perceive all the strength and suppleness of the
principles which they guard; anxious to conserve intact the heritage which has been handed to them, they become frightened when
the interior force of the principle acts to transform the world according to a plan which escapes them. Like the fright of a man who
sees the foundation of his house, an oak trunk still full of sap,
burgeon, send out branches, and rise above the roof of the house
while demolishing it. The most manifest sign of the truth of a doctrine is its ability to accommodate itself to all the developments of
humanity, without ceasing to be itself. Is that not because it contained them all in embryo? The incomparable power of religions
comes from this capacity; when orthodoxy misunderstands this,
it undermines its own raison d'être.

As a result of this misunderstanding, in which each party has
its share of responsibility, it has taken a long time to perceive this
simple truth: the world has been worked upon for the last 1800
years by a leaven, the Gospel, and the last revolution which has
come from that Gospel is its triumph and definitive achievement.
All that was overthrown had been secretly undermined by the
hidden virtue of that ferment. Bossuet, one of the rare persons who
foresaw all, knew this well: "Jesus Christ came into the world to
overthrow the order that pride had established there; it is because
of that that his politics are directly opposed to those of this world."
All the great effort of our time was predicted and commanded by
these words: *Misereor super turbam.* That drop of pity, fallen on
the harshness of the old order, has insensibly softened our blood;
it has produced the modern man with his moral and social conceptions, his aesthetics, his politics, his inclination of mind and

heart toward little things and little people. But this constant action of the Gospel, which at need we admit in the past, we deny in the present. Man walks like an evening traveler who goes toward the East; night becomes ever darker before his eyes, he has only a little light behind him on the known road where the daylight is fading. Moreover, the apparent contradiction was too strong; on the one hand the narrow interpretation of the Gospel—what we might call the Jewish meaning—on the other hand, a revolution which seemed directed against it, whereas it was the natural development of the Christian meaning. Except for a few unprejudiced minds, a Ballanche, for example, it has taken time for us to understand the relation of the effect to the cause; today these truths are in the air, as they say; their evidence is such that if I were to dwell on them longer I fear I would be taxed with ingenuousness.

These considerations were, however, necessary to determine the only moral inspiration which can bring pardon to realism for the harshness of its methods. It responds to one of our needs when it studies life with rigorous precision, when it uncovers even the tiniest roots of our actions in the fatalities that govern them; but it deceives our surest instinct when it voluntarily ignores the mystery which subsists beyond rational explanations, the possible quantity of the divine. I am content that it affirm nothing of the unknown world; but at least it ought always to tremble on the sill of that world. Since it prides itself on observing phenomena without suggesting arbitrary interpretations, it ought to accept this fact of evidence, the latent fermentation of the spirit of the Gospel in the modern world. More than to any other form of art, religious feeling is indispensable to it; this feeling brings it the charity which it needs; since it does not draw back before ugliness and misery, it ought to make them bearable by an unending flow of pity. Realism becomes hateful as soon as it ceases to be charitable. And the spirit of pity, we shall see in a moment, aborts and leads astray in literature as soon as it departs from its sole source.

Oh, I know that in giving to the art of writing a moral goal I shall bring smiles to the faces of the adepts of the doctrine now in honor: art for art's sake. I admit that I do not understand it, at least in the sense in which it is understood today. Certainly morality and beauty are synonyms in art: a song of Virgil is worth a

On Russian and French Realism

chapter of Tacitus. But we must not confuse that spiritual beauty which is born of a certain illumination of the artist's vision with the skillful hand of the prestidigitator. My reserve has to do with this confusion. I shall never believe that serious men, concerned over their dignity and public esteem, want to be reduced to the role of tumblers, or wandering clowns.

These delicate ones are singular creatures. They profess a fine disdain for the bourgeois author who is concerned about teaching and consoling people, and yet they consent to turn cartwheels before the crowd with the sole intention of making it admire their skill; they boast of having nothing to say instead of excusing themselves for this. How reconcile this abdication with the pontifical role which the literary men of our time are so quick to claim? No doubt each of us gives in on occasion to the temptation to write for our own amusement: let him who is without sin cast the first stone! But it is inconceivable that we should make a doctrine out of what ought to remain an exception, a momentary relaxation from the human duty of the poet. If that is literature, I ask for the other form a name less open to usurpation; except for the use of pen and ink—which are also used for the activities of process-servers—our noble profession has nothing in common with this commerce; it is legitimate, certainly, if uprightness and decency are brought to it, but it resembles literature about as much as a toy shop does a library. I have no intention here of derogating such and such a genre, reputed light: a novel, a comedy, can be as useful to men as a treatise on theodicy. I rise up solely against the prejudice against ever allowing a moral intention. Happily those very people who defend this heresy are the first to betray it, when they have heart and talent.

To sum up our ideas on what realism ought to be, I seek a general formula which expresses its method and its creative power at the same time. I can find only one; it is very old, but I do not know of any that is better or more scientific or comes closer to the secret of all creation: "The Lord God formed man from the clay of the earth."—See how exact and significant that word clay is! Without prejudging or contradicting anything in detail, it contains all that we can guess about the origins of life; it shows those first quiverings of humid matter in which the series of organisms slowly formed and developed. Formation out of clay, that is all that experimental science can know, the field where its power of discovery is undefined; you can study there the misery of the human animal, everything there is in him of grossness, fatality, or corruption.— Yes, but there is something besides experimental science; clay is not enough to account for the mystery of life, it is not all our *I*: this bit of mud that we are, which is becoming and will become better and better known to us, we feel to be animated by a principle forever ungraspable by our instruments of study. It is necessary to complete the formula in order to express the duality of our being; thus the text adds:—". . . and he gave it a breath of life, and man was a living soul."—This "breath," drawn from the source of universal life, is spirit, the certain and impenetrable element which moves us, which envelops us, which disconcerts all our explanations, and without which they will always be insufficient. Clay, that is in the order of positive knowledge, what we have of the universe in a laboratory, of man in a clinic; you can go a long way with it, but as long as you do not bring in the "breath," you do not create a living soul, for life begins only where we cease to understand.

The literary creator must regulate his activity by this model. How has realism conformed to this in those literatures in which it has made its experiments?

I I

Let us consider it first in our own country. Nowhere was the soil less favorable to it. Our intellectual tradition protests against the aesthetics necessary to realism. Our genius is impatient of all slowness, is enamored of brilliant and rapid effects. The art which prides itself on imitating nature like nature has need of slow preparations to produce rare and intense effects. It heaps up minute details for the composition of a face or a picture; we want to have a character or a scene drawn for us in a few strokes. Realism derives all its strength from its simplicity, from its naïveté; nothing is less simple or less naive than the taste of an ancient race, witty and saturated with rhetoric. Thus in borrowing their procedures of minute analysis from the natural sciences our realistic writers, our naturalists—it little matters which name we give them—found

On Russian and French Realism

themselves confronting a redoubtable problem: to force our literary faculties to a new use which is repugnant to them. However, these difficulties of form are not enough to explain the resistance which these writers meet with on the part of most of the public. They are reproached above all with diminishing, saddening, and dirtying the spectacle of the world; we hold it against them because they ignore half of our being, and the better half.

Is their impotence therefore inherent in their principles? Nobody would dare assert that. Long before these quarrels began, it was attested that the greatness of the universe was visible in the infinitely small, just as in the other extreme; people marveled at the mite, as prodigious as the colossus; they found immensity "within the bounds of an atom." The vice of the new school is not in that it goes after the infinite from below, that it is interested in little things and little people; it is not in the object of study but in the eye that studies that object.

We know that the realist line goes back to Stendhal. It is a by-blow rather than a lineal descendance. You do not always plan the children you have. The author of *La Chartreuse de Parme* scarcely thought at all of creating a literary line; and I do not know whether that crotchety man would have acknowledged the posthumous family which came after him. He is like one of those ancestors whom you find when you draw up a genealogy. From some standpoints Stendhal is a writer of the eighteenth century, at once behind and in advance of his contemporaries. If he happened to encounter Diderot and Flaubert during his sojourn among the shades, it is certainly the former to whom he would confidently extend his hand. It is evident that the method of the new school is in germ in the account of the Battle of Waterloo, in the depiction of the character of Julien Sorel; but when we try to call Stendhal a true realist, we are stopped by an insurmountable objection: he has infinite wit, even a fine wit; we continually catch him in the act of mocking intervention, of Voltairean persiflage. Now there is an incompatibility between that quality of wit and realism; it is indeed the big difficulty which stands in the way, among us French, of the acclimatization of this form of art. Beyle has nothing of the impassivity which is one of the dogmas of the school; he has only an abominable dryness. His heart was constructed, under the Directorate, from the same wood as the heart of a Barras or a Talleyrand; his conception of life and of the world belongs to that era. I am sure that he poured the whole content of his soul into Julien Sorel; it is an evil soul, very inferior to the average. I understand and share the pleasure people have in rereading *La Chartreuse* today; I admire the finesse of observation, the mordancy of the satire, the shamelessness of the joking: but are these the virtues held in esteem by contemporary realism? It is more difficult for me to enjoy *Le Rouge et le Noir*, a hateful, sad book; it has exercised a disastrous influence on the development of the school which claims it; yet it does not penetrate great human truth, for its tenacity in the pursuit of evil reeks of exception and artifice, like the invention of romantic satanic figures.—And indeed, why Beyle and not Mérimée? People are prudently silent about the latter; realism should have the same reasons for claiming or repudiating the one as the other.

If Stendhal's paternity is open to question, that of Balzac passes for established fact. In spite of general consent, I wish to formulate express reservations. I shall not take the liberty of passing judgment on our great novelist in a few lines; I seek only the part he plays in the origins of realism. It is considerable, if you consider only his handiwork; construction of great ensembles in which all the materials are under control, hereditary preparation of temperaments, inventory of environments and demonstration of their influence on character, Balzac has left to his successors all the resources of their art; did he use them in the same spirit? This workman of the real remains the most ardent idealist of our century, the seer who always lived in a mirage, a mirage of millions, of absolute power, of pure love, and so much else. The heroes of *La Comédie humaine* are at times only interpreters for their father, charged with translating for us the systems which haunt his imagination. Following the precepts of classical art, his chief characters are pushed entirely toward a single passion; look at Nucingen, Balthazar Claës, Béatrix, Mme de Mortsauf. . . . To grasp the fundamental difference between Balzac and the later realists we need to go back to his primary conceptions of character. Like the classical author our novelist says to himself: Given this passion, what man may I use to incarnate it? The others reason in the op-

On Russian and French Realism

posite direction: Given this man, what are the dominant passions to which he is subject? Thus among the latter, portraits are exact and sad like police descriptions; those of a Rastignac or a Marsay are transformed, glorified by the interior vision of the painter.

Certainly Balzac gives us an illusion of life, but of a life better composed and more intense than that of everyday; his actors are natural, with the naturalness of good actors on stage; when they act and speak, they know that they are being looked at and listened to; they do not live simply for themselves, like those whom we meet with other novelists. Yet if the characters come from the highest social levels, they lose a bit of their truth; Mme de Maufrigneuse and the Duchesse de Langeais are true as women, but less true as examples of the society in which they live. To sum up, it is not absolutely exact to say that Balzac describes real life; he describes his dream; but he has dreamed with such precision of detail and such force of recollection that the dream imposes itself on us as reality. And that explains a strange quality which has been often noted: the depictions of the novelist seem more accurate to the generation which followed him than to the one that sat for him. So many of his readers had modeled themselves on the ideal types which he set before them!

We come to the uncontested initiator of realism, to him who reigns today, Gustave Flaubert. We shall not have to go further. After him they will invent new names and refine on the method, but they will change nothing in the methods of the Rouen master, and certainly nothing in his conception of life. If M. Zola has imposed himself on us with undoubted power, it is, in all deference, thanks to the epic qualities of which he could not rid himself. In his novels the realistic part is weak; he subjugates us by the old means of romanticism, by creating a synthetic monster, animated by formidable instincts, which absorbs men and lives its own life above the level of reality; a garden in *La Faute de l'abbé Mouret*, a market in *Le Ventre de Paris*, a cabaret in *L'Assommoir*, a mine in *Germinal*, always something of the kind. I was going to add: a cathedral in *Notre-Dame de Paris*, to such a degree is the work of idealization identical with that of Victor Hugo. The realist apparatus seems rather to be an embarrassment to this epic poet, a concession to the tastes of the times, which are repugnant to his abstract imagination.

Let us stop with Flaubert. He has greatly increased in reputation during the last few years; he has owed this posthumous glory less to his marvelous gifts as prose writer than to the manifest influence which it is recognized he has had on all the literature of the last quarter of a century. In taking his work as the pre-eminent example of French realism, I do not think I will encounter contradiction. The author of *Madame Bovary* went quickly to the logical extremes of the principle; no one will show us better than he the nothingness of that principle.

Oh, how instructive is the study of that singular mind! As in a mirror, you see the image of the world reflected first with éclat, then falsified and distorted; it diminishes, diminishes, darkens, and is deformed in caricature. At the beginning he is a fervent devotee of romanticism, enamored of the grandiose and the sonorous. Soon he is struck by the difference between life as he sees it and the life his masters depict; he observes around him, he reproduces his direct impression. No longer anything of Stendhal's wit or Balzac's dream. But in proportion as his vision becomes more exact, it becomes more limited and more sad; no moral mainspring sustains him.

With his Norman good sense he has verified the inanity of the poor idols in which literature believed for better or worse: the divinity of passion, the conversion of scoundrels, the liberalism of Béranger, the revolutionary humanitarianism of 1848. He has understood the factitiousness of the human sympathies of his predecessors; a sympathy doubled with hate, a pure play of antitheses which raised up the miserable in order to use them as a weapon against society. This humanitarianism rightly irritates Flaubert. According to the theory offered him, you must pity the people but at the same time proclaim that they are endowed with all wisdom and all virtue; the realist who looks at men without prejudice knows how false this is; he rejects the whole theory. And since he is unaware of the existence of a higher source of charity, he gets rid of all pity; he no longer sees anything in the universe but stupid or wicked animals subject to their experiences, the world of his Bovarys and his Homais. He had been taught that reason

On Russian and French Realism

was an infallible instrument and that it should bow to no discipline; now he perceives that it stumbles at every step; and, in anger, he unmasks its ridiculousness. He conceives for men and their reason a frightful disdain; he pours it out in his favorite book, in the grotesque Iliad of nihilism, *Bouvard et Pécuchet*.

Ecce homo! Behold Bouvard, behold man as progress, science, immortal principles have made him, without a higher grace to direct him: an educated idiot, who turns in the world of ideas like a squirrel in his cage. Poor Flaubert becomes impassioned over this idiot; he forgets that moral weakness is as worthy of compassion as physical weakness; no doubt he would correct a child who was so cruel as to abuse a humpback; yet he acts like that child in his treatment of this intellectual cripple. It is logical: he does not know or disdains the Word which has commanded respect for the poor in spirit by promising them happiness.

Bouvard et Pécuchet is the last word, the necessary culmination of a realism without faith, without emotion, without charity. A critic has justly remarked that this realism is condemned to end in caricature; and Paul de Kock is in one sense its true father. Flaubert said of his book: "I want to produce such an impression of lassitude and boredom that as people read the book they will think it has been written by a cretin."—What are we to think of this inverted artistic ambition? Is it not symptomatic of advanced decadence? But let there be no mistake; in the author's mind, this book was not a farce, but the synthesis of his philosophy, the philosophy of nihilism. If I belabor this point it is with the conviction that it has had a much greater influence on our literary generation than is thought; of all the works by this novelist, it today is the one which is most savored. We are going to study nihilism among the Russians; with them we shall not find moral illness as acute or as triumphant. Flaubert and his disciples made an absolute void in the souls of their readers; in those stricken souls there is only one feeling, the fatal product of nihilism: pessimism.

Recently people have been holding forth on pessimism till their breath gives out. People with good digestions and little thought have called it reprehensible; it is what the healthy might say of fever in unhealthy regions. We have charitably been advised to be gay, with the candor of those doctors who tell a hypochondriac:

"Calm your mind with cheerful ideas." Of the doctors who gave us this advice we might have asked if they had not given some little assistance to the invasion of sceptical materialism; and pessimism came out of that, like a worm out of rotten fruit. There have been arguments whose indirect efficacy I recognize; they are of so ridiculous a nature that they ought to cure our black humors by the sovereign virtue of laughter. I have read somewhere that it took a great deal of ill will to be a pessimist after '89, after the great principles, after fifteen years of a republic; we have been shamed for our discouragement by being told that M. Thiers was not a pessimist, or M. Gambetta either. Now that is a great comfort for the eternal disquietude of the soul! Others have taken a wider view of the matter in relating it to the vast problems of evil, pain, and death;—of sin, someone has even said, and we were astonished, and did not understand what there was new and profound in the scientific use of this word.

For my part I believe that without going back to causes that are general, permanent, and as old as the world, it is enough to say, in explaining the intensity of the present crisis, that pessimism is the natural parasite of a void and that it inevitably lives where there is neither faith nor love. When you have reached that point, you invent it yourself without having read Schopenhauer. However, we must distinguish between two varieties. One is materialist pessimism, resigned as long as it has its ration of daily pleasure, determined to scorn men while taking from them whatever it can for its pleasure. We see it flower in our literature. The other is a suffering, revolted pessimism, and this conceals hope beneath its curses; the last stage in nihilist evolution, it is at the same time the first symptom of a moral resurrection. It has been rightly said of it that it is the instrument of all progress, for the world has never been transformed or improved by those whom it completely satisfies.

To conclude, our realistic literature has left us only the choice between these two forms of pessimism, because it has lacked a divine sense and a human sense. Inaugurated by Stendhal, if you wish, consummated by Flaubert, vulgarized in the same spirit by his successors, it has failed one part of its task, which was to give comfort to the humble and draw them closer to us in making us

On Russian and French Realism

know them better. From a purely literary point of view it has paid for its moral wrong by offering us only a partial and deformed representation of the world, without a surrounding atmosphere, without distant perspectives. Of the precept of creation it has kept only the first half: it has petrified the clay, it has curiously burrowed into it, it has drawn from it all that it contains; it has forgotten to inspire it with the breath which makes "a living soul." This literature thought to make up for everything by egotistical refinements of art; this bias has led it to make itself a mandarinate, to isolate it from general life, whose servant it ought to be. It dries up and perishes like the poet's verbena in the cracked vase from which the nourishing water has fled.

People are drawing away, they are looking for something else; for any disinterested observer this motion of recoil is quite evident. For twenty-five or thirty years the instinct of the new generations, weary of childish invention and famished for truth, imperiously demanded that we come back to the conscientious study of life and that we render it with great simplicity. But underneath variations of taste the basis of the human being does not change; he continues to have his eternal need of sympathy and hope; we are to be caught only by these noble weaknesses, we are to be caught only by being lifted off the earth. He who lowers us and mutilates our hopes can assuredly amuse us for an hour; but he will not keep us long. To-day people forget these truths, which are as durable as man, because we are at a period of transition and universal uncertainty. Souls belong to nobody, they whirl about, seeking a guide, just as swallows graze the marsh in a storm, frightened in the cold, the shadows, and the noise. Try to tell them that there is a retreat where wounded birds are gathered up and warmed again; you will see them assemble, all these souls, rise, depart in full flight, over your arid deserts, toward the writer who has called them with a cry from the heart.

III

While realism was painfully taking root in France, it had already conquered two great literatures, in England and in Russia. There the soil was ready to receive it, and everything was favorable to its growth. We and all our racial brothers have inherited the genius of the absolute from our Latin masters; the races of the North, Slav or Anglo-German, have the genius of the relative; whether it be a matter of religious beliefs, legal principles, or literary methods, this deep-seated division of the European family stands out all through history. Unlike our intelligence, sharp and clear, always inclined to limit its field of study, the mind of these peoples is broad and disturbed, because it sees many things at the same time. It does not have our classical education, which permits us to isolate a fact, a character, and in that character a passion, to supplement by a thousand conventions what is not shown to us; it believes that the representations of the world ought to be as complex and contradictory as the world itself; it suffers in its conscience when there is concealment of some part of this ensemble, where everything is held in tight dependency. See to what different needs dramatic compositions respond; in ours, a central figure, a few secondary ones, a rigorously delimited action, *Le Cid, Phèdre, Zaïre*; in the English and German tragic works a tumultuous multitude rushing through a series of events and, if one may say so, a piece of general life, without artifice, without mutilations: *Henry VI, Richard III, Wallenstein*. The same is true for novels; the patient readers of those countries do not fear the dense, philosophic novel, one crammed with ideas, which makes their minds work almost as much as a book of pure science.

However, the capital difference between our realism and that of the northern peoples must be sought elsewhere; we shall find it in the source of moral inspiration much more than in differences of aesthetics. On this point all critics are in agreement.

M. Taine said of Stendhal and Balzac in comparing them with Dickens: "They love art more than men . . . they do not write out of sympathy for the miserable but from love of the beautiful."— That says it all, and this distinction becomes more evident as we follow it out between our contemporary realists and Dickens' continuators or the Russian realists. M. Montégut makes it even clearer in his studies of George Eliot; he recalls and sums up earlier works in a phrase to which I fully subscribe: "It is to this religious origin that I attributed the moral spirit which has never ceased to distinguish the English novel, even in its most daring or most cynical productions, and I asserted that realism, perfectly ac-

On Russian and French Realism

ceptable when it is fecundated by this element, could not, if deprived of it, produce anything but inferior, puerile, and immoral works: I have not changed my opinion on this point."—Still in reference to Eliot, M. Brunetière says in his turn: "If it is true, as I believe I have shown, that the observation in some degree hostile, ironic, mocking at least, of our French naturalists does not go beyond the outer shell of things, whereas inversely there is scarcely a hidden recess of the human soul which English naturalism has not reached, do not take the time or trouble to seek out the cause elsewhere; it lies there. In fact, sympathy, not that banal sympathy which makes the rich man of the epigram on poor Holofernes weep, but that sympathy of an intelligence lighted up by love, which descends gently and places itself without ostentation at the reach of those whom it wishes to include: that is, that has always been, and that will always be the instrument of philosophical analysis."

I have insisted on quoting these opinions because they may be applied to Russian realism with the same accuracy as to English realism.

I shall say no more about the latter. Messers Taine, Montégut, and Schérer, to mention only those names, have exhausted the subject in France. England has the honor of having inaugurated and carried to its highest perfection the form of art which corresponds to the new needs of the minds of all Europe. Realism, proceeding from Richardson, has there made its most signal advancements with Dickens, Thackeray, and George Eliot. At the time when among us Flaubert was dragging down the doctrine in the decay of his intelligence, Eliot was giving it a serenity and grandeur which no one has equalled. In spite of my decided taste for Turgenev and Tolstoy, it is possible that I prefer that enchantress Mary Evans to them; if in a hundred years the novels of the past are still being read, I am certain that the admiration of our descendants will hesitate among those three names.

No doubt we must admit the slowness with which the English get under way; like life realism demands from us a tribute of patience in order to give us pleasure; if you press it in this respect you falsify all its dynamics. You must resign yourself to seeing a whole volume given over to the education of two children, in *The Mill on the Floss*, in order later to understand the adorable little soul of Maggie. In reading these limpid works, in which nothing makes you measure the space gone through, it seems that you are going down insensibly into deep water; there is nothing to set it apart, it is like all water; suddenly I know not what shiver warns you that it is the water of the ocean in which you are overwhelmed. Take *Adam Bede* or *Silas Marner*; you read page after page of simple words to depict simpler facts; we could have written them, you and I.—What have I to do with these things and these men? you say to yourself. And all at once, without a motive, without a tragic event, by the pressure alone of that invisible grandeur which has been piling up for the last hour, a tear falls on the book; why, I defy the most subtle to say; it is because it is as beautiful as if God were speaking, that is all.

It has the beauty of the Bible; Dinah's visit to Lisbeth and a score of other passages seem to be written by the same hand as the Book of Ruth. You feel how England is permeated to the marrow by her Bible. And with George Eliot it is clearly a case of influence of race, atmosphere, and education. Her opinions are certainly non-conformist, as we know; she has rejected the old faith for herself; no matter, it is in her blood, "that primary religious monad, placed in English souls by Protestantism, to which the superiority of the English novel over ours is to be attributed." We shall find the same phenomenon among the Russian authors; personally detached from Christian doctrine, they keep its strong stamp, bells of the church which always ring out things divine, even when turned to profane uses. The writer's doctrine of the moment has at times only a little influence on his work; what counts most with him, what we lack above all, is long unconscious preparation in a healthy environment, it is the religious quality of the heart. Whatever may be the religious beliefs on which Mary Evans will settle, she will always be able to attribute to herself these words of the Methodist Dinah Morris, in which she has concentrated the essence of her thought: "It seems to me that there is no place at all in my soul for anxieties about myself, so abundantly has it pleased God to fill my heart with compassion for the suffering of the poor people who belong to Him."

In this fashion might think and might speak several of those Russians who now vie with the English for primacy in the realistic

334

On Russian and French Realism

novel. Their arrival on the major literary scene has been sudden and unexpected. Until recent years we left it to a few Orientalists to glance over the writings of the Sarmatians. We supposed that they might have a literature there, as in Persia or Arabia, but we expected little of it. Mérimée was the first to recognize this little frequented country; he pointed out there some writers of talent and some original works. Turgenev came to us as a missionary of Russian genius; by his example he proved the high artistic value of that genius; the Western public remained sceptical. Our opinions on Russia were determined by one of those facile formulas of which we are so fond in France and with which you may crush a country as well as an individual: "A nation rotten before it was ripe," we were accustomed to say, and that took care of everything. The Russians could hardly hold it against us: we shall see that certain of them, and the most important, leveled the same judgment against themselves. Let us beware of summary judgments. Do you know that Mirabeau expressed himself about the Prussian monarchy in identical terms? He wrote in his *Histoire secrète*: "Rottenness before ripeness, I am very much afraid that will be the motto of the Prussian power."—The aftermath has proved that this idea was very badly applied. In the same way J. J. Rousseau, speaking of Russia in *Le Contrat social* did not miss the occasion to emit a paradox: "The Russian Empire will want to subjugate Europe and will itself be subjugated. The Tartars, its subjects or its neighbors, will become its masters and ours; this revolution to me appears inevitable."—Ségur, better informed by his personal experience, said with more justice: "The Russians are still what they are made to be; some day when they are more free, they will be themselves."

That day, which has been slow in coming in other respects, came for literature at least, well before Europe deigned to notice it. Toward 1840 a school which called itself the *natural school*—or naturalist, the Russian word can be translated either way—absorbed all the literary energies of the country. It devoted itself to the novel and at once produced some remarkable works. This school recalled that of England and owed a great deal to Dickens, but very little to Balzac, whose renown had not yet been established abroad; it preceded our realism in the form that Flaubert was going to fix later. Some of these Russians immediately achieved the desolating ideas and the grossness of expression to which we have come very recently through effort; if that is a merit, we must restore their priority to them. But other writers disengaged realism from these excesses and, like the English, they communicated to it a superior beauty, which was due to the same moral inspiration: compassion, filtered of all impure elements and raised by the evangelic spirit.

They do not have the intellectual solidity and virile force of the Anglo-Saxons, of that granite race who are always sure of themselves, who master themselves as they master the ocean. The floating soul of the Russians draws from all philosophies and all errors; it makes its stations in nihilism and pessimism; a superficial reader could sometimes confuse Tolstoy and Flaubert. But this nihilism is never accepted without revulsion, this soul is never impenitent, you hear it sigh and seek; it gets hold of itself finally and redeems itself by charity; charity more or less active in Turgenev and Tolstoy, with Dostoevsky unbridled to the point of becoming a painful passion. They shake in the wind of every doctrine brought to them from abroad, sceptic, fatalist, positivist; but unconsciously in the most secret fibers of the heart they always remain Christians, of whom an eloquent voice once said: "They have not ceased to share in that universal cry by which men and things, tributaries of time, water the unquenchable flood."—Going through the strangest of their books, you guess that nearby there is a regulating book toward which all the others gravitate; it is the venerable volume which you see in the place of honor in the Imperial Library at Petersburg, The Gospel of Ostromir of Novgorod (1056); in the midst of the recent products of the national literature, this volume symbolizes their source and their spirit.

After sympathy the distinctive trait of these realists is a sense of what there is of life beneath and around them. They close in on the study of the real more completely than has ever been done, they seem to be confined in it; nevertheless they meditate on the invisible; over and beyond known things which they describe exactly, they grant a secret attention to unknown things which they suspect. Their characters are disturbed by the universal mystery;

and however strongly involved they appear to be in the drama of
the moment, they lend an ear to the murmur of abstract ideas; they
people the deep atmosphere where the creatures of Turgenev, Tolstoy, and Dostoevsky breathe. The areas that these writers frequent by preference resemble coastal lands; there you enjoy hills,
flowers and trees, but every point of view is commanded by the
moving horizon of the sea, which adds to the grace of the landscape the feeling of the illimitability of the world, the ever-present
witness of the Infinite.

Like their source of inspiration their practice in literature brings
them close to the English; they make you buy interest and emotion
at the same price of patience. As we enter into their works we are
disoriented by the lack of composition and apparent action, and
are wearied by the effort of attention and memory which they demand of us. These lazy and reflective minds delay at every step,
come back in their tracks, raise up visions precise in detail and
confused in the ensemble, with ill-defined contours; they create
on too large a scale and bring in too extraneous material for our
taste; the relation of Russian words to ours is that of meter to
foot. In spite of everything we are seduced by qualities which appear to be incompatible, the most naive simplicity and a subtleness
of psychological analysis; we are amazed at a total comprehension
of the inner man such as we have never met before, at the perfection of naturalness, at the truth of feelings and language among
all the characters. Since Russian novels are nearly always written
by men of standing, we find there for the first time the manners
and tone of the best company, without a single false note; but, when
we leave the Court, these impeccable observers make the peasant
speak with the same propriety, without for a moment travestying
his humble thoughts. By the virtues of naturalness and emotion
alone, the realist Tolstoy succeeds, like George Eliot, in turning
the most banal stories into tranquil epics, striking throughout; he
forces us to salute in him the greatest evoker of life who has appeared perhaps since Goethe.

I have no desire to develop an analysis to which I shall have
occasion often to return in this volume, in connection with each
particular writer. In summing it up here my only plan was to show
the ties which bind Russian realism to English realism, and how

they both differ from ours; to make clear how this form of art, sometimes unjustly decried, has elsewhere been able to produce masterpieces as soon as it was brought back to its true sources of strength, a little light and a little warmth. For literature works like all firesides in virtue of the sovereign law which governs the physical and moral world; it changes into force all that it receives of light and heat, it gives the one in proportion as it possesses the two others. Where we have failed the English and the Russians have succeeded because they fully applied the precept of creation; they have taken man from the clay, but they have given him the breath of life and have formed "living souls."

Thus their literature has made its fortune, and it is quietly capturing the European public. It answers all needs, because by its content it satisfies the permanent needs of the human soul, and by its form the taste for realism peculiar to our era, as it has been determined by the universal inclination of the mind of which I spoke to begin with.

This leads us to sad but necessary reflections. Thanks to the frequency and rapidity of changes of all kinds, thanks to the growing solidarity which unifies the world, there is being created in our days, over and above preferences of coterie and nationality, a European spirit, a fund of culture, ideas, and inclinations common to all intelligent societies; like the costume which is everywhere uniform, we find this spirit much the same and docile to the same influences in London, in Petersburg, in Rome, or in Berlin. We find it even further away, on the steamship that crosses the Pacific, on the prairie where an immigrant is breaking the soil, in the shop which a merchant sets up in the antipodes.

This spirit escapes us; the philosophies and literatures of our rivals are slowly encompassing it. This spirit is no longer ours; we do not communicate it, we trail behind, sometimes with success; but to follow is not to lead. I am not unaware that our enormous production of novels may still boast of triumph in the book market; people buy them out of habit and respect for fashion, they are amused by them for a moment; but, with rare exceptions, the book which acts and nourishes, the one people take seriously, which is read in the family circle and which in the long run shapes minds, that book no longer comes from Paris. With heavy heart and wishing I were mistaken, I note here the observation which sums up my long experience abroad: the general ideas which are transforming Europe no longer come from the French soul. As unfortunate as our politics where we have been dispossessed of the material empire of the world, our literature through its own fault has let slip the intellectual empire which was its unchallenged inheritance.

I V

It is to be hoped that the reader will understand that in setting up these parallels, I am not seeking the impious pleasure of depreciating my own country. If I thought this momentary decay irremediable, I would be silent. I speak freely, because today more than ever, I am convinced of the contrary. After our great misfortune, we imagined that the national spirit was going to change all of a sudden and that our literature would bring testimony of that change. This showed poor knowledge of history and of nature, which act slowly. Recall the "Muse" of the years following the terrible shocks of the Revolution; she continued to languish, identical in every respect with what she had been on the eve of the drama. For her the world had not changed. Chateaubriand did not come on the scene until six years after the Terror, and he remains a unique exception; the powerful literary movement by which we can measure the shaking up of French intelligence did not assert itself until twenty years later. This is because catastrophes do not instruct and scarcely modify their witnesses who are already mature, and who come back on the morrow with their old habits of mind, prejudices, and routine. They operate in an inexplicable fashion on imaginations which are still tender, on children, who magnify them as they open before them those fine astonished eyes in which any spectacle is enlarged. These little ones grow up and are recognized as the children of the tempest.

It will work out like this for our era. For fifteen years we have been turning on the old bed where the wound caught us; we have lived on outworn formulas, literature has not varied its recipes. When you ask about it, you would think that nobody wants more healthy food. That would be a mistake. Those who keep their eyes on youth know this. They need not be judged on the basis of a few noisy and bizarre fantasies. A spirit of disquietude is working on that literary youth, it seeks for a new focal point in the world of ideas. It shows an equal repugnance for everything served up to it. The last sighs of idealist art scarcely touch it; inattentive to the soft sound of a dying thing, it refuses the elegant conventions and the light fictions which charmed even our generation. But it is no less rebellious toward materialistic, down-to-earth literature. Neither musk nor manure, but air seems to be its motto. Its native generosity seems repelled by the egotistic detachment and the intolerable dryness of the only realism which it has been offered. The brutal negations of positivism do not satisfy it. If you speak to youth about the necessity of a religious revival in letters, it listens with curiosity, without prejudice and without hatred, for, in default of faith, it has to the highest degree a sense of mystery: that is its distinctive trait. It is reproached for its pessimism, and it is offered nothing to cure this malady; its pessimists are souls which flutter around a truth.

Their situation is not new, and to see what it presages, nothing would be better than to reread that book which best lights up all the beginning of our century, those admirable *Mémoires* of Ségur. Do you recall how the young man depicts his discouragement and that of his contemporaries toward 1796?—"All belief was shaken, all sense of direction effaced and become uncertain; and the more thoughtful and ardent the young were, the more they went astray and wore themselves out without support in the vague infinite, a desert without limits, where nothing confined their strayings, where many of them finally became exhausted and fell back upon themselves in disenchantment, perceiving nothing certain, through the dust of so much debris, but death as an end! . . . I saw nothing but that everywhere and in everything. . . . Thus my soul wore itself out, ready to carry off everything else; I was languishing. . . ."—Could contemporary pessimism speak any differently? We know how the future general shook off his one day in the month of Brumaire at the grill of the swing-bridge to begin a valiant career as soldier and writer. Ours is equally curable, at the bidding of the man or the idea which will raise up these young people. People deliberately let themselves be cast down by this fateful word: *fin de siècle*. It is a snare. The century is ever beginning for people

On Russian and French Realism

twenty years old. We have divided time into artificial periods, we compare them to the decline of a human existence; the creative force of nature takes little account of our calculations; it uninterruptedly pushes generations into the world, it confides to them a new treasure of life without looking at the hour on our dial.

Perhaps these prognostics will be called illusions, and people will wonder what they have to do with Russian literature. One of the symptoms which has most struck me is the passion with which youth has fallen upon the new fruit. Somewhere Pushkin calls translators "the draft horses of civilization." One could not better depict the hardness and utility of their office. Those who first tried to introduce the French public to Russian books scarcely foresaw all the results of their enterprise. They had told themselves that France must never remain behind in an idea, and that a monopoly of a new field of study should not be left to Germany, where Messers Reinholdt, Zabel, and Brandes have for the last few years done considerable work on Slavic literatures. They thought only of awakening emulation and curiosity in lettered circles. They were the first to be surprised by the unexpected success of these novels, so different from ours and so difficult to approach. For my part, I had no hope of seeing our taste shared, and when the public showed its interest, I understood that beneath the apparent immobility of these fifteen years many changes and openings up had occurred in the national mind.

In order to explain the success of the Russians, people have talked of style and fad. Ah! what a superficial way of looking at it that is! I admit that there is a degree of fashion—it is the parasitic plant that attaches itself to any living tree—and faddishness in some salons. But the Russian novel has found its true public among studious youth of all levels. What has seduced them is not the local color and the exotic mishmash; it is the sense of life which animates these books, the accent of sincerity and of sympathy. Youth found there the spiritual nourishment which our imaginative literature denies them, and as they were very hungry, they bit into it with delight. I am by no means speaking casually; how many letters from young people, known and unknown friends, might I cite as evidence!

It is likely that so marked a favor will have two slight incon-

341

veniences. We shall see the indiscriminate translation of everything
that comes out of Russia—that has already begun—and in the heap
are some pretty poor works; we can manage this by not reading
them. On the other hand, I am told that young "decadents," moved
above all by the bizarreries which mar Dostoevsky's talent, take
his exaggerations as a model on which to reinforce their chimerical
literature. That was bound to happen; you have to let them blow
off steam. Having made these reservations, I am convinced that
the influence of the great Russian writers will be salutary for our
worn-out art; it will aid it to take flight again, to observe the real
better, while looking further away, and above all to rediscover emotion. We already see something of a totally new moral value slipping into novelistic works. I find it difficult to understand those
who take fright at these borrowings from outside and who seem
to fear the integrity of French genius. Do they then forget our
whole literary history? Like everything in existence literature is
an organism which lives on nutrition; it must ceaselessly assimilate
foreign elements in order to transform them into its own substance.
If the stomach is good, assimilation is not dangerous; if it is worn
out, it only has the choice of perishing through inertia or indigestion. If that were our case, a bit of Russian gruel would change
nothing in our sentence of death.

When the Grand Siècle began, literature was suffering its last
agonies in the affectations at the Hôtel de Rambouillet; Corneille
went to Spain for his provisions, and Molière did the same in
Italy. Then we had wonderful health, and we lived for two hundred
years on our own funds. With the nineteenth century other needs
arose; the national savings found themselves once more exhausted;
we then borrowed from England and Germany, and literature,
raised again, had the fine renewal about which we know. Now a
time of famine and anemia has come for it again: the Russians
arrive on the scene opportunely; if we are still able to digest, we
shall reconstitute our blood stream at their expense. To those who
might blush at owing anything to "Barbarians," let us remember
that the intellectual world is a vast society of mutual help and
charity. In the Koran there is a very fine verse: "By what shall we
know that the end of the world has come? asked the Prophet.—
That will be the day when one soul can no longer do anything for

On Russian and French Realism

another."—Heaven grant that the Russian soul may be able to do a great deal for ours!

While studying the expression of this Russian soul in its literature, I have spoken almost exclusively of our French literature, and I make no excuses for this. During the years I passed over there trying to get hold of foreign thought, to listen to that language, a vague, musical, and supple vesture of new ideas, I dreamed ceaselessly of what might be brought back to enrich our thought, our old language, the result of the labor and acquisitions of our ancestors. They levied on the whole world in order to adorn their queen; they knew that all was permitted in her service, that they might ransom passersby, arm corsairs, skim the seas, and appropriate all they found.

Let us imitate them. Certain men of letters pretend that French thought has no need to roam the universe and that it is sufficient for it to contemplate itself in its Parisian mirror. Others say that henceforth the language ought to be an impersonal, impassive voice, that we ought to work like mosaic-workers in the hard cold stones which the descendants of Raphael fabricate at Florence for the Americans. Poor language! I thought the centuries had melted it in fire and molded it in the furnace, a bell to send to the world its powerful ringings. To make it more resistant and more superb they tossed into it their laughter, their anger, their love, their despair, their whole souls, those rude workmen, Rabelais, Pascal, Saint-Simon, Mirabeau, Chateaubriand, Michelet! Language and thought, each age must cast them again without fail; that is why after bad times during which they failed, this task comes back to us; let us work at it in the fashion of that metal of Corinth, which came from defeat and conflagration rich with all the treasures of the world, all the relics of the fatherland, rich with its ruins and misfortunes, a metal striking and sonorous, good for the forging of both jewels and swords.

"Manifesto of Five Against
La Terre"*

THE "FIVE" who signed their names to this manifesto have received a
degree of immortality not justified by their works, which are largely
forgotten. Although they claimed to be Zola's admiring disciples, they
did not wait even for the serial publication of *La Terre* to be completed in *Gil Blas*, nor in fact were they known to Zola. There have
been many suggestions that this statement was the result of a cabal
led by Daudet or Goncourt out of jealousy toward Zola. It seems certain, however, that the manifesto was composed by J.-H. Rosny and
published in *Le Figaro* on August 18, 1887, through the good offices
of Paul Bonnetain, a member of the staff. The others signed it somewhat reluctantly.

Not the least of the ironies of this situation is that two of the signa-
tories were themselves tried for outrage against public morals. Paul
Bonnetain (1858-1899) was the author of *Charlot s'amuse* (1883),
a really scabrous book and the most scandalous product of the entire
naturalistic movement. Lucien Descaves (1861-1949) published *Sous-
Offs*, a novel about the underside of army life, in 1889 and stirred up
a row which reached the Chamber of Deputies. He was stripped of his
sergeant-major rating by the Army and was brought to trial in a civil
court, but acquitted. Zola was one of the fifty-four authors who signed
a petition demanding that the government respect the rights of the
writer.

It is difficult today to see why *La Terre*, rather than one of the earlier
novels, should have produced this explosion. No doubt the outburst
was inevitable and long overdue, since Zola had swept all before him
for the past ten years. At any rate this manifesto heralded the decline
of naturalism as a vital literary force in France and was the signal
for many to declare their disaffection or repudiation. In fact two weeks
later Ferdinand Brunetière (1849-1906), who for ten years had been
known as a critic for his implacable enmity toward naturalism, published what he hoped would be the coup de grâce in the *Revue des
Deux Mondes*, an article entitled "The Bankruptcy of Naturalism." It
begins as follows:

> "It has been a long time since we have spoken of M. Zola's
> novels. This is not because we have not read them, for that
> was our duty, but because, having read them, we had nothing
> to say that we had not already said. . . . It seemed better to
> wait; and since from novel to novel he kept getting further

* "Manifeste des Cinq contre *La Terre*," *Figaro*, August 18, 1887.

away from decency, naturalness, and truth, it would be suitable to speak of him once more, and for the last time, when he should have abandoned those qualities altogether.

"That is what has just happened: the volume has not yet appeared and M. Zola's newspaper has not even completed serial publication of the novel, yet already *La Terre* by putting the novelist beyond the pale seems at the same time to have succeeded in disqualifying *naturalism*."

◇◇

TO EMILE ZOLA

NOT so long ago it was still possible for Zola to write, without raising serious recriminations, that literary youth was on his side. Too few years had passed since the appearance of *L'Assommoir*, since the vigorous polemics which consolidated the basis of Naturalism, for the rising generation to think of revolt. Even those of them who were particularly weary of the irritating repetition of clichés remembered too well the impetuous breach made by the great writer and his routing of the romantics.

We had seen him so strong, so superbly stubborn, so audacious that our generation, nearly all of us caught in a sickness of the will, revered him if only for that strength, that perseverance, that audacity. Even his peers, even his predecessors, the original masters who had long prepared the way for the battle, were patient in recognition of past services.

However, even on the morrow of *L'Assommoir*, serious errors were committed. It seemed to the young that the master, after giving things a push, was losing ground in the manner of those revolutionary generals whose bellies make demands which their brains encourage. They had hoped for better than to sleep on the field of battle; they awaited the results of this outburst of energy; they hoped for a fine infusion of life into books and into the theatre and a stop to the decay of art.

He, however, went on deepening his furrow; he went on tirelessly, and youth followed him, accompanying him with the applause and sympathy which are so sweet even to the most stoical beings; he went on and the oldest and wisest henceforth closed their eyes, wishing to deceive themselves and avoid seeing the master's plow mired in ordure.

Certainly it was a painful surprise to see Zola desert and migrate to Médan, turning his energies—though minimally at that time—which could have been used in works to advance and consolidate the battle to satisfactions of an infinitely less aesthetic order. No matter; youth was willing to pardon the physical desertion of the man! But a more terrible kind of desertion was already becoming evident: the treason of the writer to his work.

Zola in fact every day more deeply betrayed his program. Incredibly lazy in carrying out *personal experiment*, armed with trumpery documentation gathered at second hand, full of Hugo-esque turgidity—which was all the more irritating in that he was sharply preaching simplicity—collapsing into repetitions and endless clichés, he disconcerted even the most enthusiastic of his disciples.

Moreover, even the least perspicacious had finally come to see the ridiculousness of that so-called *Natural and Social History of a Family under the Second Empire*, the tenuous nature of the thread of heredity, the childishness of the famous genealogical tree, and the profound ignorance of the Master in things medical and scientific.

No matter; they refused, even among themselves, to make an outright statement of their disappointment. There were some "Perhaps he should have . . .", "Don't you think a little less . . .", and all the timid observations of disappointed Levites who did not wish to push to the very bottom of their disillusionment. It was hard to give up the banner! And even the most daring went no further than to whisper that after all Zola was not Naturalism and that study of real life *had not been invented* after Balzac, Stendhal, Flaubert, and the Goncourts; but nobody dared to write down this heresy.

However, this disheartened feeling obdurately increased, especially as a result of the growing exaggeration of indecency in the use of dirty words in the *Rougon-Macquart*. It was vain to excuse everything on the basis of the principle set forth in the preface to *Thérèse Raquin*:

"I do not know if my novel is moral or immoral; I admit that I never concerned myself about making it more or less chaste. What I know is that I never thought for a moment about putting in it the dirtiness that moral people find there; this is because I wrote every scene, even the most heightened ones, with pure scientific curiosity."

They asked only to believe this, and indeed some of the young writers had, out of a need to exasperate the middle class, exaggerated the *curiosity of the scientist*. But it was becoming impossible to be satisfied with such arguments: the sharp, irresistible *feeling* of everyone before certain pages of the *Rougon-Macquart* was no longer one of the brutality of a document but of a violent penchant for obscenity.

Then while some attributed this to an illness of the writer's lower organs, to the manias of the solitary monk, others preferred to see it as an *unconscious* development of an insatiable appetite for sales, as *instinctive* canniness on the part of the novelist in perceiving that his big success in repeated printings depended on the fact that "the imbeciles buy the *Rougon-Macquart*, caught not so much by their literary quality as by the reputation for pornography which the popular voice has given them."

Now it is very true that Zola seems excessively concerned with sales (and those of us who have heard him talk are well aware of this); but it is also well-known that he early lived a life of isolation and exaggerated continency, first by necessity, later by principle. As a young man he was very poor and very timid with women, whom he did not experience at the age when he should have and who haunted him with a vision that was evidently false. The difficulty in maintaining balance which comes from the illness of his loins no doubt contributes to his being excessively concerned with certain functions and impels him to magnify their importance. Perhaps Charcot, Moreau (of Tours), and the doctors of the Salpêtrière Hospital who have given us studies of coprolaliacs might be able to hit upon the symptoms of his illness. And to these sickly causes should we not add the anxiety so frequently observed among misogynists, as well as among very young men, as to their competence in matters of love-making?

However that may be, until very recently people have shown themselves to be indulgent; fearful whisperings were quieted with a promise: *La Terre*. They gladly waited on the struggle of the great writer with some high subject in the expectation that he would decide to abandon a worn-out soil. They liked to imagine Zola living among the peasants, heaping up *personal documents*, intimate documents, patiently analyzing the rural temperament, in short, beginning once again the superb work of *L'Assommoir*. Hope of a masterpiece stilled all tongues. Certainly the subject, simple and broad, gave promise of interesting revelations.

La Terre appeared. The disappointment has been profound and painful. Not only is the observation superficial, the devices outmoded, the narration ordinary and flat, but dirtiness is carried still further, going so low as at times to make you think you are reading a collection of scatology: the Master has gone down to the very depths of uncleanness.

Very well, that is the end of the adventure! We vigorously repudiate this imposture of true literature, this effort toward the spicy and salacious concocted by a brain sick for success. We repudiate those good fellows decked out in Zolaesque rhetoric, those enormous, superhuman, and misshapen silhouettes which, divested of complication, are thrown brutally in heavy masses into a setting casually glimpsed through the window of an express train. Resolutely, though not without sadness, we turn away from this latest work of the great mind which gave *L'Assommoir* to the world, from this bastard *La Terre*. It pains us to push away the man whom we have too warmly loved.

Our protest is the outcry of probity, the dictate of conscience on the part of young men anxious to defend their works—good or bad—against possible identification with the aberrations of the Master. We would willingly have waited longer, but we have no more time; tomorrow it will be too late. We are convinced that *La Terre* is not the ephemeral falling-off of a great man but the last stage in a series of descents, the irremediable morbid depravity of a chaste man. We can expect nothing from the *Rougon-Macquart* hereafter; we are all too able to foresee what the novels on the Railroads and on the Army will be like: the famous genealogical tree spreads out its sickly arms and will henceforth bear no fruit.

Now let it be clearly stated once again that no hostility brings us to make this protest. We should have found it pleasant to watch the great man pursue his career in peace. Even the decline

"Manifesto of Five against *La Terre*"

of his talent is not the motive that animates us; it is the compromising anomaly of that decline. There are surrenders of principle which cannot be borne: we can no longer stand for the spontaneous labeling as realistic of every book which is drawn from reality. We would bravely face any persecution in defense of a just cause: we refuse to have any part in a shameful degeneration.

It is the misfortune of men who stand for a doctrine that it becomes impossible to spare them when they compromise that doctrine. Then what is to be said to Zola, who has provided so many examples of a frankness that was often brutal? Did he not celebrate the *struggle for life, struggle* in its simple form, incompatible with the instincts of a developed race, *struggle* authorizing violent attacks? "I am a force," he shouted, crushing both friends and enemies, closing to those who came after him the breach in the wall which he himself had opened.

For our part, full of admiration for the immense talent which the man has often displayed, we deny any idea of disrespect. But is it our fault if the celebrated formula: "A corner of nature seen through a temperament," has been transformed with respect to Zola into "a corner of nature seen through a *morbid sensory apparatus*," and if it is our duty to take the hatchet to his works? It is imperative that the judgment of the public aim straight at *La Terre* lest the sincere books of tomorrow be peppered by a general discharge of lead.

It is necessary that with all the strength of our hard-working youth, with all the loyalty of our artistic consciences, we adopt a proper demeanor and dignity toward literature without nobility, that in the name of healthy and manly ambition, in the name of our dedication, we protest our profound love, our supreme respect for art.

PAUL BONNETAIN, J.-H. ROSNY,
LUCIEN DESCAVES, PAUL MARGUERITTE,
GUSTAVE GUICHES.

Pernicious Literature*

By The National Vigilance Association

THE BASTION of British middle-class morality was the last to be breached by the new literature. When George Moore (1852-1933) returned from France determined to create the naturalistic novel in England, he found himself "subject to the censorship of a tradesman who, although doubtless an excellent citizen and a worthy father," was not competent to decide on artistic questions. He was referring to Mr. Mudie, the proprietor of Mudie's Select Library, who exercised a virtual monopoly of book circulation on a large scale. When Mudie refused to circulate Moore's novel *A Modern Lover* (1883) because two ladies in the country had expressed their disapproval, the author determined to fight the system by publishing his next novel *A Mummer's Wife* at six shillings. He thus successfully broke through the monopoly and asserted that he was no longer subject to injury from the "select" circulating libraries, that he was "now free to write as I please. . . ."

These and other comments were incorporated in a pamphlet with the title *Literature at Nurse, or Circulating Morals*, published by Vizetelly & Co. in 1885. Moore's intention is to hold British philistinism up to ridicule by showing what sort of erotic trash is allowed by "our English Academy, the Select Circulating Library," provided it is sufficiently gilded and scented, while at the same time Mr. Mudie refuses to keep naturalistic literature because it is not proper, "and thus an interesting, if not a very successful, literary experiment is stamped out of sight. . . ."

Moore's claim to have escaped the heavy hand of prudery may have been temporarily true for himself, but it was premature for literature in general. Up until 1885 the French writers of the new school had been largely ignored in England except through the avenue of clandestine importation. With Zola's fame at its height abroad, the Vizetelly firm decided to issue English translations of his and other works. Among others they published *L'Assommoir* and *Nana* in 1885, *Madame Bovary* in 1886, and *La Terre* in a cut and altered version as soon as it appeared in 1887. As a result of these translations The National Vigilance Association began an active campaign to suppress immoral literature, in particular the works of Flaubert, Zola, the Goncourts, Maupassant, Daudet, and Bourget. In Parliament it brought about a debate on the subject on May 8, 1888, and in No-

* The National Vigilance Association, *Pernicious Literature. Debate in the House of Commons. Trial and Conviction for Sale of Zola's Novels. With Opinions of the Press*, London, 1889.

vember succeeded in bringing Mr. Henry Vizetelly, the offending publisher of the Zola translations, to trial. It had been hoped to make the trial an important demonstration in favor of free speech, but the attitude of the court and jury was so evidently hostile, that the defendant speedily changed his plea to guilty and got off with a fine and suspended sentence when he voluntarily undertook to withdraw the offending works from circulation.

The National Vigilance Association published a transcript of the Parliamentary debate and the trial, along with voluminous and repetitious excerpts from the newspapers, in a pamphlet which appeared early in 1889. What this record does not show is that Vizetelly was tried again later in that year and this time received a sentence of three months in jail without respect for his advanced age and ill health.

◇◇

PERNICIOUS LITERATURE

THE National Vigilance Association earnestly invite your serious perusal of the following pamphlet, referring to the widespread circulation of pernicious literature among the young people of our nation. The peculiar and special nature of the work done by this Association affords exceptional opportunities of ascertaining the enormous amount of evil which is wrought by the circulation of immoral literature and obscene pictures, and the matter is one of such urgent and vital importance as to leave no doubt that so soon as the nation realises the dreadful havoc which is being caused by the dissemination of this vile stuff, it will rise as one man, and demand such a strengthening of the law as shall simplify the process of legally laying by the heels the scoundrels who live by its production.

A healthy public opinion is needed to enable this Association to set the law in motion—cumbersome and tedious as it is—and this pamphlet is sent forward in the strong hope that it may sound as a note of alarm, and rouse the manhood of England to action in relation to the growth of this evil, which is to-day a menace to our religious, social and national life.

The law relating to questionable literature and pictures, casts upon the Magistrates the responsibility of saying what is, and what is not indecent. Too often a lax public opinion, or the want of appreciation on the part of the Magistrate of the grave issues involved, leads him to hesitate in condemning the book or picture, when brought before him. The Association has already framed a Bill dealing with an important section of this subject, which it is hoped to bring before Parliament at an early date.

The Association appeal to all who are interested in the healthy mental and moral growth of the nation to assist them, by information and otherwise, in bringing to justice the men who are carrying on this degrading trade. The Association will conduct and take the financial responsibility for all legal proceedings in such cases, where the evidence is forthcoming. They will also be glad of any information which will enable them by means of their officers to trace the men who engage in this nefarious business, and bring them to justice.

All communications—which must be authenticated by the name and address of the writer—will be treated as private and confidential, and should be sent to

WM. ALEX. COOTE, *Secretary.*

National Vigilance Association,
267, Strand, London, W.C.
January 1st, 1889.

DEBATE IN THE HOUSE OF COMMONS, MAY 8, 1888.

[Reprinted from "Hansard"]

MR. S. SMITH (Flintshire) said, he rose to call attention to the Motion which stood in his name, and which was as follows:—

"That this House deplores the rapid spread of demoralizing literature in this country, and is of opinion that the law against obscene publications and indecent pictures and prints should be vigorously enforced, and, if necessary, strengthened." He assured the House that nothing but an imperative sense of duty had led him to take up so painful and so disagreeable a subject—nothing but the knowledge that there had of late years been an immense increase of vile literature in London and throughout the country, and that this literature was working terrible effects upon the morals of the young. Such havoc was it making that he could only look upon it as a gigantic national danger; indeed, he questioned whether at the present time the people of this country were suffering more from the effect of an excessive use of strong drink than they were from the more subtle poison of vile and obscene literature. There was nothing that so corroded the human character, or so sapped the vitality of a nation, as the spread of this noxious and licentious literature, and he believed it was at the bottom of that shocking state of the streets of London, of which they were continual witnesses. The House would readily ask him for proof of his statement that there had been of late years a great development of this evil. He would, in the first place, refer to the public confession of one whom he believed to be the chief culprit in the spread of this pernicious literature—he referred to Mr. Vizetelly, the publisher of French novels, who, in *The Pall Mall Gazette* a short time ago, boasted that his house had been the means of translating and selling in the English market more than 1,000,000 copies of French novels, some of them of the worst class. Mr. Vizetelly boasted that at the present time he was selling in England 1,000 copies of the writings of Zola weekly. He would quote a few lines from Mr. Vizetelly's statement—

"We, of course, knew of the immense popularity of Zola in France and most European countries, and were aware that there was a tolerably large sale for the wretchedly-translated and mutilated American editions of his works imported into this country. After much hesitation, we determined to issue an unabridged translation of *Nana*, suppressing nothing, and merely throwing a slight veil over those passages to which particular exception was likely to be taken. The success of the work, although not rapid, was very complete, and induced us to reproduce the whole of Zola's published novels, and to purchase the English copyrights of all his new ones."

He was quite aware it was inexpedient to advertise works of this kind, but in this case the sale was so enormous throughout the country, the facts were so generally known, that he saw no object now in preserving silence. Of the character of these works he would say that nothing more diabolical had ever been written by the pen of man. These novels were only fit for swine, and their constant perusal must turn the mind into something akin to a sty. *The Saturday Review,* a short time ago—

"Directed the attention of the police to the fact that books which no shop dare expose in Paris, or even in Brussels, are to be seen in windows in London. Books which have only escaped suppression in France through the astounding laxity which has allowed some parts of Paris to become nearly impassable to decent people —on the showing of Parisian papers themselves—are translated and openly advertised."

Some hon. Members might say that *The Saturday Review* was something of a purist, but no one would make such an accusation against *Society,* one of the society papers. This paper said, on the 21st of April last—

"But of late has come a brutal change over this spirit of not too innocent fun, and the name of the worker of the transformation is Realism, and Zola is his Prophet. Realism, according to latter-day French lights, means nothing short of sheer beastliness; it means going out of the way to dig up foul expressions to embody filthy ideas; it means not only the old insinuation of petty intrigue, but the laying bare of social sores in their most loathsome forms; it means the alteration of the brutal directness of the drunken operative of to-day with the flabby sensuality of Corinth in the past. In a word, it is dirt and horror pure and simple; and the good-humoured Englishman, who might smilingly characterize the French novel as 'rather thick,' will be disgusted and tired with the inartistic garbage which is to be found in Zola's *La Terre.* Yet Messrs. Vizetelly, of Catherine Street, Strand, are allowed with impunity to publish an almost word for word translation of Zola's bestial *chef d'oeuvre.* In the French original its sins were glaring enough in all conscience, but the English version needs but a chapter's perusal to make one sigh for something to take the nasty taste away."

He would now read a few lines as to a very painful incident; at least it struck him as a very painful incident. A writer in *The Sentinel* said—

354

"Pernicious Literature"

"The only acquaintance which the writer of this article has with Zola's novels is from two pages of one of the most notorious of them placed open in the window of a well-known bookseller in the City of London. The matter was of such a leprous character that it would be impossible for any young man who had not learned the Divine secret of self-control to have read it without committing some form of outward sin within twenty-four hours after. In this case a boy, apparently about fourteen years old, was reading the book. The writer immediately went into the shop, and accosting the manager in a loud voice, demanded that he should 'step outside and see this boy reading this infernal book in your window.' The shop was full of customers, and the manager naturally looked thunder-struck. Half-an-hour afterwards, when the writer passed, the book was gone."

Now, he asked, were they to stand still while the country was wholly corrupted by literature of this kind? Were they to wait until the moral fibre of the English race was eaten out, as that of the French was almost? Look what such literature had done for France. It overspread that country like a torrent, and its poison was destroying the whole national life. France, to-day, was rapidly approaching the condition of Rome in the time of the Caesars. The philosophy of France to-day was "Let us eat and drink, for to-morrow we die." Some might have seen the very striking article on the present state of France in *The Nineteenth Century*. Mr. Myers in the article entitled "The disenchantment of France," pointed out that this kind of literature had led to the decay of all belief in a noble ideal of life, and the degradation into which what the late Mr. Matthew Arnold called the "Worship of the great goddess of Lubricity," had plunged the country, was vividly pourtrayed. Such garbage was simply death to a nation. Were they to wait till this deadly poison spread itself over English soil and killed the life of this great and noble people? Contrast our country with Germany. He passed through Germany last autumn, and made many inquiries as to the social life of the country. Novels of the Zola type were forbidden to be sold; indeed, Germany surrounded its children with safeguards which were wholly wanting in this country. Nothing to him was more melancholy than the garbage on which the children of London fed. The chief literature on which the London children fed was what was called the penny dreadful and the penny novelette. An enormous circulation of these papers took place; they were sold by hundreds of tons weight; they were almost the entire staple of the reading of many hundreds of thousands of the children of the poor and even of respectable artizans and the middle class. He read some time ago in *The Edinburgh Review* an analysis of the type of street literature that was mainly devoured by the children of London. He would quote a few lines which he thought would impress every one in the House, as they did him, with a most painful sense of the noxious effect of this unwholesome garbage. The writer, in describing very fully the various classes of cheap penny papers, said—

"The feast spread for them is ready and abundant, but every dish is a false one, every condiment vile. Every morsel of food is doctored, every draught of wine is drugged; no true hunger is satisfied, no true thirst quenched; and the hapless guests depart with a depraved appetite, and a palate more than ever dead to every pure taste and every perception of what is good and true. Thus entertained and equipped, the wide army of the children of the poor are sent on their way, to take part in the great battle of life, with false views, false impressions, and foul aims. The pictures of men and women to whom they have been introduced are unreal and untrue. The whole drama of life as they see it is a lie from beginning to end, and in it they can play none but a vicious and unhappy part."

Could anyone be surprised at the misery and degradation and immorality that abounded in London when he pictured to himself the intellectual food upon which the children had feasted for so many years? Need they wonder that they were rearing in London a population which, to a large extent, would prove a source of weakness to the nation? He regretted to say that in a great measure the Elementary Education Act had been a failure on account of the total want of safeguards to protect the children after they left school—on account of the innumerable temptations that surrounded them on every side, and amongst these temptations he ranked the sale of licentious literature, with which we were literally surfeited. This literature penetrated everywhere. He was informed there were men employed as agents, going round to the middle class and upper schools of the country, in order to place in the hands of boys and girls, pictures of a vile kind, and advertisements of a vile kind, so as to induce them to purchase these demoralizing works. He was told there was a well-organized system of this kind which penetrated into nearly all the schools of the country. He came in contact with many persons who made it the business of their lives to try and rescue the young from these snares. Facts had been brought to his knowledge which had filled him with sadness, facts of so shocking a nature, he could scarcely state them to the House. But one which he believed to be thoroughly authentic he would state; he had it from a lady who had investigated it with care, and who had ascertained the true facts of the case. It had become the rule with a class of low booksellers in London to provide indecent literature for young girls, to offer them every inducement to come into the shops and read the books, to provide them with private rooms stocked with the vilest class of literature, where, on making the small deposit of 6d., they were supplied with this literature. And he was told that in many cases these shops were in league with houses of the worst class, to which the girls, when their minds were sufficiently polluted and depraved, were consigned. This had become a trade carried on to such an extent that he was told there was one street in London where 10 shops were devoted to this purpose. He asked what the law of this country was doing? What were they doing to allow such abominations to continue? They debated and squabbled here about many matters of secondary interest. He maintained that this was a vital matter, which lay at the very root of the nation's welfare, and he often wondered at the small amount of time this House spent on questions of this kind, and at the extreme difficulty with which any such question could be brought before the House. He could not conceive any subject with which Parliament, jealous of the highest interests of the nation, ought to be more anxious to deal wisely and rationally than such a question as this. In addition to these books—and if the Home Secretary chose to appoint a Select Committee to inquire into the subject, he would supply him with proof of all the statements he made—there was an immense circulation of lewd photographs and prints of every sort and kind of the very worst type.

There was an organized system of sending these pictures over the country. Only to-day he was told of a case in which a gentleman in the country received an advertisement of boots and shoes from a house in London, and inside that was a small notice that on application photographs would be sent. He made an application, and a parcel of most indelicate photographs of nude females was sent to him. He (Mr. Smith) asserted that in England we suffered from mistaken ideas of liberty. A class of vile scoundrels came over to England simply because the freedom of our laws enabled them to carry on their nefarious trade which their own country probably would not allow. Within his knowledge there was a large number of persons in London who had been driven from abroad, who had suffered imprisonment, and who dare not live in their own countries, because their characters were so well-known; they came here and brought with them the vilest practices, and carried them on almost untouched. He was sorry to have to add to the papers which degraded the public mind—certain of our sporting papers. He had looked over some of the sporting papers, and he was bound to say that such wretched nonsense, mixed up with a great deal of lewdness, as he found there, it had seldom been his lot to read. How any cultivated man, or rational man, could amuse himself with reading such wretched trash as was printed in some of the sporting papers, he could not understand. Again, when in India he was surprised to find on all the bookstalls an unlimited supply of English translations of French novels, and almost nothing else. He scarcely ever saw upon the stalls the book of any well-known literary man; but he was told that the worst class of French novels were bought in tens of thousands, and were regarded as samples of European civilization. He would allude very briefly to another class of books. He had spoken mainly of the cheap literature sold to the masses in immense quantities. He was told there was also a very expensive class of abominable literature now published in London, and that there was a society devoted to the publication of this depraved and lascivious literature. There was one book which had recently been published at 10 guineas. Many Members would know the book to which he referred. It contained the most abominable suggestions, and there was so large a run upon it at the present time that copies were being sold at 26 guineas each. The author, he believed, was on the point of bringing out five additional volumes. He was told that nothing more loathsome had ever been printed; but he supposed there were men of such depraved mind who were only too eager to regale themselves with such filth. Why was it the law did not touch these things? The law had been put in force against the paper called *Town Talk*, and he congratulated the Home Secretary upon the fact that a very bad number of a very bad paper had at last been prosecuted. He noticed that 17 vendors of the paper were fined last week, and very properly so. But he was not aware that the owner or publisher of the paper was fined. Somehow or other our laws touched the weaker, not the stronger; they always struck at the agent, and not the author. He asked why was this 10 guinea book, admitted by everyone to be most detestable, allowed to be purchased by the leading clubs in London, and allowed to be circulated in London without the publisher or author being prosecuted? That was a question to which he should like an answer. If there was such a demand for this class of literature, at its present high price, was it not perfectly obvious that in a few years time it would descend to the masses? If it paid the publisher to circulate it at 10 guineas, the time would come when he would publish it at a guinea, and perhaps at 1s., and then there would be an enormous overflow of this new class of poison. He was told that catalogues of these books were sent almost all over the country, that the trade was so organized that people were tempted in all parts—in the most remote parts—of the country by the agents of this vile trade. The streets were polluted with the advertisements of quack doctors. One of the greatest evils of late years had been the great increase of quack advertisements of a filthy kind. It was remarked to him the other day by a gentleman who had spent much time on the Continent, that whereas in Germany he never knew one of these indecent advertisements to be thrust into his hand, when he came to London such advertisements were thrust into his hand frequently. The well-known clauses in the Metropolitan Police Act did not in any way touch the pernicious class of literature which was strewn broadcast in the London streets—namely, pamphlets issued by quacks, and thrust into the hands of every passer-by, and which made statements with regard to secret diseases which were frequently untrue, and which were mostly intended to induce to impurity of life, and also by working upon the fears of the readers to terrify them into consulting the medical quacks whose names might be on the pamphlets. He commended to the notice of the Home Secretary this immense collection of vile literature, this social nuisance, which, he thought, ought to be dealt with in a far more stringent manner than it had been hitherto. Now he came to the daily Press. His firm conviction was that all these evils had been greatly aggravated, greatly increased, in the last few years by the action of some of our newspapers with regard to the reports of low divorce cases which they had published with such fulness. He believed that the reports of vile divorce cases, and others of an obscene character, published with loathsome plenitude, gave an immense impetus to the demand for indecent literature. They had created a taste for it; because there was this characteristic about this class of reading that the more a man read, the more he wanted to read. There was no doubt that the loathsome revelations of the Divorce Court some years ago had greatly increased the appetite for indecent literature, and would make it more difficult to stop its spread. If we, as a nation, decided upon new methods of stamping out this horrible disease, this pestilence, we must take some means of purifying the daily Press, and putting limitations on the power of publishing the details of Divorce Court proceedings. The House might ask what remedy he would apply. He would insist that the law should be put in force, for he thought it was sufficiently stringent. The Act called Lord Campbell's Act, if vigorously worked, would do a great deal to suppress this class of literature; but it was not vigorously worked, it had been allowed to fall into disuse. The administration of the law had become so lax that it was hardly of any value. Twenty years ago no London publisher dared to print and put in circulation such books as were now published; they would have been indicted at once, and sharply and severely punished. But, from a false notion of liberty, we had allowed this plague to spread on all sides, and now many people thought it was too late to do any good. He could not assent to that. He believed that was the pessimism of despair. He believed that if we had an evil to grapple with we should go forward, in the name of God, and grapple with it. Let us attempt to do so, and he believed we should not do so in vain. He was told that magistrates who formerly were perfectly willing to initiate proceedings against the publishers and vendors of this literature, now very frequently refused to do so. A case was mentioned to him yesterday in which some vile pictures were submitted to a magistrate, and he declared he could not encourage proceedings in respect of them, on the ground that it would be an interference with what he conceived to be the liberty of the British subject. He (Mr. S. Smith) believed in liberty to do right, but not in liberty to do wrong. He believed that liberty to deprave a fellow man was much more honoured in the breach than in the observance. He considered the police were very inactive, and that they allowed things to go on which ought not to be permitted. We ought to have an active Public Prosecutor. He did not know where the official called the Public Prosecutor was to be found. He believed there was some one known by that title; but he seemed to be asleep, he seemed to have had his wings clipped. It might be said to him (Mr. S. Smith) that private persons ought to institute proceedings. But it was very disagreeable for private persons to take action, because it brought them into a great deal of odium. He believed that we had not done our duty; we ought not to have stood by while this terrible pestilence was spreading throughout the country. In other countries, the State undertook this duty; and he held that, on the whole, it was a much better and thorough way of dealing with this evil. What he wanted to do was to create a sounder public opinion. He believed this House could do that. A good discussion in the House, and a strong condemnation of these detestable practices, would have immense effect on the country. There were many who were wishing to get a little encouragement to put the law in force. He was happy to think the Home Secretary thoroughly sympathised with him. He did not bring the matter forward in any attitude of opposition to the right hon. gentleman or of the Government. Indeed, he believed the debate would strengthen the hands of the Home Secretary. He was happy to think the right hon. gentleman was willing to advance so far as the House would encourage him. He hoped the House would send forth such an expression of opinion to-night as would strengthen the hands of the officers of the law in coping with this enormous evil.

Mr. T. W. Russell (Tyrone, S.) seconded the motion.

Motion made and question proposed.

"That this House deplores the rapid spread of demoralizing literature in this country, and is of opinion that the Law against obscene publications and indecent pictures and prints should be vigorously enforced, and if necessary strengthened."—(*Mr. Samuel Smith.*)

Sir Robert Fowler (London) said, he thought his hon. friend the Member for Flintshire (Mr. S. Smith) had done a great service to the country by calling attention to this subject, and he trusted the Government would accept the motion. Some years ago the then Home Secretary, Mr. Bruce, had had his attention called to obscene prints extensively circulated about the streets, and had taken effective action with regard to them.

Mr. de Lisle (Leicestershire, Mid) said, he did not propose to make a speech in supporting the motion of the hon. Member for Flintshire (Mr. S. Smith), and for the reason that he had no plan to suggest, or any counsel to give which would enable the Government to deal with this monstrous evil. But it was a matter of great satisfaction to him to be able to raise his voice along with that of his hon. friend who had preceded him in support of a motion of the kind. He believed that the greatness and the happiness of the nation depended chiefly upon the purity of its morals, and he did not know of a reason which any sane or prudent man could allege in favour of the propagation of indecent and demoralizing literature. He trusted that some endeavour would be made to see whether it was not possible to cope with the terrible evil which the motion referred to. Unfortunately the evil affected the class of persons who were least able to resist it. Those who were rich and had comfortable homes might keep the evil from their doors; but the poor, who had little scope for the higher enjoyments of life, naturally picked up the literature which was nearest at hand. It was a terrible evil that this filth should be thrown in the faces of the people day after day; and therefore he hoped that the House, if it did express an opinion on the matter, would speak most emphatically, and be prepared, if necessary, to limit that liberty of publication of which in most respects we were so justly proud. The highest duty of Conservatives was to safeguard the morals of the people; indeed, he was convinced that if they allowed the corruption of moral sentiment which had been going on for years, to continue, there was no system of government which could be erected which would long stave off the threatening clouds of revolution.

Mr. F. S. Powell (Wigan) said, he was quite sure there was quite enough in the arguments and facts brought forward to justify the introduction of the subject in that House. He expressed the satisfaction with which he had observed, as a Member for the last two sessions of the Committee on Police and Sanitary Bills, the growing desire of local authorities to take more effective powers against the distribution of demoralizing advertisements and tracts. Local authorities were taking steps in that matter, and clauses had been introduced into a considerable number of their Police Bills to enable them to deal with it, and, so far as he knew, this had been done without objection from any Member of that House. There was a kind of literature—circulars headed with Scriptural texts, and looking like religious tracts—which in effect, though not in name, was demoralizing. He must protest against the action of those well-meaning people who, in their endeavours to improve the condition of the women of India, thought it right to circulate in English homes, and among English women and girls, a class of literature that was calculated to do permanent harm. He would earnestly entreat them, while thus zealous for the purity of Indian women, not to violate the sanctity of English homes.

The Secretary of State for the Home Department (Mr. Matthews) (Birmingham, E.) said, that it was beyond doubt that there had been of recent years a considerable growth of evil and pernicious literature, and that its sale took place with more openness than was formerly the case. The French romantic literature of modern days, of which cheap editions were openly sold in this country, had reached a lower depth of immorality than had ever before been known. In comparing such literature with classical literature, it must be borne in mind that while the latter was written with no evil purpose, the former was written with the object of directing attention to the foulest passions of which human nature was capable, and to depict them in the most attractive forms. Such literature was, in his opinion, calculated to do great harm to the moral health of the country. But it was not only French literature that ought to be condemned, much harm was also done by what the hon. Member had termed the penny dreadfuls, the quack advertisements, and the full reports of divorce cases which appeared in the public daily Press. All such classes of publications were pernicious in the extreme, and they ought to be brought within the reach of the law in every civilized country. It must, however, be remembered that the law in this country was a tolerably effective weapon as it now stood, and that under the powers conferred by Lord Campbell's Act, by the Metropolitan Police Courts' Act, and by the Vagrant Act, ample powers were given which, if effectively used, would prevent the circulation of immoral literature. The reason why the law was not more frequently put in force was the difficulty that was experienced in getting juries to draw a hard and fast line and to convict in all cases that crossed that line. He had given careful attention to this question, and he should deprecate handing over to the Public Prosecutor, or anybody else, the task of deciding what was the straight and narrow line which divided what was punishable, criminal, and obscene within the meaning of the law, and what was merely indelicate and coarse. The public judgment was a safer guide than that of any official, and if the general moral sense of the community did not compel individuals to prosecute, no good would be done by trying to create an artificial moral sense by the action of the Public Prosecutor. The hon. Member had done well in directing public attention to the insidious mischief which resulted from publications which trembled on the verge of indecency and which did much to vitiate the public taste. It would be most unwise and dangerous to direct public attention to certain obscure publications of a filthy character known only to the few by instituting a State prosecution, and thus give that wide advertisement which those who brought them out would desire more than anything else. The hon. Member would do great service if he would give the public his authority for the facts which he had stated to the House, which were new to himself. It was, indeed, a most deplorable thing that literature of this kind should be supplied to little girls or circulated among boys. There could be no doubt that such acts were within the Criminal Law, and he would certainly on reasonably good evidence direct proceedings if any such facts were brought to his knowledge. He could give the same assurance with respect to advertisement of vicious literature. There was no machinery by which the Public Prosecutor could get information of this kind, and he did not believe that public opinion would tolerate any system of organized spies for the purpose. If, however, everything were brought to the knowledge of the Public Prosecutor by individuals within whose cognizance such crimes came, no time would be lost in putting the law into motion. But serious evils arose from the failure of attempts to obtain conviction upon such charges. So far, however, as he could influence the Public Prosecutor, who was, to some extent, independent of any Public Office and acted on his own discretion, he would certainly urge prosecutions in any cases in which it did not appear that more harm than good would result. He had in his official capacity to consider the case not only of obscene, but of blasphemous literature. But on inquiry he found that the offending publications were so contemptible and obscure, that much more harm than good would be done by dragging them into the light of day. He was sure, however, that the hon. Member and all those who had honest convictions would not shrink from the slight personal inconvenience of putting the law in motion in any case of real public mischief. He had no word to say against the motion so far as it expressed the hon. Member's opinion on the subject itself, though he could not accept it if it implied any censure of public officials.

Mr. Mundella (Sheffield, Brightside) said he had no desire to prolong the discussion by entering upon the legal part of it, so well expounded by the Home Secretary; but he would offer a few remarks in reference to the motion of the hon. Member for Flintshire (Mr. S. Smith) for which he, in common with every Member of the House, had entire sympathy. All were anxious to put a stop to the circulation of this abominable literature, but in this country, and in every country in Europe, the people had been educated to think, and some literature must be provided to meet the intellectual craving. He was glad to say that the spread of healthy literature in this country surpassed anything else of the kind ever known or dreamed of. Hundreds of thousands of standard works were published at so low a price as 6d. and even 3d. a volume, and the demand for such was enormous. It was not surprising that in this prolific soil some weeds grew up, but he hoped, and really believed, there was not that corruption of the mind of the country going on such as his hon. friend feared. There was a large demand and a large supply of literature of every class. On the registers of our Sunday schools were the names of 6,000,000 children, a larger number than attended day schools, notwithstanding the compulsory powers of enforcing attendance. Was it not a fact that every one of those children possessed a copy of the Scriptures, and were they not supplied with healthy literature at extremely low prices, or that it was lent to them through the libraries? Here was the antidote for this moral poison—the establishment of free libraries in all our large towns. In that respect the Metropolis was behind almost all the large towns of England—there was less public life, less civic spirit in London than anywhere else. As compared with our northern towns the difference was one hardly realised. In two or three towns with which he was best acquainted—take Nottingham, for instance—the Free Library circulated more than 1,000 volumes every day, and in Sheffield something like 500,000 books were lent every year. And that was only a part of the supply, which was supplemented by other institutions, such as mechanics' institutes, clubs, and colleges, which added a supply of healthy literature to sound teaching. Here he saw the real antidote, the supply of healthy literature, and an intellectual training to preserve the young from the pernicious effects of the poisonous stuff to be met with. Something was said by the hon. Member for Wigan (Mr. F. S. Powell) in reference to the circulation among Members of Parliament of pamphlets in reference to what was going on in India and elsewhere.

MR. F. S. POWELL said he merely alluded to publications of an apparently religious character, and which he had no doubt were earnestly and sincerely meant to promote the cause of religion and morality, but which contained matter which must be most pernicious and injurious to the moral sense of the young.

MR. MUNDELLA said he understood the hon. Member to refer

to the circulation of letters in reference to practices alleged to be carried on in India.

Mr. F. S. Powell said he mentioned no names, and would rather not mention names, because that had the effect of advertising the sheets. He was speaking of periodical publications, intended, no doubt, to be of religious character.

Mr. Mundella said he would accept the statement in the broadcast way the hon. Member would desire to make it; but this he might say, that they—the Legislators—ought to know, and ought not to be afraid to know, the truth, and the whole truth. Whatever was done within the British Empire, discreditable though it might be to our legislation and our moral nature, the House should know of it, and ought not to be afraid to know of it. They ought not to shrink from full knowledge of the facts that had been brought to the notice of Members, and though he should be sorry indeed if some of the circulars that had been placed in his hands recently should fall into the hands of young persons in his house, yet he was glad to know it if such things were done, and under the sanction of our countrymen, the rulers in our great Dependency. Every member of the House should feel the full responsibility of tolerating such infamy. ["Hear, hear!"] It was in reference to that that he wished to say a word or two. He was anxious as anyone to suppress the publication of anything suggestive of indecency, yet, if indecent practices were carried on, if such things were done with the authority of our countrymen, Members of Parliament at least ought to know of it, if only that they might put an end to the practices, rather than to put an end to the statement that such practices existed.

Mr. Mark Stewart (Kirkcudbright) said, for many years he had taken great interest in this most important question, and he sincerely thanked the hon. Member for Flintshire (Mr. S. Smith) for bringing the subject forward in the manner he had. Thanks, also, were due to the Home Secretary for the fair and candid manner in which he had met the motion and expressed his desire, speaking with legal authority, to put down the pernicious growth of impure literature among us. As to what had fallen from the hon. Member for Flintshire, he (Mr. Mark Stewart) could not help thinking—and he had mentioned it before—that we must mainly look to other than legal process to check the spread of this literature. We should look to those large agencies, those societies that had done so much in the past, and would continue their work, to spread abroad the means of becoming acquainted with healthy literature. Of course, it was difficult, when a prosecution was instituted, to obtain a conviction on the merits of the case, and failure to convict increased the evil. But in town and country those agencies to which he referred were exercising a most salutary effect by depôts in towns, by colporteurs in country districts. In too many of the lowest parts of towns unwholesome literature circulated, because it was all that was at hand; but the efforts of the associations for the spread of literature of a wholesome class were directed to inducing shops to supply the better class of reading, and there was no unwillingness on the part of traders to do this when it was shown to them that it was their interest to do so. That he had on the testimony of a friend who visited the back streets and slums with that object in view, and had paid some 20,000 visits to shops which sold the bad reading for the masses. Those interested should give every encouragement to the good work. Meanwhile, the school master was abroad; every child could read, and was eager to read, and should have within reach that which was, while interesting, instructive and religious in tone. The work was difficult, yet could be carried on by judiciously selecting centres, and providing shops, stalls, and colporteurs, to meet and to encourage demand. Much could be done in that way to promote the view expressed in the motion. With regard to what had been said about the circulation of papers in reference to matters that had been commented upon in the House, though it might be useful to bring such matters to light, yet it should be done by some less indiscriminate method than had been adopted.

MR. H. J. WILSON (York, W. R., Holmfirth) said there was much in the speech of the Home Secretary that must give general satisfaction; but his hon. friend (Mr. Smith) had made one reference to which some explanation would have been desirable. His hon. friend referred to a recent prosecution for the sale of a certain publication, and rather pointedly challenged the Home Secretary to say why he did not proceed against the publisher, instead of the lads who were selling the publication. Unless there was a good reason for it—and for aught he knew there might be a sufficient answer—it did seem to him rather unfair to allow the prosecution of the sellers, while the greater sinner, who made the larger profit, the publisher, was left untouched. He thanked the right hon. gentleman the Member for the Brightside Division of Sheffield for his remarks in reference to what had been said by the hon. Member for Wigan, and as one who had had a good deal to do with such matters, he could assure the latter that it was with the greatest regret this literature was circulated to Members in reference to the working of the Contagious Diseases Act; but it was the only way to make the truth known, and the only way to stop the dissemination of such statements was to put an end to the horrible system that rendered such dissemination necessary.

Mr. S. Smith said he desired to take the sense of the House on the question, not in the spirit of any censure whatever upon the Government, for he entirely sympathized with and heartily reciprocated the language of the Home Secretary; nothing could be more satisfactory. To the motion, he believed, there was no opposition, and it would no doubt be accepted unanimously. This unanimous judgment of the House would have a very useful effect out-of-doors.

Question Put and Agreed to.

CENTRAL CRIMINAL COURT.

November Sessions, 1888.

Mr. Henry Vizetelly surrendered to his recognizances to answer an indictment charging him with publishing an obscene libel. The book which formed the subject-matter of the indictment was an English translation of a French novel, and entitled "The Soil."

The Solicitor-General, Mr. Poland, and Mr. Asquith conducted the prosecution; Mr. B. F. Williams, Q. C., and Mr. Cluer were counsel for the defence.

The Solicitor-General, in opening the case, referred to the case of "The Queen v. Hicklin," in which Lord Chief Justice Cockburn laid it down that the test of obscenity was whether the tendency of the matter charged as obscenity was to deprave and corrupt those whose minds were open to such immoral influences and into whose hands the publication might fall. In that case a Protestant society had collected and published certain passages from Roman Catholic books, with the object of calling attention to the supposed errors of the Romish Church; but it was held that the object of the publication had nothing to do with the matter. The Solicitor-General pointed out also that it had been held that if any one published a report of the case containing the passages complained of they would be liable to be proceeded against, and the fact that it was merely the report of the case would not be a justification. He would read the extracts from the book complained of, and if any one took the opportunity of publishing the passages in a report of the case, or otherwise, the person doing so would be plainly liable to the same penalty as the defendant if the verdict should be adverse to him. It was for the jury to look at the passages complained of. He did not say that if they saw in a volume one isolated passage of an immoral tendency that that would be a sufficient justification for indicting the publisher of the book as being guilty of a misdemeanour. Undoubtedly there might be passages in works of a medical kind, intended for perusal of medical men and students, which would not be subject to a prosecution, but if the passages were collected in a book and published for the purpose of ministering to the depraved taste of casual readers, they would undoubtedly be subject to an indictment. It had been suggested that in our literature and in that of other countries there were great works whose authors were recognised as being kings in literature, which works contained certain immoral and indecent expressions. It was true that in our literature, especially in that of two or three hundred years ago, there were passages which might conflict with their judgment as to what was fit for circulation, but that was entirely a different question, and one which had been dealt with in the case of "The Queen v. Hicklin," where the suggestion was dismissed as being no excuse. If there was anything in the objection it would not in the least degree be applicable to the filthy book which he held in his hand. It was not one, two, or three passages which had been chosen, but they had twenty-one passages, taken from different parts of the work in question, some of them long passages, extending over several of its pages. There was no question before them of a book written with a wholesome purpose of teaching, or with an innocent purpose of amusing, but this book was filthy from beginning to end. He did not believe there was ever collected between the covers of a book so much bestial obscenity as was found in the passages of this book, and after he had read the passages complained of he thought the jury would be of opinion that every syllable of what he had said was justified. There was not a passage in it which contained any literary genius or the expression of any elevated thought. There was not a single scene described which could be pointed to as being free from vicious suggestions and obscene expressions. The Solicitor-General then proceeded to read the passages complained of, and after some of them had been read the jury asked if it was necessary to read all of them.

The Recorder.—They are charged in the indictment as being the substance and essence of the case. They are revolting to a degree, but they are charged in the indictment, and must be proved.

A Juryman.—But is it necessary to read them all?

The Recorder.—The Solicitor-General will exercise his own discretion.

The Solicitor-General.—I hope you will understand that it is at least as unpleasant to me to read them as it is to you to listen to them. If you think, subject to what may be said by my learned friend on the part of the defence, that these passages are obscene, I will stop reading them at once.

Mr. Williams said that his client, acting upon his advice, desired to withdraw his plea of "Not Guilty" and to plead "Guilty" to having published these books. There was no doubt that the work which formed the subject-matter of the indictment contained passages which the Jury had intimated were very disgusting and unpleasant, even in the discharge of a public duty, to have to listen to. He would remind his Lordship that these works were works of a great French author.

The Solicitor-General.—A voluminous French author.

The Recorder.—A popular French author.

Mr. Williams.—Of an author who ranks high among the literary men of France. Mr. Vizetelly had pleaded guilty to this charge, and therefore it was not for him to contend that these were not obscene. That being so, Mr. Vizetelly would undertake at once to withdraw all those translations of M. Zola's works from circulation. For a long time these works had been published—one of them had been published for four years without any intimation that there was any objection to it. This book, "The Soil," had been published for a year or more, and until this prosecution was instituted no exception was taken to the publication of it. He understood that the Solicitor-General did not ask that any imprisonment should be inflicted.

The Solicitor-General was very glad that a course had been taken which not only would result in stopping the circulation of the books in question, but which carried with it an undertaking that Mr. Vizetelly would be no party to the circulation of other works of M. Zola. He would like to point out that after this warning proceedings under the Act of Parliament would be taken in the event of any person attempting to circulate these books. The question of punishment was for the Court, but he did not ask that Mr. Vizetelly should be sent to prison.

Mr. Vizetelly asked that witnesses might be called to speak to his character, but the Recorder said it was not necessary.

The Recorder, addressing Mr. Vizetelly, said:—There is a great distinction between this case and "The Queen v. Hicklin." There the object of the publication was no doubt extremely good, but it was held, and very properly so, to be no answer. This book has been published for the sake of gain, and it is not necessary for me to say that it was deliberately done in order to deprave the minds of persons who might read the books. In my opinion they are of the most repulsive description. They are not of a seductive or a fanciful character, but repulsive and revolting to the last degree. Therefore, when a man who has a good character—which you say, and which I am quite prepared to admit you deserve—finds that the opinion is entertained by the authorities that they are of this description, he could not do otherwise than express himself as you have done and undertake to withdraw them from circulation. That is the great object of such an enquiry as this. The sentence is that you be fined £100 and enter into your own recognizances in £200 to keep the peace and be of good behaviour for twelve months.

The Recorder added that the fine of £100 was to be paid by Saturday.

"Pernicious Literature"

OPINIONS OF THE PRESS ON THE PROSECUTION

FROM *The Times*.

On October 31st, Mr. Henry Vizetelly, the publisher, pleaded guilty before the Recorder, at the Central Criminal Court, of publishing an obscene libel by the sale of an English translation of Zola's novel, "La Terre." He was sentenced to pay a fine of £100 and to enter into his own recognizances in £200 to keep the peace and to be of good behaviour for twelve months. This is a sufficiently heavy punishment when it is considered that Mr. Vizetelly had undertaken, through his counsel, at once to withdraw from circulation all the translations of Zola's works published by him, so that, in addition to paying a not inconsiderable fine, he will suffer a severe commercial loss. At the same time it is not a vindictive punishment, and, considering the looseness with which the law relating to obscene libels has been administered of late years, it would certainly have been impolitic to inflict any such punishment on a person who pleaded guilty. By pleading guilty Mr. Vizetelly may be held to have virtually admitted that when he published a translation of "La Terre" he commited an offence for which he was ready to run the risk of being prosecuted.

The question of policy involved in prosecutions of this kind is not very easy to decide, but assuredly most people will agree that the publication of cheap translations of the worst of Zola's novels is a grave offence against public morals, and that it is a good thing that the law should be invoked to restrain it. Between prudery and pruriency in such matters there is a wide debatable ground, and it is not always easy to draw the line which separates what is permissable from what is not. But if the line is not to be drawn so as to exclude translations of such works of Zola as "La Terre" and "Pot Bouille," it is plain that it cannot be drawn at all. They are published purely for the sake of gain, and for gain which cannot be realised except by the corruption of those who buy and read them. The evil wrought by literature of this vile character is immense, as was shown and acknowledged in the debate on obscene publications initiated in the House of Commons during the last Session by Mr. Samuel Smith. In any case, we fear, the law can do little to cope with this evil, but it is well that the little that it can do should be done.

FROM *The St. James's Gazette.*

With the literary aspects of the question raised by the prosecution for publishing obscene books we do not propose to meddle. Some literary persons, well-qualified and ill-qualified, were ready to take up the cudgels for Mr. Vizetelly, for Zolaism in general, and for "La Terre" in particular. But Mr. Vizetelly cut away the ground from his apologists by pleading guilty and promising not to repeat his fault. Nor shall we touch the question—raised and debated a hundred times, but never likely to be settled—how far Art is concerned with Morality. Is art above morality? or beneath it? or does it stand on an altogether different plane? The desire not to advertise them, and the probability of an unsuccessful prosecution, have influenced many persons, who detest them and would gladly suppress them, to leave them quite alone. We are not quite sure that this was not the wiser course; nor are we quite sure that the punishment of Mr. Vizetelly will have none but good effects, even in that sphere of morality which is intended to benefit by it. But purity is not the whole of morality. If the books which tend toward lubricity are to be suppressed, why should the books be allowed to go free that glorify murder, burglary, and highway robbery? Why is bloodshed and dishonesty to be preached in the streets if sexual morality is to be guarded by legal procedure? It is quite as important that the minds of boys and girls should be kept from unnecessary contact with crime which injures the community, as with dirtiness which has no influence except upon the personal character. If dirty fiction is to be suppressed, why should we not take one step further and check the sensational histories of actual crimes? This is a course which few people would be as yet prepared to recommend. But yet it is in a way the logical consequence of proceedings in the Central Criminal Court. If we are to have a censorship of public morals, let it at least be complete and thoroughgoing. But we are not sure that the nation would not be ready to support some kind of censorship, if it had any kind of certainty that its good effects would counterbalance the evils which it certainly would bring about. It is certainly a singular and significant sign of the times that it should be possible to discuss the question at all. Yet discussed it will be.

"Pernicious Literature"

FROM *The Whitehall Review.*

We must confess to looking with suspicion upon the many "vigilance" societies which have been started to look after our morals. The idea, in itself, an excellent one, has been very much abused by its connection with a vast array of irresponsible persons who have their own notoriety at stake first, and then the morals of the people. It is unfortunate that this should be so, because it tends to dwarf the good which other and really sound associations of a similar character endeavour to do. Vigilance associations, moreover, are apt to be led away by enthusiasts, and to set their wits and forces against some form of vice which, with all the influence and energy behind them, it is impracticable to reach. Enthusiasts too often grope about until they find shadows, and then make bold attack on these in an eminently visionary manner.

The step which the National Vigilance Association has taken with regard to putting down the publication and sale of impure and indecent literature is, however, worthy of the highest commendation and support. The evil is being bravely combatted by Mr. Samuel Smith, M. P., who by the recent death of Lord Mount-Temple has lost a valuable colleague and councillor in his good work. In the present day, when so many books are published, and reading has become so general, the circulation of impure literature must, of necessity, have an evil and contagious effect upon the morals of the nation. It is idle to argue that people read pernicious literature and then cast it aside, disappointed that it has not come up to expectation.

The immoral volume, which is not, as it were, up to sample, and does not give satisfaction to the prurient mind and taste, is but an appetiser to make men and women create a demand for more seasoned matter, and we know that in evil things there is always a supply to meet the demand, and this supply is cunningly contrived to meet all wants and tastes, from the juvenile to the patriarch. In his search to reach the offenders Mr. Samuel Smith has lighted on a vicious form of literature which does almost as much harm as the sensuous writings of the English and French schools.

"It will be asked" pertinently suggests the report of the Association, "why, considering that there is a law against obscene publications, are not these indecent books and photographs suppressed? The answer is that although something has been done in this direction, public opinion is not active enough to compel the magistrates to do their duty. Through the efforts of Mr. Samuel Smith, a prosecution was commenced against Messrs. Vizetelly, the publishers of a translation of a work by M. Zola. But the other day the National Vigilance Association took out a summons against the publishers of a New and Unexpurgated edition of Boccaccio's 'Decameron.' Innocent persons who have read the expurgated editions which are usually published in England will have little idea of the disgusting matter which this book contains. The case came before Mr. Alderman Phillips at the Guildhall, and the magistrate, though he thought it necessary to clear the Court of women, dismissed the summons without assigning reasons. It is of no use to say that these books are literature. It may be right that they should remain in our libraries in the original languages, or perhaps in English, accessible to students of literature or of manners. That is no reason why they should be distributed broadcast in cheap issues, unexpurgated, or in careful selections of the most indecent parts, specially for the corruption of young people." It is useless to disguise the fact that all this impure literature is published for the mere pursuance of pecuniary gain.

FROM *The Star.*

In the opinion, probably, of the majority of people Mr. Vizetelly may consider that he has done very well to have escaped from an English court with merely a moderate fine. The very able defence which Mr. Vizetelly put forth some time ago was only calculated to obscure the issue. It is true that Rabelais is obscene, that Chaucer is coarse, and that Boccaccio's ladies and gentlemen are all too frank. But M. Zola's "La Terre" has none of the charm, the humour, the style which redeem the works of the authors named. It is simply unrelieved and morbid filth. Even were it elevated by the undoubted power and realistic skill of some of the writer's earliest efforts, it is impossible to excuse its reproduction into English. Mr. Matthew Arnold once said of a translation of

"Pernicious Literature"

Homer that there was no justification for its existence. Still less could a hastily and a slovenly written translation of a filthy French novel justify its existence. Some translations, notably those of Schiller's "Wallenstein" and Carlyle's "Wilhelm Meister," have been literature in the best sense. But indifferent translations are not literature, and there is an end of the matter from the standpoint of art.

FROM *The Liverpool Mercury.*

Messrs. Vizetelly pleaded guilty at the Central Criminal Court to the charge of publishing English translations of M. Zola's French novels. This action on their part was an admission that they could not offer a valid defence to the indictment. Of course, there never was any denial that the works were issued by them in an English dress; the only point in doubt, when the prosecution commenced, was whether such versions as they produced brought them within the penal statutes. It is gratifying to find that our law is strong enough to prevent the dissemination of demoralizing literature of a certain character. There is nothing likely to be of more injury to the morals of the people than the free publication of cheap editions of works which pander to prurient tastes: and there cannot be the slightest doubt that the novels of M. Zola are amongst the worst of their kind. It is true that the English editions are expurgated, but even when the most repulsive features were gone there still remained enough of objectionable matter—in the characters, the incidents, the plot, and the moral—to justify repressive action. Where we find an inconsistency is the impunity enjoyed by those who retail the same works when clothed in the original French. If the English versions are offensive to the law, it is hard to understand why the far more revolting French versions are allowed to circulate. The effect must be as grave upon the more educated as upon the less educated. A man is not a superior person morally because he can read French, and there is no logical reason why he should be privileged on this account to touch and look on rank fruits which are wisely forbidden to the exclusively English reader.

FROM *The Globe.*

Mr. Henry Vizetelly was yesterday found guilty of the publication of an obscene libel in the form of a translation of Zola's last novel but one—"La Terre." The law in these matters has not been administered with sufficient frequency and vigour to prevent a certain amount of doubt as to where the line should be, and would be, drawn. That a line must be drawn somewhere is, however, admitted on all hands. It is idle to argue that great men have ere now written great books which have been far from free from the taint of the obscene. The eagles have, it is true, sometimes stooped to carrion, but it has not been their normal food. The bad with them has been, in the language of logic, an accident; whereas, with such a book as "La Terre," it is not an accident, but an essential property. To say that there is a wide expanse of moral ground which is debateable, and within which it would be inexpedient for the law to be dogmatic, is only common sense. But to say that the subject matter of Mr. Vizetelly's offence does not lie quite beyond the limits of that debateable ground is an outrage on common sense and common decency. There are many things in literature which are questionable, and there are also some which are unquestionable, and Mr. Vizetelly is rightly punished for having shut his eyes to the fact that the beastliness of this book is one of the latter.

FROM *The Morning Advertiser.*

There can be little difference of opinion as to the justice of the judgment of the Court. If there is such a thing as improper literature M. Zola has produced it. His books have great merits, no doubt, but their merits do not redeem them from the imputation of ministering to the lowest passions of human nature, and it is difficult to imagine that any man or woman can be the better for their perusal. The average man or woman, and, still more, the average boy or girl, must infallibly be made worse by reading them. We do not believe it would be possible to submit them to any ordinarily constituted jury in England without the certainty of their being condemned as they were yesterday at the Old Bailey. The fact that there are classic writers in our own language who have written works as objectionable in form as "Nana" and "La

"Pernicious Literature"

Terre," if for the sake of argument we admit it to be a fact, has really but little bearing on the question. The improprieties of Shakespeare and other old dramatists, and even those of some of the eighteenth century novelists, belong to a past age, and do not appeal to the imagination of readers of to-day like descriptions of wickedness whose scene is laid in our own times, and which is portrayed in current phraseology. The contention that if we are to suppress the vicious novels of our own time we must, to be consistent, make a clean sweep of a large portion of English literature cannot be maintained, and is not seriously maintained even by those who put it forth. It does not follow that traffickers in vice are to have their way, and that nothing should be done because we are unable to do all that we would fain wish to do. The function of the law in this matter is not difficult to define. It ought to maintain public decency, and it can do so. The exhibition of vicious pictures in shop windows, or in the streets, can be prevented by ordinary police vigilance, just as indecency can be repressed upon the stage. Incentives to wickedness ought not to be forced upon public notice, and it is the duty of the guardians of order to prevent it. In this respect there is great room and urgent need of a more stringent rule than has yet been established. There ought to be no difficulty in stopping the exhibition of placards in the streets advertising catch-penny publications, the wording of which is an offence to the most elementary notions of decency. The publications themselves are often innocent enough, we dare say, but the handbills which call attention to them are a disgrace to a community which professes to be civilised. Neither the liberty of the Press nor any other liberty which deserves a moment's respect ought to prevent the prompt seizure and confiscation of such papers without the formality of a prosecution. There are offences against public propriety which no police-constable would hesitate to deal with on the spot without considering whether or not they are specified in any Act of Parliament, and the exhibition of palpably indecent handbills ought to come within the same category. If the exhibitors or their employers consider themselves aggrieved, they can resort to a legal remedy. There is little fear that they would do so, or that the police authorities would not be fully sustained by public opinion. We frankly confess that we should be

379

glad to see a little despotism in this matter exercised by the Commissioners both in the City and the West-end.

FROM *The Saturday Review.*

The conviction of Messrs. Vizetelly at the Central Criminal Court on three charges of publishing obscene libels, is matter for congratulation, though it might well have been brought about earlier. The offences charged were committed in the course of publishing English translations of three of the dirtiest of M. Zola's novels. It will be well that the numerous persons who have of late years engaged in this disgusting traffic should take note of the fact that by so doing they commit a crime punishable by a heavy term of imprisonment: and it is to be hoped that they will be discouraged by the fact that there is a limit to the long-suffering timidity of the officials whose duty it is to institute prosecutions of this character. To the latter persons it may be well to point out, now that they have discovered how easy it is to do their duty, that the law has provided them with a far more summary and effectual procedure than that which they have at last adopted. The proper course is not to wait until books like "The Soil" have been sold in large numbers, but as soon as they appear to seize them by means of a warrant under Lord Campbell's Act, and procure an order for their destruction at the cost of the publisher. There is no reason to fear that the magistrates would be remiss in enforcing the law if the authorities of Whitehall and Scotland Yard would only perform their duty in putting it in motion. In this instance the latter persons have the less excuse for their laches, because the existence of the works in question, and the proper manner of dealing with them, have more than once been pointed out to them in these columns. It is probably due more to the good sense of counsel than to the proper feeling of the defendant that nothing was heard on Wednesday of the loathsome cant about a high moral purpose which suitably disfigures the introductions of some of these disgraceful volumes.

FROM *The Methodist Times.*

We have never been able to believe in the moral intentions of Zola, and it has always been a marvel to us that such a critic as

"Pernicious Literature"

Mr. James should seriously contend for them. Zolaism is a disease. It is a study of the putrid. Even France has shown signs that she has had enough of it. No one can read Zola without moral contamination, and the only plea that can be made is that the disgust inspired destroys the fascination of the evil. It is time that legislative action was taken against other authors besides Zola, who are contributing to the literature of the sewer. Let those who have a liking for the "scrofulous French novel" read it if they will, but let it at least be in the original. Broadcast translations are an offence which demands the utmost severity of punishment and repression.

FROM *The Western Morning News.*

Whatever may be said in favour of the State shutting its eyes to the circulation of Zolaesque literature, there can be no question that Zola is filthy in the extreme, and obscene to the point of bestiality. He is more unclean, and realistically so, than any other writer, not an Oriental, whose name we can record. It has been his boast that he saw the evil side of life and had described it accurately. There are many undesirable things of which all men have knowledge, and of which only the evil-minded speak. It is the shame of Zola that he has put an end to reticence. No doubt, in the older dramatists, and especially in the dramatists of the Restoration, there are obscene passages. But Zola sinks to a lower depth than any English writer ever touched. We could prove our point in a moment if by the very proof we were not likely to do the evil which we deprecate. The Court had no alternative but to make it clear that the law did not tolerate such work as "Pot Bouille," "Nana," and "La Terre." Yet what a comedy it all is when the thing is considered! The other day the unmarried heroine of a novel was described as having been the reader of the whole of Zola's works, and young ladies in a drawing room will not hesitate in these latter days to talk of realism and naturalism with reference to the latest prurient pages of the seeker after degraded aspects of life. These books, which have been debated in society for years, are now practically prohibited for their obscenity. The comedy of it cannot fail to be appreciated. Fathers and mothers in this latter day have become more tolerant of what shall be introduced into their homes than the judge at the old Bailey as to what may be sold in the streets. Unless this side of our national life be looked after a little more closely greater evils will befal than any which can arise from political changes or from other social conditions.

"The Limits of Realism in Fiction"*

By Edmund Gosse

EDMUND GOSSE (1849-1928) was one of the major English critics of the late nineteenth and early twentieth centuries. A lecturer at Trinity College, Cambridge, from 1884 to 1890, librarian of the House of Lords from 1904 to 1914, he was listened to with respect and had a major part in introducing the new writing, particularly from France and Scandinavia, into England.

The present article was never published in an English review but appeared in the *Forum* in the United States in 1890, only a few months after the noise and fury of the Vizetelly trial. It is an attempt, in a tone of quiet reason, to bring the partisans to their senses so that they may see the subject in perspective. Gosse makes no bones about his belief that Zola is "one of the leading men of genius in the second half of the nineteenth century, one of the strongest novelists in the world. . . ." He then proceeds to make sound, dispassionate criticisms of realism, though his comments on the lapses of taste to which this kind of writing is prone are heavy with irony. He ends in conciliatory fashion by asserting that realism has undoubtedly had its day, but tips the scales in its favor again by the statement that it "has cleared the air of a thousand follies, has pricked a whole fleet of oratorical bubbles."

This article should be compared with "The Moral Teaching of Zola" by Vernon Lee, which was published in England in 1893. Known as an interpreter of Italian art and letters and of the Italian scene—a taste which was essentially romantic and eminently genteel, Miss Lee carried some weight when she announced that "despite all drawbacks, real and imaginary, Zola has had to be accepted." She correctly points out that "despite all his realistic programme, the art of Zola is not simple realism but a most complex personal art. . . ." She then sketches out what was to be the most popular way of accepting Zola into the canon: the way of social prophet. His novels are likened to various divisions of Hell, each of them showing the difficulties in the way of becoming real human beings, "because, for all the pretence of schooling, religion, and political rights, there is a dead wall of want and weariness between them [the underprivileged classes] and humanising influences. . . ." She meets the charge of obscenity and vice head on by ask-

* Gosse, Edmund, "The Limits of Realism in Fiction," *Forum* 9: pp. 391-400, June 1890. Reprinted in *Questions at Issue*, London, William Heinemann Ltd., 1893, and used here by permission of that publisher.

ing whether as much could have been achieved "at a less expense of evil suggestion and loathsome detail," and she concludes that "it is well to be shown as a vast system what one's individual experience can show only in fragments. . . . It is salutary to be horrified and sickened when the horror and the sickening make one look around, pause, and reflect."

◇◇

In the last new Parisian farce, by M. Sarcey's clever young son-in-law, there is a conscientious painter of the realistic school who is preparing for the Salon a very serious and abstruse production. The young lady of his heart says, at length: "It's rather a melancholy subject; I wonder you don't paint a sportsman, crossing a rustic bridge, and meeting a pretty girl." This is the climax, and the artist breaks off his relations with Young Lady No. 1. Toward the end of the play, while he is still at work on his picture, Young Lady No. 2 says: "If I were you, I should take another subject. Now, for instance, why don't you paint a pretty girl, crossing a rustic bridge, and met by a sportsman?" This is really an allegory, whether M. Gandillot intends it or not. Thus have those charming, fresh, ingenuous, ignorant, and rather stupid young ladies, the English and American publics, received the attempts which novelists have made to introduce among them what is called, outside the Anglo-Saxon world, the experimental novel. The present writer is no defender of that class of fiction; least of all is he an exclusive defender of it; but he is tired to death of the criticism on both sides of the Atlantic, which refuses to see what the realists are, whither they are tending, and what position they are beginning to hold in the general evolution of imaginative literature. He is no great lover of what they produce, and most certainly does not delight in their excesses; but when they are advised to give up their studies and paint pretty girls on rustic bridges, he is almost stung into partisanship. The present article will have no interest whatever for persons who approve of no more stringent investigation into conduct than Miss Yonge's, and enjoy no action nearer home than Zambeziland; but to those who have perceived that in almost every country in the world the novel of manners has been passing through a curious phase, it may possibly not be un-

"The Limits of Realism in Fiction"

interesting to be called upon to inquire what the nature of that phase has been, and still more what is to be the outcome of it.

So far as the Anglo-Saxon world is concerned, the experimental or realistic novel is mainly to be studied in America, Russia, and France. It exists now in all the countries of the European Continent, but we know less about its manifestations there. It has had no direct development in England, except in the clever but imperfect stories of Mr. George Moore. Ten years ago the realistic novel, or at all events the naturalist school, out of which it proceeded, was just beginning to be talked about, and there was still a good deal of perplexity, outside Paris, as to its scope and as to the meaning of its name. Russia, still unexplored by the Vicomte de Vogüé and his disciples, was represented to western readers solely by Turgeneff, who was a great deal too romantic to be a pure naturalist. In America, where now almost every new writer of merit seems to be a realist, there was but one, Mr. Henry James, who, in 1877, had inaugurated the experimental novel in the English language, with his "American." Mr. Howells, tending more and more in that direction, was to write on for several years before he should produce a thoroughly realistic novel.

Ten years ago, then, the very few people who take an interest in literary questions were looking with hope or apprehension, as the case might be, to Paris, and chiefly to the study of M. Zola. It was from the little villa at Médan that revelation on the subject of the coming novel was to be expected; and in the autumn of 1880 the long-expected message came, in the shape of the grotesque, violent, and narrow, but extremely able volume of destructive and constructive criticism called "*Le Roman Expérimental*." People had complained that they did not know what M. Zola was driving at; that they could not recognize a "naturalistic" or "realistic" book when they saw it; that the "scientific method" in fiction, the "return to nature," "experimental observation" as the basis of a story, were mere phrases to them, vague and incomprehensible. The Sage of Médan determined to remove the objection and explain everything. He put his speaking-trumpet to his lips, and, disdaining to address the crassness of his countrymen, he shouted his system of rules and formulas to the Russian public, that all the world might hear. In 1880 he had himself proceeded far. He had published the Rougon-Macquart series of his novels, as far as *"Une Page d'Amour."* He has added to the bulk of his works since then, with six or seven novels, and he has published many forcible and fascinating and many repulsive pages. But since 1880 he has not altered his method or pushed on to any further development. He had already displayed his main qualities—his extraordinary mixture of versatility and monotony, his enduring force, his plentiful lack of taste, his cynical disdain for the weaknesses of men, his admirable constructive power, his inability to select the salient points in a vast mass of observations. He had already shown himself what I must take the liberty of saying that he appears to me to be, one of the leading men of genius in the second half of the nineteenth century, one of the strongest novelists of the world; and that in spite of faults so serious and so eradicable that they would have hopelessly wrecked a writer a little less overwhelming in strength and resource. Zola seems to me to be the Vulcan among our later gods, afflicted with moral lameness from his birth, and coming to us sooty and brutal from the forge, yet as indisputably great as any Mercury-Hawthorne or Apollo-Thackeray of the best of them. It is to Zola, and to Zola only, that the concentration of the scattered tendencies of naturalism is due. It is owing to him that the threads of Flaubert and Daudet, Dostoiefsky and Tolstoi, Howells and Henry James can be drawn into anything like a single system. It is Zola who discovered a common measure for all these talents, and a formula wide enough and yet close enough to distinguish them from the outside world and bind them to one another. It is his doing that for ten years the experimental novel has flowed in a definite channel, and has not spread itself abroad in a thousand whimsical directions.

To a serious critic, then, who is not a partisan, but who sees how large a body of carefully-composed fiction the naturalistic school has produced, it is of great importance to know what is the formula of M. Zola. He has defined it, one would think, clearly enough, but to see it intelligently repeated is rare indeed. It starts from the negation of fancy—not of imagination, as that word is used by the best Anglo-Saxon critics, but of fancy—the romantic and rhetorical elements that novelists have so largely used to embroider the homespun fabric of experience with. It starts with the exclusion of all that is called "ideal," all that is not firmly based on the actual life of human beings, all, in short, that is grotesque, unreal, nebulous, or didactic. I do not understand Zola to condemn the romantic writers of the past; I do not think he has spoken of Dumas *père* or of George Sand as Mr. Howells has spoken of Dickens. He has a phrase of contempt—richly deserved, it appears to me—for the childish evolution of Victor Hugo's plots, and in particular of that of *"Notre Dame de Paris"*; but, on the whole, his aim is rather to determine the outlines of a new school than to attack the recognized masters of the past. If it be not so, it should be so; there is room in the Temple of Fame for all good writers, and it does not blast the laurels of Walter Scott that we are deeply moved by Dostoiefsky.

With Zola's theory of what the naturalistic novel should be, it seems impossible at first sight to quarrel. It is to be contemporary; it is to be founded on and limited by actual experience; it is to reject all empirical modes of awakening sympathy and interest; its aim is to place before its readers living beings, acting the comedy of life as naturally as possible. It is to trust to principles of action and to reject formulas of character; to cultivate the personal expression; to be analytical rather than lyrical; to paint men as they are, not as you think they should be. There is no harm in all this. There is not a word here that does not apply to the chiefs of one of the two great parallel schools of English fiction. It is hard to conceive of a novelist whose work is more experimental than Richardson. Fielding is personal and analytical above all things. If France points to George Sand among its romanticists, we can point to a realist who is greater than she, in Jane Austen. There is not a word to be found in M. Zola's definitions of the experimental novel that is not fulfilled in the pages of "Emma," which is equivalent to saying that the most advanced realism may be practiced by the most innocent as well as the most captivating of novelists. Miss Austen did not observe over a wide area, but within the circle of her experience she disguised nothing, neglected nothing, glossed over nothing. She is the perfection of the realistic ideal, and there ought to be a statue of her in the vestibule of the forthcoming *Académie des Goncourts*. Unfortunately, the lives of her later brethren have not been so sequestered as hers, and they, too, have thought it their duty to neglect nothing and to disguise nothing.

It is not necessary to repeat here the rougher charges which have been brought against the naturalist school in France—charges which in mitigated form have assailed their brethren in Russia and America. On a carefully-reasoned page in the copy of M. Zola's essay *"Du Roman"* which lies before me, one of those idiots who write in public books has scribbled the remark, "They see nothing in life but filth and crime." This ignoble wielder of the pencil but repeats what more ambitious critics have been saying in solemn terms for the last fifteen years. Even as regards Zola himself, as the author of the delicate comedy of *"La Conquête de Plassans,"* and the moving tragedy of *"Une Page d'Amour,"* this charge is utterly false, and in respect of the other leaders it is simply preposterous. None the less, there are sides upon which the naturalistic novelists are open to serious criticism in practice. It is with no intention of underrating their eminent qualities that I suggest certain points at which, as it appears to me, their armor is conspicuously weak. There are limits to realism, and they seem to have been readily discovered by the realists themselves. These weak points are to be seen in the jointed harness of the strongest book that the school has yet produced in any country, *"Crime et Châtiment."*

When the ideas of Zola were first warmly taken up, about ten years ago, by the most earnest and sympathetic writers who then were young, the theory of the experimental novel seemed unassailable, and the range within which it could be worked to advantage practically boundless. But the fallacies of practice remained to be experienced, and looking back upon what has been written by the leaders themselves, the places where the theory has broken down are patent. It may not be uninteresting to take up the leading dogmas of the naturalistic school, and to see what elements of failure, or, rather, what limitations to success, they contained. The outlook is very different in 1890 from what it was in 1880; and a vast number of exceedingly clever writers have labored to no avail, if we are not able at the latter date to gain a wider perspective than could be obtained at the earlier one. Ten years ago, most ardent and generous young authors, outside the frontiers of

"The Limits of Realism in Fiction"

indifferent Albion, were fired with enthusiasm at the results to be achieved by naturalism in fiction. It was to be the Revealer and the Avenger. It was to display society as it is, and to wipe out all the hypocrisies of convention. It was to proceed from strength to strength. It was to place all imagination upon a scientific basis, and to open boundless vistas to sincere and courageous young novelists. We have seen with what ardent hope and confidence its principles were accepted by Mr. Howells. We have seen all the Latin races, in their coarser way, embrace and magnify the system. We have seen M. Zola, like a heavy father in high comedy, bless a budding generation of novel-writers, and prophesy that they will all proceed further than he along the road of truth and experiment. Yet the naturalistic school is really less advanced, less thorough, than it was ten years ago. Why is this?

It is doubtless because the strain and stress of production have brought to light those weak places in the formula which were not dreamed of. The first principle of the school was the exact reproduction of life. But life is wide and it is elusive. All that the finest observer can do is to make a portrait of one corner of it. By the confession of the master spirit himself, this portrait is not to be a photograph. It must be inspired by imagination, but sustained and confined by the experience of reality. It does not appear at first sight as though it should be difficult to attain this, but in point of fact it is found almost impossible to approach this species of perfection. The result of building up a long work on this principle is, I hardly know why, to produce the effect of a reflexion in a convex mirror. The more accurately experimental some parts of the picture are, the more will the want of balance and proportion in other parts be felt. I will take at random two examples. No better work in the naturalistic direction has been done than is to be found in the beginning of M. Zola's *"La Joie de Vivre,"* or in the early part of the middle of Mr. James's "Bostonians." The life in the melancholy Norman house upon the cliff, the life among the uncouth fanatic philanthropists in the American city, these are given with a reality, a brightness, a personal note which have an electrical effect upon the reader. But the remainder of each of these remarkable books, built up as they are with infinite toil by two of the most accomplished architects of fiction now living,

leaves on the mind a sense of strained reflection, of images blurred
or malformed by a convexity of the mirror. As I have said, it is
difficult to account for this, which is a feature of blight on almost
every specimen of the experimental novel; but perhaps it can in a
measure be accounted for by the inherent disproportion which
exists between the small flat surface of a book and the vast arch
of life which it undertakes to mirror, those studies being least
liable to distortion which reflect the smallest section of life, and
those in which ambitious masters endeavor to make us feel the
mighty movements of populous cities and vast bodies of men being
the most inevitably misshapen.

Another leading principle of the naturalists is the disinterested
attitude of the narrator. He who tells the story must not act the
part of Chorus, must not praise or blame, must have no favorites;
in short, must not be a moralist but an anatomist. This excellent
and theoretical law has been a snare in practice. The nations of
continental Europe are not bound down by conventional laws to
the same extent as we English are. The Anglo-Saxon race is now
the only one that has not been touched by that pessimism of which
the writings of Schopenhauer are the most prominent and popular
exponent. This fact is too often overlooked when we scornfully
ask why the foreign nations allow themselves so great a latitude in
the discussion of moral subjects. It is partly, no doubt, because of
our beautiful Protestant institutions; because we go to Sunday
schools and take a lively interest in the souls of other people; because, in short, we are all so virtuous and godly, that our novels
are so prim and decent. But it is also partly because our hereditary
dullness in perceiving delicate ethical distinctions has given the
Anglo-Saxon race a tendency to slur over the dissonances between
man and nature. This tendency does not exist among the Latin
races, who run to the opposite extreme and exaggerate these dis-
cords. The consequence has been that they have, almost without
exception, been betrayed by the disinterested attitude into a contemplation of crime and frailty (notoriously more interesting than
innocence and virtue) which has given bystanders excuse for saying that these novelists are lovers of that which is evil. In the same
way they have been tempted by the Rembrandtesque shadows of
pain, dirt, and obloquy to overdash their canvases with the subfusc

"The Limits of Realism in Fiction"

hues of sentiment. In a word, in trying to draw life evenly and draw it whole, they have introduced such a brutal want of tone as to render the portrait a caricature. The American realists, who were guarded by fashion from the Scylla of brutality, have not wholly escaped, on their side, and for the same reason, the Charybdis of insipidity.

It would take us too far, and would require a constant reference to individual books, to trace the weaknesses of the realistic school of our own day. Human sentiment has revenged itself upon them for their rigid regulations and scientific formulas, by betraying them into faults the possibility of which they had not anticipated. But above all other causes of their limited and temporary influence, the most powerful has been the material character which their rules forced upon them, and their excess of positivism and precision. In eliminating the grotesque and the rhetorical they drove out more than they wished to lose; they pushed away with their scientific pitchfork the fantastic and intellectual elements. How utterly fatal this was may be seen, not in the leaders, who have preserved something of the reflected color of the old romance, but in those earnest disciples who have pushed the theory to its extremity. In their somber, grimy, and dreary studies in pathology, clinical bulletins of a soul dying of atrophy, we may see what the limits are of realism, and how impossible it is that human readers should much longer go on enjoying this sort of literary aliment.

If I have dwelt upon these limitations, however, it has not been to cast a stone at the naturalistic school. It has been rather with the object of clearing away some critical misconceptions about the future development of it. Anglo-Saxon criticism of the perambulating species might, perhaps, be persuaded to consider the realists with calmer judgment, if it looked upon them, not as a monstrous canker that was slowly spreading its mortal influence over the whole of literature, which it would presently overwhelm and destroy, but as a natural and timely growth, taking its due place in the succession of products, and bound, like other growths, to bud and blossom and decline. I venture to put forth the view that the novel of experiment has had its day; that it has been made the vehicle of some of the loftiest minds of our age; that it has produced a huge body of fiction, none of it perfect, perhaps, much of it bad, but much of it, also, exceedingly intelligent, vivid, sincere, and durable; and that it is now declining, to leave behind it a great memory, the prestige of persecution, and a library of books which every highly-educated man in the future will be obliged to be familiar with.

It would be difficult, I think, for any one but a realistic novelist to overrate the good that realism in fiction has done. It has cleared the air of a thousand follies, has pricked a whole fleet of oratorical bubbles. Whatever comes next, we cannot return, in serious novels, to the inanities and impossibilities of the old "well-made" plot, to the children changed at nurse, to the madonna heroine and the god-like hero, to the impossible virtues and melodramatic vices. In future, even those who sneer at realism and misrepresent it most willfully, will be obliged to put in their effects in ways more in accord with veritable experience. The public has eaten of the apple of knowledge, and will not be satisfied with mere marionettes. There will still be novel-writers who address the gallery, and who will keep up the gaudy old convention, and the clumsy "Family Herald" evolution, but they will no longer be distinguished people of genius. They will no longer sign themselves George Sand and Charles Dickens.

In the meantime, wherever I look I see the novel ripe for another reaction. The old leaders will not change. It is not to be expected that they will write otherwise than in the mode which has grown mature with them. But in France, among the younger men, every one is escaping from the realistic formula. The two young athletes for whom M. Zola predicted ten years ago an "experimental" career more profoundly scientific than his own, are realists no longer. M. Guy de Maupassant has become a psychologist, and M. Huysmans a mystic. M. Bourget, who set all the ladies dancing after his ingenious, musky books, never has been a realist; nor has Pierre Loti, in whom, with a fascinating freshness, the old exiled romanticism comes back with a laugh and a song. All points to a reaction in France; and in Russia, too, if what we hear is true, the next step will be one toward the mystical and the introspective. Tolstoi's "Sonata," still unpublished as I write these lines, is understood to be wholly distinct from his earlier novels—to be psychological and imaginative. In America it would be rash for a

"The Limits of Realism in Fiction"

foreigner to say what signs of change are evident. The time has hardly come when we look to America for the symptoms of literary initiative. But it is my conviction that the limits of realism have been reached; that no great writer who has not already adapted the experimental system will do so; and that we ought now to be on the outlook to welcome (and, of course, to persecute) a school of novelists with a totally new aim, part of whose formula must unquestionably be a concession to the human instinct for mystery and beauty.

Naturalism in the Theatre*

By August Strindberg

JOHAN AUGUST STRINDBERG (1849-1912) was, along with Ibsen and Hauptmann, an important progenitor of the new drama in western Europe at the turn of the century. A highly rebellious and independent personality, he ran almost the full gamut of literary modes and owed allegiance to no school, though he was for a time caught up in what was essentially a naturalistic attitude. His first play, *Master Olof*, was written in 1871-1872 and showed a strong realistic quality, though it was an historical drama. The Theatre Royal in Stockholm offered to present it on condition that he rewrite it in verse and modify the realistic treatment of theme and characters. Strindberg refused and turned to the novel for his next work, *The Red Room* (1879). This was realistic in its portrayal of the contemporary scene and morality and brought the author a great popular success. It was followed in 1884 by a book of short stories or sketches entitled *Married*. The author and publisher were brought into court on a charge of impiety (over a minor incident in one of the stories) but escaped the charge of immorality which had been expected and were acquitted on the first charge.

The peak of Strindberg's activity as realistic dramatist occurred in 1886-1888, when he wrote four plays of considerable importance which brought him an international reputation. These were *The Father, Comrades, Miss Julie,* and *Creditors*. In addition to their morbid or pessimistic tone which inevitably stirred up vigorous public discussion and attack, the plays are notable for their innovations in form. The preface to *Miss Julie* reprinted here is an attempt to explain innovations in both form and content. So important did the statement seem to contemporaries that it was read aloud at the Berlin premiere at the Freie Bühne in 1892, while a translation was circulated to the Paris audience at Antoine's Théâtre Libre in 1893.

◇◇

AUTHOR'S FOREWORD

THEATRE has long seemed to me—in common with much other art—a *Biblia Pauperum*, a Bible in pictures for those who cannot read what is written or printed; and I see the playwright as a lay preacher peddling the ideas of his time in popular form, popu-

* Strindberg, August, "Author's Foreword," *Miss Julie*, 1888. Reprinted by permission of Willis Kingsley Wing. Copyright © 1955 by Elizabeth Sprigge.

Naturalism in the Theatre

lar enough for the middle-classes, mainstay of theatre audiences, to grasp the gist of the matter without troubling their brains too much. For this reason theatre has always been an elementary school for the young, the semi-educated and for women who still have a primitive capacity for deceiving themselves and letting themselves be deceived—who, that is to say, are susceptible to illusion and to suggestion from the author. I have therefore thought it not unlikely that in these days, when that rudimentary and immature thought-process operating through fantasy appears to be developing into reflection, research and analysis, that theatre, like religion, might be discarded as an outworn form for whose appreciation we lack the necessary conditions. This opinion is confirmed by the major crisis still prevailing in the theatres of Europe, and still more by the fact that in those countries of culture, producing the greatest thinkers of the age, namely England and Germany, drama—like other fine arts—is dead.

Some countries, it is true, have attempted to create a new drama by using the old forms with up-to-date contents, but not only has there been insufficient time for these new ideas to be popularized, so that the audience can grasp them, but also people have been so wrought up by the taking of sides that pure, disinterested appreciation has become impossible. One's deepest impressions are upset when an applauding or hissing majority dominates as forcefully and openly as it can in the theatre. Moreover, as no new form has been devised for these new contents, the new wine has burst the old bottles.

In this play I have not tried to do anything new, for this cannot be done, but only to modernize the form to meet the demands which may, I think, be made on this art today. To this end I chose —or surrendered myself to—a theme which claims to be outside the controversial issues of today, since questions of social climbing or falling, of higher or lower, better or worse, of man and woman, are, have been and will be of lasting interest. When I took this theme from a true story told me some years ago, which made a deep impression, I saw it as a subject for tragedy, for as yet it is tragic to see one favoured by fortune go under, and still more to see a family heritage die out, although a time may come when we have grown so developed and enlightened that we shall view with indifference life's spectacle, now seeming so brutal, cynical and heartless. Then we shall have dispensed with those inferior, unreliable instruments of thought called feelings, which become harmful and superfluous as reasoning develops.

The fact that my heroine rouses pity is solely due to weakness; we cannot resist fear of the same fate overtaking us. The hypersensitive spectator may, it is true, go beyond this kind of pity, while the man with belief in the future may actually demand some suggestion for remedying the evil—in other words some kind of policy. But, to begin with, there is no such thing as absolute evil; the downfall of one family is the good fortune of another, which thereby gets a chance to rise, and, fortune being only comparative, the alternation of rising and falling is one of life's principal charms. Also, to the man of policy, who wants to remedy the painful fact that the bird of prey devours the dove, and lice the bird of prey, I should like to put the question: why should it be remedied? Life is not so mathematically idiotic as only to permit the big to eat the small; it happens just as often that the bee kills the lion or at least drives it mad.

That my tragedy depresses many people is their own fault. When we have grown strong as the pioneers of the French revolution, we shall be happy and relieved to see the national parks cleared of ancient rotting trees which have stood too long in the way of others equally entitled to a period of growth—as relieved as we are when an incurable invalid dies.

My tragedy "The Father" was recently criticised for being too sad—as if one wants cheerful tragedies! Everybody is clamouring for this supposed "joy of life," and theatre managers demand farces, as if the joy of life consisted in being ridiculous and portraying all human beings as suffering from St. Vitus's dance or total idiocy. I myself find the joy of life in its strong and cruel struggles, and my pleasure in learning, in adding to my knowledge. For this reason I have chosen for this play an unusual situation, but an instructive one—an exception, that is to say, but a great exception, one proving the rule, which will no doubt annoy all lovers of the commonplace. What will offend simple minds is that my plot is not simple, nor its point of view single. In real life an action—this, by the way, is a somewhat new discovery—is generally caused by a whole series of motives, more or less fundamental, but as a rule the spectator chooses just one of these—the one which his mind can most easily grasp or that does most credit to his intelligence. A suicide is committed. Business troubles, says the man of affairs. Unrequited love, say the women. Sickness, says the invalid. Despair, says the down-and-out. But it is possible that the motive lay in all or none of these directions, or that the dead man concealed his actual motive by revealing quite another, likely to reflect more to his glory.

I see Miss Julie's tragic fate to be the result of many circumstances: the mother's character, the father's mistaken upbringing of the girl, her own nature, and the influence of her fiancé on a weak, degenerate mind. Also, more directly, the festive mood of Midsummer Eve, her father's absence, her monthly indisposition, her pre-occupation with animals, the excitement of dancing, the magic of dusk, the strongly aphrodisiac influence of flowers, and finally the chance that drives the couple into a room alone—to which must be added the urgency of the excited man.

My treatment of the theme, moreover, is neither exclusively physiological nor psychological. I have not put the blame wholly on the inheritance from her mother, nor on her physical condition at the time, nor on immorality. I have not even preached a moral sermon; in the absence of a priest I leave this to the cook.

I congratulate myself on this multiplicity of motives as being up-to-date, and if others have done the same thing before me, then I congratulate myself on not being alone in my "paradoxes," as all innovations are called.

In regard to the drawing of the characters, I have made my people somewhat "characterless" for the following reasons. In the course of time the word character has assumed manifold meanings. It must have originally signified the dominating trait of the soul-complex, and this was confused with temperament. Later it became the middle-class term for the automaton, one whose nature had become fixed or who had adapted himself to a particular rôle in life. In fact a person who had ceased to grow was called a character, while one continuing to develop—the skilful navigator of life's river, sailing not with sheets set fast, but veering before the wind to luff again—was called characterless, in a derogatory sense, of course, because he was so hard to catch, classify and keep track of. This middle-class conception of the immobility of the soul was transferred to the stage where the middle-class has always ruled. A character came to signify a man fixed and finished: one who invariably appeared either drunk or jocular or melancholy, and characterization required nothing more than a physical defect such as a club-foot, a wooden leg, a red nose; or the fellow might be made to repeat some such phrase as: "That's capital!" or: "Barkis is willin'!" This simple way of regarding human beings still survives in the great Molière. Harpagon is nothing but a miser, although Harpagon might have been not only a miser, but also a first-rate financier, an excellent father and a good citizen. Worse still, his "failing" is a distinct advantage to his son-in-law and his daughter, who are his heirs, and who therefore cannot criticise him, even if they have to wait a while to get to bed. I do not believe, therefore, in simple stage characters; and the summary judgments of authors—this man is stupid, that one brutal, this jealous, that stingy, and so forth—should be challenged by the Naturalists who know the richness of the soul-complex and realise that vice has a reverse side very much like virtue.

Because they are modern characters, living in a period of transition more feverishly hysterical than its predecessor at least, I have drawn my figures vacillating, disintegrated, a blend of old and new. Nor does it seem to me unlikely that, through newspapers and conversations, modern ideas may have filtered down to the level of the domestic servant.

My souls (characters) are conglomerations of past and present stages of civilization, bits from books and newspapers, scraps of humanity, rags and tatters of fine clothing, patched together as is the human soul. And I have added a little evolutionary history by making the weaker steal and repeat the words of the stronger, and by making the characters borrow ideas or "suggestions" from one another.

Miss Julie is a modern character, not that the half-woman, the man-hater, has not existed always, but because now that she has been discovered she has stepped to the front and begun to make a noise. The half-woman is a type who thrusts herself forward, selling herself nowadays for power, decorations, distinctions, diplomas, as formerly for money. The type implies degeneration; it is not a good type and it does not endure; but it can unfortunately transmit its misery, and degenerate men seem instinctively to choose their mates from among such women, and so they breed, producing offspring of indeterminate sex to whom life is torture. But fortunately they perish, either because they cannot come to terms with reality, or because their repressed instincts break out uncontrollably, or again because their hopes of catching up with men are shattered. The type is tragic, revealing a desperate fight against nature, tragic too in its Romantic inheritance now dissipated by Naturalism, which wants nothing but happiness—and for happiness strong and sound species are required.

But Miss Julie is also a relic of the old warrior nobility now giving way to the new nobility of nerve and brain. She is a victim of the discord which a mother's "crime" has produced in a family, a victim too of the day's complaisance, of circumstances, of her own defective constitution, all of which are equivalent to the Fate or Universal Law of former days. The Naturalist has abolished guilt with God, but the consequences of the action—punishment, imprisonment or the fear of it—he cannot abolish, for the simple reason that they remain whether he is acquitted or not. An injured fellow-being is not so complacent as outsiders, who have not been injured, can afford to be. Even if the father had felt impelled to take no vengeance, the daughter would have taken vengeance on herself, as she does here, from that innate or acquired sense of honour which the upper-classes inherit—whether from Barbarism or Aryan forebears, or from the chivalry of the Middle Ages, who knows? It is a very beautiful thing, but it has become a danger nowadays to the preservation of the race. It is the nobleman's *harakiri*, the Japanese law of inner conscience which compels him to cut his own stomach open at the insult of another, and which survives in modified form in the duel, a privilege of the nobility. And so the valet Jean lives on, but Miss Julie cannot live without honour. This is the thrall's advantage over the nobleman, that he lacks this fatal preoccupation with honour. And in all of us Aryans there is something of the nobleman, or the Don Quixote, which makes us sympathize with the man who commits suicide because he has done something ignoble and lost his honour. And we are noblemen enough to suffer at the sight of fallen greatness littering the earth like a corpse—yes, even if the fallen rise again and make restitution by honourable deeds. Jean, the valet, is a race-builder, a man of marked characteristics. He was a labourer's son who has educated himself towards becoming a gentleman. He has learnt easily, through his well-developed senses (smell, taste, vision)—and he also has a sense of beauty. He has already bettered himself, and is thick-skinned enough to have no scruples about using other people's services. He is already foreign to his associates, despising them as part of the life he has turned his back on, yet also fearing and fleeing from them because they know his secrets, pry into his plans, watch his rise with envy, and look forward with pleasure to his fall. Hence his dual, indeterminate character, vacillating between love of the heights and hatred of those who have already achieved them. He is, he says himself, an aristocrat; he has learned the secrets of good society. He is polished, but vulgar within; he already wears his tails with taste, but there is no guarantee of his personal cleanliness.

He has some respect for his young lady, but he is frightened of Kristin, who knows his dangerous secrets, and he is sufficiently callous not to allow the night's events to wreck his plans for the future. Having both the slave's brutality and the master's lack of squeamishness, he can see blood without fainting and take disaster by the horns. Consequently he emerges from the battle unscathed, and probably ends his days as a hotel-keeper. And even if *he* does not become a Roumanian Count, his son will doubtless go to the university and perhaps become a county attorney.

The light which Jean sheds on a lower-class conception of life, life seen from below, is on the whole illuminating—when he speaks the truth, which is not often, for he says what is favourable to himself rather than what is true. When Miss Julie suggests that the lower-classes must be oppressed by the attitude of their superiors, Jean naturally agrees, as his object is to gain her sympathy; but when he perceives the advantage of separating himself from the common herd, he at once takes back his words.

It is not because Jean is now rising that he has the upper hand of Miss Julie, but because he is a man. Sexually he is the aristocrat because of his virility, his keener senses, and his capacity for taking the initiative. His inferiority is mainly due to the social environment in which he lives, and he can probably shed it with his valet's livery.

The slave mentality expresses itself in his worship of the Count (the boots), and his religious superstition; but he worships the Count chiefly because he holds that higher position for which Jean himself is striving. And this worship remains even when he has won the daughter of the house and seen how empty is that lovely shell.

I do not believe that a love relationship in the "higher" sense could exist between two individuals of such different quality, but I have made Miss Julie imagine that she is in love, so as to lessen her sense of guilt, and I let Jean suppose that if his social position were altered he would truly love her. I think love is like the hyacinth which has to strike roots in darkness *before* it can produce a vigorous flower. In this case it shoots up quickly, blossoms and goes to seed all at the same time, which is why the plant dies so soon.

As for Kristin, she is a female slave, full of servility and sluggishness acquired in front of the kitchen fire, and stuffed full of morality and religion, which are her cloak and scape-goat. She goes to church as a quick and easy way of unloading her household thefts on to Jesus and taking on a fresh cargo of guiltlessness. For the rest she is a minor character, and I have therefore sketched her in the same manner as the Pastor and the Doctor in "The Father," where I wanted ordinary human beings, as are most country pastors and provincial doctors. If these minor characters seem abstract to some people this is due to the fact that ordinary people are to a certain extent abstract in pursuit of their work; that is to say, they are without individuality, showing, while working, only one side of themselves. And as long as the spectator does not feel a need to see them from other sides, there is nothing wrong with my abstract presentation.

In regard to the dialogue, I have departed somewhat from tradition by not making my characters catechists who ask stupid questions in order to elicit a smart reply. I have avoided the symmetrical, mathematical construction of French dialogue, and let people's minds work irregularly, as they do in real life where, during a conversation, no topic is drained to the dregs, and one mind finds in another a chance cog to engage in. So too the dialogue wanders, gathering in the opening scenes material which is later picked up, worked over, repeated, expounded and developed like the theme in a musical composition.

The plot speaks for itself, and as it really only concerns two people, I have concentrated on these, introducing only one minor character, the cook, and keeping the unhappy spirit of the father above and behind the action. I have done this because it seems to me that the psychological process is what interests people most today. Our inquisitive souls are no longer satisfied with seeing a thing happen; we must also know how it happens. We want to see the wires themselves, to watch the machinery, to examine the box with the false bottom, to take hold of the magic ring in order to find the join, and look at the cards to see how they are marked.

In this connection I have had in view the documentary novels of the brothers de Goncourt, which appeal to me more than any other modern literature.

As far as the technical side of the work is concerned I have made the experiment of abolishing the division into acts. This is because I have come to the conclusion that our capacity for illusion is disturbed by the intervals, during which the audience has time to reflect and escape from the suggestive influence of the author-hypnotist. My play will probably take an hour and a half, and as one can listen to a lecture, a sermon or a parliamentary debate for as long as that or longer, I do not think a theatrical performance will be fatiguing in the same length of time. As early as 1872, in one of my first dramatic attempts, "The Outlaw," I tried this concentrated form, although with scant success. The play was written in five acts, and only when finished did I become aware of the restless, disjointed effect that it produced. The script was burnt and from the ashes rose a single well-knit act—fifty pages of print, playable in one hour. The form of the present play is, therefore, not new, but it appears to be my own, and changing tastes may make it timely. My hope is one day to have an audience educated enough to sit through a whole evening's entertainment in one act, but one would have to try this out to see. Meanwhile, in order to provide respite for the audience and the players, without allowing

Naturalism in the Theatre

the audience to escape from the illusion, I have introduced three art forms: monologue, mime and ballet. These are all part of drama, having their origins in classic tragedy, monody having become monologue and the chorus, ballet.

Monologue is now condemned by our realists as unnatural, but if one provides motives for it one makes it natural, and then can use it to advantage. It is, surely, natural for a public speaker to walk up and down the room practicing his speech, natural for an actor to read his part aloud, for a servant girl to talk to her cat, a mother to prattle to her child, an old maid to chatter to her parrot, and a sleeper to talk in his sleep. And in order that the actor may have a chance, for once, of working independently, free from the author's direction, it is better that the monologue should not be written, but only indicated. For since it is of small importance what is said in one's sleep or to the parrot or to the cat—none of it influences the action—a talented actor, identifying himself with the atmosphere and the situation, may improvise better than the author, who cannot calculate ahead how much may be said or how long taken without waking the audience from the illusion.

Some Italian theatres have, as we know, returned to improvisation, thereby producing actors who are creative, although within the bounds set by the author. This may well be a step forward, or even the beginning of a new art-form worthy to be called *productive*.

In places where monologue would be unnatural I have used mime, leaving here even a wider scope for the actor's imagination, and more chance for him to win independent laurels. But so as not to try the audience beyond endurance, I have introduced music—fully justified by the Midsummer Eve dance—to exercise its powers of persuasion during the dumb show. But I beg the musical director to consider carefully his choice of compositions, so that conflicting moods are not induced by selections from the current operetta or dance show, or by folk-tunes of too local a character.

The ballet I have introduced cannot be replaced by the usual kind of "crowd-scene," for such scenes are too badly played—a lot of grinning idiots seizing the opportunity to show off and thus destroying the illusion. And as peasants cannot improvise their taunts, but use ready-made phrases with a double meaning, I have not composed their lampoon, but taken a little-known song and dance which I myself noted down in the Stockholm district. The words are not quite to the point, but this too is intentional, for the cunning, i.e. weakness, of the slave prevents him from direct attack. Nor can there be clowning in a serious action, or coarse joking in a situation which nails the lid on a family coffin.

As regards the scenery, I have borrowed from impressionist painting its asymmetry and its economy; thus, I think, strengthening the illusion. For the fact that one does not see the whole room and all the furniture leaves scope for conjecture—that is to say imagination is roused and complements what is seen. I have succeeded too in getting rid of those tiresome exits through doors, since scenery doors are made of canvas, and rock at the slightest touch. They cannot even express the wrath of an irate head of the family who, after a bad dinner, goes out slamming the door behind him, "so that the whole house shakes." On the stage it rocks. I have also kept to a single set, both in order to let the characters develop in their métier and to break away from over-decoration. When one has only one set, one may expect it to be realistic; but as a matter of fact nothing is harder than to get a stage room that looks something like a room, however easily the scene painter can produce flaming volcanoes and water-falls. Presumably the walls must be of canvas; but it seems about time to dispense with painted shelves and cooking utensils. We are asked to accept so many stage conventions that we might at least be spared the pain of painted pots and pans.

I have set the back wall and the table diagonally so that the actors may play full-face and in half-profile when they are sitting opposite one another at the table. In the opera AÏDA I saw a diagonal background, which led the eye to unfamiliar perspectives and did not look like mere reaction against boring straight lines.

Another much needed innovation is the abolition of foot-lights. This lighting from below is said to have the purpose of making the actors' faces fatter. But why, I ask, should all actors have fat faces? Does not this under-lighting flatten out all the subtlety of the lower part of the face, specially the jaw, falsify the shape of the nose and throw shadows up over the eyes? Even if this were not so, one thing is certain: that the lights hurt the performers' eyes, so that the full play of their expression is lost. The foot-lights strike part of the retina usually protected—except in sailors who have to watch sunlight on water—and therefore one seldom sees anything other than a crude rolling of the eyes, either sideways or up towards the gallery, showing their whites. Perhaps this too causes that tiresome blinking of the eyelashes, especially by actresses. And when anyone on the stage wants to speak with his eyes, the only thing he can do is to look straight at the audience, with whom he or she then gets into direct communication, outside the framework of the set—a habit called, rightly or wrongly, "greeting one's friends."

Would not sufficiently strong side-lighting, with some kind of reflectors, add to the actor's powers of expression by allowing him to use the face's greatest asset—the play of the eyes?

I have few illusions about getting the actors to play *to* the audience instead of *with* it, although this is what I want. That I shall see an actor's back throughout a critical scene is beyond my dreams, but I do wish crucial scenes could be played, not in front of the prompter's box, like duets expecting applause, but in the place required by the action. So, no revolutions, but just some small modifications, for to make the stage into a real room with the fourth wall missing would be too upsetting altogether.

I dare not hope that the actresses will listen to what I have to say about make-up, for they would rather be beautiful than life-like, but the actor might consider whether it is to his advantage to create an abstract character with grease-paints, and cover his face with it like a mask. Take the case of a man who draws a choleric charcoal line between his eyes and then, in this fixed state of wrath, has to smile at some repartee. What a frightful grimace the result is! And equally, how is that false forehead, smooth as a billiard ball, to wrinkle when the old man loses his temper?

In a modern psychological drama, where the subtlest reactions of a character need to be mirrored in the face rather than expressed by sound and gesture, it would be worth while experimenting with powerful side-lighting on a small stage and a cast without make-up, or at least with the minimum.

If, in addition, we could abolish the visible orchestra, with its distracting lamps and its faces turned toward the audience; if we could have the stalls raised so that the spectators' eyes were higher than the players' knees; if we could get rid of the boxes (the centre of my target), with their tittering diners and supper-parties, and have total darkness in the auditorium during the performance; and if, first and foremost, we could have a *small* stage and a *small* house, then perhaps a new dramatic art might arise, and theatre once more become a place of entertainment for educated people. While waiting for such a theatre it is as well for us to go on writing so as to stock that repertory of the future.

I have made an attempt. If it has failed, there is time enough to try again.

Naturalism Is Not Dead*

By Paul Alexis

In 1891 an enterprising journalist Jules Huret (1864-1915) conducted what was probably the first literary poll in history. Assuming that naturalism (and also the Parnassian school of poetry) was in decline, he undertook to interview the leading writers of the day and to elicit their comments on the literary situation. Sixty-four such interviews were published in *L'Echo de Paris* from March 3 to July 5, 1891, and then collected in book form.

Huret began his inquiry with the so-called psychological writers, a group who seemed to be replacing the naturalists. The first question to be addressed to Anatole France, the first interviewee, was: "Is naturalism sick?" To which came the reply: "From all that I can see it is dead."

As was to be expected, the naturalists thought this report of their death at least somewhat exaggerated. Zola said "perhaps" in a modest way. Edmond de Goncourt considered the movement on the wane and likely to be over by 1900. Maupassant exclaimed: "I beg you, don't speak to me about literature," and refused to be interviewed. Henri Céard said naturalism could not die because it had never existed. And Paul Alexis sent a telegram with the agitated message: "Naturalism not dead. Letter follows."

Paul Alexis (1847-1901) was a member of the Médan group and Zola's faithful shadow. He won a modest renown for his novels such as *Madame Meuriot* (1891). The statement on naturalism here reprinted is notable for its claim that it is a way of seeing and thinking, rather than a method of writing, and that it is being permanently assimilated into human intellectual processes, so that in fact it cannot die.

◇◇◇◇◇◇◇◇◇◇◇◇◇◇◇◇◇◇◇◇◇◇◇◇◇◇◇·◇◇◇◇◇◇◇◇◇◇◇◇◇◇◇◇◇◇◇◇◇

I asked M. Paul Alexis, the most faithful member of the Médan group, for his opinion in this inquiry. He was at Aix-en-Provence at the moment. This is the telegram I received from him:

"Naturalism not dead. Letter follows."

Then came the letter which the telegram had promised:

*Huret, Jules, *Enquête sur l'évolution littéraire*, pp. 188-195; Paris, Charpentier, 1891.

Aix, 4 April 1891

"My dear colleague,

"No, naturalism is not dead! So little dead is it that, foreseen perhaps by Bacon, and certainly by Diderot, unconsciously practiced by the author of *Manon Lescaut*, taken up again in this century by Balzac and Stendhal (whom Flaubert, the Goncourts, Duranty, Zola and others continued), it has not gone beyond its first infant stammerings. At this end of a century, when so many things are ripe, ready to collapse with age, it is still young, very young. Tomorrow belongs to it even more than today. Naturalism will be the literature of the twentieth century.

"However, my dear colleague, before making the 'detailed' judgment of our literary development for which you ask me, we must understand each other about the word—more precisely, about the thing itself. There is a general and gross ambiguity which I should like once more to attempt to remove. Naturalism is not a 'rhetoric,' as is generally believed, but something of greater seriousness, a 'method.'

"A method of thinking, seeing, reflecting, studying, experimenting, a need to analyze in order to know, but not a special way of writing. In all deference to the pretty-pretty critics for whom Europe envies us, naturalism in no sense consists of writing four-letter words clear and bold. That would be too easy. Anyway the romantics did that long before us. And if we ourselves have done it on occasion—I first of all in a series of special articles—it is possibly not the best thing that we have done. In every case it was for the sake of laughter, in order to pull the legs of a host of over-amiable colleagues who pretended to see in us only 'pornographers' and 'cleaners of privies,' not to mention other amiable terms of abuse. But let's pass over that.

"On the contrary, naturalism is broad enough to include all kinds of 'writing.' The tone of a court-record of Stendhal or the displeasing dryness of Duranty find favor with it to the same degree as the concentrated and impeccable lyricism of Flaubert, the adorable nervosity of Goncourt, the grandiose abundance of Zola, or the sly and tender insight of Daudet. All authorial temperaments may participate in it.

"Also naturalism is in no sense a sect, a brotherhood, a school,

408

Naturalism Is Not Dead

a clan, a freemasonry, or a secret rite. You do not gain entrance as you would to a mill or a beer parlor. You do not present yourself as you do to the Academy or the Mirlitons. Naturalism bursts out—and seizes us by the heart—from every page even of *Salammbô*, just as an abundance of romanticism remains in *Madame Bovary* (in the suicide at the end, for example! for the real Madame Bovarys hardly ever commit suicide) and even more in *Germinal*.

"And you, dear colleague, with your interesting inquiry about literary trends, like your comrade Xau with his on the serious question of dress rehearsals, both of you have just done an excellent naturalistic job. A breath of naturalism penetrates even into the Chamber of Deputies, not to be sure on those days when the honorable gentlemen treat each other like drunken porters, but on those rare occasions when they are in labor with some reasonable and necessary reform. Indeed you are well aware that M. Constans himself acted like a good naturalist when he managed to rid us of General Boulanger, whereas the latter was so romantic as to flee across the border in the hope of escaping a Borgia dose of poison.

"Thus it is well established that naturalism is in no way what a whole group of critics have been so snobbish as to believe. Not a special way of twisting the written word! Not a leaning toward immorality or brutality! Not a panacea remedying lack of talent! As M. Edmond de Goncourt told you, it consists in replacing the 'out-of-this-world' humanity of romanticism more and more by a humanity drawn after nature. And now a question arises: 'Are there in our time any true, complete naturalists, and do they exist in any number?'

"Well, according to one of your interviewees, M. Paul Adam (author of *Chair molle* and a simple naturalist in revolt), naturalism today would not flutter so feebly if there were more than two 'pure' naturalists. And these two would seem to be the author of *L'Argent* and . . . the author of *Madame Meuriot*.

"Here let me begin a parenthesis. On no account in the world do I wish to appear to be trying to advertise the latter work. For I don't mind admitting that it, up to the present at least, has only been seriously discussed abroad, in Russia and especially in Italy. Whereas in France, leaving aside Messers Philippe Gille, Albert

Delpit, Montorgueil, and Auguste Filon, who accorded me a few kindly lines, my colleagues have so far given *Madame Meuriot* only silence and disdain. And on top of that the Hachette publishing house has had the cruelty to ban it from railroad stations. Poor *Madame Meuriot*! And it is well written, what's more. That will teach me to be more careful of my timing. The unhappy author is being paid back for *Monsieur Betsy*.

"Thus it is true that if all by myself I have the honor to be half of naturalism—M. Paul Adam and his friends really do me too much honor—it is possible that after *Madame Meuriot* naturalism was very ill. However, these young people seem to forget one very small detail! the seventy editions of *L'Argent*! Yes, is not the mountain of volumes by Zola which was carried away in a few days a proof, a pretty 'symbol' of success and vitality? What does M. Moréas think of that, for I am sure he would be more than happy to achieve the modest 3,000 copies of *Madame Meuriot* which were sold?

"But, dear colleague, let us quickly abandon these petty matters, these miserable questions of sales and immediate success, which don't prove everything. Naturalism in sum is only a branching-out into the domain of literature of the broad general current which carries our age toward more science, more truth, and no doubt also more happiness. The true naturalists, the pure ones, are therefore not six, or two, or one; properly speaking, *there are none in existence yet*. But they will be legion, for the road is broad, the goal high and distant, and it is in this direction that in their turn our children and the children of our grandchildren will make their toilsome way. As for us, and those of our elders whom we revere as we attempt to carry on from them, neither we nor they are yet truly naturalists. Romanticism, whence we all came, is still there, too near at hand. None of us has yet succeeded in purging his blood completely of the hereditary romantic virus.

" 'So be it,' you will reply. 'But if so far there are only precursor naturalists, then what about the psychological writers? And the symbolists, what do you make of them?'

"Patience! I was coming to them. The psychological writers first. Permit me to set apart, absolutely apart, an old comrade— Paul Bourget—whom I love with all my heart and in whom I discern an immense talent, not only subtle and supple but powerful

Naturalism Is Not Dead

when he wishes it to be, for example, in *Mensonges* and even in his 'Nouveaux Pastels,' in *Monsieur Legrimaudet*, that admirable literary failure who finishes out his days in an equivocal furnished house. . . . But Bourget excepted, I find that the psychological writers are only sickly, enfeebled naturalists—little brothers to the rest of us, born prematurely, whom it is necessary to raise in cotton wool and who all their lives will suffer the effects of a sickly youth, since they have grown up in a hot house. Let them take iron, those fellows; they need it. Perhaps then they will be able to stop limiting themselves to *demi-naturalism*. Now, since we can only arrive at a complete knowledge of man through physiology and psychology, let me ask you why we should keep one of the two windows obstinately closed? The opposite error would be equally stupid. Bourget at least, even though he be placed among the psychological writers, is passionate about letters and life, a healthy and vigorous man who in no way disdains physiology. The true leader of this half-blind, anemic naturalism is without any doubt M. Edouard Rod, that astonishing professor from Geneva to whom Jules Vallès said one day in my presence with that laugh of his that rings like bronze: 'Oh, Rod! Rod! good old Rod! How is your womb trouble coming along?'

"As for the symbolists, the decadents, they don't really exist. No, there are none; I see none. Verlaine, Villiers de l'Isle-Adam, and Mallarmé were belated followers of Baudelaire, men of talent certainly who must have been completely astonished when one fine day they heard that they were leaders of a school. They went along with the idea all right, but the school was a pitiful thing. Except for Paul Adam, a fellow of merit who managed to stray into this foolishness somehow, the rest have never done anything except make a bit of noise, without producing any works. They are merely comical. Books alone amount to something, are everything. And by 1901 all these unreadable writers—decadents, symbolists, vaporizers—and a heap of other absurd schools and sub-schools will have long since disappeared.

"In the twentieth century there will be no more schools at all. For naturalism is the opposite of a school. It is the end of all schools, the liberation of individuality, the flowering of original and sincere natures.

PAUL ALEXIS"

"Guy de Maupassant"*

By Leo Tolstoy

Leo Tolstoy (1828-1910) is one of the great novelists of all time and essentially a realist. Apparently artless in composition, his works seem to present both the figured surface and the deep current of life itself. As William Dean Howells puts it in his introduction to *Sevastopol*, "In these books you seem to come face to face with human nature for the first time in fiction. All other fiction at times *seems* fiction; these alone seem the very truth always."

Of all the major writers in the realistic movement Tolstoy has least to say about his craft. It is true that at the end of the May 1855 section of *Sevastopol* he wonders if what he has shown would not have been better undepicted, since the tale does not explicitly show "the evil we must avoid, and the good towards which we must strive to go." In place of conventional hero and villain he finds that "the hero of my tale, the one I love with all the power of my soul, the one I have tried to reproduce in all his beauty, just as he has been, is, and always will be beautiful, is Truth."

The major Tolstoy works, *War and Peace* (1865-1869), and *Anna Karenina* (1873-1877), as well as a number of shorter pieces such as *The Cossacks* (1863), were completed before the author underwent a spiritual crisis of a magnitude which redirected his energies and attitudes during the last three decades of his life. During these years he did on occasion write essentially objective works, such as *The Death of Ivan Ilych* and *Hadji Murad*, but most of his writing was directed toward a didactic end, with the result that he felt bound to enunciate an aesthetic consonant with this explicit moral purpose. *What Is Art?* (1897-1898) is the result of this effort, which by its emphasis on the moral purpose of literature and its repudiation of all works (including Tolstoy's own) which fail to measure up to his criterion is in no sense a document having to do with realism. Some years earlier, however, after the death of Guy de Maupassant, Tolstoy was prevailed upon to write an article about him which is a prestudy of the later aesthetic inquiry and also an attack on some of the tenets of realism. His position is that Maupassant's work is vitiated by failure to communicate right feelings in the spheres of both personal and social morality, a failure which is all the more serious because of the author's great power to sway the mind and emotions of his readers.

* Tolstoy, Leo, "Guy de Maupassant," *Arena* 11: pp. 15-26, December 1894. The translation is by Charles Johnston. (A somewhat longer version was issued in London by the Brotherhood Publishing Company in 1898.)

"Guy de Maupassant"

Nothing could, in fact, be more striking than the confrontation of the moralistic Tolstoy and the amoral Maupassant. Emile Faguet, the eminent French critic, was quick to take advantage of this opportunity in an article "Tolstoi et Maupassant," in the *Revue Bleue* for May 23, 1896. Having called Tolstoy a "rigorous moralist," he characterizes Maupassant as "a realistic novelist, the most clearly and sharply realistic of novelists, who has wished and been able to see only middling humanity, the exclusive province of realism, without any general ideas to superimpose on reality and deform it, without any passion which might trouble the sight and make reality something other than it is, without any desire for edification or satire, without any moral goal, in short, a realist who is so impersonal that impersonality in his case seems to go, and indeed does go, to the point of unconsciousness."

A contrast so sharply drawn is instructive as to the goals, methods, and limitations of the realistic movement. Tolstoy's arguments here and at greater length in *What Is Art?* do not in fact destroy the realistic position; if anything they strengthen it by their waywardness. However, they also point up the fact that literature can have other goals and that when these are too long denied they are likely to reassert themselves explosively.

◇◇

IF I am not mistaken, it was in 1881 that Turgenev, who was staying with me at the time, brought forth a small book from his trunk, and handed it to me; the book was called *Maison Tellier*.

"Read it when you have nothing else to do!" he said, quite carelessly; in the same way that, about a year before, he had given me a number of *Russkoe Bogatstvo*, with an article by Garshin, who was just beginning to write. It was evident on both occasions that Turgenev was trying not to influence me in any way, but wished me to form an independent opinion. "He is a young French writer," he continued; "you will find him not at all bad. He knows your books and—thinks very highly of them," this as a bribe. "In his life and character he reminds me of Drujénin. Like Drujénin, he is a good son, a faithful friend, and a strong sympathizer with the working classes. And his relations with the fair sex remind me of Drujénin, too." And Turgenev told me some wonderful, almost incredible, stories of this side of Maupassant's character.

That very period, 1881, was the most fateful epoch of the rebuilding of my inner life; and while this rebuilding was going on, the activities which are generally called "artistic," and to which I had formerly dedicated all my powers, not only lost for me the high value I had once set on them, but grew even repellent to me; precisely because of the disproportionate space they had filled in my own life, and in the lives of the rich in general. And so, at that time, I took no interest at all in works like this which Turgenev had lent me. But I did not want to disappoint him, and so read the book.

The first story, "La Maison Tellier," showed me, beyond all doubt, that its author possessed a true talent, in spite of the looseness and insignificance of his theme. The author clearly had the peculiar gift, the talent of concentrating his mind on one subject or another, which gives to its possessor the power of seeing something new, something invisible to others, in what he is looking at. And without doubt Guy de Maupassant could see things invisible to others. Yet, as far as I could judge from this one book, in spite of his talent he lacked the chief of the three qualities necessary for the production of a true work of art. *These three conditions are: a true, a moral attitude towards his subject; clear expression, or, what is the same thing, beauty of form; and, thirdly, sincerity—unfeigned love or unfeigned hatred for what he depicts.*

Of these three conditions, Guy de Maupassant possessed the two last only, and was utterly devoid of the first. He had no true, no moral attitude towards his subject. From what I had read, I decided that Guy de Maupassant possessed this talent; that he could intend his mind on things, and thus discern qualities unseen by others; that he also possessed beauty of form—he could say clearly, simply, and beautifully whatever he had to say; that he also possessed the indispensable condition of effectiveness—sincerity. He did not feign love and hatred. He loved and hated sincerely. But unhappily lacking the first, the chiefest condition of true work—the right moral attitude, the discernment between good and evil—he loved and painted things that are not worthy of love; and did not love or paint things that are worthy of love. In this little book, he describes with rich detail, and evident relish, the ways in which men and women seduce each other, and even adds some hardly intelligible impurities, as in "La Femme de Paul,"

414

while at the same time he describes the village toilers not only callously but even repellently, as mere animals.

A total failure to understand the life and hopes of the toilers, while depicting them as repulsive animals, moved only by lust, wrath and greed, is a capital defect in French writers generally. Guy de Maupassant does not escape this defect; in this, as in his other books, he ever describes the masses of France as coarse, vulgar animals, worthy only of ridicule. I cannot, of course, claim to know the masses of France better than the French writers know them; but though I am a Russian, and have never lived among the masses in France, I confidently affirm that the French writers err in describing the French people as they do, and that the French people cannot be what the French writers say they are. If the France we know, with her really great men, with the endowments they have dedicated to science, art, civilization, and the moral progress of the world, really exists, then the working masses who have sustained and still sustain this gifted France on their shoulders, cannot be made up of mere animals, but must be made up of men, with great moral qualities. And so I do not believe the pictures of them in novels like *La Terre*, and the stories of Guy de Maupassant, just as I could not believe in a fine palace without foundations.

And so the general impression of the book Turgenev had given me left me completely indifferent to the young French writer. And, still more, I felt so disgusted at the time with "Une Partie de Campagne," "La Femme de Paul," and "L'Histoire d'une Fille de Ferme," that I never even noticed the two really excellent stories, "Le Papa de Simon," and "Sur l'Eau"—a wonderful description of night. It seemed to me that, in our days, there are so many people who possess a true talent prostituted to falseness. So I told Turgenev, and then forgot all about Guy de Maupassant.

The first work of his I saw after this was *Une Vie*, which somebody advised me to read. This book totally changed my opinion of Guy de Maupassant; and afterwards I always read with great interest whatever appeared over his signature. *Une Vie* is an excellent novel; not only is it beyond comparison Guy de Maupassant's best, but I think it would not be wrong to say that it is the best French novel after Hugo's *Les Misérables*.

Une Vie, besides showing a true talent, a true power of concentration on a subject, so as to reveal new and unseen relations, also unites in itself the three essential conditions of a true work of art: a true, a moral attitude towards the subject; beauty of form; and sincerity—unfeigned love for what the author describes. The author sees that the meaning of life transcends the adventures of profligates of either sex. The contents of the book, as its title shows, comprehend "A Life"; a life, innocent and ruined; a gracious woman ever open to all good influences, but brought to utter ruin by the very grossness of animal instincts which, in former days, were, in the opinion of the author, the central, dominant facts of life. But in this book, all the sympathies of the author are on the side of what is really good.

The style of his first stories is also excellent, but here it reaches such heights of perfection as have never, in my opinion, been reached by any writer of French prose. But, best of all, the author truly and sincerely loves the kindly family he describes, and really hates the coarse sensualist who destroys its happiness and peace. And this sincerity is the root of that vividness which pervades the whole work. The easy-going, good-hearted mother; the noble, weak, sympathetic father, and the still more sympathetic daughter in her simplicity and great openness to all that is good; their mutual relations; their first journey; their servants and neighbors; the stingy, sensual, trivial, and impudent bridegroom, who deceives the innocent girl with his commonplace idealization of the most brutal sides of human character; the wedding; Corsica, with its charmingly described nature; then their country life; the coarse unfaithfulness of the husband; his usurping all proprietary rights over their property; his collisions with his father-in-law; the retiring timidity of the good, and the triumph of the impudent; their relations with their neighbors; all this is life itself, with all its complex variety; and not only is it admirably and vividly described—it is pervaded by a sincere, pathetic tone, in which the reader shares, even against his will. You feel that the author loves this woman; and not for her outer beauty, but for her soul, for all that is good in her. He pities her, and suffers with her; and this feeling of his is communicated to the reader. And the questions, "Why, with what object, is this gracious being ruined;

416

and is this possibly right?" arise in the reader's heart, and force him deeper into the import and sense of human life.

The next novel of Guy de Maupassant's which I read was *Bel-Ami*. *Bel-Ami* is distinctly an impure book. The author clearly gives way to his inclination to describe what attracts him in an unworthy way; and so often loses the original negative attitude towards his hero, and goes over bodily to his side. But, in a more general way, *Bel-Ami*, as well as *Une Vie*, is based on serious thought and earnest feeling. In *Une Vie*, this fundamental thought is perplexity at the cruel purposelessness with which an excellent woman is made to suffer through the vulgar sensuality of a man. In *Bel-Ami*, it is more than perplexity. It is indignation at the success and happiness of a coarse animal, who succeeds, and wins a high social position through this very sensuality; and indignation at the profligacy of the atmosphere in which the hero wins success. In the first story, the author seems to ask: With what object, for what fault is this beautiful being ruined; why did it happen? In the second, he seems to answer these questions: everything pure and good in our society is doomed to ruin, because this society is immoral, mad and chaotic. The last scene of the novel, the wedding of a triumphant rascal, decorated with the *Légion d'Honneur*, in a fashionable church, with a pure young girl, the daughter of a once blameless mother whom he had seduced; a wedding which received an episcopal blessing, and was acknowledged universally as a thing to be respected, expresses this fundamental thought with unusual power. In this novel, you see that the author is dealing earnestly with life, in spite of its being encumbered with impure detail, which, unhappily, seems to delight him.

Read the conversation of the old poet with Duroy, after they have left the Walters' dinner party, if I mistake not:

"She holds me already, *la gueuse*," he says, of Death; "she has loosened my teeth, torn out my hair, crippled my limbs, and she is ready to swallow me; I am already in her power. She lingers, playing with me, like a cat with a mouse, and knowing that there is no escape for me. Fame and wealth—what profit is in them? when you cannot buy with them a woman's love. A woman's love is the one thing worth living for; and Death robs us of it; of love, and then of health, of strength, of our very life; and this for us all, and nothing gained."

This is the meaning of the old poet's words; but Duroy is the successful suitor of every woman that pleases him; he is so full of lust, energy, and force, that he, hearing, hears not, and understanding, understands not, the old poet's words. He certainly hears and understands, but the springs of self-indulgent life pulsate in him so strongly that this self-evident truth fails to touch him, though foreshadowing his own end.

This interior contradiction, together with its ironic purpose, forms the chief meaning of *Bel-Ami*. The same thought illumines the excellent description of the consumptive journalist's death. The author asks himself what this life is, how to explain the eternal contradiction between the love of life and the knowledge of inevitable death. But he gives no answer to this question. He seems to seek, to wait for, a solution; but gives no decision in either sense. But still his moral attitude towards life remains true in this novel.

But in the stories that follow, this moral attitude towards life becomes confused; the valuation of the incidents of life begins to be uncertain, obscured, and at last altogether dislocated. In *Mont-Oriol*, Guy de Maupassant seems to join the motives of the two preceding novels, and to go over their contents once more. This story is rich in descriptions of a fashionable health resort, with its hygienic activities; full of admirable humor. But we see the same Paul, as cruel and as worthless as the husband in *Une Vie*; the same sweet, weak, lovely, sympathetic woman, deceived and ruined; the same heartless triumph of worthless vulgarity as in *Bel-Ami*. The leading thought is certainly the same, but the author's moral attitude is considerably lower. His notions of good and evil become very uncertain. In spite of all his intellectual striving to be dispassionate and objective, the profligate Paul evidently has his sympathy, and consequently the story of Paul's passion, and his successful attempts to seduce, rings quite false. The reader does not quite know what the author intends, and whether he wishes to paint Paul's meanness and moral bankruptcy, his indifferent desertion and insults towards his victim, for the sole reason that, when pregnant with his child, she loses her grace and beauty; or wishes to show how easy and pleasant it is to live the life of this profligate.

In the stories that follow, *Pierre et Jean* and *Fort comme la mort*, the author's moral attitude towards his creations is still more uncertain; and in *Notre Coeur* it seems to be altogether lost. All these stories are stamped with indifference, haste and unreality, and, above all, with the lack of that right moral attitude towards life, which was so clearly present in the earlier story, *Une Vie*.

This deterioration seems to have begun exactly at the period when Guy de Maupassant's reputation as a fashionable writer was established; when he was led into the strong temptation belonging to our time; the temptation which is likely to come to any successful writer, and the more so, if the writer is so attractive as Guy de Maupassant. On one side, the success of his first novels; the praises of the critics; the flattery of society and especially of women; on another, increasing gains and still more rapidly increasing wants; and, lastly, the importunity of publishers, who cease to judge the quality of what the author offers them, ready to accept anything bearing a lucrative signature—all this intoxicates the author. He gives way, and though still as perfect, or even more perfect in style, and even taking delight in his descriptions, he loves what he describes from mere whim, and not because it is good and worthy of all love; or hates what he describes from mere whim, and not because it is evil and worthy of hate.

The motive in *Une Vie* is this: here is a human being, kindly, bright, sympathetic, open to all good influences; and for some reason, this human being is sacrificed first to her vulgar, worthless, stupid, sensual husband, and then to her son who is no better. Why is this being led to ruin without ever having given anything to the world? This is the question Guy de Maupassant puts, and, to all appearances, he leaves it unanswered. But the whole story, all our compassion for the victim, all our abhorrence for the causes of her ruin, are an answer to this question. If even one man could enter into, and express, her sorrows, they are justified. Such was the meaning of Job's answer to his friends, who said that none would understand his sorrow. You have learned suffering and understood it; this is its justification. And the author has seen and understood this suffering, and has unveiled its mysteries to others. The suffering is justified by the fact that, once it has been understood by mankind, its source will be inevitably removed, sooner or later.

The story that followed, *Bel-Ami*, no longer raises the question of the suffering of the innocent; the question it raises is: Why should the unworthy win wealth and fame? What, then, are this wealth and fame, and how are they acquired? This question also contains its solution within itself; its solution is the negation of everything that the mob values most highly. The theme of *Bel-Ami* is still serious; but the author's moral attitude towards his subject is far more infirm. In *Une Vie*, the sensual blots which disfigure the story were few and far between; but in *Bel-Ami*, these blots spread and expand, till whole chapters are darkened by them, without disturbing the author's complacency.

In *Mont-Oriol*, the question, Why should a gracious woman suffer, and a brutal seducer triumph? is no longer put. The author seems really to assume that this is exactly as it should be; moral requirements are hardly felt at all; but impure, sensual descriptions are frequent, though quite uncalled for by any artistic necessity or fitness. The author's moral attitude towards his subject is perfectly false; and, as a striking example of his doing violence to the laws of beauty, one may cite the very detailed description of the appearance of the heroine in her bath. This description is perfectly unnecessary; quite unconnected with either the exterior or the interior theme of the novel. Tiny bubbles cover pink flesh. What of that? asks the reader. Nothing! replies the author; I describe this because I like this kind of description.

In the two stories that follow, *Pierre et Jean* and *Fort comme la mort*, there is no moral basis at all. Both are built upon profligacy, deceit, and lying; leading the persons of the story to tragic complications. Then in *Notre Coeur*, the situation is perfectly monstrous, impossible, and immoral. Here the chief characters make no attempt at resistance; they give themselves up heart and soul to the shallowest sensual pleasures; and the author seems to sympathize with them sincerely. The only conclusion the reader can possibly draw is, that there is nothing in life worth living for but sexual indulgence, no aim but its most extended enjoyment.

I shall touch on his short stories—his chief achievement and title to fame—later on; but in all his novels after *Bel-Ami*, Guy de Maupassant is evidently enslaved by the false theory that reigned in his circle in Paris and still reigns everywhere: the theory that an artistic creation demands no defined sense of good and evil; that, on the contrary, a true artist is bound to ignore all moral questions, and that in this ignoring lies the artist's chief merit. This theory holds it to be the artist's duty to represent actuality—what actually is, or what is beautiful—that is, what pleases him or may serve as material for "science"; but that it is no part of his duty to discern between moral and immoral, good and evil. In compliance with this verdict of elect spirits, Guy de Maupassant wrote his novels under the curious belief that whatever his circle believed to be beautiful, was that true Beautiful which all art must serve.

Guy de Maupassant grew up and formed himself among those who believed that feminine beauty and feminine passion were finally and universally acknowledged by the best minds as the only true subject of real art. This theory, in all its terrible inanity, enslaved Guy de Maupassant as soon as he became a fashionable writer; and, as could have been foretold, this false ideal led him into a whole series of mistakes, in work that grew steadily weaker and weaker.

And here we come to the radical difference between a novel and a short story. The theme of a novel, interior and exterior, is the description of a whole life, or even many lives; hence the writer of a novel must clearly discern between good and evil in life—a discernment which Guy de Maupassant never possessed. Quite the opposite, for it was blazoned on the banner of his school that he must ignore this very discernment. Had he been one of the throng of talentless prophets of sensuality, he would have depicted evil as good in perfect contentment, and his novels would have been complete and interesting for readers who shared his views. But Guy de Maupassant was not talentless; he had the true talent —the power of discerning reality—and therefore, in spite of himself, depicted reality, and saw evil in what he tried to depict as good. And this is why in all his novels but *Une Vie* his sympathies are so uncertain; sometimes depicting evil as good; sometimes seeing evil in evil, and good in good; and continually changing from one to the other. And this uncertainty is fatal to the wholeness of impression, fatal to the illusion.

With the exception of his early novels, or, to speak more exactly, with the exception of his earliest one, all his novels are weak as such; and, had he left us nothing but his novels, his life would be valuable only as a striking example of a brilliant gift ruined by the false surroundings in which it developed, and the false theories of men without love for, and therefore without understanding of, art.

But, happily, Guy de Maupassant wrote short stories also, in which he did not comply with a false theory; in which he did not aim at fine writing, but simply recorded what touched his heart or repelled his moral sense. And so, in the best of these short stories, you can trace the development of his moral sense, and the gradual and unconscious dethronement of all that formerly constituted for him the whole aim and meaning of life. And the wonderful characteristic of all true talent is that, unless the author does violence to his own better nature, a true talent will teach its possessor and lead him on the road of moral unfolding, making him love the truly lovable, and hate what is worthy of hatred. An artist is an artist only in so far as he can see things, not as he wishes to see them, but as they really are. The possessor of a true talent may err, but the true talent, when given free scope—as Guy de Maupassant's was, in his short stories—will unveil and reveal the truth as it really is; will compel love for it if it be lovable, and hatred, if it be worthy of hate. What befell Balaam will befall every true artist, when, under outward influences, he seeks to represent what should not be represented; seeking to bless the accursed, he cursed, and seeking to curse the blessed, he blessed. Unwillingly, he does not what he would, but what he should.

And so with Guy de Maupassant. There was hardly another writer who felt so sincerely that the sole end and aim of life is woman, and who described woman and woman's love so powerfully and passionately from every side; and yet who showed the dark reverses of the picture so clearly and truly, though sincerely seeking to exalt his ideal, and show in it the true end and happiness of life. The deeper he penetrated into life with this ideal, the more completely all veils were torn away, leaving bare the dark consequences and still darker realities. Guy de Maupassant wished to hymn the praises of passion, but the deeper he penetrated, the deeper grew his loathing. He loathes passion for the calamities and sufferings that follow in its wake; for its many disappointments; and, most of all, because passion counterfeits true love—a counterfeit which brings the more suffering the more credulous was its victim.

The moral progress of Guy de Maupassant's life is written in ineffaceable characters through the whole series of his delicious short stories and his best books *Sur l'eau* and *Une Vie*. This growth is to be traced not only in the dethronement of sexual passion—the more significant that it is involuntary—but also in Guy de Maupassant's increasing demands from life in a moral sense. He begins to perceive the chasm between man and beast not in sexual passion alone, but in the whole fabric of life.

He sees that the material world, such as it is, is not the best of all possible worlds; that it might be far other; that it does not satisfy the demands of reason and love. He begins to perceive that another world exists; or, at least, he realizes the soul's longings for this other world. And this thought is strikingly expressed in "Le Horla." He is tortured by the material world's unreason and ugliness; by its lack of love, its separation. I know no other cry of despair that goes straighter to the heart, coming from one who from chaos had found conscience, than the expression of this thought in the charming story, "Solitude." The fact that tortured Guy de Maupassant most keenly, and to which he returns again and again, is this very loneliness, this consciousness of a spiritual barrier shutting him off from all mankind; a barrier that grows more palpable as physical intercourse grows closer. What makes him suffer so? What is he longing for? What could break down the barrier, and bring this utter loneliness to an end? What but love? Yet not the *mirage* of woman, of sexual passion: but true love—pure, spiritual, and divine. And this Guy de Maupassant thirsts for. This true love, long clearly recognized as the salvation of life, is the goal of his struggles from the toils he feels drawn round him. He has not yet found the name of what he seeks; nor will he name it with the lips alone, through fear of bringing pollution to the shrine. Yet unnamed as is his impulse, his horror of loneliness is so intense that it is communicated to the reader, who is far more touched by this upward struggle than by all the idyls of passion that have flowed eloquent from Guy de Maupassant's lips. The tragedy of his life is in the fact that, though plunged in a life and tide of moral chaos, the power and luminousness of his talent was making for his liberation from this chaos; his release was definitely sure; he was already breathing the free air. Yet, having spent his strength in the struggle, he failed in the last needed effort, and perished unreleased.

According to the thought that surrounded him, in which he was formed, and which the young lust of his passionate nature strengthened and confirmed, life was for indulgence alone, and the chiefest indulgence was sexual love; and this false tendency gained force and color from his wonderful power of depicting passion and communicating it to others.

But the more he bent his eyes on this indulgence, the more there struggled to the light elements foreign and hostile to passion and beauty; woman grew strangely repellent; then the pains of pregnancy, of childbirth; the unwelcome children; then deceit, cruelty, moral suffering; then—old age, and—death. Then again —is this "beauty" real beauty? Of what use is it? This ideal of his might hold, if we could bind the wings of time; but life hurries on—and what does this mean? The hurry of life means this— thin and grizzled hair, toothlessness, wrinkles, tainted breath; even long before the end all becomes ugly and repellent; visible paint, sweat, foulness, hideousness. Where, then, is the god of my idolatry? Where is beauty? Beauty is all, and is—vanished. Nothing is left. Life is gone. Nor is it only that life has gone from where you beheld it. You yourself begin to lag behind. You yourself grow weak, dull, decrepit. Others cull the sweets before your eyes.

And even this is not all. You begin to see the glimmer of another life; something different; another communion with life, and with mankind; a communion with no place for these deceits; a communion not to be destroyed, but ever true and ever beautiful. But this may not be. It is but the gleam of an oasis, where we know no oasis is, but sand only. Guy de Maupassant has reached the tragic hour of struggle between the lies around him, and the truth he was beginning to see. The throes of the new birth were close at hand. And these throes are expressed in his most excellent works, and more than all in his short stories. Had he not been doomed to death in the birth-struggle, he would have given us great evangels; yet even what he gave us in his pain is much already. Therefore let us thank this strong, truthful writer for what he has given.

Part Three

Twentieth Century Revisions

and Evaluations

"A Natural History
of American Naturalism"*

By Malcolm Cowley

MALCOLM COWLEY (1898—   ) has considerable importance as an
historian of American literature since the First World War. A member of the expatriate group of the 1920's, he returned to become literary editor of the *New Republic* from 1929 to 1944. He is the author
of *Exile's Return* (1934), of three chapters in the *Literary History
of the United States*, and of many critical articles. He has been the
editor of *After the Genteel Tradition* (1937) and a number of volumes
in the Viking "portable" series.

As he has said in "Naturalism: No Teacup Tragedies," realism is
not his tradition, since he disagrees "with its doctrines and even more
with the slipshod manner in which they are applied. Nevertheless, it
has produced some admirable novels, not all of them by European authors, and it has contributed to our picture of the modern world." He
tends in his discussion to place too much emphasis on Frank Norris's
conception of "bigness and romance" as inherent in naturalism and
therefore gathers some unlikely specimens into the realist-naturalist
net. Nonetheless his discussion gives a good idea of the *general* influence which realism has had on American writing in this century.

◇◇

THERE have been too many unfruitful arguments over naturalism in American fiction. Now that the movement has flourished
for half a century, we can forget to attack or defend it and instead
can look back in an objective or naturalistic spirit at the work of
the many authors it has inspired. We can note that their line
extends from Norris and the early Dreiser through Farrell and
Steinbeck. We can describe their principles, note how these were
modified in practice, and finally try to reach some judgment of
their literary remains.

Naturalism has been defined in two words as pessimistic de-

* Cowley, Malcolm, "A Natural History of American Naturalism," *Kenyon
Review*, Summer 1947. In expanded form this appeared under the title "Naturalism in American Literature," in Persons, Stow (ed.), *Evolutionary Thought in
America*, Yale University Press, 1950. The article, reprinted by permission of
the author and the Yale University Press, corresponds to pages 313-333.

terminism and the definition is true so far as it goes. The naturalistic writers were all determinists in that they believed in the omnipotence of abstract forces. They were pessimists so far as they believed that men and women were absolutely incapable of shaping their own destinies. They regarded the individual as "a pawn on a chessboard"; the phrase recurs time and again in their novels. They felt that he could not achieve happiness by any conscious decision and that he received no earthly or heavenly reward for acting morally; man was, in Dreiser's words, "the victim of forces over which he has no control."

In some of his moods, Frank Norris carried this magnification of forces and minification of persons to an even greater extreme. "Men were nothings, mere animalculae, mere ephemerides that fluttered and fell and were forgotten between dawn and dusk," he said in the next-to-last chapter of *The Octopus*. "Men were naught, life was naught; FORCE only existed—FORCE that brought men into the world, FORCE that made the wheat grow, FORCE that garnered it from the soil to give place to the succeeding crop." But Norris, like several other naturalists, was able to combine this romantic pessimism about individuals with romantic optimism about the future of mankind. "The individual suffers, but the race goes on," he said at the very end of the novel. "Annixter dies, but in a far distant corner of the world a thousand lives are saved. The larger view always and through all shams, all wickednesses, discovers the Truth that will, in the end, prevail, and all things, surely, inevitably, resistlessly work together for good." This was, in its magniloquent way, a form of the belief in universal progress announced by Herbert Spencer, but it was also mingled with native or Emersonian idealism, and it helped to make naturalism more palatable to Norris' first American readers.

Zola had also declared his belief in human perfectibility, in what he called "a constant march toward truth"; and it was from Zola rather than Spencer or any native sources that Norris had borrowed most of his literary doctrines. Zola described himself as "a positivist, an evolutionist, a materialist." In his working notes, which Norris of course had never seen, but which one might say that he divined from the published text of the novels, Zola had indicated some of his aims as a writer. He would march through

430

the world observing human behavior as if he were observing the forms of animal life. "Study men as simple elements and note the reactions," he said. And again, "What matters most to me is to be purely naturalistic, purely physiological. Instead of having principles (royalism, Catholicism) I shall have laws (heredity, atavism)." And yet again, "Balzac says that he wishes to paint men, women and things. I count men and women as the same, while admitting their natural differences, and *subject men and women to things.*" In that last phrase, which Zola underlined, he expressed the central naturalistic doctrine: that men and women are part of nature and subject to the same indifferent laws.

The principal laws, for Zola, were those of heredity, which he assumed to be as universal and unchanging as the second law of thermodynamics. He fixed upon the hereditary weakness of the Rougon-Macquart family as a theme that would bind together his vast series of novels. Suicide, alcoholism, prostitution, and insanity were all to be explained as the result of the same hereditary taint. "Vice and virtue," he said, "are products like vitriol and sugar." Norris offered the same explanation for the brutality of McTeague. "Below the fine fabric of all that was good in him," Norris said, "ran the foul stream of hereditary evil, like a sewer. The vices and sins of his father and of his father's father, to the third and fourth and five hundredth generation, tainted him. The evil of an entire race flowed in his veins. Why should it be? He did not desire it. Was he to blame?" Others of the naturalistic school, and Norris himself in his later novels, placed more emphasis on environmental forces. When Stephen Crane sent a copy of *Maggie* to the Reverend Thomas Dixon, he wrote on the fly-leaf: "It is inevitable that this book will greatly shock you, but continue, pray, with great courage to the end, for it tries to show that environment is a tremendous thing and often shapes lives regardlessly. If I could prove that theory, I would make room in Heaven for all sorts of souls (notably an occasional street girl) who are not confidently expected to be there by many excellent people." Maggie, the victim of environment, was no more to blame for her transgressions than McTeague, the victim of hereditary evil. Nobody was to blame in this world where men and women are subject to the laws of things.

A favorite theme in naturalistic fiction is that of the beast within. As the result of some crisis—usually a fight, a shipwreck, or an expedition into the Arctic—the veneer of civilization drops or is stripped away and we are faced with "the primal instinct of the brute struggling for its life and for the life of its young." The phrase is Norris', but it might have been written by any of the early naturalists. When evolution is treated in their novels, it almost always takes the opposite form of devolution or degeneration. It is seldom that the hero evolves toward a superhuman nature, as in Nietzsche's dream; instead he sinks backward toward the beasts. Zola set the fashion in *L'Assommoir* and *La Bête humaine* and Norris followed him closely in the novel he wrote during his year at Harvard, *Vandover and the Brute*. Through yielding to his lower instincts, Vandover loses his humanity; he tears off his clothes, paddles up and down the room on his hands and feet and snarls like a dog.

A still earlier story, *Lauth,* was written at the University of California after Norris had listened to the lectures of Professor Joseph Le Conte, the famous evolutionist. The action takes place in medieval Paris, where Lauth, a student at the Sorbonne, is mortally wounded in a brawl. A doctor brings him back to life by pumping blood into his veins, but the soul had left the body and does not return. Without it, Lauth sinks back rapidly through the various stages of evolution: he is an ape, then a dog, then finally "a horrible shapeless mass lying upon the floor. It lived, but lived not as the animals or the trees, but as the protozoa, the jellyfish, and those strange lowest forms of existence wherein the line between vegetable and animal cannot be drawn." That might have been taken as a logical limit to the process of devolution; but Jack London, who was two parts naturalist, if he was also one part socialist and three parts hack journalist, tried to carry the process even further, into the realm of inanimate nature. Here, for example, is the description of a fight in *Martin Eden*:

> Then they fell upon each other, like young bulls, in all the
> glory of youth, with naked fists, with hatred, with desire
> to hurt, to maim, to destroy. All the painful, thousand
> years' gains of man in his upward climb through creation

were lost. Only the electric light remained, a milestone on the path of the great human adventure. Martin and Cheese-Face were two savages, of the stone age, of the squatting place and the tree refuge. They sank lower and lower into the muddy abyss, back into the dregs of the raw beginnings of life, striving blindly and chemically, as atoms strive, as the star-dust of the heavens strives, colliding, recoiling and colliding again and eternally again.

It was more than a metaphor when London said that men were atoms and star dust; it was the central drift of his philosophy. Instead of moving from the simple to the complex, as Herbert Spencer tells us that everything does in this world, the naturalists kept moving from the complex to the simple, by a continual process of reduction. They spoke of the nation as "the tribe," and a moment later the tribe became a pack. Civilized man became a barbarian or a savage, the savage became a brute and the brute was reduced to its chemical elements. "Study men as simple elements." Zola had said; and many years later Dreiser followed his advice by presenting love as a form of electromagnetism and success in life as a question of chemical compounds; thus he said of his brother Paul that he was "one óf those great Falstaffian souls who, for lack of a little iron or sodium or carbon dioxide in his chemical compost, was not able to stride the world like a Colossus."

There was a tendency in almost all the naturalistic writers to identify social laws with biological or physical laws. For Jack London, the driving force behind human events was always biology —"I mean," says his autobiographical hero, Martin Eden, "the real interpretative biology, from the ground up, from the laboratory and the test tube and the vitalized inorganic right on up to the widest esthetic and social generalizations." London believed that such biological principles as natural selection and the survival of the fittest were also the laws of human society. Thomas Hardy often spoke as if men's destinies were shaped by the physical sciences. He liked to say that his characters were doomed by the stars in their courses; but actually they were doomed by human conflicts or by the still Puritan conventions of middle-class England. Nor-

ris fell into the same confusion between the physical and the social
world when he pictured the wheat as "a huge Niagara . . . flowing
from West to East." In his novels wheat was not a grain improved
by men from various wild grasses and grown by men to meet
human needs; it was an abstract and elemental force like gravity.
"I corner the wheat!" says Jadwin, the hero of *The Pit*. "Great
heavens, it is the wheat that has cornered me." Later, when he is
ruined by the new grain that floods the market, Jadwin thinks to
himself,

> The Wheat had grown itself: demand and supply, these
> were the two great laws that the Wheat obeyed. Almost
> blasphemous in his effrontery, he had tampered with
> these laws, and roused a Titan. He had laid his puny
> human grasp upon Creation and the very earth herself,
> the great mother, feeling the touch of the cobweb that
> the human insect had spun, had stirred at last in her
> sleep and sent her omnipotence moving through the
> grooves of the world, to find and crush the disturber of
> her appointed courses.

Just as the wheat had grown itself, so, in the first volume of
Norris' trilogy, the Pacific and Southwestern Railroad had built
itself. This octopus that held a state in its tentacles was beyond
human control. Even Shelgrim, the president of the railroad, was
merely the agent of a superhuman force. At the end of the novel
he gives a lecture to Presley which overwhelms the poet and leaves
him feeling that it ran "with the clear reverberation of truth."
"You are dealing with forces," Shelgrim says, "when you speak
of Wheat and the Railroads, not with men. There is the Wheat,
the supply. It must be carried to the People. There is the demand.
The Wheat is one force, the Railroad, another, and there is the
law that governs them—supply and demand. Men have little to do
with the whole business." If the two forces came into conflict—if
the employees of the railroad massacred the wheat ranchers and
robbed them of their land—then Presley should "blame conditions,
not men."

The effect of naturalism as a doctrine is to subtract from literature the whole notion of human responsibility. "Not men" is its constant echo. If naturalistic stories had tragic endings, these were not to be explained by human wills in conflict with each other or with fate; they were the blind result of conditions, forces, physical laws, or nature herself. "There was no malevolence in Nature," Presley reflects after meeting the railroad president. "Colossal indifference only, a vast trend toward appointed goals. Nature was, then, a gigantic engine, a vast, cyclopean power, huge, terrible, a leviathan with a heart of steel, knowing no compunction, no forgiveness, no tolerance; crushing out the human atom standing in its way, with nirvanic calm." Stephen Crane had already expressed the same attitude toward nature in a sharper image and in cleaner prose. When the four shipwrecked men in *The Open Boat* are drifting close to the beach but are unable to land because of the breakers, they stare at a windmill that is like "a giant standing with its back to the plight of the ants. It represented in a degree, to the correspondent, the serenity of nature amid the struggles of the individual—nature in the wind, and nature in the visions of men. She did not seem cruel to him, then, nor beneficent, nor treacherous, nor wise. But she was indifferent, flatly indifferent."

These ideas about nature, science, and destiny led to the recurrent use of words and phrases by which early naturalistic fiction can be identified. "The irony of fate" and "the pity of it" are two of the phrases; "pawns of circumstance" is another. The words that appear time and again are "primitive," "primordial" (often coupled with "slime"), "prehensile," "apelike," "wolflike," "brute" and "brutal," "savage," "driving," "conquering," "blood" (often as an adjective), "master" and "slave" (also as adjectives), "instinct" (which is usually "blind"), "ancestor," "huge," "cyclopean," "shapeless," "abyss," "biological," "chemic" and "chemism," "hypocrisy," "taboo," "unmoral." Time and again we read that "The race is to the swift and the battle to the strong." Time and again we are told about "the law of claw and fang," "the struggle for existence," "the blood of his Viking ancestors," and "the foul stream of hereditary evil." "The veneer of civilization" is always being "stripped away," or else it "drops away in an instant." The characters in early naturalistic novels "lose all resemblance to humanity," reverting to "the abysmal brute." But when they "clash together like naked savages," or even like atoms and star dust, it is always the hero who "proves himself the stronger"; and spurning his prostrate adversary he strides forward to seize "his mate, his female." "Was he to blame?" the author asks his readers; and always he answers, "Conditions, not men, were at fault."

All these characteristics of the earlier American naturalists might have been deduced from their original faith in Darwinian evolution and in the need for applying biological and physical laws to human affairs. But they had other characteristics that were more closely connected with American life in their own day.

The last decade of the nineteenth century, when they started their literary careers, was an age of contrasts and sudden changes. In spite of financial panics, the country was growing richer, but not at a uniform rate for all sections: the South was hopelessly impoverished and rural New England was returning to wilderness. Cities were gaining in population, partly at the expense of the Eastern farms, industry was thriving at the expense of agriculture, and independent factories were being combined into or destroyed by the trusts. It was an age of high interest rates, high but uncertain profits, low wages and widespread unemployment. It was an age when labor unions were being broken, when immigrants were pouring through Ellis Island to people the new slums and when the new American baronage was building its magnificently ugly chateaux. "America," to quote again from Dreiser's memoirs, "was just entering upon the most lurid phase of that vast, splendid, most lawless and most savage period in which the great financiers were plotting and conniving at the enslavement of the people and belaboring each other." Meanwhile the ordinary citizen found it difficult to plan his future and even began to suspect that he was, in a favorite naturalistic phrase, "the plaything of forces beyond human control."

The American faith that was preached in the pulpits and daily reasserted on editorial pages had lost its connection with American life. It was not only an intolerable limitation on American writing, as all the rebel authors had learned; it also had to be disregarded by anyone who hoped to rise in the business world and by anyone who, having failed to rise, wanted to understand the reasons for his failure. In its simplest terms, the American faith was that things were getting better year by year, that the individual could solve his problems by moving, usually westward, and that virtue was rewarded with wealth, the greatest virtue with the greatest wealth. Those were the doctrines of the editorial page; but reporters who worked for the same newspaper looked around them and decided that wealth was more often the fruit of selfishness and fraud, whereas the admirable persons in their world—the kind, the philosophic, the honest, and the open-eyed—were usually failures by business standards. Most of the early naturalistic writers, including Stephen Crane, Harold Frederic, David Graham Phillips, and Dreiser, were professional newspaper men; while the others either worked for short periods as reporters or wrote series of newspaper articles. All were more or less affected by the moral atmosphere of the city room; and the fact is important, since the newspaper men of the 1890's and 1900's were a special class or type. "Never," says Dreiser, speaking of his colleagues on the Pittsburgh *Dispatch*, "had I encountered more intelligent or helpful or companionable albeit more cynical men than I met here"; and the observation leads to general remarks about the reporters he had known:

> One can always talk to a newspaper man, I think, with the full confidence that one is talking to a man who is at least free of moralistic mush. Nearly everything in connection with those trashy romances of justice, truth, mercy, patriotism, public profession of all sorts, is already and forever gone if they have been in the business for any length of time. The religionist is seen by them for what he is: a swallower of romance or a masquerader looking to profit and preferment. Of the politician, they know or believe but one thing: that he is out for himself.

Essentially the attitude forced upon newspaper men as they interviewed politicians, evangelists, and convicted criminals was the same as the attitude they derived or might have derived from popular books on evolution. Reading and experience led to the same convictions: that Christianity was a sham, that all moral professions were false, that there was nothing real in the world but force and, for themselves, no respectable role to play except that of detached observers gathering the facts and printing as many of them as their publishers would permit. They drank, whored, talked shop, and dreamed about writing cynical books. "Most of these young men," Dreiser says, "looked upon life as a fierce, grim struggle in which no quarter was either given or taken, and in which all men laid traps, lied, squandered, erred through illusion: a conclusion with which I now most heartily agree." His novels one after another would be based on what he had learned in his newspaper days.

In writing their novels, most of the naturalists pictured themselves as expressing a judgment of life that was scientific, dispassionate, and, to borrow one of their phrases, completely unmoral; but a better word for their attitude would be "rebellious." Try as they would, they could not remain merely observers. They had to revolt against the moral standards of their time; and the revolt involved them more or less unconsciously in the effort to impose new standards that would be closer to what they regarded as natural laws. Their books are full of little essays or sermons addressed to the reader; in fact they suggest a naturalistic system of ethics complete with its vices and virtues. Among the vices those most often mentioned are hypocrisy, intolerance, conventionality, and unwillingness to acknowledge the truth. Among the virtues perhaps the first is strength, which is presented as both a physiological and a moral quality; it implies the courage to be strong in spite of social restraints. A second virtue is naturalness, that is, the quality of acting in accordance with one's nature and physical instincts. Dreiser's Jennie Gerhardt was among the first of the purely natural heroines in American literature, but she had many descendants. A third virtue is complete candor about the world and oneself; a fourth is pity for others; and a fifth is tolerance, especially of moral rebellion and economic failure. Most of the characters presented sympathetically in naturalistic novels are either the victors over moral codes which they defy (like Cowperwood in *The Financier* and Susan Lenox in the novel by David Graham Phillips about her fall and rise) or else victims of the economic struggle, paupers and drunkards with infinitely more wisdom than the respectable citizens who avoid them. A great deal of naturalistic writing, including the early poems of Edwin Arlington Robinson, is an eloquent hymn to loneliness and failure as the destiny, in America, of most superior men.

There are other qualities of American naturalism that are derived not so much from historical conditions as from the example of the two novelists whom the younger men regarded as leaders or precursors. Norris first and Dreiser after him fixed the patterns that the others would follow.

Both men were romantic by taste and temperament. Although Norris was a disciple of Zola's, his other favorite authors belonged in one way or another to the romantic school; they included Froissart, Scott, Dickens, Dumas, Hugo, Kipling, and Stevenson. Zola was no stranger in that company, Norris said; on one occasion he called him "the very head of the Romanticists."

> Terrible things must happen [he wrote], to the characters of the naturalistic tale. They must be twisted from the ordinary, wrenched from the quiet, uneventful round of everyday life and flung into the throes of a vast and terrible drama that works itself out in unleashed passions, in blood and sudden death. . . . Everything is extraordinary, imaginative, grotesque even, with a vague note of terror quivering throughout like the vibration of an ominous and low-pitched diapason.

Norris himself wished to practice naturalism as a form of romance, instead of taking up what he described as the "harsh, loveless, colorless, blunt tool called Realism." Dreiser in his autobiographical writings often refers to his own romantic temper. "For all my modest repute as a realist," he says, "I seem, to my self-analyzing eyes, somewhat more of a romanticist." He speaks of himself in his youth as "a creature of slow and uncertain response to anything practical, having an eye to color, romance, beauty. I was but a half-baked poet, romancer, dreamer." The other American naturalists were also romancers and dreamers in their fashion, groping among facts for the extraordinary and even the grotesque. They believed that men were subject to natural forces, but they felt those forces were best displayed when they led to unlimited wealth, utter squalor, collective orgies, blood, and sudden death.

Among the romantic qualities they tried to achieve was "bigness" in its double reference to size and intensity. They wanted to display "big"—that is, intense—emotions against a physically large background. Bigness was the virtue that Norris most admired in Zola's novels. "The world of M. Zola," he said, "is a world of big things; the enormous, the formidable, the terrible, is what counts; no teacup tragedies here." In his own novels, Norris looked for big themes; after his trilogy on Wheat, he planned to write a still bigger trilogy on the three days' battle of Gettysburg, with one novel devoted to the events of each day. The whole notion of writing trilogies instead of separate novels came to be connected with the naturalistic movement, although it was also adopted by the historical romancers. Before Norris there had been only one planned trilogy in serious American fiction: *The Littlepage Manuscripts*, written by James Fenimore Cooper a few years before his death; it traces the story of a New York state landowning family through a hundred years and three generations. After Norris there were dozens of trilogies, with a few tetralogies and pentalogies: to mention some of the better known, there were Dreiser's trilogy on the career of a financier, T. S. Stribling's trilogy on the rise of a poor-white family, Dos Passos' trilogy on the United States from 1900 to 1930, James T. Farrell's trilogy on Studs Lonigan and Eugene O'Neill's trilogy of plays, *Mourning Becomes Electra*. Later O'Neill set to work on a trilogy of trilogies, a drama to be complete in nine full-length plays. Farrell wrote a pentalogy about the boyhood of Danny O'Neill and then attacked another theme that would require several volumes, the young manhood of Bernard Clare. Trilogies expanded into whole cycles of novels somehow related in theme. Thus, after the success of *The Jungle*, which had dealt with the meat-packing industry in Chicago, Upton Sinclair wrote novels on other cities (Denver, Boston) and other industries (oil, coal, whisky, automobiles); finally he settled on a character, Lanny Budd, whose adventures were as endless as those of Tarzan or Superman. Sinclair Lewis dealt one after another with various trades and professions: real estate, medicine, divinity, social service, hotel management, and the stage; there was no limit to the subjects he could treat, so long as his readers' patience was equal to his own.

With their eyes continually on vast projects, the American naturalists were careless about the details of their work and indifferent to the materials they were using; often their trilogies resembled great steel-structural buildings faced with cinder blocks and covered with cracked stucco ornaments. Sometimes the buildings remained unfinished. Norris set this pattern, too, when he died before he could start his third novel on the Wheat. Dreiser worked for years on *The Stoic*, which was to be the sequel to *The Financier* and *The Titan*; but he was never satisfied with the various endings he tried, and the book had to be completed by others after his death. Lewis never wrote his novel on labor unions, although he spent months or years gathering material for it and spoke of it as his most ambitious work. In their effort to achieve bigness at any cost, the naturalists were likely to undertake projects that went beyond their physical or imaginative powers, or in which they discovered too late that they weren't interested.

Meanwhile they worked ahead in a delirium of production, like factories trying to set new records. To understand their achievements in speed and bulk one has to compare their output with that of an average novelist. There is of course no average novelist, but there are scores of men and women who earn their livings by writing novels, and many of them try to publish one book each year. If they spend four months planning and gathering material for the book, another four months writing the first draft (at the rate of about a thousand words a day), and the last four months in revision, they are at least not unusual. Very few of the naturalists would have been satisfied with that modest rate of production. Harold Frederic wrote as much as 4,000 words a day and often sent his manuscripts to the printer without corrections. At least he paused between novels to carry on his work as a foreign correspondent; but Jack London, who wrote only 1,000 words a day, tried to fulfill that quota six days a week and fifty-two weeks a year; he allowed himself no extra time for planning or revision. He wrote fifty books in seventeen years, and didn't pretend that all of them were his best writing. "I have no unfinished stories," he told an interviewer five years before his death. "Invariably I complete every one I start. If it's good, I sign it and send it out. If it isn't good, I sign it and send it out." David Graham Phillips finished his first novel in 1901 and published sixteen others before his death in 1911, in addition to the articles he wrote for muckraking magazines. He left behind him the manuscripts of six novels (including the two-volume *Susan Lenox*) that were published posthumously. Upton Sinclair set a record in the early days when he was writing half-dime novels for boys. He kept three secretaries busy; two of them would be transcribing their notes while the third was taking dictation. By this method he once wrote 18,000 words in a day. He gained a fluency that helped him later when he was writing serious books, but he also acquired a contempt for style that made them painful to read, except in their French translations. Almost all the naturalists read better in translation; that is one of the reasons for their international popularity as compared with the smaller audience that some of them have found at home.

The naturalistic writers of all countries preferred an objective or scientific approach to their material. As early as 1864 the brothers Goncourt had written in their journal, "The novel of today is made with documents narrated or selected from nature, just as history is based on written documents." A few years later Zola defined the novel as a scientific experiment; its purpose, he said in rather involved language, was to demonstrate the behavior of given characters in a given situation. Still later Norris advanced the doctrine "that no one could be a writer until he could regard life and people, and the world in general, from the objective point of view—until he could remain detached, outside, maintain the unswerving attitude of the observer." The naturalists as a group not only based their work on current scientific theories, but tried to copy scientific methods in planning their novels. They were writers who believed, or claimed to believe, that they could deliberately choose a subject for their work instead of being chosen by a subject; that they could go about collecting characters as a biologist collected specimens; and that their fictional account of such characters could be as accurate and true to the facts as the report of an experiment in the laboratory.

"A Natural History of American Naturalism"

It was largely this faith in objectivity that led them to write about penniless people in the slums, whom they regarded as "outside" or alien subjects for observation. Some of them began with a feeling of contempt for the masses. Norris during his college years used to speak of "the canaille" and often wished for the day when all radicals could be "drowned on one raft." Later this pure contempt developed into a contemptuous interest, and he began to spend his afternoons on Polk Street, in San Francisco, observing with a detached eye the actions of what he now called "the people." The minds of the people, he thought, were simpler than those of persons in his own world; essentially these human beings were animals, "the creatures of habit, the playthings of forces," and therefore they were ideal subjects for a naturalistic novel. Some of the other naturalists revealed the same rather godlike attitude toward workingmen. Nevertheless they wrote about them, a bold step at a time when most novels dealt only with ladies, gentlemen, and faithful retainers; and often their contemptuous interest was gradually transformed into sympathy.

Their objective point of view toward their material was sometimes a pretense that deceived themselves before it deceived others. From the outside world they chose the subjects that mirrored their own conflicts and obsessions. Crane, we remember, said his purpose in writing *Maggie* was to show "that environment is a tremendous thing and often shapes lives regardlessly." Yet, on the subjective level, the novel also revealed an obsessive notion about the blamelessness of prostitutes that affected his career from beginning to end; it caused a series of scandals, involved him in a feud with the vice squad in Manhattan and finally led him to marry the madam of a bawdy house in Jacksonville. Norris's first novel, *Vandover and the Brute*, is an apparently objective study of degeneration, but it also mirrors the struggles of the author with his intensely Puritan conscience; Vandover is Norris himself. He had drifted into some mild dissipations and pictured them as leading to failure and insanity. Dreiser in *Sister Carrie* was telling a story based on the adventures of one of his sisters; that explains why Carrie Meeber in the novel is "Sister" Carrie, even though her relatives disappear after the first few pages. "My mind was a blank except for the name," Dreiser said when explaining how he came

443

to write the novel. "I had no idea who or what she was to be. I have often thought that there was something mystic about it, as if I were being used, like a medium." In a sense he was being used by his own memories, which had become subconscious. There was nothing mystic to Upton Sinclair about his fierce emotion in writing *The Jungle*; he knew from the beginning that he was telling his own story. "I wrote with tears and anguish," he says in his memoirs,

> pouring into the pages all that pain which life had meant to me. Externally, the story had to do with a family of stockyard workers, but internally it was the story of my own family. Did I wish to know how the poor suffered in Chicago? I had only to recall the previous winter in a cabin, when we had only cotton blankets, and cowered shivering in our separate beds. . . . Our little boy was down with pneumonia that winter, and nearly died, and the grief of that went into the book.

Indeed, there is personal grief and fury and bewilderment in all the most impressive naturalistic novels. They are at their best, not when they are scientific or objective, in accordance with their own theories, but when they are least naturalistic, most personal and lyrical.

If we follow William James and divide writers into the two categories of the tough and the tender-minded, then most of the naturalists are tender-minded. The sense of moral fitness is strong in them; they believe in their hearts that nature *should* be kind, that virtue *should* be rewarded on earth, that men *should* control their own destinies. More than other writers, they are wounded by ugliness and injustice, but they will not close their eyes to either; indeed, they often give the impression of seeking out ugliness and injustice in order to be wounded again and again. They have hardly a trace of the cynicism that is often charged against them. It is the quietly realistic or classical writers who are likely to be cynics, in the sense of holding a low opinion of life and human beings; that low estimate is so deeply ingrained in them that they never bother to insist on it—for why should they try to make converts in such a hopeless world? The naturalists are always

444

trying to convert others and themselves, and sometimes they build up new illusions simply to enjoy the pain of stripping them away. It is their feeling of fascinated revulsion toward their subject matter that makes some of the naturalists hard to read; they seem to be flogging themselves and their audience like a band of penitentes.

So far I have been trying to present the positive characteristics of a movement in American letters, but naturalism can also be defined in terms of what it is not. Thus, to begin a list of negations, it is not journalism in the bad sense, merely sensational or entertaining or written merely to sell. It has to be honest by definition, and honesty in literature is a hard quality to achieve, one that requires more courage and concentration than journalists can profitably devote to writing a novel. Even when an author holds all the naturalistic doctrines, his books have to reach a certain level of observation and intensity before they deserve to be called naturalistic. Jack London held the doctrines and wrote fifty books, but only three or four of them reached the required level. David Graham Phillips reached it only once, in *Susan Lenox*, if he reached it then.

Literary naturalism is not the sort of doctrine that can be officially sponsored and taught in the public schools. It depends for too many of its effects on shocking the sensibilities of its readers and smashing their illusions. It always becomes a threat to the self-esteem of the propertied classes. *Babbitt*, for example, is naturalistic in its hostile treatment of American businessmen. When Sinclair Lewis defended Babbittry in a later novel, *The Prodigal Parents*, his work had ceased to be naturalistic.

For a third negative statement, naturalism is not what we have learned to call literature "in depth." It is concerned with human behavior and with explanations for that behavior in terms of heredity or environment. It presents the exterior world, often in striking visual images; but unlike the work of Henry James or Sherwood Anderson or William Faulkner—to mention only three writers in other traditions—it does not try to explore the world within. Faulkner's method is sometimes described as "subjective naturalism," but the phrase is self-contradictory, almost as if one spoke of "subjective biology" or "subjective physics."

Naturalism does not deal primarily with individuals in themselves, but rather with social groups or settings or movements, or with individuals like Babbitt and Studs Lonigan who are regarded as being typical of a group. The naturalistic writer tries not to identify himself with any of his characters, although he doesn't always succeed; in general his aim is to present them almost as if they were laboratory specimens. They are seldom depicted as being capable of moral decisions. This fact makes it easy to distinguish between the early naturalists and some of their contemporaries like Robert Herrick and Edith Wharton who also tried to write without optimistic illusions. Herrick and Wharton, however, dealt with individuals who possessed some degree of moral freedom; and often the plots of their novels hinge on a conscious decision by one of the characters. Hemingway, another author whose work is wrongly described as naturalistic, writes stories that reveal some moral quality, usually stoicism or the courage of a frightened man.

Many naturalistic works are valuable historical documents, but the authors in general have little sense of history. They present each situation as if it had no historical antecedents, and their characters might be men and women created yesterday morning, so few signs do they show of having roots in the past. "Science" for naturalistic writers usually means laboratory science, and not the study of human institutions or patterns of thoughts that persist through generations.

With a few exceptions they have no faith in reform, whether it be the reform of an individual by his own decision or the reform of society by reasoned courses of action. The changes they depict are the result of laws and forces and tendencies beyond human control. That is the great difference between the naturalists and the proletarian or Marxian novelists of the 1930's. The proletarian writers—who were seldom proletarians in private life—believed that men acting together could make a new world. But they borrowed the objective and exterior technique of the naturalists, which was unsuited to their essentially religious purpose. In the beginning of each book they portrayed a group of factory workers as the slaves of economic conditions, "the creatures of habit, the playthings of forces"; then later they portrayed the conversion of one or more workers to Communism. But conversion is a psychological, not a biological, phenomenon, and it could not be explained purely in terms of conditions or forces. When the conversion took place, there was a shift from the outer to the inner world, and the novel broke in two.

It was not at all extraordinary for naturalism to change into religious Marxism in the middle of a novel, since it has always shown a tendency to dissolve into something else. On the record, literary naturalism does not seem to be a doctrine or attitude to which men are likely to cling through their whole lives. It is always being transformed into satire, symbolism, lyrical autobiography, utopian socialism, Communism, Catholicism, Buddhism, Freudian psychology, hack journalism or the mere assembling of facts. So far there is not in American literature a single instance in which a writer has remained a naturalist from beginning to end of a long career; even Dreiser before his death became a strange mixture of Communist and mystic. There are, however, a great many works that are predominantly naturalistic; and the time has come to list them in order to give the basis for my generalities.

I should say that those works, in fiction, were *Maggie* and *George's Mother* by Stephen Crane, with many of his short stories; *The Damnation of Theron Ware* by Harold Frederic; *Vandover, McTeague* and *The Octopus* (but not *The Pit*) by Frank Norris; *The Call of the Wild*, which is a sort of naturalistic Aesop's fable, besides *The Sea Wolf* and *Martin Eden* by Jack London; *The Jungle* by Upton Sinclair, as far as the page where Jurgis is converted to socialism; *Susan Lenox* by David Graham Phillips; all of Dreiser's novels except *The Bulwark* which has a religious ending written at the close of his life; all the serious novels of Sinclair Lewis between *Main Street* (1920) and *Dodsworth* (1929), but none he wrote afterward; Dos Passos' *Manhattan Transfer* and *U.S.A.*; James T. Farrell's work in general, but especially *Studs Lonigan*; Richard Wright's *Native Son*; and most of John Steinbeck's novels, including *In Dubious Battle* and all but the hortatory passages in *The Grapes of Wrath*. In poetry there is Robinson's early verse (*The Children of the Night*) and there is Edgar Lee Masters' *Spoon River Anthology*. In the drama there are the early plays of Eugene O'Neill, from *Beyond the Horizon* to *Desire under the Elms*. Among essays there are H. L.

Mencken's *Prejudices* and Joseph Wood Krutch's *The Modern Temper*, which is the most coherent statement of the naturalistic position. There are other naturalists in all fields, especially fiction, and other naturalistic books by several of the authors I have mentioned; but these are the works by which the school is likely to be remembered and judged.

And what shall we say in judgment?—since judge we must, after this long essay in definition. Is naturalism true or false in its premises and good or bad in its effect on American literature? Its results have been good, I think, in so far as it has forced its adherents to stand in opposition to American orthodoxy. Honest writing in this country, the only sort worth bothering about, has almost always been the work of an opposition, chiefly because the leveling and unifying elements in our culture have been so strong that a man who accepts orthodox judgments is in danger of losing his literary personality. Catullus and Villon might be able to write their poems here; with their irregular lives they wouldn't run the risk of being corrupted by the standards of right-thinking people. But Virgil, the friend of Augustus, the official writer who shaped the myth of the Roman state—Virgil would be a dubious figure as an American poet. He would be tempted to soften his values in order to become a prophet for the masses. The American myth of universal cheap luxuries, tiled bathrooms, and service with a smile would not serve him as the basis for an epic poem.

The naturalists, standing in opposition, have been writers of independent and strongly marked personalities. They have fought for the right to speak their minds and have won a measure of freedom for themselves and others. Yet it has to be charged against them that their opposition often takes the form of cheapening what they write about; of always looking for the lowdown or the payoff, that is, for the meanest explanation of everything they describe. There is a tendency in literary naturalism—as distinguished from philosophical naturalism, which is not my subject—always to explain the complex in terms of the simple: society in terms of self, man in terms of his animal inheritance, and the organic in terms of the inorganic. The result is that something is omitted at each stage in this process of reduction. To say that man is a beast of prey or a collection of chemical compounds omits most of man's special nature; it is a metaphor, not a scientific statement.

This scientific weakness of naturalism involves a still greater literary weakness, for it leads to a conception of man that makes it impossible for naturalistic authors to write in the tragic spirit. They can write about crimes, suicides, disasters, the terrifying, and the grotesque; but even the most powerful of their novels and plays are case histories rather than tragedies in the classical sense. Tragedy is an affirmation of man's importance; it is "the imitation of noble action," in Aristotle's phrase; and the naturalists are unable to believe in human nobility. "We write no tragedies today," said Joseph Wood Krutch in his early book, *The Modern Temper*, which might better have been called "The Naturalistic Temper." "If the plays and novels of today deal with littler people and less mighty emotions it is not because we have become interested in commonplace souls and their unglamorous adventures but because we have come, willy-nilly, to see the soul of man as commonplace and its emotions as mean." But Krutch was speaking only for those who shared the naturalistic point of view. There are other doctrines held by modern writers that make it possible to endow their characters with human dignity. Tragic novels and plays have been written in these years by Christians, Communists, humanists, and even by existentialists, all of whom believe in different fashions and degrees that men can shape their own fates.

For the naturalists, however, men are "human insects" whose brief lives are completely determined by society or nature. The individual is crushed in a moment if he resists; and his struggle, instead of being tragic, is merely pitiful or ironic, as if we had seen a mountain stir itself to overwhelm a fly. Irony is a literary effect used time and again by all the naturalistic writers. For Stephen Crane it is the central effect on which almost all his plots depend: thus, in *The Red Badge of Courage* the boy makes himself a hero by running away. In *A Mystery of Heroism* a soldier risks his life to bring a bucket of water to his comrades, and the water is spilled. In *The Monster* a Negro stableman is so badly burned in rescuing a child that he becomes a faceless horror; and the child's father, a physician, loses his practice as a reward for sheltering the stableman. The irony in Dreiser's novels depends on the contrast between conventional morality and the situations he describes: Carrie Meeber loses her virtue and succeeds in her career; Jennie Gerhardt is a kept woman with higher principles than any respectable wife. In Sinclair Lewis the irony is reduced to an obsessive and irritating trick of style; if he wants to say that a speech was dull and stupid, he has to call it "the culminating glory of the dinner" and then, to make sure that we catch the point, explain that it was delivered by Mrs. Adelaide Tarr Gimmitch, "known throughout the country as 'the Unkies' Girl.'" The reader, seeing the name of Gimmitch, is supposed to smile a superior smile. There is something superior and ultimately tiresome in the attitude of many naturalists toward the events they describe. Irony—like pity, its companion—is a spectator's emotion, and it sets a space between ourselves and the characters in the novel. They suffer, but their cries reach us faintly, like those of dying strangers we cannot hope to save.

There is nothing in the fundamental principles of naturalism that requires a novel to be written in hasty or hackneyed prose. Flaubert, the most careful stylist of his age, was the predecessor and guide of the French naturalists. Among the naturalistic writers of all countries who wrote with a feeling for language were the brothers Goncourt, Ibsen, Hardy, and Stephen Crane. But it was Norris, not Crane, who set the standards for naturalistic fiction in the United States, and Norris had no respect for style. "What pleased me most in your review of 'McTeague,'" he said in a letter to Isaac Marcosson, "was 'disdaining all pretensions to style.' It is precisely what I try most to avoid. I detest 'fine writing,' 'rhetoric,' 'elegant English'—tommyrot. Who cares for fine style! Tell your yarn and let your style go to the devil. We don't want literature, we want life." Yet the truth was that Norris' novels were full of fine writing and lace-curtain English. "Untouched, unassailable, undefiled," he said of the wheat, "that mighty world force, that nourisher of nations, wrapped in Nirvanic calm, indifferent to the human swarm, gigantic, resistless, moved onward in its appointed grooves." He never learned to present his ideas in their own clothes or none at all; it was easier to dress them in borrowed plush; easier to make all his calms Nirvanic and all his grooves appointed.

"A Natural History of American Naturalism"

Yet Norris wrote better prose than most of his successors among the American naturalists. With a few exceptions like Dos Passos and Steinbeck, they have all used language as a blunt instrument; they write as if they were swinging shillelaghs. O'Neill is a great dramatist, but he has never had an ear for the speech of living persons. Lewis used to have an ear, but now listens only to himself. He keeps being arch and ironical about his characters until we want to snarl at him, "Quit patronizing those people! Maybe they'd have something to say if you'd only let them talk." Farrell writes well when he is excited or angry, but most of the time he makes his readers trudge through vacant lots in a South Chicago smog. Dreiser is the worst writer of all, but in some ways the least objectionable; there is something native to himself in his misuse of language, so that we come to cherish it as a sign of authenticity, like the tool marks on Shaker furniture. Most of the others simply use the oldest and simplest phrase.

But although the naturalists as a group are men of defective hearing, they almost all have keen eyes for new material. Their interest in themes that others regarded as too unpleasant or ill-bred has immensely broadened the scope of American fiction. Moreover, they have had enough vitality and courage to be exhilarated by the American life of their own times. From the beginning they have exulted in the wealth and ugliness of American cities, the splendor of the mansions and the squalor of the tenements. They compared Pittsburgh to Paris and New York to imperial Rome. Frank Norris thought that his own San Francisco was the ideal city for storytellers: "Things happen in San Francisco," he said. Dreiser remarked of Chicago, "It is given to some cities, as to some lands, to suggest romance, and to me Chicago did that hourly. . . . Florence in its best days must have been something like this to young Florentines, or Venice to the young Venetians." The naturalists for all their faults were embarked on a bolder venture than those other writers whose imaginations can absorb nothing but legends already treated in other books, prepared and predigested food. They tried to seize the life around them, and at their best they transformed it into new archetypes of human experience. Just as Cooper had shaped the legend of the frontier and Mark Twain the legend of the Mississippi, so the naturalists have been shaping the harsher legends of an urban and industrial age.

"The Naturalism of Mr. Dreiser"*

By Stuart P. Sherman

STUART PRATT SHERMAN (1881-1926) was a member of the New Humanist group of Paul Elmer More and Irving Babbitt, to whom the doctrines of naturalism were anathema for their insistence on the animality of man. Strongly influenced by Babbitt at Harvard, where he received his Ph.D. in 1906, Sherman later became a contributor to the *Nation* under the editorship of More.

This article, which appeared in *The Nation* in 1915 at the time of the furore over *The "Genius,"* is significant primarily for the repetition of the general line of attack which had been used against Zola thirty years before. The arguments are 1) that realism is not a new thing; 2) that it is not possible to avoid selection and bias; 3) that it provides a false theory of life; 4) that Dreiser oversimplifies and therefore casts no light on fundamental human concerns; and 5) that he is monotonous and repetitious. To this is added, in all such attacks, a general comment on Dreiser's "heavy hand" and mawkishness—in short, on his bad writing.

In the last years of his life Sherman reversed his position in part, made handsome amends to Dreiser, and brought consternation to the camp of the New Humanists when he wrote in praise of *An American Tragedy*†. He admits that it is "the worst written great novel in the world," but he considers that in it the author has made "a long stride toward a genuine and adequate realism." For the first time Dreiser is telling the truth in comprehensive and balanced fashion and is proving himself to be a moralist. "I do not know where else in American fiction one can find the situation here presented dealt with so fearlessly, so intelligently, so exhaustively, so veraciously, and *therefore* with such unexceptionable moral effect."

◇◇

THE layman who listens reverently to the reviewers discussing the new novels and to the novelists discussing themselves can

* Sherman, Stuart P., "The Naturalism of Mr. Dreiser" (*Nation*, December 8, 1915), appeared as "The Barbaric Naturalism of Theodore Dreiser" in *On Contemporary Literature*, 1917, by Stuart P. Sherman, and is reprinted by permission of Holt, Rinehart and Winston, Inc.

† Sherman, Stuart P., "Mr. Dreiser in Tragic Realism," *The Main Stream*, pp. 134-144; New York, Charles Scribner's Sons, 1927.

"The Naturalism of Mr. Dreiser"

hardly escape persuasion that a great change has rather recently taken place in the spirit of the age, in the literature which reflects it, and in the criticism which judges it. The nature of the supposed revolution may be briefly summarized.

The elder generation was in love with illusions, and looked at truth through a glass darkly and timorously. The artist, tongue-tied by authority and trammelled by aesthetic and moral conventions, selected, suppressed, and rearranged the data of experience and observation. The critic, "morally subsidized," regularly professed his disdain for a work of art in which no light glimmered above "the good and the beautiful."

The present age is fearless and is freeing itself from illusions. Now, for the first time in history, men are facing unabashed the facts of life. "Death or life," we cry, "give us only reality!" Now, for the first time in the history of English literature, fiction is become a flawless mirror held up to the living world. Rejecting nothing, altering nothing, it presents to us—let us take our terms from the bright lexicon of the reviewer—a "transcript," a "cross-section," a "slice," a "photographic" or "cinematographic" reproduction of life. The critic who keeps pace with the movement no longer asks whether the artist has created beauty or glorified goodness, but merely whether he has told the truth.

Mr. Dreiser, in his latest novel, describes a canvas by a painter of this austere modern school: "Raw reds, raw greens, dirty gray paving stones—such faces! Why, this thing fairly shouted its facts. It seemed to say: 'I'm dirty, I am commonplace, I am grim, I am shabby, but I am life.' And there was no apologizing for anything in it, no glossing anything over. Bang! Smash! Crack! came the facts one after another, with a bitter, brutal insistence on their so-ness." If you do not like what is in the picture, you are to be crushed by the retort that perhaps you do not like what is in life. Perhaps you have not the courage to confront reality. Perhaps you had better read the chromatic fairy-tales with the children. Men of sterner stuff exclaim, like the critic in this novel, "Thank God for a realist!"

Mr. Dreiser is a novelist of the new school, for whom we have been invited off and on these fourteen years to thank God—a form of speech, by the way, which crept into the language before the

dawn of modern realism. He has performed with words what his
hero performed with paint. He has presented the facts of life "one
after another with a bitter, brutal insistence on their so-ness,"
which marks him as a "man of the hour," a "portent"—the successor of Mr. Howells and Mr. James. In the case of a realist, biographical details are always relevant. Mr. Dreiser was born of
German-American parents in Terre Haute, Indiana, in 1871. He
was educated in the Indiana public schools and at the State University. He was engaged in newspaper work in Chicago, St. Louis,
New York, and elsewhere, from 1892 to 1910. He has laid reality
bare for us in five novels published as follows: "Sister Carrie,"
1901; "Jennie Gerhardt," 1911; "The Financier," 1912; "The
Titan," 1914; and "The Genius," 1915. These five works constitute a singularly homogeneous mass of fiction. I do not find
any moral value in them, nor any memorable beauty—of their
truth I shall speak later; but I am greatly impressed by them
as serious representatives of a new note in American literature,
coming from that "ethnic" element of our mixed population which,
as we are assured by competent authorities, is to redeem us from
Puritanism and insure our artistic salvation. They abundantly illustrate, furthermore, the methods and intentions of our recent
courageous, veracious realism. Before we thank God for it, let
us consider a little more closely what is offered us.

I

The first step towards the definition of Mr. Dreiser's special
contribution is to blow away the dust with which the exponents of
the new realism seek to becloud the perceptions of our "reverent
layman." In their main pretensions, there are large elements of
conscious and unconscious sham.

It should clear the air to say that courage in facing and veracity
in reporting the facts of life are no more characteristic of Theodore
Dreiser than of John Bunyan. These moral traits are not the peculiar marks of the new school; they are marks common to every
great movement of literature within the memory of man. Each
literary generation detaching itself from its predecessor—whether
it has called its own movement Classical or Romantic or what not
—has revolted in the interest of what it took to be a more ade-

quate representation of reality. No one who is not drunken with the egotism of the hour, no one who has penetrated with sober senses into the spirit of any historical period anterior to his own, will fall into the indecency of declaring his own age preëminent in the desire to see and to tell the truth. The real distinction between one generation and another is in the thing which each takes for its master truth—in the thing which each recognizes as the essential reality for it. The difference between Bunyan and Dreiser is in the order of facts which each reports.

It seems necessary also to declare at periodic intervals that there is no such thing as a "cross-section" or "slice" or "photograph" of life in art—least of all in the realistic novel. The use of these catchwords is but a clever hypnotizing pass of the artist, employed to win the assent of the reader to the reality of the show, and, in some cases, to evade moral responsibility for any questionable features of the exhibition. A realistic novel no more than any other kind of a novel can escape being a composition involving preconception, imagination, and divination. Yet, hearing one of our new realists expound his doctrine, you might suppose that writing a novel was a process analogous to photographing wild animals in their habitat by trap and flashlight. He, if you will believe him, does not invite his subjects, nor group them, nor compose their features, nor furnish their setting. He but exposes the sensitized plate of his mind. The pomp of life goes by, and springs the trap. The picture, of course, does not teach nor preach nor moralize. It simply re-presents. The only serious objection to this figurative explanation of the artistic process is the utter dissimilarity between the blank impartial photographic plate, commemorating everything that confronts it, and the crowded inveterately selective human mind, which, like a magnet, snatches the facts of life that are subject to its influence out of their casual order and redisposes them in a pattern of its own.

In the case of any specified novelist, the facts chosen and the pattern assumed by them are determined by his central theory or "philosophy of life"; and this is precisely criticism's justification for inquiring into the adequacy of any novelist's general ideas. In vain, the new realist throws up his hands with protestations of innocence, and cries: "Search me. I carry no concealed weapons.

I run life into no preconceived mould. I have no philosophy. My business is only to observe, like a man of science, and to record what I have seen." He cannot observe without a theory, nor record his observations without betraying it to any critical eye.

As it happens, the man of science who most profoundly influenced the development of the new realistic novel—Charles Darwin —more candid than the writers of "scientific" fiction—frankly declared that he could not observe without a theory. When he had tentatively formulated a general law, and had begun definitely to look for evidence of its operation, then first the substantiating facts leaped abundantly into his vision. His "Origin of Species" has the unity of a work of art, because the recorded observations support a thesis. The French novelists who in the last century developed the novel of contemporary life learned as much, perhaps, from Darwin's art as from his science. Balzac emphasized the relation between man and his social *milieu*; the Goncourts emphasized the importance of extensive collection of "human documents"; Zola emphasized the value of scientific hypotheses. He deliberately adopted the materialistic philosophy of the period as his guide in observation and as his unifying principle in composition. His theory of the causes of social phenomena, which was derived largely from medical treatises, operated like a powerful magnet among the chaotic facts of life, rejecting some, selecting others, and redisposing them in the pattern of the *roman naturaliste*. Judicious French critics said: "My dear man," or words to that effect, "your representations of life are inadequate. This which you are offering us with so earnest an air is not reality. It is your own private nightmare." When they had exposed his theory, they had condemned his art.

Let us, then, dismiss Mr. Dreiser's untenable claims to superior courage and veracity of intention, the photographic transcript, and the unbiassed service of truth; and let us seek for his definition in his general theory of life, in the order of facts which he records, and in the pattern of his representations.

II

The impressive unity of effect produced by Mr. Dreiser's five novels is due to the fact that they are all illustrations of a crude and naïvely simple naturalistic philosophy, such as we find in the mouths of exponents of the new *Real-Politik*. Each book, with its bewildering masses of detail, is a ferocious argument in behalf of a few brutal generalizations. To the eye cleared of illusions it appears that the ordered life which we call civilization does not really exist except on paper. In reality our so-called society is a jungle in which the struggle for existence continues, and must continue, on terms substantially unaltered by legal, moral, or social conventions. The central truth about man is that he is an animal amenable to no law but the law of his own temperament, doing as he desires, subject only to the limitations of his power. The male of the species is characterized by cupidity, pugnacity, and a simian inclination for the other sex. The female is a soft, vain, pleasure-seeking creature, devoted to personal adornment, and quite helplessly susceptible to the flattery of the male. In the struggles which arise in the jungle through the conflicting appetites of its denizens, the victory goes to the animal most physically fit and mentally ruthless, unless the weaklings, resisting absorption, combine against him and crush him by sheer force of numbers.

The idea that civilization is a sham Mr. Dreiser sometimes sets forth explicitly, and sometimes he conveys it by the process known among journalists as "coloring the news." When Sister Carrie yields to the seductive drummer, Drouet, Mr. Dreiser judicially weighs the advantages and disadvantages attendant on the condition of being a well-kept mistress. When the institution of marriage is brushed aside by the heroine of "The Financier," he comments "editorially" as follows: "Before Christianity was man, and after it will also be. A metaphysical idealism will always tell him that it is better to preserve a cleanly balance, and the storms of circumstance will teach him a noble stoicism. Beyond this there is nothing which can reasonably be imposed upon the conscience of man." A little later in the same book he says: "Is there no law outside of the subtle will and the power to achieve? If not, it is surely high time that we knew it—one and all. We might then agree to do as we do; but there would be no silly illusion as to divine regulation." His own answer to the question, his own valuation of regulation, both divine and human, may be found in the innumerable contemptuous epithets which fall from his pen whenever he has occasion to mention any power set up against the urge of instinct and the indefinite expansion of desire. Righteousness is always "legal"; conventions are always "current"; routine is always "dull"; respectability is always "unctuous"; an institution for transforming schoolgirls into young ladies is presided over by "owl-like conventionalists"; families in which parents are faithful to each other lead an "apple-pie order of existence"; a man who yields to his impulses yet condemns himself for yielding is a "rag-bag moralistic ass." Jennie Gerhardt, by a facile surrender of her chastity, shows that *"she could not be readily corrupted by the world's selfish lessons* on how to preserve oneself from the evil to come." Surely, this is "coloring the news."

By similar devices Mr. Dreiser drives home the great truth that man is essentially an animal, impelled by temperament, instinct, physics, chemistry—anything you please that is irrational and uncontrollable. Sometimes he writes an "editorial" paragraph in which the laws of human life are explained by reference to the behavior of certain protozoa or by reference to a squid and a lobster fighting in an aquarium. His heroes and heroines have "cat-like eyes," "feline grace," "sinuous strides," eyes and jaws which vary "from those of the tiger, lynx, and bear to those of the fox, the tolerant mastiff, and the surly bulldog." One hero and his mistress are said to "have run together temperamentally like two leopards." The lady in question, admiring the large rapacity of her mate, exclaims playfully: "Oh, you big tiger! You great, big lion! Boo!" Courtship as presented in these novels is after the manner of beasts in the jungle. Mr. Dreiser's leonine men but circle once or twice about their prey, and spring, and pounce; and the struggle is over. A pure-minded serving-maid, who is suddenly held up in the hall by a "hairy, axiomatic" guest and "masterfully" kissed upon the lips, may for an instant be "horrified, stunned, *like a bird in the grasp of a cat.*" But we are always assured that "through it all something tremendously vital and insistent" will be speaking to her, and that in the end she will not resist the urge of the *élan vital.* I recall no one of all the dozens of obliging women in these books who makes any effective resistance when summoned to capitulate. "The *psychology of the human animal,* when confronted by these

458

tangles, these ripping tides of the heart," says the author of "The Titan," "has little to do with so-called reason or logic." No; as he informs us elsewhere with endless iteration, it is a question of chemistry. It is the "chemistry of her being" which rouses to blazing the ordinarily dormant forces of Eugene Witla's sympathies in "The Genius." If Stephanie Platow is disloyal to her married lover in "The Titan," "let no one quarrel" with her. Reason: "She was an unstable chemical compound."

Such is the Dreiserian philosophy.

III

By thus eliminating distinctively human motives and making animal instincts the supreme factors in human life, Mr. Dreiser reduces the problem of the novelist to the lowest possible terms. I find myself unable to go with those who admire the powerful reality of his art while deploring the puerility of his philosophy. His philosophy quite excludes him from the field in which a great realist must work. He has deliberately rejected the novelist's supreme task—understanding and presenting the development of character; he has chosen only to illustrate the unrestricted flow of temperament. He has evaded the enterprise of representing human conduct; he has confined himself to a representation of animal behavior. He demands for the demonstration of his theory a moral vacuum from which the obligations of parenthood, marriage, chivalry, and citizenship have been quite withdrawn or locked in a twilight sleep. At each critical moment in his narrative, where a realist like George Eliot or Thackeray or Trollope or Meredith would be asking how a given individual would feel, think, and act under the manifold combined stresses of organized society, Mr. Dreiser sinks supinely back upon the law of the jungle or mutters his mystical gibberish about an alteration of the chemical formula.

The possibility of making the unvarying victoriousness of jungle-motive plausible depends directly upon the suppression of the evidence of other motives. In this work of suppression Mr. Dreiser simplifies American life almost beyond recognition. Whether it is because he comes from Indiana, or whether it is because he steadily envisages the human animal, I cannot say; I can only note that he never speaks of his men and women as "educated" or "brought up."

Whatever their social status, they are invariably "raised." Raising human stock in America evidently includes feeding and clothing it, but does not include the inculcation of even the most elementary moral ideas. Hence Mr. Dreiser's field seems curiously outside American society. Yet he repeatedly informs us that his persons are typical of the American middle class, and three of the leading figures, to judge from their names—Carrie Meeber, Jennie Gerhardt, and Eugene Witla—are of our most highly "cultured" race. Frank Cowperwood, the hero of two novels, is a hawk of finance and a rake almost from the cradle; but of the powers which presided over his cradle we know nothing save that his father was a competent official in a Philadelphia bank. What, if anything, Carrie Meeber's typical American parents taught her about the conduct of life is suppressed; for we meet the girl in a train to Chicago, on which she falls to the first drummer who accosts her. Eugene Witla emerges in his teens from the bosom of a typical middle-class American family—with a knowledge of the game called "post office," takes the train for Chicago, and without hesitation enters upon his long career of seduction. Jennie Gerhardt, of course, succumbs to the first man who puts his arm around her; but, in certain respects, her case is exceptional.

In the novel "Jennie Gerhardt" Mr. Dreiser ventures a disastrous experiment at making the jungle-motive plausible without suppressing the evidence of other motives. He provides the girl with pious Lutheran parents, of fallen fortune, but alleged to be of sterling character, who "raise" her with the utmost strictness. He even admits that the family were church-goers, and he outlines the doctrine preached by Pastor Wundt: right conduct in marriage and absolute innocence before that state, essentials of Christian living; no salvation for a daughter who failed to keep her chastity unstained or for the parents who permitted her to fall; Hell yawning for all such; God angry with sinners every day. "Gerhardt and his wife, and also Jennie," says Mr. Dreiser, "accepted the doctrines of their church without reserve." Twenty pages later Jennie is represented as yielding her virtue in pure gratitude to a man of fifty, Senator Brander, who has let her do his laundry and in other ways has been kind to her and to her family. The Senator suddenly dies; Jennie expects to become a mother; Father Gerhardt is brokenhearted, and the family moves from Columbus to Cleveland. This first episode is not incredibly presented as a momentary triumph of emotional impulse over training—as an "accident." The incredible appears when Mr. Dreiser insists that an accident of this sort to a girl brought up *under the conditions stated* is not necessarily followed by any sense of sin or shame or regret. Upon this simple pious Lutheran he imposes his own naturalistic philosophy, and, in analyzing her psychology before the birth of her illegitimate child, pretends that she looks forward to the event "without a murmur," with "serene, unfaltering courage," "the marvel of life holding her in trance," with "joy and satisfaction," seeing in her state "the immense possibilities of racial fulfillment." This juggling is probably expected to prepare us for her instantaneous assent, perhaps a year later, when a healthy, magnetic manufacturer, who has seen her perhaps a dozen times, claps his paw upon her and says, "You belong to me," and in a perfectly cold-blooded interview proposes the terms on which he will set her up in New York as his mistress. Jennie, who is a fond mother and a dutiful daughter, goes to her pious Lutheran mother and talks the whole matter over with her quite candidly. The mother hesitates—not on Jennie's account, gentle reader, but because she will be obliged to deceive old Gerhardt; "the difficulty of telling this lie was very great for Mrs. Gerhardt"! But she acquiesces at last. "I'll help you out with it," she concludes—"with a little sigh." The unreality of the whole transaction shrieks.

Mr. Dreiser's stubborn insistence upon the jungle-motive results in a dreary monotony in the form and substance of his novels. Interested only in the description of animal behavior, he constructs his plot in such a way as to exhibit the persistence of two or three elementary instincts through every kind of situation. He finds, for example, a subject in the career of an American captain of industry, thinly disguised under the name of Frank Cowperwood. He has just two things to tell us about Cowperwood: that he has a rapacious appetite for money, and that he has a rapacious appetite for women. In "The Financier" he "documents" those two truths about Cowperwood in seventy-four chapters, in each one of which he shows us how this hero made money or how he captivated women in Philadelphia. Not satisfied with the demonstration, he returns to the same theses in "The Titan," and shows us in sixty-two chapters how the same hero made money and captivated women in Chicago and New York. He promises us a third volume, in which we shall no doubt learn in a work of sixty or seventy chapters—a sort of huge club-sandwich composed of slices of business alternating with erotic episodes—how Frank Cowperwood made money and captivated women in London. Meanwhile Mr. Dreiser has turned aside from his great "trilogy of desire" to give us "The Genius," in which the hero, Witla, alleged to be a great realistic painter, exhibits in 101 chapters, similarly "sandwiched" together, an appetite for women and money indistinguishable from that of Cowperwood. Read one of these novels, and you have read them all. What the hero is in the first chapter, he remains in the hundred-and-first or the hundred-and-thirty-sixth. He acquires naught from his experience but sensations. In the sum of his experiences there is nothing of the impressive mass and coherence of activities bound together by principles and integrated in character, for all his days have been but as isolated beads loosely strung on the thread of his desire. And so after the production of the hundredth document in the case of Frank Cowperwood, one is ready to cry with fatigue: "Hold! Enough! We believe you. Yes, it is very clear that Frank Cowperwood had a rapacious appetite for women and for money."

If at this point you stop and inquire why Mr. Dreiser goes to such great lengths to establish so little, you find yourself once more confronting the jungle-motive. Mr. Dreiser, with a problem similar to De Foe's in "The Apparition of Mrs. Veal," has availed himself of De Foe's method for creating the illusion of reality. The essence of the problem and of the method for both these authors is the certification of the unreal by the irrelevant. If you wish to make acceptable to your reader the incredible notion that Mrs. Veal's ghost appeared to Mrs. Bargrave, divert his incredulity from the precise point at issue by telling him all sorts of detailed credible things about the poverty of Mrs. Veal's early life, the sobriety of her brother, her father's neglect, and the bad temper of Mrs. Bargrave's husband. If you wish to make acceptable to your reader the incredible notion that Aileen Butler's first breach of the seventh article in the decalogue was "a happy event," taking

"The Naturalism of Mr. Dreiser"

place "much as a marriage might have," divert his incredulity by describing with the technical accuracy of a fashion magazine not merely the gown that she wore on the night of Cowperwood's reception, but also with equal detail the half-dozen other gowns that she thought she might wear, but did not. If you have been for three years editor-in-chief of the Butterick Publications, you can probably perform this feat with unimpeachable verisimilitude; and having acquired credit for expert knowledge in matters of dress and millinery, you can now and then emit unchallenged a bit of philosophy such as "Life cannot be put in any one mould, and the attempt may as well be abandoned at once. . . . Besides, whether we will or no, theory or no theory, the large basic facts of chemistry and physics remain." None the less, if you expect to gain credence for the notion that your hero can have any woman in Chicago or New York that he puts his paw upon, you had probably better lead up to it by a detailed account of the street-railway system in those cities. It will necessitate the loading of your pages with a tremendous baggage of irrelevant detail. It will not sound much like art. It will sound more like one of Lincoln Steffens's special articles. But it will produce an overwhelming impression of reality, which the reader will carry with him into the next chapter where you are laying bare the "chemistry" of the human animal.

I V

It would make for clearness in our discussions of contemporary fiction if we withheld the title of "realist" from a writer like Mr. Dreiser, and called him, as Zola called himself, a "naturalist." While asserting that all great art in every period intends a representation of reality, I have tried to indicate the basis for a working distinction between the realistic novel and the naturalistic novel of the present day. Both are representations of the life of man in contemporary or nearly contemporary society, and both are presumably composed of materials within the experience and observation of the author. But a realistic novel is a representation based upon a theory of human conduct. If the theory of human conduct is adequate, the representation constitutes an addition to literature and to social history. A naturalistic novel is a representation based upon a theory of animal behavior. Since a theory of

463

animal behavior can never be an adequate basis for a representation of the life of man in contemporary society, such a representation is an artistic blunder. When half the world attempts to assert such a theory, the other half rises in battle. And so one turns with relief from Mr. Dreiser's novels to the morning papers.

"A Literary
Manifesto: The Populist Novel"*

By Léon Lemonnier

LÉON LEMONNIER (1890-1953) was, along with André Thérive, the founder of the short-lived populist school which dominated literary discussion for two or three years at the beginning of the 1930's. Both Lemonnier and Thérive were scholars, critics, and novelists. The movement began with an article by Thérive in *Comoedia* in 1927 in defense of naturalism, or, better, attacking the literature of snobs, inverts, aesthetes, and bourgeois. In the summer of 1929 Lemonnier drafted the present manifesto, which was published in *L'Oeuvre* on August 27. In 1931 his book *Populisme* was published by La Renaissance du Livre. At the height of the movement there was great activity of literary polls—Bernard Shaw, Sinclair Lewis, and Heinrich Mann were among those replying to one of international scope; a populist salon was opened in 1933. A prize for a populist novel was founded and awarded in the first instance to Eugène Dabit for his *Hôtel du Nord*. Populism appeared in the theatre with the première of Marcel Achard's *La Belle Marinière* at the Comédie Française. Although writers of the stature of Eugène Dabit, Georges Simenon, Georges Duhamel, Jules Romain, Romain Rolland, Henri Barbusse, and Louis Aragon adhered to the movement or expressed sympathy for its aims, it was of comparatively short duration.

Lemonnier's numerous pronouncements help expand the present statement. He suggests that the term has two meanings: it indicates works which treat of the people, in any sense of the word, and in a wider sense works which seem to continue the realist tradition. He feels that his group is separated from the naturalists in at least two respects, however: they find mysticism of value and they consider that "Petty pessimism is out of date, and the petty and niggling antipathy the naturalists show toward their characters is shocking to us, as is their sickly need to diminish, straiten, and dirty everything." Thérive had earlier suggested that morals and society are so subject to change that they constitute an ever-changing model. The attention and love given to depiction of that changing reality is what he calls "the true and indispensable naturalism."

* Lemonnier, Léon, "Un Manifeste Littéraire. Le Roman Populiste," *L'Oeuvre*, August 27, 1929. Translated by permission of Madame Léon Lemonnier.

ARE literary manifestos coming back into style? They had their finest hour a century ago; then a school popped up every two or three years. A few authors drew up a profession of faith under three headings which some review or other piously printed. That was the official birth announcement. When the school died, there was likewise a death notice; five or six authors sweepingly repudiated the principles which they had defended.

It seems to me that these proclamations provided contemporaries with highly diverting news. When you hear that a new airplane has just been tested, you shudder as you think of the catastrophe to come. When a group of more or less youthful authors inform you that they have just founded a new school, you permit yourself a quiet smile at the thought of the probable outcome of their hopes. However, I must say that such declarations support an intellectual atmosphere and that art would be unable to live without occasional theoretical discussions and even battles in which the cudgels of style are taken up.

That is the way the Naturalists succeeded in imposing themselves upon literary history. For we are forced to remember the dates which they chose themselves. The school was born officially with the publication of *Les Soirées de Médan* (1880) and died shortly after *Le Manifeste des Cinq* (1887). Léon Deffoux states this in his book *Le Naturalisme*. He shows, moreover, that "naturalism is not dead," to use a famous phrase. And he indicates in what sense its influence continues: "Thanks to the brake provided by naturalistic descriptions, the writers who sought to write living and true were led to a more careful examination of reality and to a more rigorous choice of materials."

Now Thérive has never concealed his sympathy for naturalism or his faith in the future of the school if it would only give up certain timeworn principles. Indeed, on May 3, 1927, he published a manifesto. But he timidly called it: *A Plea for Naturalism*, and he modestly neglected to mention himself. He was afraid of ridicule, which is an error, indeed a grave fault, on the part of the leader of a school. . . .

Is there any need, in view of what he has said, to indicate the principles of populism? The word should naturally be taken in a broad sense. We have had enough of chic characters and of snob literature; we wish to depict the people. But above all, what we undertake to do is to study reality with close attention.

We are opposed, in a certain sense, to the naturalists. Their language is out of date, and it is important to imitate neither the bizarre neologisms of which some of them are guilty nor their way of using the vocabulary and slang of all occupations. Nor do we any longer wish to be embarrassed by those social doctrines which have a tendency to distort works of literature.

Two things are left: First, daring in the choice of subjects: we should not be put to flight by affected cynicism or a certain finicking good taste, if I may risk the phrase. Above all, let us have done with characters from high society, those trivial sinners who have nothing else to do but put on rouge; the leisured ones who seek to practice the so-called elegant vices. We wish to go to the little people, to the ordinary people who make up the mass of society and whose lives also contain drama. Therefore certain ones of us have decided to form a group around André Thérive under the name of "populist novelists."

As I have said, the word is to be taken in a broad sense. We wish to depict the people, but we are above all ambitious to study reality with care. In this way we are sure to prolong the great tradition of the French novel, which always disdains pretentious acrobatics in favor of writing simply and true.

On Portuguese Neo-Realism*

By Jaime Brasil

ARTUR JAIME BRASIL LUQUET NETO (1896—) is known as a brilliant journalist and editor. He is currently editor of *O Primeiro de Janeiro* in Lisbon. He has translated Zola's *J'Accuse* into Portuguese and in 1943 published *Vida e obras de Zola*, several chapters of which are concerned with realism.

The following essay is more important for its symptomatic qualities than for the information which it gives about Portuguese writers. It bespeaks a sense of continuity with the nineteenth-century tradition, even though Zola is officially taboo. It turns to the observed and experienced in Portuguese life of the present day for subject matter, but conceives of the expected literary renovation in formal as well as contentual terms. It carries interesting implications of social betterment as one of the purposes of the new writing, which echoes the goals of late nineteenth-century realists in other countries. Because of Senhor Brasil's emphasis on the importance of reportage with style, the contemporary reader is forced to reflect on the importance of newspaper reporting in the development of realism in the United States at the turn of the century.

◇◇◇

THESE crucial years of war have been, paradoxically, favorable to the development of letters in Portugal. We say paradoxically, because neither is the internal climate favorable to the flowering of literary talent, nor is the external situation such as to permit to the intellect the calm necessary for maturation of works of art. The stimulus felt by young Portuguese writers must be very strong for them to surmount all the obstacles and limitations and fulfill themselves, if not completely, at least with great power.

Certainly with respect to works produced in the last five years there was no opportunity for long and serene incubation. The Portuguese have never been distinguished for works of thought, for the construction of systems, even for simple essays. Their originality is lyrical in nature. Even in prose fiction lyricism breaks

---

* Brasil, Jaime, *Os novos escritores e o movimento chamado NEO-"REALIS-MO,"* Oficinas Gráficas de "O Primeiro de Janeiro," Porto, 1945. Translated by permission of the author.

On Portuguese Neo-Realism

out irrepressibly. Nonetheless Portuguese fiction has deep roots in the past. Both the *Amadis* and the *Diana* of Jorge de Montemor, as well as *Saüdades* or *Menina e Moça* of Bernardim Ribeiro, preceded by a long time *La Princesse de Clèves* of Madame de la Fayette, who, moreover, was probably influenced by the *Lettres d'une religieuse portugaise*, attributed rightly or wrongly to Mother Dona Mariana Alcoforado, a professed religious who died full of years in the Convent of the Conception in Beja.

Portuguese fiction, moreover, has its ancient texts. When it burst out in a torrent with Camilo and flourished in formal elegance and subtlety of intellect with Eça it was the product of its time but also had its roots in the past. It has always been thus, and it would be naive to assert that artistic movements, especially in literature, have a spontaneous generation and issue fully armed from the brow of Minerva. Each work of art as it comes forth— apparently in one burst—from the genius who creates it is the product of a long development which in our day goes back for millennia.

Whether they wish it or not the writers of today are the heirs of all the thought of those who preceded them. It is indeed a great glory to know how to make good use of this inheritance, how to transform it into new riches. It is great ingratitude to deny it and to pretend that we are original and new when we are merely one link in an eternal chain.

It is in no way shameful to be a link in a chain, to feel the embrace of the link that comes before and to clasp it firmly in order to embrace the link that comes after. Without going beyond Portugal we can see this intellectual solidarity manifested in all eras and among all the great men of Portuguese letters.

The wonderful poetry of the "Cancioneiros" is impregnated with the measures and themes dear to the trouvères and minstrels of France. In the Renaissance the Vincentine theatre took inspiration from the Spanish theatre, the poetry of Sá de Miranda from Italian poems, and that unequaled genius Camoens borrowed his techniques here and there—for his epic even from classical writers —in order to discipline his exuberant imagination.

But nearer to our day, the Arcades were Italianate; the Romantics, if they did not know the German *Romantik*, were impregnated with English and French romanticism. The Portuguese realists, with Eça at their head, were disciples, sometimes too literally so, of the masters of French realism, even making use of some of the ideas of naturalism. All of them, however, were able to imprint their own genius on the current tendency and, if they did undergo influences, they were not simple imitators. They could not be: climate and blood, the internal and external landscape, were bound to give a distinct character to themes and a different vibration to form. It is for this reason that in two novels as similar as *Madame Bovary* and *O primo Basilio* Emma and Luisa are so different.

This young Portuguese literature, carrying the weight of all these external and internal influences, in spite of the world's woes and its own difficulties, has brought forth some works which, if they are not definitive, at least give reason for great hopes. They make us believe that Portuguese letters will again attain the prestige given them by the so-called "generation of the seventies"—a rather chronologically inexact designation—which contained a brilliant constellation of writers whose centenary falls in this decade of the 1940's: Antero, Teófilo, Oliveira Martins, Eça de Queiroz, etc.

The young Portuguese writers drew from these predecessors the sap of rebellion, the anxious desire for conceptual and formal renewal. It is not possible to deny this. The decisive impulse was given, however, by the young Brazilian literature which, disorderly and still uncouth in form, burst forth with all the vigor of tropical vegetation in the beginning of the second quarter of this century. More than a stimulus, it appears to have been a cause of emulation. It looked as though the torch of literary creation was about to pass out of our hands to the other shore of the Atlantic. Then by a great effort, without previous agreement and, we repeat, without a favorable atmosphere, the young intellectuals on this side took back the torch to raise it high.

We cannot observe this almost sportive competition without a shiver of emotion. The heroism of these youths entitles them to the respect of all. The mind of the West does not want to die; Europe does not relinquish her primacy. However, respect for the team that fights in order to win a trophy or in order not to lose a banner does not prevent us from criticizing the game or pointing out infractions of the rules.

Certainly in the ardor of the game the players do not want to pay any attention to critics. The latter disturb them in their creative work and appear to give comfort to their enemies. A clan psychosis shouts: "who is not for us is against us." Now the truth is that unconditional approbation, stupid admiration, irrational conformity are characteristic of those areas where "the leader is always right." In the intellectual realm, fortunately, all space is free and there are no boundaries or leaders. The spirit of the tribe is incompatible with intelligence.

In spite of the opposition of the artists criticism cannot, after all, abdicate its function—almost always irritating, but still necessary—in order to avoid going overboard or exaggerating. Whoever by demand of his conscience or through lack of creative power undertakes this type of magistracy must fulfill it like a priesthood. He must not be afraid to proclaim what he believes to be the truth; but he must not be intolerant toward those whom he believes to be in error. The artist, the creator, is incapable of judging his own work or that of his peers. It is necessary to be outside it, to be almost a spectator, if one is to judge whether the characters fulfill their roles perfectly. This judgment must be made without acrimony, however. Never does the French proverb: "You are angry, you are wrong" have more value as a dogma than in the realm of the intellect.

An independent criticism, confronted by the brilliant flowering of the young Portuguese writers, must study the process that made this possible. To do this we must go back to the currents that have polarized the Portuguese mind from the beginning of this century until now. The first was made up of writers who were grouped around the "Renascença" and afterwards continued their labors in the "Seara Nova." Of progressive inclination the elements in this current formed the intellectual basis of the nascent republican regime. Later but parallel was a retrogressive current inspired by the political doctrines of the "Action Française." When today we assess these forces, it is evident that in spite of the existence of some brilliant individuals their effect on the Portuguese mind was nil. This is because their politics limited it, indeed, sullied it.

Art and politics are values not only different but antagonistic.

There is scarcely need to mention the effort at merely formal renewal—since conceptually it contained nothing—sketched out in the review *Orfeu* and continued later in *Contemporânea*. One of the editors of the former, Fernando Pessoa, left his imprint on the poetic renascence which has since taken place in Portugal. This, however, was a case of personal influence, independent of the program outlined in the review.

Since then there has occurred a movement remote from politics, one of almost pure aesthetic renewal, centered around the review *Presença*. Having the impact and exaggerations of all young movements, it gave Portuguese letters a breath of fresh air. This movement also sought a renewal of form, particularly in poetry, but it also enlarged and opened up the field of criticism. It clarified aesthetic doctrine, permitting wider information about what was going on in the world. The most representative of its adherents did not yet have the courage to make a choice. They maintained, and still maintain today, the same adolescent uncertainty, vacillating between creation and criticism, which prevents them from serving either one or the other well. Nonetheless these most representative members of the "presencista" movement are the ones who today have the widest public, and some of them, by their dynamic qualities, by their constant "presence" in books and newspapers, have shown themselves able to maintain the combativity of the heroic times of the first battles.

Within the *Presença* group and its followers and sympathizers there was initiated the movement which today looms large in Portuguese letters. It was there that arose the quarrel between "pure art and social art," between the individualism of the artist—internal, everything in psychological reactions—and the artist preoccupied with the collectivity, with the common good, peering with open eyes at the harsh realities of life.

To tell the truth, these two extremes never existed. They served merely as banners for opposing forces. Every work of art is a purely individual creation and must reflect the individual who created it with his interior vibrations; but it is also, and chiefly, a reflection of that individual's acquisitions from the milieu in which he lives. If poetry can on occasion be practically interior soliloquy, prose fiction never ceases to be the product of observation, of analysis of the things around. There is no such thing as fiction without characters; but there is also no such thing as characters without what we conventionally call psychology, or what have you, an intimate, deep way of being.

It would seem that since we have no *corpus delicti*—that is, no works in which we can see the two tendencies—there is no ground for a quarrel and the case ought to be arbitrated. However, it has not worked out that way. A fiery debate still goes on, sustained enthusiastically by the group that defend social art, art put in the service of the collectivity, who are interested above all in human problems, in actual real events. However, the acolytes of this school do not document with their works the theories which they defend. They almost always analyze individual cases which, while they may on occasion reflect collective phenomena, have sharply individualistic solutions.

Young Portuguese writers, more inclined toward the new aesthetic or simply literary attitude, have not yet attempted so-called literature of the masses or proletarian literature, novels of a group in action, such as Barbusse, Fadaev and, more recently, Silone and Steinbeck have written. To give the collective background, they limit themselves to documentaries which have rather the character of successive pieces of reporting almost without conflicts. They insist, however, on calling their works novels, a genre which has its rules which are not to be broken.

This new aesthetic attitude, although it is only manifested in literature, derives from new-humanism. They chose for it a hybrid and unsatisfactory term that had already been applied twenty years ago to a renewal of dramatic technique in Germany: "neo-realism." This designation, which its own followers consider inadequate, seems destined to survive, thanks to the battle carried on by the detractors of the idea which it contains.

Without this battle it would be doomed to disappear, since such an attitude has nothing at all to do with a renewal of realism as Duranty and Champfleury defined it or Flaubert and the Goncourts practiced it. Possibly it comes closer to naturalism. If they had adopted the term "neo-naturalism," the movement would have the merit of not becoming confused with movements already in existence and it would correspond more closely to the ideas of those who defend it, since analysis of social phenomena, criticism of the bad organization of society, exaltation of the value of the workingman in contrast with the inferiority of those who exploit him were, in addition to being the scientific preoccupations of the day, the aims of Zola, the founder of the school.

It appears, however, that naturalism is taboo in Portugal. The term never took root, but was replaced by realism. Nonetheless the works of the creator of the naturalistic movement are those with the widest public among the Portuguese masses that are able to read. Zola is in bad odor among men of letters in general and the new generation in particular. Certainly he scorned adornment and "floweriness." Yet this seems to have its attraction, for literary youth feel, or acknowledge, that he is their predecessor and master in this respect.

We do not exaggerate in calling Zola the precursor of the new Portuguese literary generation and of a certain class of writers who are appearing all over the world. In addition to the lesson of his works, he left them advice to be followed at their risk. It appears that a certain young writer asked the master of Médan what was necessary for the writing of novels, how he went about it. Zola is said to have answered: "Be a reporter!" The anecdote may be apocryphal. But that undoubtedly is the formula. One of the great discoveries of naturalism was reportage, observation, "experiment," as Zola called it.

Now what is characteristic of the new Portuguese prose writers —it is these we wish particularly to discuss—is the discovery of reportage. Apparently they don't like to have their works described in these terms. Their scorn of journalism extends to its most brilliant form: reportage. As they see it, reporting is only the obscure work of a reporter and a statement in banal words about banal occurrences. True reporting, however, is relating true facts with art, accenting a line here or softening a harshness there. The events are real; the artist's part is to touch them with beauty, to give them value. Thus reportage, so scorned, rises to the level of an independent literary genre.

Reportage is the French "récit" or particularly the Russian "ocherk." Certainly Ilya Ehrenburg in defining this genre in his

On Portuguese Neo-Realism

essay on modern Russian literature (in *Encyclopédie Française*, vol. XVII, pp. 1754-1759) says it is difficult to translate it by the word reportage because the artistic problem plays a big part in it. He adds: "We can, however, compare it to certain documentary films which have their own style and their own artistic quality." It is surprising that the great writer, journalist, and reporter of genius, does not see the role that artistry can play in reportage, not least in his own reportages. He, however, judges the Russian "ocherk" a definite creation to be seen as the basis of the new Russian novel which is still being developed, and he considers himself as the great developer of this genre.

Now the genre practiced by the young Portuguese writers is precisely the "ocherk," artistic reportage, documentary with style. In general they write with great formal elegance and organize their compositions with art. Their reportages of rural life, of certain painful, lowly toils, of fishing or other hard and dangerous work, are pictures, a succession of scenes, barely tied together by a tenuous thread, and almost without conflict or plot.

There are some very fine productions in this genre, which is entirely new in Portuguese literature. The strange thing is that their authors, without the courage to break the old molds, persist in calling them *romances, short stories, tales*, when they belong to a mode of literary art that is substantially different. The documentary, spoken, colored, emotional, at times charming, which the young Portuguese writers prefer, is already able to demand autonomy, since it has reached its literary majority and has its own life.

In spite of youth's tendency to be generous and confident, the new Portuguese writers react with reserve and distrust, indeed with hostility, toward anyone who seeks to examine critically the content of their art, or to show that it is independent and contemporary, freed from the formulas and conceptions of the past. Perhaps they are not sufficiently informed and their lack of confidence comes from unjust attacks which disturb them, when they are not iniquitous persecutions which harass them. They take umbrage readily and sin by excess of legitimate defense in considering as hostile the hands which, bare and unarmed, do not applaud them unconditionally.

Who are these young writers to whom we have been vaguely referring? Are they all the Portuguese writers born in this century and now about thirty years old? Not at all. Among these men of "thirty more or less" there are many octogenarians, bonzes lost in contemplation of the navel of the past who write to win prizes for excellence and know how to get a place reserved for them in some learned society, illustrious circle, or banqueting club. It is not these who interest us. We might call them scribblers, since they write on ruled paper at so much per signature.

We are interested in disturbed youth, which has come to the surface during these tragic years of the war, which tries strenuously to swim above the slime and guards its Faith with manacled hands. This progressive and renascent youth, some of them hardly out of school, still adolescent in ideas and as eager for a fight as street urchins, is what provides hope for those of us over forty, survivors from the last century, who will never see the dreams of our youth realized.

Before putting down their names, we should like to name here the precursor of this young literature, the writer who, in themes and form, introduced the new genre into Portugal. We are referring to Ferreira de Castro. This novelist was the first to treat social problems in the Portuguese language. He reported the drama of the workers and sketched out the human documentary. Ferreira de Castro entered literature by way of journalism. His first important works, *Emigrantes* and *A selva*—masterpieces which today have a worldwide public—what are they fundamentally? Reporting. Vivid and deeply felt reporting, since the author lived, in his nerves and flesh, the situations evoked by his masterly fiction. He was an emigrant and an employe of an airfield lost in the forest of the Amazon. He himself carried out the "experiment" outlined by Zola.

We have already written, and take pleasure in repeating, that *A selva* is the *Germinal* of the virgin forest. This monumental documentary has as its main thread the struggle of man against hostile forces: those of untamed nature and capitalistic exploitation. If the central figure is the Forest, the action consists of a dialogue between Man and her. This action is overshadowed, however, by the grandeur of the document. This novel, almost without intrigue

On Portuguese Neo-Realism

or novelistic movement, is a genial piece of reportage, given value by the art of the narrator. *Emigrantes* is also a social document, a vivid piece of reporting, as are the other works of this author, particularly the still unpublished novel—provisionally entitled *Intervalo*, but the true title of which should be *Luta de classes*—a work which, when it comes out, will show Ferreira de Castro to have been the discoverer of the new reality in Portuguese literature.

We say of Portuguese literature and not merely in Portugal, for Ferreira de Castro preceded the modern Brazilian novelists, some of whom nobly acknowledge his primacy, for they know that he was the first to take the new attitude.

Let us see now who are the most representative writers of this new generation, which, disturbed and tormented, seeks its own direction and—in the area of the human documentary touched up with art, of reportage of the painful aspects of social life evoked in clear style—has already produced significant works. Not all of them belong, or wish to belong, to the avant garde which calls itself "neo-realist." All of them, however, suffer from the same anxieties and participate in the new techniques. Since the avant garde will shortly give up this inexpressive title, we can group them all together, for it is the task of criticism to make syntheses of artistic movements, no matter where their leaders come from or what aims they have.

Face to face with Portuguese reality, the principal activities of which are rural, these writers have not yet attempted to call the attention of the collective conscience to the drama of the rural worker. They have also not yet reported on the proletariat of factory and office, which appears only episodically in a few short stories. Once again it is Ferreira de Castro who is going to attempt this in the novel on which he is working and in which he hopes to evoke the life of those who work in the wool industry, in spinning and weaving mills.

Of the young writers the one who seems best endowed and who has produced the most works is Alves Redol. Since an ethnographic essay and a volume of short stories which he published in 1941, he has produced four novels: *Gaibéus, Marés, Avieiros,* and *Fanga.* It is the last undoubtedly which best indicates the talent of the writer. In it he presents the drama of the rural worker whose lot it is to cultivate the land of others, scarcely getting a minimal part of what he produces or maintaining the illusion of independence. It is a powerful work, though unbalanced, with pages of great vehemence.

Another writer who arouses great hopes is Pereira Gomes. He has published only one book, *Esteiros*, in which he documents the life of those who work on the banks of the Tagus in the small construction-materials industry. The organization of this reportage is beautifully balanced, the language is vigorous, and the deep feeling of this inquiry is vibrant with humanity.

Still another writer with the quality of a novelist is Afonso Ribeiro, who in addition to a volume of short stories has published three novels: *Plano inclinado, Aldeia,* and *Trampolim.* Of the three it is probably *Aldeia* that is most sharply characteristic of the new genre. It is a piece of reporting like a geological cross-section of the various strata that make up a village, a veritable microcosm of the passions.

The three writers just mentioned come directly to prose fiction without passing along the road of poetry—at least so far as is known. Hence the vigor with which they confront their themes and model their characters. One might say that they are much more sculptors than painters. There are others of whom the same thing is true, that is, they entered into literature by the broad highway of prose, ignoring or scorning the impassable or tortuous ways of poetry, above all those of modern poetry, which is mathematical, abstract, and esoteric. They are not equal, however, to those mentioned in the vigor of their creations.

Among the new writers who came to prose fiction by way of poetry an outstanding case is Manuel da Fonseca, an admirable novelist who in his one novel *Cerromaior*—a documentary of life in a small provincial town—brings out both his poetic imagination and his qualities as novelist, for each scene of his reportage is a complete short story. They are linked together by the heavy atmosphere of a sleepy town. Another poet, Fernando Namora, in his one novel *Fogo na noite escura*, chose as scene of his reportage a provincial city, the university city of Coimbra, whose intellectual tone does not remove its provincial character. In a series of scenes

On Portuguese Neo-Realism

he makes this work a documentary, albeit a bit fanciful—that is, poetic—of student life.

A poet but also a prosewriter of talent is Carlos de Oliveira, the author of *Casa na duna* and of *Alcateia*, works in which, after choosing the sand dunes as a setting, he does not successfully portray the tormented lives of those who live there. He is much closer to certain other writers already mentioned in his use of the older formulas of the novel, above all the romantic ones, which brings a great disequilibrium to his works, which are neither novels nor artistic reportage. He is the youngest of all, we believe—little more than twenty years old—and all his vacillations and uncertainties are explicable. Since he is an admirably talented prosewriter, with more experience and more discipline he will certainly be equal to the best.

Of the young writers who did not come by way of poetry—so far as is known—we wish also to mention Vergilio Ferreira, whose first novel, *O camino fica longe*, was not published. We know that it is in part an evocation of academic life in Coimbra. His second work of fiction, *Onde tudo foi morrendo*, is reportage of the life of a family in a little settlement, though not a typical rural village. Another of these writers is Manuel do Nascimento, who in his first work, *Eu queria viver*, analyzes a sentimental and social drama in which tuberculosis plays a certain role in the action. His second work *Mineiros*, written before the other, has a sharper quality of reportage, too sharp indeed, for it is limited to the account of a writer of memoirs in the form of a diary. We await the publication of this writer's *Onde o aço perdeu a têmpera*.

We shall mention the short story writers José Loureiro Botas and António Vitorino, who, while apparently not associating themselves with the tendency we have been discussing, have many points of contact with it. They are both from the same region and for their works have chosen scenes collected there. The former in *Litoral a oeste* and *Frente ao mar* gives us scenes and episodes from the maritime verge of Estremadura; the latter in *Gente de Vieira* and *A vida começou assim* sets forth aspects of maritime labor in the same region and in addition portrays the work of sawyers, recording experiences of his youth. These works would be more properly called reportage than tales. They are true artistic reportage, precious documents with style.

Proletarian life in the great centers has not yet had its reporter. Only Ramos da Cunha in a volume of short stories *Lá fora o sol brinca* gives us some aspects of this life, which he treats, however, in the naturalistic manner. We are informed that Assis Esperança, a vigorous novelist, though of small output, has in hand a novel which will analyze various aspects of women's work. The action of this novel *E a noite não acaba* takes place among the suffering laboring population of a great city.

The drama of adolescence, about which there recently appeared an excellent documentary, *Ilha doida* by Joaquim Ferrer, is also the subject of a novel *Jardim fechado* being written by the critic Roberto Nobre; with it he will make his debut into fiction. We also know that this writer has in preparation a reportage, *Caminho do Levante*, in which he will show the life of contraband runners. This work, at any rate, is in line with the new tendency.

This tendency, clear-cut, without circumlocution, has so far had its most representative product in the book *Fogo no mar* of João Falcato, who in pages of great intensity gives us a picture of a fire on board a cargo ship in open ocean with forceful scenes and characters of rare vigor. It is a simple piece of reporting of an event, as it might have been written by a very talented reporter who was on board. Even if we were to be given the name of the burned ship and official data about the men on board, it would remain one of the most beautiful and most human works of fiction written in Portugal in recent years. Which means that there is nothing like experience, one's own experience, to give a feeling of life to artistic creation.

There is one type of subject that few have treated in literature, and this is strange. It is the colonials, the life of the so-called primitive peoples of Africa. Only Julião Quintinha gives us on this subject some pieces of reporting and some short stories of value, and he has in preparation a novel in which the Negro is the hero. Fausto Duarte in *Aúa* and *Revolta* also has evoked the African background.

In this rapid account of the young Portuguese literature, we have limited ourselves to prose fiction, although the so-called "neo-realists" come in part from the group of young poets of "Novo

On Portuguese Neo-Realism

Cancioneiro," a group of Coimbran origin, for Coimbra has been the cradle of the many artistic movements and efforts at aesthetic renewal which have occurred in Portugal since the campaign of "Bom Senso e Bom Gosto." We do not cite, however, any women. If we were concerned with the creation of poetry, it would not be difficult to give some women's names. But so far as we know in prose fiction there is no woman writer to single out for her inclination toward reportage with style.

In Portugal, by chance, the designation of "neo-realism" was given to artistic new-humanism—an old philosophy which we are not interested in discussing here. Its practitioners and theorists are the first to recognize that the name does not correspond to the idea which it seeks to represent. We shall not belabor them on this point. After all the name does not matter, but rather the movement in itself. Now this movement is certainly not "neo-realistic," but it is new and and of flagrant reality. It seeks to reduce everything to human terms and to analyze collective phenomena rather than individual cases. It hopes to alleviate the burden of labor and to prepare the man of tomorrow for the progress of the future. All who love life, human liberty, the exaltation of human dignity, cannot help viewing this movement with unconcealed sympathy. It has not yet produced fully matured fruits. Perhaps it will only succeed in doing so with the new humanity, forged in the pain and horror of the last war. More than the men of today still burdened with the many defects of their time and class, they look forward to the future and wish to give expression to it, those writers to whom in admiration we have tried to point.

That it has been possible in the midst of the limitations and convulsions of these times to establish the basis of a movement reaching out to the future, although it is formed by acquisitions of the past, is truly worthy of note and gives dignity to the young Portuguese literature. This literature, however, confines itself to prose fiction, a genre which while it finds a large public among those who read does not reach the lowest levels of the populace. They are the foundation of culture, however elementary, and those who seek to minister to them will be well advised. The young writers certainly understand this and, once they have satisfied their anxieties in the artistic realm, they must direct their energies to raising the masses to that level of culture without which all aspirations for future amelioration will be frustrated. Those who feel themselves better fitted for the obscure labor of diffusing knowledge will have to give up literary fame for this worthy mission. The zeal that they put into their struggle today will not be limited to the destruction of evils of the past but will go also to the building of the future society.

On Socialist Realism*

By Friedrich Engels

THIS letter by Friedrich Engels (1820-1895) is the acknowledged fountainhead of Marxist literary theory, as will be seen from other selections on the same subject. The original of this letter is preserved in the Marx-Engels-Lenin Institute at Moscow.

The comments of Marx and Engels on literature incline more to a materialist interpretation of history as explanation of literary products than to consideration of literary forms as such. Engels does, however, support the general realistic tenet of objectivity, suggesting that tendentiousness is not the first aim of the socialist writer, since "the bias should flow by itself from the situation and action" without author intrusion. He believes that "a socialist-biased novel fully achieves its purpose . . . if by consciously describing the real mutual relations, breaking down conventional illusions about them, it shatters the optimism of the bourgeois world, instills doubt as to the eternal character of the existing order, although the author does not offer any definite solution or does not even line up openly on any particular side." (Letter to Minna Kautsky, November 26, 1885)

◇◇◇

THANK you very much for sending me your *City Girl* through Mr. Vizetelly. . . .

What strikes me most in your tale, besides its realistic truth, is that it exhibits the courage of the true artist. Not only in the way you treat the Salvation Army, in your sharp repudiation of the conception of the self-satisfied philistines, who will learn from your story, perhaps for the first time, why the Salvation Army finds such support among the masses of the people, but above all in the unembroidered form in which you have clothed the fundamental basis of the whole book—the old, old story of the proletarian girl seduced by a man from the middle class. A mediocre writer would have attempted to disguise the trite character of the plot under a heap of artificial details and embellishment, and his design would

---

*Engels, Friedrich, Letter to Margaret Harkness, April 1888, in *Literature and Art by Karl Marx and Friedrich Engels: Selections from their Writings*, pp. 41-43; New York, International Publishers, 1947. Reprinted by permission of the publisher; the translator is not indicated.

have been seen through, nonetheless. But you felt that you could tell an old story because you were in a position to make it new by the truthfulness of your presentation.

Your Mr. Grant is a masterpiece.

If I have any criticism to make, it is only that your story is not quite realistic enough. Realism, to my mind, implies, besides truth of detail, the truthful reproduction of typical characters under typical circumstances. Now your characters are typical enough, to the extent that you portray them. But the same cannot be said of the circumstances surrounding them and out of which their action arises. In *City Girl* the working class appears as a passive mass, incapable of helping itself or even trying to help itself. All attempts to raise it out of its wretched poverty come from the outside, from above. This may have been a valid description around 1800 or 1810 in the days of Saint Simon and Robert Owen, but it cannot be regarded as such in 1887 by a man who for almost fifty years has had the honor to participate in most of the struggles of the fighting proletariat and has been guided all the time by the principle that emancipation of the working class ought to be the cause of the working class itself. The revolutionary response of the members of the working class to the oppression that surrounds them, their convulsive attempts—semiconscious or conscious—to attain their rights as human beings, belong to history and may therefore lay claim to a place in the domain of realism.

I am far from finding fault with your not having written a purely socialist novel, a *Tendenzroman*, as we Germans call it, to glorify the social and political views of the author. That is not at all what I mean. The more the author's views are concealed the better for the work of art. The realism I allude to may creep out even in spite of the author's views. Let me refer to an example.

Balzac, whom I consider a far greater master of realism than all the Zolas, past, present, or future, gives us in his *Comédie Humaine* a most wonderfully realistic history of French "society," describing, chronicle fashion, almost year by year from 1816 to 1848, the ever-increasing pressure of the rising bourgeoisie upon the society of nobles that established itself after 1815 and that set up again, as far as it could (*tant bien que mal*) the standard of the *vieille politesse française*. He describes how the last remnants of this, to him, model society gradually succumbed before the intrusion of the vulgar moneyed upstart or was corrupted by him. How the *grande dame*, whose conjugal infidelities were but a mode of asserting herself, in perfect accord with the way she had been disposed of in marriage, gave way to the bourgeoise, who acquired her husband for cash or cashmere. And around this central picture he groups a complete history of French society from which, even in economic details (for instance, the redistribution of real and private property after the French Revolution) I have learned more than from all the professional historians, economists and statisticians of the period together.

Well, Balzac was politically a legitimist; his great work is a constant elegy on the irreparable decay of good society; his sympathies are with the class that is doomed to extinction. But for all that, his satire is never keener, his irony never more bitter, than when he sets in motion the very men and women with whom he sympathizes most deeply—the nobles. And the only men of whom he speaks with undisguised admiration are his bitterest political antagonists, the republican heroes of the Cloître Saint Méry, the men who at that time (1830-1836) were indeed representatives of the popular masses.

That Balzac was thus compelled to go against his own class sympathies and political prejudices, that he *saw* the necessity of the downfall of his favorite nobles and described them as people deserving no better fate; that he *saw* the real men of the future where, for the time being, they alone were to be found—that I consider one of the greatest triumphs of realism, and one of the greatest features in old Balzac.

I must own, in your defense, that nowhere in the civilized world are the working people less actively resistant, more passively submitting to fate, more depressed than in the East End of London. And how do I know whether you have not had your reasons for contenting yourself, for once, with a picture of the passive side of working class life, leaving the active side for another work?

Comments on Socialist Realism

By Maxim Gorky and Others

MAXIM GORKY (1868-1936) was the most influential literary figure of Soviet Russia in the period between the Revolution and the Second World War and was its chief link with the Tsarist regime. His first statement is contained in a letter to Chekhov written in January 1900; the other statements were made during the 1930's. They serve to underline the movement from strict realist objectivity to a conception of the writer as concerned with purposive social activity.

The last two statements are made by party officials, not men of letters, and constitute the rigid party line against which Abram Tertz inveighs in his *On Socialist Realism*, since he considers it stultifying to the mind and to the potential development of Russian literature in this century. The official position has had considerable influence outside of Russia since the 1930's, when the vogue of proletarian literature arose in western Europe and the United States. Ralph Fox, an important English spokesman for this tendency, put the attitude very well when he asserted that among modern realists "the lack of dialectic, of a philosophy which enables them really to understand and to perceive the world has led them along the false trail," finding that in our day the supreme humiliation of the artist lies in not knowing what to think about life.* Marxism, it is clear, remedies the latter deficiency but at a cost of aesthetic uniformity and philosophical rigidity which Tertz, for one, feels no longer tolerable.

◇◇

INDEED a time has come when we need the heroic: everyone wants the stimulating, the colorful—something, you know, that would not resemble life, but would be higher than life, better, more beautiful. It is absolutely necessary that today's literature begin to embellish life somewhat, and as soon as it does so, life will be embellished, i.e., people will begin to live more swiftly, more brightly. . . .†

Personally, it seems to me that realism would best cope with

---

* Fox, Ralph, *The Novel and the People*, p. 106; London, Laurence and Wishart, 1937.

† Gorky, Maxim, from a letter to Chekhov, January 1900, in *Chekhov i Gorki, sbornik materialov*, pp. 61-62; Moscow, 1954. This and the following six selections from the Russian are translated by Linda Gordon.

On Socialist Realism

its task if, in analyzing an individual in the process of finding his true place on the road from petty bourgeois, animal individualism to socialism, it would describe man not as he is today, but also as he must be—and will be—tomorrow.*

Revolutionary romanticism—this essentially is a pseudonym for socialist realism, the purpose of which is not only to depict the past critically, but chiefly to promote the consolidation of revolutionary achievement in the present and a clearer view of the lofty objectives of the socialist future.†

I think that a mixture of realism and romanticism is necessary. Not a realist, not a romantic, but a realist and a romantic—they are like two facets of a single being. . . .‡

And it seems to me that the union of these two principles characterizes Gorky himself best of all—from his romanticism come his dreams of a great future, from his realism comes his building of that future.§

Comrade Stalin has called our writers the engineers of human souls. What does this mean?. . .

It means, in the first place, to know life, in order to depict it truthfully in works of art, to depict it not scholastically, not lifelessly, not simply as "objective reality," but to depict actuality in its revolutionary development.

Moreover, the truthfulness and historical concreteness of artistic description must be combined with the task of the ideological transformation and education of the working people in the spirit of socialism. This method of literature and of literary criticism is what we called the method of socialist realism.**

---

* Gorky, Maxim, *Gorki o literature*, p. 492; Moscow, 1957.
† *Ibid.*, p. 656.
‡ A statement made by Gorky in the editorial office of *Krasnaya Nov* in 1928 and quoted by Konstantin Fedin in *Gorki sredi nas*, Moscow, 1943-44.
§ Fedin, Konstantin, in comment on the preceding statement; quoted in Brainin, B., *Konstantin Fedin*, p. 184; Moscow, 1951.
** A. A. Zhdanov at the First All-Soviet Congress of Writers, August 17, 1934.

Our artists, writers, and others active in the field of art . . . must constantly remember that the typical is not only that which is most frequently met, but also that which expresses most fully and precisely the nature of existing social forces. In the Marxist-Leninist understanding the typical by no means denotes any kind of statistical mean. Typicalness corresponds to the substance of the actual social-historical phenomenon, and is not simply the most widespread, the frequently repeated, the usual. Conscious exaggeration or stressed images do not exclude the typical, but reveal and emphasize it more fully. The typical is the principal arena for the manifestation of the party spirit in realistic art. The problem of the typical is always a political problem.*

* G. Malenkov at the Nineteenth Party Congress, October 5, 1952.

"A Defense of Realism"*

By Héctor P. Agosti

THIS intricate and often exasperating article attempts to describe a realism which will be a fusion of traditional realism and the formalism which followed it, given shape and direction by a kind of Marxist dialectic. Agosti qualifies the older way of writing as "a flat and soulless realism" which fails to get beneath the surface of phenomena. In another essay, "Las Problemas de la Novela," he suggests that in addition to being negative, anti-romantic, and anti-lyrical, it "was a realism without perspective, limited to seeing *what is,* but incapable of seeing *what is to be,* that is, incapable of understanding and reflecting in creation the grand lines of social development."

The most useful part of this article is the perspective it gives to the anti-objectivist reaction as inevitable but ultimately insufficient. He clearly will not stop with the insistence of the surrealists, for example, that it is enough for imagination to reassume its rights and that in literature the marvelous alone is capable of producing fecund works of art. André Breton in the first surrealist manifesto (1924) asserted that the realist attitude, "inspired by positivism from St. Thomas to Anatole France," had been hostile to any moral or intellectual soaring. Agosti's position would seem to be that an adequate dialectic will make possible a specific soaring which is necessary for the renovation of man and society.

◇◇

I. THE TORMENTS OF THE ARTISTIC CONSCIOUSNESS

WHENEVER the subject of realism is mentioned, the words of André Lothe come to mind. The great painter said in his famous *Discurso de Venecia*: "If the modern artist, he who seeks to be 'of his time' and who, in fact, has found means of expression worthy of this era, would consent to give up trite and unpleasing subjects such as the studio model, the guitar, and the dish of fruit, in favor of those demanded by contemporary life, wrung as it is by disquietude and marvelous aspirations, he would be able to arouse

* Agosti, Héctor P., "Defensa del realismo" (a lecture before the faculty of architecture, December 1, 1944), *Defensa del realismo,* pp. 9-25; Montevideo, Editorial Pueblos Unidos, 1945. The text here presented is a revision prepared by the author for the third edition of this work published by Editorial Lautaro of Buenos Aires and is translated with his permission.

very great curiosity and emotion. Then we would be at the dawn of a new Renaissance."

Who could deny that we are at the first confused light of the dawning of a new Renaissance? Disturbed by events which have distinctly shown the emptiness of certain ways of life which have been assumed to be inalterable, it takes no great effort for us to discover that a new and integrated way of life must be formed among the rubble. And this integrated way of life will have to be distinguished —is already being distinguished—by an exaltation of man, of his disquietudes and his secret or glowing aspirations, not unlike the return of that human obscuration which abstract art proclaimed with challenging voice.

Where was the drama in that period before World War I, which now seems so remote to us, if not in that "dehumanization" which deprived art of its most generous resonances? A flat and soulless realism had by reaction provoked that optical revolution foreseen by Cézanne and Van Gogh, that redeeming search for forms pursued by the Cubists, that anxious desire for dynamic simultaneity in representation which tortured the Futurists, that turning inward to the forbidden zone of dream and irrationality which the Surrealists opened up and added to the domain of art. But if form was rescued, on the other hand art fell into the almost perverse vortex of dehumanization. All the painter's art seemed to be reduced to the skillful disposition of mass and color; all the poet's art seemed to be limited to the tortuous assembling of bits of automatic writing. Subject was proscribed and cursed, since the artists believed that the triumph of mind over matter would be accomplished by volatilizing, almost extinguishing, the feeling of the object, emptying it of all human substance and making it ever more esoteric. To the insipid objectivity of the academies was opposed an intransigent subjectivity which held reality in abomination and turned the artist into the supreme demiurge of objects, which had their birth in him before having a material existence outside of him, and were aureoled by him with a cold abstract vibration which aspired to emotional eternity. Thenceforth realism was a dirty word and was uttered with all the pejorative weight of the commonplace.

That anti-objectivist reaction was not separated, however, from the course of general ideas. The scientific splendor of the nineteenth

"A Defense of Realism"

century was followed by the spiritualist metaphysic of "anxious consciousness" as instrument of knowing, with intuition taking the place of experiment. And when some desperate philosopher asserted the necessity of a new Middle Ages as a consequence of the social chaos, was there anything surprising in this dematerialization of art, this dehumanization of the object, so similar to that of a Middle Ages at pains to deny the sensory objectivity of man? The constant relation with general ideas makes it possible to follow the vicissitudes of the artistic consciousness. In that world corrupted by the banal fin-de-siècle prosperity of great industry, artists had to protest against a social structure that was alien and opposed to imagination. Plekhanov said with great certainty that "the tendency toward art for art's sake appears and develops where there exists an insoluble discordance between the people who are concerned with art and the social milieu which surrounds them." Blocked by the counterfeit and anti-poetic realism of the academies, the artists in their rebellion clamored for liberty carried to the extreme of an absolute break with the past—a formalist break fecund to this extent, that as a result of it painters will no longer be able to paint pictures as they did before the Cubists, or poets write as they did before the Surrealists. Perhaps we can explain the removal of all objective content in abstract art most accurately if we relate it to that gnosiology of the imperceptible that in essence is the basis of the spiritualist reaction of 1900. Gleizes and Metzinger, two disciples of Cubism, sum up the theory of knowledge of their school in a book published in 1906. "There exists nothing real outside of us," they write. "We cannot doubt the existence of those objects that act on our senses; but rational existence is possible only in respect to the images that the objects bring to our minds." From that it is to be deduced that those objects, which it is impossible to know in their true reality, acquire real existence only when the thinking subject, like a god of modern times, decides to blow upon them with his divine breath and give them form. That is the cloak of subjectivism which explains the insistence on form and on withdrawal from the real conflicts of the world, from the subjects "demanded by contemporary life," according to Lothe's expressive formulation.

II. REALISM AND VERISM

Such a gnosiology of the imperceptible is repugnant to the new realism. But the new realism also begins by repudiating that other way of knowing which the traditional realists arrogated to themselves, prisoners of a pedestrian objectivity and subject to a blind and irreducible determinism which kept them from reacting to objects in a valid way.

Unlike a realism in the modern sense of the word, it was rather a verism caught in the surface of phenomena. Its adherents sought the truthful representation of the phenomenon, without recognizing that the phenomenon is scarcely more than the external, sudden, and fluid revelation of a more profound and stable reality. They took their position before reality as if it had to give itself passively and simply in a spontaneous and automatic reflection. They were caught in a mechanical determinism from which they could not escape: man was subject to nature, quietly caught in a spell by external objects which imposed upon him their ineluctable law. When the Médan disciples rose up against Zola, for example, they were no doubt attacking the master, but they were certainly also protesting against the suffocation which stultified their creative force. That is what Huysmans thought when he asserted that naturalism found itself "in a blind alley, or better, a tunnel to which the exit was blocked," with no recourse but to narrate over and over "the love affair of a nondescript wine merchant with the first nondescript shopgirl he encountered." The difficulty is fundamental in criticism of the old realism, which was limited in its subject matter and made banal by its formal inquiries. Tied to a philosophical scientism with a purely biological basis, that realism frequently fell into coarseness, although on occasion it was saved by a painter of the stature of Courbet or a novelist of the magnitude of Flaubert.

Courbet also shouted to the skies the realist theory of knowledge which is so opposed to that affirmed by Gleizes and Metzinger: "Yes, it is necessary to make art coarse! . . . Why should I try to see in the world what isn't there and through efforts of the imagination disfigure what is to be found there?" Flaubert in turn wrote: "You must treat men as if they were mastodons or croco-

"A Defense of Realism"

diles. Isn't it possible to become enthusiastic over the horns of the former and the mandibles of the latter? Show them to us; dissect them for us; put them in solution: that is all there is to it. But don't pronounce moral judgments over them, for who are you to do that, you shapeless little toads?" And the shapeless little toad, a part of nature, gives himself up to the "healthy mania of the document" with objective ardor. But the document only gives him the face of the phenomenon—I should say the painted face of the phenomenon—while the subtle and diabolically dialectical tissue of essential reality is hidden behind the simple data of the senses. The neutral objectivism of Zola consists of this. Although at times it is exalted to the almost romantic utopia of the *Gospels*, its strict feet-on-the-ground-of-the-object doctrine limits its vision. And this feet-on-the-ground position is more notorious still in the realists following Courbet, for their ambition is nothing more than subservience to nature, which they have set up as the supreme patron of beauty.

III. THE BASIS OF THE NEW REALISM

From this flow of affirmations and negations the new realism emerges. Its philosophical basis is nothing other than dialectical knowledge of external reality, in the emotive content of whose contemplation Hegel had seen an "alienation" of semi-religious character. Inverting this Hegelian scheme on a material base, this brand-new realism comes to grips with a nature which appears to it as a totality of reciprocal actions. No longer, as in traditional realism, is the subject placed in the position of a receptacle submissive to influences.* Artistic creation, in so far as it is a particular form of knowing, now appears as judge of the interplay between the action of reality and the reaction of consciousness. Set in the midst of his world, the artist, contrary to the situation of the scientist, undertakes to reproduce the essence of reality in particular

* As Lefebvre points out: "Even when he humbly believed that he was imitating or reproducing nature, the true artist did not submit to a slice of nature, to a piece of life stretched out before him like a slab of bloody, dead meat. Every true artist has been mistaken about himself when he believed that he was simply describing, observing, and confining himself to the near at hand. He was expressing nature through a man (of such and such an epoch and class) and man through nature." (Henri Lefebvre, *Contribution à l'esthétique*, Editions Sociales, Paris, 1953; p. 132.)

form. He does not set himself up as the demiurge of objects, but aspires to know the objects which have being outside of him with majestic—albeit controlled—autonomous life. But if knowledge is a reflection of reality, it would be stupid on the part of the artist to believe in the possibility of a simple, immediate, and pure reflection on a strictly sensory basis, as if his were an action similar to the making of an impression on a photographic plate. His greatness lies in the certainty of transforming his condition as servant into one of master of objects. By its dialectic of mobility this realistic theory of knowledge saves us from impassive metaphysical fixity and at the same time liberates us from the eternal coercion of objects. For thought—having taken wing from action on the real to arrive at the most daring patterns of abstraction—is in the final analysis a dominion over the real, but also an anticipation of the real in the fleeting framework of the possible. Reality is thus elevated to mythological dimensions by these infinite possibilities which seethe in its contradictory heart.

And here we find ourselves at a point of total contradiction. The old fixed realism reflected the world as it appears in the surface of phenomena, and that world—as Franz Roh indicated with great sensitivity—was "asserted . . . and even magnified with a certain demonic pride." In the new realism, with its discursive and dialectical basis, the possible world aspires to abstract itself from among the premonitions of the real world. The real world is furnished to the artist as a confused mass of events, whose recondite meaning is frequently disfigured by extrinsic appearances which it is necessary to remove with utmost rigor. The new realism assumes that these events act on the artist, but that the artist, in his turn, translates the reaction of his consciousness on the external reality which stimulates it, almost always in harmony with the general ideas of his times, which are in turn the anticipatory, simultaneous, or belated expression of a system of social relations. Reality contains a multiplicity of coherent representations, and in the selection of each one of these, in the artist's efforts at expression or in the modifications a work of art undergoes from the first outline to the finished conception, that dramatic conflict between the world of objects and the sensitive subject which seeks to penetrate it, that tremendous combat of interchanges between the

494

reality of the world and the consciousness of the artist, that rending substitution for signs learned by signs which it is necessary to invent in order to capture essences, all that constitutes, so to speak, the psychological mechanism of the creative process which has ever been the painful nurture of the true artist. Such a process necessarily implies a psychology and sociology of the creative act, since the individual consciousness of the artist is submerged in a social complex, the consequences of which bear upon him though on occasion he may think that he escapes them.

The difference between the new realism and any other theory of art consists in the fact that it hopes to make conscious that consciousness at times unconscious with which the artist approaches objects. If consciousness works by reaction on the material which it tries to know, it would seem to be an unnecessary tautology to assert the desirability of the artist's being conscious of that consciousness. And this, far from impelling him to an art of frozen rational projections, on the contrary hurls him into the boiling whirlpool of living ideas. Has it not been said that the science of knowledge, abstracted from an ideal isolated man, must be integrated with multitudinous human experience? The influences of theoretical reason still impose themselves in practice in a schema emptied of vitality. If on this account a philosophical renascence will have to herald itself, preferably by breaking down the metaphysical barriers between rational abstractions and the lively and even picturesque content of experience, the new realism begins by assigning to art a primordial gnosiological role. Art will be able to seize "directly, in things themselves, conceptions which in the present state of society and of consciousness are apprehended apart from things, outside of them." Such a future role for knowledge replaces the immobility of the old naturalism, which was subject to nature. By the very fact that things are not given once and for all, this new realism finds its distinctive character in the incessant movement of penetration into unstable matter, in the tenacity with which it seeks to discover the possible world amid the apparent rigors of the real world.

The objectivity of the old realism was passive and silent; the objectivity of the new realism is variable and informative. Its method might be summed up in Engels's formula: typical characters in typical situations, with those situations harboring within them the possibility of a new reality ready to come into being. For that reason, in default of a better name, I propose, provisionally, that we call this realism *dynamic realism*.

IV. OBJECTIVITY AND SUBJECTIVITY

Passive to the point of nausea, that objectivity was bound to become torpid in its impotence, unable to reproduce or to reflect changing reality. And this nauseous content condemned it to the annihilation of form, which was restricted within narrow bounds where all daring of invention was completely frowned upon. Now when we consider the historical circumstances in which the revolution of abstract art took place, we can discern a satisfactory explanation. To the fundamental discord between society and the artist, the romantics had replied by exalting the individual hero sovereignly endowed with all the virtues which bourgeois civilization had undermined; the realists had replied by abandoning the superhuman hero and shriveling the soul from a point of view essentially anti-poetic; then the disciples of abstract art replied by escaping from the reality of the world of objects and forging their own subjective world of things. An arch-exemplar of this stubborn subjectivism which seeks to arrive at the real by way of magic is Schrimpf, the painter who fabricated his landscapes within the studio without ever making preliminary sketches from nature, raising himself to the level of architect of his own personal nature. In reaction to an existence cluttered with triviality the Cubists made the discovery of primordial arch-forms which suddenly enabled them to take themselves off beyond the concrete world of objects. They give notice, in fact, that the new emotional content of life can no longer be adequately conveyed by the old forms of expression; but instead of placing themselves fully in the world with a lucid consciousness able to divine its laws, they preferred to take flight and fall back first into the most extreme subjectivity and then into the irrational delirium of Surrealism. It is always a matter of polar opposites that cannot be reconciled: a straitened objectivism on the one hand, a haughty subjectivism on the other.

Dynamic realism aspires to place itself between extremes in order to fuse them in a brand-new aesthetic category which will take its inheritance from both and join them together. If the process of knowing is a judging of reciprocal actions and reactions between reality and consciousness, this dynamic realism has no idea of constructing objects *within itself*, but neither is it resigned to receiving them with the passive receptivity of a mirror. Its aesthetic ideal is the translation of reality through a temperament, since man in the last analysis has come once more to see himself as the measure and the end of things. But in spite of everything this man is not the absolute being that the followers of subjectivism imagined. Man is a real man, caught up in the conflicts of his time, modified in his innermost thoughts by his social relations, constrained to mold his individual consciousness in conjunction with or opposition to the prevailing order, although in the end he is a part of that reality which he will succeed in preserving or modifying in accordance with his impulses and his interest. That man of flesh and bone is he who sets forth for the artistic conquest of the material world, which is exterior and anterior to him. But if that man, converted into artist, is no longer the demiurge of objects that the abstract artists assert him to be, neither is he the register of objects as the naturalists claim. He ceases to be both in opposition in order to be both simultaneously. Having risen to a consciousness of his goals as artist and as man, he is now a "transformer" of energy, since his realism—in accordance with Aragon's very precise definition—has ceased to be dominated by nature and takes hold of the social realities which seek to modify nature itself.

The aesthetic ideal of dynamic realism consists, then, in the translation of reality through a temperament, although this temperament seems to be determined and conditioned by the circumstances which I have just indicated. Yes, that social consciousness —solidarity—of goals is fundamental in the doctrine of dynamic realism. But the artist breaks in also with his own psychological tonality, for artistic creation is, in fact, a very subtle process of reaching individual conclusions. The constant interpenetration of the individual and the collectivity is an attribute of this dynamic realism, for which we need to find another name. Since it is neither ignominiously objective nor extravagantly subjective, I would suggest, rather than dynamic, that we call it *super-subjective*. (And it seems to me, in passing, that this term acquires a certain conceptual value capable of clarifying the interminable debate about the hermeticism and transparency of language. If realism consists in the translation of reality through a temperament, those categories of expression also lose their dogmatic rigidity in their subordination to the development of individual psychologies. What is interesting is that the artist rises to consciousness of the object, and when he has reached that consciousness then he can allow himself freedom in the means of expression, which will be dense or translucent in accordance with his individual psychological quality, unless he falls into a hateful treason toward himself, premonitory of certain treason toward his fellows. . . .)

V. ARTISTIC CREATION

If all artistic creation amounts to transforming substantial or formal realities into material for representation, the manner of realistic representation can on no account be confined to the boring meanness of the copy.

Art is a way of knowing; but, different from knowledge through universal laws which is exclusive to the sciences, here we have knowledge of the singular, although that singularity does not necessarily indicate the excessive exaltation of the individual. Such knowledge of the singular has validity only when the husk of reality is stripped away. The copy—the "document" of the old inert naturalists—was scarcely able to provide us with the appearance of the real. On the other hand, dynamic realism disdains that external figuration which frequently pushes away true reality; or to speak more exactly, it only considers those appearances in their relation with the internal causes that produce them. Just as knowledge is not an exact and continuous reflection of being, dynamic realism presupposes simultaneously a subjection and a liberation of thought in respect to things. Being determines thought, but thought is not a blind suicidal operation which annihilates itself at the moment it comes into operation. When confronted with the things that stimulate it, thought rises, on the contrary, to a dignity which no determinism whatsoever could ever give it. Having its origin in things, thought takes power over things and imposes its magnificent dominion upon them.

"A Defense of Realism"

But artistic realism does not work with things that are constantly manipulatable, visible, or present. In contrast with the old naturalism, this realism introduces into its bloodstream a capacity to dream, that imaginary, whole vision of reality which seeks to dominate its rebellious and protean materials. And the capacity to dream really—to dream *in* things and *among* things—assumes in dynamic realism an invention of the concrete adequate to the reproduction of the concrete. The concrete can be reproduced; but the concrete can also be artistically invented as an anticipation of the possible among the tight meshes of the real. In a thoughtful essay, Max Raphael asserts that works of art may "contain more than what their time provides them concretely to the degree that they reproduce materially or formally collectivities which belong to the past or are imaginary." Under the heading of "imaginary collectivities," is there not included that prevision of the future which dynamic realism derives from the present by means of a forward projection of its dialectical consciousness? And is it not to be inferred from this that in the doctrine of the new realism art is not only a reproduction but also a revelation from which the lucid forms of knowledge often receive the impulse and the anticipation of certain seminal intuitions? This revelatory intuition—which is like a sudden ray of light in the harsh quarrel between form and matter—is joined with that abstraction of essential reality without the exercise of which reality would slip away from us or would become deformed by the endless multitude of phenomena. How could we know true reality if we were not capable of abstracting, by an act of reflective consciousness, its primordial and definitive essence?

On this level the method of artistic creation according to the criteria of dynamic and super-subjective realism begins to become clear. The artist finds his material in the world of objects, outside himself. The world of objects unfolds by means of social relationships which the artist undergoes as object, but which he also seeks to modify in his more elevated position as subject. This incessant movement between the action of things and the reaction of his consciousness provides him with a multitude of appearances through which he necessarily seeks to discover essential reality. Then he has recourse to abstraction, to the separation of the accessory by

499

a deliberate act of reflective will. But abstraction, although it sketches out the primordial reality, is not yet a work of art but only knowledge. Such knowledge of the real will become a work of realistic art when it is transformed into sensible substance, that is, when that reality is translated through the temperament of the artist. However much it may be influenced or modified by social milieu or ideological inclinations, that individual temperament is after all obliged to provide the personal psychological tone in the vast tumult of voices that fill the universe. Then in the process of judging reciprocal actions and reactions, knowledge is converted into a work of art: then the capacity to dream appears, which is somewhat like prevision of the future in the present, somewhat like the recapture of the present in the past.

I do not need to defend myself by stating that what I have just said is a purely logical schema. You are well aware that in real life aesthetic emotion may come before knowledge. The new realism, however, prefers that the artist be conscious of his means of expression rather than give himself up to the spontaneous fury of inspiration.* If I were not afraid of falling into Bergsonian error, I would say that "immediate data" of sensibility are not enough for the artist, according to the new realism. Such "data" will have to bring him into contact with the real world which is more closely linked to his personal temperament. Once this occurs—what we might call the choice of the angle of focus—the artist is in need of some clarifying principle so as to impose himself on objects rather than let himself be dominated by them. At the heart of the new realism—as I believe I have shown—there exists a coherent system of clarifying principles. For instead of immuring itself within the apparent real it goes forward with bold creativity to-

* I notice an almost identical position in Lefebvre (*Contribution à l'esthétique*, pp. 154-158). He takes a stand against the supposition—at times supported by Lukacs—that unconsciousness in art is favorable to aesthetic creation, and although he admits that some *transitions*, that is, where unconsciousness plays a part, are always possible, he does not fail to emphasize that the necessity of internal coherence in the work of art reduces such unconsciousness to an agent of sterility. "The basic error in aesthetics," he says, "would be to propagate the belief in the fecundity of the unconscious." Lefebvre does not believe (and rightly so) that retarded development of artistic consciousness is fatal, but he thinks that the function of criticism and aesthetics lies precisely in speeding up the removal of that retardation.

"A Defense of Realism"

ward the possible real; it has scarcely more in common with previous "realisms" than the tendency to consider the world of objects as universally valid and basic.

Opposed to abstract art because the latter implies dehumanization and evasion, realism, however, does turn toward abstraction in its primordial method in order to get hold of reality. This amounts to giving to consciousness a function which is very special and at times dramatic. Modern realism rejects the empty sterile desperation of self-centered consciousness. In its place it postulates a consciousness at the same time retrospective and anticipatory, in the sense that unfolding the past illuminates and broadens the realm of its origins. Rather than formulate a theory of consciousness in itself, realism brings speculation about the objective conditions of consciousness back to its fundamentals. Immersed in the world, open to nature and social conditions, consciousness is, in Hegel's felicitous allegory, like Minerva's owl which comes out at nightfall. Consciousness takes its triumphal flight in the ripeness of being. But consciousness, subordinate to the being of man, is not only a consciousness of being but even more a consciousness of doing, and almost always a consciousness of doing preceding and permitting consciousness of being. On that account consciousness is at once retrospective and forward-looking. When it has freed itself from the idealistic illusion that it is creative in itself, consciousness becomes really creative. It is not a cosmic and depersonalized consciousness, but one that is intimately personal and human, immersed in things, which throws light on the individual and social interplay of thought and act.

VI. RECIPROCAL ACTION

The human and personal nature of consciousness necessitates allusion also to its psychological basis, an indispensable element in the artist, as I have said.

Modern realism—need I repeat it—in no way means the abrogation of the person, as is customarily asserted without further thought. Perhaps those who have done it most harm in its normal spread are the vulgar adherents who deform it and make it ridiculous on the pretext of defending a merely social result. These would-be defenders adopt a method of investigation and representation in contradiction to the doctrine they preach. They strive to forge a reality which *a priori* will serve their "will to prove" and thus fall into that idealistic position which discovers in history only a confirmation of preconceived ideas. The critics label as "external method" (or exaltation of the individual) the approach which sees in external reality a simple reflection of thoughts, and customarily contrast to it what they call the "internal method" (or omission of the individual) in which the subject, nullifying himself by an act of will so as to get into the reality which confronts him, forgets the living existence of truth in order to seek it solely in the history of thought. Weak and fallacious by reason of their unilateral approach, the two methods are joined by the new realism into a synthesis or internal-external graft which neither leaves out the thinking subject nor exalts him above all other relationships. Hence the reciprocal action between reality and consciousness serves to penetrate that reality by means of a criticism directed inward, while adapting that consciousness by a criticism directed outward. The conjunction of the two extremes, which seems to contradict traditional logic, is the only method by which to translate the phenomenon of the world in its infinite mobility, unceasingly rhythmic and plastic.

Yet the artist is not only a reflective consciousness, but also an emotive consciousness, obliged to respond as an individual in spite of the burdens that may weigh on him as a member of a group. Personal response does not indicate a fugitive or neutral art. Through its repudiation of objectivity as a system, the new realism consciously incorporates a will for the purposive. If this direction is consonant with the general ends of the work of art, in no way does it demand uniformity of means of expression, a fearfully depersonalizing idea by which the most noble intentions of the old naturalism were nullified. In the permanent play of reciprocal actions such a psychological tonality is fundamental in the choice of language. Although a common aesthetic nurtures them, a stable temperament and an impulsive temperament do not react in the same way to the same external stimulus. And while at first sight this seems to be a simple platitude, if you reflect on it for a moment, you will perceive its importance in the redemption of realism, which has been injured by so many extravagant defenders and so many uncomprehending adversaries.

VII. THE RECONQUEST OF MAN

By realism, in the last analysis, man comes once more to be seen as the center of the world, and it is in this anthropomorphic sense that we may speak of a new renascence, of a new submission to earthly essences.

Dehumanization meant nothing less than a fertile revolt against the triviality of the old anti-poetic realism. But in virtue of that reaction the recapture of aesthetic values of form was flawed by the abandonment of ethical values of content. The depreciation of subject matter, especially in painting, resulted from a considerable confusion between anecdote, which is the transitory exterior of subject, and subject itself, which is the opening through which to reach the ultimate essence of reality. The revolution of abstract art* was thus, for a long time, an heroic asceticism of form, an endless torture in order to remove from form all carnal substance, in order to make it vibrate by the pure and absolute necessity of abstraction. But art could not persist in this stubborn divorce from the real world without running the risk of abdicating its own transforming role. The relation between the artist and the spectator—that functional element of the work of art which covers such a lofty hierarchy for dynamic realism—was it possible to achieve it, let us say, by the extremes of the Cubist evasion?

Brought to meditate on these matters as theoretician and as painter, André Lothe proclaimed a return to man "violently demanding a smoker at the end of the everlasting Cubist pipe or someone with inspired arms around the obsessive soundless gui-

* Although the idea is self-evident in the text, I should like to make clear here, in order to avoid ambiguity, that I use the word *abstract* in opposition to *real*, while admitting the heavy dosage of the figurative with which the "pure abstractionists" reproach Cubism. I am aware that to some theoreticians Cubism is *the most real* representation of reality; for example, Daniel-Henry Kahnweiler (*Les Années héroiques du cubisme*, Braun et Cie., Paris, 1954; p. 6) says: "The realism of the synthetic phase of Cubism is, certainly, that of the medieval philosophers. The *essence*, not the *appearance*, of objects is what those painters seek to capture." I prefer to hold to the definition by Gleizes and Metzinger which has already been set down (*Du cubisme*, Figuière, Paris, 1906) and to use the word *abstraction* to evoke all those currents of art not concerned with a direct reflection of reality.

tar." Very well, this return to men is what I would say realism
should have received as its historical mandate, if the formula had
not been so discredited. But this realism is certainly not a polar
opposite of abstract art, since it gathers up all the results of its
technical experiments and enriches them with the proud pomp of
a brand-new humanized content. Are we to say then that the
tumult of the abstract schools has been in vain? Much of what
we have said thus far serves to make it clear that this new realism
would be incomprehensible if it were deprived of that richness of
analysis which the subjectivists brought to modern art. That richness took the subjectivists out of the world; but on the contrary
it is of use to the realists in putting themselves into the world, in
penetrating it more deeply, in rising to a consciousness of the world
and in making of their art of representation also an instrument for
the transformation of the world.

For none of man's experiences is ever lost. The "cultural heritage" is a mound which could never be laid waste unless beforehand
the historical consciousness of man as a passionate and contempla-
tive being were extinguished. Perhaps in the last analysis the
iconoclastic break means nothing but a failure of light on that zig-
zagging line of interpenetrations which marks the course of social
evolution. When Stravinsky, in a frenzied gesture, denied all value
to the German classicists, Busoni hit the mark in his reply that
he would consider them better if he could hear them with new ears.
Those "new ears," those "new eyes," are the possibility of rescuing from the past the elements that continue to have value for
our tortured present; they are that function of the retrospective
consciousness capable of disentangling the present emotion from
what at first sight seems dead forever. Referring to the tendency
of contemporary music toward equilibrium, through what was in
its day the extremist revolution of atonality, this same Busoni has
been able to speak of a "modern classicism." "I call *new classicism*," he wrote in 1921, "to its domain, the selection, the purifica-
tion, and the exploitation of all the conquests achieved by previous
experiments, and their embodiment in solid and beautiful forms.
. . . That art will be, at once, new and old. Toward it we make our
way—with luck—consciously or unconsciously, willingly or perforce." I do not go along with the whole of Busoni's analysis; but

it is necessary to agree that the feeling of "inheritance" and of the union of what is simultaneously new and old, at certain points coincides with the basis of a realistic theory of art which is dynamic and super-subjective, a theory which this afternoon I have tried to make clear in its basic elements.

Let us return to the words with which we began. "If the modern artist, he who seeks to be of 'his time' and who, in fact, has found means of expression worthy of this era, would consent to give up trite subjects . . . in favor of those demanded by contemporary life, wrung as it is by disquietude and marvelous aspirations, he would be able to arouse very great curiosity and emotion. Then we would be at the dawn of a new Renaissance."

In order to affirm that renascence of the whole man in our twentieth century—as actor in the most vast and resounding transformations of history—the new realism demands a robust participation in the marvelous aspirations and disquietudes of the present world. It does not impose a formula on the artist; it offers him a philosophical framework. It knows that not *all* of reality can be expressed; but it is satisfied if the artist translate that which is nearest his heart, that which he feels most intimately as a man; provided that this be in accord with the deep pulse of other men who, like him, undergo their own sufferings, creativity, and dreams. Is this indeed a proclamation of another redemptive humanism? Perhaps it may be. And perhaps also the reply may already be heard with the bright splendor of dawn through the obdurate darkness of daily events.

"Emile Zola"*

By Henry James

THIS ESSAY is the next to the last of the substantial articles by James on his nineteenth-century predecessors; appearing in the *Atlantic Monthly* for August 1903 (only a few months after Zola's death), it was followed in 1905 by an article on Balzac. He uses what he calls the *case* of Zola both for observations on the latter's art and for a discussion of the novel in general. Considering the difference of his own practice, his remarks are remarkably generous.

On the whole James accepts Zola's choice of the coarser side of human experience, based on the community of all the instincts, which, he points out as novelist, is also the more practicable side. Indeed he doubts that there has ever been "a more totally represented world." In the depiction numbers, crowds, breadth, and energy take the place of penetration and give a picture of bourgeois society grossly materialized. The result is shallow and simple with psychology subordinated to the material manifestation. It is at this point that James protests that "Science accepts surely *all* our consciousness of life." Nonetheless he considers Zola's works "one of the few most constructive achievements of our time," thus making a notable advance beyond the supercilious and grudging response which he had made to *Nana*.

◇◇◇

IF IT BE TRUE that the critical spirit today, in presence of the rising tide of prose fiction, a watery waste out of which old standards and landmarks are seen barely to emerge, like chimneys and the tops of trees in a country under flood—if it be true that the anxious observer, with the water up to his chin, finds himself asking for the *reason* of the strange phenomenon, for its warrant and title, so we likewise make out that these credentials rather fail to float on the surface. We live in a world of wanton and importunate fable, we breathe its air and consume its fruits; yet who shall say that we are able, when invited, to account for our preferring it so largely to the world of fact? To do so would be to make some adequate statement of the good the product in question does

* James, Henry, "Emile Zola" (*Atlantic Monthly*, August 1903) is reprinted with the permission of Charles Scribner's Sons from *Notes on Novelists with Some Other Notes* by Henry James and also by permission of John Farquharson Ltd.

"Emile Zola"

us. What does it do for our life, our mind, our manners, our morals —what does it do that history, poetry, philosophy may not do, as well or better, to warn, to comfort and command the countless thousands for whom and by whom it comes into being? We seem too often left with our riddle on our hands. The lame conclusion on which we retreat is that "stories" are multiplied, circulated, paid for, on the scale of the present hour, simply because people "like" them. As to why people *should* like anything so loose and mean as the preponderant mass of the "output," so little indebted for the magic of its action to any mystery in the making, is more than the actual state of our perceptions enables us to say.

This bewilderment might be our last word if it were not for the occasional occurrence of accidents especially appointed to straighten out a little our tangle. We are reminded that if the unnatural prosperity of the wanton fable cannot be adequately explained, it can at least be illustrated with a sharpness that is practically an argument. An abstract solution failing we encounter it in the concrete. We catch in short a new impression or, to speak more truly, recover an old one. It was always there to be had, but we ourselves throw off an oblivion, an indifference for which there are plenty of excuses. We become conscious, for our profit, of a *case*, and we see that our mystification came from the way cases had appeared for so long to fail us. None of the shapeless forms about us for the time had attained to the dignity of one. The one I am now conceiving as suddenly effective—for which I fear I must have been regarding it as somewhat in eclipse—is that of Emile Zola, whom, as a manifestation of the sort we are considering, three or four striking facts have lately combined to render more objective and, so to speak, more massive. His close connection with the most resounding of recent public quarrels; his premature and disastrous death; above all, at the moment I write, the appearance of his last-finished novel, bequeathed to his huge public from beyond the grave—these rapid events have thrust him forward and made him loom abruptly larger; much as if our pedestrian critic, treading the dusty highway, had turned a sharp corner.

It is not assuredly that Zola has ever been veiled or unapparent; he had, on the contrary been digging his field these thirty years, and for all passers to see, with an industry that kept him, after the fashion of one of the grand grim sowers or reapers of his brother of the brush, or at least of the canvas, Jean-François Millet, duskily outlined against the sky. He was there in the landscape of labor—he had always been; but he was there as a big natural or pictorial feature, a spreading tree, a battered tower, a lumpish round-shouldered useful hayrick, confounded with the air and the weather, the rain and the shine, the day and the dusk, merged more or less, as it were, in the play of the elements themselves. We had got used to him, and, thanks in a measure just to this stoutness of his presence, to the long regularity of his performance, had come to notice him hardly more than the dwellers in the marketplace notice the quarters struck by the town-clock. On top of all accordingly, for our skeptical mood, the sense of his work—a sense determined afresh by the strange climax of his personal history—rings out almost with violence as a reply to our wonder. It is as if an earthquake or some other rude interference had shaken from the town-clock a note of such unusual depth as to compel attention. We therefore once more give heed, and the result of this is that we feel ourselves after a little probably as much enlightened as we can hope ever to be. We have worked round to the so marked and impressive anomaly of the adoption of the futile art by one of the stoutest minds and stoutest characters of our time. This extraordinarily robust worker has found it good enough for him, and if the fact is, as I say, anomalous, we are doubtless helped to conclude that by its anomalies, in future, the bankrupt business, as we are so often moved to pronounce it, will most recover credit.

What is at all events striking for us, critically speaking, is that, in the midst of the dishonor it has gradually harvested by triumphant vulgarity of practice, its pliancy and applicability can still plead for themselves. The curious contradiction stands forth for our relief—the circumstance that thirty years ago a young man of extraordinary brain and indomitable purpose, wishing to give the measure of these endowments in a piece of work supremely solid, conceived and sat down to *Les Rougon-Macquart* rather than to an equal task in physics, mathematics, politics or economics. He saw his undertaking, thanks to his patience and courage, practically to a close; so that it is exactly neither of the so-called constructive sciences that happens to have had the benefit, intellectually speaking, of one of the few most constructive achievements of our time. There then, provisionally at least, we touch bottom; we get a glimpse of the pliancy and variety, the ideal of vividness, on behalf of which our equivocal form may appeal to a strong head. In the name of what ideal on its own side, however, does the strong head yield to the appeal? What is the logic of its so deeply committing itself? Zola's case seems to tell us, as it tells us other things. The logic is in its huge freedom of adjustment to the temperament of the worker, which it carries, so to say, as no other vehicle can do. It expresses fully and directly the whole man, and big as he may be it can still be big enough for him without becoming false to its type. We see this truth made strong, from beginning to end, in Zola's work; we see the temperament, we see the whole man, with his size and all his marks, stored and packed away in the huge hold of *Les Rougon-Macquart* as a cargo is packed away on a ship. His personality is the thing that finally pervades and prevails, just as so often on a vessel the presence of the cargo makes itself felt for the assaulted senses. What has most come home to me in reading him over is that a scheme of fiction so conducted is in fact a capacious vessel. It can carry anything—with art and force in the stowage; nothing in this case will sink it. And it is the only form for which such a claim can be made. All others have to confess to a smaller scope—to selection, to exclusion, to the danger of distortion, explosion, combustion. The novel has nothing to fear but sailing too light. It will take aboard all we bring in good faith to the dock.

An intense vision of this truth must have been Zola's comfort from the earliest time—the years, immediately following the crash of the Empire, during which he settled himself to the tremendous task he had mapped out. No finer act of courage and confidence, I think, is recorded in the history of letters. The critic in sympathy with him returns again and again to the great wonder of it, in which something so strange is mixed with something so august. Entertained and carried out almost from the threshold of manhood, the high project, the work of a lifetime, announces beforehand its inevitable weakness and yet speaks in the same voice for its admirable, its almost unimaginable strength. The strength was in the young man's very person—in his character, his will, his passion, his fighting temper, his aggressive lips, his squared shoulders (when he "sat up") and overweening confidence; his weakness was in that inexperience of life from which he proposed not to suffer, from which he in fact suffered on the surface remarkably little, and from which he was never to suspect, I judge, that he had suffered at all. I may mention for the interest of it that, meeting him during his first short visit to London—made several years before his stay in England during the Dreyfus trial—I received a direct impression of him that was more informing than any previous study. I had seen him a little, in Paris, years before that, when this impression was a perceptible promise, and I was now to perceive how time had made it good. It consisted, simply stated, in his fairly bristling with the betrayal that nothing whatever had happened to him in life but to write *Les Rougon-Macquart*. It was even for that matter almost more as if *Les Rougon-Macquart* had written *him*, written him as he stood and sat, as he looked and spoke, as the long, concentrated, merciless effort had made and stamped and left him. Something very fundamental was to happen to him in due course, it is true, shaking him to his base; fate was not wholly to cheat him of an independent evolution. Recalling him from this London hour one strongly felt during the famous "Affair" that his outbreak in connection with it was the act of a man with arrears of personal history to make up, the act of a spirit for which life, or for which at any rate freedom, had been too much postponed, treating itself at last to a luxury of experience.

I welcomed the general impression at all events—I intimately entertained it; it represented so many things, it suggested, just as it was, such a lesson. You could neither have everything nor be everything—you had to choose; you could not at once sit firm at your job and wander through space inviting initiations. The author of *Les Rougon-Macquart* had had all those, certainly, that this wonderful company could bring him; but I can scarce express how it was implied in him that his time had been fruitfully passed with *them* alone. His artistic evolution struck one thus as, in spite of its magnitude, singularly simple, and evidence of the simplicity seems further offered by his last production, of which we have just come into possession. *Vérité* truly does give the measure, makes the author's high maturity join hands with his youth, marks

"Emile Zola"

the rigid straightness of his course from point to point. He had seen his horizon and his fixed goal from the first, and no cross-scent, no new distance, no blue gap in the hills to right or to left ever tempted him to stray. *Vérité*, of which I shall have more to say, is in fact, as a moral finality and the crown of an edifice, one of the strangest possible performances. Machine-minted and made good by an immense expertness, it yet makes us ask how, for dis-interested observation and perception, the writer had used so much time and so much acquisition, and how he can all along have han-dled so much material without some larger subjective consequence. We really rub our eyes in other words to see so great an intellectual adventure as *Les Rougon-Macquart* come to its end in deep desert sand. Difficult truly to read, because showing him at last almost completely a prey to the danger that had for a long time more and more dogged his steps, the danger of the mechanical all confident and triumphant, the book is nevertheless full of interest for a reader desirous to penetrate. It speaks with more distinctness of the au-thor's temperament, tone and manner than if, like several of his volumes, it achieved or enjoyed a successful life of its own. Its heavy completeness, with all this, as of some prodigiously neat, strong and complicated scaffolding constructed by a firm of builders for the erection of a house whose foundations refuse to bear it and that it is unable therefore to rise—its very betrayal of a method and a habit more than adequate, on past occasions, to similar ends, carries us back to the original rare exhibition, the grand assurance and grand patience with which the system was launched.

If it topples over, the system, by its own weight in these last applications of it, that only makes the history of its prolonged success the more curious and, speaking for myself, the spectacle of its origin more attaching. Readers of my generation will remember well the publication of *La Conquête de Plassans* and the portent, indefinable but irresistible, after perusal of the volume, conveyed in the general rubric under which it was a first installment,* "Natural and Social History of a Family under the Second Em-pire." It squared itself there at its ease, the announcement, from the first, and we were to learn promptly enough what a fund of

* James's memory is at fault. *La Fortune des Rougon* is the first novel in the Rougon-Macquart series.

life it masked. It was like the mouth of a cave with a signboard hung above, or better still perhaps like the big booth at a fair with the name of the show across the flapping canvas. One strange animal after another stepped forth into the light, each in its way a monster bristling and spotted, each a curiosity of that "natural history" in the name of which we were addressed, though it was doubtless not till the issue of *L'Assommoir* that the true type of the monstrous seemed to be reached. The enterprise, for those who had attention, was even at a distance impressive, and the nearer the critic gets to it retrospectively the more so it becomes. The pyramid had been planned and the site staked out, but the young builder stood there, in his sturdy strength, with no equipment save his two hands and, as we may say, his wheelbarrow and his trowel. His pile of material—of stone, brick and rubble or whatever—was of the smallest, but this he apparently felt as the least of his difficulties. Poor, uninstructed, unacquainted, unintroduced, he set up his subject wholly from the outside, proposing to himself wonderfully to get into it, into its depths, as he went.

If we imagine him asking himself what he knew of the "social" life of the second Empire to start with, we imagine him also answering in all honesty: "I have my eyes and my ears—I have all my senses: I have what I've seen and heard, what I've smelled and tasted and touched. And then I've my curiosity and my pertinacity; I've libraries, books, newspapers, witnesses, the material, from step to step, of an *enquête*. And then I've my genius—that is, my imagination, my passion, my sensibility to life. Lastly I've my method, and that will be half the battle. Best of all perhaps even, I've plentiful lack of doubt." Of the absence in him of a doubt, indeed of his inability, once his direction taken, to entertain so much as the shadow of one, *Vérité* is a positive monument—which again represents in this way the unity of his tone and the meeting of his extremes. If we remember that his design was nothing if not architectural, that a "majestic whole," a great balanced façade, with all its orders and parts, that a singleness of mass and a unity of effect, in fine, were before him from the first, his notion of picking up his bricks as he proceeded becomes, in operation, heroic. It is not in the least as a record of failure for him that I note this particular fact of the growth of the long series as on the whole the liveliest interest it has to offer. "I don't know my subject, but I must live into it; I don't know life, but I must learn it as I work"—that attitude and program represent, to my sense, a drama more intense on the worker's own part than any of the dramas he was to invent and put before us.

It was the fortune, it was in a manner the doom, of *Les Rougon-Macquart* to deal with things almost always in gregarious form, to be a picture of *numbers*, of classes, crowds, confusions, movements, industries—and this for a reason of which it will be interesting to attempt some account. The individual life is, if not wholly absent, reflected in coarse and common, in generalized terms; whereby we arrive precisely at the oddity just named, the circumstance that, looking out somewhere, and often woefully athirst, for the taste of fineness, we find it not in the fruits of our author's fancy, but in a different matter altogether. We get it in the very history of his effort, the image itself of his lifelong process, comparatively so personal, so spiritual even, and, through all its patience and pain, of a quality so much more distinguished than the qualities he succeeds in attributing to his figures even when he most aims at distinction. There can be no question in these narrow limits of my taking the successive volumes one by one—all the more that our sense of the exhibition is as little as possible an impression of parts and books, of particular "plots" and persons. It produces the effect of a mass of imagery in which shades are sacrificed, the effect of character and passion in the lump or by the ton. The fullest, the most characteristic episodes affect us like a sounding chorus or procession, as with a hubbub of voices and a multitudinous tread of feet. The setter of the mass into motion, he himself, in the crowd, figures best, with whatever queer idiosyncrasies, excrescences and gaps, a being of a substance akin to our own. Taking him as we must, I repeat, for quite heroic, the interest of detail in him is the interest of his struggle at every point with his problem.

The sense for crowds and processions, for the gross and the general, was largely the *result* of this predicament, of the disproportion between his scheme and his material—though it was certainly also in part an effect of his particular turn of mind. What the reader easily discerns in him is the sturdy resolution with

which breadth and energy supply the place of penetration. He rests
to his utmost on his documents, devours and assimilates them,
makes them yield him extraordinary appearances of life; but in his
way he too improvises in the grand manner, the manner of Walter
Scott and of Dumas the elder. We feel that he *has* to improvise
for his moral and social world, the world as to which vision and
opportunity must come, if they are to come at all, unhurried and
unhustled—must take their own time, helped undoubtedly more or
less by blue-books, reports and interviews, by inquiries "on the
spot," but never wholly replaced by such substitutes without a
general disfigurement. Vision and opportunity reside in a personal sense and a personal history, and no short cut to them in the
interest of plausible fiction has ever been discovered. The short
cut, it is not too much to say, was with Zola the subject of constant
ingenious experiment, and it is largely to this source, I surmise,
that we owe the celebrated element of his grossness. He was *obliged*
to be gross, on his system, or neglect to his cost an invaluable aid
to representation, as well as one that apparently struck him as lying close at hand; and I cannot withhold my frank admiration
from the courage and consistency with which he faced his need.

His general subject in the last analysis was the nature of man;
in dealing with which he took up, obviously, the harp of most
numerous strings. His business was to make these strings sound
true, and there were none that he did not, so far as his general economy permitted, persistently try. What happened then was
that many—say about half, and these, as I have noted, the most
silvered, the most golden—refused to give out their music. They
would only sound false, since (as with all his earnestness he must
have felt) he could command them, through want of skill, of practice, of ear, to none of the right harmony. What therefore was
more natural than that, still spendidly bent on producing his illusion, he should throw himself on the strings he might thump with
effect, and should work them, as our phrase is, for all they were
worth? The nature of man, he had plentiful warrant for holding,
is an extraordinary mixture, but the great thing was to represent
a sufficient part of it to show that it was solidly, palpably, commonly the nature. With this preoccupation he doubtless fell into
extravagance—there was clearly so much to lead him on. The

coarser side of his subject, based on the community of all the instincts, was for instance the more practicable side, a sphere the vision of which required but the general human, scarcely more than the plain physical, initiation, and dispensed thereby conveniently enough with special introductions or revelations. A free entry into this sphere was undoubtedly compatible with a youthful career as hampered right and left even as Zola's own.

He was in prompt possession thus of the range of sympathy that he *could* cultivate, though it must be added that the complete exercise of that sympathy might have encountered an obstacle that would somewhat undermine his advantage. Our friend might have found himself able, in other words, to pay to the instinctive, as I have called it, only such tribute as protesting taste (his own dose of it) permitted. Yet there it was again that fortune and his temperament served him. Taste as he knew it, taste as his own constitution supplied it, proved to have nothing to say to the matter. His own dose of the precious elixir had no perceptible regulating power. Paradoxical as the remark may sound, this accident was positively to operate as one of his greatest felicities. There are parts of his work, those dealing with romantic or poetic elements, in which the inactivity of the principle in question is sufficiently hurtful; but it surely should not be described as hurtful to such pictures as *Le Ventre de Paris*, as *L'Assommoir*, as *Germinal*. The conception on which each of these productions rests is that of a world with which taste has nothing to do, and though the act of representation may be justly held, as an artistic act, to involve its presence, the discrimination would probably have been in fact, given the particular illusion sought, more detrimental than the deficiency. There was a great outcry, as we all remember, over the rank materialism of *L'Assommoir*, but who cannot see today how much a milder infusion of it would have told against the close embrace of the subject aimed at? *L'Assommoir* is the nature of man—but not his finer, nobler, cleaner or more cultivated nature; it is the image of his free instincts, the better and the worse, the better struggling as they can, gasping for light and air, the worse making themselves at home in darkness, ignorance and poverty. The whole handling makes for emphasis and scale, and it is not to be measured how, as a picture of conditions, the thing would have suffered from timidity. The qualification of the painter was precisely his stoutness of stomach, and we scarce exceed in saying that to have taken in and given out again less of the infected air would, with such a resource, have meant the waste of a faculty.

I may add in this connection moreover that refinement of intention did on occasion and after a fashion of its own unmistakably preside at these experiments; making the remark in order to have done once for all with a feature of Zola's literary physiognomy that appears to have attached the gaze of many persons to the exclusion of every other. There are judges in these matters so perversely preoccupied that for them to see anywhere the "improper" is for them straightway to cease to see anything else. The said improper, looming supremely large and casting all the varieties of the proper quite into the shade, suffers thus in their consciousness a much greater extension than it ever claimed, and this consciousness becomes, for the edification of many and the information of a few, a colossal reflector and record of it. Much may be said, in relation to some of the possibilities of the nature of man, of the nature in especial of the "people," on the defect of our author's sense of proportion. But the sense of proportion of many of those he has scandalized would take us further yet. I recall at all events as relevant—for it comes under a very attaching general head—two occasions of long ago, two Sunday afternoons in Paris, on which I found the question of intention very curiously lighted. Several men of letters of a group in which almost every member either had arrived at renown or was well on his way to it, were assembled under the roof of the most distinguished of their number, where they exchanged free confidences on current work, on plans and ambitions, in a manner full of interest for one never previously privileged to see artistic conviction, artistic passion (at least on the literary ground) so systematic and so articulate. "Well, I on my side," I remember Zola's saying, "am engaged on a book, a study of the *mœurs* of the people, for which I am making a collection of all the 'bad words,' the *gros mots*, of the language, those with which the vocabulary of the people, those with which their familiar talk, bristles." I was struck with the tone in which he made the announcement—without bravado and without apology, as an interesting idea that had come to him and that he was working, really to arrive at character and particular truth, with all his conscience; just as I was struck with the unqualified interest that his plan excited. It was *on* a plan that he was working—formidably, almost grimly, as his fatigued face showed; and the whole consideration of this interesting element partook of the general seriousness.

But there comes back to me also as a companion-piece to this another day, after some interval, on which the interest was excited by the fact that the work for love of which the brave license had been taken was actually under the ban of the daily newspaper that had engaged to "serialize" it. Publication had definitively ceased. The thing had run a part of its course, but it had outrun the courage of editors and the curiosity of subscribers—that stout curiosity to which it had evidently in such good faith been addressed. The chorus of contempt for the ways of such people, their pusillanimity, their superficiality, vulgarity, intellectual platitude, was the striking note on this occasion; for the journal impugned had declined to proceed and the serial, broken off, been obliged, if I am not mistaken, to seek the hospitality of other columns, secured indeed with no great difficulty. The composition so qualified for future fame was none other, as I was later to learn, than *L'Assommoir*; and my reminiscence has perhaps no greater point than in connecting itself with a matter always dear to the critical spirit, especially when the latter has not too completely elbowed out the romantic —the matter of the "origins," the early consciousness, early steps, early tribulations, early obscurity, as so often happens of productions finally crowned by time.

Their greatness is for the most part a thing that has originally begun so small; and this impression is particularly strong when we have been in any degree present, so to speak, at the birth. The course of the matter is apt to tend preponderantly in that case to enrich our stores of irony. In the eventual conquest of consideration by an abused book we recognize, in other terms, a drama of romantic interest, a drama often with large comic no less than with fine pathetic interweavings. It may of course be said in this particular connection that *L'Assommoir* had not been one of the literary things that creep humbly into the world. Its "success" may be cited as almost insolently prompt, and the fact remains true if the idea of success be restricted, after the inveterate fashion, to the idea of circulation. What remains truer still, however, is that for the critical spirit circulation mostly matters not the least little bit, and it is of the success with which the history of Gervaise and Coupeau nestles in *that* capacious bosom, even as the just man sleeps in Abraham's, that I here speak. But it is a point I may better refer to a moment hence.

Though a summary study of Zola need not too anxiously concern itself with book after book—always with a partial exception from this remark for *L'Assommoir*—groups and varieties none the less exist in the huge series, aids to discrimination without which no measure of the presiding genius is possible. These divisions range themselves to my sight, roughly speaking, however, as scarce more than three in number—I mean if the ten volumes of the *Œuvres critiques* and the *Théâtre* be left out of account. The critical volumes in especial abound in the characteristic, as they were also a wondrous addition to his sum of achievement during his most strenuous years. But I am forced not to consider them. The two groups constituted after the close of *Les Rougon-Macquart*— *Les Trois Villes* and the incomplete *Quatre Evangiles*—distribute themselves easily among the three types, or, to speak more exactly, stand together under one of the three. This one, so comprehensive as to be the author's main exhibition, includes to my sense all his best volumes—to the point in fact of producing an effect of distinct inferiority for those outside of it, which are, luckily for his general credit, the less numerous. It is so inveterately pointed out in any allusion to him that one shrinks, in repeating it, from sounding flat; but as he was admirably equipped from the start for the evocation of number and quantity, so those of his social pictures that most easily surpass the others are those in which appearances, the appearances familiar to him, are at once most magnified and most multiplied.

To make his characters swarm, and to make the great central thing they swarm about "as large as life," portentously, heroically big, that was the task he set himself very nearly from the first, that was the secret he triumphantly mastered. Add that the big central thing was always some highly representative institution or industry of the France of his time, some seated Moloch of custom, of commerce, of faith, lending itself to portrayal through its abuses and excesses, its idol-face and great devouring mouth, and we embrace the main lines of his attack. In *Le Ventre de Paris* he had dealt with the life of the huge Halles, the general markets and their supply, the personal forces, personal situations, passions, involved in (strangest of all subjects) the alimentation of the monstrous city, the city whose victualing occupies so inordinately much of its consciousness. Paris richly gorged, Paris sublime and indifferent in her assurance (so all unlike poor Oliver's) of "more," figures here the theme itself, lies across the scene like some vast ruminant creature breathing in a cloud of parasites. The book was the first of the long series to show the full freedom of the author's hand, though *La Curée* had already been symptomatic. This freedom, after an interval, broke out on a much bigger scale in *L'Assommoir*, in *Au bonheur des dames*, in *Germinal*, in *La Bête humaine*, in *L'Argent*, in *La Débâcle*, and then again, though more mechanically and with much of the glory gone, in the more or less wasted energy of *Lourdes, Rome, Paris*, of *Fécondité, Travail* and *Vérité*.

Au bonheur des dames handles the colossal modern shop, traces the growth of such an organization as the Bon Marché or the Magasin-du-Louvre, sounds the abysses of its inner life, marshals its population, its hierarchy of clerks, counters, departments, divisions and subdivisions, plunges into the labyrinth of the mutual relations of its staff, and above all traces its ravage amid the smaller fry of the trade, of all the trades, pictures these latter gasping for breath in an air pumped clean by its mighty lungs. *Germinal* revolves about the coal mines of Flemish France, with the subterranean world of the pits for its central presence, just as *La Bête humaine* has for its protagonist a great railway and *L'Argent* presents in terms of human passion—mainly of human baseness—the fury of the Bourse and the monster of Credit. *La Débâcle* takes up with extraordinary breadth the first act of the Franco-Prussian war, the collapse at Sedan, and the titles of the six volumes of The Three Cities and the Four Gospels sufficiently explain them. I may mention, however, for the last lucidity, that among these *Fécondité* manipulates, with an amazing misapprehension of means to ends, of remedies to ills, no less thickly peopled a theme than that of the decline in the French birth rate, and that *Vérité* presents a fictive equivalent of the Dreyfus case, with a vast and elaborate picture of the battle in France between lay and clerical instruction. I may even further mention, to clear the ground, that with the close of *Les Rougon-Macquart* the diminution of freshness in the author's energy, the diminution of intensity and, in short, of quality, becomes such as to render sadly difficult a happy life with some of the later volumes. Happiness of the purest strain never indeed, in old absorptions of Zola, quite sat at the feast; but there was mostly a measure of coercion, a spell without a charm. From these last-named productions of the climax everything strikes me as absent but quantity (*Vérité*, for instance, is, with the possible exception of *Nana*, the longest of the list); though indeed there is something impressive in the way his quantity represents his patience.

There are efforts here at stout perusal that, frankly, I have been unable to carry through, and I should verily like, in connection with the vanity of these, to dispose on the spot of the sufficiently strange phenomenon constituted by what I have called the climax. It embodies in fact an immense anomaly; it casts back over Zola's prime and his middle years the queerest gray light of eclipse. Nothing moreover—nothing "literary"—was ever so odd as in this matter the whole turn of the case, the consummation so logical yet so unexpected. Writers have grown old and withered and failed; they have grown weak and sad; they have lost heart, lost ability, yielded in one way or another—the possible ways being so numerous—to the cruelty of time. But the singular doom of this genius, and which began to multiply its symptoms ten years before his death, was to find, with life, at fifty, still rich in him, strength only to undermine all the "authority" he had gathered. He had not grown old and he had not grown feeble; he had only grown all too wrongly insistent, setting himself to wreck, poetically, his so massive identity—to wreck it in the very waters in which he had formally arrayed his victorious fleet. (I say "poetically" on purpose to give him the just benefit of all the beauty of his power.) The process of the disaster, so full of the effect, though so without the intention, of perversity, is difficult to trace in a few words; it may best be indicated by an example or two of its action.

The example that perhaps most comes home to me is again connected with a personal reminiscence. In the course of some talk that I had with him during his first visit to England I happened to ask him what opportunity to travel (if any) his immense application had ever left him, and whether in particular he had been able to see Italy, a country from which I had either just returned or which I was luckily—not having the "Natural History of a Family" on my hands—about to revisit. "All I've done, alas," he replied, "was, the other year, in the course of a little journey to the south, to my own *pays*—all that has been possible was then to make a little dash as far as Genoa, a matter of only a few days." *Le Docteur Pascal*, the conclusion of *Les Rougon-Macquart*, had appeared shortly before, and it further befell that I asked him what plans he had for the future, now that, still *dans la force de l'âge*, he had so cleared the ground. I shall never forget the fine promptitude of his answer—"Oh, I shall begin at once *Les Trois Villes*." "And which cities are they to be?" The reply was finer still— "Lourdes, Paris, Rome."

It was splendid for confidence and cheer, but it left me, I fear, more or less gaping, and it was to give me afterwards the key, critically speaking, to many a mystery. It struck me as breathing to an almost tragic degree the fatuity of those in whom the gods stimulate that vice to their ruin. He was an honest man—he had always bristled with it at every pore; but no artistic reverse was inconceivable for an adventurer who, stating in one breath that his knowledge of Italy consisted of a few days spent at Genoa, was ready to declare in the next that he had planned, on a scale, a picture of Rome. It flooded his career, to my sense, with light; it showed how he had marched from subject to subject and had "got up" each in turn—showing also how consummately he had reduced such getting-up to an artifice. He had success and a rare impunity behind him, but nothing would now be so interesting as to see if he could again play the trick. One would leave him, and welcome, Lourdes and Paris—he had already dealt, on a scale, with his own country and people. But was the adored Rome also to be his on such terms, the Rome he was already giving away before possessing an inch of it? One thought of one's own frequentations, saturations—a history of long years, and of how the effect of them had somehow been but to make the subject too august. Was *he* to find it easy through a visit of a month or two with "introductions" and a Baedeker?

It was not indeed that the Baedeker and the introductions didn't show, to my sense, at that hour, as extremely suggestive; they were positively a part of the light struck out by his announcement. They defined the system on which he had brought *Les Rougon-Macquart* safely into port. He had had his Baedeker and his introductions for *Germinal*, for *L'Assommoir*, for *L'Argent*, for *La Débâcle*, for *Au bonheur des dames*; which advantages, which researches, had clearly been all the more in character for being documentary, extractive, a matter of *renseignements*, published or private, even when most mixed with personal impressions snatched, with *enquêtes sur les lieux*, with facts obtained from the best authorities, proud and happy to co-operate in so famous a connection. That was, as we say, all right, all the more that the process, to my imagination, became vivid and was wonderfully reflected back from its fruits. There *were* the fruits—so it hadn't been presumptuous. Presumption, however, was now to begin, and what omen mightn't there be in its beginning with such complacency? Well, time would show—as time in due course effectually did. *Rome*, as the second volume of The Three Cities, appeared with high punctuality a year or two later; and the interesting question, an occasion really for the moralist, was by that time not to recognize in it the mere triumph of a mechanical art, a "receipt" applied with the skill of long practice, but to do much more than this— that is really to give a name to the particular shade of blindness that could constitute a trap for so great an artistic intelligence. The presumptuous volume, without sweetness, without antecedents, superficial and violent, has the minimum instead of the maximum of *value*; so that it betrayed or "gave away" just in this degree the state of mind on the author's part responsible for its inflated hollowness. To put one's finger on the state of mind was to find out accordingly what was, as we say, the matter with him.

It seemed to me, I remember, that I found out as never before when, in its turn, *Fécondité* began the work of crowning the edifice. *Fécondité* is physiological, whereas *Rome* is not, whereas *Vérité* likewise is not; yet these three productions joined hands at a given moment to fit into the lock of the mystery the key of my meditation. They came to the same thing, to the extent of permitting me to read into them together the same precious lesson. This lesson may not, barely stated, sound remarkable; yet without being in possession of it I should have ventured on none of these remarks. "The matter with" Zola then, so far as it goes, was that, as the imagination of the artist is in the best cases not only clarified but intensified by his equal possession of Taste (deserving here if ever the old-fashioned honor of a capital), so when he has lucklessly never inherited that auxiliary blessing the imagination itself inevitably breaks down as a consequence. There is simply no limit, in fine, to the misfortune of being tasteless; it does not merely disfigure the surface and the fringe of your performance— it eats back into the very heart and enfeebles the sources of life. When you have no taste you have no discretion, which is the conscience of taste, and when you have no discretion you perpetrate books like *Rome*, which are without intellectual modesty, books like *Fécondite*, which are without a sense of the ridiculous, books like *Vérité*, which are without the finer vision of human experience.

It is marked that in each of these examples the deficiency has been directly fatal. No stranger doom was ever appointed for a man so plainly desiring only to be just than the absurdity of not resting till he had buried the felicity of his past, such as it was, under a great flat leaden slab. *Vérité* is a plea for science, as science, to Zola, is *all* truth, the mention of any other kind being mere imbecility; and the simplification of the human picture to which his negations and exasperations have here conducted him was not, even when all had been said, credible in advance. The result is amazing when we consider that the finer observation is the supposed basis of all such work. It is not that even here the author has not a queer idealism of his own; this idealism is on the contrary so present as to show positively for the falsest of his simplifications. In *Fécondité* it becomes grotesque, makes of the book the most muscular mistake of *sense* probably ever committed. Where was the judgment of which experience is supposed to be the guarantee when the perpetrator could persuade himself that the lesson he wished in these pages to convey could be made immediate and direct, chalked, with loud taps and a still louder commentary, the sexes and generations all convoked, on the blackboard of the "family sentiment"?

I have mentioned, however, all this time but one of his categories. The second consists of such things as *La Fortune des Rougon* and *La Curée*, as *Eugène Rougon* and even *Nana*, as *Pot-Bouille*, as *L'Œuvre* and *La Joie de vivre*. These volumes may rank as social pictures in the narrowest sense, studies, comprehensively speaking, of the manners, the morals, the miseries—for it mainly comes to that—of a bourgeoisie grossly materialized. They deal with the life of individuals in the liberal professions and with that of political and social adventures, and offer the personal character and career, more or less detached, as the center of interest. *La Curée* is an evocation, violent and "romantic," of the extravagant appetites, the fever of the senses, supposedly fostered, for its ruin, by the hapless second Empire, upon which general ills and turpitudes at large were at one time so freely and conveniently fathered. *Eugène Rougon* carries out this view in the high color of a political portrait, not other than scandalous, for which one of the ministerial *âmes damnées* of Napoleon III, M. Rouher, is reputed, I know not how justly, to have sat. *Nana*, attaching itself by a hundred strings to a prearranged table of kinships, heredities, transmissions, is the vast crowded *epos* of the daughter of the people filled with poisoned blood and sacrificed as well as sacrificing on the altar of luxury and lust; the panorama of such a "progress" as Hogarth would more definitely have named—the progress across the high plateau of "pleasure" and down the facile descent on the other side. *Nana* is truly a monument to Zola's patience; the subject being so ungrateful, so formidably special, that the multiplication of illustrative detail, the plunge into pestilent depths, represents a kind of technical intrepidity.

There are other plunges, into different sorts of darkness; of which the esthetic, even the scientific, even the ironic motive fairly escapes us—explorations of stagnant pools like that of *La Joie de vivre*, as to which, granting the nature of the curiosity and the substance labored in, the patience is again prodigious, but which make us wonder what pearl of philosophy, of suggestion or just of homely recognition, the general picture, as of rats dying in a hole, has to offer. Our various senses, sight, smell, sound, touch, are, as with Zola always, more or less convinced; but when the particular effect upon each of these is added to the effect upon the others the mind still remains bewilderedly unconscious of any use for the total. I am not sure indeed that the case is in this respect better with the productions of the third order—*La Faute de l'Abbé Mouret, Une Page d'amour, Le Rêve, Le Docteur Pascal* —in which the appeal is more directly, is in fact quite earnestly, to the moral vision; so much, on such ground, was to depend precisely on those discriminations in which the writer is least at home. The volumes whose names I have just quoted are his express tribute to the "ideal," to the select and the charming—fair fruits of invention intended to remove from the mouth so far as possible the bitterness of the ugly things in which so much of the rest of his work had been condemned to consist. The subjects in question then are "idyllic" and the treatment poetic, concerned essentially to please on the largest lines and involving at every turn that salutary need. They are matters of conscious delicacy, and nothing might interest us more than to see what, in the shock of the potent forces enlisted, becomes of this shy element. Nothing might interest us more, literally, and might positively affect us more, even very nearly to tears, though indeed sometimes also to smiles, than to see the constructor of *Les Rougon-Macquart* trying, "for all he is worth," to be fine with fineness, finely tender, finely true—trying to be, as it is called, distinguished—in face of constitutional hindrance.

The effort is admirably honest, the tug at his subject splendidly strong; but the consequences remain of the strangest, and we get the impression that—as representing discriminations unattainable —they are somehow the price he paid. *Le Docteur Pascal*, for instance, which winds up the long chronicle on the romantic note, on the note of invoked beauty, in order to sweeten, as it were, the total draught—*Le Docteur Pascal*, treating of the erotic ardor entertained for each other by an uncle and his niece, leaves us amazed at such a conception of beauty, such an application of romance, such an estimate of sweetness, a sacrifice to poetry and passion so little in order. Of course, we definitely remind ourselves, the whole long chronicle is explicitly a scheme, solidly set up and intricately worked out, lighted, according to the author's pretension, by "science," high, dry, and clear, and with each part involved and necessitated in all the other parts, each block of the edifice, each "morceau de vie," *physiologically* determined by previous combinations. "How can I help it," we hear the builder of the pyramid ask, "if experience (by which alone I proceed) shows me certain plain results—if, holding up the torch of my famous 'experimental method' I find it stare me in the face that the union of certain types, the conflux of certain strains of blood, the intermarriage, in a word, of certain families, produces nervous conditions, conditions temperamental, psychical and pathological, in which nieces *have* to fall in love with uncles and uncles with nieces? Observation and imagination, for any picture of life," he as audibly adds, "know no light but science, and are false to all intellectual decency, false to their own honor, when they fear it, dodge it, darken it. To pretend to any other guide or law is mere base humbug."

That is very well, and the value, in a hundred ways, of a mass of production conceived in such a spirit can never (when robust execution has followed) be small. But the formula really sees us no further. It offers a definition which is no definition. "Science" is soon said—the whole thing depends on the ground so covered. Science accepts surely *all* our consciousness of life; even, rather, the latter closes maternally round it—so that, becoming thus a force within us, not a force outside, it exists, it illuminates only as we apply it. We do emphatically apply it in art. But Zola would apparently hold that it much more applies *us*. On the showing of many of his volumes then it makes but a dim use of us, and this we should still consider the case even were we sure that the article offered us in the majestic name is absolutely at one with its own pretension. This confidence we can on too many grounds never have. The matter is one of appreciation, and when an artist answers for science who answers for the artist—who at the least answers for art? Thus it is with the mistakes that affect us, I say, as Zola's penalties. We are reminded by them that the game of art has, as the phrase is, to be played. It may not with any sure felicity for the result be both taken and left. If you insist on the common you must submit to the common; if you discriminate, on the contrary, you must, however invidious your discriminations may be called, trust to them to see you through.

To the common then Zola, often with splendid results, inordinately sacrifices, and this fact of its overwhelming him is what I have called his paying for it. In *L'Assommoir*, in *Germinal*, in *La Débâcle*, productions in which he must most survive, the sacrifice is ordered and fruitful, for the subject and the treatment harmonize and work together. He describes what he best feels, and feels it more and more as it naturally comes to him—quite, if I may allow myself the image, as we zoologically see some mighty animal, a beast of a corrugated hide and a portentous snout, soaking with joy in the warm ooze of an African riverside. In these cases everything matches, and "science," we may be permitted to believe, has had little in the business. The author's perceptions go straight, and the subject, grateful and responsive, gives itself wholly up. It is no longer a case of an uncertain smoky torch, but of a personal vision, the vision of genius, springing from an inward source. Of this genius *L'Assommoir* is the most extraordinary record. It contains, with the two companions I have given it, all the best of Zola, and the three books together are solid ground—or would be could I now so take them—for a study of the particulars of his power. His strongest marks and features abound in them; *L'Assommoir* above all is (not least in respect to its bold free linguistic reach, already glanced at) completely genial, while his misadventures, his unequipped and delusive pursuit of the life of the spirit and the tone of culture, are almost completely absent.

It is a singular sight enough this of a producer of illusions whose interest for us is so independent of our pleasure or at least of our complacency—who touches us deeply even while he most "puts us off," who makes us care for his ugliness and yet himself at the same time pitilessly (pitilessly, that is, for *us*) makes a mock of it, who fills us with a sense of the rich which is none the less never the rare. Gervaise, the most immediately "felt," I cannot but think, of all his characters, is a lame washerwoman, loose and gluttonous, without will, without any principle of cohesion, the sport of every wind that assaults her exposed life, and who, rolling from one gross mistake to another, finds her end in misery, drink and despair. But her career, as presented, has fairly the largeness that, throughout the chronicle, we feel as epic, and the intensity of her creator's vision of it and of the dense sordid life hanging about it is one of the great things the modern novel has been able to do. It has done nothing more completely constitutive and of a tone so rich and full and sustained. The tone of *L'Assommoir* is, for mere "keeping up," unsurpassable, a vast deep steady tide on which every object represented is triumphantly borne. It never shrinks nor flows thin, and nothing for an instant drops, dips or catches; the high-water mark of sincerity, of the genial, as I have called it, is unfailingly kept.

For the artist in the same general "line" such a production has an interest almost inexpressible, a mystery as to origin and growth over which he fondly but rather vainly bends. How after all does it so get itself *done*?—the "done" being admirably the sign and crown of it. The light of the richer mind has been elsewhere, as I have sufficiently hinted, frequent enough, but nothing truly in all fiction was ever built so strong or made so dense as here. Needless to say there are a thousand things with more charm in their truth, with more beguilement of every sort, more prettiness of pathos, more innocence of drollery, for the spectator's sense of truth. But I doubt if there has ever been a more totally *represented* world, anything more founded and established, more provided for all round, more organized and carried on. It is a world practically workable, with every part as functional as every other, and with the parts all chosen for direct mutual aid. Let it not be said either that the equal constitution of parts makes for repletion or excess; the air circulates and the subject blooms; deadness comes in these matters only when the right parts are absent and there is vain beating of the air in their place—the refuge of the fumbler incapable of the thing "done" at all.

The mystery I speak of, for the reader who reflects as he goes, is the wonder of the scale and energy of Zola's assimilations. This wonder besets us above all throughout the three books I have placed first. How, all sedentary and "scientific," did he get so *near*? By what art, inscrutable, immeasurable, indefatigable, did he arrange to make of his documents, in these connections, a use so vivified? Say he was "near" the subject of *L'Assommoir* in imagination, in more or less familiar impression, in temperament and humor, he could not after all have been near it in personal experience, and the copious personalism of the picture, not to say its frank animalism, yet remains its note and its strength. When the note had been struck in a thousand forms we had, by multiplication, as a kind of cumulative consequence, the finished and rounded book; just as we had the same result by the same process in *Germinal*. It is not of course that multiplication and accumulation, the extraordinary pair of legs on which he walks, are easily or directly consistent with his projecting himself morally; this immense diffusion, with its appropriation of everything it meets, affects us on the contrary as perpetually delaying access to what we may call the private world, the world of the individual. Yet since the individual—for it so happens—is simple and shallow our author's dealings with him, as met and measured, maintain their resemblance to those of the lusty bee who succeeds in plumping for an instant, of a summer morning, into every flower-cup of the garden.

Grant—and the generalization may be emphatic—that the shallow and the simple are *all* the population of his richest and most crowded pictures, and that his "psychology," in a psychologic age, remains thereby comparatively coarse, grant this and we but get another view of the miracle. We see enough of the superficial among novelists at large, assuredly, without deriving from it, as we derive from Zola at his best, the concomitant impression of the solid. It is in general—I mean among the novelists at large— the impression of the *cheap*, which the author of *Les Rougon-Macquart*, honest man, never faithless for a moment to his own stiff standard, manages to spare us even in the prolonged sandstorm of *Vérité*. The Common is another matter; it is one of the forms of the superficial—pervading and consecrating all things in such a book as *Germinal*—and it only adds to the number of our critical questions. How in the world is it made, this deplorable democratic malodorous Common, so strange and so interesting? How is it taught to receive into its loins the stuff of the epic and still, in spite of that association with poetry, never depart from its nature? It is in the great lusty game he plays with the shallow and the simple that Zola's mastery resides, and we see of course that when values are small it takes innumerable items and combinations to make up the sum. In *L'Assommoir* and in *Germinal*, to some extent even in *La Débâcle*, the values are all, morally, personally, of the lowest—the highest is poor Gervaise herself, richly human in her generosities and follies—yet each is as distinct as a brass-headed nail.

What we come back to accordingly is the unprecedented case of such a combination of parts. Painters, of great schools, often of great talent, have responded liberally on canvas to the appeal of ugly things, of Spanish beggars, squalid and dusty-footed, of martyred saints or other convulsed sufferers, tortured and bleeding, of boors and louts soaking a Dutch proboscis in perpetual beer; but we had never before had to reckon with so literary a treatment of the mean and vulgar. When we others of the Anglo-Saxon race are vulgar we are, handsomely and with the best conscience in the world, vulgar all through, too vulgar to be in any degree literary, and too much so therefore to be critically reckoned with at all. The French are different—they separate their sympathies, multiply their possibilities, observe their shades, remain more or less outside of their worst disasters. They mostly contrive to get the *idea*, in however dead a faint, down into the lifeboat. They may lose sight of the stars, but they save in some such fashion as that their intellectual souls. Zola's own reply to all puzzlements would have been, at any rate, I take it, a straight summary of his inveterate professional habits. "It is all very simple—I produce, roughly speaking, a volume a year, and of this time some five months go to preparation, to special study. In the other months, with all my *cadres* established, I write the book. And I can hardly say which part of the job is stiffest."

The story was not more wonderful for him than that, nor the job more complex; which is why we must say of his whole process and its results that they constitute together perhaps the most extraordinary *imitation* of observation that we possess. Balzac appealed to "science" and proceeded by her aid; Balzac had *cadres* enough and a tabulated world, rubrics, relationships and genealogies; but Balzac affects us in spite of everything as personally overtaken by life, as fairly hunted and run to earth by it. He strikes us as struggling and all but submerged, as beating over the scene such a pair of wings as were not soon again to be wielded by any visitor of his general air and as had not at all events attached themselves to Zola's rounded shoulders. His bequest is in consequence immeasurably more interesting, yet who shall declare that his adventure was in its greatness more successful? Zola "pulled it off," as we say, supremely, in that he never but once found himself obliged to quit, to our vision, his magnificent treadmill of the pigeonholed and documented—the region we may qualify as that of experience by imitation. His splendid economy saw him through, he labored to the end within sight of his notes and his charts.

The extraordinary thing, however, is that on the single occasion when, publicly—as his whole manifestation was public—life did swoop down on him, the effect of the visitation was quite perversely other than might have been looked for. His courage in the Dreyfus connection testified admirably to his ability to live for himself and out of the order of his volumes—little indeed as living at all might have seemed a question for one exposed, when his crisis was at its height and he was found guilty of "insulting" the powers that were, to be literally torn to pieces in the precincts of the Palace of Justice. Our point is that nothing was ever so odd as that these great moments should appear to have been wasted, when all was said, for his creative intelligence. *Vérité*, as I have intimated, the production in which they might most have been reflected, is a production unrenewed and unrefreshed by them, spreads before us as somehow flatter and grayer, not richer and more relieved, by reason of them. They really arrived, I surmise, too late in the day; the imagination they might have vivified was already fatigued and spent.

I must not moreover appear to say that the power to evoke and present has not even on the dead level of *Vérité* its occasional minor revenges. There are passages, whole pages, of the old full-bodied sort, pictures that elsewhere in the series would in all likelihood have seemed abundantly convincing. Their misfortune is to have been discounted by our intensified, our finally fatal sense of the *procédé*. Quarreling with all conventions, defiant of them in general, Zola was yet inevitably to set up his own group of them—as, for that matter, without a sufficient collection, without their aid in simplifying and making possible, how could he ever have seen his big ship into port? Art welcomes them, feeds upon them always;

no sort of form is practicable without them. It is only a question of what particular ones we use—to wage war on certain others and to arrive at particular forms. The convention of the blameless being, the thoroughly "scientific" creature possessed impeccably of all truth and serving as the mouthpiece of it and of the author's highest complacencies, this character is for instance a convention inveterate and indispensable, without whom the "sympathetic" side of the work could never have been achieved. Marc in *Vérité*, Pierre Froment in *Lourdes* and in *Rome*, the wondrous representatives of the principle of reproduction in *Fécondité*, the exemplary painter of *L'Œuvre*, sublime in his modernity and paternity, the patient Jean Macquart of *La Débâcle*, whose patience is as guaranteed as the exactitude of a well-made watch, the supremely enlightened Docteur Pascal even, as I recall him, all amorous nepotism but all virtue too and all beauty of life—such figures show us the reasonable and the good not merely in the white light of the old George Sand novel and its improved moralities, but almost in that of our childhood's nursery and schoolroom, that of the moral tale of Miss Edgeworth and Mr. Thomas Day.

Yet let not these restrictions be my last word. I had intended, under the effect of a reperusal of *La Débâcle, Germinal* and *L'Assommoir*, to make no discriminations that should not be in our hero's favor. The long-drawn incident of the marriage of Gervaise and Cadet-Cassis and that of the Homeric birthday feast later on in the laundress's workshop, each treated from beginning to end and in every item of their coarse comedy and humanity, still show the unprecedented breadth by which they originally made us stare, still abound in the particular kind and degree of vividness that helped them, when they appeared, to mark a date in the portrayal of manners. Nothing had then been so sustained and at every moment of its grotesque and pitiful existence lived into as the nuptial day of the Coupeau pair in especial, their fantastic processional pilgrimage through the streets of Paris in the rain, their bedraggled exploration of the halls of the Louvre museum, lost as in the labyrinth of Crete, and their arrival at last, ravenous and exasperated, at the *guinguette* where they sup at so much a head, each paying, and where we sit down with them in the grease and the perspiration and succumb, half in sympathy, half in shame, to their monstrous pleasantries, acerbities and miseries. I have said enough of the mechanical in Zola; here in truth is, given the elements, almost insupportably the sense of life. That effect is equally in the historic chapter of the strike of the miners in *Germinal*, another of those illustrative episodes, viewed as great passages to be "rendered," for which our author established altogether a new measure and standard of handling, a new energy and veracity, something since which the old trivialities and poverties of treatment of such aspects have become incompatible, for the novelist, with either rudimentary intelligence or rudimentary self-respect.

As for *La Débâcle*, finally, it takes its place with Tolstoy's very much more universal but very much less composed and condensed epic as an incomparably human picture of war. I have been rereading it, I confess, with a certain timidity, the dread of perhaps impairing the deep impression received at the time of its appearance. I recall the effect it then produced on me as a really luxurious act of submission. It was early in the summer; I was in an old Italian town; the heat was oppressive, and one could but recline, in the lightest garments, in a great dim room and give one's self up. I like to think of the conditions and the emotion, which melt for me together into the memory I fear to imperil. I remember that in the glow of my admiration there was not a reserve I had ever made that I was not ready to take back. As an application of the author's system and his supreme faculty, as a triumph of what these things could do for him, how could such a performance be surpassed? The long, complex, horrific, pathetic battle, embraced, mastered, with every crash of its squadrons, every pulse of its thunder and blood resolved for us, by reflection, by communication from two of the humblest and obscurest of the military units, into immediate vision and contact, into deep human thrills of terror and pity—this bristling center of the book was such a piece of "doing" (to come back to our word) as could only shut our mouths. That doubtless is why a generous critic, nursing the sensation, may desire to drop for a farewell no term into the other scale. That our author was clearly great at congruous subjects— this may well be our conclusion. If the others, subjects of the private and intimate order, gave him more or less inevitably "away," they yet left him the great distinction that the more he could be promiscuous and collective, the more even he could (to repeat my imputation) illustrate our large natural allowance of health, heartiness and grossness, the more he could strike us as penetrating and true. It was a distinction not easy to win and that his name is not likely soon to lose.

"A Defense of Naturalism"*

By Roger Sherman Loomis

ROGER SHERMAN LOOMIS (1887—) is emeritus professor of English literature at Columbia University. An eminent authority on the Arthurian legend and on medieval literature in general, he taught at Columbia for most of his life, capping his career with the Eastman professorship at Oxford in 1955-1956. He remarks of the present article that "As an instructor in English at the University of Illinois I wrote the essay as an expression of my ideas, and, having said my say, I have not published anything more directly on the subject, but my views are substantially unchanged." He recalls that when he went to Oxford as a Rhodes scholar early in the century he became a Fabian and a rationalist and states that he is now a member of the New York Ethical Culture Society.

In this article Mr. Loomis approaches the subject from a philosophical rather than a literary standpoint. He accepts the distinction between realism, which has become acceptable, and naturalism, which is still execrated because of its insistence on pessimism and bestialism and its denial of the demi-god in man. He justifies the position of naturalism on these points and further defends its major philosophic tenets: "a cosmic order without justice, a morality without sanction or stability, and a will, free within limits to choose what it likes best, but determined as to what it likes best." His conclusion is that naturalism has gradually been making over our morality and that it is visibly working in the social sphere for increased human happiness—which is its goal.

<hr />

NATURALISM is a word with as many phases of meaning as pacifism or patriotism, and about it rages nearly as fierce a conflict. When Zola issued his well-known pronunciamento that Naturalistic art was Nature seen through a temperament, he stressed the word "Nature." Nature and Nature only must be the subject of art: to face Nature frankly and openly, to present her dulnesses and stupidities and shames with scrupulous impartiality must be the aim of the artist. Now modern English criticism has preferred

* Loomis, Roger Sherman, "A Defense of Naturalism," *International Journal of Ethics* 29: pp. 188-201, January 1919. Reprinted by permission of the author and the University of Chicago Press.

to call such full-length and unflattering portraiture of Dame Nature, even the emphasis upon her wry neck, bow legs, and squint eyes, by the name of Realism. Accordingly, when the critic nowadays quotes Zola's definition of Naturalism, he stresses the word "temperament." Naturalistic art is Nature seen through a certain temperament, or through a certain formula created by that temperament. Naturalism, we are told, is not simply a reproduction of the homely and repulsive side of Nature's physiognomy, but an attempt to read in it a certain character.

With Zola's profession faithfully to portray Nature the critics have now no quarrel, but with his practice of giving a certain interpretation of her character they and a great body of readers beg leave, more or less politely, to differ. Realism, though not admitted to so high a seat as idealizing poetry and romance, has been received into the company of the immortals, and Howells and Bennett are permitted to sit down to dinner with self-respecting critics. But Naturalism, Zola's interpretation of Nature, the high priests of criticism hold up to mocking and execration. Flaubert, Ibsen, Hardy, Moore, Brieux, and Masters were all at first denounced in the reputable journals as devils from the pit: and they are still ostracized by good society as if a sulphurous vapor hung around them.

To the question, "What is this interpretation, this formula which brings down upon its enunciators the formidable wrath of the critics?" we are likely to receive several answers. The first genial and rubicund gentleman of letters whom we interrogate over a bottle of Burgundy is apt to reply simply: "These fellows are arrant pessimists. They do not assure us that 'God's in his heaven, all's right with the world.' They are notoriously addicted to depressing surroundings and unhappy endings. Literature should not upset one's ideas about anything, and should be either soothing, inspiring, or funny." Apparently, for all his assumed superiority the genial critic demands just about the same remoteness from the workaday world and the same comfortable ending as the tired business man, whom he professes to despise.

If we approach some gentleman who has perhaps felt a little more than our genial friend the brunt of pain and perplexity, we are likely to get a somewhat more illuminating answer. "Natural-

536

"A Defense of Naturalism"

ism is Bestialism. Man is not a beast." To be sure, Zola has much to say of the Bête Humaine, and undoubtedly does stress in us the ape and tiger strains. But will anyone deny that the strains are there? Now and then a human being sprouts an atavistic tail or fell of hair. So, too, now and then, human beings commit atrocities at Louvain or East St. Louis. Let him that is without a streak of the beast in him cast the first stone at the Bête Humaine. After all, what most critics of this class object to is not the recognition of the animal, but the recognition of the animal as a serious problem. The emphasis on the beast in *L'Assommoir, Jude the Obscure*, and *Spoon River* shocks the conventional critic, who is accustomed to hear such things mentioned only over his after-dinner cigar: he feels it very deeply when he sees them in print where they can be read by ladies, and where apparently they are treated not as jests to roll under his tongue but as grit to break his teeth on. He is ready enough to recognize the beast, but only as a joke or a German. So long as it can be laughed away or blown to bits with high explosive, he is quite ready to appreciate it in his Boccaccio or his Bryce reports. But when the naturalistic author shows him the beast everywhere about him, in the office, the church, and the home, and by no means to be got rid of by such simple methods as laughter or trinitrotoluol, and he realizes that only a reorganization of all his ideas in the light of what sociological, economic, and psychological experts tell him can make this abundant *élan vital* galvanize rather than blast our society, he kicks like a Missouri mule and refuses to recognize the Bête Humaine.

Perhaps, however, we have put our question to some more rational critic and he replies that he confesses the beast in man, but that he also finds a demigod: Naturalism denies the demigod. True enough, if by the demigod is meant some infusion of a supernatural or mystical element into the beast. But if by the demigod be meant simply those qualities which men have ascribed to gods as their chief and worthiest title to worship—justice and love, beauty and reason—then, of course, the Naturalist does not deny the demigod, though like the Nazarene he often discovers him in the less reputable circles of society. Furthermore, he finds embryonic even in the beast all that is popularly considered peculiar to man—art, altruism, remorse, some of the simpler forms of reasoning and foresight. In the most primitive types of humanity he finds a religion claiming as much supernatural sanction as the Roman Church or Bahaism. When confronted, then, with the fact that even animals possess the supposedly divine traits, and that as divine revelation the totem pole and the Cross claim equal authority, the Naturalist comes to the conclusion that the supernatural is only a development of the natural, and that mystical experience, however valuable as a dynamic, is worthless as a directive. Only reason acting upon the facts supplied by experience can guide us to the truth.

Accordingly the Naturalist discards as obsolete three supernaturalistic concepts—Providence, absolute morality, and freedom of the will. In his novels and plays Providence is represented as a blind bungler, conventional morality is scouted and even flouted, and man is displayed as a puppet worked by the forces of Heredity and Environment. It is about these three phases of the Naturalistic interpretation of Nature that the battle of the critics still rages. What may be said in defense of these tenets of Naturalistic doctrine—a cosmic order without justice, a morality without sanction or stability, and a will, free within limits to choose what it likes best, but determined as to what it likes best?

The idea of a Providence in the affairs of men, working out a sort of poetical justice, has, to be sure, a certain basis in fact. No one can help observing that certain acts cause pain, directly to himself or indirectly through others. The relation is far from being uniform and inevitable, but despite the exceptions certain general causal relations are recognized. It is obvious that to overindulge in Welsh rarebit or to spoil a child with petting brings its own retribution with it. But Nemesis as an instrument of God's jealous vengeance upon the mortal who dares disobey his fiat seems a superfluous explanation of these facts. For it occurs to the Naturalist that a sane ethics calls only those deeds evil which generally bring suffering in their train: and if occasionally that suffering falls upon the evil-doer there is no occasion for seeking an explanation in some mysterious Nemesis. Surely never was an absurder piece of writing than Emerson's dithyramb on *Compensation*. To him it would be a cause for wonder and awful speculation that Providence had provided a dark brown taste in the mouth to balance

"A Defense of Naturalism"

the exhilaration of drunkenness, and had made fire burn to punish the child for putting its finger in the flame. The fundamental idea is worthy of the good old lady who thanked the dear Lord for providing such excellent harbors where the cities of New York and San Francisco were to spring up. Nemesis is a law, just as gravitation is a law; but like gravitation it is offset a billion times a minute by other laws: and inasmuch as it is therefore less successful than any human penal system in saddling the heaviest penalty on the worst offender, it scarcely deserves all the mystified veneration that has been lavished upon it.

Let us turn next to the Naturalist's morality. We have noted that whether an act is right or wrong depends upon whether joy or pain in the long run follows. This, in turn, depends upon the human and other sentient beings involved. These, in turn, will be affected by climate, heredity, education, and a thousand other things. Naturalistic morality differs, then, from orthodox morality in its relativity. The notion of an eternal code, confided by Infallible Wisdom to the visions of seers and the conscience of every individual, does not appeal to the Naturalistic thinker. If conscience be an infallible guide to right conduct, why did the conscience of 1700 encourage duelling, the conscience of ancient Sparta stealing, the conscience of the devout Mohammedan polygamy, and why was what we now regard as a loathsome sexual perversion practised unblushingly in Periclean Athens? The Naturalist has come to believe that conscience, an emotional assurance of the rightness of one's action, varies so uniformly with the social conventions about it that it can no more be relied on than a compass in the neighborhood of masses of iron. If the moral law is carved on tables of adamant for all times and all places, why is it that when the moral law interferes too severely with the right to life or happiness, we all by common consent make and approve exceptions thereto? We agree that the starving child cannot be blamed for stealing, the invalid must be kept alive by falsehoods, self-defense justifies killing, a noble purpose takes the taint from suicide. I know a clergyman, who had one of the greatest shocks of his life when I wrote him that I believed in comparative freedom of divorce, who yet not long after met with a case of domestic unhappiness, which not only led him to approve a divorce but actually to officiate at the remarriage of the divorced wife. The unpardonable sin, to use a manner of speaking, for the Naturalist is to let a taboo stand in the way of human happiness.

Naturalistic ethics, then, are hedonistic. The greatest happiness of the greatest number is the end and criterion of action. But the Naturalistic thinker does not believe that to obey each moment's passing whim brings the maximum of happiness either for the individual or for the group. He perceives that man is a highly complex organism, whose nature includes, besides the passions, a social instinct, an artistic instinct, and a reason. In the harmonizing of all these factors lies happiness. To give controlled expression to the passions and to sublimate them, to enjoy the pleasures of social intercourse and social approval, to do all things beautifully, and viewing all these things in their relation, to harmonize them by reason,—this is the art of living. Individuals here and there may attain degrees of happiness in spite of, even by the partial denial of one or another of these four elements. One may even kill the artistic impulse and yet live in moderate pleasure. But to deny the fundamental passions or the claims of society or of reason is to court destruction. On the other hand, to follow too eagerly the seductions of any one is to distort the growth of the organism, and evil results appear either in the later development of the individual or in the society which imitates him.

What does duty mean to the Naturalistic thinker? The root of the word supplies the key. Duty is simply the debt which the individual owes to society. If society gives him much,—wealth, power, education,—society has a right to demand much. If it gives him little, it should demand little. The product of the slum, the ten hour day, and the gin palace, owes nothing to society. Society's demand that he make himself an intelligent human being and refrain from burglary, rape, and murder is an impossible impertinence on the part of society; though society will doubtless continue to enforce the payment of loans which it never made. Duty, then, is simply a claim by society upon the individual.

Since, however, the individual craves happiness and the way to complete happiness does not lie in antagonism to society and wholesale infringement of social interests, it will always be expedient for him, no matter how little society has done for him, to work for social ends. On the whole, it pays to cash up when society sends in a bill.

What have the Naturalistic writers done for morality? We may admit at once that they have done more to throw down rotting conventions than to build up new moral and social laws. But the former service is not to be minimized. Zola built his ponderous engines of destruction up against the walls of clerical imposture and vice in many forms; Hardy battered at the undemocratic walls of Oxford colleges and laid bare the shallowness of revivalism; Wells in his Naturalistic period exploded the bladder of the patent medicine and the whole vast imposture of advertising; Galsworthy attacked a jingoistic patriotism, and enacted for us the farce-tragedy that is sometimes played under the title of "Justice"; and Masters in his *Spoon River Anthology* has pierced to the root of nearly every wrong and folly and sham that festers in the modern social body.

Greatest has been the service of the Naturalistic school to the cause of labor and the cause of women. There are Naturalists who have been indifferent or hostile to both, but they form a small minority. From Zola to Verhæren, from Arthur Morrison to Ernest Poole, the majority of Naturalists have insistently claimed for labor that right to the pursuit of happiness which is so tantalizingly offered in our revolutionary Declaration of Independence.

For women Naturalistic literature has done the enormous service of telling the truth and the whole truth about sex. Conventional literature gave glimpses of purple mountain peaks, encircled with clouds of gold; it told besides of a vast tract hidden by sulphurous vapors, where the unwary wanderer felt the earth's crust crumble beneath him, and sank into a seething cauldron. Conventional literature charted only the most obvious parts of this region: where the concealed dangers were perhaps greatest it gave no direction. It prescribed for women one entrance only, a gate called marriage, and gave many details of the route thither. But for all the tract that lay beyond or outside of it the details were meagre and sometimes false. Now all this region has been faithfully charted and published abroad. I venture to say the reading of half a dozen novels of the Naturalist school will exhibit more of the rationale of sex than any other body of literature ever written. Wifely subjection, the double standard of morals, prostitution, the seduction of working-girls, long sanctioned or condoned in much conventional literature, have received no quarter here. Among what school of writers are we to find one particular form of criminal folly so scarified as in *Ghosts, Damaged Goods*, and "Willard Fluke" of the *Spoon River Anthology*? Burke's famous generalization that no discoveries are to be made in morality breaks down before such a case. For while, doubtless, the ethical principle of which this is an application is as old as society, yet the perception of its application and the forcible presentation of the evil and its consequences, leading at last to recognition in our legislatures, is new and may be placed in large measure to the credit of the Naturalists.

Look at Tom Jones, the hero of what has been called by the conventionalists the greatest English novel. Tom is scarcely more than a slave of the moment's appetite. To be sure, he has too much sense of fair play ever to seduce women, but women have not the slightest difficulty in seducing him. The possibility that any of his adventures may have dire consequences is never faced, except when the sensational possibility of committing incest for a time horrifies him. This amiable gentleman, rather than soil his hands, resolves to sell himself to a lady in return for his keep. At last, he marries the chaste Sophia and rears a lusty brood. I should like to know what those who charge the Naturalistic novel with a predilection for feeble heroes and heroines have to say for this flabby protagonist of their greatest English novel. As a picture of random sex relations it betrays a facile optimism that no realist would be capable of.

Now by way of contrast let us look at a novel of the Naturalistic extreme,—*Sanine*, by Artzybasheff. The book is not a typical example of Naturalism, for the author derides the exercise of reason and humanitarian effort. But even though in these respects it falls short of the saner Naturalism characteristic of Zola, Ibsen, Hardy, and Masters, even though it glorifies sexual experiences as the greatest thing in the world, yet it is so far superior to *Tom Jones* as a criticism of life that it does not flinch from the tragic possibilities in such experience, and it makes a sharp differentiation between the putrescent koprophagy of the garrison town and the artistic

542

"A Defense of Naturalism"

expression of a healthy desire. While in my opinion the author does not sufficiently recognize that human nature has other summits than those reached in the culmination of the mightiest elemental passion, and does not realize the limitations which society has a right to place upon mating, yet in his demand that passion be beautiful as a Greek statue is beautiful, and in his recognition of the woman, not as a plaything but as a personality, he admits the place of the artistic and social impulses and justifies his classification as a Naturalist. Neither *Sanine* nor *Tom Jones* gives us anything like an exhaustive study of sex, but *Sanine* penetrates beneath the crust of convention; *Tom Jones* does not: *Sanine* has an idealism of sex; *Tom Jones* has none.

The larger Naturalism, then, founded upon the view of happiness as the goal of life, of the all round development of the individual as the way, and of the golden mean as the guiding principle, has been gradually making over our morality, ridding it of the relics of primitive taboos, and establishing it upon the demands of human nature.

But the third fundamental principle of Naturalism, determinism, is a stumbling block to many. The conventionalist is sure to object. "Granted that Naturalism has laid bare the ulcers and cancerous growths in the body of society, and has been as plain-spoken as the Old Testament or Shakespeare about things that are never mentioned in polite society, it destroys all incentive to salve those sores because it denies the freedom of the human will. It so impresses on us the thorough corruption of society that we feel that it is condemned to an eternity of disease. We see these men, as one reverend critic phrases it, 'concentrating attention on the shadiness and seaminess of life, exploiting sewers and cesspools, dabbling in beastliness and putrefaction, dragging to light the ghastly and gruesome, poring over the scurvy and unreportable side of things, bending in lingering analysis over every phase of mania and morbidity, going down into the swamps and marshes to watch the phosphorescence of decay and the jack-o'-lanterns that dance on rottenness'; and we conclude forsooth that if this is life, there is no hope for the world."

Naturalism may at once plead guilty to the doctrine of determinism: but it does not admit that the doctrine is inconsistent

543

with optimism of the future or that it robs man of incentive to moral action. The argument that optimism can be justified only by belief in an outside power pumping virtue into humanity by slow degrees is not convincing to anyone who realizes what is meant by potential energy. It is not necessary to believe that if a pound of radium could emit electrical energy for thousands of years it must be connected with a celestial dynamo. Neither is it necessary to believe that the human race is incapable of improving itself, however unhappy its present condition. No man can tell the potential energies latent in the human race, energies that may express themselves through reason, social feeling, and the love of beauty to make the superman. Determinism is no foe to an optimism of the future. Professor Santayana puts the theory admirably: "We are a part of the blind energy behind Nature, but by virtue of that energy we impose our purposes on that part of Nature which we constitute or control. We can turn from the stupefying contemplation of an alien universe to the building of our own house, knowing that, alien as it is, that universe has chanced to blow its energy also into our will and to allow itself to be partially dominated by our intelligence. Our mere existence and the modicum of success we have attained in society, science and art, are the living proofs of this human power. The exercise of this power is the task appointed for us by the indomitable promptings of our own spirit, a task in which we need not labor without hope."

The conventionalist pursues his point. "This all sounds mighty fine. But experience shows that a belief in the freedom of the will and moral responsibility is all that keeps us from wallowing in a sensual sty." As the Rev. Dr. S. Law Wilson puts it, "What, we ask, would be the effect of persuading the masses of mankind to believe that all the evil of which they are guilty is necessitated, and all the blame must be laid to the door of blood, or birth, or environment, or the tyranny of impulse? Indoctrinate the masses of our population with this pestiferous teaching, and there be some of us who shall not taste of death till we see the reign of moral anarchy and disintegration set in."

Now let us see what the real effect of acting upon the doctrine of free will is as contrasted with the effect of acting upon its denial. The theory of the freedom of the will, apart from its incompatibil-

544

ity with the generally accepted law of causation as implying an agent that, without being itself caused, initiates or causes action, involves the doctrine of complete responsibility. For if the will could have refrained just as well as not from the immoral act, no matter how powerful the pressure of heredity and environment, the man is absolutely responsible. His guilt has no extenuation. Punishment heavy and merciless is but his due. The only thing for society to do is impress upon him the enormity of his crime and urge him to repentance.

Now the old penal methods were in entire accord with this theory. Criminals were in prison to be punished. No treatment was too bad for them. The prison chaplain dilated on their essential wickedness, and told them that they had only themselves to thank for the plight in which they found themselves. If they would freely confess their guilt and accept the inspiration of religion, though society would not forgive them, God would. Now the results of such a logical application of the doctrine of moral responsibility to the criminal class are notorious. Everyone knows that the men who went to the penitentiary did not come out penitent, far less did they come out with any propensity to good. These men had learned what the doctrine of free will was in its application to them. Somehow there seems to have been a perverse conspiracy among criminals throughout the world to discredit the doctrine of free will and its corollary, moral responsibility.

What, however, are the results of determinism as applied to these same men? Mr. Osborne, whose work at Sing Sing we all know, has without knowing it acted upon this principle. He has brought into the prison pleasure and social life and a system of stimuli in the form of rewards. He has created a society where the criminal naturally did his duty to society because society had done something for him. He has taught the men trades and made openings for them in the world, and as a result he has made citizens out of outlaws. Of his success there can be no question. What here the individual could not do for himself, environment did for him. It mattered little whether he thought his will free or not: it responded inevitably to the right stimuli. Little need have we to fear the spread of the determinist theory among the masses, if only we have intelligence enough to practice as well as to preach it.

The conventionalist once more objects. "But turn away from life to your own Naturalistic novels. Are they not shrieking in our ears that man is feeble and doomed to failure? Are not their heroes and heroines weaklings who fall unresisting under the bludgeonings of Fate?"

Now it may well be admitted that the Naturalists, in order to show where the rocks lie, have usually represented their human barks as breaking upon the reefs rather than gliding smoothly into harbor. But in doing so the Naturalists have done only what every tragic writer has done. If the Mayor of Casterbridge or Madame Bovary fell through a combination of defects of character with adverse circumstances, what else may we say of Hamlet and Lear? Are we to despise Tess of the D'Urbervilles because though she often showed great strength of character, at certain crises of her fate timidity prevailed over purpose? When the conventionalists begin to call the great tragedies decadent on the same grounds that they condemn the Naturalistic novels; when they scorn Desdemona because when her husband suspected her she did not call up the Pinkerton's detective agency of Cyprus and probe the matter to the bottom, and because on her deathbed she did not wrestle courageously, but murmured merely, "A guiltless death I die," then we may listen patiently when they apply these standards to works not in the classic tradition. Until then some of us are inclined to believe that these critics unconsciously act upon the principle that any stick is good enough to beat a dog with.

Dr. Johnson once said that if he had no duties and no reference to futurity he would spend his life in driving briskly in a post-chaise with a pretty woman. To such a declaration the appropriate Johnsonian reply is, "You lie, sir." If the Doctor would permit of any further explanation, we might go on to say: "In the first place, Fate might refuse. Fate, in the form of the pretty woman, might politely decline the invitation. She might prefer other company to that of the hectoring oracle of the Mitre, the polysyllàbic proser of the *Rambler* papers: she might object to being referred to as an unidea-ed girl. In the second place, if the woman found it agreeable, the Doctor himself would soon have found it disagreeable. It may be an impertinence to presume that we know the Doctor better than he knew himself, but Boswell has made the claim possible.

"A Defense of Naturalism"

Now the Doctor had certain hereditary traits that would never have been satisfied for long with sitting in a post-chaise beside a pretty woman. He had too active a brain, he was too much of a clubman, and, as a matter of fact, despite all his complaints of indolence, he had an instinct for work. Moreover, it is difficult to imagine that Samuel Johnson would have let the American Revolution go by without leaping from the post-chaise and scratching off *Taxation No Tyranny*. At the very least, he would have had to stop for a moment, stretch his limbs, and perhaps roll down a hill for the fun of it. Without disparaging the worthy Doctor's sincerity, one may say that, granted his pecuniary and other restrictions, he would have lived much the same life if he had had no theories of duty beyond what every social being holds, and no more reference to futurity than the desire that the rest of life contain as much happiness as he could put into it.

Moreover, one cannot help thinking that if Doctor Johnson had exerted his great influence, not as a conventionalist and Tory, but as a Naturalist and democrat, the whole course of events in Europe might have been changed. His posthumous power might have offset the Bourbonism of Burke; England might not have thrown her strength on the side of that Holy Alliance of Prussian, Austrian, and Russian despotisms; the contagion of a liberal England and France might have liberalized Europe; and the world might have been made safe for democracy a hundred years ago. But it was not to be.

There are people who see in Naturalism the origin of this war and in the triumph of the Allies the vindication of Providence. Such a view is only possible through a misconception of the facts. The insane policies of German imperialism found ready support throughout the ranks of the German supernaturalists, and palliation in that inviolate citadel of supernaturalism, the Vatican. On the other hand, the bitterest and most courageous of the foes of German imperialism were a small group of atheistic socialists in Germany, whose creed was the creed of Naturalism. As for the victory of the Allies I can see nothing but a confirmation of the blunt statement erroneously attributed to Napoleon that God is always on the side of the heaviest battalions. The feeble succor afforded by St. Michael at Mons hardly leads one to rely much upon the heav-

enly powers for aid. The despairing prayers of millions went unheeded until material force came to the aid of spiritual yearnings.
One who can believe in supernaturalism after this war possesses,
indeed, a faith which serves as an evidence of things not seen.
Let him have his angels of Mons and be happy. But the rest
of us, in this time momentous and critical as scarcely any other
time in the world's history, can hardly afford to base our hopes for
the future on any efforts but our own, or afford to direct those
efforts by any but Naturalistic principles: for these must bring
happiness in their wake, or *ipso facto* cease to be the principles of
Naturalism.

On the Falsity of Realism*

By Marcel Proust

MARCEL PROUST (1871-1922) was a novelist of essentially a single work, the vast and daedal *A la recherche du temps perdu* (*Remembrance of Things Past*), 1913-1927. Impressionistic, poetic, and above all concerned with inner states, this work is the very antithesis of what the realists sought, and its author is therefore one of the great innovators of the twentieth century.

Already in his critical essay "Contre Sainte-Beuve" Proust revealed his anti-realistic attitude. He begins the essay by asserting that the value of the intellect becomes visibly less with the passage of each day, since it cannot restore the past to us, which is the "private essence of ourselves" alongside of which the truths of the intellect seem scarcely to contain any reality. Proust's approach deserts the logical, analytic process of the great nineteenth-century novelists and strives for some sort of synthetic recreation of essences, of an absolute which is concealed under the transitory world of appearances, which must be disengaged from them and ultimately given body as a work of art. One of the consequences of this position is the dissolution of personality in the characters of a novel. Proust sees man as many, not one; knowledge of another person is always relative; social forms, which are aggregations of people, are therefore in flux as well. What remains is those moments of truth—out of time—which are all that is truly real.

The passage here presented occurs toward the end of the novel when the narrator, who, after many years, has occasion to visit the Duke de Guermantes' house, undergoes three sudden flashes of involuntary memory occasioned by stepping on uneven paving stones, by the sound of a spoon against a glass, and by the starched texture of a napkin. Enraptured by this experience, which he had undergone long before in the famous episode of the madeleine and the cup of tea, he attempts to understand the nature of the true reality and formulates a highly particular but sweepingly anti-realistic credo. The passage ends with the flat assertion that "Nothing takes us further away from what we have perceived in reality" than a cinematographic view of things, that the literature called realistic is the one "farthest removed from reality, the one which impoverishes and saddens us the most. . . ."

* Proust, Marcel, *Remembrance of Things Past* II: pp. 993-1004, New York, Random House, 1932 (copyright renewed 1959). The translation is by Frederick A. Blossom and is reprinted by permission of Random House, Inc., and Chatto & Windus Ltd., publishers of the English translation of Proust in the British Commonwealth.

. . . THE piece they were playing was likely to finish at any moment and I be obliged to enter the salon. Therefore I made an effort to try as quickly as possible to see clearly into the nature of the identical pleasures I had just felt three separate times within a few minutes, and then to draw from them the lesson they had to give. The great difference there is between the actual impression we received from something and the artificial impression we create for ourselves when we endeavour by an effort of the will to bring the object before us again, I did not pause to consider; remembering only too well the comparative indifference with which Swann used to be able to speak of the period in his life when he was loved (because this expression suggested something so different to him) and the sudden pain caused him by Vinteuil's little phrase, which brought to mind those days themselves just as he had felt them, I understood too clearly that the sensation of the uneven flagstones, the stiffness of the napkin and the savour of the *madeleine* had awakened in me something that had no relation to what I used to endeavour to recall to mind about Venice, Balbec, Combray with the aid of a colourless, undistinguishing memory. And I understood how one can come to judge life to be mediocre, when at certain times it seems so beautiful, because this judgment and this disparaging conclusion are based on something entirely different from life itself, on mental images which have retained no trace of life. At the most, I noted incidentally that the difference between each of these real impressions and the corresponding artificial one—differences which explain why an even-toned painting of life cannot be a true likeness—was probably due to this cause, namely, that the slightest word we have spoken or the most insignificant gesture we have made at a certain moment in our life was surrounded and illumined by things that logically had no relation to it and were separated from it by our intelligence, which had no need of them for reasoning purposes; and yet, in the midst of these irrelevant objects—here, the rosy glow of eventide on the flower-covered wall of a rustic restaurant, the feeling of hunger, the yearning for women, the pleasant sensation of luxury; there, blue volutes of the morning sea, wrapped in spirals around strains of music which only partly emerge, like mermaids' shoulders—the most insignificant gesture, the simplest act remain enclosed, as it were, in a thousand sealed jars, each filled with things of an absolutely different colour, odour and temperature. Furthermore, these jars, ranged along the topmost levels of our bygone years—years during which we have been constantly changing, if only in our dreams and thoughts—stand at very different altitudes and give us the impression of strangely varied atmospheres. It is true that we have gone through these changes imperceptibly, but between our present state and the memory that suddenly comes back to us, just as between two recollections of different years, places or hours, there is such a wide difference that that fact alone, regardless even of any specific individuality, would suffice to make comparison between them impossible. Yes, if, thanks to our ability to forget, a past recollection has been able to avoid any tie, any link with the present moment, if it has remained in its own place and time, if it has kept its distance, its isolation in the depths of a valley or on the tip of a moutain peak, it suddenly brings us a breath of fresh air—refreshing just because we have breathed it once before—of that purer air which the poets have vainly tried to establish in Paradise, whereas it could not convey that profound sensation of renewal if it had not already been breathed, for the only true paradise is always the paradise we have lost. And, in passing, I noted that the work of art which I already felt myself prepared to undertake, but without my having made any conscious resolution to that effect, would present great difficulties. For I would be obliged to execute the different parts of it in somewhat different mediums. The medium suitable for recalling mornings by the sea would be very different from that required to describe afternoons in Venice, a medium distinct and new, of a very special transparence and sonority, compact, refreshing and rosy-hued. And then, different again would be the medium, if I essayed to depict the evenings at Rivebelle in the dining-room opening on the garden, when the heat seemed to disintegrate, to condense and settle to the ground, while the falling twilight still tinted the roses on the wall of the restaurant and the sky still glowed with the pastel tints of dying day. But I passed quickly over all that, under the more imperious urge which I felt to seek the reason for this feeling of happiness and the air of certainty with which it came over me, a search I had hitherto postponed. I caught an inkling of this reason when I compared these various happy impressions with one another and found that they had this in common, namely, that I felt them as if they were occurring simultaneously in the present moment and in some distant past, which the sound of the spoon against the plate, or the unevenness of the flagstones, or the peculiar savour of the *madeleine* even went so far as to make coincide with the present, leaving me uncertain in which period I was. In truth, the person within me who was at that moment enjoying this impression enjoyed in it the qualities it possessed which were common to both an earlier day and the present moment, qualities which were independent of all considerations of time; and this person came into play only when, by this process of identifying the past with the present, he could find himself in the only environment in which he could live and enjoy the essence of things, that is to say, entirely outside of time. That explained why my apprehensiveness of death vanished the moment I instinctively recognised the savour of the little *madeleine*, because at that moment the person within me was a timeless person, consequently unconcerned with the vicissitudes of the future. That person had never come to me, never manifested himself, except independently of all immediate activity, all immediate enjoyment, whenever the miracle of a resemblance with things past enabled me to escape out of the present. He alone had the power to make me recapture bygone days, times past, which had always balked the efforts of my memory and my intelligence.

And perhaps a moment ago, when I considered that Bergotte had been mistaken in speaking of the satisfactions of the intellectual life, this was because at that time I applied the term "intellectual life" to logical processes of reasoning which had no connection with it or with what was then taking place within me—just as the reason I found society and even life tiresome was because I appraised them on the basis of false impressions of the past, whereas in reality I had now such an eager desire to live that an actual moment from the past had just been revived within me on three distinct occasions.

Merely a moment from the past? Much more than that, perhaps; something which, common to both past and present, is far more essential than either.

On the Falsity of Realism

How many times in the course of my life had I been disappointed by reality because, at the time I was observing it, my imagination, the only organ with which I could enjoy beauty, was not able to function, by virtue of the inexorable law which decrees that only that which is absent can be imagined. And now suddenly the operation of this harsh law was neutralised, suspended, by a miraculous expedient of nature by which a sensation—the sound of the spoon and that of the hammer, a similar unevenness in two paving stones—was reflected both in the past (which made it possible for my imagination to take pleasure in it) and in the present, the physical stimulus of the sound or the contact with the stones adding to the dreams of the imagination that which they usually lack, the idea of existence—and this subterfuge made it possible for the being within me to seize, isolate, immobilise for the duration of a lightning flash what it never apprehends, namely, a fragment of time in its pure state. The being that was called to life again in me when, with such a thrill of joy, I heard the sound that characterises both a spoon touching a plate and a hammer striking a car wheel, or when I felt under foot the unevenness of the pavement in the court of the Guermantes residence, similar to that in the baptistry of Saint Mark's, draws its sustenance only from the essence of things, in that alone does it find its nourishment and its delight. It languishes in the contemplation of the present, where the senses cannot furnish this essential substance, or in the study of the past, rendered barren for it by the intelligence, or while awaiting a future which the will constructs out of fragments of the past and the present from which it has withdrawn still more of their reality, retaining only that part of them which is suited to the utilitarian, narrowly human purpose for which it designs them. But let a sound already heard or an odour caught in bygone years be sensed anew, simultaneously in the present and the past, real without being of the present moment, ideal but not abstract, and immediately the permanent essence of things, usually concealed, is set free and our true self, which had long seemed dead but was not dead in other ways, awakes, takes on fresh life as it receives the celestial nourishment brought to it. A single minute released from the chronological order of time has re-created in us the human being similarly released, in order that he may sense that minute.

And one comprehends readily how such a one can be confident in his joy; even though the mere taste of a *madeleine* does not seem to contain logical justification for this joy, it is easy to understand that the word "death" should have no meaning for him; situated outside the scope of time, what could he fear from the future?

But this illusion, which brought close to me a moment from the past, incompatible with the present, never lasted any length of time. One can, it is true, prolong the visions evoked by voluntary recollection, which do not engage more of our faculties than flipping the pages of a picture book. Thus, for example, on that day long gone by, when I was to call for the first time on the Princesse de Guermantes, from the sun-bathed court of our Paris house I had idly called up before me at will, now the Place de l'Eglise at Combray, now the beach at Balbec, very much as I might have illustrated the kind of day it was by turning the pages of a book of watercolour sketches made in the different places I had visited, saying to myself, with the selfish pleasure of a collector, as I thus catalogued the illustrations in my memory, "Just the same, I have seen some beautiful things in my life!" At that time, no doubt my memory asserted the differences between the sensations, but all it did was to combine homogeneous elements. Such had not been the case, however, with the three memories of the past which had just come over me, from which, instead of conceiving a more flattering idea of my inner self, I had on the contrary almost come to doubt the present reality of this self. Just as on the day when I had dipped the *madeleine* in the hot tea, at the very heart of the place where I happened to be (whether, as then, it was my room in Paris or, as to-day, at this very moment, the library of the Prince de Guermantes or, a moment ago, the court in front of the residence) there had been within me, radiating outward around me from a small zone, a sensation—the taste of a *madeleine* dipped in tea, a metallic sound, the feeling of uneven steps—which was common both to the place where I happened to be and also to some other place—the bedroom of my Aunt Léonie, a railway carriage, the baptistry of Saint Mark's. And at the moment I was reasoning thus, the shrill noise of a hot-water pipe, exactly like the long blasts we sometimes heard of a summer evening from pleasure boats off Balbec, made

On the Falsity of Realism

me feel (as I had already felt once before in a large restaurant in Paris at the sight of the luxurious dining-room, half empty, hot and summery) much more than merely a sensation similar to the one I felt at Balbec toward the end of one afternoon when, the tables already covered with their linen and silverware, the vast windows wide open on the embankment without a single interruption, a single intervening plenum of glass or stone, and the sun slowly setting over the ocean, where boats were beginning to move about, I could join Albertine and her friends, strolling on the embankment, by merely stepping over the wooden window frame, scarcely higher than my ankle, in the groove of which they had slid back the sectional windows in order to ventilate the hotel. Moreover, it was not merely an echo or a duplication of a past sensation which the sound of the hot-water pipe had just made me experience, but that very sensation itself. In that case, as in all the preceding ones, the sensation common to both occasions had sought to re-create about itself the former setting, while the present setting, which was occupying its space, opposed with all the resistance of its mass this invasion of a Paris residence by a Normandy beach or a railway embankment. The dining-room by the sea at Balbec, with its damask linen laid like altar cloths to receive the setting of the sun, had sought to shatter the solidity of the Guermantes mansion and force open its doors, and it had for an instant made the sofas rock about me, as it had, on another day, the tables in a Paris restaurant. Always, in these resurrections of the past, the distant place, evoked about the common sensation, had grappled for a moment, like a wrestler, with the present scene. The latter had always been the victor but it was ever the vanquished that seemed to me the more beautiful, so that I was in a state of ecstasy as I stood on the uneven pavement—as I had been when I sat before the cup of tea—seeking to perpetuate as soon as they appeared, or to bring back to mind after they had escaped me, that Combray, that Balbec, that Venice which rose out.of the past and invaded the very heart of these places in the present (which, however, the past can permeate) only to be forced to retreat and abandon me. And if the present scene had not been immediately victorious, I believe I should have fainted; for, during the instant that they last, these resurrections of the past are so

complete that they do not merely oblige our eyes to become oblivious to the room before them and contemplate instead the rising
tide or the railway track edged with trees; they also force our
nostrils to inhale the air of places which are, however, far remote,
constrain our will to choose between the various plans they lay
before us, compel our entire being to believe itself surrounded by
them, or at least to vacillate between them and the present scenes,
bewildered by an uncertainty similar to that which one sometimes
experiences before an ineffable vision at the moment of losing
consciousness in sleep.

Thus it was that what the being three and even four times revived within me had just enjoyed was perhaps, it is true, fragments of existence removed outside the realm of time, but this
contemplation, although part of eternity, was transitory. And yet
I felt that the pleasure it had bestowed on me at rare intervals
in my life was the only one that was fecund and real. Is not the indication of the unreality of the others sufficiently evident either
in their inability to satisfy us—as, for example, social pleasures,
which at best produce the discomfort caused by partaking of
wretched food; or friendship, which is a delusion, because, for
whatever moral reasons he may do it, the artist who gives up an
hour of work for an hour's conversation with a friend knows that
he is sacrificing a reality for something which is non-existent
(friends appearing to be such only thanks to that gentle madness
from which we suffer throughout our lives and to which we give
way, though, in the depth of our intelligence, we know it to be
the error of a mind unbalanced enough even to believe the chairs
and tables alive and to carry on a conversation with them)—or in
the despondency that follows whatever satisfaction they may give,
like the sadness I felt the day I was introduced to Albertine because I had gone to that trouble (very slight, it is true) to accomplish something—making a young girl's acquaintance—which
seemed unimportant now only because I had accomplished it?
Even a profounder pleasure, such as I might have experienced
when I was in love with Albertine, was realised only inversely by
the distress I felt when she was not there, for, whenever I was
certain she was coming, like the day she returned from the Troca-
déro, it seemed to me I experienced only a vague ennui; whereas

On the Falsity of Realism

I became more and more exalted as I analysed more and more deeply the sound of the spoon against the plate or the taste of the herb tea, with an ever increasing joy which had transported into my room the bedroom of my Aunt Léonie and, in its wake, all Combray and the two walks, Guermantes way and Méséglise way.

And so I was decided to consecrate myself to this study of the essence of things, to establish its true nature, but how should I do this, by what means? It is true that, when the stiffness of the napkin called up Balbec before me and for a moment caressed my imagination not only with a mental picture of the sea as it was that morning long ago, but also with the odour of the room, the force of the wind, the desire for luncheon, the hesitation which walk to choose—all of that attached to the sensation of the open sea, like the wings of a water wheel in its dizzy course; and again, when the unevenness of the two paving stones extended in every direction and all dimensions the bare and barren impressions I had of Venice and Saint Mark's and likewise all the sensations I had experienced there, connecting the *piazza* with the church, the *imbarcadero* with the *piazza*, the canal with the *imbarcadero* and, with all that the eyes see, that world of desires which is perceived only with the mind—it is true that at those moments I was tempted —if not, on account of the season, to go and idly glide over the waters of Venice, which I associated more especially with the springtime—at any rate to return to Balbec. But I did not tarry an instant with this idea; not only did I know that distant places were not what was suggested to me by the names they bore when I imagined them to myself. (It was now almost exclusively in my dreams, while sleeping, that a place would spread itself out before me composed of pure matter, entirely distinct from the common things one sees and touches.) But even with regard to those mental images of another sort, those of memory, I knew that I had not found the beauty of Balbec when I went there, and even the beauty it had left me, that of memory, was no longer the same as that which I found on my second visit there. I had too often experienced the impossibility of discovering in physical form what was in the depths of my being. It was not in the Piazza San Marco, any more than it had been on my second visit to Balbec or on my return to Tansonville to see Gilberte, that I would recapture past Time, and the journey which was merely suggested to me once more by the illusion that these old impressions existed outside myself, at the corner of a certain square, could not be the means I was seeking. I did not want to follow another false trail, for the important thing for me was at last to determine whether it was really possible to attain what, because of my constant disappointment in places and persons, I had believed to be unrealisable (although at one time the concert piece by Vinteuil had seemed to tell me the opposite). Therefore I was not going to attempt another experiment along the path which I had long known led nowhere. Impressions such as those which I was endeavouring to analyse and define could not fail to vanish away at the contact of a material enjoyment that was unable to bring them into existence. The only way to get more joy out of them was to try to know them more completely at the spot where they were to be found, namely, within myself, and to clarify them to their lowest depths. I had not been able to grasp the happiness at Balbec any more than I had that of living with Albertine, as it had not been perceptible to me until the occasion had come and gone. And if I recapitulated the disappointments in my life, as far as it had been lived, which led me to believe that its real essence must lie somewhere else than in action, and compared different disappointments, but not in a haphazard manner or merely following the vicissitudes of my existence, I came to realise clearly that disappointment in a journey and disappointment in a love affair were not different in themselves but merely the different aspects assumed in varying situations by our inability to find our real selves in physical enjoyment or material activity. And thinking over again that timeless joy caused by the sound of the spoon or the taste of the *madeleine*, I said to myself, "Was that the happiness suggested by the little phrase of the sonata to Swann, who made the mistake of confusing it with the pleasure of love and was unable to find it in artistic creation—that happiness which I came to sense dimly was even farther removed from everything earthly than the little phrase of the sonata had suggested, when I caught the red, mysterious call of that septet which Swann had never known, having died, like so many others, before the truth intended for them had been revealed?" But it would have availed him nothing in any case, for that phrase may, indeed, have been able to symbolise a call, but it could not have created talents and made of Swann the writer he never was. However, after having meditated a short while over these resurrections of past memories, I became aware that in another way obscure impressions had sometimes, even as far back as Combray along the Guermantes way, engaged my thoughts after the manner of those subjective recollections, but these others concealed within themselves, not a sensation of bygone days, but a new truth, a priceless image, which I sought to discover by efforts like those one makes to recall something forgotten, as if our most beautiful ideas were like musical airs that would come back to us without our ever having heard them and which we would make an effort to seize and transcribe. I remembered with pleasure, because it shewed me that I was already the same then as now and it was an indication of a fundamental trait of my nature (but also with sadness when I reflected that I had made no progress since then) that even when I was at Combray, I used to hold attentively before my mind some object that had forced itself upon my attention— a cloud, a triangle, a steeple, a flower, a pebble—because I felt there might be underneath these signs something quite different which I ought to try to discover, a thought which they transcribed after the manner of those hieroglyphics which one might think represented only material objects. Most assuredly this deciphering was difficult but it alone offered some truth to be read. For the truths that the intelligence grasps directly and openly in the full-lighted world are somehow less profound, less indispensable than those which life has communicated to us without our knowledge through the form of impressions, material because they have come to us through our senses, but the inner meaning of which we can discern. In short, in this case as in the other, whether objective impressions such as I had received from the sight of the spires of Martinville, or subjective memories like the unevenness of the two steps or the taste of the *madeleine*, I must try to interpret the sensations as the indications of corresponding laws and ideas; I must try to think, that is to say, bring out of the obscurity what I had felt, and convert it into a spiritual equivalent. Now this method, which seemed to me the only one, what was it other than to create a work of art? And already the consequences came crowding into my mind; for, whether it was subjective memories of the type of the sound made by the spoon or the taste of the *madeleine*, or those truths recorded with the aid of external objects, the significance of which I sought to find within my head, where, jumbled together, steeples, wild flowers, they made up a complicated, flower-bedecked medley, their first characteristic was that I was not free to choose them but they came to my mind pell-mell. And I felt that that must surely be the hall mark of their genuineness. I had not set out to seek the two paving stones in the court which I struck my foot against. But it was precisely the fortuitous, unavoidable way in which I had come upon the sensation that guaranteed the truth of a past which that sensation revived and of the mental images it released, since we feel its effort to come up into the light and also the thrill of recapturing reality. That sensation is the guarantee of the truth of the entire picture composed of contemporary impressions which the sensation brings in its train, with that unerring proportion of light and shadow, emphasis and omission, remembrance and oblivion, which conscious memory and observation will never know.

To read the subjective book of these strange signs (signs standing out boldly, it seemed, which my conscious mind, as it explored my unconscious self, went searching for, stumbled against and passed around, like a diver groping his way), no one could help me with any rule, for the reading of that book is a creative act in which no one can stand in our stead, or even collaborate with us. And therefore how many there are who shrink from writing it; how many tasks are undertaken in order to avoid that one! Each happening, the Dreyfus case, the war, supplied fresh excuses to the writers for not deciphering that book—they wished to assure the triumph of right, rebuild the moral unity of the nation, and they had no time to think of literature. But these were only excuses; they had no talent, that is to say, no instinct, or had lost what they formerly had. For instinct dictates the duty to be done and intelligence supplies the excuses for evading it. But in art excuses count for nothing; good intentions are of no avail; the artist must at every instant heed his instinct; so that art is the most real of all things, the sternest school in life and truly the

On the Falsity of Realism

Last Judgment. This book, the most difficult of all to decipher, is also the only one dictated to us by reality, the only one the "imprinting" of which on our consciousness was done by reality itself. No matter what idea life may have implanted within us, its material representation, the outline of the impression it has made upon us, is always the guarantee of its indispensable truth. The ideas formed by pure intellect have only a logical truth, a potential truth; the selection of them is an arbitrary act. The book written in symbolic characters not traced by us is our only book. Not that the ideas we form ourselves may not be logically correct, but we do not know whether they are true. Only the subjective impression, however inferior the material may seem to be and however improbable the outline, is a criterion of truth and for that reason it alone merits being apprehended by the mind, for it alone is able, if the mind can extract this truth, to lead the mind to a greater perfection and impart to it a pure joy. The subjective impression is for the writer what experimentation is for the scientist, but with this difference, that with the scientist the work of the intelligence precedes, and with the writer it comes afterwards. Anything we have not had to decipher and clarify by our own personal effort, anything that was clear before we intervened, is not our own. Nothing comes from ourselves but that which we draw out of the obscurity within us and which is unknown to others. And since art is a faithful recomposing of life, around these truths that one has attained within oneself there floats an atmosphere of poetry, the sweetness of a mystery, which is merely the semi-darkness through which we have come. An oblique ray of the setting sun instantly recalls to me a period in my early childhood that I had never thought of since—when my Aunt Léonie had an illness which Dr. Percepied feared might be typhoid fever, so they moved me for a week into the little room Eulalie had on the Place de l'Eglise, which had only a grass rug on the floor and a muslin curtain at the window and always hummed with a sunshine I was not accustomed to. And as I saw how the remembrance of that little room of a former servant suddenly added to my past life a long stretch of time so different from the rest and so delightful, I thought by contrast of the utter nullity of the impressions that the most sumptuous affairs in the most princely mansions had contributed to my life. The only slightly unpleasant thing about that room of Eulalie's was that, owing to the nearness of the railway bridge, you could hear the shrieking whistles of the trains at night. But since I knew that these cries came from machines under control, I was not frightened, as I might have been in a prehistoric age by the howlings of some nearby mammoth in his free and unregulated wanderings.

Thus I had already come to the conclusion that we are not at all free in the presence of the work of art to be created, that we do not do it as we ourselves please, but that it existed prior to us and we should seek to discover it as we would a natural law because it is both necessary and hidden. But when art enabled us to make this discovery, was it not disclosing to us, after all, what we ought to hold most precious but what usually remains forever unknown to us, our true life, reality as we have felt it, so different from what we think that we are filled with great happiness when chance brings back to us the true remembrance of it? I convinced myself of this by the falseness of even the art that calls itself "realist," which would not be so untruthful if we had not formed in life the habit of giving to our sensations an outward expression so different from them, which after a short while we take for reality itself. I realised that I would not have to trouble myself about the various literary theories that had disturbed me for a time, more especially those the critics developed at the time of the Dreyfus case and revived during the war, which sought to "make the artist come out of his ivory tower," scorn frivolous or sentimental subjects, depict great working-class movements and, if not huge crowds, at any rate no more insignificant idlers ("I confess that the portrayal of these useless persons is of no particular interest to me," Bloch said) but high-minded intellectuals or heroes. Moreover, leaving to one side for the present the consideration of their logical content, these theories seemed to me a proof of inferiority on the part of those who advanced them, just as a really well bred child, hearing some people with whom he has been sent to have luncheon say, "We speak right out, we are frank," feels that this remark indicates a moral quality inferior to the good deed, pure and simple, which says nothing. True art has no use for so many proclamations and is produced in silence. Moreover, those who

theorised thus used ready-made expressions which bore a marked
resemblance to the very ones they branded as imbecile. And perhaps it is more by the quality of the language used than by the
aesthetic principles observed that one can determine to what level
an intellectual or moral effort has been carried. But inversely, this
quality of language which the theoreticians believe they can disregard (and even when it comes to studying the laws of character,
one can do this quite as well on a frivolous as a serious subject,
just as a prosecutor can study the laws of anatomy precisely as
well on the body of an imbecile as on that of a man of talent, for
the great moral laws, like those governing the circulation of the
blood or renal elimination, vary but little with the intellectual
worth of the individual) is readily believed by those who admire
these theoreticians not to be a proof of intellectual value, which
they cannot infer from the beauty of an image and can discern
only if they see it expressed in direct form. From this comes the
vulgar temptation for the writer to produce intellectual works. A
grave lack of fine feeling! A book in which there are theories is
like an article from which the price mark has not been removed.
And even at that, a price mark merely expresses value, whereas
in literature logical reasoning lessens it. We reason, that is to say,
we wander about aimlessly, whenever we lack the power to compel ourselves to pass a subjective impression through all the successive stages that shall finally lead to its comprehension and definition and to the expression of its reality. The reality to be expressed, I now understood, was to be found, not in the outward
appearance of the subject, but in the extent to which this impression
had penetrated to a depth where that appearance was of little importance, as was symbolised by that sound of a spoon against a
plate, that starchy stiffness of the napkin, both of more priceless
value for my spiritual renewal than any number of conversations
on humanitarianism, patriotism or internationalism. "No more
style!" I had heard them say in those earlier days. "No more
literature! Give us life!" One may imagine how extensively even
the simple theories of M. de Norpois "against the flute-players"
had blossomed forth again since the beginning of the war. For
everyone who, having no artistic sense—that is to say, no submission to subjective reality—may have the knack of reasoning about

art till doomsday, especially if he be, in addition, a diplomat or financier in contact with the "realities" of the present day, is only too ready to believe that literature is an intellectual game which is destined to be gradually abandoned as time goes on. Some wished the novel to be a sort of cinematographic parade. This conception was absurd. In reality, nothing is farther removed than this cinematographic view from what we have perceived.*

* A bit further on (p. 1009) Proust reiterates his dissatisfaction with realistic literature in these terms:

". . . The literature that is satisfied merely to 'describe things,' to furnish a miserable listing of their lines and surfaces, is, notwithstanding its pretensions to realism, the farthest removed from reality, the one that most impoverishes and saddens us, even though it speak of nought but glory and greatness, for it sharply cuts off all communication of our present self with the past, the essence of which the objects preserve, and with the future, in which they stimulate us to enjoy the past again. But there was more than that, I reflected. If reality were merely that by-product of existence, so to speak, approximately identical for everybody—because, when we say 'bad weather, war, cab-stand, brightly lighted restaurant, garden in bloom,' everyone knows what we mean—if reality were that, then naturally a sort of cinematographic film of these things would be enough and the 'style' or the 'literature' that departed from their simple theme would be an artificial *hors d'oeuvre*."

"Conclusions and Applications"*

By Arthur McDowall

ARTHUR MCDOWALL, then a fellow of All Souls College, Oxford, brought out what is perhaps the last full-length treatment of modern realism in English in 1918. There have been other more limited studies since that time, and Erich Auerbach's *Mimesis* is a work of magnitude which covers the whole sweep of western literature. McDowall, however, was a philosopher, and his title, *Realism: A Study in Art and Thought*, is of comprehensive interest to students of literature, the plastic arts, and philosophy.

He points out in his preface that so little has been done, at least in English, to discover the theory of realism in art, and its connection, if any, with realism in thinking, that such an inquiry is overdue. He finds that "A vivid reflection of the world we know and live in, from every side that our intuition or experience can grasp, has been and is increasingly the characteristic of modern art, so far as it deals with representation. The range of matter for representation has widened; the depth of what it is possible to represent has been increased." Granting the many claims for importance of realistic thought and art, he is yet somewhat doubtful about its ultimate value: "Realism in thought rejects many interesting and enticing explanations of the universe, just as realism in art leaves on one side many fruitful types of creation."

This author makes a sharp distinction between realism and naturalism, and between external and psychological realism. His preference is for the formula which includes the most of experience and his most scathing words are for what he calls "The Fallacy of Naturalism," the title of one of the chapters, though not the most original one. The selection here printed is the concluding chapter; it attempts both to sum up and to explore some of the semantic implications of the term realism.

◇◇

REALISM, whether as philosophy or art, will seem to many to be wanting in the chief conditions of great art and thinking—the power of a ruling sentiment or idea and the true freedom of creation. It has a fatal opposition to romanticism, and to the idealistic thought which is often a romance in thinking.

* McDowall, Arthur, *Realism: A Study in Art and Thought*, pp. 267-294; London, Constable and Company Ltd, 1918. Reprinted by permission of the publisher.

Romance casts a spell in art, and we all yield to it from time to time, and for some it is the only thing which is profoundly moving. It is the sense of escape which thrills us. Not an escape, always, from ourselves, but from what limits or fetters us. In romance the self may be unfolded, spread out to dream over, free from the pressure of material things. It can turn them to Chopin's music, or in poetry to Lamartine's cadences, or shape itself into bizarre and haunting images like Poe's. In such a mood it

> "may not hope from outward form to win
> The passion and the life, whose fountains are within."

But there are moments when the mind tires of its own kingdom, and desires one that is palpable, only more glorious than the world it knows. It feels an impulse towards the rich and strange. So Flaubert, sitting in his study, yearned for the rhythmical tread of camels, pointed Chinese roofs, and a tiger's eyes glittering through the jungle. So Coleridge discovered the "sunny pleasure dome with caves of ice"; a symbol of the splendours which we half imagine and half remember from a dream. This romantic beauty of imagined forms sets us free from our surroundings, and has been the secret, or half the secret, of the fascination of the Russian ballet.

Another mood—which some hold to be the very core of the romantic feeling—sets us free even from ourselves. This is the movement towards the vague and the infinite, which Rousseau, still more Wordsworth, rediscovered in unwonted places. It has led the modern man, as long before it led his primitive fathers, on to mountain-tops and among solitary wastes. There, in the "unfrequented haunts of shepherds and abodes of unearthly calm," the self can be transcended and forgotten. This vision is akin to what Nietzsche calls the Dionysiac view of things, the source of music and tragedy. Lastly, there is the mood of the great storytellers. Dreaming, ecstasy, and contemplation, passionate or passionless, are forsaken for the delight of action. In the spirit of that delight, under the spell of adventure, the old sagas were made; and the spirit descends afresh on those who, like Scott or Dumas or Stevenson, love the story for its own sake, for the unrolling of swift deeds and strange events and the brilliant words which tell them. Sometimes it is the pure revel of adventure, and sometimes it has a great suggestiveness, as when the curtain of *Redgauntlet* rises on the crimson sunset, the wet sands of Solway, and the horsemen with salmon spears galloping to and fro. These romances, we are in the habit of saying, "take us out of ourselves"; perhaps they do; but what is more certain is that we escape by means of them from all known surroundings, and slake, vicariously, our thirst for change and action.

Art has other forms of the ruling sentiment even beyond the limits of romanticism. There is, for instance, a type of inspiration which is more defined, and yet is too elusive to be confused with a system. The novels of Thomas Hardy have an undercurrent of this kind. Rich as they are in realistic detail and unflinching in their candour, they do not leave the impression of a thoroughly realistic art. That feeling, curiously enough, is left rather by his poems, with their faithful perpetuation of chance moments. But both novels and poems give a sense of "something far more deeply interfused." So far as this "something" is born of an understanding sympathy with nature, it might certainly be the feat of a higher realism to have placed human things and natural things—for the first time in the novel's history—on an equal plane of interest. But there is more than that. It would be too harsh an emphasis to describe as a philosophy the point of view revealed not only in chance sentences but in the whole structure of *The Return of the Native* and *The Mayor of Casterbridge*, given again with a different implication in *Tess* and *Jude*, and repeated almost avowedly in so many of the poems. Yet all this art is quickened by a philosophic impulse; it is as near to incarnate thinking as a great artist can safely go. It shows a world of people and events fashioned in harmony with a pervading view of things. We do not expect to find in this world a perfect correspondence with the actual. It is rather the embodiment, in Mr. Hardy's words, of "a series of personal seemings or impressions"; too deeply tinged with a certain colour to be realistic, or even merely personal, and reaching, by its completeness, a kind of universal truth.

There are parallels to almost all these types of art in the world of thinking, and all of them seem to lie outside the borders of realism. The romantic art which delights to exhibit and contemplate the self finds an analogue in the philosophical theories which centre round the idea of self-realisation. For these theories, while aiming at universal truth, draw everything within the circle of the mind and its thoughts. It is the self, and not the things that lie beyond it, which is the real interest; and the universe is only a duplication of it, since it proves to be a second Self, enlarged and glorified. Certainly these theories are based generally on reason, while personal romance luxuriates, as a rule, in feeling; but none the less they start from the scarcely veiled presupposition that everything is subordinate to consciousness. In this sense all idealism, if not "personal," is human or subjective. Again, the idealist's longing for perfection, or rather his assumption that the universe is implicitly perfect, reminds us of that romantic mood which turns from the ugly or unfinished to build a sunny pleasure dome. Granting the fascination of such a view, and its possible stimulus to effort, we may still feel tempted to exclaim, as the poet does, Beware!

> "Weave a circle round him thrice
> And close your eyes with holy dread."

The instinct for the vague and mysterious is, or should be, satisfied abundantly in philosophy by the conception of the Absolute. The Whole which is the only Real, and yet is only known and manifested through appearances, which combines not only the values of truth and beauty and goodness, but the "disvalues" of falsehood, ugliness, and evil, with an unexplained balance on behalf of the former, so that the Absolute is its only possible description—this, as I have said already, is a conclusion which realism does not regard as profitable or clear.

Another school of modern thought has appealed to essentially the same instinct as the romance of action. This is pragmatism, with its view of truth as the right way of meeting a situation, its constant assimilation of thought to action, and its emphasis on the adventurous hazards of thinking. As a philosophy of *life* realism is distinctly in sympathy with pragmatism. Both agree as to the difference which action, here and now in time, may make to the sum of things; both are theories of experience rather than of completion. But in the matter of truth and knowledge there is a certain antagonism between them. The emphasis which the pragmatist lays on the claims of practical satisfaction leads him to a point where the realist cannot follow him. For pragmatism, like idealism, seems committed in the end to the view that knowledge makes reality, only without the safeguards which the modern idealist introduces. This view would take all stability and independence out of the world, and make it the creature of individual thoughts and actions.

Finally, just as there is a form of art which regards life as the embodiment of some one guiding thought or feeling, so it has been a common trait of philosophers to choose one element of the universe and look in it for the meaning of the whole. So Spinoza chose substance, Schopenhauer chose will, while modern theorists who start from physical science interpret everything in terms of activity or force. This point of view realism also repudiates as deceptive in its assumptions and its simplicity. It is too easy and too consistent with the prepossessions of the thinker to be true. Theories of this kind borrow a term which has a definite meaning in its own context, and exalt it to the position of a universal predicate, without seeing that their principle is thus emptied of meaning, though it may go on trading upon its former associations.

Realism in thought rejects many interesting and enticing explanations of the universe, just as realism in art leaves on one side many fruitful types of creation. Indeed, when we consider the other possible directions which activity may take in thought or art—and we have only considered some of them—realism may appear more remarkable for what it does not do than for what it does. The negative side of realism—the restrictions under which the realist puts himself—seems to be the characteristic element of it, and perhaps the only one which its manifestations in art and thinking have in common. Of course, this is the kind of impression that is naturally made when we are looking at the limits of anything, for, as Spinoza said, "all determination is negation." Yet it is perfectly true that realism *is* restricted in a sense in which romance or idealism are not. It does debar itself, in one case, from imaginations, and in the other from the hypotheses, which might be suggested by the free creativeness of the mind. "The temper of realism is to deanthropomorphise; to order man and mind to their proper place among the world of finite things; on the one hand, to divest physical things of the colouring which they have received from the vanity or arrogance of mind; and on the other to assign them along with minds their due measure of self-existence."* This description, which a philosophic realist gives of the method of realistic thinking, applies quite equally to the realistic form of art.

But as art is one kind of activity and speculative thinking is another, the limitations are also different in the two cases. The sphere of realism in art is limited to the actual, that is to say, to the world of our common experience or to what we recognise as possible there. Though the realistic artist may say, as we have seen, that all subjects are equal and indifferent, these possible subjects only exist for him inside the range of possible experiences through which we may live. And within these he tends to return to the familiar, partly because it is the central core of experience which interests him most, and partly because it is there that he and we are in the best position to recognise what is true. But we have seen that one aspect of life after another asserts its claims for realism, and that the matter rests finally in the artist's hands. Realism lies essentially in the *treatment* of the actual, and it is for the artist to make the unique experience take its place as a vivid and intelligible part of our ordinary world. His method of doing it, whether highly conscious, as in Flaubert's case, or quite instinctive, is "by letting speak, himself kept out of view," the scene or situation or character which has become his subject. In this sense he "deanthropomorphises" like the philosopher; "se dépersonnaliser" is the phrase which Faguet actually uses of the artist. He sheds not only the personal bias, but so far as possible all bias which besets the human mind as such.

The philosopher is not limited to the actual in the way the artist is, for his business is not with the particular things which happen in the world, but with the laws or forms or general characteristics which make such things possible. And though he is a discoverer and his work is in a sense creative, he does not deal with his material as the artist does, for his task is to understand rather than to vivify; he appeals to the discursive and not the aesthetic reason. But when these reservations have been made, his general attitude is the same as that of the realistic artist. He also feels himself in

* Alexander, *The Basis of Realism*, p. 1.

presence of a world which the mind has not made by its own thinking. The actuality or reality of which art persuades us by making it vivid, he can only demonstrate by showing that it is something independent of ourselves, something which includes us and our reason. There will always be minds and temperaments for which a realism of this kind is by no means "real"; which prefers the feeling of creativeness to the feeling of a solid framework; and for them the realistic way of approaching ultimate problems seems not only to provide no answer, but to make any answer of an illuminating kind impossible. For besides being pledged, like other thinkers, to avoid personal caprices and distortions, the realist is also bound to hold that the most fashionable and reassuring philosophy, that which interprets the world in terms of mind or spirit or will, is itself a fallacy of human thought—an idolon, as Bacon would have called it. This is his restriction, debarring him from the flattering solution, as he is debarred from the opposite conclusion of the "naturalists," that nature is simply a machine. Realism thus has an air of being mainly negative. As it has been revived in the form of a theory of knowledge, directed against other theories which are highly affirmative, this is almost inevitable. But this is only the reverse side of the doctrine, and on the other it might be said to appear as the most positive of theories, since it affirms the being or existence of divers orders of things, and investigates their nature and connections. Nor would it be quite fair to charge it with stopping on the threshold, and remaining agnostic upon the final problems of metaphysics, until its argument has been fully worked out.

The answer to the question about reality, for instance, still hangs in the air. Realists have told us what they mean by being and by existence, but they have been less inclined to commit themselves on the subject of reality. Perhaps they regard it, not without reason, as a hallmark of ambiguous meaning, which each theorist stamps on the principle that finds most favour in his eyes. We have seen that the independence of things is the chief clue of their theory, but we cannot identify independence with reality. For in that case all the products which depend wholly or partly on consciousness, such as history, ethics, art and "values" generally, would be pronounced unreal. It would be most consistent with the first inspiration of realism, and with the more concrete form of the theory, to say, as common sense does, that the real is what exists—including in that both individual things and universal forms, so far as the latter are embodied in the existent. Existence, as more full and complex, would be more real than the being which abstract forms and principles are declared to enjoy. On the other hand, to declare simply that the real is the perfect, as it is also popular to do, would be a matter of some difficulty for realism. For realists assert that imperfection and evil exist as persistently as anything else, and that they are not mere appearances, swallowed up and transmuted in an Infinite Whole.

It is characteristic of realistic thought to believe that truth is attainable by mortals, without waiting for the completion of an ideal experience. And for realistic art, too, truth has a significance which it does not have for art of other kinds. It is not that the deliberate statement of truth is the realist's first inspiration. His original interest, if we have guessed it rightly, is a vivid appreciation of the shapes and forms of existence. It is a poetic joy in life. But as soon as the artist's mind becomes ever so little sophisticated, and reflection on error begins, it generates that critical apprehension which Flaubert describes as driving him to scoop and dig into the fact. No doubt, as truth is practically meaningless except among a society of men, the realist only begins to contemplate it expressly when he has become aware of rival ways of regarding and representing life. He then reacts against the sentimentalism, romanticism, idealism, and in general the "pathetic fallacy," which infects the views of others. Where ancient realism remained pictorial, modern realism tends to be critical and analytic. But here again there is no finality; at any moment a new temperament may strike out a new type or throw back to a forgotten one.

Though modern realistic art has been affected deeply by science, the truth it aims at is not, as Zola thought it was, scientific truth. It is a truth of impression in which feeling and imagination play the essential part. For this reason truth for the realistic artist can never consist in what many people believe to be its essence—a simple correspondence with facts. He is an observer, but he is not a reporter. He does not copy, but he creates a world which refers us back to our own world and shows it to us more truly. The world he makes must be congruous with ours, but it does not correspond with it bit by bit, as a literal imitation. If it does, the vivid truth of impression is defeated; for art cannot hold us with a stale second-hand replica of what we can have in life at first hand. It has been noticed how in Stendhal's greatest novel the one fact which seems unreal is the fact which was actually incorporated from "real life."

The reason why it seems unreal is because of the incongruous mixture of imitation with creation. But the phrase "seeming unreal" may suggest a further dilemma for the realist. Does not the adventure of life actually consist in those startling, undreamt-of experiences which at the moment of happening seem unreal because they are so unexpected? These, we say sometimes, give us a glimpse of reality or are the real thing. Yet apparently it is just these that realism is incompetent to deal with, if it always has to refer us back, for emotional verification, to the commonplace routine of life. Say what we will, it is tethered to a stake, and the really exciting things take place outside the circle of its tether.

The realist's reply to this might be that his art is not so tied to the routine of life as the objection supposes. Its truth is tested by our whole reach of experience, not by the trivial part of it; and it is only for the commonplace mind or the stunted life that the whole of experience is trivial. The belief in fantastic, exceptional occurrences, which Dostoevsky among others cherished, is elusive, because it is characteristic of these occurrences to seem unreal, and yet, we are told, they reveal a deeper reality to us. This is the ambiguity about the "real" again. It would be truer to say that the strange experience seems impossible, but that it drives us to think of what is most important—namely, what it means to live and die. Whether it actually makes us do this will depend on how it is handled. It brings, at any rate, a sudden compulsion to revise our conclusions; it is the point where we have to make a join in our experience between the new and old. And for this reason, if it is an opportunity for the realist, it is a difficult one. All art is an affair of seeming, and his art deals in what seems true of life. It is because the rare event has not been assimilated to the rest of our experience that it makes, aesthetically, a larger demand on him.

It goes without saying that one of the greatest of these rifts

in experience which has ever confronted art and life is presented
by the war. So long as armies were professional and their numbers
were counted by thousands, the rest of the world might affect a
vague callousness to their experiences. Now that they are counted
by millions and comprise the manhood of whole peoples, this has
become impossible. There arises a burning desire to comprehend,
but at that very moment we find something which bars comprehension. There are two worlds of experience, and they seem hopelessly divided. The following fragment of a letter quoted in a weekly paper expresses this sense of cleavage, rather temperately than
otherwise :—

"I have often heard it said that the curious thing about those who
have been to the front is their complete indifference. They appear
to be practically untouched by what they have seen and gone
through, they talk of war in a callous and humorous way, they
even joke about its horrors. The impression one has from them is
that it is, on the whole, a dreary and unpleasant business, with
its anxious moments and its bright moments, but not nearly such
a hell as one really knows it to be. In the case of the vast majority,
however, this is an attitude, a screen—I speak of educated, thinking men—and it is not granted to many who have not shared the
same experiences to see behind this screen. The reason for this,
as the article (the article was called 'On Leave') points out, is
the practical impossibility of the uninitiated to realise or imagine
even dimly the actual conditions of war. And a man who has been
through it and seen and taken part in the unspeakable tragedies
that are the ordinary routine, feels that he has something, possesses
something, which others can never possess. It is morally impossible for him to talk seriously of these things to people who cannot
even approach comprehension. It is hideously exasperating to hear
people talking the glib commonplaces about the war and distribut-
ing cheap sympathy to its victims."*

It is impossible to read a testimony of this kind without asking
oneself more than one question about experience and truth. For
here is an exceptional experience which persists in its exception,
to the point of not assimilating itself in any way to the experience
of those who have not shared it, nor even, perhaps, to the rest of

* The *Nation*, 23rd June 1917, p. 299.

"Conclusions and Applications"

the experience of those who have. It seems to defy expression by any method that we can call representative. For if the artist has not been within the horror his work must be untrue; and if he has, how can he make the world outside feel or believe his experiences? The art, therefore, that expresses the war may not be a realistic one. Or if the war is expressed by realism, it will be a realism concerned with states of mind rather than sequences of action. *The Dark Forest* of Mr. Walpole occurs to the mind as a work of great beauty, which uses realistic detail in a certain measure and is evidently prompted by a personal experience, and yet is not realistic as a whole, since its main interest lies not so much in representation as in the working out of an idea. The only type of "war novel" which can appeal directly or realistically to the experience of the civilian public is that which represents the war at home or behind the front, and one or two successes show that in this form the war is already amenable to art.*

There is obviously a social or ethical motive which, apart from the aesthetic one, makes it desirable that truth should be told, whether this is done realistically or otherwise. No virtue suffers more severely in war than truth. The story goes that a Russian statesman, since distinguished as one of the most sagacious heads in the Revolution, told a parliamentary colleague in one of the darker moments before that change that he was going down to the Duma to tell the truth. "What? truth in war-time?" was the horrified reply. It was the one thing which was evidently out of place. Truth does not suffer only from the official suppression of disagreeable facts. It is sapped by the idealised or conventional descriptions of those engaged in "writing up" the war, and by the obsession of mind which makes it almost impossible for any nation to realise other points of view than its own. Detachment may be impracticable while history is in the making, but there is a degree of coolness and comprehension which is needed for judging how to act. There is a realism of the understanding which tries to put the facts in their places and see them as they are.

It may be worth while to emphasise this, because there is a

* Since this was written there has been a rush of books attempting to reproduce the sensations of war; but only Mr. Siegfried Sassoon's poems seem to bridge the gulf between the two experiences.

575

strong tendency to use realism as a mere term of prejudice in politics, just as it has been used disparagingly in the criticism of art. The abuse of the word has come from a mixture of two judgments, one of which is a true conviction and the other an error of thought. It is from German *Realpolitik* that we tend to derive political realism, and in our discussions it is generally the Germans who figure as the "realists." There are two characteristics which in this way we ascribe to realism; one is the habit of building on facts and refusing to be taken in by appearances, and the other is the determination to pursue material interests only and to get your own way. We rightly condemn the second, but there is no reason why we should suppose it to be an ingredient in the first. It is clear that the two things have no necessary connection with each other. They may have been united in the Germans—with a large alloy of fixed ideas and false calculations—but it does not follow that they must be found together in every one else. Realism is not materialism in politics, any more than it is materialism in philosophy or Zolaesque naturalism in art. No doubt, as used of politics, the word is a metaphor, and one so often misleading that it might be better discarded; but if it is used at all, it must be used consistently with its original meaning.

Only so could we hope to describe its relation to political idealism. To one kind of idealism, the false or deluded or subjective, it is certainly opposed. What, then, of the "sentimental idealist"? It is sometimes forgotten that feelings are facts, no less than material objects or institutions. They are indeed, as has been explained already, the most important of all facts in the region of values—the region where we make those choices which alter the face of our world. "Sentimental idealist" is a phrase generally applied by those who think in terms of power or tradition to those who think in terms of feeling or ideas; but for the realist it could only mean one whose wishes have blinded him to circumstance, who thinks that what he desires is already actual, or that it is possible under conditions which, as a fact, forbid it. It seems natural to say that the realist is a person who is mainly influenced by what exists, and the idealist one who is governed by the thought of what may exist. This is true, in a sense, but it does not mean that the realist is satisfied by things as they are. It is rather idealism which, as Professor Perry says, is the "all-saving philosophy," while realism is a "philosophy of extermination." Between the realist and the practical idealist there is no quarrel. The conflict of realism is with that theoretic or optimistic idealism which declines to see the imperfection of things, or uses it, like Browning, as actually evidence for perfection; which props what is tottering or obsolete because of a latent good which may possibly counterbalance its patent evil. Acting on one temperament realism may make a sceptic or a désenchanté; acting on another it will make a ruthless revolutionary. The "existing things" to which the realist pays attention are not only the material conditions which limit action, but the felt wants and hopes which inspire it; and his war is not only with reluctant matter but with codes, formulas, and doctrines which prescribe what one ought to think and feel. The test will be, as it has always been, what satisfies; and the realist, as a believer in the school of experience, is confident that ideals and values will grow richer rather than poorer. He distrusts only dictated values, fixed standards, and the assumption that all is for the best.

It is perhaps on lines like these that a practical realism might be expected to develop. It should not be confused with that revival of abstract, medieval realism which would attribute a "real personality" to groups or associations, such as churches, trade unions, or other organised societies. As a legal formula—and it is the legal side of the question which is apt to be the pressing one—this has its special application, on which lawyers must be left to pronounce. As a political or metaphysical theory it seems to exaggerate the recognition of an undoubted fact.* This fact is the existence of other groups beside the State, which divide with the State the interests and perhaps even the allegiance of their members. They may range from the family to the Amalgamated Society of Engineers, and include all those associations which, whether shadowy or definite, transcend the borders of the State, such as the "International" and the Roman Catholic Church. The importance of these groupings is not to be denied. We are finding more and more that the chief problem of political theory is not, as it used to be, the relation of one and all, the individual and the State, but the ad-

* A brilliant article by Mr. Ernest Barker on "The Discredited State," in the *Political Quarterly* for February 1915, discusses the topic comprehensively.

justment of one group and one range of interests to others. Even now, when a colossal war seems to have restored to the State an omnipotence which it had lost for centuries, we are busily devising schemes to limit that sovereignty, as between State and State, more definitely than it has ever been limited before. The establishment of a league of nations, in however loose a form, would recognise that States themselves are groups or constituents of a larger commonwealth, and that their authority is not plenary or uncontrolled.

But this is a different thing from saying that there is a "real personality" in all these groups. This doctrine, originated to defend the lesser groups against the greater, may be easily turned against the weak. If a Church has the will and consciousness of a real person, the State should have it too. It is the ground of our complaint against Prussia that she has menaced Europe by assuming a personality of this kind, and reducing human souls to insignificance beside the all-transcending State. The "abstract universal" of the Middle Ages has taken possession of a people and clothed itself with new and terrible force. And what we have learned to our cost in this case is always a delusion and a snare. If the group is treated as a real person, the individuals who compose it cease to have the rights of persons, and the uniting principle gets a fictitious strength. We begin to fight for personified interests, crystallised ideas—exactly the things which, as explained above, the realist would analyse remorselessly. The best chance of securing the flexible adjustment of competing interests is to recollect that in every case of a group we are dealing with individuals whom some organising principle has united. In those individuals the will and personality remain. The tie which unites them, whether it is race or interest or simply an idea, may have a passionately compelling effect, but so long as no existence is ascribed to it apart from the members whom it unites, reason has a weapon to temper its exclusive dominion. For the individuals of the group are also susceptible to other "universals," other principles of combination, and in the name of these we may appeal to them to recognise the common right of all.

"Notes on the Decline of Naturalism"*

By Philip Rahv

PHILIP RAHV (1908—) has as critic attempted both to define the aims of contemporary writers and to analyze writing of the nineteenth century in terms of its meaning to those writers. Editor of the *Partisan Review*, fellow of the Indiana School of Letters, he can be said to stand for the commitments and approaches of the post-realistic school. Thus this article is particularly informative about the current evaluation of realism-naturalism by writers and about the substance which they still draw from it.

Although the article suggests that philosophical system and fictional practice should not be confused, it nonetheless makes clear the relationship of contemporary writing to a changed view of reality. The orthodox naturalist method, Rahv says, can be used only when reality is taken for granted. This is no longer possible, and the crisis of art today is the crisis of "the dissolution of the familiar world." He may err in making that dissolution too recent a phenomenon, since it has been suggested that what brought an end to nineteenth-century realism was radical changes in physics at the end of the century which profoundly altered, if they did not destroy, the certified structure of reality. In any event the world he describes as normative for the artist today is one which cannot be handled or conceived of by the realists whom we have been examining in this volume.

◇◇

QUITE a few protests have been aired in recent years against the sway of the naturalist method in fiction. It is charged that this method treats material in a manner so flat and external as to inhibit the search for value and meaning, and that in any case, whatever its past record, it is now exhausted. Dissimilar as they are, both the work of Franz Kafka and the works of the surrealist school are frequently cited as examples of release from the routines of naturalist realism, from its endless book-keeping of existence.

* Rahv, Philip, "Notes on the Decline of Naturalism," *Image and Idea*, pp. 128-138; New York, New Directions, 1949. First published in *Partisan Review* 9: pp. 483-493, 1942. Copyright © 1957 by Philip Rahv. Reprinted by permission of New Directions, Publishers.

Supporting this indictment are mostly those writers of the younger group who are devoted to experimentation and who look to symbolism, the fable, and the myth.

The younger writers are stirred by the ambition to create a new type of imaginative prose into which the recognizably real enters as one component rather than as the total substance. They want to break the novel of its objective habits; some want to introduce into it philosophical ideas; others are not so much drawn to expressing ideas as to expressing the motley strivings of the inner self—dreams, visions, and fantasies. Manifestly the failure of the political movement in the literature of the past decade has resulted in a revival of religio-esthetic attitudes. The young men of letters are once again watching their own image in the mirror and listening to inner promptings. Theirs is a program calling for the adoption of techniques of planned derangement as a means of cracking open the certified structure of reality and turning loose its latent energies. And surely one cannot dispose of such a program merely by uncovering the element of mystification in it. For the truth is that the artist of the avant-garde has never hesitated to lay hold of the instruments of mystification when it suited his purpose, especially in an age such as ours, when the life about him belies more and more the rational ideals of the cultural tradition.

It has been remarked that in the long run the issue between naturalism and its opponents resolves itself into a philosophical dispute concerning the nature of reality. Obviously those who reject naturalism in philosophy will also object to its namesake in literature. But it seems to me that when faced with a problem such as that of naturalist fiction, the critic will do well not to mix in ontological maneuvres. From the standpoint of critical method it is impermissible to replace a concrete literary analysis with arguments derived from some general theory of the real. For it is plainly a case of the critic not being able to afford metaphysical commitments if he is to apply himself without preconceived ideas to the works of art that constitute his material. The art-object is from first to last the one certain datum at his disposal; and in succumbing to metaphysical leanings—either of the spiritualist or materialist variety—he runs the risk of freezing his insights in some kind of ideational schema, the relevance of which to the task in hand is hardly more than speculative. The act of critical evaluation is best performed in a state of *ideal aloofness* from abstract systems. Its practitioner is not concerned with making up his mind about the ultimate character of reality but with observing and measuring its actual proportions and combinations within a given form. The presence of the real affects him directly, with an immediate force contingent upon the degree of interest, concreteness, and intensity in the impression of life conveyed by the literary artist. The philosopher can take such impressions or leave them, but luckily the critic has no such choice.

Imaginative writing cannot include fixed and systematic definitions of reality without violating its own existential character. Yet in any imaginative effort that which we mean by the real remains the basic criterion of viability, the crucial test of relevance, even if its specific features can hardly be determined in advance but must be *felt anew* in each given instance. And so far as the medium of fiction is concerned, one cannot but agree with Henry James that it gains its "air of reality"—which he considers to be its "supreme virtue"—through "its immense and exquisite correspondence with life." Note that James's formulation allows both for analogical and realistic techniques of representation. He speaks not of copies or reports or transcripts of life but of relations of equivalence, of a "correspondence" which he identifies with the "illusion of life." The ability to produce this illusion he regards as the storyteller's inalienable gift, "the merit on which all other merits . . . helplessly and submissively depend." This insight is of an elementary nature and scarcely peculiar to James alone, but it seems that its truth has been lost on some of our recent catch-as-catch-can innovators in the writing of fiction.

It is intrinsically from this point of view that one can criticise the imitations of Kafka that have been turning up of late as being one-sided and even inept. Perhaps Kafka is too idiosyncratic a genius to serve as a model for others, but still it is easy to see where his imitators go wrong. It is necessary to say to them: To know how to take apart the recognizable world is not enough, is in fact merely a way of letting oneself go and of striving for originality at all costs. But originality of this sort is nothing more than a professional mannerism of the avant-garde. The genuine innovator is always trying to make us actually experience his creative contradictions. He therefore employs means that are subtler and more complex: *at the very same time that he takes the world apart he puts it together again.* For to proceed otherwise is to dissipate rather than to alter our sense of reality, to weaken and compromise rather than change in any significant fashion our feeling of relatedness to the world. After all, what impressed us most in Kafka is precisely this power of his to achieve a simultaneity of contrary effects, to fit the known into the unknown, the actual into the mythic and vice versa, to combine within one framework a conscientiously empirical account of the visibly real with a dreamlike and magical dissolution of it. In this paradox lies the pathos of his approach to human existence.

A modern poetess has written that the power of the visible derives from the invisible; but the reverse of this formula is also true. Thus the visible and the invisible might be said to stand to each other in an ironic relation of inner dependence and of mutual skepticism mixed with solicitude. It is a superb form of doubletalk; and if we are accustomed to its exclusion from naturalistic writing, it is all the more disappointing to find that the newly-evolved "fantastic" style of the experimentalists likewise excludes it. But there is another consideration, of a more formal nature. It seems to be a profound error to conceive of reality as merely a species of material that the fiction-writer can either use or dispense with as he sees fit. It is a species of material, of course, and something else besides: it also functions as the *discipline of fiction*, much in the same sense that syllabic structure functions as the discipline of verse. This seeming identity of the formal and substantial means of narrative-prose is due, I think, to the altogether free and open character of the medium, which prevents it from developing such distinctly technical controls as poetry has acquired. Hence even the dream, when told in a story, must partake of some of the qualities of the real.

Whereas the surrealist represents man as immured in dreams, the naturalist represents him in a continuous waking state of prosaic daily living, in effect as never dreaming. But both the surrealist and the naturalist go to extremes in simplifying the human condition. J. M. Synge once said that the artist displays at once the difficulty and the triumph of his art when picturing the dreamer leaning out to reality or the man of the real lifted out of it. "In all the poets," he wrote, and this test is by no means limited to poetry alone, "the greatest have both these elements, that is they are supremely engrossed with life, and yet with the wildness of their fancy they are always passing out of what is simple and plain."

The old egocentric formula, "Man's fate is his character," has been altered by the novelists of the naturalist school to read, "Man's fate is his environment." (Zola, the organizer and champion of the school, drew his ideas from physiology and medicine, but in later years his disciples cast the natural sciences aside in favor of the social sciences.) To the naturalist, human behavior is a function of its social environment; the individual is the live register of its qualities; he exists in it as animals exist in nature.* Due to this emphasis the naturalist mode has evolved historically in two main directions. On the one hand it has tended towards passive documentation (milieu-panoramas, local-color stories, reportorial studies of a given region or industry, etc.), and on the other towards the exposure of socio-economic conditions (muckraking). American fiction of the past decade teems with examples of both tendencies, usually in combination. The work of James T. Farrell, for instance, is mostly a genre-record, the material of which is in its very nature operative in producing social feeling, while such novels as *The Grapes of Wrath* and *Native Son* are exposure-literature, as is the greater part of the fiction of social protest. Dos

---

* Balzac, to whom naturalism is enormously indebted, explains in his preface to the *Comédie Humaine* that the idea of that work came to him in consequence of a "comparison between the human and animal kingdoms." "Does not society," he asks, "make of man, in accordance with the environment in which he lives and moves, as many different kinds of man as there are different zoological species? . . . There have, therefore, existed and always will exist social species, just as there are zoological species."

Zola argues along the same lines: "All things hang together: it is necessary to start from the determination of inanimate bodies in order to arrive at the determination of living beings; and since savants like Claude Bernard demonstrate now that fixed laws govern the human body, we can easily proclaim . . . the hour in which the laws of thought and passion will be formulated in their turn. A like determination will govern the stones of the roadway and the brain of man. . . . We have experimental chemistry and medicine and physiology, and later on an experimental novel. It was an inevitable evolution." (*The Experimental Novel*)

Passos' trilogy, *U.S.A.*, is thoroughly political in intention but has the tone and gloss of the methodical genre-painter in the page by page texture of its prose.

I know of no hard and fast rules that can be used to distinguish the naturalist method from the methods of realism generally. It is certainly incorrect to say that the difference is marked by the relative density of detail. Henry James observes in his essay *The Art of Fiction* that it is above all "solidity of specification" that makes for the illusion of life—the air of reality—in a novel; and the truth of this dictum is borne out by the practice of the foremost modern innovators in this medium, such as Proust, Joyce, and Kafka. It is not, then, primarily the means employed to establish verisimilitude that fix the naturalist imprint upon a work of fiction. A more conclusive test, to my mind, is its treatment of the relation of character to background. I would classify as naturalistic that type of realism in which the individual is portrayed not merely as subordinate to his background but as wholly determined by it—that type of realism, in other words, in which the environment displaces its inhabitants in the role of the hero. Theodore Dreiser, for example, comes as close as any American writer to plotting the careers of his characters strictly within a determinative process. The financier Frank Cowperwood masters his world and emerges as its hero, while the "little man" Clyde Griffiths is the victim whom it grinds to pieces; yet hero and victim alike are essentially implements of environmental force, the carriers of its contradictions upon whom it stamps success or failure—not entirely at will, to be sure, for people are marked biologically from birth—but with sufficient autonomy to shape their fate.

In such a closed world there is patently no room for the singular, the unique, for anything in fact which cannot be represented plausibly as the product of a particular social and historical complex. Of necessity the naturalist must deal with experience almost exclusively in terms of the broadly typical. He analyzes characters in such a way as to reduce them to standard types. His method of construction is that of accretion and enumeration rather than of analysis or storytelling; and this is so because the quantitative development of themes, the massing of detail and specification, serves his purpose best. He builds his structures out of literal fact

"Notes on the Decline of Naturalism"

and precisely documented circumstance, thus severely limiting the variety of creative means at the disposal of the artist.

This quasi-scientific approach not only permits but, in theory at least, actually prescribes a neutral attitude in the sphere of values. In practice, however, most naturalists are not sufficiently detached or logical to stay put in such an ultra-objective position. Their detractors are wrong in denying them a moral content; the most that can be said is that theirs is strictly functional morality, bare of any elements of gratuity or transcendence and devoid of the sense of personal freedom.* Clearly such a perspective allows for very little self-awareness on the part of characters. It also removes the possibility of a tragic resolution of experience. The world of naturalist fiction is much too big, too inert, too hardened by social habit and material necessity, to allow for that tenacious self-assertion of the human by means of which tragedy justifies and ennobles its protagonists. The only grandeur naturalism knows is the grandeur of its own methodological achievement in making available a vast inventory of minutely described phenomena, in assembling an enormous quantity of data and arranging them in a rough figuration of reality. *Les Rougon-Macquart* stands to this day as the most imposing monument to this achievement.

But in the main it is the pure naturalist—that monstrous offspring of the logic of a method—that I have been describing here. Actually no such literary animal exists. Life always triumphs over methods, over formulas and theories. There is scarcely a single novelist of any importance wearing the badge of naturalism who is all of a piece, who fails to compensate in some way for what we miss in his fundamental conception. Let us call the roll of the leading names among the French and American naturalists and see wherein each is saved.

The Goncourts, it is true, come off rather badly, but even so, to quote a French critic, they manage "to escape from the crude painting of the naked truth by their impressionistic mobility" and, one might add, by their mobile intelligence. Zola's case does not rest solely on our judgment of his naturalist dogmas. There are

* Chekhov remarks in one of his stories that "the sense of personal freedom is the chief constituent of creative genius."

entire volumes by him—the best, I think, is *Germinal*—and parts
of volumes besides, in which his naturalism, fed by an epic imagination, takes on a mythic cast. Thomas Mann associates him with
Wagner in a common drive toward an epic mythicism:

> They belong together. The kinship of spirit, method, and
> aims is most striking. This lies not only in the ambition
> to achieve size, the propensity to the grandiose and the
> lavish; nor is it the Homeric leitmotiv alone that is com-
> mon to them; it is first and foremost a special kind of nat-
> uralism, which develops into the mythical. . . . In Zola's
> epic . . . the characters themselves are raised up to a plane
> above that of every day. And is that Astarte of the Sec-
> ond Empire, called Nana, not symbol and myth? (*The
> Sufferings and Greatness of Richard Wagner*)

Zola's prose, though not controlled by an artistic conscience, over-
comes our resistance through sheer positiveness and expressive
energy—qualities engendered by his novelistic ardor and avidity
for recreating life in all its multiple forms.* As for Huysmans,
even in his naturalist period he was more concerned with style than
with subject-matter. Maupassant is a naturalist mainly by alliance,
i.e. by virtue of his official membership in the School of Médan;
actually he follows a line of his own, which takes off from naturalism never to return to it. There are few militant naturalists among
latter-day French writers. Jules Romains is sometimes spoken of
as one, but the truth is that he is an epigone of all literary doctrines,
including his own. Dreiser is still unsurpassed so far as American
naturalism goes, though just at present he may well be the least
readable. He has traits that make for survival—a Balzacian grip
of the machinery of money and power; a prosiness so primary in
texture that if taken in bulk it affects us as a kind of poetry of the
commonplace and ill-favored; and an emphatic eroticism which
is the real climate of existence in his fictions—Eros hovering over
the shambles. Sinclair Lewis was never a novelist in the proper
sense that Zola and Dreiser are novelists, and, given his gift for

---

* Moreover, it should be evident that Zola's many faults are not rectified but
merely inverted in much of the writing—so languidly allusive and decorative—
of the literary generations that turned their backs on him.

exhaustive reporting, naturalism did him more good than harm by providing him with a ready literary technique. In Farrell's chronicles there is an underlying moral code which, despite his explicit rejection of the Church, seems to me indisputably orthodox and Catholic; and his Studs Lonigan—a product of those unsightly urban neighborhoods where youth prowls and fights to live up to the folk-ideal of the "regular guy"—is no mere character but an archetype, an eponymous hero of the street-myths that prevail in our big cities. The naturalism of Dos Passos is most completely manifested in *U. S. A.*, tagged by the critics as a "collective" novel recording the "decline of our business civilization." But what distinguishes Dos Passos from other novelists of the same political animus is a sense of justice so pure as to be almost instinctive, as well as a deeply elegiac feeling for the intimate features of American life and for its precipitant moments. Also, *U. S. A.* is one of the very few naturalist novels in which there is a controlled use of language, in which a major effect is produced by the interplay between story and style. It is necessary to add, however, that the faults of Dos Passos' work have been obscured by its vivid contemporaneity and vital political appeal. In the future, I think, it will be seen more clearly than now that it dramatizes social symptoms rather than lives and that it fails to preserve the integrity of personal experience. As for Faulkner, Hemingway, and Caldwell, I do not quite see on what grounds some critics and literary historians include them in the naturalist school. I should think that Faulkner is exempted by his prodigious inventiveness and fantastic humor. Hemingway is a realist on one level, in his attempts to catch the "real thing, the sequence of motion and fact which made the emotion"; but he is also subjective, given to self-portraiture and to playing games with his ego; there is very little study of background in his work, a minimum of documentation. In his best novels Caldwell is a writer of rural abandon—and comedy. His *Tobacco Road* is a sociological area only in patches; most of it is exotic landscape.

It is not hard to demonstrate the weakness of the naturalist method by abstracting it, first, from the uses to which individual authors put it and, second, from its function in the history of modern literature. The traditionalist critics judge it much too one-sidedly in professing to see in its rise nothing but spiritual loss—an invasion of the arcanum of art by arid scientific ideas. The point is that this scientific bias of naturalism was historically productive of contradictory results. Its effect was certainly depressive in so far as it brought mechanistic notions and procedures into writing. But it should be kept in mind that it also enlivened and, in fact, revolutionized writing by liquidating the last assets of "romance" in fiction and by purging it once and for all of the idealism of the "beautiful lie"—of the long-standing inhibitions against dealing with the underside of life, with those inescapable day-by-day actualities traditionally regarded as too "sordid" and "ugly" for inclusion within an aesthetic framework. If it were not for the service thus rendered in vastly increasing the store of literary material, it is doubtful whether such works as *Ulysses* and even *Remembrance of Things Past* could have been written. This is not clearly understood in the English-speaking countries, where naturalism, never quite forming itself into a "movement," was at most only an extreme emphasis in the general onset of realistic fiction and drama. One must study, rather, the Continental writers of the last quarter of the 19th century in order to grasp its historical role. In discussing the German naturalist school of the 1880's, the historian Hans Naumann has this to say, for instance:

> Generally it can be said that to its early exponents the doctrine of naturalism held quite as many diverse and confusing meanings as the doctrine of expressionism seemed to hold in the period just past. Imaginative writers who at bottom were pure idealists united with the dry-as-dust advocates of a philistine natural-scientific program on the one hand and with the shameless exploiters of erotic themes on the other. All met under the banner of naturalism—friends today and enemies tomorrow. . . . But there was an element of historical necessity in all this. The fact is that the time had come for an assault, executed with glowing enthusiasm, against the epigones . . . that it was finally possible to fling aside with disdain and anger the pretty falsehoods of life and art. (*Die Deutsche Dichtung der Gegenwart*, Stuttgart, 1930, p. 144)

"Notes on the Decline of Naturalism"

And he adds that the naturalism of certain writers consisted simply in their "speaking honestly of things that had heretofore been suppressed."

But to establish the historical credit of naturalism is not to refute the charges that have been brought against it in recent years. For whatever its past accomplishments, it cannot be denied that its present condition is one of utter debility. What was once a means of treating material truthfully has been turned, through a long process of depreciation, into a mere convention of truthfulness, devoid of any significant or even clearly definable literary purpose or design. The spirit of discovery has withdrawn from naturalism; it has now become the common denominator of realism, available in like measure to the producers of literature and to the producers of kitsch. One might sum up the objections to it simply by saying that it is no longer possible to use this method *without taking reality for granted*. This means that it has lost the power to cope with the ever-growing element of the problematical in modern life, which is precisely the element that is magnetizing the imagination of the true artists of our epoch. Such artists are no longer content merely to question particular habits or situations or even institutions; it is reality itself which they bring into question. Reality to them is like that "open wound" of which Kierkegaard speaks in his *Journals*: "A healthy open wound; sometimes it is healthier to keep a wound open; sometimes it is worse when it closes."

There are also certain long-range factors that make for the decline of naturalism. One such factor is the growth of psychological science and, particularly, of psychoanalysis. Through the influence of psychology literature recovers its inwardness, devising such forms as the interior monologue, which combines the naturalistic in its minute description of the mental process with the anti-naturalistic in its disclosure of the subjective and the irrational. Still another factor is the tendency of naturalism, as Thomas Mann observes in his remarks on Zola, to turn into the mythic through sheer immersion in the typical. This dialectical negation of the typical is apparent in a work like *Ulysses*, where "the myth of the *Odyssey*," to quote from Harry Levin's study of Joyce, "is superimposed upon the map of Dublin" because only a myth could "lend shape or meaning to a slice of life so broad and banal." And from a social-historical point of view this much can be said, that naturalism cannot hope to survive the world of 19th-century science and industry of which it is the product. For what is the crisis of reality in contemporary art if not at bottom the crisis of the dissolution of this familiar world? Naturalism, which exhausted itself in taking an inventory of this world while it was still relatively stable, cannot possibly do justice to the phenomena of its disruption.

One must protest, however, against the easy assumption of some avant-gardist writers that to finish with naturalism is the same as finishing with the principle of realism generally. It is one thing to dissect the real, to penetrate beneath its faceless surface and transpose it into terms of symbol and image; but the attempt to be done with it altogether is sheer regression or escape. Of the principle of realism it can be said that it is the most valuable acquisition of the modern mind. It has taught literature how to take in, how to grasp and encompass, the ordinary facts of human existence; and I mean this in the simplest sense conceivable. Least of all can the novelist dispense with it, as his medium knows of no other principle of coherence. In Gide's *Les Faux-Monnayeurs* there is a famous passage in which the novelist Edouard enumerates the faults of the naturalist school. "The great defect of that school is that it always cuts a slice of life in the same direction: in time, lengthwise. Why not in breadth? Or in depth? As for me, I should like not to cut at all. Please understand: I should like to put everything into my novel." "But I thought," his interlocutor remarks, "that you want to abandon reality." Yes, replies Edouard, "my novelist wants to abandon it; but I shall continually bring him back to it. In fact that will be the subject; the struggle between the facts presented by reality and the ideal reality."

"The Realistic Fallacy"*

By Erich Heller

ERICH HELLER (1911—), currently professor of German literature at Northwestern University, has made significant contributions to the study of nineteenth and twentieth-century literature. He is the author of *The Disinherited Mind* (1952), *The Hazard of Modern Poetry* (1953), *The Ironic German, a Study of Thomas Mann* (1958), and the chapter on "Imaginative Literature 1830-1870" in the new *Cambridge Modern History*.

The essay included here was originally given as a talk on the BBC Third Program. It makes an interesting distinction between the orthodox realism which this volume traces and the pretensions of writers as far back as the romantics to the revelation or creation of a mystical essence which is the only real reality, one in which the word takes precedence over the fact. In this way Professor Heller exposes one area of semantic confusion which besets discussion of this subject and also shows the bias and source of much twentieth-century irrealistic writing—for example, the passage from Proust above or the kind of literature espoused by André Breton's surrealist manifestos.

◇◇

DANTE claimed that the world of the *Divine Comedy* was the truly real world. Cervantes meant his *Don Quixote* to rehabilitate the true sense of reality in his readers' minds which had been perverted by manufacturers of abstruse unreality. In the literary debates of the eighteenth century in Germany, Shakespeare was held up before the adolescent poetical genius of the nation as the supreme example of realistic insight and natural spontaneity, qualities that put to shame the high-flown artificialities of French classicism. Yet it was these two "realists," Cervantes and Shakespeare, that the early German romantics regarded as essential luggage when they prepared their bid for the freedom of the imagination. To them they were the quintessence of romanticism.

Goethe praised Homer for his realism. Ortega y Gasset blamed

---

* Heller, Erich, "The Realistic Fallacy: A Discussion of Realism in Literature," *The Listener* 53: pp. 888-889, May 19, 1955. The text as presented here has undergone slight corrections and additions by the author and is reprinted with his permission and that of The *Listener*.

Goethe for his obstinate refusal to face his true reality. Nietzsche extolled Goethe as a "convinced realist" who had conquered and transcended the deeply anti-realistic instincts of his age.

Much could be added to this list, but little to the confusion which could hardly be worse confounded. A mere index giving the varied uses of the term "realism" in literature would render the belief that, say, Balzac is closer to "reality" than Homer highly improbable. For the confused history of man is largely the history of conflicting senses of reality, and the scope for bewilderment becomes infinite if we include the history of literature. Our grasp of reality being as insecure as it is, we are indeed asking for trouble if we try to define imaginative literature, which is, whatever else it is, a sort of make-believe, in terms of what manifestly it is not, namely, reality.

Or is it? Or rather, has such a question any meaning at all? And if it has no meaning, are we to dismiss that large section of European philosophy and aesthetic which deals with this problem as yet another outcome of man's indiscreet habit of satisfying his excessive desire for sense by talking nonsense? Plato, it seems, was in no uncertainty about it. To him the world which we inhabit, and habitually regard as the real world, was itself unreal enough. It was a mere imitation, imperfect throughout, of that perfect reality which resides in the Ideas; therefore the work of art, in imitating what was in itself an imperfect imitation, was at two removes from reality. Thus the poetic activity was intellectually unworthy and morally suspect, and the ideal republic was advised to do without the corrupting machinations of the poet.

In the face of this denunciation Aristotle, it is true, advanced his *moral* apologia for tragedy, but not until very much later in the history of European thought did it occur to anyone to claim for literature and the arts a higher degree of actual *reality* than that possessed by the so-called real world. This enormous claim for a product of the human imagination could hardly have hoped for as much as a glimmer of understanding before the nineteenth century. It was Schopenhauer who, in terms of Plato himself, completely reversed the Platonic view of the arts. Yet when this happened, it seemed merely the philosophical consummation of what artists and the lovers of the arts had come to feel with ever in-

"The Realistic Fallacy"

creasing conviction: the artistic creation was closer to reality than the world as it appeared to the uninitiated human mind. For although Plato was right, so the argument ran, in judging the world of appearances to be the mere copy-book of reality, blotted, as Schopenhauer added, by the crude scribblings of the self-willed creature, he was yet blind to the fact that the work of the artists, in being the outcome of pure self-less contemplation, bore the authentic imprint of the Ideas, that is, of Truth, that is, of Reality; and the artistic product was bound to be the greater, the more energetically it cut through the tangled trappings and frivolous futilities of the shadow-realm of appearances, the less it was distracted by personal bias and prejudice from its awful conversation with that which is truly true and really real. In other words and two senses: the more the work of art is like real life, the less it is like "real life." The German painter Max Liebermann once summed up, in his homely-aggressive Berlin idiom, this Schopenhauerian view of the arts. A banker who had commissioned his portrait from him, complained that the unflattering vision on the canvas was not a bit like him. "My dear man," said Liebermann, "this is more like you than you yourself."

Schopenhauer's philosophy is an aesthetic gnosis, a secular apocalypse: the world is worthless; art is good. Life is no life; letters are the real thing. Music is Reality, poetry is the vision of a creature that has escaped from the cave, standing now in the clear light of the Eternal Forms. Small wonder that so tenuous a salvation should first have been preached with irony. Some time before Schopenhauer became known, the German romantics had founded their ironical church. They too wished to believe in the ultimate reality of poetry, but never quite succeeded in shutting out the harsh voice of the ultimately unreal yet, alas, ever so present real world. The result was irony, that irony which is the idiom of the peculiarly romantic divided disloyalty towards reality as well as poetry. The early German romantics cultivated irony as the mysticism of these two half-beliefs. Like all mysticism, romantic irony seems fathomless and unspeakable, but unlike the mysticism of the believer, it is often shallow and loquacious. For the ironical romantic fixes the eyes of poetry upon the world, and the eyes of the world upon poetry; and by virtue of this romantic squint it is now poetry and now the world that comes to nothing.

In turns amused and agonized by this incongruous spectacle, some of the romantics arrived at the concept of *Universalpoesie*, universal poetry. It is an extraordinary notion, never clearly expressed but often hinted at with intellectual passion and aphoristic force. If we piece together many fragments on the subject, there emerges the scintillating manifesto of absolute poetic imperialism: poetry must conquer the world, the world must become poetry. Every aspect of the community of men—religion, science, politics —must, by direct attack or peaceful penetration, become infused with the poetic spirit and in the end be transformed into a work of art. For everything that poetry can do within poetry itself has been done; now the infinite poetical yearning yearns for the world. Remaining poetry, it will yet become science, psychology, politics, knowledge and power; and science, psychology, politics, knowledge and power will become poetry. The world will be the body of poetry, and poetry will be the body of the world. In this new incarnation both the world and poetry will be saved.—Madness? Well, if it is madness, it has yet, with no more than an ironical shift of emphasis, taken very methodical form in the philosophy of the dominant thinker of the age: Hegel. And his was indeed a philosophy with very real consequences.

Hegel was a romantic. He supplied the systematic theology of the new incarnation. But he differed from his romantic compatriots in holding somewhat old-fashioned views about poetry. He conversed with a mightier emissary of the Absolute: with the world-spirit itself, and he believed that its final unfolding would render poetry redundant. Soon the poetic faculty would be seen to be a mere atavistic survival from a stage of as yet incomplete consciousness where man had to rely on the imagination for a few glimpses of Truth, and on the power of casually divined symbols for some mediation between ignorance and Reality. Now, however, the world-spirit was getting ready for the ultimate illumination in which mankind would celebrate the unveiling of the mystery. It is a piece of profound romantic irony that Hegel should have summed up and superseded all romantic philosophizing with this excess of rationality, casting the suspicion of poetic and intellectual

594

"The Realistic Fallacy"

irresponsibility—read his attack on Friedrich Schlegel—on the imperialists of poetry. Yet the Hegelian world-spirit and the universalized poetry of the romantics are closer to each other than the conventional enmity between reason and imagination would seem to allow. In both the early romantics and Hegel the human mind puts forward a total claim for itself, a claim in which revolution and eschatology are uneasily mingled. The world must become imagination and poetry, say the romantics; and Hegel says, the world must become rational consciousness. But the poetry meant by the romantics, and the rational consciousness meant by Hegel have much in common: above all the ambition of the human mind to dominate reality to the point of usurping its place. This situation is reflected in the *two realisms* that have ever since held sway over European literature.

The two realisms. The first is, of course, the realism of the great nineteenth-century novel, acknowledged under this heading by all text-books of literature. If it is concerned with man's reality, it certainly shares this concern with the great literature of any other age. The name "realism" merely betrays the particular superstition of the age, which flattered itself with the notion that it had found the key to what really is. But, in fact, the realistic writer is only, like any other writer, fascinated by certain aspects of reality, and uses the selective scheme of his fascination for the aesthetic ordering of his chosen materials. For, alas, we seem to get to know one thing at the price of losing sight of another; and however wide our interest, the sharp edge of our perception in one sphere is but in contrast to the bluntness of our sensibility in another. "Realism in art is an illusion," said Nietzsche, addressing the realist writers, "all the writers of all the ages were convinced they were realistic." And equating any artistic vision with a specific vision of happiness, he added: "What, then, is it that the so-called realism of our writers tells us about the happiness of our time? . . . One is indeed led to believe that our particular happiness does not spring from what really is, but from our *understanding of reality*. . . . The artists of our century willy-nilly glorify the scientific beatitudes."

This, I think, hits upon the distinctive quality of nineteenth-century realism—a Hegelian quality. For the "realistic" subject-mat-

ter of the great realistic novels is by no means new. From Petronius
to the English eighteenth century many writers have given us massive literary documents of life as it was lived, enjoyed or bungled
by people in the unheroic and unspectacular regions of the world.
What is new, is the particular passion haunting the pages of
Stendhal, Balzac, Flaubert, Dostoevsky or Tolstoy. It is the passion of understanding, the desire for rational appropriation, the
driving force towards the expropriation of the mystery. How tedious would be Balzac's descriptions if they were not alive with the
zeal for absolute rational possession of the things described; how
cheap would be Stendhal's melodramas if the emotions were merely
evoked without being completely controlled by the analytical intelligence and made transparent by the master-eye that sees through
everything. And Dostoevsky's genius is closely allied to the spirit
of detection, his singular greatness being due to the fact that the
light by which he searches is also the fire by which he is consumed.
Nor is it a mere accident that Tolstoy—who certainly was not a
Hegelian—repeatedly protested Reason, that is, good—almost as
if he were Hegel himself. The apparent quietness and equipoise of
Tolstoy's prose is yet vibrant with the imperialist enthusiasm of
rational understanding, and, even before his conversion, shot
through with the dark glitter of that vision in which is revealed
the vanity of all things. This vision is perhaps bound to emerge at
the end of the total exploration of man by man. For the "realistic"
sense of reality which possessed so many minds in the nineteenth
century was such that it lured them towards the rational conquest
of the human world only in order to prove to them its absolute
meaninglessness. Hence it is that the temper of realistic writing
is pessimism, at best that pessimistic humour which makes for
realism's finest appeal, at worst frustration and *ennui*. It was this
pessimism in which Nietzsche saw the surest sign of a nihilistic
age in the making. The great novelists of the nineteenth century
were to provide him with the material for the first chapter of the
book on nihilism which he planned and never wrote. He would
have used the literature of realism in order to show, as a posthumous note suggests, how "between 1830 and 1850 the romantic faith in love and in the future turned into the craving for
nothingness." Flaubert would have marked the climax of this

change at the very point where the streams of romanticism and realism join.

Flaubert, indeed, blatantly gives away the conspiracy of realism. Through him, the late-comer, its hidden aim comes into the open. To describe reality? To mirror it? Artistically to represent it? This is nothing but the innocently respectable surface of realistic literature. Somewhere in its heart quivers the hatred of reality and the lust for conquest. Even the "reality" of the person who does the writing becomes a hateful obstacle to the ultimate rational and aesthetic triumph. If only the human subject could be reduced to nothing but seeing, understanding, and writing; if only the real object could be transmuted into nothing but words! Reality? No, it must be dissolved by insight and style. Yet again and again Flaubert was dismayed by the undue resistance offered by reality, although there were times when he modestly believed that the rational penetration of the real world could suffice. "The two muses of the modern age," he said, "are history and science," and realistically allowed himself to be inspired by them. This was before he wrote his *Sentimental Education*. But after it was finished, he denounced it—in a mood not unlike that of Tolstoy after his conversion—as "a series of analyses and mediocre gossip." "For beauty," he added, "is incompatible with modern life, and this is the last time I will have anything to do with it. I have had enough." The flesh of reality proved too solid after all to be melted in the aesthetic fire. No purity of style could prevail against the infection that realism contracted by letting itself in with reality at all; and even the most sublime triumphs won by the art of writing over the barren material might not be entirely safe from the scorn which Flaubert in the end poured upon the campaigns of his Bouvard and Pécuchet to establish their petty rational dominion over a disturbing world. Perhaps the immaculate victory over reality could only be achieved by writing, as Flaubert once said, "a book about nothing at all, a book without any external connection, and which would support itself entirely by the internal force of style."

But this, clearly, would no longer be realism, at least not the one realism which we usually call by this name. Yet it anticipates the other realism, the realism which, discarding the strategy of Hegel's rational world-spirit, seems to follow the rules of war evolved by the romantics when they planned the attack of "universal poetry" upon reality. This realism does indeed sever "any external connection," as Flaubert put it, and "supports itself by internal force alone." Emerging from romanticism and leading through Baudelaire, Mallarmé, and Rimbaud to Valéry, it culminates in Rilke's *Duino Elegies* and *Sonnets to Orpheus*. Now external reality has no claims any more to being real. The only real world is the world of human inwardness. The concrete form of this reality is the poem in its pure absoluteness. *Gesang ist Dasein.* Song is existence. Hamlet's soul has at last abolished the rotten state. What is within, no longer passes show. It is for all to see and is a work of art. Imagination is reality. We know not "seems." The world is dead. The rest is poetry; or even a new kind of epic prose: the prose of *Ulysses, Finnegan's Wake*, or *The Death of Vergil*.

Neither reality nor literature, neither the world nor the word have yet recovered from this strange exertion. For nothing is more exhausting than the effort of proving fallacies true. After these extreme achievements of literature we may have to be realistically modest in our aesthetic expectations. The economy of the world cannot support forever the expensive households of so many creators competing with creation itself.

A Short Bibliography of
History and Criticism

Agosti, Hector P., *Defensa del realismo*, Montevideo, Editorial Pueblos Unidos, 1945

Åhnebrink, Lars, *The Beginnings of Naturalism in American Fiction*, Harvard University Press, 1950

Anisimov, I. I., and Elsberg, Ya. E. (eds.), *Problemy realisma*, Moscow, 1959

Antoine, André, *Mes Souvenirs sur le Théâtre-Libre*, Paris, 1921

Arrighi, Paul, *Le Vérisme dans la prose narrative italienne*, Paris, 1937

Auerbach, Erich, *Mimesis, the Representation of Reality in Western Literature*, Princeton University Press, 1953

Bab, Julius, *Fortinbras; oder, Der Kampf des 19. Jahrhunderts mit dem Geiste der Romantik*, Berlin, 1914

Bahr, Hermann, *Die Überwindung des Naturalismus*, Berlin, 1891

Beardsley, Monroe C., and Becker, George J., "Naturalism," "Realism," in Shipley, Joseph T. (ed.), *Dictionary of World Literature*, revised edition, Philosophical Library, 1953

Beuchat, Charles, *Histoire du naturalisme français*, in two volumes, Paris, Corrêa, 1949

Boas, George (ed.), *Courbet and the Naturalistic Movement*, Johns Hopkins University Press, 1938

Bölsche, Wilhelm, *Die naturwissenschäftlichen Grundlagen der Poesie: Prolegomena zu einer realistischen Aesthetik*, Leipzig, 1887

Bornecque, J. H., and Cogny, Pierre, *Réalisme et naturalisme. L'Histoire, la doctrine, les oeuvres*, Paris, Hachette, 1958

Bouvier, E., *La Bataille réaliste, Champfleury et le passage du romantisme au naturalisme 1844-57*, Fontemoing, n.d.

Bowron, Bernard R., Jr., "Realism in America," *Comparative Literature* 3: pp. 268-285, Summer 1951

Brandes, Georg M. C., *Main Currents in Nineteenth Century Literature*, in six volumes, London, W. Heinemann, 1901-1905 (originally published in Danish, 1872-1890)

Brandes, Georg M. C., *Naturalism in Nineteenth Century English Literature*, New York, Russell & Russell, 1957

Braun, Maximilian, *Der Kampf um die Wirklichkeit in der russischen Literatur*, Göttingen, Vandenhoeck & Ruprecht, 1958

Brinkmann, Richard, *Wirklichkeit und Illusion; Studien über Gehalt und Grenzen des Begriffs Realismus für die erzählende Dichtung des neunzehnten Jahrhunderts*, Tübingen, M. Niemeyer, 1957

Brunetière, Ferdinand, *Le Roman naturaliste*, Paris, 1896

599

Cady, Edwin H., *The Road to Realism*, Syracuse University Press, 1942

Champfleury (Jules Fleury), *Le Réalisme*, Paris, 1857

Cogny, Pierre, *Le Naturalisme*, Paris, Presses Universitaires de France, 1953

Colum, Mary, *From These Roots*, New York, Charles Scribner's Sons, 1937

Courtney, W. L., "Realistic Drama," *Old Saws and Modern Instances*, pp. 161-217; London, Chapman and Hall, 1919

David-Sauvageot, A., *Le Réalisme et le naturalisme dans la littérature et dans l'art*, Paris, 1889

Davies, Hugh S., *Realism in the Drama*, Cambridge University Press, 1934

Davis, Robert Gorham, "The Sense of the Real in English Fiction," *Comparative Literature* 3: pp. 200-217, Summer 1951

Decker, C. R., "Maiden Tribute: The Naturalists in England," *The Victorian Conscience*, pp. 79-114; New York, Twayne, 1952

Deffoux, Léon, *Le Naturalisme avec un florilège des principaux écrivains naturalistes*, Paris, Les Oeuvres Représentatives, 1929 (originally published in 1909)

Deffoux, Léon, *La Publication de L'Assommoir*, Paris, 1931

Desprez, Louis, *L'Evolution naturaliste*, Paris, 1884

Dneprov, Vladimir, *Problemy realisma*, Leningrad, 1960

Doménech, Jaime, *Las formas del ideal artístico*, Madrid, J. M. Yagües, 1932

Dumesnil, René, *L'Epoque réaliste et naturaliste*, Paris, Tallandier, 1945

Dumesnil, René, *La Publication de "Madame Bovary,"* Paris, 1928

Dumesnil, René, *La Publication des Soirées de Médan*, Paris, 1933

Dumesnil, René, *Le Réalisme et le naturalisme*, Paris, Del Duca de Gigord, 1955

Fingerit, Julio, *Realismo*, Buenos Aires, 1930

Frierson, W. C., "The English Controversy over Realism in Fiction," *PMLA* 43: pp. 533-550, June 1928

Frierson, W. C., *The English Novel in Transition*, University of Oklahoma Press, 1942

Frierson, W. C., *L'Influence du naturalisme français sur les romanciers anglais de 1885 à 1900*, Paris, 1925

Garland, Hamlin, *Crumbling Idols*, Chicago, Stone & Kimball, 1894

Goncourt, Edmond and Jules de, *Journal*, in 22 volumes, Fasquelle and Flammarion, 1956

Goncourt, Edmond and Jules, *Préfaces et manifestes littéraires*, Paris, 1888

Graaf, Jacob de, *Le Réveil littéraire en Hollande et le naturalisme français, 1880-1900*, Amsterdam, H. J. Paris, 1938

Bibliography

Hatfield, Henry C., "Realism in the German Novel," *Comparative Literature* 3: pp. 234-252, Summer 1951

Hemmings, F. W. J., *The Russian Novel in France 1884-1914*, Oxford University Press, 1950

Henriot, Emile, *Réalisme et naturalisme*, Paris, A. Michel, 1954

Holz, Arno, *Die neue Wortkunst: Eine Zusammenfassung ihrer ersten grundlegenden Dokumente, Das Werk von Arno Holz* 10, Berlin, 1925

Howells, William Dean, *Criticism and Fiction*, Harpers, 1891

Huret, Jules, *Enquête sur l'évolution littéraire*, Paris, 1891

James, Henry, *The Art of the Novel*, New York, Charles Scribner's Sons, 1934

James, Henry, *The Future of the Novel*, New York, Vintage Books, 1956

James, Henry, *The House of Fiction*, London, Hart-Davis, 1957

James, Henry, *Notes on Novelists*, New York, Scribner, 1914

Karganov, Alexander, *Chernishevskii i Dobroliubov o realisme*, Moscow, 1955

Kazin, Alfred, *On Native Grounds*, New York, Reynal & Hitchcock, 1942

Krutch, Joseph Wood, *The Modern Temper*, New York, Harcourt Brace, 1929

Lacher, Walter, *Le Réalisme dans le roman contemporain*, Geneva, Imprimerie Centrale, 1940

LeBlond, Maurice, *La Publication de La Terre*, Paris, 1937

Lemonnier, Léon, *Populisme*, Paris, La Renaissance du Livre, 1931

Lessing, O. E., *Die neue Form: Ein Beitrag zum Verständnis des deutschen Naturalismus*, Dresden, 1910

Levin, Harry, *Toward Stendhal*, New York, New Directions, 1945

Levin, Harry, "What Is Realism?", *Comparative Literature* 3: pp. 193-199, Summer 1951

Lubbock, Percy, *The Craft of Fiction*, New York, Scribner, 1921

Lucas, F. L., *The Decline and Fall of the Romantic Ideal*, New York, Macmillan, 1936

Lukacs, György, *Deutsche Realisten des 19. Jahrhunderts*, Berlin, Aufbau Verlag, 1951

Lukacs, György, *Essays über Realismus*, Berlin, Aufbau Verlag, 1947

Lukacs, György, *Probleme des Realismus*, Berlin, Aufbau Verlag, 1955

Lukacs, György, *Der russische Realismus in der Weltliteratur*, Berlin, Aufbau Verlag, 1952

Lukacs, György, *Studies in European Realism*, London, Hillway Publishing Company, 1950

Lukacs, György, *Wider den missverstandenen Realismus*, Hamburg, Claasen, 1958

Magny, Claude-Edmonde, *Les Sandales d'Empédocle; Essai sur les limites de la littérature*, Neuchâtel, 1945

Martino, Pierre, *Le Naturalisme français (1870-1895)*, Paris, 1923

Martino, Pierre, *Le Roman réaliste sous le second empire*, Paris, 1913

Maynial, Edouard, *L'Epoque réaliste*, Paris, Les Oeuvres Représentatives, 1931

McDowall, Arthur, *Realism: A Study in Art and Thought*, London, Constable, 1918

Montesinos, José Fernández, *Costumbrismo y novela; ensayo sobre el redescubrimiento de la realidad española*, University of California Press, 1960

Morrow, Christine, *Le Roman irréaliste dans les littératures contemporaines de langues française et anglaise*, Toulouse, 1941

Muscetta, Carlo, *Realismo e contro-realismo; saggi e polemichi*, Milano, Cino del Duca, 1958

Nordau, Max, *Degeneration*, pp. 473-535; (translated from the second edition of the German work), New York, D. Appleton and Company, 1895

O'Connor, Frank, *The Mirror in the Roadway: A Study of the Modern Novel*, New York, Knopf, 1956

Ortega y Gasset, José, *The Dehumanization of Art and Notes on the Novel*, Princeton University Press, 1948

Pardo Bazán, Emilia, *La cuestión palpitante*, Madrid, 1883

Pérez Petit, Víctor, *Las tres catedrales del naturalismo*, Montevideo, 1943

Pinto, V. de Sola, "Realism in English Poetry," *Essays and Studies by Members of the English Association* 25 (1939), Oxford University Press, 1940

Poggioli, Renato, "Realism in Russia," *Comparative Literature* 3: pp. 253-267, Summer 1951

Remak, H. H., "The German Reception of French Realism," *PMLA* 69: pp. 410-431, June 1954

Root, W. H., *German Criticism of Zola, 1875-1893*, Columbia University Press, 1931

Salvan, Albert J., "L'Essence du réalisme français," *Comparative Literature* 3: pp. 234-252, Summer 1951

Salvan, Albert J., *Zola aux Etats-Unis*, Brown University Press, 1943

Smith, Bernard, "Democracy and Realism," *Forces in American Criticism*, pp. 134-184, New York, Harcourt Brace, 1939

Sovietskii pisateli, *Problemy sotsialist-chekovo realisma*, Moscow, 1961

Stang, Richard, *The Theory of the Novel in England 1850-1870*, Columbia University Press, 1959

Taine, Hippolyte, *Essais de critique et d'histoire*, tenth (definitive) edition, Paris, 1904

Bibliography

Tertz, Abram, *On Socialist Realism*, New York, Pantheon Books, 1960

Vinogradov, Viktor, *Evolutsia russkovo naturalisma; Gogol i Dostoevskii*, Leningrad, 1929

Vogüé, E. M. de, *Le Roman russe*, Paris, 1886

Walcutt, C. C., *American Literary Naturalism, A Divided Stream*, University of Minnesota Press, 1956

Weinberg, Bernard, *French Realism: The Critical Reaction, 1830-1870*, Oxford University Press, 1937

Zola, Emile, *Documents littéraires*, Paris, 1881

Zola, Emile, *Les Romanciers naturalistes*, Paris, 1881

Zola, Emile, *Le Roman expérimental*, Paris, 1880

Index

Achard, Marcel, 465
Adam, Paul, 409, 410, 411
Addison, Joseph, 143
Aeschylus, 305
Agosti, Hector P., 489
Alarcón, Pedro de, 264, 266, 267
Alas, Leopoldo, 14, 266
Alcoforado, Mariana, 469
Alexis, Paul, 407
Anderson, Sherwood, 18, 445
Antoine, André, 394
Aragon, Louis, 465, 497
Arenal, Concepción, 270
Aristotle, 67, 197, 198, 254, 449, 592
Arnold, Matthew, 355, 376
Artzybashev, Mikhail, 542-543
Auerbach, Erich, 565
Augier, Emile, 216-218, 219, 222, 223
Austen, Jane, 387

Babbitt, Irving, 452
Bacon, Francis, 289, 571
Balzac, Honoré de, 4, 7, 21, 90, 95, 97,
    105, 106-111, 134, 135, 136, 166-167,
    179, 193, 202, 203, 204, 205, 206, 214,
    218, 222, 223, 225, 234, 249, 257, 258,
    265, 279, 282, 283, 284, 287, 290, 293,
    304-305, 306-307, 309, 326-327, 332,
    335, 346, 408, 431, 456, 484-485, 530,
    583, 592, 596
Barbusse, Henri, 465, 473
Barker, Ernest, 575
Baudelaire, Charles, 98, 411, 598
Beaumarchais, Pierre de, 210
Belinsky, Vissarion, 10, 37, 38, 41
Bennett, Arnold, 16, 25
Bergson, Henri, 500
Bernard, Claude, 150, 162-196, 256,
    258, 268, 284, 286,
Björnson, Björnsterne, 11, 142, 302
Blake, William, 127
Bleibtreu, Carl, 12, 251
Boccaccio, Giovanni, 255, 376
Boileau, Nicolas, 99, 197
Bölsche, Wilhelm, 13, 251
Bonnetain, Paul, 344, 349
Botas, José Loureiro, 479
Bourget, Paul, 9, 350, 392, 410-411
Brahm, Otto, 251
Brandes, Georg, 11, 341
Brasil, Jaime, 21, 468

Breton, André, 489, 591
Brieux, Eugène, 122, 155, 536, 542
Browning, Robert, 143
Brunetière, Ferdinand, 9, 273, 333, 344
Bunyan, John, 454
Burke, Edmund, 132, 133, 547
Burne-Jones, Edward, 128
Busnach, William, 274-275
Busoni, Ferruccio, 505
Byron, George Gordon, Lord, 50, 57,
    140

Caldwell, Erskine, 19, 587
Camoens, Luis Vaz de, 469
Camp, Max du, 283
Campoamor, Ramón de, 267-268
Capuana, Luigi, 14
Carlyle, Thomas, 143, 291, 377
Carrache, Annibal, 24
Castro, Ferreira de, 476-477
Catullus, 448
Céard, Henri, 407
Cecil, David, 112
Cela, Camilo, 20
Cervantes, Miguel de, 153, 261, 264,
    265, 266, 591
Cézanne, Paul, 490
Champfleury, 7, 80, 97, 98, 473
Chateaubriand, René de, 201, 339, 343
Chaucer, Geoffrey, 376
Chekhov, Anton, 11, 31, 35, 122, 155,
    486, 585
Chénier, André, 85
Chernishevsky, N. G., 10, 37, 41, 44
Chopin, Frédéric, 566
Churchill, Winston, 18
Cicero, 279
Coleridge, S. T., 566
Colet, Louise, 89
Conrad, M. G., 12
Cooper, James F., 16, 72, 440, 451
Corneille, Pierre, 57, 58, 85, 210, 225,
    342
Courbet, Gustave, 7, 80, 86, 87-88, 492,
    493
Courtney, W. L., 28
Cowley, Malcolm, 429
Cozzens, James G., 30
Crane, Stephen, 431, 435, 437, 443, 447,
    449, 450
cubism, 490, 491, 496, 503

Cunha, Ramos da, 480
Cuvier, Georges, 170

Dabit, Eugène, 465
Dante, 292, 309, 591
Darwin, Charles, 8, 173, 456
Daudet, Alphonse, 12, 117, 301, 302, 344, 350, 386, 408
David-Sauvageot, A., 15
Davis, Rebecca Harding, 17
Day, Thomas, 532
Deffoux, Léon, 466
Defoe, Daniel, 462
Delille, Jacques, 225
Delpit, Auguste, 410
Democritus, 67
Descaves, Lucien, 344, 349
Desnoyers, Fernand, 7, 80
Dickens, Charles, 15, 71, 134, 143, 235, 265, 332, 333, 335, 387, 392, 439
Diderot, Denis, 4, 84, 202, 210, 211, 282, 325, 408
Dixon, Thomas, 18, 431
Dos Passos, John, 18, 30, 440, 447, 451, 584, 587
Dostoevsky, Fyodor, 10, 11, 17, 26, 30, 31, 35, 310, 336, 337, 342, 386, 387, 388, 573, 596
Dreiser, Theodore, 18, 19, 29, 154-155, 429, 430, 433, 436, 437, 438, 439, 440, 441, 443-444, 447, 449-450, 451, 452-464, 584, 586
Dreyfus, Alfred, 9, 160, 520, 531, 560
Duarte, Fausto, 480
Duhamel, Georges, 465
Dumas, Alexandre (père), 136, 204, 234, 257, 387, 439, 566
Dumas, Alexandre (fils), 103, 214-216, 217, 219, 222, 223, 227, 228-229, 294
Dupanloup, F.-A.-P., 105-106
Dupuy, Ernest, 310
Duranty, Edmond, 7, 24, 97, 98, 408, 473
Dürer, Albrecht, 82

Eça de Queiroz, José, 14, 21, 469, 470
Edgeworth, Maria, 532
Eggleston, Edward, 145
Ehrenburg, Ilya, 473-474
Eliot, George, 6, 8, 15, 23, 112, 238, 290, 291, 332-334, 337, 459
Emerson, Ralph W., 289-290, 538
Engels, Friedrich, 21, 44, 483, 495

Esperança, Assis, 480
Euripedes, 305

Fadaev, Alexander, 473
Faguet, Emile, 413, 570
Falcato, João, 480
Farrell, James T., 25, 32, 429, 440, 447, 451, 583, 587
Faulkner, William, 445, 587
Ferreira, Vergilio, 479
Ferrer, Joaquim, 480
Feuerbach, Ludwig, 44, 45-48
Feuillet, Octave, 204
Feydeau, Ernest, 8
Fielding, Henry, 387, 542, 543
Filon, Auguste, 410
Flaubert, Gustave, 7, 8, 15, 21, 23, 25, 26, 28, 30, 32, 35, 89-90, 91, 94, 98-104, 117, 130, 155, 205, 206, 219, 227, 236, 247, 248, 269, 282, 283, 292, 325, 327-329, 330, 333, 335, 336, 346, 350, 386, 408, 409, 450, 473, 492, 536, 546, 566, 570, 596-597, 598
Flower, B. O., 137
Fonseca, Manuel da, 478
Fox, Ralph, 486
France, Anatole, 407, 489
Frederic, Harold, 437, 441, 447
Frierson, W. C., 7
futurism, 490

Galsworthy, John, 541
Garland, Hamlin, 137-138
Gide, André, 590
Gille, Philippe, 409
Gleizes, Albert, 491, 492, 503
Goethe, Johann W. von, 50, 52, 53, 74, 234, 238, 251, 252, 254, 258, 260, 265, 279, 309, 337, 591, 592
Gogol, Nikolai, 7, 41, 54, 59, 254, 310
Gomes, Pereira, 478
Goncharov, Ivan, 10
Goncourt, Jules and Edmond de, 8, 9, 23, 24, 25, 117, 155, 206, 219, 227, 244, 344, 346, 350, 402, 407, 408, 409, 442, 450, 456, 473, 585
Gorky, Maxim, 11, 22, 25, 34, 122, 486
Gosse, Edmund, 383
Gottschall, Rudolf, 255
Goya, Francisco de, 264
Guiches, Gustave, 349

Halévy, J. F., 218

Index

Hardy, Thomas, 433, 450, 536, 537, 541, 542, 546, 567
Hart, Heinrich and Julius, 251
Hauptmann, Gerhart, 13, 14, 155
Hawthorne, Nathaniel, 134
Hazlitt, William, 99
Hegel, G. W. F., 41, 44, 45, 46, 47, 252, 492, 501, 594-595, 597
Heine, Heinrich, 305
Heller, Erich, 37, 591
Hemingway, Ernest, 446, 587
Herrick, Robert, 446
Holz, Arno, 13, 251
Homer, 82, 279, 591, 592
Howells, W. D., 8, 17, 25, 129-130, 137, 142, 143, 237, 296-302, 385, 386, 387, 389, 454
Hugo, Victor, 5, 84, 204, 205, 211, 257, 282, 283, 327, 387, 415, 439
Huret, Jules, 9, 407
Huysmans, J.-K., 9, 230-232, 392, 586

Ibsen, Henrik, 11, 13, 15, 122, 126, 127, 142, 143, 155, 450, 536, 542

James, Henry, 4, 8, 236-237, 296, 304, 381, 385, 386, 389, 445, 454, 506, 581, 584
James, William, 444
Johnson, Samuel, 99, 143, 275, 546-547
Jones, James, 16, 20
Joyce, James, 18, 32, 236, 584, 588, 589, 598

Kafka, Franz, 18, 579, 581-582, 584
Kahnweiler, Daniel-Henry, 503
Kant, Immanuel, 46-47
Kazin, Alfred, 27
Keats, John, 132
Keller, Gottfried, 260
Kierkegaard, Soren, 589
Kipling, Rudyard, 439
Kirkland, Joseph, 145
Kock, Paul de, 90, 329
Krutch, Joseph W., 35, 448, 449

Labiche, Eugene, 218
La Bruyère, Jean de, 100
La Fayette, Madame de, 469
Laharpe, Jean-François de, 99
Lamartine, Alphonse de, 566
La Rochefoucauld, François de, 126
Leconte de Lisle, Charles, 93
Lee, Vernon, 383

Lefebvre, Henri, 493, 500
Legouvé, Ernest, 234
Lemonnier, Léon, 465
Lenin, Nikolai, 44
Leopardi, Giacomo, 268
Lermontov, Mikhail, 54, 314
Lessing, G. E., 305
Levin, Meyer, 32
Lewes, G. H., 6
Lewis, Sinclair, 18, 19, 440-441, 445, 447, 450, 451, 465, 586
Liebermann, Max, 593
Lilly, W. S., 274
Lindau, Paul, 255
Littré, Emile, 106
London, Jack, 19, 32, 432-433, 441, 445, 447
Longfellow, H. W., 126
Loomis, Roger S., 535
Lothe, André, 489, 491, 503
Loti, Pierre, 392
Lowell, J. R., 140
Lukacs, György, 500

Mabie, H. W., 296
Mailer, Norman, 16
Mallarmé, Stéphane, 411, 598
Mandeville, Bernard, 126
Mann, Heinrich, 465
Mann, Thomas, 18, 586, 589
Margueritte, Paul, 349
Martin du Gard, Roger, 10
Martins, Oliveira, 470
Marx, Karl, 33, 44
Masters, E. L., 447, 536, 537, 541, 542
Maugham, Somerset, 16
Maupassant, Guy de, 8, 9, 15, 25, 29, 89, 127, 155, 247-248, 350, 392, 407, 412-425, 586
Maury, Alfred, 106
McCarthy, Mary, 27
McDowall, Arthur, 34, 565
Meilhac, Henri, 218
Mencken, H. L., 18, 448
Mercier, Sébastien, 210, 211
Meredith, George, 120, 459
Mérimée, Prosper, 5, 326, 335
Metzinger, Jean, 491, 492, 503
Meyerbeer, Giacomo, 128
Michelangelo, 133, 283, 303
Michelet, Jules, 343
Miller, Joaquin, 140, 145
Millet, Jean-François, 508
Mirabeau, H.-G., 335, 343

Mistral, Frédéric, 140
Molière, 85, 210, 216, 225, 342, 398
Monet, Claude, 139
Montégut, Emile, 332, 333
Montemor, Jorge de, 469
Monti, Vincenzo, 136
Montorgueil, Georges, 410
Moore, George, 8, 15, 16, 248, 350, 385, 536
Moravia, Alberto, 20, 30
More, Paul Elmer, 452
Morrison, Arthur, 541
Müller, Johannes, 58
Musset, Alfred de, 314

Namora, Fernando, 478
Nascimento, Manuel do, 479
Naumann, Hans, 588
Nietzsche, Friedrich, 432, 566, 592, 595, 596
Nobre, Roberto, 480
Norris, Frank, 19, 32, 429, 430, 431, 432, 434-435, 439, 440, 441, 442-443, 447, 450

Oliveira, Carlos de, 479
O'Neill, Eugene, 440, 447, 451
Ortega y Gasset, José, 591
Ovid, 255
Owen, Robert, 128, 484

Palacio Valdés, Armando, 14
Pardo Bazán, Emilia, 14, 18, 251, 261, 266, 268, 270-273
Pascal, Blaise, 343
Pereda, José de, 264
Pérez Galdós, Benito, 14, 17, 25, 147, 261, 264
Perrier, Charles, 80
Perry, Bliss, 576
Perry, Thomas S., 8
Persius, 82
Pessoa, Fernando, 472
Petronius, 596
Phillips, D. G., 437, 442, 445, 447
Pindar, 99
Pisemsky, A. F., 10
Plato, 36, 67, 95, 127, 592-593
Plekhanov, G., 491
Plevier, Theodor, 30
Poe, E. A., 566
Poole, Ernest, 541
Pope, Alexander, 99, 140, 278
populism, 10, 465-467

Prévost, Abbé, 408
Proust, Marcel, 18, 36, 38, 236, 549, 584, 588, 591
Pushkin, Alexander, 7, 41, 50, 52, 54, 57, 314, 341

Quintinha, Julião, 480

Rabelais, François, 82, 343, 376
Racine, Jean, 57, 58, 71, 85, 210
Rahv, Philip, 579
Raphael, 82
Raphael, Max, 499
Read, Opie, 145
Redol, Alves, 477
Rembrandt, 82
Renan, Ernest, 106
Renard, Georges, 184, 244
Restif de la Bretonne, N.-E., 4
Ribeiro, Afonso, 478
Richardson, Samuel, 238, 333, 387
Richter, Jean Paul, 252, 259
Rilke, Rainer, 598
Rimbaud, Arthur, 598
Robbe-Grillet, Alain, 10
Robinson, E. A., 439, 447
Rod, Edouard, 411
Roh, Franz, 494
Rolland, Romain, 465
Romains, Jules, 10, 30, 465, 586
romanticism, 4-6, 16, 18, 22, 24, 31, 83, 84, 86, 89, 97, 201-203, 204, 209, 211, 231, 318-319, 410, 593-595, 598
Rosny, J.-H., 344, 349
Rousseau, J.-J., 200, 201, 282, 335, 566
Rubens, 82, 253
Rumi, Oschelalledin, 252
Ruskin, John, 128, 143, 290
Rutherford, Mark, 16

Sainte-Beuve, Charles, 90, 97-98, 155
Saint-Pierre, Bernardin de, 100
Saint-Simon, Claude-Henri de, 343, 484
Sanctis, Francesco de, 38
Sand, George, 4, 50, 71, 100, 282, 290, 387, 392, 532
Sandeau, Jules, 234
Santayana, George, 544
Sarcey, Francisque, 248, 273
Sardou, Victorien, 212-214, 219, 222, 223
Sarraute, Nathalie, 10
Sartre, Jean-Paul, 23, 37
Sassoon, Siegfried, 577

Index

Schelling, Friedrich, 41, 47, 252
Schérer, Edmond, 333
Schiller, Friedrich, 43, 50, 53, 303, 377
Schlegel, Friedrich, 595
Schopenhauer, Arthur, 290, 330, 569, 592-593
Schreiner, Olive, 15, 120
Scott, Walter, 71, 134, 140, 142, 143, 387, 439, 566, 567
Scribe, Eugène, 87, 212, 218
Ségur, P.-P., 335, 340
Serrano, González, 268
Shakespeare, 53, 57, 82, 107, 134, 142, 143, 267, 309, 379, 546, 591
Shaw, G. B., 6, 15, 122, 155, 465
Shelley, Percy B., 126, 127
Sheridan, Richard B., 275
Sherman, Stuart P., 452
Silesius, Angelus, 252
Silone, Ignazio, 20, 473
Simenon, Georges, 465
Sinclair, Upton, 440, 442, 444, 447
socialist realism, 21-23, 34, 483-485, 486-488
Sophocles, 305
Spencer, Herbert, 430, 433
Spinoza, Baruch, 569
Staël, Madame de, 282
Steele, Richard, 132
Steinbeck, John, 33, 429, 447, 451, 473, 583
Stendhal, 4, 5, 7, 30, 95, 97, 105, 193, 203, 204, 205, 206, 258, 282, 283, 325, 326, 330, 332, 346, 408, 573, 596
Stevenson, R. L., 439, 566
Stravinsky, Igor, 505
Stribling, T. S., 440
Strindberg, August, 122, 394
Sue, Eugène, 234, 257
surrealism, 4, 490, 491, 496
Symonds, J. A., 130, 132
Synge, J. M., 582

Tacitus, 322
Taine, Hippolyte, 9, 25, 94-95, 103, 105-106, 139, 155, 169-170, 283, 310, 332, 333
Tennyson, Alfred, Lord, 126, 140
Tertz, Abram, 22, 23, 486
Thackeray, W. M., 134, 290, 309, 333, 459
Thanet, Octave, 145
Thérive, André, 465, 466-467
Thompson, Maurice, 129

Thurber, James, 19
Tolstoy, Leo, 7, 8, 10, 11, 17, 21, 25, 30, 31, 35, 122, 129, 142, 143, 310, 333, 336, 337, 386, 392, 412-413, 533, 596
Trollope, Anthony, 8, 459
Turgenev, Ivan, 8, 10, 21, 41, 117, 155, 160, 302, 310, 333, 335, 337, 385, 413, 415
Twain, Mark, 451

Valera, Juan, 261
Valéry, Paul, 598
Vallès, Jules, 411
Van Gogh, Vincent, 490
Velásquez, 264, 265
Verga, Giovanni, 14, 18
Verhaeren, Emile, 541
Verlaine, Paul, 411
Véron, Louis, 139, 143, 273
Veronese, 82
Villemain, François, 85
Villiers, de l'Isle-Adam, Auguste, 411
Villon, François, 448
Virgil, 321, 448
Vitorino, António, 479
Vizetelly, Frank, 15, 350-355, 369-382, 383, 483
Vogüé, E.-M. de, 5, 7, 11, 310, 385
Voltaire, 84, 210, 282

Wagner, Richard, 122, 128
Walpole, Hugh, 575
Wells, H. G., 541
Wharton, Edith, 446
Whitman, Walt, 8, 16, 142, 143
Whittier, J. G., 140
Wolff, Albert, 248
Woolf, Virginia, 38
Wordsworth, William, 5, 140, 566
Wright, Richard, 20, 447, 583

Zola, Emile, 4, 6, 8, 9, 10, 11, 12, 15, 18, 19, 21, 24, 25, 27, 29, 30, 32, 33, 35, 96, 105, 117, 127, 128, 135, 154, 155, 159-160, 160-161, 230, 232-235, 237-243, 244, 245, 247, 251-260, 263, 264, 268, 272, 274-295, 296, 304-305, 306, 327, 344-349, 350, 352-355, 369, 371, 372, 373-382, 383, 385-393, 408, 410, 415, 430, 431, 432, 433, 439, 440, 442, 452, 456, 463, 466, 468, 474, 476, 484, 492, 493, 506-534, 535, 536, 537, 541, 542, 572, 576, 583, 585-586, 589